Metric Conversion

Canadians now shop readily in metric sizes, although some remain more comfortable with the imperial system. Fortunately, labels on many products have both metric and imperial measurements. In some cases, it is useful to know how to make a rough conversion, if, say, a supplier still sells an item in an imperial size. To convert basic units in both systems, use the table (*right*), or follow the rules of thumb (*below*). The linear conversion table (*below, right*) is designed to help you calculate equivalents for the imperial measurements in *New Fix-It-Yourself Manual*.

SOME RULES OF THUMB

The "10 Percent and up" Rule:
1 metre is 10 percent longer than 1 yard
1 litre is 10 percent less than 1 quart
1 kilogram is 10 percent more than 2 pounds
1 square metre (m²) is 20 percent greater than 1 square yard
1 cubic metre (m³) is 30 percent greater than 1 cubic yard

The "30" Rule:
1 foot is slightly more than 30 centimetres
1 ounce is just under 30 grams
1 fluid ounce is almost 30 millilitres

The "About" Rule:
1 inch is about 25 millimetres or 2.5 centimetres
4 inches are about 10 centimetres
A 2-inch by 4-inch piece (a 2" x 4") of lumber is about 5 centimetres by 10 centimetres
3 feet are about 1 metre
10 yards are about 9 metres
1 pound is about 0.5 kilogram
1 imperial gallon is about 4.5 litres
1 U.S. gallon is about 4 litres
1 quart is about 1 litre (the imperial quart is 1.136 litres; the U.S. quart is 0.946 litre)
1 pint is about 0.5 litre (the imperial pint is 0.568 litre; the U.S. pint is 0.473 litre)

CONVERSION FACTORS

Imperial system to metric system

To change:	Into:	Multiply by:
Inches	Millimetres	25.4
Inches	Centimetres	2.54
Feet	Metres	0.305
Yards	Metres	0.914
Miles	Kilometres	1.609
Square inches	Square centimetres	6.452
Square feet	Square metres	0.093
Square yards	Square metres	0.836
Cubic inches	Cubic centimetres	16.387
Cubic feet	Cubic metres	0.028
Cubic yards	Cubic metres	0.765
Pints	Litres	0.568
Quarts	Litres	1.136
Gallons	Litres	4.546
Ounces	Grams	28.412
Pounds	Kilograms	0.454
Tons	Tonnes	0.907

Metric system to imperial system

To change:	Into:	Multiply by:
Millimetres	Inches	0.039
Centimetres	Inches	0.394
Metres	Feet	3.281
Metres	Yards	1.093
Kilometres	Miles	0.621
Square centimetres	Square inches	0.155
Square metres	Square feet	10.8
Square metres	Square yards	1.196
Cubic centimetres	Cubic inches	0.061
Cubic metres	Cubic feet	35.3
Cubic metres	Cubic yards	1.307
Litres	Pints	1.759
Litres	Quarts	0.879
Litres	Gallons	0.22
Grams	Ounces	0.035
Kilograms	Pounds	2.204
Tonnes	Tons	1.1

LINEAR CONVERSION TABLE

Inches (in.)	1/64	1/32	1/25	1/16	1/8	1/4	3/8	2/5	1/2	5/8	3/4	7/8	1	2	3	4	5	6	7	8	9	10	11	12	36	39.4
Feet (ft)																								1	3	3¼†
Yards (yd)																									1	1½†
Millimetres* (mm)	0.40	0.79	1	1.59	3.18	6.35	9.53	10	12.7	15.9	19.1	22.2	25.4	50.8	76.2	101.6	127	152	178	203	229	254	279	305	914	1000
Centimetres* (cm)							0.95	1	1.27	1.59	1.91	2.22	2.54	5.08	7.62	10.16	12.7	15.2	17.8	20.3	22.9	25.4	27.9	30.5	91.4	100
Metres* (m)																								0.30	0.91	1.00

To find the metric equivalent of quantities not in this table, add together the appropriate entries. For example, to convert 2⅝ inches to centimetres, add the figure given for the centimetre equivalent of 2 inches, 5.08, and the centimetre equivalent of ⅝ inch, 1.59, to obtain 6.67 centimetres.

*Metric values are rounded off.
†Approximate fractions.

NEW
FIX-IT-YOURSELF
MANUAL

READER'S DIGEST

NEW FIX-IT-YOURSELF MANUAL

The Reader's Digest Association (Canada) Ltd., Montreal

New Fix-It-Yourself Manual

CANADIAN STAFF

Project Editor
Andrew Byers

Project Art Editor
John McGuffie

Designer
Andrée Payette

Research Supervisor
Wadad Bashour

Copy Preparation
Gilles Humbert

AMERICAN STAFF

Project Editor
Joseph Gonzalez

Project Art Editor
Virginia Wells Blaker

Senior Editor
Don Earnest

Editor
Carolyn Chubet

Senior Associate Editors
Theresa Lane
Nancy Shuker

Associate Editor
Tracy O'Shea

Research Associate
Willard Lubka

Art Associates
Ed Jacobus
Tomaso Milian
Jason L. Peterson
Bob Steimle, Jr., illustrator

Art Reference Photography
James McInnis

Editorial Assistant
Dolores Damm

Assistant Production Supervisor
Michael Gallo

Quality Control Manager
Ann Kennedy Harris

CONTRIBUTORS

Project Manager
Mark Feirer

Editor
Roy Barnhart

Designers
Ed Johnston
Lynn Yost
Elizabeth Tunnicliffe

Production Assistant
Tery Montalvo

Photographers
Stephen Mays, chief
Andres Palomino, art reference

Copy Editor
Katherine G. Ness

Indexer
Northwind Editorial Services

Writers
Don Best
Jeff Carroll
Fiona Gilsenan
Wade Hoyt
Melanie Hulse
Barbara H. Jacksier
Stephanie Bernardo Johns
Wendy B. Murphy
Matthew Phair
Gerry Schremp
Laura Tringali
John Warde
Charles Wardell

Illustrators
Sylvia Bokor
Steve Ferris
Todd Ferris
Mario Ferro
Tom Moore
Jacques Perrault
Ray Skibinski
Eric Starstrom
Bob Steimle, Sr.
Ian Worpole

CONSULTANTS

Evan A. Powell, chief
Arthur Arrigo
Charles W. Avoles
Steve Beatty
Malinda H. Bell, M.D.
James M. Benton
Janet Brady
Timothy D. Brown
Rick Carp
Philip Chaitman
Phillip Costikyan
Michael J. Dale
George Daniti
Buddy Dinan
Anthony L. DiVietri
Sal Dulcamaro, CML
Phil Englander

Richard J. Finnen
Jonathan Mark Gershen
Ira Gladstone
Leon R. Greenman
Mustafa Hacili
Gene and Katie Hamilton
Margaret Hamos
Jeffrey Hirsch
Fred H. Hull, Jr.
George Kaye
Jack S. Land
R. Thaddeus Lech
Tom Lloyd
Harvey B. Loomis
Jim McCann
Arthur McCracken
Frank Micela

Carl Miller, Jr.
Rob M. Muessel
Robert A. Nelson
Alec Nesbitt
Susan Perry
Marvin Rosen
Michael J. Roviello
Mark S. Russo
Nathan Shasho
Stanley H. Smith, Ph.D.
Bruce Solomon
Jim Tagliavia
Joseph Todd
Paul Weissler
Thomas L. Zera, CSP

The acknowledgments that appear on page 448 are hereby made a part of this copyright page.

Canadian Cataloguing in Publication Data

Main entry under title:

New fix-it-yourself manual

2nd ed.
ISBN 0-88850-535-3

1. Do-it-yourself work.   2. Dwellings–Maintenance and repair–Amateurs' manuals.   I. Reader's Digest Association (Canada).

TT151.N45 1996   643'.7   C96-900161-4

Printed in the United States of America

Address any comments about New Fix-it-yourself Manual to Project Editor, Book and Home Entertainment Department, Reader's Digest, 215 Redfern, Westmount, Quebec H3Z 2V9.

To order additional copies of New Fix-it-yourself Manual, call 1-800-465-0780.

Warning
All do-it-yourself activities involve a degree of risk. Skills, materials, tools, and site conditions vary widely. Although the editors have made every effort to ensure accuracy, the reader remains responsible for the selection and use of tools and methods. Always obey local codes and laws, follow manufacturers' operating instructions, and observe safety precautions.

About this book

With so much stuff in a typical household, sooner or later something will break, leak, sputter, or stop. If you've ever waited for the repairman to show up (or just tried to locate one), lost sleep worrying if the drain's gurgle foretold a flood, or groaned at a great, whopping surprise of a repair bill, you'll find this book invaluable. Millions of readers have relied on earlier versions for help in fixing everything from table legs to toasters. So what's "new" in the NEW FIX-IT-YOURSELF MANUAL? Everything.

Under guidance from a team of consultants, each one an expert in his or her field, the editors have replaced every photo, drawing, and troubleshooting chart. We've added new sections and profiled the newest appliances, explained new techniques, and identified the latest materials. The text has been completely revised and updated. Despite many changes, however, the message of the NEW FIX-IT-YOURSELF MANUAL is simple: You *can* take care of your household and you *can* fix things yourself. Even if you have no intention of making your own repairs, the knowledge of what's involved may save you money when the time comes to call in a professional.

Let this book serve as your troubleshooting companion whenever things go wrong. The charts will guide you quickly from symptom to solution, and the step-by-step illustrations will show you exactly what to do. Be sure to read the special features as well. They'll give you essential safety information, tips from the pros, and a whole lot more good, useable advice.

–The Editors

Contents

Tools and techniques

The right tools often determine how successful you are in making your own repairs, whether you're steadying a wobbly table, rewiring a toaster, or winterizing an outboard motor. Good tools, employed properly, can spell the difference between enjoying a fix-it job and feeling all thumbs. Look over the basic tool kit and the explanations of specialized tools on the following pages (pay particular attention to techniques for using the tools). Cutting and shaping tools have to be sharp to be effective; how to hone different types of edges is explained step-by-step. Finally, the dilemma of which fastener or adhesive to choose in a given situation is addressed in three pages of clear, comprehensive charts.

Tools and techniques ▪ The basic tool kit

A set of good-quality tools can simplify home repair jobs and help you handle emergencies with confidence. The tools shown here cover the general needs of most households. More specialized tools and materials are discussed in later chapters: woodworking tools (p.56), upholstery tools (p.97), plumbing tools (pp.108 and 120), appliance repair tools (p.124), and electronics repair tools (p.300). See also *Adhesives,* pp.18–20, and *Tapes,* p.20.

Buy tools as you need them rather than in a kit of dubious quality. Well-crafted tools are easier and safer to use than bargain ones, and they make the work go faster. Expensive tools that you're unlikely to need on a regular basis can usually be rented.

Properly cared for, top-quality tools can last a lifetime. Store them in a dry place (if your basement is damp, consider using an upstairs closet). Keep your tools clean and, where appropriate, oiled and sharp. Protect the edges of cutting tools with sheaths rather than storing them unprotected in a tool chest where other tools can nick the blades.

FOR YOUR SAFETY

Always use appropriate safety gear—dust mask, ear protectors, gloves, and goggles—when you work. Keep a fire extinguisher and a flashlight handy. Hang a safety light over your work to free your hands. Always plug power tools into a ground fault circuit interrupter receptacle (p.128), and if you must use an extension cord, make it a heavy-duty one.

Dust mask   Work gloves   Safety goggles

Ear protectors   Safety light   Fire extinguisher

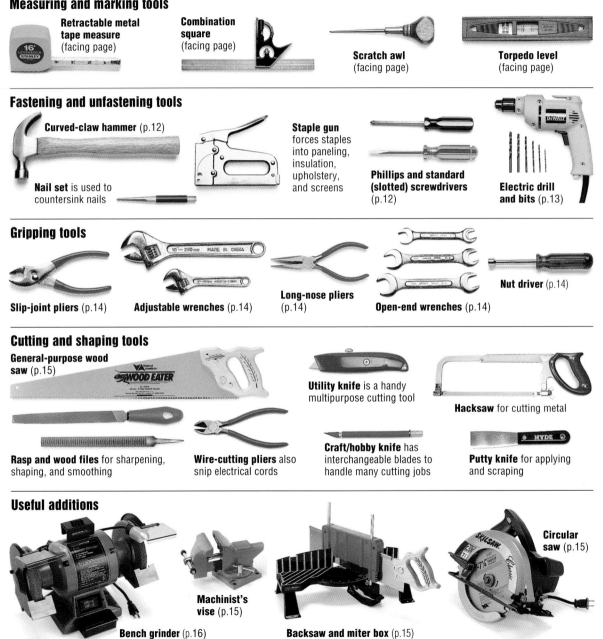

Measuring and marking tools

Retractable metal tape measure (facing page)

Combination square (facing page)

Scratch awl (facing page)

Torpedo level (facing page)

Fastening and unfastening tools

Curved-claw hammer (p.12)

Staple gun forces staples into paneling, insulation, upholstery, and screws

Nail set is used to countersink nails

Phillips and standard (slotted) screwdrivers (p.12)

Electric drill and bits (p.13)

Gripping tools

Slip-joint pliers (p.14)

Adjustable wrenches (p.14)

Long-nose pliers (p.14)

Open-end wrenches (p.14)

Nut driver (p.14)

Cutting and shaping tools

General-purpose wood saw (p.15)

Utility knife is a handy multipurpose cutting tool

Hacksaw for cutting metal

Rasp and wood files for sharpening, shaping, and smoothing

Wire-cutting pliers also snip electrical cords

Craft/hobby knife has interchangeable blades to handle many cutting jobs

Putty knife for applying and scraping

Useful additions

Bench grinder (p.16)

Machinist's vise (p.15)

Backsaw and miter box (p.15)

Circular saw (p.15)

Measuring and marking

Accurate measuring and marking are essential to the success of many home projects, from hanging a picture to replacing a length of pipe. Precisely measured parts fit together easily and smoothly. Badly measured parts require fudging and may never make a workable union. The old carpenter's adage "Measure twice and cut once" applies to all types of repairs. Learn to take accurate measurements, and make it a habit to use the same measuring tools throughout any project you undertake. The calibration of two seemingly identical measuring tools can be off by up to ⅛ inch, enough to adversely affect even simple repairs.

Steel tape

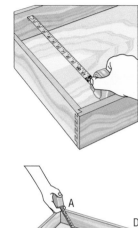

To measure an internal dimension, brace tape hook against one side and tape case against the other. Add length of case (marked on its exterior) to reading on tape.

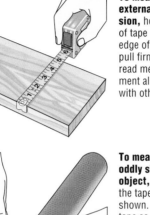

To measure an external dimension, hook end of tape over one edge of object, pull firmly, and read measurement aligned with other edge.

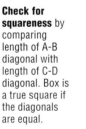

Check for squareness by comparing length of A-B diagonal with length of C-D diagonal. Box is a true square if the diagonals are equal.

To measure any oddly shaped object, overlap the tape as shown. Read the tape as it aligns with the 2-in. mark. Then subtract 2 in. from the reading.

Using a torpedo level

Level vial

Plumb vial

To see if a surface is level, rest a level on it; level bubble should be centered. To test a vertical surface for plumb, hold level beside it; plumb bubble should be centered.

Using an awl

Mark a cut line on metal pipe with an awl supported at correct height on a block of wood. Turn pipe against point of awl. Coloring pipe first with felt marker makes line clearer.

Using a combination square

Outside square — Miter square

Horizontal level

90°

45°

Inside square

Plumb level

Depth gauge

Ruler

Marking gauge

Eight tools in one, a combination square includes a ruler, 45° and 90° angles, and a level. Its many faces—plumb level, marking gauge, depth gauge, horizontal level, ruler, inside square, outside square, and miter square—are shown in use.

TIPS FROM THE PROS

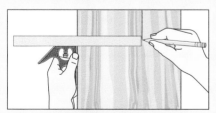

To quickly draw a line parallel to an edge, set blade of a combination square to desired width. Hold flat side of square to edge of surface and hold a pencil to end of blade. Pull the square and the pencil down the surface simultaneously to create the parallel line.

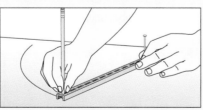

To draw a circle, use shelving standard (or a rule with holes) as a compass. Drive a nail through slot at one end of standard into workpiece at center of circle. Put a pencil through a second slot so that distance between nail and pencil equals desired radius. Scribe circle.

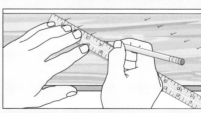

To divide a board lengthwise into equal strips, tilt a ruler across it until you get a measurement that is easily divided by the number of strips you want. To divide a 7-inch board into 5 equal strips, for example, tilt the ruler until it reads 0 at one end and 10 inches at the other.

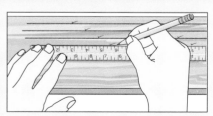

Since 10 divided by 5 is 2, mark off 2-inch increments along the tilted ruler onto the board. Move the ruler down the board a few inches and repeat the same exercise. Connect the marks to create the parallel cutting lines for 5 equal strips of wood.

Tools and techniques ▪ Hammers and screwdrivers

Both hammers and screwdrivers come in a variety of shapes and sizes to handle diverse jobs. For general maintenance and repairs, a 16-ounce curved-claw hammer is a good choice. Heavier hammers are for construction work; lighter, specialized hammers, for delicate jobs. A good hammer has a cleanly finished head of drop-forged steel and a comfortable tightly fitted or one-piece solid handle. Although hammering (below) appears to jeopardize only fingers, wear goggles; a miss-hit can send a nail flying.

A good screwdriver has a comfortable nonslip handle and a crisply machined blade tip. Start with large and small Phillips and standard models (bottom, left); add others as they are needed. Most screws require pilot holes for starting. Use an awl to make pilot holes in wood for screws up to ¾ inch long and No.6 gauge; for larger screws and for making pilot holes in masonry, use a drill.

Turn awl to make a pilot hole.

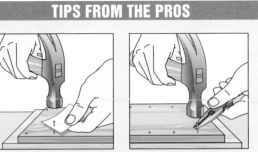

Hammering basics

Grip hammer near end, lightly but firmly. Keeping wrist straight, let hammer fall naturally, aided by shoulder and upper arm.

Use nail set to conceal nailheads. Hammer nail to within ⅛ in. of surface; countersink head with nail set; then fill hole with putty.

Pull nails with claw hammer by placing scrap block under hammerhead. Block protects wood and increases leverage.

Screwdrivers

Standard blade fits slotted screws. Tip should be smooth, not nicked.

Phillips blade has blunt tip; screw slots curve where they intersect.

Torx blade has star-shaped tip for screws in appliances and garden equipment.

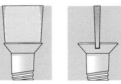

Square-drive, or Robertson, blade will not slip despite strong twisting.

Tip is too wide and too thick.

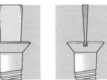

Tip is too narrow and too thin.

Tip fits properly.

Finding the right-size screwdriver. Blade should be same width as screwhead and should fit slot snugly. If too large, blade may not fit slot and can damage surrounding surface; if too small, blade may slip and damage slot. The best blade for wood screws has parallel sides.

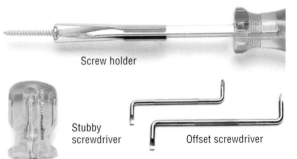

Screw holder

Stubby screwdriver

Offset screwdriver

Special screwdrivers make it easier to install screws in awkward places. Use a stubby or an offset screwdriver where space is limited. Screw holder grips screws for starting in deep, inaccessible holes. It also lets you start a screw one-handed.

Using an electric drill

An electric drill is easier to use than a hand drill, even for a beginner. While its primary purpose is boring holes, a power drill can also drive screws, sand and polish surfaces, remove rust, and strip paint.

The most versatile electric drill for general use is a variable-speed reversible drill with a chuck (jaw) capacity of ⅜ inch. Other standard chuck sizes are ¼ inch, suitable for light-duty work, and ½ inch, strong enough for heavy jobs like drilling in masonry and making large holes. Plug-in drills are more powerful than comparably priced cordless models; but if convenience and portability are important, consider buying a cordless drill.

The essential drill accessories are twist bits in assorted sizes. Buy additional bits and other accessories as needed. While twist bits are versatile, some jobs require specialized bits for best results.

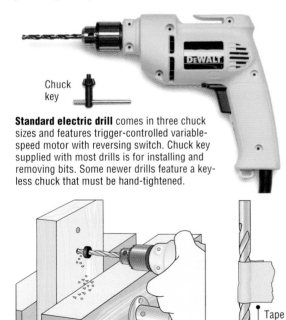

Standard electric drill comes in three chuck sizes and features trigger-controlled variable-speed motor with reversing switch. Chuck key supplied with most drills is for installing and removing bits. Some newer drills feature a keyless chuck that must be hand-tightened.

Depth stop accessory prevents drilling holes too deep. Improvise a stop by wrapping bit with masking tape at desired depth. Free ends of tape wipe dust from surface as proper depth is reached.

Picking the right drill bit

Twist bit. Best all-purpose bit. Choose high-speed steel variety; lubricate when drilling metal.

Screw pilot bit. Use with twist bit to bore pilot holes for wood screws. Diameter matches screwhead and shank.

Brad-point bit. Best choice for wood. Center point keeps bit from wandering; wide flutes clear hole of chips.

Spear-point bit. For drilling glass and ceramic tile. Use low drill speed; flood hole constantly with turpentine.

Masonry bit. Bores easily into brick, concrete, slate, and plaster. Use low drill speed (under 400 rpm).

Spade bit. Use for drilling large holes in wood. Back up work with scrap to avoid splintering; if possible, drill wood from both sides.

Accessories

Flexible shaft separates bit and drill. Permits drilling in cramped places; also makes bit manageable for intricate work like carving.

Clutch allows you to drive screws to preset depths with standard electric drill. Speeds repetitive tasks like installing drywall.

Drum sander smooths concave surfaces. Core is hard rubber; replaceable abrasive sleeves come in all grits.

Disc sander smooths flat surfaces. Replaceable abrasive discs attach to hard rubber core.

Right-angle drive allows drilling in narrow confines.

Wire brush quickly removes rust and paint from metal surfaces. Comes in several sizes.

Buffer pad of lamb's wool polishes finished surfaces including furniture, metalwork, jewelry, and shoes.

Screwdriver attachment fits over drill chuck and lets you change bits quickly. The bits come in standard screwdriver blade shapes (facing page).

Hole saw, mounted on a hole saw arbor with a bit to find the center, cuts holes for pipes and ducts in wood, metal, and masonry.

Rotary files and rasps, often attached to flexible shaft (above, left), facilitate carving and shaping in many materials.

Bit extender increases length of ordinary bit, allowing you to bore deep holes and to make holes in hard-to-reach places.

Electric sharpener for drill bits

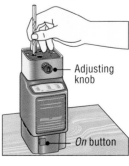

Adjusting knob

On button

To use a bit sharpener, set adjusting knob straight up; insert bit into the hole that best fits it. Twist the bit clockwise until it stops. Pressing down on the bit slightly, engage *On* button for 1 to 3 seconds. Withdraw bit, rotate it 180°, and repeat.

Tools and techniques ▪ Pliers and wrenches

Types of pliers

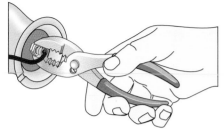

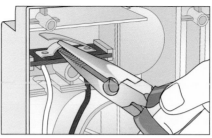

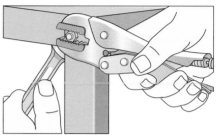

Slip-joint pliers adjust to two or more positions to accommodate different-size work. Combination jaws grip flat or curved objects. Some models include a crimper.

Groove-joint, or channel-type, pliers can grip larger objects than slip-joint pliers, and their long handles give better leverage. They are also less likely to slip as you squeeze the handles.

Long-nose pliers are used to bend wire, handle small parts, and reach into tight spaces. Similar to long-nose pliers but smaller, needle-nose pliers are also handy for eyeglass and jewelry repair.

Locking pliers serve as pliers or as a clamp, vise, or wrench. Place jaws around object, turn adjusting knob, and close handles until they lock. To unclamp, use release lever to open handles.

Wrenches

Wrenches provide the leverage necessary to tighten and loosen nuts, bolts, and pipe joints. Be sure to match the jaw's shape to that of the work. A wrench that is too big or the wrong shape can ruin a fastener. Fixed wrenches—open-end, box-end, hex, and nut drivers—come in both standard and metric sizes corresponding to specific nut and bolt sizes. Open-end wrenches (see *Tips from the pros,* right) come with offset jaws to facilitate working in tight spots.

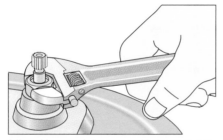

Adjustable wrench fits nuts and bolts up to maximum opening of its jaws. Worm gear adjusts size of jaw opening. When possible, turn wrench so that load is applied to fixed jaw, which is stronger than movable jaw.

Box wrench surrounds a nut or bolt, applying pressure to all corners (open-end wrenches bear on only two corners). A 6-point or 12-point wrench bears against all faces of a hexagonal fastener; an 8-point wrench fits square nuts and bolts.

TIPS FROM THE PROS

To use an open-end wrench in a narrow space, take advantage of the slight offset angle of the head and proceed as follows:

1 Slip open end of wrench onto the bolt at the best possible angle from the right-hand side.

2 Rotate the bolt until the wrench hits the obstruction on the left. Remove the wrench.

3 Turn the wrench over and slip it onto the bolt again at the best angle from the right.

4 Rotate wrench to left again, remove it, and repeat sequence until bolt is loose.

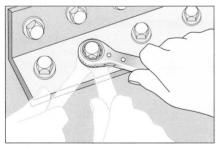

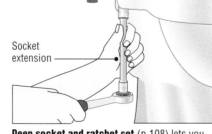

Ratchet box wrench lets you turn a fastener without constantly lifting and replacing wrench. To use it, fit head over fastener and turn tool. When turning is blocked, pull wrench in opposite direction; head will remain in position.

Both ends of a hex, or Allen, wrench fit hexagonal recess in head of hex screws (setscrews).

Nut driver has a screwdriver handle and socket end for turning hexagonal nuts and bolts.

Socket extension

Deep socket and ratchet set (p.108) lets you create a wrench to fit a particular job. Sockets can be driven by a ratcheting or a nut-driver handle. Socket extension makes it easier to reach nuts and bolts in recessed or tight spots.

Vises and saws

Types of vises

When you're cutting or shaping a workpiece with sharp tools, the success of the project—and your safety—depend on the piece not moving. A vise that attaches to a bench holds a workpiece steady for sawing and planing. The most common types of vises are shown below. For a discussion of clamps and clamping, see pages 59–61. Be sure to match the vise to the workpiece and to protect the latter by inserting a soft jaw face between it and the vise.

Machinist's vise is permanently bolted to workbench for metalworking. Some models include a small anvil and a lockable swivel base. The jaws of a woodworker's vise have holes for attaching protective wood faces.

Machinist's vise

Woodworker's vise

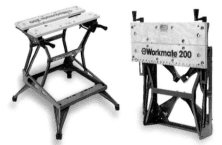

Bench-size vise combines the functions of a small workbench, a vise, a clamp, and a sawhorse. As an added convenience, it folds flat for easy storage in a closet.

Saws and sawing

Sawing wood involves cutting along the grain (ripping), across the grain (crosscutting), or at an angle to it (miter or bevel cutting). A ripsaw's teeth are designed like tiny chisels to cut along the grain; the standard blade is 26 inches long and has 4 to 7 teeth per inch. A crosscut saw has knifelike teeth designed to slice through wood fibers; its standard 26-inch blade has 7 to 12 tpi. A general-purpose saw (9 tpi) makes rough crosscuts and slow rips, but it's a good choice if you want only one saw.

To prevent binding, saw teeth are set (bent) alternately left and right so that the kerf (channel) that the saw creates as it cuts is wider than the blade. The best saw blades are made of flexible tempered or stainless steel and give a clear ringing sound when tapped.

Other saws. A backsaw is a crosscut saw with a squared-end blade (8 to 14 inches long, 11 to 14 tpi) and a stiffened rib along its back. It is often used in a miter box to cut miters and other joints. The usual metal-cutting handsaw is a hacksaw with several blades to cut different metals. If you do a lot of sawing, consider buying a circular power saw. Its interchangeable blades allow you to rip and crosscut wood and to cut metal. **CAUTION:** Use goggles and ear protection when power-sawing. Keep clothes and hands away from the blade. Unplug the saw before adjusting positions or changing blades.

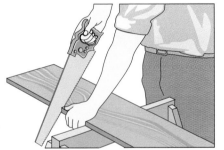

To crosscut with a handsaw, mark cut line on good side of work. Place saw on waste side of cut line; pull saw toward you to mark kerf in waste. Hold blade at a 45° angle to board as you draw saw back with a few short pulls.

Miter box holds backsaw in the right position to make angled cuts, often in molding. Box shown here has angle gauge and guides to lock saw at various angles. Wooden miter box with only 90° and 45° angle guides is less accurate.

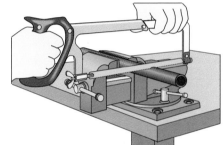

To cut metal pipe with a hacksaw, secure it in a machinist's vise (or use a miter box as on page 121). Pick blade with right tooth size for thickness of work (blade should have three teeth touching edge of metal). Hold saw with both hands.

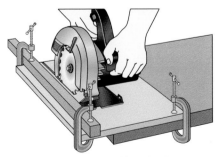

To make a clean rip cut with a circular saw, mark cut line on back of work and clamp work face down over scrap of wood. Run baseplate of saw against 2 x 4 straightedge clamped to work (not to waste side). Hold saw with both hands.

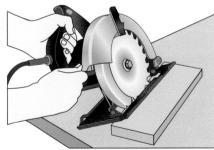

To adjust depth of cut on a circular saw, unplug saw and loosen knob holding motor in place. Move motor in an arc as shown (or up and down, depending on model) to match desired number on saw's depth-of-cut scale.

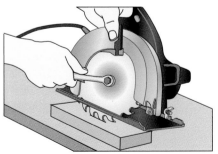

To change a circular saw blade, unplug saw and pull back blade guard, pushing teeth into scrap wood. Loosen locknut and remove old blade. Install new blade with teeth facing up; retighten locknut.

Make your tools safer and more efficient by sharpening them regularly with a stone or an electric bench grinder. Buy a combination stone with a fine grit on one side and a medium grit on the other; use a medium-grit wheel on a bench grinder. Coarse grits are used to repair knicks in damaged blades.

Sharpening techniques. The first step in sharpening most tools is to create a flat bevel on the edge of the blade with a medium-grit sharpening stone. Honing on finer and finer grits increases the blade's sharpness. At each grit, you must remove the metal burr created as you hone. Finish sharpening by stropping the tool edge in one direction on an extra-fine-grit stone or on a piece of leather wiped with polishing compound.

The bench grinder. Hollow-grinding a blade on a grinder creates a concave bevel, which is often preferred for chisels and planes. To hollow-grind a blade, set the grinder's tool rest at a 25° angle and hold the blade to the wheel briefly. Use a flat fine-grit stone to further hone a hollow-ground blade (below, right).

Before mounting a grinding wheel, follow the manufacturer's testing directions or suspend the wheel on a rod and strike it with a piece of wood. A good wheel rings; discard one that buzzes. Hold a tool to the wheel with bare hands so you can feel the blade get warm. Cool the blade in water; too much heat can ruin the metal's temper. **CAUTION:** Wear safety goggles when you work at a bench grinder; the grinder's shields do not offer enough protection. Metal wheel guards protect you in case a rapidly spinning wheel should shatter; never remove the guards.

Using a bench grinder to shape a tool

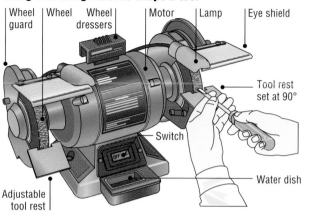

Wheel guard | Wheel | Wheel dressers | Motor | Lamp | Eye shield
Tool rest set at 90°
Switch
OFF
Water dish
Adjustable tool rest

To restore a rounded screwdriver tip with a bench grinder, use a medium-grit wheel and set tool rest at 90°. Hold screwdriver shaft with both hands as shown, and slide tip from side to side against wheel. Remove burr with a single stroke at each end of tip. If tip is now too broad, grind each of its side edges equally. Never grind flat surfaces of screwdriver shaft.

Preparing the stone

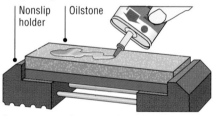

Nonslip holder | Oilstone

To prepare an oilstone, apply a little light machine oil to it. Soak a waterstone in water. To make sharpening easier, place stone in a nonslip holder.

Sharpening a curved blade

Slipstone

To sharpen a gouge or other curved blade, rotate outside edge against a stationary stone (left). Use a slipstone to remove burr (right).

Sharpening a chisel or plane blade

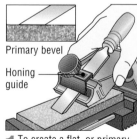

Primary bevel
Honing guide

1 To create a flat, or primary, bevel, set honing guide (or firmly hold blade) so that blade touches medium-grit stone at a 25° angle. Push blade down length of stone several times.

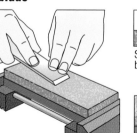

2 To remove resulting burr, turn over blade and push it once down stone. To further hone blade, repeat Step 1 using fine-grit stone. Remove burr.

Secondary bevel
30° angle

Secondary bevel strengthens blade edge. To create bevel, set up blade as in Step 1 but at a 30° angle on fine-grit stone. Push blade in one direction a few times. Deburr and strop.

Choose fasteners to suit the materials you want to join and the pressures the joint may be subjected to. Replacement fasteners should match the originals in type and strength but may need to be larger in size.

Nails are normally used in permanent joints where the pull-apart pressure is low. Common and finishing nails are the most widely used; other types have special applications (facing page). A nail's length and shaft diameter are described by its penny weight. Common nails come in sizes from 1 inch (2 penny or 2d) to 6 inches (60d).

Size | 2d 3d 4d 5d 6d 7d 8d 9d 10d 12d 16d | 20d | 30d | 40d | 50d 60d

CAUTION: Always wear safety goggles when driving nails. Hardened nails can splinter. Miss-hits can fly into your face.

Screws. In joints where a stronger bond is needed, use screws. When buying screws, specify the length in inches and the diameter by gauge number (diameters larger than ¼ inch are expressed in inches).

16 gauge

Bolts, nuts, and washers combine to create the strongest bonds. They also let you disassemble the piece without damaging it. Machine and stove bolts are used with metals, carriage bolts with metals and wood. A bolt's size is described by three numbers: diameter (in fractions of an inch), pitch (threads per inch), and length (in inches).

Special-use fasteners include hooks and eyes, staples, glazier's points, corrugated and pronged joiners, anchors, Molly bolts, and toggle bolts.

Nails

Common nails are for general heavy-duty use in rough wood-frame construction.

Finishing nails, used on trim and cabinets, are normally sunk and concealed.

Drywall nails secure wallboard to wood with ringed or barbed shanks.

Boat nails are rust-resistant and useful for outdoor furniture and fences as well as boats.

Double-headed nails have upper heads for easy removal after temporary use.

Box nails, a lighter version of the common nail, are used in wood that splits easily.

Paneling nails, in matching colors, are used to secure wall panels to studs.

Ringed nails have ridged shanks for extra holding power in soft or medium woods.

Roofing nails, often galvanized, have wide heads to hold down asphalt shingles.

Cut nails are flat with blunt tips to prevent splitting when blind-nailing floors.

Wire nails, the smallest of the common nails, are sized by length and wire gauge.

Wire brads, which are sunk and concealed in moldings, are sized by length and gauge.

Spiral nails turn like screws when driven in. The tight grip reduces squeaks in floors.

Masonry nails are forged and hardened fasteners used in concrete and masonry.

Tacks, with square or round shafts, are used in upholstery and to hold carpet to wood.

Other fasteners

Staples and glazier's points. Staples hold fabric, insulation, and wiring; glazier's points hold glass in window frames.

Corrugated and pronged joiners, hammered straight in, strengthen wood joints on picture frames and screen doors.

Picture hangers, hooks, and eyes are used to hang mirrors, paintings, plants, cups, and decorations.

Anchors and plugs fit in holes just large enough to accommodate them. Inserting a screw makes them expand and grip.

Molly and toggle bolts have wings that open inside a hollow wall, bracing against it to hold the fastener securely.

Screws, bolts, nuts, and washers

Phillips, star, and square screw sockets are designed for power-driving. One-way screwheads are driven in easily but are hard to remove. Hex-head screws can be turned with a wrench.

Flat washers distribute pressure. Split-ring and toothed washers prevent nuts from working loose. Tighten hex or square nuts with a wrench. Wing and knurled nuts are designed for hand-gripping.

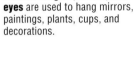

| Hex nut | Square nut | Flat square nut | Wing nut | Knurled nut |

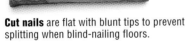

| Flat | Round | Oval | Hex | Pan | Slotted | Phillips | Square | Star | One-way | Hex |

| Flat washer | Split-ring washer | Toothed washer | Decorative washer |

Wood screws, available in many sizes, are good all-purpose wood fasteners.

Drywall screws are hard and sharp. The heads dimple wallboard to allow filling.

Sheet-metal screws fasten metal to metal or metal to wood. They require a pilot hole.

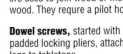

Lag bolts are heavy-duty fasteners used to join wood or metal to wood. They require a pilot hole.

Dowel screws, started with padded locking pliers, attach legs to tabletops.

Hanger bolts have wood threads on one end and accept nuts on the other.

Machine bolts have hex or square heads and take hex or square nuts.

Carriage bolts are unslotted. Shoulders sink into wood to prevent turning.

Stove bolts have flat or round slotted heads and are used to join metal pieces.

Tools and techniques ▪ Adhesives

With more and more specialized glues on the market, choosing the best adhesive for a particular project can be tricky. The chart below is designed to help you find the right adhesive for a given job.

Setting and curing time. A glue's setting time is how long it takes to harden; its curing time is how long it

takes it to reach maximum strength. Instant and other fast-setting glues are useful for bonding hard-to-clamp objects (you can hold the pieces together by hand while the glue sets). Always keep clamps on a bond for the entire setting time, and don't use any glued object until the adhesive has cured.

The water resistance of adhesives varies. Allow even waterproof adhesive bonds to cure fully before exposing them to rain or to soap and water.

Preparation. Always make sure that surfaces to be bonded are completely clean. Wood should be free of paint, varnish, and wax, as well as dirt.

Apply glue from a squeeze bottle to the bonding surface in a zigzag pattern. Brush on thicker glues or spread them with a putty knife.

To apply hot glue, plug in gun; wait 5 min. for glue stick to melt. Dot surfaces to be bonded with glue. Press pieces together; wipe off excess.

A caulk gun delivers urethane and other glues packaged in caulk-gun tubes. Pressure on the trigger keeps the rope of glue flowing evenly.

Mix two-part glues according to label directions on disposable aluminum foil or wood scraps that can be discarded with the unused glue.

Adhesives

TYPE		SAMPLE BRAND NAMES	USES AND PROPERTIES	MIXING AND APPLICATION	CURING AND SETTING	REMOVAL AND CLEANUP
Acrylic		Acrylic Latex Sealant, Devcon Plastic Welder, 3 Ton Adhesive	For wood (outdoor furniture), metal, glass. Waterproof, rigid, strong.	Most brands come in a mixing dispenser. With liquid-and-paste types, apply liquid to one surface, paste to the other.	Sets in about 5 min.; cures overnight.	Acetone (the main ingredient in some brands of nail polish remover)
Aliphatic resin (yellow glue)		Elmer's Carpenter's, Titebond	For cabinetwork, furniture making, furniture repair (p.58). Water-resistant, rigid, strong.	Squeeze from bottle directly onto both surfaces.	Sets in about 30 min.; cures overnight.	Warm water
Anaerobic resin (bolt-locking compound)		Perma-Lok Liquid Lock Washer, Scotch-Weld Epoxy Adhesive, Pronto Instant Bond	For locking threads of bolts and screws. Hardens in absence of air between tight-fitting metal parts.	Squeeze from tube or use bottle applicator.	Sets in 15 min.; usually cures overnight (longer for steel-to-steel bonds).	Soap and water before glue hardens
Cellulose		Ambroid, Duco Cement, LePage's China Weld	For bonding wood, china, cloth, glass, and some plastics (if a drop of cement etches a plastic surface, cement will likely bond that plastic).	Apply directly from tube, or from can with wood strip. For increased strength, apply 2 coats to each surface, allowing first to get tacky before adding second.	Sets to 60% of strength in 2 hr.; cures to 90% of strength in 2 days.	Acetone (the main ingredient in some brands of nail polish remover)
Construction mastic		LePage's Tile & Tub, Scotch-Grip Industrial Mastic, Poly Fix	For bonding ceiling, wall, and floor tiles, plywood panels, concrete, asphalt, leather, fabric.	Apply directly from tube, or from can with stick or notched trowel.	Sets in 5 to 15 min.; cures in 24 hr.	Usually mineral spirits or turpentine. Consult product label.
Contact cement		Elmer's Premium Contact Cement, LePage's Household Cement, Pres-Tite Contact Cement	For bonding plastic to countertops and veneers to cabinets; also works with rubber, glass, metal, and leather (e.g., shoe soles to tops). Waterproof.	Apply with disposable brush or roller to both surfaces. Let stand 15 min. or until dry before joining surfaces.	Sets instantly; cures in minutes.	Acetone (the main ingredient in some brands of nail polish remover)

TYPE	SAMPLE BRAND NAMES	USES AND PROPERTIES	MIXING AND APPLICATION	CURING AND SETTING	REMOVAL AND CLEANUP
Cyanoacrylate (super glue)	Hot Stuff, InstaBond Super Glue, Krazy Glue, Wonder Bond Plus	Liquid form for plastic, metal, rubber, and nonporous ceramics; gel form for porous materials like wood and leather. Water-resistant, rigid, very strong.	Apply a drop or two directly from tube. **CAUTION:** Wear rubber gloves to keep fingers from bonding to each other. Never point tube toward your face.	Sets in 10 to 30 sec.; cures in 30 min. to 12 hr.	Acetone (the main ingredient in some brands of nail polish remover) or special solvent
Epoxy	Cold Cure Poxy, Elmer's Expoxy Glue, 5 Minute Expoxy Glue, Scotch-Weld Adhesive, Super-Fast Epoxy	For most materials (glass, metal, wood, plastic) and for bonding two dissimilar materials such as metal to wood or plastic to glass. Waterproof, rigid, very strong.	Mix equal amounts of liquid or putty immediately before using. Wear gloves and use disposable applicator, such as a toothpick or wood paddle.	Sets in 5 min. to overnight; cures in 3 hr. to several days.	Soap and water before curing; otherwise, acetone (the main ingredient in some brands of nail polish remover)
Hide glue	Behlen Pearl Hide Glue, flake and granular forms carry retailer's name	For repairing furniture originally assembled with hide glue, including many antiques.	Apply liquid directly. Soak flakes in warm water until smooth; heat in double boiler to 130°F. Apply hot mixture with brush.	Sets in 15 to 30 min.; cures in 24 hr.	Warm water
Hot melt	Thermogrip Hot Melt, 3M Jet Melt	For fast repairs of leather and fabrics. Fills gaps in loose joints on furniture. Waterproof but weak.	Apply with glue gun (see facing page).	Sets as soon as cool; cures in minutes.	Acetone (the main ingredient in some brands of nail polish remover)
Latex-base	Elmer's SAFG-T, Multi-Purpose Latex Adhesive, Scotch-Grip Plastic Adhesive	For bonding fabric, carpet, paper, and cardboard. Water-resistant, flexible, but weak; not effective at freezing or lower temperatures.	Apply to both surfaces directly from tube, or from can with brush or wood strip.	Sets instantly; cures in 5 to 15 min.	Lighter fluid
Liquid solder	LePage's Liquid Solder, Liquid Steel, Scotch-Seal Sealant, Plastic Steel	For bonding metals as well as wood and concrete. (*Note:* Not for making electrical connections.) Water-resistant, moderately flexible, strong.	Apply directly from tube, or from can with wood paddle.	Sets in 15 to 30 min.; cures in 12 to 24 hr.	Acetone (the main ingredient in some brands of nail polish remover)
Polyester	Fiberglass Resin, Scotch-Seal Marine Adhesive	Used with matting and roving to repair fiberglass boats and to patch fiberglass sinks and porch roofs. Waterproof, rigid.	Mix with activator according to directions, and apply with brush or stick.	Consult label.	Acetone (the main ingredient in some brands of nail polish remover)
Polyvinyl acetate (PVA, white glue)	Elmer's Glue-All, GF Glue, LePage's Bondfast, LePage's Supergrip	For general interior use on wood, ceramics, and paper. Water-soluble, rigid, strong.	For small jobs, use bottle applicator; for larger jobs, use a brush.	Sets in 8 hr.; cures in 24 hr.	Soap and warm water
Polyvinyl chloride (PVC)	Scotch Super Strength Adhesive	For quick repairs of china, marble, porcelain, glass, wood, metal.	Apply directly from tube or use a wood paddle.	Sets in minutes; cures in 24 hr.	Acetone (the main ingredient in some brands of nail polish remover)
Resorcinol	Scotch-Grip Plastic Adhesive, Weldwood Waterproof Glue	For strong repairs of wood indoors and outdoors (patio furniture and boats, for example). Waterproof, rigid, strong.	Mix needed amount of liquid and powder just before use. Wear gloves and apply with brush or roller. Clean joints before glue sets; it leaves a dark glue line.	Sets and cures in about 10 hr. at room temperature, faster if warmer.	Cool water before glue hardens; difficult to remove afterward
Styrene butadiene (rubber-base cement)	LePage's Butyl Sealant Caulk, Weather Ban Butyl Sealant	For bonding metal, glass, leather, rubber, and many plastics. Waterproof, flexible, strong.	Apply directly from tube for small jobs; for larger jobs use spatula, putty knife, or trowel.	Sets and cures in 1 to 2 days.	Peel or rub (from hands, for example) or scrape off with a knife

continued

Tools and techniques ▪ Adhesives

Adhesives

TYPE		SAMPLE BRAND NAMES	USES AND PROPERTIES	MIXING AND APPLICATION	CURING AND SETTING	REMOVAL AND CLEANUP
Urea formaldehyde (plastic resin)		Aerolite 306, LePage's Panite Plastic Resin Glue	For very strong bonding in furniture and cabinetry repair. Water-resistant, rigid, strong.	Mix with water just before use. Apply with brush, roller, or spatula.	Sets in 9 to 13 hr.; cures in 24 hr.	Soap and warm water before glue hardens
Urethane-silicone		Dow Corning Urethane Bond, Elmer's Stix-All	For strong but flexible joints between pieces of wood or between wood and metal or glass. Waterproof, flexible.	Apply directly from small tube; with larger tubes, use a caulk gun (p.18).	Starts setting in 20 min.; cures in 3 days.	Alcohol before glue hardens

Tapes

TYPE		DESCRIPTION	USES	APPLICATION
Anti-slip tape		Heavy weatherproof plastic with rough-textured surface on top and strong adhesive on bottom.	For improving footing in bathtubs and showers, and on steps, skateboards, and ladders.	Remove backing and apply to clean dry surface.
Carpet tape		Plastic or cloth with moderately strong adhesive on both sides. Also made in waterproof version for outdoor use.	For bonding carpets and rugs to floors and patios.	Apply to clean dry floor first; then remove backing and press carpet or rug to top side.
Cloth tape		Coated cloth with moderately strong adhesive on one side. Available in many colors.	For repairing books, albums, plastic upholstery, and other household items. Also used to color-code items.	Hold edges of tear together and apply.
Duct tape		Strong silver-colored, plastic-coated cloth with moderately strong adhesive on one side. Resistant to moisture, heat, and cold.	For sealing joints in ductwork and for temporary patching of many items from camping equipment to cracked glass. *Note:* Flue tape (see below) is more heat-resistant than duct tape and should be used on hot-air ducts near the furnace.	Apply to clean dry surface.
Electrical tape		Thin heat-resistant, stretchable vinyl with moderately strong adhesive on one side.	For temporarily insulating household electrical cords and automotive wiring and for securing wire connectors (p.124). **CAUTION:** Do not use tape alone to join electrical wires.	Carefully wrap around wires in overlapping spirals, making sure wires are insulated from each other.
Flue tape		Heat-resistant metal tape with a strong adhesive on one side.	For metal flue-pipe joints on furnaces, and for stopping leaks in hot-air ducts.	Apply to clean dry surface.
Foam mounting tape		Flexible foam-core tape with strong adhesive on both sides.	For mounting lightweight items, particularly on rough-textured surfaces like brick and concrete.	Remove backing from one side, press tape against wall; then remove backing from other side, press item against tape.
Masking tape		Beige crepe paper or white flat paper with moderately strong adhesive on one side.	For masking windows and other surfaces while painting, for holding glued pieces together while they cure, and for many other household jobs.	Apply by pressing lightly. *Note:* Buy fresh tape every year; old tape becomes extremely difficult to remove.
Metal foil tape		Heavy aluminum foil with strong adhesive on one side.	For sealing and repairing gutters, ducts, and aluminum siding.	Apply to clean dry surface.
Plastic tape		Thin stretchable, waterproof vinyl with moderately strong adhesive on one side.	For repairing plastic upholstery and other plastic products.	Hold clean dry sides of a tear together and apply.
Reflective tape		Waterproof plastic with adhesive on one side and a reflective finish on the other that shines when hit by light.	For marking bicycles and children's and joggers' clothing so car drivers can see them at night. Can also be used to mark projecting corners and stair edges.	Apply to clean dry surface.

Around the home

With continued use and the passage of time, almost everything around the home needs attention—whether it be sharpening a knife to make it cut like new, replacing the screens in your windows, or installing a new doorbell. Drawing on many basic skills, including sewing, gluing, and nailing, this chapter provides practical, lasting solutions to the myriad problems that can crop up. You'll learn, for instance, how to mend a favorite toy, refasten loose wall-to-wall carpeting, salvage a broken bracelet, fix a door lock, extend the life of your luggage, and rewire a lamp. By using the clear step-by-step instructions on the following pages, you'll get the satisfaction of fixing something yourself and save the expense of hiring someone else.

Carpet care

Keeping a carpet clean is essential to prolonging its life and maintaining its appearance. Depending on how much traffic a carpet bears, vacuum it as often as several times a week; shampoo it at least once a year.

Distributing wear patterns will also help prolong a carpet's life. To do this, periodically rotate the carpet or reposition the furniture.

Direct sunlight may fade a carpet's color. If possible, keep draperies or blinds shut during peak sunlight hours.

Shampooing. To deep-clean a carpet, either hire a professional carpet cleaning service or do it yourself using supermarket spray-on carpet cleaner or a shampooing machine. Apply spray-on cleaner to the carpet one section at a time, then work it into the fibers with a damp sponge. When the cleaner dries, vacuum the residue away. Before using any cleaner, test it in a hidden area to be sure it won't affect the carpet's color (see *Use and care,* p.24).

A shampooing machine, which you can rent at a supermarket or hardware store, scrubs the pile with rotating brushes. Shampoo applied by machine cleans more effectively than sprayed-on cleaner but takes longer to dry.

Odors and stains. To deodorize a carpet, sprinkle baking soda over it, wait 30 minutes, then vacuum. For strong odors, rinse the area with a 20-80 solution of vinegar and water. When possible, clean spills immediately, blotting them with a clean white cloth instead of scrubbing them. The longer a stain sits, the harder it is to remove. For more on stain removal, see page 46.

Laying wall-to-wall carpeting

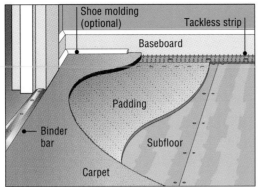

Shoe molding (optional)
Tackless strip
Baseboard
Padding
Binder bar
Subfloor
Carpet

A wall-to-wall carpet is laid over padding (underlayment), which rests on a plywood subfloor or on hardwood strips or planks that cover the subfloor. Tackless strips (wood strips with metal teeth) are nailed around room's perimeter to grip back of carpet and hold it in place. Power stretchers and knee-kickers (available for rent at carpet dealers) are used to stretch carpet and hook it onto tackless strips. Binder bars installed at doorways create a smooth edge between carpet and flooring in adjoining rooms. Shoe molding may cover the gap between carpet and baseboard.

Refastening wall-to-wall carpeting

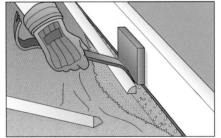

1 Gently pull shoe molding, if any, from baseboard with pry bar or putty knife. Use scrap wood to protect the baseboard. Work slowly to avoid damaging molding. As each piece is removed, mark its original location on the back.

2 Follow manufacturer's directions to set knee-kicker's teeth to correct depth. Set tool perpendicular to wall, a few inches from edge of carpet. Hold tool with one hand; thrust knee against heel of tool to reseat carpet. Repeat as needed.

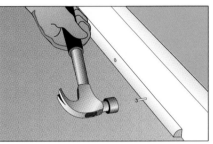

3 After carpet is firmly reseated on tackless strips, follow your markings on the back of the molding and refasten it using 1½-in. finishing nails. Cover nailheads with wood filler; sand if necessary; stain or paint if desired.

Replacing a tackless strip

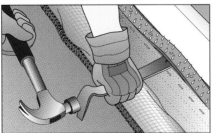

1 If tackless strip won't grip carpet, replace it. Remove molding, if any; pull back carpet. Use pry bar and hammer to lift up damaged strip.

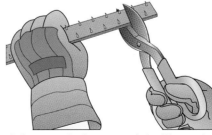

2 Buy new strips from carpet dealer. Wear work gloves and safety glasses. Cut strips with heavy shears. Place strips so teeth point toward wall.

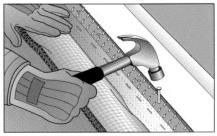

3 Use 2d ring underlay nails to fasten strips; if strips are prenailed, just tap them into place with hammer. Secure carpet with knee-kicker.

Patching a carpet

If area to be patched is near carpet perimeter, tack down carpet around damage with nails (this isn't necessary if damage is in middle of carpet). Lay a carpenter's square alongside damage and use it as a guide to cut through carpet backing with a utility knife. Lift out damaged section.

Use damaged piece as template to cut patch; be sure pile lies in same direction as surrounding carpet. If needed, fit new padding, stapling it along edges. Place strips of 2¼-in. cloth binding (sold in fabric stores) around edges of hole so half of cloth is under existing carpet and half is exposed.

Lay a bead of latex seam adhesive, available at carpet supply stores, over binding (be sure to wear gloves). Use a disposable paintbrush to spread out the adhesive so it covers all of binding, including part that lies under existing carpet. Carefully place patch in prepared opening.

Use tip of an awl or an old screwdriver to free and fluff any tufts that may be caught under patch. Blot any excess adhesive with a clean damp cloth. Weight down patch with a stack of books or another heavy object for time specified by adhesive manufacturer.

Shifting a worn stair runner

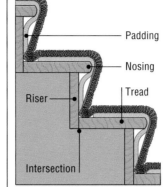

Padding

Nosing

Riser

Tread

Intersection

1 If staircase is straight, as shown, runner was probably laid as a single length. If so, the folded hem at either end can be used to shift the runner, hiding worn sections and increasing its life. If staircase curves or if steps are irregular, carpeting should be cut to fit each step.

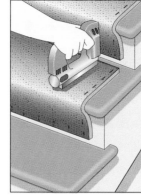

2 Remove runner, starting at top of staircase. Use a pry bar or hammer claw to lift out any tacks; if tackless strips were used, free carpeting with a rented knee-kicker. After runner is free, spread a thin bead of latex adhesive on underside of edges to prevent unraveling; let it dry thoroughly.

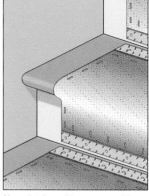

3 If padding is damaged, remove it and staple a new section on each tread. If using tacks to reattach runner, leave a ¾-in. gap between edge of padding and riser above; if using tackless strips, leave a 1½-in. gap. Butt padding to any strips that are already in place.

If you're installing new tackless strips, place one on each riser and one on each tread. Leave a ¼-in. gap between intersection of riser and tread and edge of each tackless strip. Make sure strips' teeth face each other at each intersection. If not using tackless strips, proceed to Step 4.

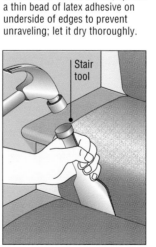

Keep tacks 1" apart

4 If hem was at top, increase it 6 to 8 in.; if at bottom, fold top under 6 to 8 in. Butt folded edge to underside of top nosing and tack it in place, working from center out. Keeping runner taut and again working from center out, tack runner to each riser and tread, ⅜ in. from riser/tread intersections.

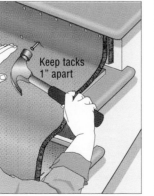

Stair tool

To stretch carpet over tackless strips, use a stair tool (a blunt chisel-like tool you can rent at a carpet store or home center). Tack down top of runner as in Step 4; then keeping carpet taut, place stair tool in the riser/tread intersection and tap it with a hammer until runner is snug.

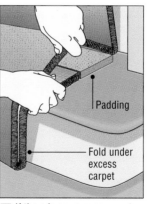

Padding

Fold under excess carpet

5 If there is any excess carpet at bottom of runner, fold it under to create a hem. Be sure that fold is straight and neat. If necessary, create a smooth, even layer on the bottom tread by cutting a piece of the padding to fit gap between the end of the excess and the riser.

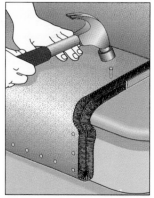

6 Tack bottom end of runner to bottom riser at 1-in. intervals, starting at center and working toward sides. Place tacks at side edges of runner halfway up bottom riser. Secure sides of runner with two evenly spaced tacks on each tread.

23

Resewing a seam or tear in a carpet

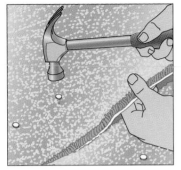

1 Pull the sides of the carpet together until they meet. To keep the carpet from gapping open again, and to avoid placing stress on the seam, hold the carpet in place by tacking it down with a few nails or tacks. Position the nails at least 6 in. away from the torn edges of the carpet.

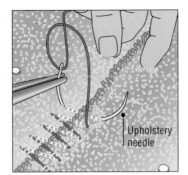

Upholstery needle

2 Using a curved upholstery needle threaded with light-weight monofilament, sew the carpet back together. Move needle through carpet backing with needle-nose pliers. Upon reaching end, double back over stitching to secure seam. Brush fibers to fluff them up and cover the repair.

Burn marks

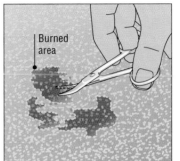

Burned area

To remove shallow burns or other stubborn disfiguring surface marks on rugs or carpets, snip off the charred or discolored fiber tips with curved manicure scissors. Cut off as little of the pile as possible. Variation in tuft height probably won't be noticed. Deep burns require a patch (p.23).

Rug repairs

Minor rug repairs can be done at home; major repairs and all repairs to valuable rugs are best left to a professional. However, if a rug frays, stitch the area to halt the damage until it can be professionally repaired.

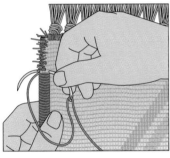

Mend a frayed edge with curved upholstery needle and heavy-duty matching thread. Start about ¼ in. away from damage; sew over edge, wrapping thread around frayed area until covered. Don't sew too close to frayed area, or you may catch loose threads with needle and increase damage.

Binding a jute carpet

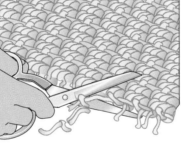

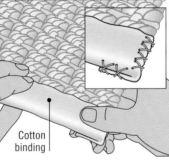

Cotton binding

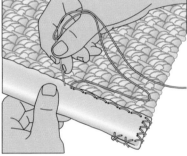

1 To keep damage from spreading, repair the fraying edge of a jute carpet as soon as possible. Trim the frayed edge with heavy-duty shears, making the cut neat and straight.

2 Cut strip of cotton binding 2 in. longer than raw edge of carpet. Fold binding evenly over raw edge of carpet. Fold one end of binding under carpet and secure it with a series of cross-stitches (inset).

3 Sew down the length of binding, penetrating through the carpet and both layers of binding. After folding the opposite end of the binding underneath the carpet, use cross-stitches to secure it.

Area rugs need regular vacuuming, periodic deep cleaning, and shampooing. Twice a year, spread the rug out upside down over an old sheet on a flat surface. With the vacuum cleaner's beater bar on its lowest setting, vacuum the back of the rug. Move the rug aside, and turn the sheet over. Replace the rug on the sheet, face up, and vacuum the pile.

Shampooing. Have a professional shampoo a valuable rug. For other rugs, use a commercial cleaner, sold at carpet stores, but first test the rug for colorfastness. Dampen a corner with water; blot it with a white towel. If color comes off, the rug should be cleaned by a professional.

Repairing a worn braided rug

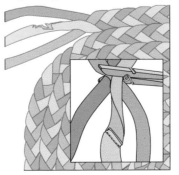

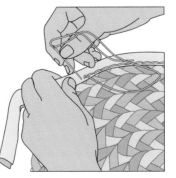

Braided rugs consist of three long strips of fabric braided together; braid is then coiled and stitched to itself. When a section wears out, pick out stitches holding coil together and unwind rug. Cut off worn portion. Undo braid and splice new strips to old on the bias, right sides facing each other (inset). Rebraid strips; then recoil braid.

Resew coil with a heavyweight needle and linen thread of a coordinating color. Make stitches small and tight. To complete repair, reinforce outer edges by attaching a strip of cotton binding tape to the perimeter. Choose tape of a complementary color. Stitch tape directly to outside of coil, again with small, tight stitches.

Cutlery, pocketknives, and scissors

Knife blades become dull as a result of repeated contact with hard cutting surfaces, such as countertops and metal or ceramic plates. A wood or plastic cutting board helps reduce dulling.

If used daily, a conventional chef's steel or an even more effective diamond steel will keep unserrated blades sharp. If an edge becomes badly dulled, however, sharpen the blade with a stone, as shown below.

The basic sharpening tool is a combination stone with a medium grit on one side and a fine grit on the other. Knives seldom require sharpening on a coarse stone. Before using a stone,

lubricate it with oil or water, depending on the type of stone; wipe it clean afterward. Sharpen on the medium-grit side, then on the fine-grit side. Press down firmly at first, less so as the edge becomes fine. Finish by lightly stropping both sides of the blade (with the edge trailing) on leather or rough cloth. For more on sharpening with a stone or with a bench grinder, see *Keeping tools sharp*, p.16.

Scissors and shears. The blades of scissors and shears are designed to break through fibers, not slice them, so their edges should not be honed smooth. Use only a coarse stone to sharpen the

blades. After sharpening, only the tips of the blades should meet and bear lightly on one another. If they don't, tighten the pivot (see below).

Electric sharpeners quickly produce a high-quality uniform edge on both knives and scissors. Many models have a magnetic device that guides the blades through the slots and holds them at the proper angle against the grinding stone.

When sharpening scissors with an electric sharpener, follow the manufacturer's directions closely; remember that left- and right-handed scissors should be sharpened at opposite angles.

Regluing a knife handle

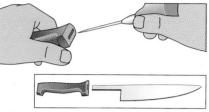

1 If the handle and blade of a knife come apart, scrape the old glue from the inside of the handle with a screwdriver or an awl.

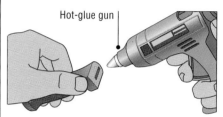

Hot-glue gun

2 Fill the handle approximately two-thirds full with epoxy (see *Adhesives*, p.18). Or use a hot-glue gun instead.

3 Push the tang firmly into the handle. Make sure the blade is firmly seated, with the heel of the blade touching the top of the handle.

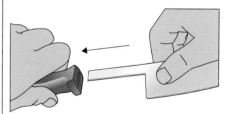

Masking tape

4 Wipe off any excess adhesive that oozes from the handle. Clamp the assembly with masking tape. Let the adhesive dry for 24 hr.

Sharpening a knife with a stone

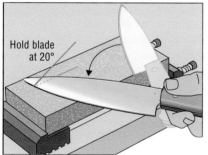

Hold blade at 20°

Begin on medium-grit side of combination stone; finish on fine-grit side. Hold blade at a 20° angle to stone. Pull blade along stone, using a pivoting motion to turn it toward you. Repeat on other side of blade, this time pushing away as you pivot. Keep angle and pressure consistent; stroke each side same number of times.

Using a steel

A steel rubs away bent lip on edge of a dull blade. Begin by placing base of blade near rod's handle. Without moving steel, wipe blade along rod in an arcing motion; rub entire length of blade against rod. Wipe other side of blade along underside of rod. Stroke both sides equally; maintain same angle and pressure.

Sharpening and repairing scissors

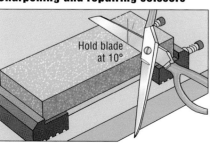

Hold blade at 10°

To find correct whetting angle, open scissors wide; place one blade on stone with inner face vertical. Tip it back slightly less than 10°.

To sharpen, pull blade across stone with a slight arcing motion. Always use a pulling motion; never push the blade.

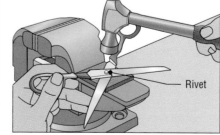

Rivet

If blades are loose, tighten pivot with screwdriver. If pivot is a rivet, put rivet head on metal surface (like a vise) and strike with hammer.

Around the home ▪ Doorbells, buzzers, and chimes

Signaling systems such as doorbells, buzzers, and chimes consist of the sounding device, one or more push buttons, and a transformer, usually located on a basement or attic joist. The transformer steps down household current to between 12 and 24 volts for bells and buzzers and to about 16 volts for chimes. Pressing a push button closes the circuit, allowing current to flow and activate the sounding device.

Although it's usually safe to work on a live signaling system circuit, it's best to turn off power to the circuit at the service panel (p.127) just in case a malfunctioning transformer isn't reducing the voltage. If you suspect a faulty transformer, restore power to the cir-

cuit and *carefully* test the transformer for voltage (below, right). Turn off the power again to replace a defective transformer. The new transformer must match the voltage of it's replacment.

CAUTION: If you are inspecting components on a live signaling system circuit, touch only the insulated parts of the wiring. *If you use a pacemaker,* never handle live wiring, no matter what the voltage may be. Always turn off the power first.

The push button is a common source of signaling system problems. To test the button, short it with a screwdriver (below). Other signaling system problems include broken wiring and dirt in the sounding device.

Troubleshooting

Problem	CAUSE? / Solution
Unit does not sound	NO POWER TO CIRCUIT? See *General troubleshooting*, p.144.
	LOOSE WIRES? Tighten wire connections behind push button, inside signaling unit, and at transformer (see *Making connections: Wire to terminal*, p.134). ◇
	DAMAGED OR BROKEN WIRES? Check circuit wiring for breaks and any visible signs of wear. Turn off power to the circuit (p.127); then splice breaks by stripping both ends of the wire and joining them with a wire connector (see *Making connections: Wire to wire*, p.135). ◆
	CORRODED TERMINALS? Remove button plate and inspect for corrosion. Spray terminals with electrical contact cleaner, or remove wires from the screws and sand off all corrosion with fine sandpaper. ◇
	FAULTY PUSH BUTTON? Remove plate and test button (below, left). ◇
	FAULTY SOUNDING DEVICE? To test a sounding device, remove transformer lead from its terminal in the device. With VOM on RX100, probe transformer terminal and each push-button terminal in turn. A reading of infinity or zero ohms means sounding device is defective and should be replaced. ◆ ▣
	FAULTY TRANSFORMER? Test transformer; replace if defective (below). ◆
Faint or muffled sound	DIRTY SOUNDING DEVICE? Clean the sounding mechanism with a cotton swab or toothbrush dipped in rubbing alcohol. Because oil attracts dust, do not lubricate the unit. ◇
	OLD OR DETERIORATED GROMMETS? *(Mechanical chimes only)* Inspect pads (the grommets) supporting metal chime plates. If worn, get replacements from hardware or electrical supply store. ◇
	HAMMER ARM BENT? *(Bells only)* Restore shape by gently bending arm with pliers; if this fails, replace bell. ◇
Continuous sound	SHORT CIRCUIT? Remove button plate and look for touching or pinched wires. Tighten screws and make sure wires are separated. ◇

Degree of difficulty: Simple ◇   Average ◆   Complex ◆   Volt-ohm meter required: ▣

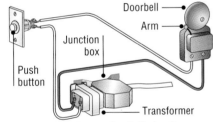

A typcial single-button doorbell circuit

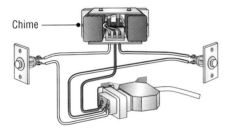

A two-button chime circuit

Testing the push button

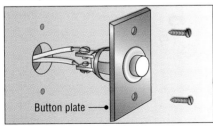

1 To remove the push button, loosen the screws securing the button plate. If the plate is not held in place with screws, use a screwdriver or a flat kitchen knife to gently pry it up.

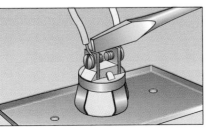

2 Test the push button by holding the blade of a screwdriver across the terminals. If the sounding device sounds, the button is defective and must be replaced. If you don't hear a sound, test the other components.

Testing and replacing the transformer

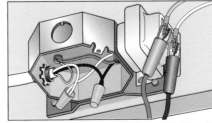

1 To test transformer, set VOM on ACV, 50-volt range. Attach tester probes to terminal screws holding signaling system wires. Reading under 6 volts or over 24 volts means transformer is faulty; replace it with one of equal voltage.

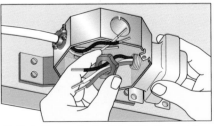

2 Shut off power to circuit (p.127); disconnect signaling system and house cable wires from transformer. Undo transformer locknut. Run new transformer leads through knockout. Secure transformer with locknut; reattach wires.

Doorknobs, locks, and hinges

Many lock problems can be solved by either cleaning and lubricating the lock, having a new key cut, or making a simple adjustment (see *Troubleshooting locks,* p.28). Even if a repair is beyond your skills, you can save the cost of a service call by removing the lock and taking it to a locksmith.

Common residential locks. Exterior doors in most homes are equipped with both a key-in-knob lock and an auxiliary lock—a deadbolt or a rim lock—for added security. Deadbolts and knob locks are examples of bored locks; that is, they require a hole bored through the face of the door (the cross bore) to hold the lock body and a connecting hole through the edge of the door (the edge bore) for the latch or bolt mechanism.

Rim locks require only a cross bore for the cylinder. The lock case is mounted on the inside surface of the door; the bolt slides into a receptacle on a strike plate mounted on the jamb.

Expensive and rarely installed today, mortise locks fit into a recess cut in the edge of the door.

Knob lock construction. There are two basic types of key-in-knob locks: cylindrical and tubular. Nearly all the working parts of a cylindrical lock are contained in a chassis that fits in the cross bore and intersects with the latch mechanism mounted in the edge bore.

In a tubular lock, the latch mechanism is also mounted in the edge bore, but it extends nearly all the way into the cross bore. The outer knob in an exterior-door lock—or the inner knob in a privacy lock (right)—has a central spindle and two screw posts that fit through the latch mechanism.

Privacy locks. Normally used on interior bedroom and bathroom doors to prevent inadvertent entry, a privacy lock has a push button or thumb turn on the inside knob that keeps the door from being opened from the outside. In an emergency (a locked-in child, for example), a hole in the outside knob allows you to open the door with an "emergency key," often a simple probe. Privacy locks are available in both cylindrical and tubular models.

Knob locks

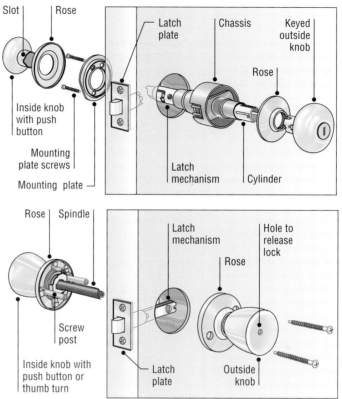

Cylindrical key-in-knob lock is locked with push button or thumb turn on inside knob or with key on outside knob. To remove knobs, push a nail into slot at base of inside knob; pull off knob. Look for spring tab holding rose; press it to slide off rose. Undo mounting plate screws; remove outer knob.

Tubular privacy lock, used on interior doors to prevent inadvertent entry, is not a security device. In the tubular model shown here, two screws fit through the outside knob's rose into screw posts attached to inside knob. Since screws are exposed, knobs are easily removed.

Auxiliary locks

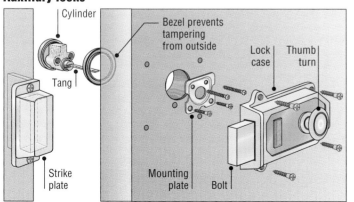

Rim locks may be keyed on both sides or keyed outside and have a thumb turn inside; when either is turned, the bolt slides into a strike plate mounted on the jamb. To access cylinder, remove lock case screws and unfasten mounting plate screws that hold cylinder in place.

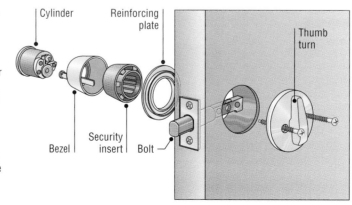

Single-cylinder deadbolt locks with a key from outside and with thumb turn on the inside. (Double-cylinder locks are keyed inside and out; some building codes prohibit their use.) To remove the cylinder, unscrew the mounting plate screws next to the thumb turn.

Common lock mechanisms

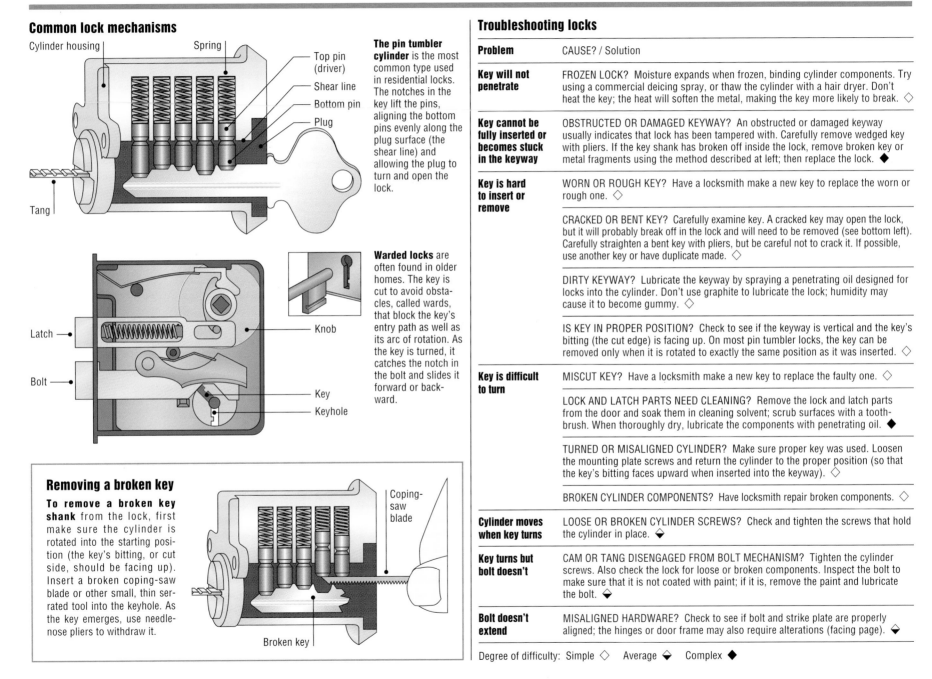

Cylinder housing
Spring
Top pin (driver)
Shear line
Bottom pin
Plug
Tang

The pin tumbler cylinder is the most common type used in residential locks. The notches in the key lift the pins, aligning the bottom pins evenly along the plug surface (the shear line) and allowing the plug to turn and open the lock.

Latch
Bolt
Knob
Key
Keyhole

Warded locks are often found in older homes. The key is cut to avoid obstacles, called wards, that block the key's entry path as well as its arc of rotation. As the key is turned, it catches the notch in the bolt and slides it forward or backward.

Removing a broken key

To remove a broken key shank from the lock, first make sure the cylinder is rotated into the starting position (the key's bitting, or cut side, should be facing up). Insert a broken coping-saw blade or other small, thin serrated tool into the keyhole. As the key emerges, use needle-nose pliers to withdraw it.

Coping-saw blade

Broken key

Troubleshooting locks

Problem	CAUSE? / Solution
Key will not penetrate	FROZEN LOCK? Moisture expands when frozen, binding cylinder components. Try using a commercial deicing spray, or thaw the cylinder with a hair dryer. Don't heat the key; the heat will soften the metal, making the key more likely to break. ◇
Key cannot be fully inserted or becomes stuck in the keyway	OBSTRUCTED OR DAMAGED KEYWAY? An obstructed or damaged keyway usually indicates that lock has been tampered with. Carefully remove wedged key with pliers. If the key shank has broken off inside the lock, remove broken key or metal fragments using the method described at left; then replace the lock. ◆
Key is hard to insert or remove	WORN OR ROUGH KEY? Have a locksmith make a new key to replace the worn or rough one. ◇
	CRACKED OR BENT KEY? Carefully examine key. A cracked key may open the lock, but it will probably break off in the lock and will need to be removed (see bottom left). Carefully straighten a bent key with pliers, but be careful not to crack it. If possible, use another key or have duplicate made. ◇
	DIRTY KEYWAY? Lubricate the keyway by spraying a penetrating oil designed for locks into the cylinder. Don't use graphite to lubricate the lock; humidity may cause it to become gummy. ◇
	IS KEY IN PROPER POSITION? Check to see if the keyway is vertical and the key's bitting (the cut edge) is facing up. On most pin tumbler locks, the key can be removed only when it is rotated to exactly the same position as it was inserted. ◇
Key is difficult to turn	MISCUT KEY? Have a locksmith make a new key to replace the faulty one. ◇
	LOCK AND LATCH PARTS NEED CLEANING? Remove the lock and latch parts from the door and soak them in cleaning solvent; scrub surfaces with a toothbrush. When thoroughly dry, lubricate the components with penetrating oil. ◆
	TURNED OR MISALIGNED CYLINDER? Make sure proper key was used. Loosen the mounting plate screws and return the cylinder to the proper position (so that the key's bitting faces upward when inserted into the keyway). ◇
	BROKEN CYLINDER COMPONENTS? Have locksmith repair broken components. ◇
Cylinder moves when key turns	LOOSE OR BROKEN CYLINDER SCREWS? Check and tighten the screws that hold the cylinder in place. ◆
Key turns but bolt doesn't	CAM OR TANG DISENGAGED FROM BOLT MECHANISM? Tighten the cylinder screws. Also check the lock for loose or broken components. Inspect the bolt to make sure that it is not coated with paint; if it is, remove the paint and lubricate the bolt. ◆
Bolt doesn't extend	MISALIGNED HARDWARE? Check to see if bolt and strike plate are properly aligned; the hinges or door frame may also require alterations (facing page). ◆

Degree of difficulty: Simple ◇   Average ◆   Complex ◆

Door and door frame alignment

Problems with a door's latch are often caused by misaligned hardware or warped woodwork. To swing well, a door needs an exactly vertical pivot point,

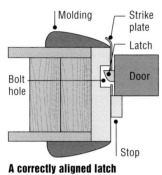

meaning that the hinge pins have to be carefully aligned. The hardware must be positioned so that when the door is flush with the doorstop, the latch makes contact with the strike plate.

A correctly aligned latch

If the latch does not meet the strike plate, realign them. A slight misalignment can sometimes be corrected by filing the strike plate to restore clearance; but if the latch bolt misses the strike plate by more than ⅛ inch, move the plate (right). If the latch does engage the strike plate but the door rattles when shut, reposition the stop closer to the bolt hole.

Shimming, chiseling, and planing. If the door keeps popping open, the latch may not be extending far enough into the bolt hole. As long as the latch and the strike plate align, this problem can be solved by placing a thin wood or cardboard shim underneath the

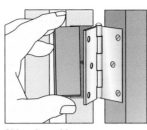

Shimming a hinge

hinges or underneath the strike plate. If a hinge mortise isn't flat and plumb, place a partial shim underneath the hinge. To ensure an accurate fit, use the plate or hinge as a template for cutting out the shim (see *Shimming a cabinet door hinge,* p.74).

If a door resists closing or rubs or sticks against the jamb, look for paint buildup on the door and jamb. If paint is the problem, remove it with paint remover, a scraper, and sandpaper (see *Stripping wood,* p.81). If not, use a chisel to slightly deepen the hinge mortises (see *Planing a door,* p.74).

Also examine the hinges themselves for signs of wear. Shim worn hinge knuckles (below). Tighten any loose screws; if necessary, fill enlarged holes (below) and reset the screws.

Doors that bind in only one corner can usually be corrected by shimming the hinge diagonally opposite the bind—providing this will align the hinge pins. If the hinges are OK, the house may have settled and the jamb may no longer be square and plumb. In this case, planing the door's high spots may be the only solution.

Realigning the strike plate

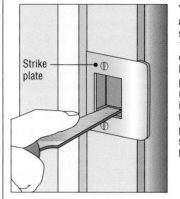

To correct a slight misalignment (latch misses strike plate by less than ⅛ in.), file the strike plate on the side closest to the latch. Although the strike plate can be filed without removing it, you may find it easier to do so in order to allow the file greater play. It may also be necessary to enlarge the latch hole behind strike plate.

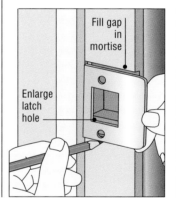

To correct a more serious misalignment (latch misses strike plate by more than ⅛ in.), reposition plate. Take out plate screws; then move plate so that latch will engage hole. Mark new position with a pencil. Use a wood chisel to extend mortise and latch hole as needed. Before securing strike plate in place, fill old screw holes (see below); use wood filler to fill gaps around plate. Let the filler harden; reinstall plate.

Misaligned hinge

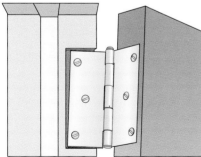

For proper latch and strike plate alignment (and smooth swing), hinge pins must be plumb, top and bottom. This one needs resetting (p.75).

Shimming hinge knuckles

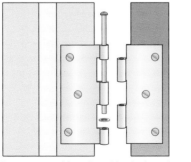

Restore worn hinge knuckles by inserting metal washers as needed between knuckles. After inserting washers, lubricate with penetrating oil.

Filling enlarged screw holes

1 Plug stripped screw holes with golf tees. Dip the tees into carpenter's glue and drive them into the holes.

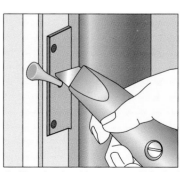

2 After the glue dries, cut tee off flush with surface. Center screw point in the new material. Tee will expand as screw is driven into it.

Around the home ▪ Fabric, leather, and zippers

The usual way to repair torn fabric is to seam it. If the material is too heavy to be sewn or if a seam will distort the shape of the piece, try patching. In general, patch heavy materials such as leather, vinyl, and canvas; sew thinner materials unless the damage is very extensive or a piece is missing.

Patches may be sewn, glued, or ironed on to either side of the material. Sewing is the most secure means of applying a patch. Gluing and ironing are easier, but adhesives for fabric and leather (see *Adhesives,* p.18) are rarely permanent—laundering, dry cleaning, or even wear will eventually weaken their bond. And because of the high heat needed to apply iron-on patches, use them only on natural-fiber fabrics.

Because a wrong-side, or flush, patch is meant to hide the defect, cut it from material that closely matches the original in color, texture, and flexibility. In some cases, it may even be possible to use a piece of material from a hem or facing.

Right-side patches, put over the flaw, can be cut from contrasting fabrics for a decorative touch. These patches may be glued on, but stitching adds interest and strength. Buy fabric and leather adhesives, precut patches, and appliqués at fabric and craft stores.

Flush patching

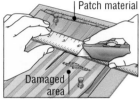 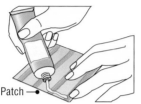 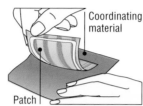 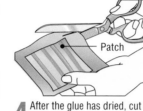 

1 Place patch material between cardboard and damaged area. Using a utility knife, cut around damage, through patch material.

2 Discard damaged piece. Apply fabric adhesive to the wrong side of patch; be careful not to apply too much.

3 Press patch onto a coordinating material. Let adhesive dry before touching the assembly.

4 After the glue has dried, cut around patch, leaving a ⅛-in. edge of the coordinating material on all sides.

5 Apply a thin bead of fabric adhesive around the entire edge of assembly. Don't get any adhesive on patch.

6 Turn item inside out. Place assembly so patch is centered in cutout and coordinating material is hidden. Let dry.

Zippers

While some plastic zippers have teeth, most are made of continuous nylon coils. As long as the coils aren't damaged, this type of zipper can usually be fixed. But if the coils are crushed, or if the stitching holding the coils to the tape unravels, replace the zipper. To fix a zipper whose coils have pulled apart, rezip it by running the slider down the tracks and then back up.

Metal zippers have individual teeth. To keep both metal- and plastic-toothed zippers sliding smoothly, periodically lubricate them by rubbing a dry cake of soap across the teeth. If the zipper becomes dirty, clean it with a toothbrush dipped into a solution of dishwashing detergent and water.

If the slider comes loose from the tracks of either type of zipper, pry off the bottom stop and rethread the track through the slider. If possible, reattach the stop and crimp it into place; but if the stop is damaged, use a needle and heavy thread to sew a new one (see right). To replace a missing handle from a slider, attach a very small key ring to the slider.

Reattaching a loose slider

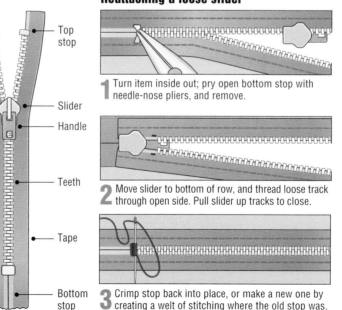

— Top stop
— Slider
— Handle
— Teeth
— Tape
— Bottom stop

1 Turn item inside out; pry open bottom stop with needle-nose pliers, and remove.

2 Move slider to bottom of row, and thread loose track through open side. Pull slider up tracks to close.

3 Crimp stop back into place, or make a new one by creating a welt of stitching where the old stop was.

USE AND CARE

Read the manufacturer's label before cleaning or repairing fabric or leather items. Although some synthetics closely resemble natural materials, they require different treatment. For more on stains, see *Stain removal,* p.46.

Leather and suede need to breathe; don't store them in airtight wraps or in damp or hot areas. Leather absorbs odors; keep it away from mothballs and cedar chips.

Suede. Imitation suede may be machine-washable; hand-wash natural suede with suede shampoo. Brush suede with a terry-cloth towel to raise the nap. To clean spots, rub them with a fine emery board.

Leather. Keep leather from drying and cracking by regularly applying leather conditioner (available at shoe repair stores). Have leather cleaned by a professional. Buff small marks with shoe polish.

Handbags and luggage

Although handbags, garment bags, and soft totes vary greatly in style, most share a common design feature: the shoulder strap is secured to the body of the bag by means of D-shaped rings attached to looped pieces of leather, called chapes, which are sewn or riveted to the outside of the bag or into slots in the bag's side. The handles of many sports bags, travel bags, and car-ryalls are also secured by D-rings and chapes and are repaired in the same way as handbags.

Handbag

If a shoulder strap is torn in mid-length, cut it off the bag and replace it. If the damage is closer to one end, cut the strap just above the damage and re-attach it (right); the resulting strap will be shorter but otherwise fine.

Travel bag

To make sure you get the right replacement parts, take the bag to a luggage dealer or repair shop. Your supplier should also be able to pro-vide rivets and other replacement hardware. If the end of a rivet will be hidden, use a split rivet, whose two prongs fold over a washer. If the end of the rivet will be exposed, use a solid rivet, which has a hollow tube and is secured by hammer-ing the end of the shaft over a washer.

If a bag tears, patch it as soon as possible to avoid further damage (see facing page). To make patches less noticeable, try incorporating them into the bag's design. Tint leather patches with shoe polish so they match the original color.

Briefcase

Briefcase handles are usually secured to the case by two brack-ets. Each side of the handle loops over a pin that fits between two posts. In some cases, these pins can be removed and the handle reat-tached with replacement pins (use brads if duplicate pins aren't available). But if the pins are not accessible from the outer sides of the posts, have a professional replace the entire handle unit.

Reattaching a broken strap

 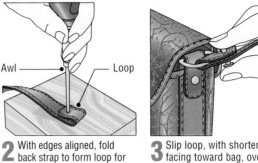 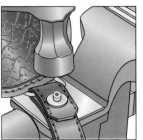

1 Cut damaged portion of strap from D-ring. For a neat repair, trim off corners of cut edge with a utility knife.

2 With edges aligned, fold back strap to form loop for D-ring. Punch hole through both parts of strap with a sharp awl.

3 Slip loop, with shorter end facing toward bag, over D-ring. Insert solid rivet through holes with shaft toward bag.

4 Slide washer onto rivet shaft; use tin snips to cut shaft to ¼ in. Brace against vise; hammer shaft flat against wash-

Replacing a damaged chape

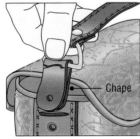 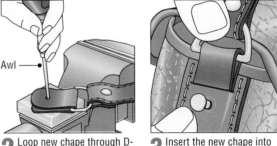 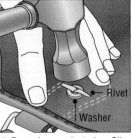

1 Cut off rivet with tin snips. Pull old chape from slot, and use it as a template to cut a replacement chape.

2 Loop new chape through D-ring on strap. Using a vise to support chape, align edges and punch hole for new rivet.

3 Insert the new chape into slot, aligning holes in bag and chape. Insert a split rivet from the outside of bag.

4 Brace bag against vise. Slip a washer over the rivet's prongs; then hammer the prongs flat against the washer.

Replacing a briefcase handle

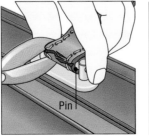 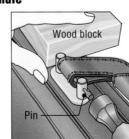

Cut pin holding handle to posts with tin snips. Insert a thin blade between handle and post to push pin through post.

Drive new pin through posts and replacement handle. Seal both ends of pin with a drop of instant glue.

Luggage maintenance and repair

The shell of a soft-sided suitcase may be made of tweed, cotton, tapestry, or other fabric, but the most durable shells are made of leather, nylon, or polyester that is rated over 1,000 denier. Regardless of the material, remove stains and repair tears as soon as possible (see *Fabric, leather, and zippers*, p.30). Hard-sided cases have a durable plastic shell that is not usually subject to damage; maintain them by washing the exterior occasionally with mild soap and water.

Soft cases often have wheels that are mounted and secured with rivets, whereas the wheels on hard cases are screwed or bolted into the shell. Sometimes the wheels wear out, or the brackets that hold them in place break off. If possible, remove and store the wheels and pulls inside the case when not in use.

Handles secured with D-rings or rivets can be replaced in the same manner as handbag straps (p.31), but if a recessed or retractable handle breaks, replace the entire handle unit (below, left).

To keep wheel and handle fasteners from catching on the contents of the case, they are usually hidden beneath a lining that's either sewn or glued into place. To remove a sewn lining, unpick the stitches; after making the repair, sew the lining back in place.

If the lining is glued down, gently tug at its edge to loosen the glue bond, then carefully pull the lining down to expose the shell of the case. Reattach the lining with rubber cement (apply the adhesive sparingly; too much may stain the lining).

If a soft case's metal or plastic frame becomes bent, brace the outside of the frame with a block of wood and gently tap against the inside with a mallet.

Purchase replacement parts from a luggage repair shop or from the manufacturer. To make sure you get the right part, keep a record of the case's style number, size, color, and the year it was purchased.

Replacing a recessed handle

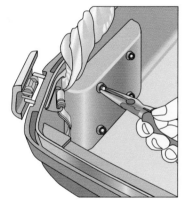

Pull back the lining to access the handle fasteners. Use pliers or a socket wrench to remove the bolts. Pull off the damaged handle unit. Fit the replacement handle, and reinstall the bolts.

Replacing a retractable handle

Clamp
Handle

From inside the case, locate screws securing handle unit and remove them. Clamp the replacement handle in place; install screws from inside the case.

Replacing bolted wheels

Wheel cap

Washer
Nut

To replace a bolted wheel, gently pry off wheel cap with a flat-bladed tool, such as an old screwdriver.

Remove nut, pry up washer, and then pull wheel off bolt. Reverse procedure to install replacement wheel.

Replacing riveted wheels

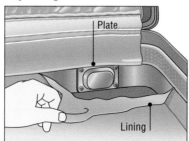

Plate
Lining

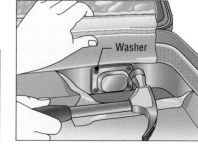

Washer

1 Pull back or unstitch the lining to access the wheel mounting plate; be careful not to damage lining.

2 Using a bit slightly larger than rivet shaft, drill out end of each rivet from inside of case. Push rivets from holes.

3 With new wheel in place, insert solid rivets from case exterior. Slide washer over shaft and hammer the end flat.

Replacing screwed-on wheels

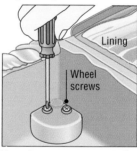

Lining
Wheel screws

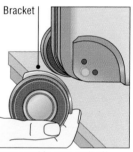

Bracket

To replace a screw-mounted wheel, pull back the lining to reveal the wheel screws. Remove the screws.

From outside case, pull off wheel and bracket. Replace with new wheel and bracket, and reinstall screws.

Jewelry

Precious gems are durable but not indestructible; pearls, opals, emeralds, and other soft stones are especially prone to damage if handled roughly. Clean your jewelry regularly (see *Use and care,* below), and examine it periodically through a magnifying glass or jeweler's loupe. Take jewelry (especially expensive or delicate pieces such as knotted pearls and items with pronged settings) to a jeweler once a year; a professional can detect signs of wear, cracks, or loose stones that are not readily apparent.

Although the clasps are the most vulnerable part, all of the components that make up a piece of jewelry—known collectively as the *findings*—are subject to damage. Replacement findings are available from craft and jewelry suppliers or from your jeweler. Replace gold findings with new ones of the same karat rating; when possible, replace a clasp with an exact duplicate.

Gold. All gold jewelry is stamped with a karat (k) rating: 24-karat is 100 percent gold; gold labeled 18k, 14k, and 10k is blended with increasingly greater amounts of other metals, making it more durable. Costume jewelry is made either entirely of base metal or of base metal combined with a minimal amount of gold.

Silver and platinum. Silver is a soft metal that reacts with oxygen and becomes discolored, or tarnished. Although tarnish is easily removed (see below), wearing silver jewelry regularly may help reduce discoloration. Because platinum is such a valuable metal, it should be repaired only by a professional jeweler.

Repair tools. Using regular household tools to repair a piece of jewelry can result in permanent damage. A jewelry repair kit should include special pliers for gripping and manipulating findings, abrasives for smoothing, a 5X or 10X loupe, a lint-free cleaning cloth (some cloths are impregnated with cleaning solution), a leather or wooden mallet, a mandrel for shaping rings, and small cutters. A special spring bar tool with a notched screwdriver blade on one end and a point on the other is invaluable for watch repair.

Working with jump rings

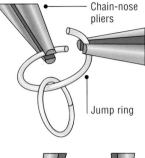

Chain-nose pliers

Jump ring

Jump rings are basic items in jewelry making and repair. To open a jump ring, grip each end with chain-nose pliers, and gently twist the ends in opposite directions until the resulting gap is large enough to slip the jump ring over an adjacent ring or other element.

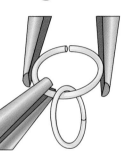

Close a jump ring by twisting the ends in opposite directions until realigned. Close the gap between the the ends by gently squeezing the sides of the jump ring with pliers until the ends meet. For a more secure link, seal a jump ring with a drop of instant glue.

Jewelry repair tools

Chain-nose pliers are used to manipulate findings.

Flat-nose pliers have smooth flat jaws that are ideal for flattening and straightening metal.

Cutters or snippers are invaluable for cutting metal in tight spots.

Round-nose pliers have smooth tapered round jaws that are used to shape loops.

Hole-punching pliers create neat holes in leather and fabric watch bands.

Sanding stick smooths rough edges.

Loupe magnifies items so that they can be closely inspected for damage.

Polishing cloth keeps jewelry bright and clean.

Tweezers grasp and hold small findings.

Ring mandrel is used to shape rings. The taper allows you to achieve the proper ring size.

Leather mallet is used to pound jewelry without damaging the metal.

Spring bar tool manipulates spring bars and friction pins in watch repair.

Awl is used to pry open clasps and move friction pins.

Around the home ▪ Jewelry

Repairing clasps

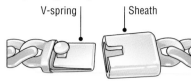
V-spring | Sheath

Box snap has a V-shaped spring that slides into boxlike sheath. If V is flattened or sheath is bent, the clasp won't lock.

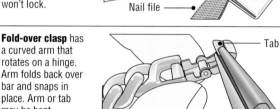
Nail file

Pry open leaves of the V with a nail file or other flat tool. Reshape a bent sheath by manipulating it with flat-nose pliers.

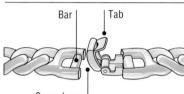
Bar | Tab
Curved arm

Fold-over clasp has a curved arm that rotates on a hinge. Arm folds back over bar and snaps in place. Arm or tab may be bent.

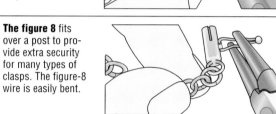
Tab

If clasp doesn't snap closed, bend tab back onto itself; test clasp and repeat if needed. Reshape arm with chain-nose pliers.

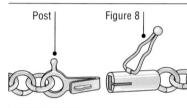
Post | Figure 8

The figure 8 fits over a post to provide extra security for many types of clasps. The figure-8 wire is easily bent.

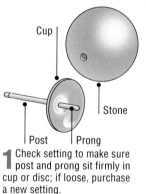

To restore its shape, gently squeeze the center of the 8 with round-nose pliers; test and repeat until the 8 fits snugly over the post.

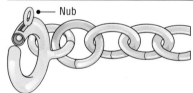
Nub

Spring ring contains a spring that compresses when you pull back nub. If spring breaks or nub snaps off, replace the entire ring.

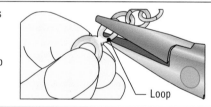
Loop

Open loop holding spring ring to jewelry piece; remove ring. Position new ring; close loop as you would a jump ring (p.33).

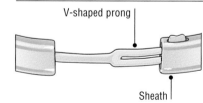
V-shaped prong
Sheath

Banger snap clasp has a V-shaped prong that widens as it slides into sheath, securing clasp. The prong may lose tension.

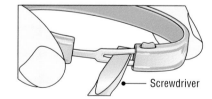
Screwdriver

Widen V by inserting the blade of a small screwdriver and gently twisting; keep testing clasp until it snaps securely into place.

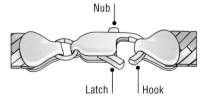
Nub
Latch | Hook

Pulling back nub of a lobster clasp causes latch to pivot back, opening clasp. If latch or nub breaks off, replace the clasp.

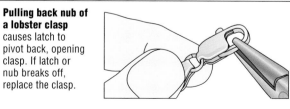

If latch bends, realign hook and latch of clasp by gently manipulating them with chain-nose pliers until parts meet.

Earrings: Post

Post earrings are held in place with a clutch back, usually butterfly-shaped, that slides onto a post. Rough treatment may cause the post to break off from the earring. Take valuable pieces to a jeweler, who can solder on a new post. To repair inexpensive earrings, use wire snippers to clip off any remaining part of the post. Purchase a replacement post equipped with a flat disc or a cup to provide a wide surface for the adhesive. Apply epoxy to both the setting and the stone; hold them together for a few minutes. To keep the earring from moving while the adhesive sets, wedge it (post facing upward) into a small box densely packed with tissue.

Reattaching a post setting

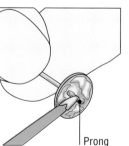
Cup
Stone
Post | Prong

Pin

1 Check setting to make sure post and prong sit firmly in cup or disc; if loose, purchase a new setting.

2 If setting is OK, remove any old adhesive by gently scraping the cup and stone with a pin or an awl.

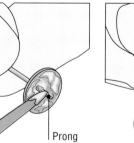
Prong

3 Dab epoxy onto cup with a wooden toothpick. Be sure to completely cover the prong with adhesive.

4 Slide the stone onto prong. Hold tightly for 5 min.; then wedge earring into box stuffed with tissue to complete drying.

Earrings: Clip-on

The clip that holds the earring in place may become bent, affecting the earring's tension. Too much tension causes discomfort to the wearer; too little loosens the earring.

A clip-on earring consists of a clip with a flat spring that pivots against a stationary neck. The spring maintains tension.

If the clip falls off, reinsert the clip into the holes; then use pliers to gently sqeeze the flanges toward each other.

To adjust spring tension, gradually bend neck forward or backward with pliers until desired tension is reached.

For further adjustment, first remove clip from earring. Bend spring down to increase tension, up to decrease it.

Earrings: Hoop

Hoop earrings are usually fastened by a pivoting wire that snaps into a V-like notch. If this pivot breaks, take the earring to a jeweler for repair.

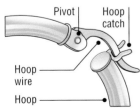

The hinged hoop wire locks into a V-shaped catch on other side of the hoop.

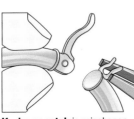

If wire or catch is misshapen, gently bend back into shape with flat-nose pliers.

Pins and brooches

A bent pin stem on a brooch can tear fabric or cause the brooch to work loose as the pin slips from the ball clasp. With regular use, the ball clasp or ball joint can separate from the brooch backing. If this happens, purchase a new ball clasp or ball joint that is attached to a backing; secure the clasp or ball joint to the brooch with epoxy.

A pin catch consists of a pin stem that is held by two flanges, forming a ball joint. It is held closed by securing the pin stem in the ball clasp. All of the parts are subject to wear and can become damaged or loose.

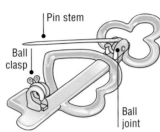

To straighten a pin stem, hold the brooch firmly and gently pull the stem through the jaws of flat-nose pliers (left). If the tip is bent, first straighten it, then file the end to a point with a fine emery board.

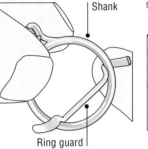

Tighten a loose or wobbly pin stem by gently squeezing the flanges of ball joint together with flat-nose pliers as shown. To increase tension, grasp pin stem near ball joint and carefully bend it behind ball clasp.

To tighten the latch on a ball clasp, position latch so nubs point up; firmly squeeze both sides of clasp together with flat-nose pliers as shown. Test by rotating latch to closed position; if latch stays closed, clasp is secure.

Rings

Rings often catch on fabric or other materials, bending the shank or loosening the stones. Have expensive rings, channel-set rings, or those with hollow shanks repaired by a jeweler. Minor repairs to pronged or bezel-set rings can be made at home.

If a ring is too big, use a ring guard to keep it in place. Guards are available from jewelry suppliers.

Pronged setting   Channel setting   Bezel setting

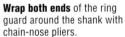

Fit a ring guard through the ring and position it on the bottom half of shank.

Wrap both ends of the ring guard around the shank with chain-nose pliers.

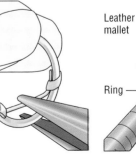

If guard is too tight, use pliers to gently bend center of guard toward bottom of shank.

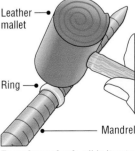

To reshape shank, slide it onto mandrel; rotate mandrel while pounding with leather mallet.

35

Watches

A bracelet-type watchband consists of metal links held together by friction pins or clip springs, and is fastened by a three-fold clasp. Other common bands consist of a leather, cloth, or plastic strap fastened by a buckle. Periodically check bands and clasps for wear; buy replacement parts at a jewelry store. A spring bar tool is handy for fixing watchbands, but you can also use an awl, paper clip, or thin, stiff wire.

Never repair the inner workings of a watch yourself; it's easy to damage delicate parts. And unless you have a sport watch that has a separate, easily accessed battery cavity, let a professional replace the battery.

Adjusting a three-fold clasp

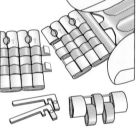

Spring bar tool
Spring bar (within clasp)

1 Push on one end of the spring bar with the pointed end of a spring bar tool; slide bar from the holes.

2 Align bar with new holes. Insert one end of spring bar, squeeze bar, and snap it into the opposite hole.

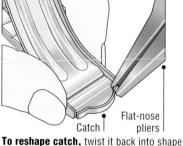

Catch Flat-nose pliers

To reshape catch, twist it back into shape with flat-nose pliers. Make sure it bends slightly inward so clasp will remain locked.

Adjusting a friction pin bracelet

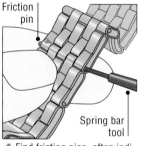

Friction pin

Spring bar tool

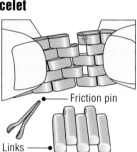

Friction pin

Links

1 Find friction pins, often indicated by tiny arrows on inside of bracelet. Push pin out of link in direction of arrow.

2 Separate bracelet links and remove or insert links as needed to adjust bracelet length. Realign links.

3 Reinsert friction pins in opposite direction of arrows. If pin is stiff, use spring bar tool to push it in.

Adjusting a clip spring bracelet

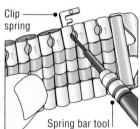

Clip spring

Spring bar tool

1 Locate F-shaped clip springs (look for arrows). Insert tool into hole; press slightly while pushing pin up and out.

2 To separate links, gently twist band and unhook. Remove or insert links as needed to resize the bracelet.

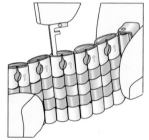

3 Join two ends of bracelet, aligning links and reinserting clip springs in the opposite direction from Step 1.

Replacing a watchband or spring bar

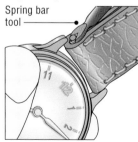

Spring bar tool

Spring bar

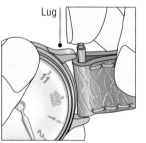

Lug

1 Press notched end of tool against outer sheath of spring bar; depress bar and twist it away from watch face.

2 Slide spring bar from loop on band. If bar is bent, try straightening it with pliers; or buy a new one.

3 Place spring bar through loop in band; insert one end of bar into lug; use spring bar tool to maneuver bar into place.

Repairing eyeglasses

Have eyeglasses fitted by a professional; ill-fitting glasses can impair vision and are likely to break. To make minor repairs to the frame, such as tightening a screw or reattaching an arm, you'll need a repair kit (sold at eyeglass shops and drugstores) consisting of a jeweler's screwdriver and screws. Use a drop of instant glue or clear nail polish to keep screws in place. Clean lenses by wiping them with soapy water mixed with a drop of vinegar or rubbing alcohol; polish with a soft cloth.

Screw

Lamps and lighting

Incandescent lamps

When a lamp flickers or won't light, make sure the bulb isn't loose or damaged. If the bulb is OK but the lamp still doesn't light, check for a tripped circuit breaker or a blown fuse (p.127). If that's not the problem, suspect the lamp's power cord, socket, or switch.

Unplug the lamp and examine the cord and plug for visible signs of damage (see *General troubleshooting*, p.144). To replace a defective plug, see page 135; to replace a defective cord, see below.

If the cord and plug look OK, remove the socket and switch unit and test the cord with a continuity tester (Step 4, below). To test a cord with a polarized plug (one wide prong, one narrow prong), see *Rewiring a desk lamp*, Step 2, p.38. If the cord is faulty, replace it. If it's good, replace the socket and switch (Step 8, below). Always replace defective parts with duplicates. To ensure a match, take along the old parts when shopping for replacements.

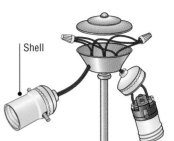

Lamps with multiple sockets are repaired in much the same way as single-socket lamps. The socket wires are joined to the cord by wire connectors (p.135).

An incandescent table lamp

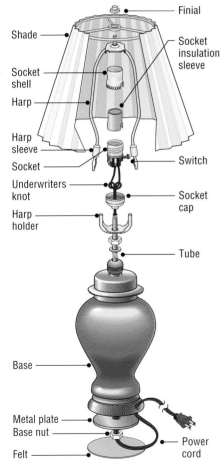

- Finial
- Shade
- Socket insulation sleeve
- Socket shell
- Harp
- Harp sleeve
- Socket
- Switch
- Underwriters knot
- Socket cap
- Harp holder
- Tube
- Base
- Metal plate
- Base nut
- Felt
- Power cord

Rewiring a table lamp

1 Unplug lamp and remove bulb. Unscrew finial; lift off shade. Slide up harp sleeves to expose clips at ends of harp holder; squeeze harp arms to release harp.

2 Depress outer shell of socket where it is marked *Press*. Pull off socket shell and insulating sleeve to expose socket.

3 Tighten any loose wire connections on socket terminals. Reassemble lamp; try again. If problem persists, unplug lamp and free socket by loosening terminal screws.

Continuity tester

4 Clip continuity tester (p.125) on one plug prong; probe each wire in turn while flexing cord. Repeat with clip on second prong. Tester should light once at each prong.

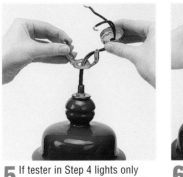

5 If tester in Step 4 lights only once or not at all, cord is faulty. Untie Underwriters knot and unscrew socket cap. Pull off harp holder and any other hardware.

6 Remove felt from base; cut off plug. Pull cord through hole in base; untie knot, if any. Splice new cord to old (inset); secure with tape. Pull cord up tube until tape emerges.

7 Remove old cord. Split top 3 in. of new cord; strip ¾ in. of insulation from ends. Replace harp holder and socket cap; then tie Underwriters knot (p.135). Install new plug on cord end.

8 Connect cord's ridged (neutral) wire to socket's silver terminal (p.135); connect smooth wire (hot) to brass terminal. Reassemble lamp in reverse order it was taken apart.

37

Incandescent desk lamps

Because a desk lamp traps more heat than a table lamp (p.37), its socket has a plastic or ceramic insulating sleeve that may or may not be removable. In some lamps, cord wires are soldered rather than screwed to the socket terminals. To disconnect soldered wires, simply snip them off. To attach the cord to a new socket, strip ¾ inch of insulation from the ends of the wires and hook them to the screw terminals of the replacement socket.

Rewiring a desk lamp

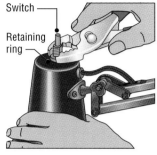

Switch

Retaining ring

1 Unplug lamp and remove bulb. With pliers, twist off socket retaining ring on top of lamp. Push cord up through lamp from base to create slack at elbow. Remove strain-relief fitting (p.170) to free cord at head. Carefully pull socket from lamp. Remove insulating sleeve, if possible; disconnect cord from socket terminal screws.

Continuity tester

2 If plug is polarized (one wide prong, one narrow), attach continuity tester clip to bare end of ridged (neutral) wire; touch probe to wide prong. Repeat test with smooth (hot) wire and narrow prong. Tester should light each time. To test a cord with a standard plug (prongs same size), see *Re-wiring a table lamp*, Step 4, p.37.

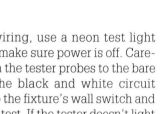

Old

New

3 To replace a faulty cord, use old cord to guide new one through lamp. Cut off old plug; splice cords at base of lamp. Tape over splice; pull cords through lamp (see Step 6, p.37). Undo splice before feeding new cord through lamp head. Secure neutral wire to silver terminal screw, hot wire to brass screw. Reassemble lamp.

A wall-switched ceiling fixture

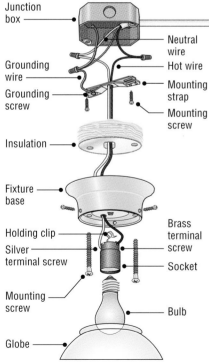

Junction box

Neutral wire

Grounding wire

Hot wire

Grounding screw

Mounting strap

Mounting screw

Insulation

Fixture base

Holding clip

Silver terminal screw

Brass terminal screw

Socket

Mounting screw

Bulb

Globe

Incandescent ceiling fixtures

Ceiling fixture wires and house circuit wires are joined by wire connectors inside a ceiling box; in some fixtures, the house wires connect directly to screw terminals in the fixture. Ceiling fixtures may be mounted directly to a mounting strap (left) or to a threaded nipple (facing page); they shouldn't be screwed directly to the box.

If a ceiling fixture fails, first make sure that the problem isn't the bulb, the circuit (p.37), or the switch (p.129). **CAUTION:** Turn off power to the fixture at the service panel (p.127). Before touching any wiring, use a neon test light (p.125) to make sure power is off. Carefully touch the tester probes to the bare ends of the black and white circuit wires. Flip the fixture's wall switch and repeat the test. If the tester doesn't light at all, the wires are safe to work on.

Testing and replacing the socket

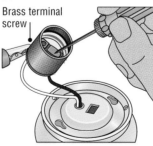

1 Turn off power to fixture at service panel; remove globe and bulb. Loosen mounting screws; rotate fixture until screws align with keyhole openings; pull it from box. Have an assistant hold fixture while you undo wire connectors or terminal screws.

Brass terminal screw

2 To test socket, clip continuity tester to socket's hot (black) lead or brass terminal screw; touch probe to tab in socket base. Clip tester to neutral (white) lead or silver screw; probe socket threads. If tester does not light both times, replace socket.

3 If socket is held in place by a holding clip (as above), remove socket by prying clip up from base with a screwdriver. In some fixtures, socket may screw into base or to a bracket. Remove all wires attached to socket.

4 Replace socket with duplicate. Connect neutral circuit wire to socket's white lead or silver screw terminal (see *Making connections*, p.134). Attach hot circuit wire to black lead or brass screw. Reassemble fixture; restore power.

Fluorescent fixtures

When a fluorescent light is switched on, electricity flows through a ballast, which boosts the household current and charges the gasses inside the tube (bulb), causing the gasses and the tube's phosphor lining to glow. After this burst of current, the ballast reduces the voltage to a level just high enough to keep the tube lit.

When a tube flickers or only partly lights, examine the tube and replace it if its ends are discolored; if they're not, make sure the tube is properly seated in the sockets. Rotating the tube may help; but if its pins are bent or broken, replace the tube.

If a fixture won't light at all, make sure there is power to the circuit (p.144) and that the wall switch is OK (p.129). Then shut off power to the fixture at the

service panel (p.127) and remove the diffuser and tubes. Look for broken sockets and bent or corroded contacts. Replace defective sockets. If the fixture

still fails, replace the ballast (a bad ballast may also cause the fixture to hum). Before doing so, check prices; it may be cheaper to replace the whole fixture.

Fluorescent tubes are fragile and may explode if dropped: *handle them carefully*. Tubes will last longer if they are not turned on and off repeatedly.

Starter-type fixtures

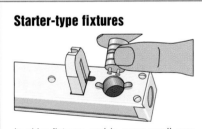

In older fixtures, and in many small new ones, a starter (a small metal cylinder located near one of the sockets) provides the initial surge of voltage needed to light the tube. If the tube in a starter-type fixture flickers or fails, check the power supply and examine the tube. If the power supply and tube are OK, replace the starter. To remove it, turn off power to the fixture. Push down on the starter and rotate it counterclockwise a quarter turn; then pull it out. Reverse the procedure to install a new starter (be sure the replacement has the same rating).

Rapid- or instant-start fixture

Socket   Ballast

Cover plate

Tube   Pins

Diffuser

Replacing the ballast

Ballast

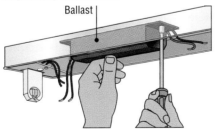

1 Turn off power to circuit at main service panel. After removing diffuser, tubes, and cover plate, make a diagram of the wiring to facilitate reassembly. Disconnect wires by removing wire connectors. With a screwdriver or nut driver, disconnect the ballast from the fixture; make sure to support ballast so it doesn't fall.

2 Replacement ballast should have same rating as the old one. While holding new ballast in position, replace screws or mounting nuts. Following your diagram, reconnect wires with wire connectors (see *Making connections*, p.134). Replace cover plate, tubes, and diffuser; then restore power to fixture.

Circular rapid-start fixture

Threaded nipple
Grounding wire
Fixture strap
Ballast
Cover plate
Tube socket
Tube pins
Circular tube
Diffuser
Cap nut

Replacing a socket

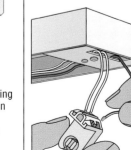

Socket

1 Turn off power to fixture at service panel. Remove diffuser, tubes, and cover plate. Remove socket from fixture—some are held in place with screws; others snap into place.

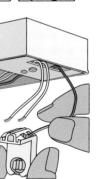

2 Disconnect wires from socket. For push-in terminals, insert a straightened paper clip into each terminal slot and pull out wire. If socket has screw terminals, loosen screws and unhook wires.

3 Replace socket with duplicate. Push wire ends into push-in terminal slots, or hook them on terminal screws (see *Making connections*, p.134). Reassemble fixture; restore power to circuit.

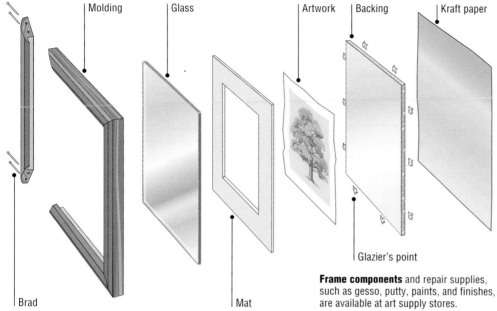

Molding   Glass   Artwork   Backing   Kraft paper

Brad   Mat   Glazier's point

Frame components and repair supplies, such as gesso, putty, paints, and finishes, are available at art supply stores.

Picture frames usually consist of four lengths of hardwood molding that meet to form simple miter joints. The back of the molding is rabbeted (cut away) to accommodate a piece of single-strength window glass, a cardboard mat, the artwork, and a foam-core or hardboard backing. Brads or glazier's points hold the assembly in place. Kraft paper glued to the back of the frame keeps out dust. Screw eyes or D-rings for hanging the picture are installed one-fourth to one-third of the way down the sides of the frame; felt pads in the frame's lower corners protect both frame and wall.

Because improper hanging may cause a frame's joints to pull apart or the glass to break, always make sure a picture is hung correctly (far right). To repair separated or weak joints, simply insert dowels or nails diagonally through the joint. Even if the joints appear secure, reinforcing them before hanging can prevent problems in the future (facing page).

Repairing gesso. Gold, silver, or other colors are often applied to a frame over a layer of gesso—a white plaster-like material that can be carved into ornate designs. If a piece of gesso falls off, glue it back on. If this isn't possible, take a putty impression of the design from elsewhere on the frame and make a cast. On gilded frames, keep the putty from pulling off the gilding by coating the area with three thin coats of shellac. Let the shellac dry between coats. After making the cast, remove the shellac with isopropyl (rubbing) alcohol.

Gilding is a very thin layer of gold leaf that's applied to a frame with a water- or an oil-base adhesive. Because it's hard to identify the type of adhesive used, don't dampen a gilded frame (moisture ruins water gilding). For minor touch-ups, use gold opaque watercolor paint. Slowly mix water into the paint until it's the consistency of thick ink. Dab it on sparingly, avoiding the surrounding gilding.

Replacing broken glass

Cut away the kraft paper by running a utility knife around the inside back edge of the frame. Use pliers to pull out the brads or glazier's points. Remove the other components; wear gloves to protect your hands from the broken glass. Measure between the inside back edges of the frame to find the size of the new glass, or take the frame to a glazier to have the glass custom-fitted.

To reassemble the frame, stack the backing, artwork, mat, and glass. Lay the frame over the stack. Flip over the assembly so that its back faces you. Secure the components with glazier's points or ¾-inch brads (below). Coat the back of the frame with PVA (see *Adhesives*, p.18); put a sheet of kraft paper on the frame and cut away the excess paper.

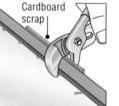

Cardboard scrap

Press brads into frame with groove-joint pliers every 1½ to 2 in. Protect frame with cardboard.

Push glazier's points into place with a wide screwdriver. Position the points 1½ to 2 in. apart.

USE AND CARE

Don't hang pictures in direct sunlight, in hot or humid areas, or where the temperature changes quickly.

Dust gilded frames with a dry cloth. Use a small brush to clean ornate detailing (don't brush a frame with damaged gilding); then vacuum the frame after covering the nozzle with fine mesh.

Clean glass with glass cleaner; wipe dry with crumpled newspaper. Use a commercial cleaner (sold by plastics suppliers) on acrylic. Don't spray solutions directly on surfaces; spray cloth.

Hanging a picture

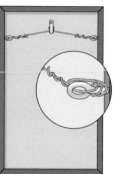

Thread braided wire (or nylon fishing line) through screw eye on one side of frame. Wrap wire around screw eye's base; then double back, wrapping wire around itself (inset). Repeat on other side.

Double wire loops help distribute the weight of heavy frames evenly. Thread wire through screw eyes, loop wires together (inset), and twist each end around itself. Hang picture from two wall hangers as shown.

Repairing loose frame joints

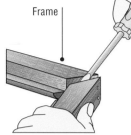

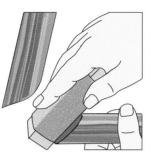

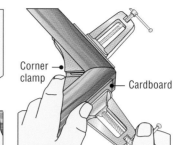

1 With frame contents removed, pry open loose corner of frame with screwdriver. If other joints loosen up, continue opening bad joint by hand.

2 Tap end of brad or dowel until head emerges; use pliers to pull out fastener. Replacement nail should be a bit longer than original.

3 Scrape off adhesive from joint faces with utility knife. Sand off any light residue with sanding block (p.77). Wipe off dust.

4 Coat faces of joint with carpenter's glue, and close joint. Clamp joint with corner clamp; use cardboard to protect frame. Let dry 1 hr.

Frame

Corner clamp — Cardboard

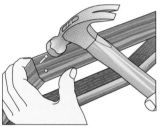

Nail set

Vinyl spackle

5 Insert new brads or dowels into existing holes. If fasteners were not used before, drill two pilot holes into joints before inserting fasteners.

6 Leave dowels flush with wood's surface. To hide brad heads, clamp frame in vise and use nail set to sink heads slightly below surface.

7 To fill depressions left by countersunk brads, apply a dab of vinyl spackle over each nail. Wear gloves when working with spackle.

8 After the spackle has dried, smooth the area with a damp cotton ball. Use an opaque watercolor paint to hide spackle.

Mirrors

Polish mirrors regularly with a commercial cleaner and a lint-free cloth. Because cleaning solution can dissolve a mirror's silver coating, don't let the cleaner come into contact with the edges or back of the mirror.

Remove grease from a mirror with a solution of 2 tablespoons vinegar, 2 tablespoons ammonia, and 1 quart water. Sponge the solution onto the mirror, let it sit for 30 seconds (be sure the cleaner does not drip onto the edges), and then wipe it off.

To remove small scratches from a mirror, apply a paste of ¼ cup glycerine, ¼ cup jeweler's rouge (available at jewelry supply stores), and ¼ cup water; gently rub with a soft cloth. Repeat until marks disappear. Don't let jeweler's rouge dry on mirror.

If small patches of silvering flake off the back of a mirror, conceal damage (right) with a thin layer of silver paint. If the damaged area is extensive, take the mirror to a glazier for repair.

Artist's brush

Reinforcing frame joints

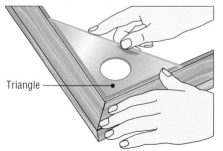

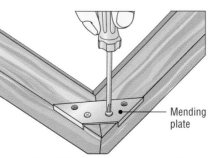

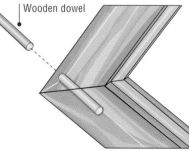

Triangle

Mending plate

Finishing nail

Wooden dowel

Before reinforcing frame, check that corners form 90° angles by measuring with a triangle. If angle is not true, repair any loose frame joints (see above); then check joints again.

One way to reinforce frames is with metal frame-mending plates, sold at hardware stores. Drill pilot holes before securing plates; be sure screws provided will not protrude through front of frame.

To reinforce small frame, use a finishing nail instead of a mending plate. Drill a pilot hole; then drive nail through joint. Countersink nailhead; fill depression with vinyl spackle (above).

Strengthen very large frames with ⅛-in. dowels. Drill holes 1⁄16 in. deeper than dowels (for glue). Coat dowels with carpenter's glue, slip them into holes, and cut flush with frame's surface.

Types of ceramic ware

Household items made of fired clay are ceramic, and can be divided into three categories: pottery (also known as earthenware), ironstone (sometimes called stoneware), and porcelain. The term "china" was first used by early European importers of Chinese products to describe what was actually the first authentic porcelain. Today the term is used loosely to describe items made of almost any type of fired clay.

Pottery, or earthenware, is lightweight, porous, and opaque. An exposed edge reveals a grainy texture that is easily scratched with a knife.

Ironstone, or stoneware, is heavier, nonporous, and opaque. An exposed edge has a fine-grained texture that is difficult to scratch with a knife.

Porcelain is of moderate weight, nonporous, and translucent. An exposed edge has a glassy texture that can't be scratched with a knife.

With modern adhesives, it's possible to make nearly invisible repairs to damaged ceramic and glass items. However, if the damaged piece is of monetary or sentimental value, have the repair done by a professional restorer to ensure the best possible job.

Adhesives. Two kinds of adhesives are generally used to mend ceramics and glass: polyvinyl acetate (PVA), also known as white glue, and clear, slow-setting two-part epoxy (see *Adhesives*, p.18). In order to choose the correct adhesive for a ceramic repair, you must first identify the type of ceramic involved (see above). Use PVA for repairing pottery; use epoxy for ironstone, porcelain, and glass. Because an exact fit is essential in repairing ceramics and glass, you must adjust the pieces precisely before the glue sets. Five-minute epoxies and instant glues dry too fast and are not recommended for this type of repair.

Preparation

The most important step in repairing a broken glass or ceramic item is to make sure the pieces are clean. If the item has been fixed before, undo the old repair (see right), or the new adhesive may not bond. Before handling the pieces, put on clean gloves to protect your hands from sharp edges. Clean the pieces with a mixture of mild dishwashing liquid and warm water; gently loosen dirt with a plastic scrubbing pad. Rinse the pieces and let them dry completely.

If stains persist, fill a plastic basin with warm water and add 1 cup of liquid chlorine bleach. Carefully submerge the pieces in the liquid. Cover the basin with plastic wrap to contain the fumes and let it sit undisturbed for 2 to 3 days. Remove the pieces, rinse them under running water, and let them dry overnight.

Repairing chipped glass rims

Gloves

Chips along the rim are a common problem with glassware. Fixing larger chips (or any chip on a valuable piece) is a job best left to a professional glass restorer. To fix small chips, tape a piece of 320-grit wet/dry sandpaper around a pencil and rub the

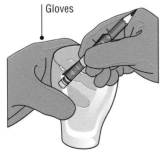

damaged area. Next, sand the area with 400-grit sandpaper; then switch to 600-grit sandpaper. Polish the area by rubbing the rim with a cloth dipped in silver polish.

Undoing an old repair

Protect hands with gloves

1 Fill a plastic basin with boiling water, and soak the object for 1 hr. It may be necessary to repeat the process several times until the adhesive bond weakens enough so the pieces can be separated.

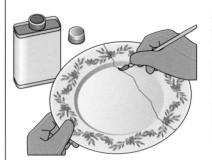

2 If repeated soaks don't loosen the old glue bond, brush paint remover onto all glued joints and let it sit for 1 hr. Check periodically to see if the pieces are loosening. If not, repeat the process.

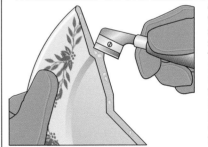

3 Once the pieces have loosened, soak them again to soften the glue on the exposed edges. Use paint remover if needed. Rub off glue with plastic scrubbing pad; rinse pieces well. Scrape off remaining glue with a razor blade.

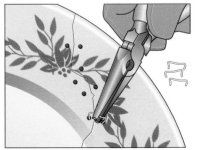

If metal staples set in drilled holes were used in old repair, soak item in boiling water until staples can be wiggled. Next, use needle-nose pliers to carefully pull staples from the object. Clean edges as above.

Applying the adhesive

To repair a piece of pottery with a single break, use a disposable brush to apply PVA (white glue) to only one of the broken edges. Quickly join the pieces together while applying light pressure. Avoid shifting the pieces; small particles may come loose, ruining the repair. Any glue that oozes from the joint can be removed later. Place the object in a positioning box (see below); let the glue dry for at least 1 hour. After taking the item out of the box, use a razor blade and hot water to remove any adhesive that oozed from the joint. Return the item to the positioning box until the glue is completely dry—usually 24 hours.

For a single break in porcelain, ironstone, or glass objects, mix a small amount of clear, slow-setting two-part epoxy; then proceed as described above. Once the object is in the positioning box, let it cure overnight before using a razor and lacquer thinner to remove any epoxy residue (see below).

Use only enough adhesive to cover the edge. Too little will leave gaps, resulting in a weak repair; too much will make it difficult to achieve a tight joint.

Place repaired item in a positioning box so that the item stays balanced. To make the box, fill a shallow container three-quarters full of uncooked rice or beans.

Gently scrape off excess adhesive with a razor blade. Then use cotton swabs dipped in hot water to remove remaining PVA; use lacquer thinner for epoxy.

Fixing an object with multiple breaks

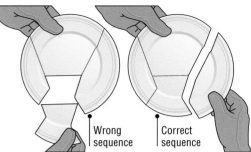

Wrong sequence   Correct sequence

To avoid locking out a piece, establish the order of assembly before applying the glue. After determining the sequence, number each piece with a nonpermanent marker. Bond two pieces at a time, using the technique at left. Allow each joint time to dry before continuing the repair.

Because the glue itself takes up space, any that seeps onto the inside edges where another piece will attach should be removed before it hardens. Otherwise, the remaining pieces won't fit tightly together, weakening the bond and distorting the repair.

Filling in small chips

To repair chips that are 1/8 inch or less in depth, mix a small amount of slow-setting clear epoxy. Blend oil-base hobby enamels to create a shade that matches the item; then stir a small amount of the paint into the epoxy with a toothpick. Use only enough paint to tint the glue; too much will thin it. Dab epoxy on the chip; then smooth it until it's flush with the surrounding area. Let the repair dry for 48 hours.

Caring for repaired objects

Because temperatures over 200°F (93°C) soften most adhesives, don't use repaired objects in the oven or on the stove. Although the temperature inside a dishwasher is below 200°F (93°C), repeated exposure to hot water and detergents may weaken bonds. Instead, hand-wash these items with mild soap and warm water. Don't use harsh chemical cleaners on items whose paint has been touched up; they could dissolve the paint. Even though it may be safe to use repaired items with food, it is not recommended.

Touching up decorations

To touch up a faded or worn design, you'll need a set of fast-drying hobby enamel paints (oil-base) and a small, good-quality artist's brush. For cleanup, and to thin the paints, use mineral spirits or paint thinner.

On the bottom surface of an inverted paper cup, mix small amounts of different-colored paints until you come as close as possible to the color of the original decoration. If during the mixing the paint becomes too thick, use an eyedropper (available at pharmacies) to add tiny amounts of mineral spirits to the paint until it reaches the desired consistency.

Brush on the paint so that it blends in with the adjacent designs. If you're not happy with the result, you can wipe it off with a rag dipped in mineral spirits and begin again. Before adding any more colors, let the paint dry overnight; otherwise you may smudge the first color. Once the design is completed, set the item aside for a week to dry completely before using it.

Installing and replacing screening

Screening is usually made of either aluminum or fiberglass. Although stronger than fiberglass, aluminum is subject to corrosion and trickier to install. Unless you're planning to replace all of your screening, use material of the same type and color as currently in place. Screening is sold in several widths, either by the foot or in rolls of various lengths. Purchase enough material to cover the entire screen frame with a 2-inch overhang on all sides.

In metal frames, the screening is held in place by a spline pressed into a groove. Some screens have reusable metal splines; most have splines made of vinyl or rubber. As long as a vinyl or rubber spline is in good condition, you can reuse it; replace the spline if it's dry, brittle, or damaged. Available either smooth or serrated, spline ranges in diameter from ⅛ to ¼ inch. To ensure a good fit, bring a piece of the old spline with you when buying the new spline.

In wood frames, screening is stapled directly to the wood. Molding is used to cover the staples and the edges of the screening to create a neat appearance.

Replacing screening in a metal frame

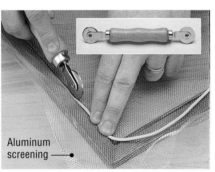

Aluminum screening

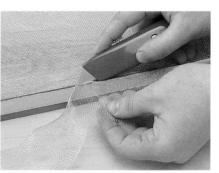

1 Pry out the end of old spline with an awl (or a nail); then pull up rest of spline. Lift the screening out of the frame. Once the frame is empty, lay new screening over it; make sure pattern is correctly aligned.

2 Press aluminum screening into groove with *convex* end of a spline roller (inset); maintain tension by pulling screening taut on opposite side. Roll in spline with *concave* end of roller. Roll fiberglass screening and spline into place at same time.

3 As you near each corner, cut a slit in the screening at a 45° angle to the corner; this prevents the material from bunching up. Use a screwdriver to press the spline into the corner; then continue rolling in spline around the frame.

4 After the spline is in place, cut off the excess screening with a sharp utility knife. Holding the knife at an angle, cut carefully along the outside edge of the groove so you won't damage the screening (or cut your fingers) if the blade slips.

Replacing screening in a wooden frame

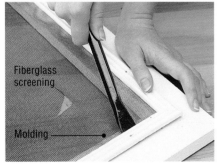

Fiberglass screening

Molding

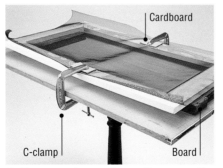

Cardboard

C-clamp   Board

BRAD'S

1 Pry off the molding with a pry bar or a stiff-bladed putty knife. Start at the corners and move toward the middle; work slowly to avoid damaging the molding. Use a screwdriver to remove the staples that secure the screening.

2 Place screening over frame; align pattern. To make sure screening will be taut, place boards under the ends of frame and clamp the middle to work surface until the frame bows. Use scraps of cardboard to protect frame.

3 Use staple gun to secure one end of screening. Place first staple in middle of frame; then staple toward each corner. After completing both ends, release clamps and staple sides, holding screening taut to maintain tension.

4 Use a tack hammer to gently tap in any staples that are not fully set. Cut off the excess screening with a utility knife (don't cut too close to the staples). Remove old nails from molding; reattach molding (above) with brads.

Patching screens

You can buy a kit to patch aluminum screens, or make a patch from a spare piece of screening cut 2 inches larger all around than the damage. Remove several strands of wire from all edges of the patch; then bend the remaining wires at a 90° angle as shown at right.

Fix small holes in a fiberglass screen by realigning the threads with an awl. If the threads are broken, dab epoxy (p.19) over the area. For larger holes, cut a patch slightly larger than the damage from a piece of spare screening; proceed as shown at far right.

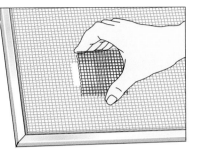

To patch aluminum screening, neatly cut out the damaged area. Center the patch over the hole; press bent wire ends through the screening. Turn the screen over and flatten the protruding wires to secure the patch.

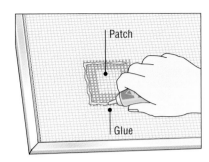

To patch fiberglass screening, cut out the damaged area. Lay patch over hole; check to make sure the pattern aligns. Apply a thin bead of epoxy around all edges of patch; smooth glue and blot excess with a rag before it dries.

Storm windows and doors

To keep storm windows operating smoothly, spray the metal frame and channels once a year with a silicone lubricant; wipe off the excess with a rag. Remove corrosion with steel wool. If the corrosion is particularly bad, use aluminum jelly (follow the manufacturer's directions; wear heavy rubber gloves and eye protection). To keep storm windows from sticking, never paint the frames or the channels.

The most common type of storm window features a flexible spline that wedges a glass or acrylic panel into place against a metal frame (below). The glazing can be replaced without disassembling the frame. On other types of storm windows, the frame is held together with metal or plastic corner keys or with spring-insert corner clips (right). To disassemble a frame with corner keys, loosen any setscrews at the corners and pull apart the frame. A frame with corner clips comes apart once you pry out the clips with an awl. Once either type of frame is apart, reassembly is simply a matter of sliding a U-shaped gasket onto the edges of the glazing, then putting the frame back together using the keys or clips.

On spline-type windows, new glazing should be ¹⁄₁₆ inch smaller in length and width than the rabbet in which it will sit. On gasket-type windows, the glazing ought to be ⅛ inch smaller in length and width than the groove it will sit in. Have a glazier cut the new glass to size. When handling glass, wear gloves and eye protection.

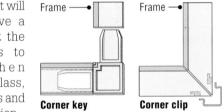

Corner key   **Corner clip**

Most storm doors have a mounting system that lets you switch between storm and screen panels; look for knurled retaining screws on the inside of the door. For safety reasons, use acrylic panels instead of glass panes in doors.

Replacing glazing in a splined frame

1 Pry out end of spline with an awl; then grasp end and pull slowly to remove it. If spline is still flexible, save it for reuse; if it's old and brittle, replace it. **CAUTION:** Wear heavy gloves and eye protection when handling glass.

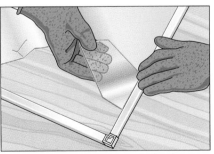

2 If old glass was glued to frame, brush on paint remover to free it; then run a screwdriver around groove to remove bits of stuck glass. There is no need to replace glue; the pressure from the spline will hold glass in place.

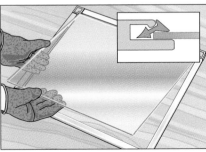

3 At the corners, measure inside dimension of frame between lips that spline fits into (inset). New glass should be ¹⁄₁₆ in. smaller to allow for expansion and contraction. Carefully lay the new glass in the frame.

4 Miter-cut one end of new spline with utility knife. Starting at one corner, press spline against glass and under lip of frame. As you near next corner, miter-cut spline to length; repeat process on all sides. Stretch reused spline to fit.

Before treating any stain, identify the stained material and check the label, if any, for cleaning instructions. Always spot-test fabrics for colorfastness by dabbing a small amount of the cleaner in an inconspicuous area. If the color runs or fades, have the item dry-cleaned. Don't mix cleaning agents; combining chlorine bleach and ammonia, for instance, will form a poisonous gas.

Treat stains quickly; blotting a stain immediately often removes enough so that normal laundering will clean the rest. Some stains require special cleaners. For example, the best way to treat oily stains is with an oil solvent (such as K2R); on protein-base stains, use an enzyme detergent (such as Javex 2 or Wisk); on combination stains, use a combination solvent (such as Shout or Spray 'N' Wash). These and other cleaning agents mentioned below are available at supermarkets, drugstores, or home centers.

Removing fabric stains

STAIN	WASHABLE FABRICS	NON-WASHABLE FABRICS
Alcoholic beverages (except beer)	Apply glycerine; let sit 15–20 min. Dab liquid dish detergent over glycerine; then gently rub in a few drops of water. Rinse and let dry. Apply oil solvent to any remaining stain.	Apply 50-50 solution of vinegar and water. Follow with oil solvent; feather and let dry. **Note:** To feather, wipe stain from outer edge to center with a clean cloth.
Antiperspirant, deodorant	Put a combination solvent over stain and let it sit 20 min. Apply liquid dish detergent and launder.	Rub on oil solvent; repeat. If safe for fabric, use 50-50 solution of vinegar and water; rinse.
Ballpoint pen	Apply glycerine; rub area. Let sit 20 min. Add liquid dish detergent, rub, and let sit 10 min. Add a few drops of water; then rub. Keep adding water and rubbing until stain is gone.	Apply gycerine directly to stain; let sit for 20 min. Follow with an oil solvent; feather and let dry.
Chewing gum	Apply ice to freeze gum; crack off as much as possible. Apply oil solvent, blot, let dry. Follow with liquid dish detergent; rinse.	Follow procedure for washable fabrics; use minimal amount of detergent and water.
Coffee and tea	Flush area with cool water; then apply a combination solvent. Let sit for 15–20 min. Apply liquid dish detergent and launder.	Use a 50-50 solution of vinegar and water; follow with an oil solvent. Feather and let dry.
Combination stains: candle wax, crayon, lipstick, tar, etc.	Dab oil solvent onto stain; follow by rubbing in liquid dish detergent. If it's safe for fabric (check label), use solution of 1 tbsp. bleach to ¼ cup water. Launder.	Cover stain with oil solvent; then blot. Repeat. Apply 50-50 solution of vinegar and water. Rinse with water, feather, then let dry.
Combination stains: chocolate, makeup, tomato sauces, etc.	Gently rub in a combination solvent; let sit 15–20 min. Follow with an application of liquid dish detergent; let sit 15–20 min. Rinse well; launder.	Use oil solvent, blot, repeat. Dab on liquid dish detergent and 1–2 drops water. Rinse, feather.
Dyes: food stains, grass, soft drinks, tempera paint, etc.	Apply 50-50 solution of vinegar and water; let sit 5 min. Dab on liquid dish detergent, rub. Let sit for 10–15 min. Add water 1 drop at a time, rub gently; rinse. If stain remains, apply enzyme detergent; let sit 15–20 min.; rinse.	Apply oil solvent directly to stain. Follow with a 50-50 solution of vinegar and water; blot. Flush area with water and blot. Feather and let dry. Then have item dry-cleaned.
Fruit stains	Dab glycerine on stain and let sit 10–15 min. Follow with 50-50 solution of alcohol and water; let sit 10 min. Add 2–3 drops of vinegar; wash as usual. Do not place detergent directly on stain; it may set the stain.	Apply oil solvent over stain. Follow with a 50-50 solution of vinegar and water; blot. Flush area with water and blot. Feather and let dry. Then have item dry-cleaned.
Oils: butter, face cream, grease, etc.	Blot with an oil solvent. Dab on a laundry presoak. Let sit for 15 min.; work in liquid dish detergent; launder.	Place oil solvent on stain. Repeat as needed. On last application, feather and let dry.
Proteins: blood, egg, feces, milk, etc.	Apply a small amount of an enzyme detergent with just enough water to keep spot moist, let sit 15 min., rinse; launder. Do not use enzyme detergents on wool or silk.	Apply a liquid dish detergent and 1–2 drops of water. Rub; let sit 5 min.; rinse with cool water. Feather and let dry.
Urine	Soak fresh stains with a 50-50 solution of vinegar and water. Treat old stains with 1 tbsp. ammonia and 1 cup water. Follow both treatments with liquid dish detergent; blot and rinse.	Rinse with water, apply a dab of liquid dish detergent, let sit 5 min., then flush with water. Feather and let dry.

Removing stains from household materials

Brick, stone, concrete. Scrub with a mild detergent and warm water. Use muriatic acid on stubborn stains; be sure to follow manufacturer's instructions and protect your eyes, face, and hands. Soak up grease or oil by applying cat litter, cornmeal, or sawdust over the area; follow with an application of muriatic acid. Remove mildew by scrubbing with a soft brush; then apply a solution of 1 part bleach to 2 parts water. Rinse the area with water. To remove algae or moss, sprinkle powdered lime over the area, scrub well with water, then rinse.

Carpeting. Spot-test (see text above) before treating stains. Apply commercial cleaning foam. Treat protein stains with a solution of 2 cups lukewarm water and 1 cup vinegar. Use a solution of 2 tbsp. ammonia and 1 cup water on tough stains. (For more on carpet care, see *Carpets and rugs*, pp.22–24.)

Leather. Spot-test (see text above) before treating stains. Wipe item with hot water and clean rag. Treat oily stains by dusting the area with cornstarch; let it sit overnight, then brush off the residue. (For more on leather, see *Fabric, leather and zippers*, p.30.)

Marble. Use a marble cleaning kit (available at home centers) or apply borax with a damp cloth. Rinse with warm water and buff dry.

Metals. Use a commercial metal cleaner. Follow the manufacturer's directions.

Plastic laminate. Use a nonabrasive commercial cleaner or a paste of baking soda and water. Rinse with water and wipe with a soft cloth. Don't use steel wool; it may cause scratches.

Porcelain. See *Pottery, porcelain, and glass*, p.42.

Suede. See *Fabric, leather, and zippers*, p.30.

Tile. Scrub the area with chlorine bleach; rinse with water.

Vinyl flooring. If commercial cleaners fail, wipe stain with alcohol and soft cloth. If stain remains, rub stain with mineral spirits; let area dry for 30 min. before walking on it.

Wood. See *Reviving a finish*, p.80.

Toys / teddy bears and other stuffed toys

With time and heavy use, a stuffed toy will inevitably show signs of wear. Repairing an antique toy is a job for a doll hospital; to fix ordinary stuffed toys, all you need to master is a few simple stitches (see *Stitches,* far right). Torn seams are a common problem for stuffed toys, but they can be fixed with slip stitches. Replace a nose with satin stitches; secure ears with overhand stitches.

Replacement parts (such as eyes, noses, and sound boxes) are available at craft supply stores. Use only nontoxic parts that lock securely into place. Buy replacement plush (fur) and stuffing at sewing or notions shops.

Where possible, patch holes from inside the toy; open a seam and remove enough stuffing to allow you room to work. If you can't access the inside, sew the patch over the hole with overhand stitches; fluff up the fur with a brush to hide the seams. For more on patching, see *Fabric, leather, and zippers,* p.30.

If a limb comes loose and it's not jointed, reattach it to the torso as you would an ear (see right). If a pivoting limb is broken, you'll have to replace the joint (often a rotating disc held by a cotter pin; newer toys may have a one-piece molded plastic joint). Replacement kits are available at doll and craft supply stores; follow the installation instructions that come with the kit.

Stuffed toys tend to lose their shape with use. To restore plumpness, open a seam and push in fresh stuffing. Try to match the original material, but if you can't, use polyester wadding. Older toys may be stuffed with a gray plastic foam or a white polystyrene pellet mix, which, when ignited, releases toxic fumes. Keep such toys away from children.

Restitching a seam

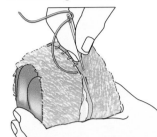

Close open seams with slip stitches. Poke leaking stuffing back in as you sew. Use a soft brush to fluff up the fur over completed stitches.

Reattaching an ear

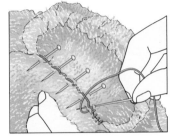

Pin the ear to the head to keep it from slipping. Sew it into place with overhand stitches; for added security, stitch along both sides of ear.

Replacing an eye

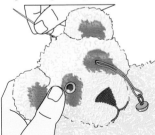

To reattach button eyes, stitch through head. Pull thread tightly and knot securely in back of head. Don't use button eyes on children's toys.

Replacing a stitched nose and mouth

1 First mark outline of nose; then fill in the area with satin stitches. Use embroidery thread for a neat look. Keep stitches close together.

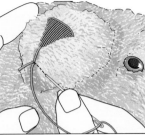

2 Finish the nose with one horizontal stitch across the top. Sew an inverted Y underneath the nose to create a mouth.

Replacing a paw pad

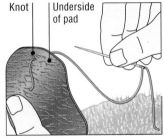

Knot | Underside of pad

1 Cut pad from felt or leather; make it slightly larger than existing one. Tie knot in thread and pull through pad; catch knot on underside.

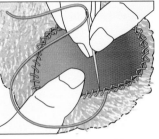

2 Position new pad over old one. Attach pad to toy with tiny cross stitches. Comb fur over seam to hide completed stitching.

Replacing a sound box

Rear seam

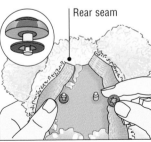

Lock-in eyes (inset) are held by washers. Open seam and take out stuffing. Push eye through material; attach washer from underneath.

Sound box
Rear seam

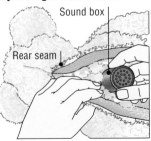

Open rear seam and insert sound box. Press stuffing securely around the box. Stitch up seam; don't let stuffing come between box and fur.

Stitches

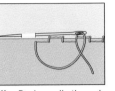

Slip. Push needle through material on one side of gap, then on other side. Alternate sides until seam is completed.

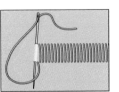

Satin. This is a long, straight, solid stitch meant to fill in open areas. Place satin stitches close together.

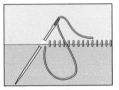

Overhand. Push needle diagonally from back edge to front. Insert needle behind previous stitch; bring it out a stitch length away.

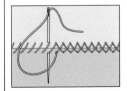

Cross. Sew series of angled stitches. When end of seam is reached, reverse direction, sewing back over the stitches.

Types of dolls

Soft dolls (or rag dolls) can be made of any durable fabric. Hair is usually made of yarn.

Cloth-body dolls have a cloth torso; heads and limbs are plastic or vinyl. Hair is rooted or a wig.

Plastic or vinyl dolls are held together by flanged limbs or elastic (right). Hair is rooted or a wig.

If an antique doll (one that's at least 50 years old) needs to be repaired, have a doll hospital evaluate its worth and the amount of work required to fix it. (Extensive repairs may actually decrease the value of an antique doll.) In most cases, newer dolls can be repaired quickly and easily. Replacement parts (hooks, elastic, wigs, etc.) are available from craft or doll supply stores. The most common repairs required on soft dolls are resewing ripped seams (p.47) and patching holes. (For more on patching, see *Fabric, leather, and zippers,* p.30). If a soft doll loses its shape, open a central seam and add fresh stuffing in the form of polyester wadding.

Plastic and vinyl dolls

Plastic and vinyl dolls are made in two basic ways. Some have flanges on the head and limbs that fit into sockets in the torso. Others have elastic loops inside the body that hold the head and limbs in place. If the head or a limb comes off a doll with push-in limbs, push it back into place. To make replacement easier, warm the flange by holding it over a kettle of steaming water for a few minutes to make it pliable. If the elastic inside a doll breaks, replace it (right).

Wash dolls with a mild detergent and a damp rag; dry with a clean rag. If the doll's hair is rooted (fed through the scalp), you can shampoo it. Don't shampoo dolls with wigs; water may damage the glue.

Doll diagram labels: Hooks, Head bar, Elastic loop, Knot, Elastic loop, Hooks

Doll with elastic loops

Repairing a cloth-body doll

If the torso is too damaged to patch (p.30), replace it (below). Cloth-body dolls have rooted hair (plugs of hair fed through the scalp) or wigs. If a wig comes loose, reglue it with PVA (p.18). If rooted hair is damaged, cut it close to the scalp and glue a wig over it.

1 Undo stitching holding head and limbs to torso. Unstitch body; use it as pattern for the new one. Add 1 in. of fabric to limb and neck openings.

2 Sew torso inside out; leave rear seam open. To attach plastic pieces, turn up 1 in. of fabric; sew through holes at base of each piece.

3 Turn torso right side out. Use polyester wadding to stuff the doll. Then stitch up the rear seam with small, tight overhand stitches.

Restringing a plastic or vinyl doll

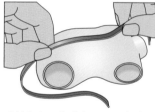

1 Make two elastic loops: one for legs and head, a shorter one for arms. Loop sizes depend on doll size and elastic's resiliency; they should hold limbs and head securely yet allow smooth movement. Knot elastic ends tightly.

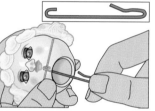

2 If the hanging hook is missing, make new one from a wire coat hanger. Cut off a section with wire-cutting pliers and bend it into shape (inset). Attach hook to head bar; it should extend into the neck cavity.

3 Secure the larger elastic loop to the hanging hook. Push the loop down through the neck cavity and into the doll's torso. Position doll's head on top of body.

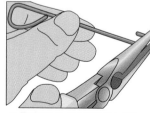

4 To help in stringing the doll, make a stringing hook from a wire coat hanger. Use wire-cutting pliers to snip off a section of wire. Twist one end into a small hook, the other into a looped handle.

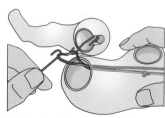

5 To attach legs, use stringing hook to reach into torso and grasp loop. Pull loop down through leg hole and secure it to hook on leg. Pull out the stringing hook and repeat the process for other leg.

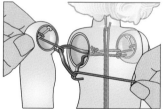

6 Use smaller loop to secure arms. Hook one end of loop to arm; feed loop through arm hole. Use stringing hook to pull loop through opposite arm hole. Attach loop to hook on arm; remove stringing hook.

Toys / miscellaneous

Plastic toys

Gluing plastic to plastic rarely results in a lasting repair, especially if the joint has to sustain pressure or strain during use. Reattach decorative elements with an adhesive specially formulated for bonding plastics, such as epoxy or cyanoacrylate (see *Adhesives,* pp.18–19). Very lightly roughen both edges of the break with sandpaper, and wipe off any dust. Apply the glue to both of the surfaces to be joined. To keep the pieces from

Clamping a repair

moving while the glue hardens, improvise a clamp from an elastic band, string, or tape (don't let the glue come into contact with the clamp). Let the repair sit overnight before releasing the clamp.

If a plastic part comes loose from a piece of wood or metal, drill holes through both surfaces and fasten them with bolts or rivets.

Battery-powered toys

Before assuming a toy is broken, test it with fresh batteries. Next, make sure the batteries are inserted correctly—the negative end usually fits against a tab or spring. Verify that the batteries are in all the way, touching the contacts. If they're not, pry up the contacts a little (right). Look for corrosion on the terminals (especially if the toy has been sitting idle for months); clean them if needed (far right). If the toy is operated by a rechargeable battery, examine the battery as well as the charger (see *Cordless tools and appliances,* pp.142–143).

Wheeled toys

Most problems with wheeled toys involve the wheels, axles, or handle. If a wood wheel splits, reinforce it with dowels. Drill holes in each piece for the dowels; add wood glue to the dowels, and clamp the wheel together with masking tape. If a metal wheel is bent or damaged, replace it; metal wheels are hard to straighten. Replace broken axles (right).

To repair a crushed handle loop on a wagon or other pull toy, position a block of scrap wood behind the damaged area and pound the area back into shape with a mallet.

Mending leaks in sports balls

Inflatable balls often lose pressure when they haven't been used in a while, so don't automatically assume a deflated ball is leaky. Instead, reinflate it with a hand pump, then toss it around for a while to see if it retains air. If it doesn't, test the ball for a leak (right). If you don't find a leak, suspect the valve—it could be clogged with dirt, allowing air to escape. To clean a dirty valve, plunge a moistened inflating needle through the valve hole several times. If this doesn't solve the problem, plug the valve by breaking off a toothpick in the hole.

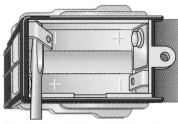

A battery's contact may flatten out over time, interfering with the function of the toy. If the contact isn't touching the battery, use a screwdriver to pry it up; be careful not too bend it too far.

Clean corroded contacts with a piece of sandpaper or steel wool wrapped around the eraser end of a pencil. Wipe battery compartment free of all debris with cotton swab dipped into glass cleaner.

Replacing a broken axle

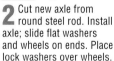

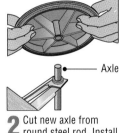

1 With pliers, pry off push nuts and unscrew lock washers (inset). Remove wheels and flat washers; slide out axle.

2 Cut new axle from round steel rod. Install axle; slide flat washers and wheels on ends. Place lock washers over wheels.

3 Rest one wheel on scrap wood. Install push nut over opposite wheel; tap it into place with hammer. Repeat on other side.

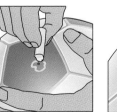

1 Submerge ball in a tub of water and rotate it slowly; escaping air bubbles will indicate a hole. Dry the area, then mark the leak with chalk or a piece of masking tape.

2 Heat the blade of an old screwdriver by moving it back and forth over a flame. Rub hot blade over leaky area until vinyl melts. Let vinyl harden for at least 5 min.

3 To reinflate the ball, moisten the inflator needle and push it straight down through the ball's valve. Use hand pump to inflate ball to the recommended pressure.

Kinds of typewriters

In standard (nonelectronic) typewriters, a raised typeface strikes a sheet of paper wrapped around a rubber cylinder, or *platen*. An inked ribbon placed between the typeface and the platen leaves the impression of the character on the paper. After each strike, the ribbon advances, presenting fresh ink.

Standard typewriters come in two basic styles: electric type-element units (below) and type-bar units (electric or manual). Electronic typewriters (p.52) are also available.

Type-element typewriters

In a type-element typewriter, the characters are arranged on the face of a spherical metal element the size of a Ping-Pong ball. A carrier assembly and a system of spring clutches and cords move the element back and forth across the paper, tilting and rotating it with each keystroke to direct the appropriate character toward the platen.

Type-element typewriters have several advantages over type-bar typewriters (facing page): they're faster and easier to use, and they allow greater flexibility since you can change typefaces and type sizes by switching elements. And because the element is driven by a motor, the darkness of the characters is uniform, rather than varying with the amount of pressure placed on the keys. They do have some drawbacks, however. A common problem is "flicking"—if the typist presses a key only partway down, the machine will print a dash rather than the right character. The only remedy for this is to press the keys firmly. Type-element typewriters don't work well on standard envelopes (or other thick items); using the very thin envelopes designed for them will help. The thin correctable-film ribbons found in these machines don't work well with coated or porous paper; use uncoated bond instead.

Because most problems in type-element typewriters are caused by a build-up of dirt and debris, cleaning is an essential part of maintenance. Excessive oiling is also a problem, as oil tends to hold dirt in place.

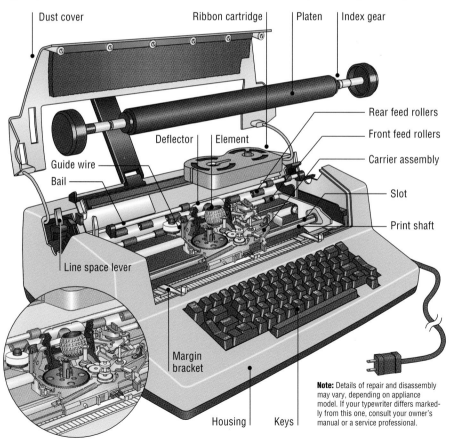

Dust cover | Ribbon cartridge | Platen | Index gear

Rear feed rollers
Front feed rollers
Deflector | Element
Carrier assembly
Guide wire
Bail
Slot
Print shaft
Line space lever
Margin bracket
Housing | Keys

Note: Details of repair and disassembly may vary, depending on appliance model. If your typewriter differs markedly from this one, consult your owner's manual or a service professional.

Troubleshooting: Type-element typewriter's

Problem	CAUSE? / Solution
Paper slips	DIRTY PLATEN? Clean platen (Step 1, facing page). ◇
	HARDENED RUBBER ON PLATEN? An eroded platen won't firmly grip the paper. Lightly rub the platen with sandpaper or emery cloth. Then vacuum the area and wipe the platen with lacquer thinner or denatured alcohol. ◇
Some letters not clear	LETTER ON TYPE ELEMENT CLOGGED? Remove debris from the affected character with a sharp pin (Step 5, facing page). ◇
Ribbon keeps breaking	RIBBON INSTALLED INCORRECTLY? Make sure the ribbon goes around the ribbon release lever. ◇
Tops of letters not being erased	CORRECTION TAPE INCORRECTLY INSTALLED? Make sure the correction tape runs behind the separator wire. ◇
Bottom half of every third character missing	RIBBON FOLDED OR TWISTED? Examine the ribbon; if it is folded or twisted, remove it and then reinstall it. Make sure the ribbon lies flat between the ribbon guides. ◇
Carrier moves sluggishly	SLOT IN PRINT SHAFT CLOGGED? Slide the carriage to one side and clean out groove in print shaft (Step 8, facing page). Slide carriage to the opposite side; repeat cleaning process. ◆
Letters overprint	SLOT IN PRINT SHAFT CLOGGED? See *Carrier moves sluggishly*, above. ◆
Half of one letter and half of another print together	TYPE ELEMENT BROKEN? Examine the base of the element for cracks and broken or missing teeth. Replace the element if necessary. ◇
Type cuts paper	PLATEN HARDENED? Place a backing page beneath original. Or consult an authorized service center to see if your platen can be reconditioned. ◇
All print blurry	WORN RIBBON? Replace ribbon. ◇
	DIRTY ELEMENT? Clean the element (Step 5, facing page). ◇

Degree of difficulty: Simple ◇ Average ◆ Complex ◆

Cleaning a type-element typewriter

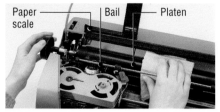

Paper scale — Bail — Platen

1 Lift the cover, bail, and paper scale. Pull the paper release lever. Clean the platen and paper scale with an alcohol-dampened cloth.

Release lever

Index gear

2 Press platen release levers and remove platen. Note location of index gear; platen must be reinstalled with gear in same place.

3 Remove ribbon. Wipe deflector and card holder with alcohol-dampened cloth. Clean all feed rollers; move carrier as needed to access them.

Tab

4 After making sure that the capital lock is off, lift the element's locking tab and pull the element from the carrier.

5 Wipe element with alcohol-dampened cloth. Dab petroleum jelly inside to prevent binding (left). Pick debris from letters with pin (right).

6 With a clean dry paintbrush, brush off any dust and debris from the carrier assembly, housing, and keys.

7 Clean guide wire (above) with an alcohol-dampened cloth. Move carrier aside; brush dust cover with paintbrush.

8 Use an alcohol-dampened cloth to clean rail and margin brackets. Use a cotton swab dipped in alcohol to clean slot in print shaft.

Type-bar typewriters

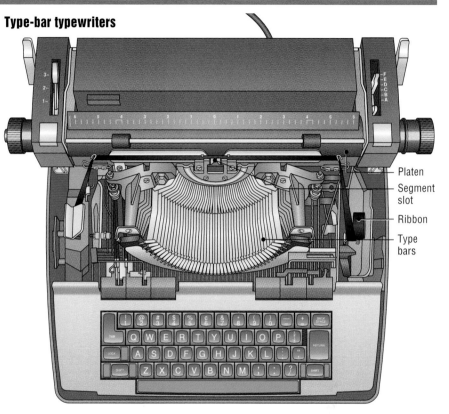

Platen
Segment slot
Ribbon
Type bars

The characters in an electric or manual type-bar typewriter are secured to metal bars arranged in a semicircle in front of the platen. When you press a key, a lever pushes the corresponding bar forward until it hits the paper. After each keystroke, a system of belts and pulleys advances the carriage and the paper. A common problem with type-bar typewriters occurs when you press two keys at once—the resulting clash between bars can knock the characters out of alignment or chip the typeface. If this occurs often, try regulating your typing rhythm or typing more slowly. To diagnose other type-bar typewriter problems, consult the *Troubleshooting* chart on page 52. As with type-element typewriters, it's essential to clean all of the typewriter's components on a regular basis (see *Servicing a type-bar typewriter*, p.52).

A critical part of electric type-bar machines is the power roll, a rubber-faced metal roller attached via a pulley to the typewriter's motor. When the typewriter is turned on, the power roll spins, transferring power from the motor to the carriage return, tab, and other moving parts. To keep the typewriter in good working order, periodically clean the power roll (p. 52, Step 5).

Troubleshooting: Type-bar typewriters

Problem	CAUSE? / Solution
Paper slips	RUBBER ON PLATEN STARTING TO HARDEN? Lightly rub platen with sandpaper or emery cloth. Vacuum area and wipe platen with lacquer thinner or denatured alcohol. ◇
Type cuts paper	HARDENED PLATEN? Place another sheet of paper under original as backing. Or consult an authorized service center to see if your platen can be reconditioned. ◇
Blurry print	WORN RIBBON? Replace ribbon. ◇
	DIRTY TYPEFACE? Clean the type bars (Step 2, right). ◇
Keys hard to press or type bar sticks in guide	BENT TYPE BAR? Grip bar with pliers and gently bend it back into shape. Or make several small bends; check alignment after each bend until bar is centered in guide. ◆
	BENT LINK? Gather the bars together into a group; secure with rubber band to hold them out of the way. Use needle-nose pliers to bend the link back into position. ◇
	OBJECT LODGED BENEATH TYPE BARS? Gather all the bars together into a group and secure them with rubber band. Use tweezers to remove object lodged beneath them. ◆
	CLOGGED SEGMENT SLOT? Use thin nail file or knife to scrape dirt from the slot. Clean slot with 50-50 mix of typewriter oil and nail polish remover. Drop solution into slot with an eyedropper and move type bar back and forth by hand to work it in. ◆
Margin or tab won't work	MECHANICAL STOPS DIRTY? *(Manual typewriters only)* Pry out the stops. Soak them in denatured alcohol or nail polish remover. ◇
	LEVER-TYPE TABS STUCK? *(Electric typewriters only)* Lubricate tabs with a 50-50 solution of nail polish remover and typewriter oil. ◇
Faulty space bar movement	CARRIAGE TRACK DIRTY? Clean the track with alcohol-dampened cloth; then lubricate it sparingly using a thin artist's brush dipped in typewriter oil. ◇

Degree of difficulty: Simple ◇   Average ◈   Complex ◆

Electronic typewriters

Resembling basic word processors more than they do traditional typewriters, electronic typewriters offer features such as changeable typefaces and built-in spell checkers. Most have a liquid crystal display (LCD) that shows the last few typed lines. Other than cleaning these units and maintaining the battery, there's not much you can do to repair them. A battery-powered memory stores all of the settings, including tabs and margins. When the battery dies, all the settings must be reset; avoid this by replacing the battery every 2 years. On most units, however, the battery must be replaced by a professional. If one of the typewriter's special functions works intermittently, make sure that all the cables are firmly attached to the circuit board. Move the carriage to one side to expose the board; then disconnect and reseat each of the cables. If the problem persists, take the typewriter to an authorized service center for repair. Because dirt and debris will interfere with an electronic typewriter's performance, periodically dust the housing and the carrier assembly with a soft artist's brush.

Servicing a type-bar typewriter

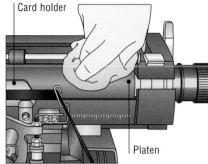
Card holder
Platen

1 Remove front cover. Brush off exposed areas with a clean soft paintbrush. Clean the platen and card holder with an alcohol-dampened cloth.

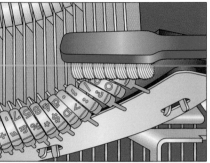

2 Clean the type bar faces with an alcohol-dampened cloth or with a stiff toothbrush. Use a straight pin to dig debris from clogged letters.

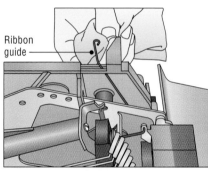
Ribbon guide

3 Remove the ribbon. Use a cloth to wipe any ink or carbon from the ribbon guides. Lightly scrape very dirty areas with thin nail file.

Dust pan

4 Turn electric machine onto its back and remove dust pan. Carefully brush dust from inside machine; clean dust pan.

Power roll pulley
Power roll

5 Clean electric machine's power roll with alcohol-dampened cloth. Turn power roll pulley to access entire surface of roll. Replace dust pan.

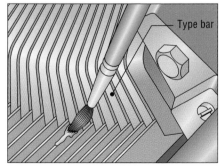
Type bar

6 Oil pivot points with a small artist's brush. Don't spray on oil; it will scatter. Lightly oil nuts and linkages underneath type bars.

Window blinds and shades

Venetian, mini, and micro blinds

The tape or string ladders that hold together the slats of a venetian, mini, or micro blind and the cords that lift them can wear with age and eventually break. To replace broken ladder tapes and lift cords, see below, right. Buy replacement parts at a hardware store, but make sure the tape is right for your blinds.

If a venetian blind sticks, look for a tangled cord inside the headbox; straightening the cords usually solves the problem. If the blind does not rise evenly, adjust the equalizing buckle on the lift cord.

Vertical blinds

The vanes of vertical blinds rotate to provide privacy and control light. They may part in the center or open to either side. Vertical blinds can be mounted on the wall, the ceiling, or against the inside surface of window or door jambs. A headrail hides the mounting brackets, the carriers that hold the vanes, the track that the carriers ride on, and the pulleys that move the vanes. Weights or chains used to connect the bottoms of the vanes keep them straight. Vertical blinds seldom fail; if they do, the problem is most likely related to the track. If you suspect a problem with the track, contact the manufacturer—attempting to fix the track yourself will usually void the warranty.

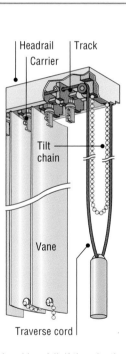

Headrail / Track / Carrier / Tilt chain / Vane / Traverse cord

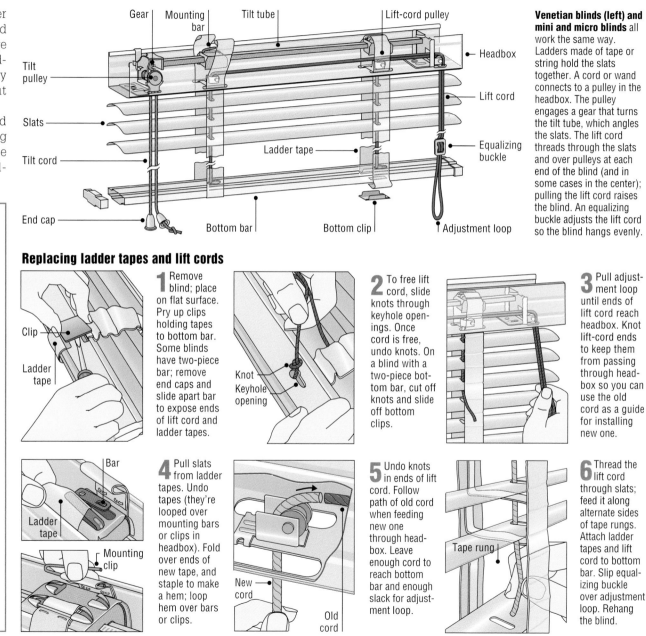

Gear | Mounting bar | Tilt tube | Lift-cord pulley | Headbox

Tilt pulley

Slats

Tilt cord

End cap

Lift cord

Ladder tape

Equalizing buckle

Bottom bar | Bottom clip | Adjustment loop

Venetian blinds (left) and mini and micro blinds all work the same way. Ladders made of tape or string hold the slats together. A cord or wand connects to a pulley in the headbox. The pulley engages a gear that turns the tilt tube, which angles the slats. The lift cord threads through the slats and over pulleys at each end of the blind (and in some cases in the center); pulling the lift cord raises the blind. An equalizing buckle adjusts the lift cord so the blind hangs evenly.

Replacing ladder tapes and lift cords

1 Remove blind; place on flat surface. Pry up clips holding tapes to bottom bar. Some blinds have two-piece bar; remove end caps and slide apart bar to expose ends of lift cord and ladder tapes.

Clip / Ladder tape

2 To free lift cord, slide knots through keyhole openings. Once cord is free, undo knots. On a blind with a two-piece bottom bar, cut off knots and slide off bottom clips.

Knot / Keyhole opening

3 Pull adjustment loop until ends of lift cord reach headbox. Knot lift-cord ends to keep them from passing through headbox so you can use the old cord as a guide for installing new one.

4 Pull slats from ladder tapes. Undo tapes (they're looped over mounting bars or clips in headbox). Fold over ends of new tape, and staple to make a hem; loop hem over bars or clips.

Bar / Ladder tape / Mounting clip

5 Undo knots in ends of lift cord. Follow path of old cord when feeding new one through headbox. Leave enough cord to reach bottom bar and enough slack for adjustment loop.

New cord / Old cord

6 Thread the lift cord through slats; feed it along alternate sides of tape rungs. Attach ladder tapes and lift cord to bottom bar. Slip equalizing buckle over adjustment loop. Rehang the blind.

Tape rung

53

Window shades

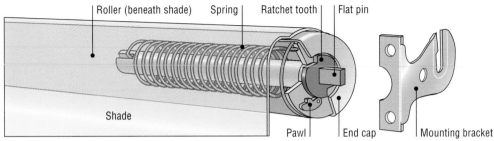

Roller (beneath shade) — Spring — Ratchet tooth — Flat pin
Shade — Pawl — End cap — Mounting bracket

Easy to install and maintain, window shades are sold by the width, measured from the tip of the round pin at one end of the roller to the tip of the flat pin at the other end. The pins fit into mounting brackets placed inside the window frame, on the face of the frame, or on the wall. One mounting bracket accepts the round pin; the other accepts the flat one.

The shade itself is stapled or taped to the roller, which is usually made of wood or cardboard and has metal end caps. One end of the roller is hollow and contains the shade's spring. The lower the shade is pulled, the more the spring's tension increases. When the shade is raised, the spring uncoils rapidly, wrapping the shade around the roller. Sluggish rewinding caused by insufficient spring tension is a common problem; too much tension also causes trouble. To fix these and other shade problems, see the chart at right.

Roll-up blinds

These blinds are a cross between venetian blinds (p.53) and roller shades (above). Like venetian blinds, they have slats and pulleys with a cord to lock them in place; but like roller shades, they only move up and down—there is no tilt mechanism to angle the slats.

If the cord slides off the blind, roll the blind by hand and slip the cord back into place. Replace a broken cord with the same type used in venetian blinds (available at hardware stores). Cut the knots above the headbox, and remove the old cord; save the buckle. Let the blind hang to full length. Feed the new cord through the headbox and knot it. Drop the cord down behind the blind and pull it underneath to the front. Feed the cord straight up the blind and through the pulley, across the headbox, and through the locking pulley on the other side. Allowing extra cord for the adjustment loop, then bring the cord back through the pulley. Bring the cord down the front, and up behind the blind. Knot it at the top. Slide the buckle over the loop and adjust.

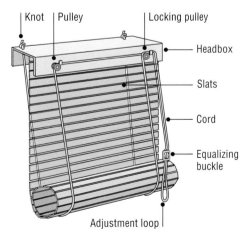

Knot — Pulley — Locking pulley
Headbox
Slats
Cord
Equalizing buckle
Adjustment loop

How the latching mechanism works

A small latching device at one end of the roller (called a pawl) locks onto the ratchet tooth to keep the roller from turning.

When shade is pulled down, pawl is rotated away from tooth, freeing roller. Spring tension then causes shade to rise.

As shade rolls up, centrifugal force keeps pawl pivoted outward, preventing it from engaging tooth and stopping roller.

When shade stops, centrifugal force ceases. Pawl then drops down onto tooth, locking shade in new position.

Troubleshooting window shades

Problem	CAUSE? / Solution
Shade rolls up too fast	SPRING TOO TIGHT? To loosen tension, roll up shade and remove roller from brackets. By hand, unroll the shade halfway. Replace roller in brackets. Repeat if necessary. ◇
Shade rolls up too slowly	SPRING TOO LOOSE? Pull shade down halfway. Remove roller from brackets. Roll up shade by hand; then replace roller on brackets. Repeat if necessary. ◇
Shade can't be raised	SPRING FULLY UNCOILED? Remove roller from brackets. Unroll shade halfway, twist flat pin with pliers until you feel tension, then back off so pawl hooks onto ratchet. Adjust tension (above). ◆
Shade can't be pulled down	SPRING LOCKED IN COIL? Remove roller from brackets. Grip flat pin with pliers, twist clockwise to free the pawl, then release quickly. As the coil unwinds, the pin will spin counterclockwise. Adjust the tension as needed (above). ◆
Shade doesn't stay down	RATCHET NOT LOCKING? Remove roller from brackets. Take off metal dust cap. Brush dirt off pawl and ratchet. Lubricate them with penetrating oil. ◇
Shade is crooked	BRACKETS NOT LEVEL? Place a carpenter's level on the roller. If the level's bubble is not centered, remove and reposition one of the mounting brackets. ◆
Shade binds	BRACKETS TOO CLOSE TOGETHER? If possible, reposition brackets farther apart. Or flatten inside mounting brackets by tapping them with a hammer; bend outside mounting brackets away from window. As a last resort, shorten round pin with hacksaw. ◆
Shade wobbles	BENT ROUND PIN? Remove roller; straighten pin with pliers. ◇
Shade falls from brackets	BRACKETS LOOSE? Tighten mounting screws. ◇
	BRACKETS TOO FAR APART? Reposition mounting brackets. Shim one or both inside mounting brackets to move them closer. ◆

Degree of difficulty: Simple ◇   Average ◆   Complex ◆

Furniture repair

You can prevent small problems from growing into big ones by maintaining the frame and finish of your wooden furniture and by making repairs promptly. Luckily, most of this work is within the reach of a typical do-it-yourselfer using common hand tools.

Furniture repair sometimes calls for a combination of skills. To refurbish a cherished club chair, for example, you may have to strip off the old finish, strengthen the frame, patch nicks or gouges in the legs, reupholster the seat, and (finally) apply a stain and sealer to any exposed wood. Before you attempt such projects, review this entire section to identify the woodworking, finishing, and sewing skills you'll need for the work. Most furniture repairs involve gluing and clamping, so read those pages with particular care. Because stains, strippers, and finishes can be hazardous to work with, follow the manufacturer's instructions when dealing with these products and consult *For your safety,* p.81, before you get started.

Saws and sawing 15
Keeping tools sharp 16
Clamps and clamping 59

Furniture repair ▪ Woodworking tools

Enlarging your tool kit

A standard tool kit (p.10) already contains many of the tools you'll need for basic furniture repair: a utility knife, a hammer, pliers, screwdrivers, a combination square, and an electric drill. In addition, you may need to acquire some or all of the woodworking tools shown at right. Consider adding specialized tools, such as a dowel center (p.67) or a veneer saw (p.79), as necessary for a particular job. Because most furniture repairs involve gluing and clamping, it's a good idea to have several types and sizes of clamps on hand. Although each clamp is designed for a specific function, one type can often be substituted for another, or two small clamps can do the job of a large one. For more on clamping, see pages 59–61.

Before buying a tool, make sure it's the right one for the job. To avoid harming yourself or your work, never use a tool for a task that it wasn't intended to perform. For example, the coarse teeth of a ripsaw are no substitute for the finer teeth of a tenon saw. It's best to purchase the highest quality tool that you can afford. In most cases, a good-quality tool will perform better than a cheaper model; and with proper use, care, and storage, it will last a lifetime.

You'll need a flat, uncluttered surface on which to work and a way to secure the work. Large objects can be set on the floor. To avoid back strain, place smaller objects on a waist-level work surface. While a workbench with a woodworker's vise is ideal, a sturdy table with a clamp-on vise will do. In some cases, you can hold down the work with a clamp instead of a vise.

Tools for the furniture restorer

Tenon saw makes fine, clean cuts. Its stiff blade makes it ideal for cutting tenons and dovetails.

Wooden mallet is used to assemble and dismantle joints. To prevent marring, use with a wood block.

Chisel shaves off small areas of wood; it's especially useful for making recesses and for trimming a joint to make it fit flush. Match blade's width to that of wood to be removed.

Hand plane shaves down swollen or warped wood and smooths edges and surfaces. The block plane shown is ideal for cramped spots. Use a plane with a longer body for larger areas.

Pipe clamp is a heavy-duty variation of the bar clamp at right. Jaws come in two sizes, to fit ½-in.- or ¾-in.-diameter pipe. One end of pipe must be threaded. Squeeze disc to slide movable jaw along pipe. To apply pressure, turn handle on other jaw.

C-clamp comes in various sizes. Used alone or in combination with other clamps, it can hold glued pieces together or hold work to a surface.

Spring clamp functions as an extra hand to hold parts. Squeeze the handles to open the jaws; a spring will force them closed. Vinyl-coated tips protect against marring.

Scraper shears paper-thin shavings from a wood surface. It can be used instead of sandpaper to prepare wood for first coat of finish.

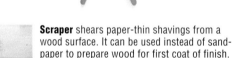

Clamp-on vise turns any sturdy work surface into a workbench. To adjust jaws on clamp or vise, simply turn handle. To protect furniture finish, insert scrap wood between vise jaws and work.

Band clamp wraps around rectangular, curved, and irregular shapes, applying pressure to several joints at once. Tighten the nylon band with the accompanying wrench. Brackets protect corners of work.

Hand-screw clamp adjusts to hold work at many angles. Its flat wooden jaws won't damage furniture surfaces.

Quick-Grip clamp has one fixed jaw and a trigger-action adjustable jaw. You can use it to apply light pressure, with only one hand on the clamp.

Fast-action clamp is a short version of the bar clamp (below). It's ideal for holding work to a table.

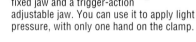

Bar clamp, available in several lengths, is suitable for most clamping jobs. The longer clamps are good for extra-wide repairs such as gluing a tabletop. One bar-clamp jaw is fixed; the other slides along the bar. Once the clamp is set, apply pressure by turning the handle.

Working with wood

Analyzing the job

Before starting a repair, look over the entire piece of furniture closely; the more familiar you are with its construction, the easier it will be to make the repair properly. Pay particular attention to the joints between parts. Try to determine whether the damaged element has weakened other sections. An unstable chair back, for example, may cause the arms to work loose. Look for damage to the hardware and veneer, if any, as well as to the finish. Plan to repair all the damage at the same time. If you find that there is much work to be done, make a list to put the steps in sequence.

When possible, select a repair technique that conforms to the original construction method. For example, if a broken leg was originally attached with a mortise-and-tenon, attach the replacement leg the same way. Avoid using nails or other hardware. They are likely to split and weaken the wood.

Organize your work area so that everything you need will be within reach. Place clean towels or other cloth under the piece to protect its finish; cover the floor with a drop cloth. For a glue-up job, be sure you have enough glue, and keep a damp rag and a container of water at hand to wipe away excess glue.

Dismantle parts carefully to avoid damaging the wood. The less dismantling you do the better, but some furniture repairs call for taking apart the whole piece to fix one joint. For easier reassembly, use a grease pencil or ink on masking tape to number parts as you remove them. Before regluing, remove all the old glue from the joints, and test-fit the pieces to make sure the reassembly goes smoothly.

To prolong the life of your furniture, regularly examine it for loose joints or hardware, for small breaks or splits, and for other damage. Always fix minor problems before they have a chance to become major ones.

Identifying the wood

Although most furniture is made of hardwood, such as mahogany, maple, or oak, softwood is also used in furniture construction. For example, chests and outdoor furniture may be made of cedar, fir, or redwood; inexpensive utilitarian furniture is often constructed of pine. Reproductions of traditional pieces are frequently made of softwoods.

If a repair entails replacing a furniture part, make sure the new part matches the wood of the piece. If you don't know the species, study the wood for clues. Even though individual pieces of the same species will vary, depending on growing conditions, age, and cutting methods, pieces of the same type of wood should share certain characteristics.

The best way to identify wood is by grain patterns. Pore size (called texture) is another good indicator—red and white oak, for example, have large pores; the pores of cherry are smaller. You'll find that the color of a wood is seldom a reliable guide in identifying it. Furniture is usually stained or finished to imitate a more expensive or rare wood; and even untreated wood will often darken with age. Try looking for an untreated section, such as the underside of a desk; but make sure the entire piece is constructed of the same wood.

Maple. Cream to light reddish brown. Dense wood with fine texture. Grain is straight or highly figured in bird's-eye, curly, or quilted patterns. Difficult to work. Finishes well.

Oak. Hard wood with distinct grain patterns. Red oak is pinkish red; has coarse texture. White oak is tan; has medium-coarse texture. Moderately easy to work. Finishes well.

Walnut. Light gray-brown to purplish black. Hard and fine-textured. Grain may be straight or wavy. Easy to work. Finishes well.

Mahogany. Light pink to reddish brown. Fine-textured, great variety of grain patterns. Moderately soft hardwood. Easy to work. Finishing turns wood deep red; may be blotchy.

Ash. Cream to light yellowish brown. Coarse-textured and straight-grained. A hard wood. Moderately easy to work. Finishes well.

Cherry. Light to dark reddish brown veins. Darkens with age. Moderately hard and fine-textured. Grain is straight but may have delicate patterns. Moderately easy to work. Finishes well.

Teak. Tawny yellow to rich dark brown; lighter streaks. Coarse-textured and moderately hard; can be brittle. Has straight or wavy grain. Moderately easy to work; hard to sand. Finishes well.

White pine. Light cream to pale brown softwood. This lightweight wood is fine-textured and straight-grained. It often has knots. Easy to work. Finishes well.

Dismantling joints

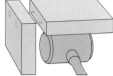

Butt. Tap joint apart with mallet. Hammer nail tips to expose heads; pull nails out with hammer claws.

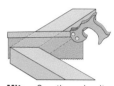

Miter. Saw through miter. Before reassembling, glue wood shim as thick as saw kerf to one side of joint.

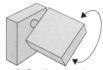

Dowel. Gently twist single dowel apart; saw through multiple dowels.

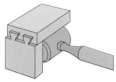

Dovetail (and mortise-and-tenon). Tap joint apart with wood mallet.

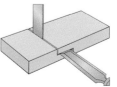

Rabbet. Tap chisels into glue lines; pull apart.

Furniture repair ▪ Gluing

Whether you're mending a split or fixing a loose joint, you can rely on glue to produce a strong, lasting repair. The woodworking purist may prefer traditional hot hide glue, especially on older pieces constructed with it. However, this opaque brown glue (which may still be available from some woodworker's catalogs) hasn't been a popular choice since the early 1900's. Today's widely available aliphatic resin, or yellow, glue is your best bet. Yellow glue is easy to clean up, its bonding power on wood is superior to that of other types of glue, and once it dries it becomes translucent. But because yellow glue begins to set in 8 to 10 minutes, that is all the time you have to assemble and clamp your repair.

Glue works by soaking in and attaching itself to the wood fibers. Because a film of old glue will prevent fresh glue from penetrating the wood and forming a strong bond, remove all old glue before starting the repair. Be careful not to damage the wood; a strong joint requires snug-fitting parts. When you're ready to reassemble any parts separated for a repair, dry-fit them by assembling the work without the glue. This allows you to make sure all joints fit properly and to make any necessary adjustments. Dry-fitting also lets you establish the types of clamps you'll need and the most efficient assembly sequence.

Apply glue to both surfaces of the joint or repair. A little glue should squeeze out during clamping; excessive glue will result in a messy cleanup job. No visible glue along the joint line means the joint is "starved" and will have little strength. Quickly unclamp the pieces, add glue, and reclamp the work.

Wipe off excess glue with a clean wet cloth. Occasionally rinse out the cloth in water. Leave clamps on for the time indicated on the glue label, but remember that glue takes longer to dry in humid weather.

Removing glue

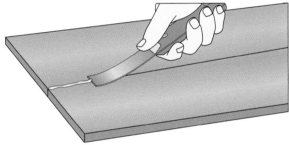

To lift off fresh semihard glue before it completely cures, use a flexible-bladed putty knife. (In some cases, this method is preferable to wetting the wood with a rag.) To prevent accidental nicks, round off the corners of the knife with a bench grinder or file.

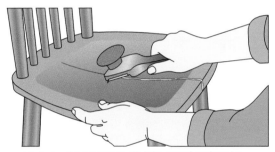

Scrape dried glue from a flat or slightly curved surface by pulling a paint scraper along the glue line. Work carefully to avoid removing wood fibers along with the glue. If the old glue is loose and flaky, you can sand it off with a sheet of coarse sandpaper.

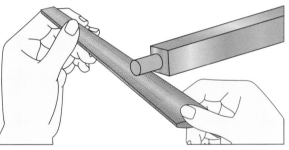

Remove old glue from a dowel with a fine wood rasp or a utility knife. Clean old glue from sockets and mortises with a narrow chisel, then with coarse sandpaper wrapped around a rod. When choosing a rod, allow room to accommodate the sandpaper.

Applying glue

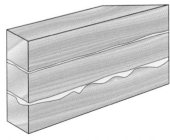

A continuous bead of glue (top) along a clamped joint signals a good bond. A dripping glue joint (bottom) is messy; too much glue won't allow the joint to join properly, causing a weak joint.

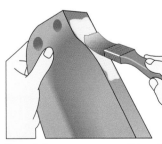

Spread glue on a narrow surface with a brush, completely covering the surface. For a simple joint, let the glue dry 1 min. before mating the pieces. To glue a dowel joint, see page 62.

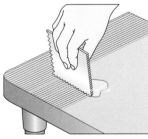

Cover large flat areas with a notched spreader (or piece of broken hacksaw blade). The teeth will spread the glue easily and keep its depth consistent.

To avoid dismantling a joint, inject glue into drilled hole with a syringe-type injector (available from woodworker's catalogs). Inspect the joint regularly to make sure it's holding up.

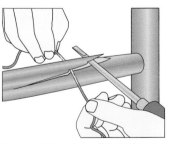

To spread glue in a split, gently pry split open with a screwdriver or awl. Dab glue on mating surfaces of split; spread glue by pulling a length of string as far as possible into split.

Clamps and clamping

A clamp used alone or in combination with others can securely hold work being chiseled or planed. Clamps prove their real value, however, when you're gluing parts together. Clamping until the glue dries is essential for ensuring a strong bond. C-clamps, hand-screw clamps, bar clamps, and pipe clamps will work for a variety of repairs. Because a job can require clamps of different types and sizes, the more you have, the better. Build up your collection by acquiring clamps as needed. Before buying specialized clamps, consider if standard clamps can do the same job.

Some clamps have two adjustable jaws; most have a stationary jaw and a movable one. To use a clamp, set the stationary jaw against the work, then tighten the movable jaw. Because the jaws can apply great pressure, protect the wood from dents by placing scrap wood blocks or rubber pads between the work and the jaws. For a large project, use wood blocks to spread the clamping pressure. Since metal parts leave stains if they touch glue, place a piece of wax paper or a bit of plastic bag between the glue and the clamp.

For smooth assembly, rehearse the clamping sequence before applying glue. Preadjust the clamps so that during the actual clamping job you can simply tighten them with a few twists. Set each clamp so that the pressure it exerts is at an exact right angle to the glue line. Even a slight misalignment can cause the joint to slip or distort. Once the clamp is in place,

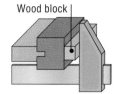
Wood block

Correctly aligned block

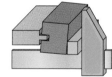

Misaligned block

tighten it. If a job requires several clamps, tighten the middle one first, then work outward to the ends. This forces trapped air out and creates a strong glue bond. Don't overtighten the clamps; too much pressure will squeeze out all the glue and crush the wood fibers. Too little pressure results in a thick glue line and a weak joint. An even ridge of glue indicates the right amount of glue and correct clamp pressure.

Hand-screw clamp

Often referred to as a hand screw, this versatile clamp may be used in several ways. The independent jaw design permits you to adjust the jaws to apply parallel pressure along their length or to apply pressure only at the tips. The jaws may also be offset. The handle farthest from the clamping action applies the most pressure, so you should tighten that one last. Because the jaws are wood, they won't mar a wood surface, making scrap pads unnecessary.

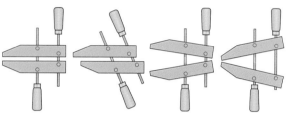

Set the clamp jaws in any of four basic positions: Clamp parallel surfaces with parallel jaws. Adjust one jaw to extend beyond the other to clamp offset parallel faces. Open the jaws to the desired angle for irregular contours. For small elements, angle the jaw tips.

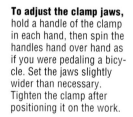

To adjust the clamp jaws, hold a handle of the clamp in each hand, then spin the handles hand over hand as if you were pedaling a bicycle. Set the jaws slightly wider than necessary. Tighten the clamp after positioning it on the work.

C-clamp

Named for the shape of its body, the C-clamp comes in a range of jaw capacities (the distance between the jaws when they're completely open) and throat depths (the distance from the front to the back of the clamp). Deep-throat C-clamps can apply pressure toward the center of a wide piece. Measure your job requirements carefully before buying clamps. Securing a small repair with a large clamp could misalign the joint. When using several C-clamps, make sure that you space them evenly along the work.

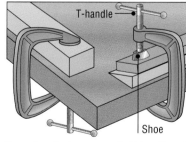
T-handle
Shim
Shoe

To apply a C-clamp, turn the T-handle until the jaws grip the work snugly, then tighten it an additional quarter turn. The swivel shoe of the adjustable jaw automatically tilts on angled surfaces.

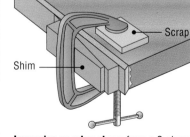
Scrap
Shim

Improvise an edge clamp from a C-clamp by driving wedge-shaped shims between the edge to be clamped and the clamp's frame. Scrap wood keeps the top and bottom surfaces of the wood from denting.

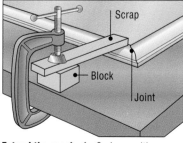
Scrap
Block
Joint

Extend the reach of a C-ciamp with a wood block and a long piece of scrap. To transfer the clamping pressure to the glue joint, make sure that the block is thicker than the piece being glued.

Offset clamp jaws to clamp parallel but offset surfaces, as when repairing a veneer bubble in a tabletop. To prevent adhesive from sticking to the wood jaw, slip a piece of paper, a small section of a plastic shopping bag, or a double layer of heavy-duty wax paper between the work and the jaw.

Furniture repair ▪ Clamps and clamping

When a repair calls for a clamp that can span a large area, the bar clamp and pipe clamp are the ones to use. They're especially good for gluing boards edge-to-edge to form a large flat surface.

The jaws of a bar clamp are mounted on a flat steel bar. Notches on the bar let you lock in the movable jaw at regular intervals. Turning the handle on the fixed jaw allows you to adjust the pressure applied to the work. To use a bar clamp, set the fixed jaw against one side of the work, slide the movable jaw against the other side, and tighten the clamp. The small version of the bar clamp, also called a fast-action clamp, is ideal for jobs requiring lightweight clamps.

Pipe clamps are used in the same way as bar clamps. The clamp heads come in two sizes, to fit ½-inch or ¾-inch black iron threaded-end pipes of any length. The jaws are available in two sizes: the standard size is for typical glue-up jobs; the deep-jaw size allows more clearance for the work between the jaw tips and the pipe. The fixed jaw screws onto one end of the pipe; the movable jaw slides over the other end. Because pipe is relatively inexpensive, buy pipes of various lengths and use the heads interchangeably.

Spring clamps. Fast and easy to use, spring clamps work much like clothespins. They are suitable for light-duty work where clamps should be applied quickly, as when you're clamping a split picture frame or a cracked chair rail. Position spring clamps carefully: If not placed at an exact right angle to the glue line, they can push the joint out of alignment. If the jaws have vinyl protective tips, it's not necessary to slip scrap pads between the work and the jaws.

Band and web clamps. To put pressure on round or irregular objects or to secure several joints at once, use band clamps or web clamps. These clamps are especially useful for repairing chairs and gluing mitered frames. To use either clamp, wrap the length of fabric or webbing around the work. Tighten the band clamp with the wrench it comes with, the web clamp with its built-in crank. When clamping, be sure that pressure is evenly distributed and that the band does not slip out of place as you tighten the clamp.

Bar and pipe clamps

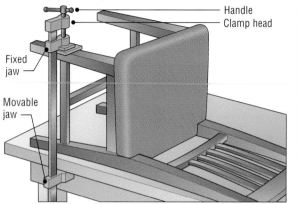

Handle
Clamp head

Fixed jaw

Movable jaw

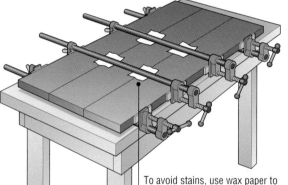

To avoid stains, use wax paper to separate clamp and glue at joint.

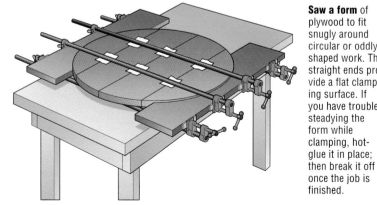

Bar clamp is excellent for large jobs (gluing chair rails, for example) and for clamping wide flat areas. Here the bar clamp, acting as a large woodworker's vise, braces the chair against the workbench.

Pipe clamp, which can often be substituted for a bar clamp, is useful for clamping edge-glued boards. When a job requires three or more clamps, stagger them above and below the work to equalize clamping pressure and to keep the wood from bowing.

Saw a form of plywood to fit snugly around circular or oddly shaped work. The straight ends provide a flat clamping surface. If you have trouble steadying the form while clamping, hot-glue it in place; then break it off once the job is finished.

Spring clamps

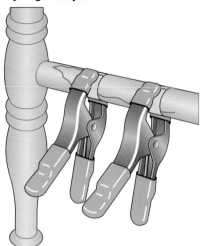

Spring clamp applies narrowly focused pressure. To reduce slippage, hold the repair together with masking tape until the glue is tacky, then apply the clamp.

Band and web clamps

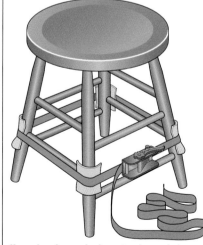

Use a band or web clamp to clamp chair or stool legs. To close a stubborn joint, try wiggling parts as you increase clamping pressure. To clamp splayed legs, see page 65.

Improvised clamping

Even if you do not own a large selection of clamps, you can still manage a wide range of furniture repairs with just a little improvisation. Clamps can be combined in different configurations to exert exactly the right pressure on the work. Or you can fabricate your own clamping devices from such common household materials as masking tape, rubber bands, cord, rope, and bungee cords. Even an ordinary automotive hose clamp can be used to repair a split in the end of a chair leg. As with a more conventional clamp, position an improvised clamp to distribute pressure evenly over the components being glued together. In most cases, you'll need to protect the furniture surface by sliding some sort of padding—a scrap piece of wood, rubber, cloth, or cardboard—between the clamp and the wood. (Masking tape and hand-screw clamps don't require pads.)

Masking tape is ideal for securing straight or curved repairs where only light pressure is required. It also comes in handy when regluing veneer repairs.

Whatever the repair, apply glue to both surfaces, press the pieces together by hand, and wrap them with the tape. (If the repair is on a turning, overlap the edges of the tape on each turn.) Make sure you keep the pieces of the repair aligned as you apply the tape. Allow the glue to dry overnight before removing the tape. Then sand off the gummy residue, or wipe it off with a rag dampened with turpentine, mineral spirits, or other solvent.

If you don't have a band or web clamp, use a length of rope, twine, or sturdy string. Any of these items can be made into a tourniquet for clamping together several joints at one time or for clamping an irregularly shaped object. Because it is soft, strong, and less stretchy than other types of rope and twine, heavy cotton clothesline is the best choice for clamping. Use a double strand when possible. Exert pressure on the work by twisting a dowel rod, wooden spoon, or stick in the rope. Bungee cords are also a suitable substitute for a band or web clamp.

Clamping with masking tape

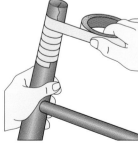

To mend a split in a furniture part, apply glue to both surfaces, then tightly overlap masking tape around the repair.

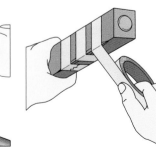

Reglue a chip or sliver by applying glue to loose piece and fitting it back in place. Securely tape repair until glue dries.

Ensure proper positioning of pieces in a repair by anchoring them in place with masking tape before applying clamps.

Combining two or more clamps

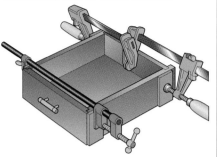

Combine two fast-action or C-clamps to span wide workpiece when only light clamping pressure is required. Hook the jaws firmly so that they can't be jarred apart.

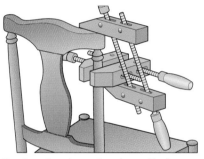

Create a clamping surface by positioning a hand-screw clamp above the jaw of a second clamp. To properly align pressure over joint, offset the jaws of the second hand-screw clamp.

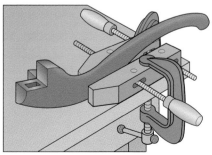

Improvise a vise to hold a workpiece for planing, sanding, or chiseling with a combination of hand-screws, C-clamps, or bar clamps. Position clamps so they're out of the way of your tools.

Tourniquets

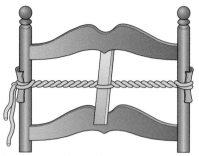

To make a tourniquet clamp, knot the rope around the parts to be glued, insert a rod, and twist until the pressure is right. Wedge the rod in place to keep the cord from unwinding.

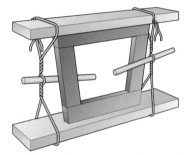

Clamp odd-shaped structure, such as this chair seat, with cord-and-board clamp. Boards distribute pressure evenly over structure. Twist rods to exert pressure; wedge them against work.

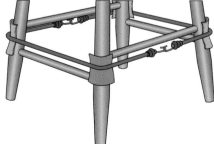

Bungee cords work like web or band clamps. They can't be adjusted, so keep several lengths on hand. Combine short cords to make longer ones; wrap too-long cords in a figure-8 pattern.

Furniture repair ▪ Dowels

One way to create a strong joint is to use one or more dowels, or wooden rods, in combination with glue. The dowel rests in sockets drilled in the mating surfaces of the joint. In furniture repair (especially in chair repair), dowels are also used to strengthen a loose joint or to replace a broken one. While inserting a dowel or dowels through a joint won't provide as much strength as replacing the original joint, this repair is quicker to perform and is adequate in most cases. Because dowel reinforcement remains visible, use it only where appearance is not critical.

An old dowel joint can work loose with time, causing a furniture piece to wobble or even break. While a loose joint can sometimes be reglued in place using a syringe-type glue injector (p.58), the repair will be more durable if you disassemble the joint, replace the worn or broken dowel, and then reglue the joint. If possible, twist out the old dowel or pull it free with pliers, being careful not to break the dowel. Don't pry around the dowel with a knife or screwdriver as this could damage or enlarge the socket. If a broken dowel is stuck in its socket, chisel the exterior part flush to the surface, then drill out the embedded piece with a drill bit that matches the diameter of the dowel. Carefully estimate the depth you will need to drill, and mark this depth on the bit with masking tape (p.13).

To clean the old glue out of the sockets, gently sand the sockets with a piece of medium-grit sandpaper wrapped around a smaller-diameter dowel. Before inserting the new dowel into the socket, blow out any sawdust (make sure you wear eye protection). Before gluing the joint, test the new dowel in the sockets. If the dowel fits loosely, use a larger dowel or wrap the dowel with thread (see right).

You can purchase precut dowels in a variety of sizes or cut your own from dowel stock. Available in diameters ranging from ⅛ to 1 inch, dowel stock is sold at most home centers in 36-inch lengths. Precut dowels have fluted sides to allow excess glue to escape. If you cut dowels from dowel stock, saw one or two lengthwise flutes in the dowel's surface for this purpose; also round off the dowel ends.

Reinforcing a loose joint with dowels

1 Measure and mark placement for dowel sockets centered on the joint. Drill through first half of the joint and about 1 in. into the mating piece, using a brad-point bit of the same diameter as the dowel. Clean out sawdust with a small brush, or blow it out (wear goggles).

Placement mark

2 Insert the dowel into the socket, and mark it ⅛ in. away from the work surface. Cut the dowel at the mark with a fine-tooth backsaw. Remove the dowel and squeeze glue into the socket—not on the dowel. Spread the glue around with a long thin sliver of wood.

3 Insert the dowel into the socket, and tap it with a mallet or hammer. Clamp the joint until the glue dries; then pare off the stub with a sharp chisel. If necessary, sand the dowel flush with the surface of the work. Finally, stain or paint the area.

TIPS FROM THE PROS

Wrap an undersize dowel with thread or string so that it will fit snugly in its socket. If a dowel joint comes loose, dismantle it. Wrap the dowel with thread, and apply glue on the thread and in the socket. Reassemble the joint and clamp it until the glue dries.

Replacing a broken dowel

1 After dismantling the joint, drill out the dowel recessed in the socket using a drill bit the same size as the dowel. Mark the depth of the socket on the bit with a piece of masking tape. (A dowel socket in a chair leg should be no deeper than half the thickness of the leg.)

2 On the mating piece, saw off the protruding part of the dowel flush to the joint line. Then make a socket by marking the center for the new dowel and carefully drilling a hole to the same depth as the first socket.

3 Cut the new dowel to size. Its length should be equal to the combined depth of both sockets, less ⅛ in. to leave space for excess glue. Test the fit. The new dowel should fit snugly with no gaps around the sides.

4 Apply glue to the inner surface of both dowel sockets with a long thin sliver of wood. Insert the dowel. Quickly assemble the joint and any others that were disassembled for the repair. Clamp the parts firmly in place, and let the glue dry thoroughly.

Mortise-and-tenon joints

In this type of joint, a tenon protruding from one end of a workpiece fits into a mortise recessed into the mating piece. A loose mortise-and-tenon joint can be reglued by using a syringe-type glue injector, but the repair may not last very long. A better strategy is to dismantle the joint and build up the size of the tenon—by adding either wood shims or wedges—so that it once again fits snugly in its mortise. Make tenon shims out of thin pieces of wood, one or more layers of wood veneer, or iron-on veneer tape. Make sure you remove all traces of the old glue before gluing and clamping the repaired joint.

Tightening the joint by inserting wedges can be difficult. If the wedges are too large, the joint won't close properly; if they're too small, the tenon will not expand enough for a tight joint. For an extremely tight joint, chisel the narrow sides of the mortise to angle wider toward the bottom of the recess. When the tenon is inserted and expands, there is little chance it will pop out.

A tenon that has broken off at its base can sometimes be reattached as long as you can remove it from the mortise in one piece. If this is not possible, the best solution is to remove the broken tenon and replace it with a new loose tenon. This is a strong repair that's relatively easy to carry out. First drill out any remaining pieces of tenon from the original mortise. Then cut a new mortise in the part of the joint that previously was tenoned, and glue a new hardwood loose tenon into both mortises. Another alternative is to fill the mortise with a piece of hardwood and reconstruct the joint using dowels.

Tightening a loose mortise-and-tenon

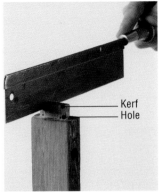

Kerf
Hole

1 Drill two holes near the base of the tenon, ½ in. from the sides. Use a drill bit that is slightly wider than the blade of the dovetail or tenon saw you'll be using to cut the kerfs. Then make two kerfs by sawing down the length of the tenon to each hole. (The holes stop the kerfs from creeping down any further.)

2 Cut thin wood wedges and insert them into the kerfs. Gently tap the wedges into place with a hammer or mallet. The tenon's new width should equal that of the mortise. Saw or chisel the ends of the wedges about ⅛ in. from the tenon. Pull out the wedges; reinsert them partway without tapping them in.

3 Apply glue to the mortise and the tenon, and reassemble the joint by lightly tapping it together. (Protect the work with a scrap block of wood.) As the tenon reaches the back of the mortise, the wedges will be forced into the tenon, thus expanding the tenon. Clamp the joint until the glue is dry.

If you need to increase the thickness of a tenon rather than its width, glue a thin wood shim to its side. Cut shim to exact size of tenon. Before gluing joint together, test the fit. If tenon is still too small, add a second shim to the opposite side; if it's too big, sand down the shim with coarse-grit sandpaper.

Replacing a broken tenon

1 Remove the broken tenon from the mortise by carefully drilling with a bit the same width as the mortise; clean out the mortise. Using a tenon saw or other small fine-tooth backsaw, cut the remains of the protruding tenon flush with the wood surface.

2 Measure and mark placement for a new mortise in the old tenon area; it should be the same size as the original mortise. Using a drill bit as wide as the mortise, drill out the wood without overlapping holes. Use masking tape around the bit to act as a depth guide (p.13).

3 Chisel out the long sides of the mortise with a wide chisel. (Hold the chisel so that the beveled ends of the blade face inside the mortise.) Clean out the narrow sides and the bottom of the mortise using a small chisel. Be careful not to change the shape of the mortise.

4 Saw a hardwood tenon to snugly fit new and old mortises. Apply glue to one end of the tenon and inside one mortise. Tap the tenon into the glued mortise with a mallet and clamp. Once the glue dries, glue and clamp together the opposite tenon end and mortise.

Furniture repair ▪ Chairs

Frame chair

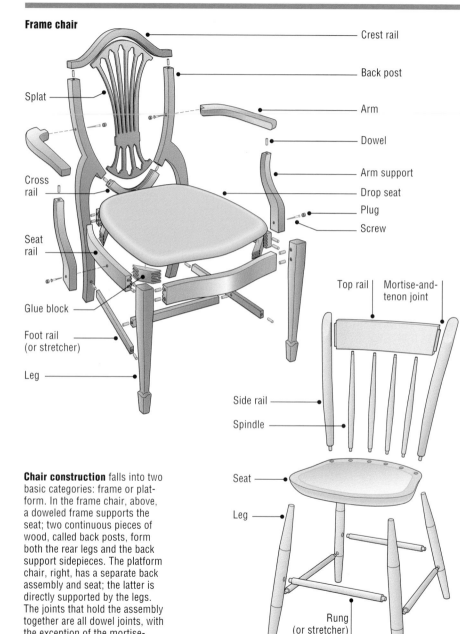

Crest rail

Back post

Arm

Dowel

Arm support

Drop seat

Plug

Screw

Splat

Cross rail

Seat rail

Glue block

Foot rail (or stretcher)

Leg

Top rail | Mortise-and-tenon joint

Side rail

Spindle

Seat

Leg

Rung (or stretcher)

Platform chair

Chair construction falls into two basic categories: frame or platform. In the frame chair, above, a doweled frame supports the seat; two continuous pieces of wood, called back posts, form both the rear legs and the back support sidepieces. The platform chair, right, has a separate back assembly and seat; the latter is directly supported by the legs. The joints that hold the assembly together are all dowel joints, with the exception of the mortise-and-tenon joint that is sometimes found at the top rail.

A wood chair suffers more everyday strain than most other types of furniture. Its lightweight structure, made up of many interlocking elements, has to provide sturdy support for a person's weight. Most well-made chairs endure a lifetime of heavy loads (and even occasional misuse) with only routine repairs. But if these repairs are neglected, minor problems will soon escalate into major ones. A small split may turn into a break, or a joint may loosen and shift its burden to neighboring joints, causing several others to fail.

All but the finest chairs can often be repaired at home with simple tools. The repairs you can expect to make depend in part on the way the chair is constructed. In platform chairs, for example, the joints between the rungs and the legs are most vulnerable to damage; frame chairs are prone to break at the joints near the back of the seat.

If you notice play in a frame chair during use, see whether the frame is working loose around the seat. If it is, try strengthening the structure by installing glue blocks. Cut a block of hardwood to fit snugly into each corner of the frame. Make the blocks about 1½ inches thick and 5 to 6 inches long. Drill two holes through each block and into the frame. Glue the mating surfaces and screw the blocks into place.

Where glue blocks are already a part of the assembly, reinstall them with fresh glue and slightly larger diameter screws to increase their holding power.

Before taking a chair apart, examine it carefully; plan to correct any previous quick-fix repairs. Before disassembly, remove all fasteners. If there are any wood plugs, pry or drill them out and remove the screws they conceal. Label the chair's components to ensure that you reassemble them correctly. This is especially important with spindles, which may be graduated in size.

In any chair, the best way to fix loose joinery is to dismantle only the damaged part of the chair and reglue the joints. Dismantle the whole chair only as a last resort for serious repairs; try to avoid taking sound joints apart. If a joint is only slightly loose, you may be able to fix it by injecting a liquid wood sweller into it. But never substitute screws, nails, metal plates, or angle irons for a good glue job.

When disassembling a joint (p.57), use the least amount of pressure possible. Because mortise-and-tenon joints can be easily damaged, it's best to saw off the tenon rather than risk damaging the mortise.

Before reassembling the chair, test-fit the pieces without glue to be sure the joints fit tightly.

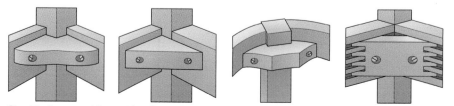

Glue blocks support the seat in a frame chair. They fit snugly below the seat at the leg-rail joints.

Disassembling a chair

To remove glue block, first remove any screws. Give the edge of the block a sharp tap with a hammer or wood mallet. If the block is joined to the frame with an interlocking joint, insert a wedge behind the block; tap wedge with a mallet.

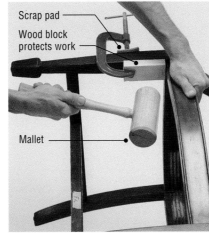

Separate a loose dowel joint by manually twisting and turning a leg, rail, or spindle from its socket. If you hear a cracking sound, don't be alarmed. It's not unusual to leave part of the dowel in the joint. To remove it, see page 62.

Gentle tapping with a wood mallet or a hammer can coax apart a joint that won't separate by twisting. If necessary, use a syringe-type glue injector to apply a glue-softening solution made of equal parts of hot water and white vinegar.

Free a stubborn joint by springing it apart with a ¾-in.-thick bowed wood strip slightly longer than the rail or spindle. To bow the wood, wet it; then clamp it and let sit overnight. Slowly apply pressure with a hand screw until the joint separates.

Reassembling a platform chair

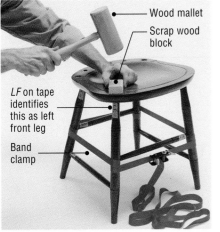

1 Glue the legs and rails; secure with a band clamp. If legs splay out, stop band from slipping by looping it around each leg. Firm up seat by alternately tapping each joint with a mallet (protect the finish with a block). Let glue dry.

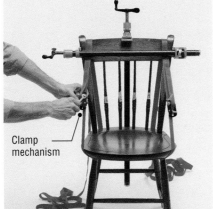

2 Add and clamp the back, with band clamp mechanisms facing front. Firm up spindle joints with the mallet, tightening the clamps as you work. If the chair has arms, add them last. Cinch a band clamp under seat and around arms.

Reassembling a frame chair

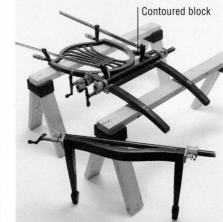

1 Glue and clamp back assembly; if needed, add blocks to create flat clamping surface. To square work, lay it on flat surface; adjust until diagonal measurements from corner to corner are equal. Clamp front assembly. Let glue dry.

2 Glue and clamp front and back assemblies with sidepieces. Place chair on level surface; firm up joints. All legs should touch level surface. Let glue dry. Screw and clamp arms to chair (inset). Spacer between arms aids alignment.

A rail, leg, spindle, or other chair part may work loose because the glue has dried out, the wood has shrunk, or damage to another part of the chair has put a strain on the joint. Many loose joints can be repaired by pulling the joint apart and removing the old glue, then applying new glue and reclamping the pieces. In some cases, the dowel or tenon may need to be enlarged to fit snugly in its housing. If the joint is badly damaged, replace it.

A break that runs along the wood grain of a chair part can often be fixed by gluing and clamping it. Because wood that is sawn or steam-bent into a curved shape tends to split along the grain at the peak of the curve, repairs there must be reinforced with a dowel after gluing and clamping. A bentwood repair usually requires that the split be softened with steam before you can coax it back into position and glue it.

Because cross-grain breaks do not glue well, they require bracing for strength. (Bracing may also be necessary if a split along the grain leaves little surface area for gluing or if the area of the split must withstand heavy use.) External bracing, in the form of a glue block (p.64) or wood splint, is usually easy to install. Internal bracing, which often consists of a dowel, is more time-consuming to install, but the finished repair is less noticeable.

Uneven legs cause a chair to wobble and can result in damage to the chair structure. Saw, rasp, or sand the bottom of the legs until they are even; or add a proper-size glide to the short leg. If the chair already has glides, insert washers between the glide and the short leg.

Gluing a split rung

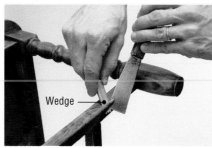

1 Carefully pry apart the split with a putty knife or old screwdriver. Insert a small wooden wedge to prop the split open for gluing.

2 Using a small brush, apply glue to both surfaces of the split; cover the surfaces evenly and completely. Immediately remove the wedge.

3 Clamp the repair until the glue dries; pad the work with scrap wood blocks to distribute clamping pressure and to protect the surface.

Gluing a split seat

1 Wedge the split open and chisel off the old glue. If chair was assembled with hide glue (an opaque brown glue used in old chairs), dissolve it with a 1:1 mix of ammonia and hot water.

2 Squeeze new glue onto both surfaces of the split; spread the glue into narrow areas with a toothpick. Apply just enough glue so that it beads along the glue line when the joint is clamped.

3 Remove the wedge. Clamp the seat with pipe or bar clamps (pad jaws with scrap blocks). Tighten the clamps alternately, making sure the seat sections stay aligned. Wipe off excess glue.

Repairing a split in a bentwood chair

1 To rebend split to proper shape, wrap it with a wet cloth; steam with a hot iron on all sides for 15 min. or more. Rewet cloth as necessary.

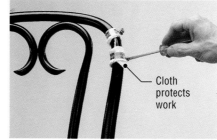

2 Clamp split with automotive hose clamps for 24 hr. When dry, slowly open split; apply glue with toothpick. Press split together; reclamp it.

3 After glue dries, drill ¼-in. hole perpendicular to split. Insert a dowel; trim it flush (see facing page). For long splits, add dowel every 2 in.

Bracing a break

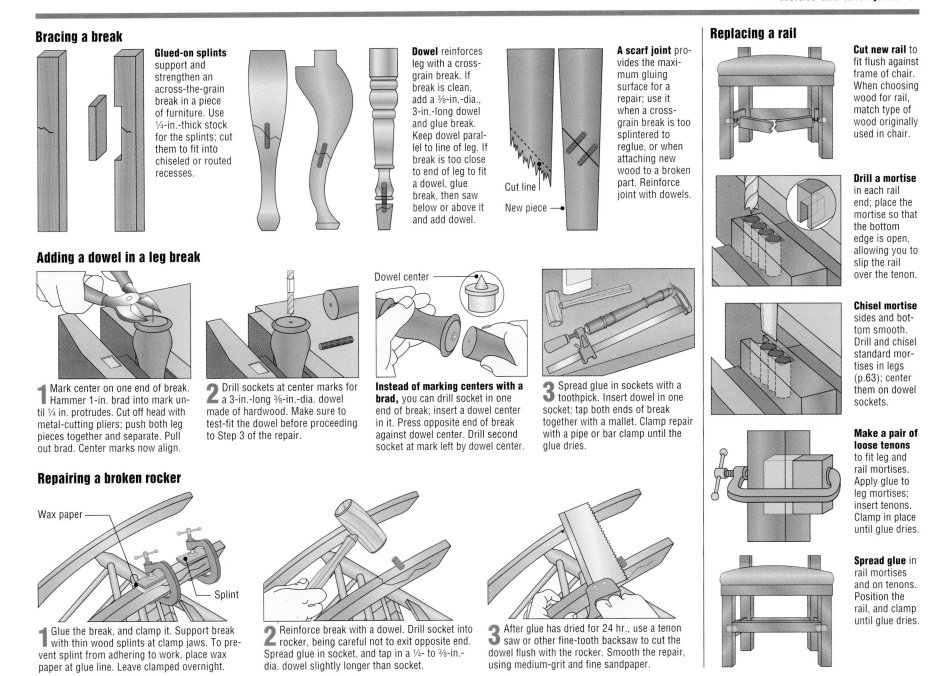

Glued-on splints support and strengthen an across-the-grain break in a piece of furniture. Use ¼-in.-thick stock for the splints; cut them to fit into chiseled or routed recesses.

Dowel reinforces leg with a cross-grain break. If break is clean, add a ⅜-in.-dia., 3-in.-long dowel and glue break. Keep dowel parallel to line of leg. If break is too close to end of leg to fit a dowel, glue break, then saw below or above it and add dowel.

Cut line
New piece

A scarf joint provides the maximum gluing surface for a repair; use it when a cross-grain break is too splintered to reglue, or when attaching new wood to a broken part. Reinforce joint with dowels.

Replacing a rail

Cut new rail to fit flush against frame of chair. When choosing wood for rail, match type of wood originally used in chair.

Drill a mortise in each rail end; place the mortise so that the bottom edge is open, allowing you to slip the rail over the tenon.

Chisel mortise sides and bottom smooth. Drill and chisel standard mortises in legs (p.63); center them on dowel sockets.

Make a pair of loose tenons to fit leg and rail mortises. Apply glue to leg mortises; insert tenons. Clamp in place until glue dries.

Spread glue in rail mortises and on tenons. Position the rail, and clamp until glue dries.

Adding a dowel in a leg break

1 Mark center on one end of break. Hammer 1-in. brad into mark until ¼ in. protrudes. Cut off head with metal-cutting pliers; push both leg pieces together and separate. Pull out brad. Center marks now align.

2 Drill sockets at center marks for a 3-in.-long ⅜-in.-dia. dowel made of hardwood. Make sure to test-fit the dowel before proceeding to Step 3 of the repair.

Dowel center

Instead of marking centers with a brad, you can drill socket in one end of break; insert a dowel center in it. Press opposite end of break against dowel center. Drill second socket at mark left by dowel center.

3 Spread glue in sockets with a toothpick. Insert dowel in one socket; tap both ends of break together with a mallet. Clamp repair with a pipe or bar clamp until the glue dries.

Repairing a broken rocker

Wax paper
Splint

1 Glue the break, and clamp it. Support break with thin wood splints at clamp jaws. To prevent splint from adhering to work, place wax paper at glue line. Leave clamped overnight.

2 Reinforce break with a dowel. Drill socket into rocker, being careful not to exit opposite end. Spread glue in socket, and tap in a ¼- to ⅜-in.-dia. dowel slightly longer than socket.

3 After glue has dried for 24 hr., use a tenon saw or other fine-tooth backsaw to cut the dowel flush with the rocker. Smooth the repair, using medium-grit and fine sandpaper.

Furniture repair ▪ Tables

The most common table problems involve the leg joints. A four-legged table will typically show wear and tear where the legs meet the apron. Dowel or mortise-and-tenon joints are often used at this location and where horizontal stretchers, if any, support the legs. Corner brace-and-bolt assemblies may also be used to secure the legs to the apron. (The brace may be a wood block or a metal plate.) Check the bolts periodically and tighten if necessary; replace a worn or split wood block with one made of hardwood. If a bolt has worn away the wood at the bolt hole, remove the bolt and plug the hole with a dowel (p.76). Then drill a hole of the same diameter as the bolt into the dowel and screw in the bolt.

A pedestal table is inherently weak where the legs meet the center column. Although dowel joints are common here, you may find dovetails in some tables. These joints often loosen or break, and need to be repaired or replaced. If you don't fix the damaged joint, the top of the leg may break near the joint.

Whatever the type of table, inspect it regularly for loose joints and damaged wood. If a joint appears just slightly loose but otherwise sound, you may be able to reglue it without disassembly, using a syringe-type glue applicator. To enlarge an undersize tenon, add wedges or shims; replace a damaged tenon with a new one (p.63). If a leg or stretcher splits along the wood grain, glue and clamp it (p.66). A break that runs across the grain should be doweled for strength (p.67).

Disassembly. If several joints are loose or broken, dismantle as much of the structure as necessary before making repairs. But remember: It's always best to dismantle as few joints as possible. Before starting the disassembly, apply a piece of masking tape to the mating pieces of each joint and label their positions. This will help you reassemble the table correctly.

Search at each joint for hidden fasteners that pin it in place. Some mortise-and-tenon joints are pegged with dowels. Drill or tap out any dowels before disassembling the joint. Pull the joints apart (p.57), and continue with the proper repair procedure.

You may have to remove the tabletop to make a repair. To do so, turn the table upside down and place it on a soft surface. Then remove all fasteners, such as glue blocks, metal brackets, and screws. If the top won't come off, invert the table to its upright position and gently tap the underside of the top upward, using a wood mallet against a scrap wood block.

Four-legged table

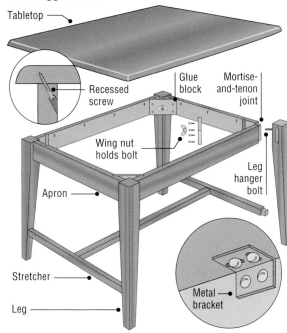

Determining a table's assembly method requires detective work. A tabletop may be held in place by glue blocks (p.64), recessed screws at bottom or side of apron, or metal brackets.

Pedestal table

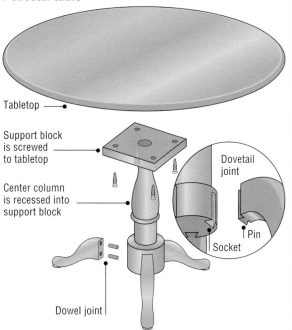

Stabilize a loose leg by first removing old dried-out glue from dowels and sockets or from dovetail pin and socket. Then apply fresh glue and clamp until the glue dries.

Pedestal leg repairs

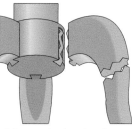

1 Remove broken dowel (p.62) or dovetail (use method shown on page 63 for removing tenon from mortise).

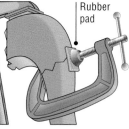

2 Scrape away old glue. If necessary, glue and clamp leg pieces. Let glue dry before continuing with joint repair.

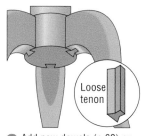

3 Add new dowels (p.62) or a loose tenon (p.63) made with one dovetail end. Test-fit the pieces.

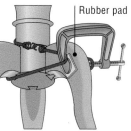

4 To clamp leg to column, wrap a tie-down or rope as shown; C-clamp helps stabilize pressure on shaped leg.

Split tabletop

A tabletop often splits along the grain or separates along a glue joint. A simple split along the grain is easily fixed: Pry the split apart with a putty knife, squeeze glue into the entire length of the split, and clamp it. To prevent further splitting, shape a bed for a butterfly patch (p.76) across the split and glue in the patch.

Separated glue joints can likewise be repaired by gluing and clamping. Clean away dirt and old glue, apply fresh glue, and clamp. Replace worn dowels, or add dowels (p.62) or biscuits for strength, if needed. If a split is so splintered that it can't be glued back together, saw or chisel off the damage and insert a snug-fitting wood strip. Be sure that the grain of the strip runs in the same direction as that of the top.

Patching a splintered tabletop

1 Clean edges of splinter with a chisel or sandpaper. Shape a wedge of matching wood slightly longer and taller than split.

2 Glue wedge in split; clamp it until glue dries. Chisel or plane wedge flush with surface. Add butterfly patch across split.

Regluing a split along a joint

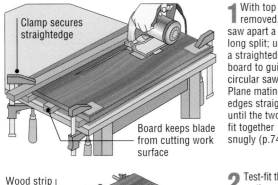

Clamp secures straightedge

Board keeps blade from cutting work surface

1 With top removed, saw apart a long split; use a straightedge board to guide circular saw. Plane mating edges straight until the two fit together snugly (p.74).

Wood strip

2 Test-fit the mating pieces. If necessary, maintain the original width of the top by inserting a strip of wood. When the proper fit is established, glue and clamp for 24 hr.

For added strength, use plate joiner to install a biscuit every 6 in. along mating edges before gluing and clamping. (Do not do this if inserting wood strip.)

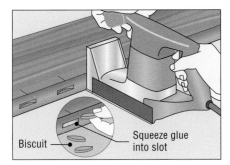

Biscuit

Squeeze glue into slot

Repairing a warped tabletop

Wood warps when it absorbs moisture unevenly or when it is subjected to seasonal humidity changes. Tabletops (and other wood items) that are finished on only one side are vulnerable to warping; the unfinished side absorbs and loses moisture at a faster rate than the finished side. But even tabletops that are finished on both sides can warp if the wood endures wide swings in humidity. If you suspect seasonal warping, wait until the next season and see whether the warp corrects itself. If it does, seal any unfinished surfaces with varnish or refinish the entire piece. Have a professional deal with warping in fine furniture.

To fix a tabletop with a cupped warp (the wood curves along its width), remove the top from the table, soak its concave side, then apply clamps (see below). To keep the top from warping again, add cleats to the underside. If the top has a waterproof or shellac finish, strip it before soaking it; refinish it as the last step.

To fix a persistent warp in a table of little value, try sawing kerfs along the grain halfway into the bottom side of the tabletop. Space the kerfs 4 inches apart (avoid fastener locations), and end them 1 inch from the top's edges. If the cup curves up, squeeze glue into the kerfs and clamp the work. If the cup curves down, square the ends of the kerfs with a chisel; glue wood strips into the kerfs and apply clamps.

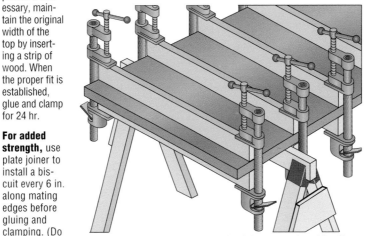

Straighten a warped top by clamping it between pairs of 2 x 4's placed on edge at 10-in. intervals. Soak concave side of top with wet rags for 24 hr., then apply clamps until top dries. Tighten clamps gradually over a period of time to avoid cracking the wood.

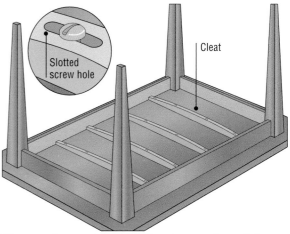

Slotted screw hole

Cleat

When warp is corrected, keep tabletop from warping again by screwing 2 x 2 cleats to its underside every 18 to 24 in., perpendicular to the wood grain. Taper the cleats at the ends. Slotted screw holes (inset) allow the top to contract and swell with the seasons.

Some tables are designed with a drop leaf or extension, allowing you to expand or reduce the surface of the table. Problems with a drop leaf can often be traced to a hinge or support. Keep hinges tight, making repairs as required (p.75). Sand or plane off any sharp edges on the support to prevent damaging the underside of the leaf. Loose or worn bearers or rails are a common source of problems in extension tables.

Pivot support. To support the drop leaf, a section cut out of the apron pivots on a dowel inserted into the apron. If the dowel is loose, remove the tabletop and replace the dowel with one of a slightly larger diameter. If the support is damaged, replace it with one made of straight-grained hardwood. Use the original support as a cutting pattern.

Hinged support. A knuckle joint secured by a metal pin or a dowel allows you to move the support. Eventually the joint may wear down, resulting in a wobbly tabletop. To repair it, remove the pin and replace it with a new larger pin or dowel. If the joint is broken, replace the entire support; you can substitute a metal hinge for the knuckle joint.

Gate-leg support. This type of support swings out like a gate to brace the leaf. Check the support for loose joints, worn or broken parts, or wear at the base of the leg. Separate and reglue any loose joints (pp.62–63); repair or replace worn or broken parts (pp.66–67). Examine the pivot points of the support. If you find a broken dowel, replace it (see right); insert a larger dowel in a worn socket.

Extension leaves. Some tables have side leaves supported by wood bearers. If a leaf tilts or wobbles, the bearers have become worn or warped. Shim a worn bearer. Replace a warped one with a duplicate made of hardwood (use the original as a pattern).

Another type of table has one or more leaves that fit in the center of the table; a rail assembly allows you to pull the tabletop apart to insert the leaf. Metal latches may hold the leaf in place. If the tabletop sags, reinforce the rail assembly with triangular glue blocks made of hardwood. Replace a damaged rail assembly with one purchased from a home center.

Drop-leaf supports

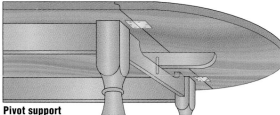
Pivot support

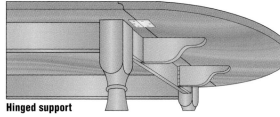
Hinged support

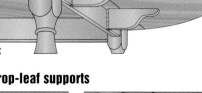
Gate-leg support

Repairing drop-leaf supports

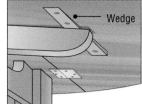
If leaf droops, position a hardwood wedge perpendicular to support, and screw it securely to the underside of the leaf.

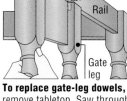
Clamp a loose hinged support against the apron. Drill hole to accept a larger-diameter dowel. Insert new dowel; glue in plug.

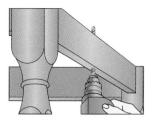
To replace gate-leg dowels, remove tabletop. Saw through dowels between rails and gate-leg support. Pull out gate leg.

Drill out dowels; continue sockets through rails. Replace gate leg; insert dowels. Glue plug into bottom socket end; attach top.

Extension tables

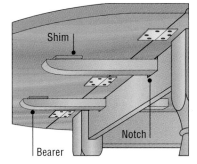

Build up a worn wood bearer by gluing a wood shim of the correct thickness to its top. If a notch in the apron through which a bearer slides becomes too large, you can build it up too by gluing on a wood shim.

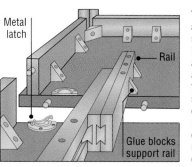

To keep a rail assembly working smoothly, periodically inspect screws that attach both assembly and latches to tabletop. Tighten loose screws. Rebuild enlarged screw holes (p.75). With table completely open, remove dirt or debris caked onto rails.

Bed frames

Most wood bed frames consist of a headboard, a footboard, two sidepieces called rails, and four bedposts (or legs). A wood or metal ledge runs along the inside face of each rail to support either the box spring and mattress directly or the slats on which the box spring and mattress rest. The rails are usually attached to the headboard and footboard with knock-down fittings that allow you to easily dismantle the bed frame.

If a bed creaks and wobbles, look for and tighten any loose fittings. If necessary, rebuild enlarged screw holes (p.75). If a recessed hook-and-plate fastener is loose, consider replacing it with a surface-mounted hook-and-plate fastener. (Plug the mortises first.) To make sure the fastener is positioned correctly, test-fit it with the halves linked together. If properly placed, the rail will fit snugly against the bedpost.

In an old bed frame the rails and bedposts may be held together by a long bolt, which is held in place by a nut recessed within the rail. Over time the bolt may wear away the wood and become loose. To tighten the bolt, insert a few washers between the bolt head and the bedpost. If the bolt turns without tightening,

look for and remove a wood plug in the rail to gain access to the nut. Then decrease the size of the nut's housing by gluing thin wood shims to its sides. Reinsert the nut; make a new plug to hide it.

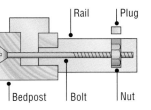

Bolt joint

The joints between the bedposts and the head- and footboards are usually mortise-and-tenons or dowels. Fix loose or faulty joints at once (pp.62–63). Glue and clamp a split rail as you would a split in a chair (p.66). Replace a badly damaged rail with one made of straight-grained hardwood; install it with surface-mounted fasteners.

A sagging or tilting mattress usually means a loose or broken wood ledge. If the ledge is sound, take it off the rail, clean off the old glue, then glue and screw the ledge in place (avoid old screw holes). Add glue blocks every 18 inches for strength. Replace a broken ledge with one made of straight-grained hardwood.

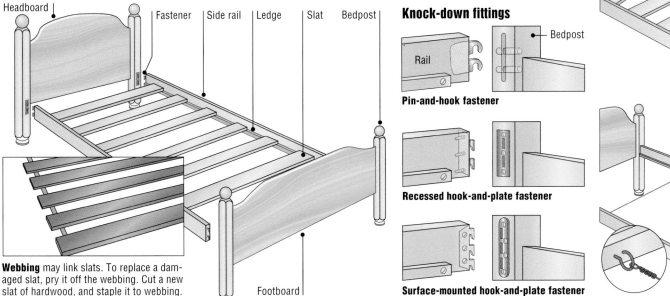

Webbing may link slats. To replace a damaged slat, pry it off the webbing. Cut a new slat of hardwood, and staple it to webbing.

Knock-down fittings

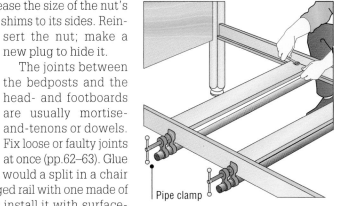

Pin-and-hook fastener

Recessed hook-and-plate fastener

Surface-mounted hook-and-plate fastener

Straightening bulging side rails

1 Pull a slightly warped rail into place with pipe clamps. Then bolt two center slats to the ledges with ³/₁₆-in.-dia. bolts (position slats so that all of them will be evenly spaced). Leave a ⅛-in. gap between the ends of the slats and the rail face.

2 Remove the clamps. Then rest the remaining slats along the ledges, spacing them evenly between the head- and footboards. Don't fasten these slats to the ledge. Replace the box spring and the mattress.

To fix a badly bulging rail (or if bed lacks slats), use turnbuckles. Screw two screw eyes into each rail (through ledges). Hook turnbuckles to screw eyes opposite bulging rail. Run heavy picture wire from turnbuckles to screw eyes in bulging rail. Turn turnbuckle sleeve to pull in rail.

All case furniture—chests, desks, cabinets, and bookshelves—is based on box construction. The frame of the box can be made of solid wood, plywood, or other manufactured material, or of wood panels contained within frames consisting of rails (horizontal components) and stiles (vertical components). The panels are sometimes veneered for a better appearance. The joinery holding the case together may be simple (butt, rabbet, and dado joints are commonly used in case furniture) or complex (mortise-and-tenon joints are often used at legs and dovetail joints at the corners of drawers). Because much of the strength of a case comes from its rigidity, check periodically that all joints

are tight. Reinforce joints with glue blocks where necessary (p.64); or disassemble, clean, and reglue the joints.

Before starting a repair, remove any shelves, drawers, doors, and if necessary, hardware and molding. For access to the piece's interior, remove the back panel, which is usually a thin board screwed or nailed into grooves in the frame. (Support the piece while working on it with light battens nailed diagonally across the back of the case.) Examine the back panel carefully—if it's warped, the furniture piece can shift out of alignment, resulting in sticking doors or drawers and weak joints. Straighten the back (p.69) or replace it with a piece of ¼-inch-thick plywood.

Before removing a cabinet top, examine it from underneath to see how it's attached (usually with screws, glue blocks, or dowels). Remove any screws; then gently tap upward from below with a wood mallet against a scrap block. If the top is split, repair it as you would a tabletop (p.69).

Whether you repair or replace a split panel depends on the amount of damage and on how easy it is to disassemble the panel's frame. A rabbet joint is easy to separate; but a mortise-and-tenon joint may have to be chiseled and sawn apart, then reassembled with a loose tenon (p.63). If the frame is joined with dowels, drill out the old dowels and replace them with new ones (p.62).

Repairing a framed panel

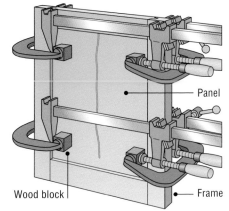

Repair a split panel within its frame by inserting glue into the split and clamping it together at top and bottom with bar clamps. The bar clamps grip wood blocks held to the panel by C-clamps.

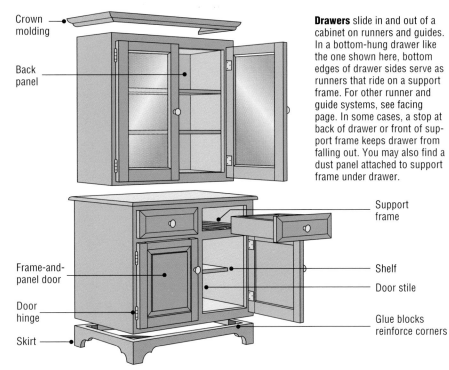

Drawers slide in and out of a cabinet on runners and guides. In a bottom-hung drawer like the one shown here, bottom edges of drawer sides serve as runners that ride on a support frame. For other runner and guide systems, see facing page. In some cases, a stop at back of drawer or front of support frame keeps drawer from falling out. You may also find a dust panel attached to support frame under drawer.

Restoring a tambour door

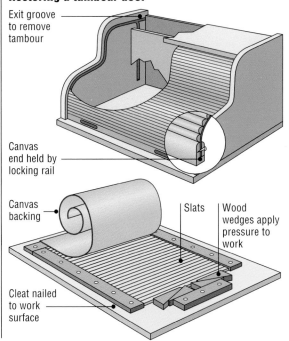

1 A tambour door, often used in desk construction, consists of narrow wooden slats glued to a canvas backing. The door runs in grooves in the cabinet's sides. The most common problem with a tambour door is the deterioration of the canvas backing. When this happens, the slats often come loose, jamming the door in its grooves. To remove the door, take off the back of the desk and slide the door through the exit groove.

2 To replace the backing, slip the slats face down in a frame made of cleats. Apply pressure to the work by sliding wedges between the last slat and a short cleat. Wet the canvas; strip off the canvas and glue with a putty knife and sandpaper. Cut the new canvas 1 in. narrower than the slats on each side and slightly longer than the door (so you can attach the canvas to the locking rail). Glue on the canvas; weight it with a heavy board until the glue dries.

Drawers

A drawer may stick because the wood has swollen in response to humid conditions. Simply wait for drier weather, then seal all wood surfaces with a coat of finish. To free a drawer that is jammed shut, remove the drawer below it, press upward on the bottom of the stuck drawer, and slide it forward. If there is no access to the drawer bottom but the drawer will open a crack, wiggle a long spatula blade in the crack. After you remove the drawer, examine its bottom to make sure it isn't warped. While a slightly bulging bottom can be cured by removing it and reinstalling it upside down, replace a drawer bottom that's badly warped.

Check wooden slide systems (see *Runner variations,* far right) for worn or loose components. Shiny spots on wood rails or runners indicate areas of friction; lightly sand them with 100-grit sandpaper, and apply a lubricant such as silicone spray or candle wax. Don't sand or plane parts that are swollen from temporary dampness; they will not fit properly when dry weather returns.

If the drawer slides on plastic or metal hardware, check it for proper alignment. Replace loose screws that won't tighten with larger ones or drill screw holes at new locations. If rollers don't work smoothly, clean them with ammonia. Replace worn or broken runners with new ones of similar length.

An out-of-square drawer can sometimes stick. To square it, examine the rear edge of the drawer bottom. If it's loose, secure it with nails; add glue blocks to support the structure. If the glue in the joints has dried out, disassemble and reglue the drawer.

Repairing wooden runners

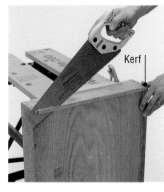 

1 Remove the damaged or worn section of the runner with a backsaw. To prevent overcutting, first saw a kerf at front of drawer. Plane or sand sawn area until it's smooth and straight. Cut a new runner section of knot-free maple or oak.

Kerf

Scrap wood

Runner

2 Glue new runner section to drawer with yellow glue. Clamp the work, using a length of scrap wood to distribute clamping pressure and to protect the drawer. Test-fit the drawer; if it doesn't slide smoothly, sand the runner.

Realigning guides and tracks

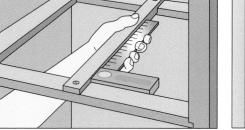 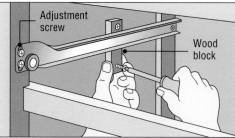

Adjustment screw

Wood block

Realign a loose wooden guide perpendicular to the drawer front using a try square. Apply yellow glue, and secure the guide with recessed screws. If a screw hole has enlarged, plug it before replacing the screw (p.75).

To realign a metal track, look for adjustment screws to move it vertically or horizontally. To correct a bow in the track (a roller falling off track indicates a bow), screw a wood block to the side of the cabinet or partition.

Squaring drawers

To check squareness of a drawer, measure diagonally with a straightedge between inside corners. Repeat on opposite diagonal. If measurements are unequal, remove all fasteners before securing back or taking apart drawer.

Reassemble the drawer by gluing and clamping with bar or pipe clamps. Check the drawer's squareness during and after clamping; adjust the clamps until the diagonals are equal. Pad the clamp jaws to protect the work.

Runner variations

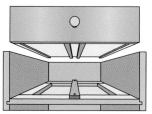

Bottom-hung drawer has side runners that ride on support frame. On wide drawers, runners also slide along center guide in frame.

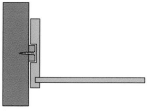

Side-hung drawer may ride on wood runners attached to the sides of the cabinet frame.

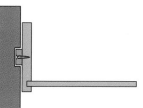

In another version of side-hung drawer, runners screwed to drawer ride in cabinet-frame grooves.

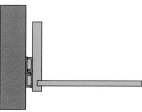

A third type of side-hung drawer has rollers that ride on runners.

Inspection and maintenance

If a cabinet door binds or sags, inspect the hinges. Tighten loose ones; rebuild worn screw holes (facing page). If a hinge is recessed too deeply, build up the recess with a shim. If the gap between the cabinet door and its frame is larger at the top than at the bottom, shim the bottom hinge; shim the top hinge if the gap is larger at the bottom.

A door that is swollen because of humidity should settle down when the weather changes. But if the door sticks because of paint buildup, strip and repaint the edges. If the door is warped, sand or plane it to fit its opening. Rub chalk on the door's edges, then open and close it a few times; the chalk will rub off on the tight spots. The latch edge of the door is the easiest to plane. If you must plane the hinged edge, deepen the hinge beds to compensate for the planing. When planing, remove as little wood as possible.

If a glass pane breaks in a cabinet door, remove the glass (be sure to wear heavy work gloves and safety goggles) before removing the door. Cut a new pane, or have it cut at a home center.

To flatten a warped shelf, reinstall it upside down; reinforce it with supports. Replace a badly warped or cracked shelf with one of the same measurements—you can veneer it to match the cabinet (p.78). If the holes used with peg-type supports are worn, plug them with dowels and drill new holes.

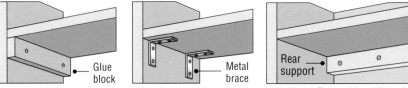

Reinforce a weak shelf with glue blocks or metal braces at each shelf end. To provide additional support for a shelf that is more than 1 ft. deep, glue and screw a 1- x 2-in. wood strip along the rear edge.

Shimming a cabinet door hinge

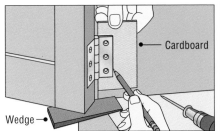

1 Make shim from a thin piece of cardboard or wood. Prop door with wedge, unscrew hinge from frame, and slide in cardboard. With pencil, trace outline of hinge; punch out screw holes with awl. Cut shim slightly smaller than outline.

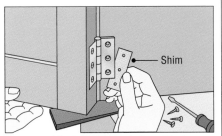

2 Insert shim behind hinge leaf, positioning punched holes under screw holes. Screw hinge leaf to frame (facing page); hinge leaf should be flush with surface of wood. Remove wedge; test hinge by opening and closing door.

Planing a door

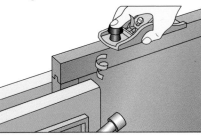

Remove thin shavings from edge of door with a block or jack plane. Use smooth strokes, applying pressure to front of plane at start of pass, to both ends of plane in mid pass, and to heel of plane at end of pass.

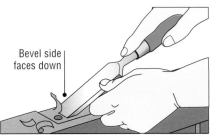

When planing hinge edge of door, deepen hinge beds with a chisel; work in short strokes and keep recessed surfaces flat. Keep both beds at an equal depth. Test-fit hinges to make sure they sit flush with door; reinstall hinges.

Replacing a glass pane

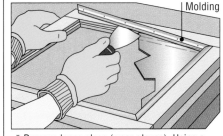

1 Remove loose glass (wear gloves). Using a stiff putty knife near brad locations, pry out molding that anchors remaining glass in door. Remove glass, wrap it in newspaper, and discard. Vacuum groove with crevice tool.

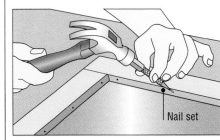

2 Insert new pane. Place molding over edges of pane, and secure it with finishing brads every 6 in. Tap brads in place, angling them to avoid hitting glass. Use a nail set for last few taps.

Repairing sliding doors

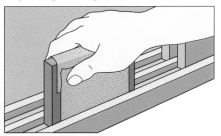

If a sliding door binds, widen its channel by sanding. Fold a piece of medium-grit sandpaper over a wood block slightly thinner than channel. Carefully sand channel, using long strokes.

Decrease an enlarged channel by shimming its edges or base with a strip of waxed hardwood. (Use paste wax on strip.) Cut strip to fit and secure it with recessed brads (see left). Wax will reduce friction of door against base of channel.

Casters and hinges

The wheels or ball bearings of casters attached to the base of a piece of furniture make it easy to move the piece. Because it is screwed to the furniture, a plate-mounted caster rarely needs repair. By contrast, a stem caster, which slides into a socket fitted in the end of a leg, often loosens and drops out. You must adjust wings on the socket to pin the caster back in place.

Sometimes a caster splits the leg it's in. To repair the leg, wrap it with masking tape, then use a drill to enlarge the socket hole. Glue in a dowel (p.62) and glue the split (p.66). After the glue dries, add a glide to the bottom of the leg or reinsert the stem caster into a new hole.

Hinges. Like caster repairs, hinge-related repairs are fairly easy to make. Hinges that do not pivot smoothly may need to be lubricated with a drop of household oil. Screws may require tightening or replacement. If a screw spins in its hole without gripping, plug the hole with a dowel (p.76), drill a new hole smaller than the screw being used, and reinsert the screw. If a hinge pin is lost or damaged, make a replacement pin from a nail or replace the hinge.

A loosened drop-leaf hinge can cause the leaf to rub at the joint. Try tightening or replacing any loose screws; be sure to center the knuckle of the hinge on the fillet line.

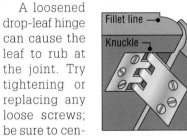

Drop-leaf hinge

When removing a hinge, take care not to damage the hinge or the wood around it. Check the hinge beds (the recesses where the hinge rests) for wear; make repairs before reinstalling the hinges. If a hinge bed is so damaged that it can't be fixed, make a new recess in a different location and move the hinge. Because hinges work in sets of two or more, you'll have to move more than one hinge to maintain symmetry and balanced support. Fill the old hinge beds with patches (p.78); finish them to match the surrounding wood.

Refitting a stem caster

1 To remove caster socket, pry its collar off leg with thin-edged prying tool. Pull out socket with slip-joint pliers.

2 Gently bend socket wings inward with pliers so they will grip the end of caster stem.

3 Using mallet and wood block, tap socket into hole, pushing collar teeth into leg. Insert caster stem in socket.

Repairing a split hinge bed

Gently pry split apart, blow out splinters (wear safety goggles), and apply glue along crack (p.58). Clamp split (use wood blocks to spread pressure) and let dry.

To reinstall hinge, tighten first screw a few twists; then go on to other screws, giving each a few twists. Continue this way until all screws are tight. Install opposite leaf as shown in Step 4 below.

Installing a recessed hinge

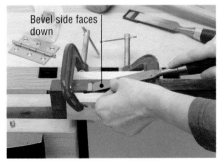
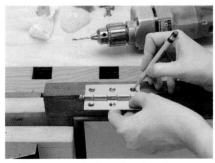

1 Mark hinge position. Cut along outline with mallet and chisel (bevel facing bed). To avoid cutting past recess, remove some wood along outline.

2 Shave hinge bed to exact hinge depth, a section at a time. Periodically test-fit hinge; it should fit snugly in the bed.

3 Slip hinge into bed; mark position for screws with a pencil or awl. Remove hinge; drill pilot holes for screws.

4 Screw hinge leaf in place on smaller piece (see above). Secure opposite leaf of each hinge with top screw before adding other screws.

Dents, nicks, and gouges often mar furniture surfaces. If you plan to refinish the piece, first repair the damaged wood. If you must also make a structural repair, wait until you disassemble the piece before taking care of the damaged surface. How you treat the surface depends on the damage it has received.

To fix a shallow dent, prick it with a pin a few times at the deepest part of the depression. Then steam it: Place a few drops of water in the dent, cover it with a damp towel, and press it with the tip of a hot iron for a few seconds. You may have to repeat the procedure a few times. If the dent refuses to rise, try filling it with a shellac stick (p.80).

Filling in a damaged area. A crack, gouge, or nick can be camouflaged with a wood filler. Latex wood filler or water-base putty is best for a coarse repair; use a precolored plastic wood filler for a delicate repair. Before using latex wood filler, stain it to match the work.

Fill any holes from an old joint or hardware with dowels; drill out an old dowel if necessary (p.62). Repair a large damage in solid wood by gluing in a patch of matching wood—irregularly shaped patches angled into the wood grain are the least conspicuous. After the glue dries, plane or sand the surface smooth and refinish the piece. If there are signs of wood beetles, inject insecticide into the holes. Chisel out the damaged section, then patch it.

Standard abrasive paper, generally known as sandpaper, consists of a cloth or paper backing coated with particles of an abrasive grit. For sanding wood, select garnet, aluminum oxide, or silicon carbide paper. Garnet paper cuts quickly, but it also wears quickly. Aluminum oxide paper is harder than garnet paper, making it a good choice as a general-purpose abrasive. Silicon carbide paper, also known as wet-or-dry paper, is expensive but ideal for sanding finishes; it may be used with water or oil to keep it from clogging.

Sandpaper comes with either a closed or open coat. Closed-coat papers are completely covered with abrasive particles; they are preferable for fast sanding. Because open-coat papers have large gaps between particles, they clog less readily, making them better suited for sanding softwoods.

Sandpaper is graded according to its grit size. The higher the number, the smaller, or finer, the particle. For light repairs, start with 120-grit paper, then move up to 180-grit paper. If necessary, finish the job with 220- or 240-grit paper. For rougher work, such as a raw surface, start with 80- to 100-grit paper, then progress to the finer grades.

Sanding basics. When you hand-sand a surface, use straight strokes and work with the grain; sanding at an angle to the grain leaves scratches. Move the paper with even pressure. On a flat surface, use a sanding block padded with cork, rubber, or felt to protect the work.

For a large job (or if you do a lot of sanding), invest in a power sander. A light hand-sanding will remove any scratches left by a power sander.

Filling a crack, gouge, or nick

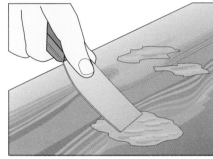

1 To fill a deep gouge, apply wood filler or putty slightly higher than the surrounding surface. Because wood putty shrinks, you may have to apply another layer after the first one dries.

2 After the filling material dries and hardens, sand it smooth. Paint on wood grain using artist's acrylic paints (p.80). Spray the repair with a compatible finish, or refinish the entire surface.

Patching a flat surface

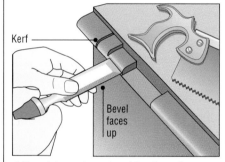

Plug a round hole with a dowel slightly longer than depth of hole. Apply glue to dowel and hole; tap in dowel with hammer or mallet. After glue dries, chisel end of dowel flush with surface.

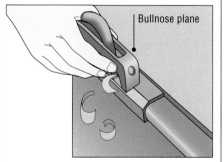

Wood glue

Grains of patch and wood run in same direction

Utility knife

For a large area, make a patch from matching wood. Place patch on damage; trace around it with a knife. Chisel cavity to shape and thickness of patch. Glue patch in place; refinish surface.

Patching a curved surface

Kerf

Bevel faces up

1 To patch wood on edge of furniture piece, saw kerfs on each side of damaged area, then remove the damaged area with a chisel. Use a square or straightedge to check bed for flatness.

Bullnose plane

2 Test-fit a patch of matching wood; use a plane or chisel to shape patch. Glue patch in place. After glue dries, round edges of patch with bullnose or block plane. Sand and finish.

Sanding tools and materials

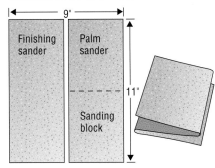

Finishing sander

Palm sander

Sanding block

9"

11"

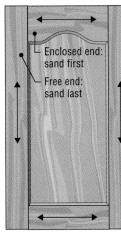

Cork pad

To size a sheet of sandpaper for a finishing sander, crease it in half along the longer dimension and tear it. To fit a palm sander or sanding block (see below), tear one of these half sheets of paper into quarter sheets. If you plan to do hand-sanding, use a quarter sheet folded into thirds.

Make a sanding block from a 6- x 3¼- x 1-in. block of wood. To avoid marring the work, glue a cork pad to bottom and top of block. Wrap a quarter sheet of sandpaper around the bottom and up the sides. Hold ends of paper against block as you sand. (You can also make a 3- x 3¼- x 1-in. block.)

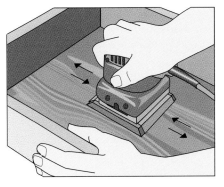

Use a palm sander to sand small areas or areas with tight corners. Move it with the wood grain in slightly overlapping parallel strokes. Guide the sander without exerting downward pressure.

Use a finishing sander on large flat surfaces. Move the sander with the grain; overlap strokes slightly. Apply just enough pressure for guidance without slowing motor. Move sander at a slow, uniform speed; a slight hesitation can create an unwanted depression.

A hand scraper removes thin wood shavings, minimizing—and even eliminating—the need for sanding. To smooth uneven surfaces, push the scraper in long strokes along the wood grain. Keeping your thumbs in the middle of the scraper, angle the tool so it tilts away from you at a 75° angle. If you create dust instead of shavings, sharpen the blade or increase its angle. The hand scraper is also available in a paisley shape with a continuous cutting edge to fit moldings and other curved surfaces.

Sanding techniques

Enclosed end: sand first

Free end: sand last

To avoid cross-grain scratches on an assembly with perpendicular sections, first sand the sections with enclosed ends (always sanding with the grain); when you sand the sections with free ends, you'll remove any scratches. Repeat for each change in size of paper grit.

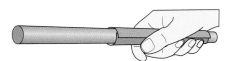

To sand cylindrical components, such as spindles or dowels, tear off a piece of sandpaper, wrap it around the component (grit side down), and move it up and down with the grain.

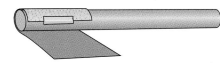

Cylindrical sanding block allows you to smooth hard-to-reach areas and to remove glue from sockets. Tape one end of a strip of sandpaper to a dowel; wrap paper around it with grit exposed.

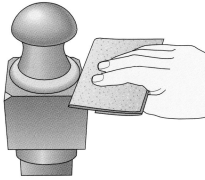

Sand tight grooves in turnings and carvings with the fold of a sheet of sandpaper. Work gently in a back-and-forth motion. For even sanding, alternate pressure along each side of groove.

Sand short sections of intricate turnings and hard-to-reach areas with a long, narrow strip of sandpaper. Pull the sandpaper back and forth over the wood in "shoeshine" fashion.

Furniture repair ▪ Restoring damaged veneer

Veneer is a thin layer of hardwood that is glued over a plywood or solid wood base, called a substrate, to create an attractive finish. As fragile as it is beautiful, veneer chips easily, especially at corners and edges. A hot object placed on a veneered surface can melt the glue and create a blister. With age, the glue bonding the veneer to the substrate may dry out, causing the veneer to lift in places. While you can repair ordinary furniture with a few simple tools, take valuable pieces to a professional refinisher.

With an older piece of furniture, in which hide glue adheres the veneer to the substrate, you can sometimes reattach a lifted section of veneer by softening the glue and allowing it to reharden. First place a damp towel over the problem area and heat it with an iron; then weight the area for 12 hours with books placed over waxed paper. (Don't try this if the piece has been finished with shellac.) On a newer furniture piece, remove the old glue and reattach the lifted area with liquid hide glue, veneer glue, or yellow glue (see right).

Remove damaged veneer and replace it with a patch of the same wood species. Buy veneer that closely matches the grain of the original veneer. (For more on buying veneer, see facing page.) The patch needn't match the original's color since the piece will be refinished. The patch will be less visible if you angle its ends into the existing veneer grain.

When making a repair, keep the substrate smooth and free of old glue and debris—even a speck of sawdust will show through the veneer. Before patching a section of veneer, check the substrate for damage; make sure you fill any dents or gouges (p.76). After gluing the veneer to the substrate, weight it with at least 20 pounds of books set on wax paper, or secure it with clamps, until the glue dries—about 12 hours.

Flattening a blister

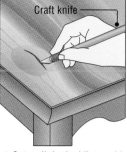

1 Cut a slit in the blister with a craft knife, following the wood grain.

2 Push the glue beneath the veneer with a toothpick or glue injector.

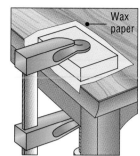

3 Smooth repair with your fingers. Clamp until the glue dries.

Regluing lifted veneer

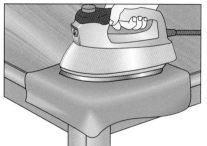

1 To make veneer pliable, place a damp towel over the veneer. Set an iron on low; apply heat in 5 to 10 sec. cycles, checking the work for scorching. Repeat until veneer is pliable.

2 Sand off the old glue, using 80-grit paper; avoid rounding the edges of the substrate. Or if you can lift the veneer without breaking it, scrape off the old glue with a craft knife.

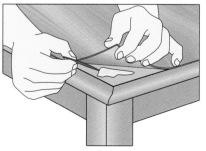

3 Spread new glue on the substrate with a toothpick. Press down the veneer and smooth it with your fingers; then wipe off any excess glue with a damp rag.

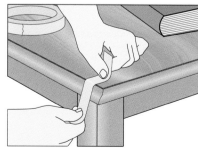

4 Secure the repair with masking tape, and weight it down. For a large repair, place wax paper between the repair and a scrap block of wood, then apply clamps.

Patching veneer

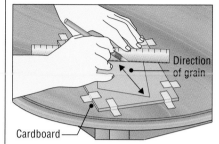

Tape thin cardboard over damaged area. Use a craft knife to cut a diamond shape through cardboard (which will serve as a template) and veneer. (Diamond should be parallel to grain.) Remove veneer in diamond outline with chisel.

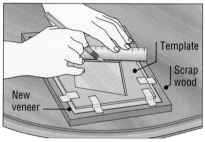

To cut patch, place new veneer on scrap wood. Position template over veneer so that grain direction of patch will match that of old veneer. Tape down template. Using a craft knife guided by a straightedge, cut out patch.

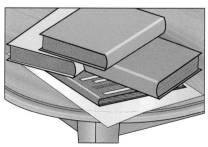

Clean out old glue from the damaged area; apply a thin coat of fresh glue to it. Quickly press the patch in place. Wipe off any excess glue with a damp cloth; cover the repair with wax paper and weight it down.

Replacing veneer

If damaged veneer requires more than localized repairs, reveneer the entire surface. Available from woodworking supply houses or catalogs, veneer comes in rigid or thinner flexible form and in sizes ranging from small iron-on strips for trimming edges to sheets as large as 36 x 96 inches. Sheets of veneer are sold in the order in which they were cut so you can match the wood grain. Number each sheet to keep track of the order. To allow for errors, buy a little more veneer than you think you'll need.

Highly figured veneers, such as those cut from a tree crotch or burl, often wrinkle and become brittle. To flatten these before use, spray them lightly with water and stack them on a piece of plywood with sheets of brown craft paper in between. Top off the stack with another piece of craft paper

and plywood, and weight the assembly for 24 hours with a stack of books.

After removing the old veneer and sanding the substrate, fill in any dents (p.76). Cut the veneer to a size slightly larger than the substrate; then trim the veneer to fit with a veneer saw or a utility knife. When veneering a surface made of solid wood, always align the veneer grain with the wood grain.

Reveneer flat surfaces (see right) with either rigid or flexible veneer. Use flexible veneer on curved surfaces. When attaching flexible veneer to the substrate, align the pieces carefully. Once the two cemented surfaces come in contact with each other, separating them will be difficult. To flatten the veneer evenly and to eliminate air bubbles, smooth over the veneer with a veneer roller or a rolling pin.

Replacing veneer inlay

1 Pry off old inlay strips with a sharp woodworker's chisel, held bevel side up. Use the chisel to scrape out any remaining old glue.

2 Make a pattern by taping tracing paper over the old imprint (or over a matching veneer inlay that is still in good shape); then carefully trace the outline of the inlay.

3 Strengthen new veneer by applying veneer tape to backside. Tape pattern to veneer. Carefully cut along outline with a craft knife. Smooth the edges with medium-grit sandpaper.

4 Brush yellow glue within the imprint. Position the inlay; secure it with masking tape. Clamp a block of scrap wood over the inlay until the glue completely dries. Refinish the whole surface.

Reveneering a flat surface

Remove old veneer with a chisel, held bevel side up. Be careful not to gouge wood underneath veneer. (To make removal easier, try softening glue with an iron, as described on facing page.)

Smooth the substrate surface with 60-grit sandpaper and a sanding block (p.77). The surface should be completely flat and clean of all debris before applying the adhesive and veneer.

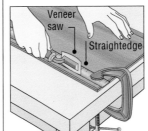

Veneer saw
Straightedge

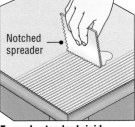

Notched spreader

To join two pieces of veneer, lay them on top of each other, face to face; clamp straightedge along cut line. Cut with several light strokes of veneer saw.

Place pieces side by side. Tape across top of joint with damp veneer tape every 6 in.; then tape along joint. Hold joint to a light; no light should be visible.

To apply standard rigid veneer, use a brush or notched spreader to completely coat substrate with yellow or veneer glue. Set veneer on substrate.

Pull out craft paper
Hold end down

To apply flexible veneer, brush contact cement on substrate and back of veneer; wait 15 min. Place two sheets of paper on substrate, overlapping ends. Lay veneer on paper, cement side down. Remove one sheet of paper, then the other. Smooth with roller.

Once veneer is in place, remove any veneer tape; wipe off excess glue or cement. Clamp work between boards. After adhesive has set for several hours, trim overhanging edges of veneer, using a veneer saw held against a straightedge; sand edges lightly.

A drab, lifeless wood finish can often be spruced up fairly easily, provided the finish is sound (i.e., no blisters, cracking, or peeling). It's even possible to spot-repair minor scratches and blemishes as long as the damage doesn't penetrate the wood. Because repairing or removing the finish on an antique decreases its value, let a professional restorer deal with valuable pieces.

Cleaning. A thorough cleaning is the first step in restoring the luster to a dark, dull, or sticky finish. (If nothing more, it allows you to evaluate the full extent of the damage and decide if stripping and refinishing are necessary.) A combination of 1 part gum turpentine and 1 part boiled linseed oil, slightly warmed, makes an excellent cleaning agent. While heating a pot of water, mix the turpentine and oil in a metal can. When the water boils, remove it from the heat and place the can in the water; leave it until the mixture is warm to the touch. Dip a pad of No. 00 steel wool in the mixture and lightly rub down the piece with the grain of the wood, rewetting the steel wool as necessary. Allow 15 to 30 minutes for the mixture to penetrate; then wipe it off with a clean rag.

Reamalgamation. If cleaning fails to revive a shellac, lacquer, or varnish finish, try reamalgamation. (A polyurethane finish can't be reamalgamated.) In this process, illustrated above, a solvent is used to liquefy the top of the old finish, which then hardens to a smooth surface. Use denatured alcohol as a solvent for shellac, lacquer thinner for lacquer, and either one or a combination of the two for varnish. If you aren't sure

Reamalgamating a damaged finish

To reamalgamate a small scratch, clean area with mineral spirits. Brush a tiny amount of solvent on the scratch; reapply a dozen or so times. After finish dries, rub with steel wool, then wax.

Repairing a severe blemish

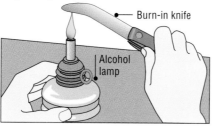

1 Fill severe blemishes with stick shellac. First mask perimeter of repair with masking tape (see Step 2). To melt the shellac, heat burn-in or grapefruit knife over soot-free alcohol lamp.

of the type of finish on the piece, experiment by dabbing various solvents and combinations on a hidden area until you find one that works. After the finish dries, lightly scrub the entire surface with No. 0000 steel wool; then rub it with paste wax.

Reamalgamation is an effective technique for removing light stains and small scratches; it will even restore an alligatored surface. But reamalgamation won't remove a white ring or a dark stain. The latter will require refinishing; to remove a white ring, rub it with a fine abrasive. Try toothpaste first. If that

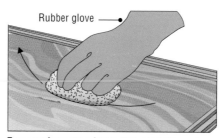

Rubber glove

To reamalgamate a large area of shellac or lacquer finish, dab a small amount of solvent into a folded and tightly wadded cheesecloth. Apply solvent, using a sweeping motion, several times.

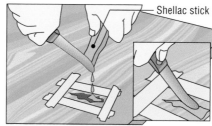

Shellac stick

2 Hold shellac stick over blemish; touch its end to hot knife blade. Shellac will drip into blemish; overfill it slightly. (Or use soldering iron to melt shellac.) Press in shellac with knife; let dry.

does not work, sprinkle salt on the ring and rub it in with a rag dipped in mineral oil; or use a rag to apply a mixture of rottenstone (p.82) and mineral oil to the white ring.

Repairing scratches. If a scratch is shallow but still too deep to be repaired by reamalgamating the finish, use a wax stick or touch-up stick to hide the scratch. For a deep scratch or a crack that enters the wood, use a shellac stick. Before filling in a cigarette burn or other blemish with a shellac stick, carefully scrape the damage down to clean wood, using a utility knife.

Restoring finish at a worn edge

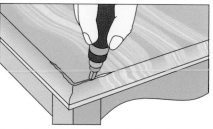

For a temporary fix, use a matching-color touch-up pen to color a worn spot. Clean area with mineral spirits; scuff with 400-grit sandpaper. Apply color and blend with finger; repeat several times.

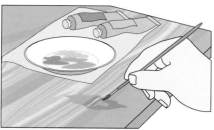

3 Carefully scrape dried shellac level with wood surface, using a woodworker's chisel. Paint in grain lines using artist's acrylic colors and a delicate paintbrush. When dry, seal with lacquer.

Choose a stick that matches the stain on the piece as closely as possible. Wax, touch-up, and shellac sticks as well as other supplies are available from woodworker's suppliers and catalogs.

TIPS FROM THE PROS

As long as a worn finish isn't lifting or peeling, here's a way to revive it without stripping the work. First cut the gloss of the old finish by gently rubbing it with No. 0 steel wool in the direction of the grain. Then apply a coat of diluted stain before applying the new top coat. The stain should be compatible with the finish (pp.84–85).

Stripping wood

If the finish on a piece of furniture is cracked, flaking, or blistering, or if you want to change its color, you'll have to strip the piece. Wood strippers are available in two types. Solvent-base strippers, which contain methylene chloride, work quickly and thoroughly on a wide range of finishes. But they emit toxic vapors as they evaporate, requiring you to take safety precautions (see right). Because a solvent-base stripper will melt nylon bristles, use a natural-bristle brush to apply it. Water-base strippers are as effective as the solvent types and are safer to use. But they take longer to work: several hours or overnight compared to the 10 to 30 minutes required by a solvent-base stripper. In addition, water-base strippers raise the wood grain, which means that you must sand the piece after stripping it. It's best to buy either type of wood stripper in paste, not liquid, form. The paste clings to vertical surfaces; the liquid does not.

Before you begin, remove all drawers, doors, and hardware; strip the drawers and doors separately. Use masking tape to cover areas you don't want to strip. Read the instructions on the stripper packaging carefully—all manufacturers' formulations differ.

Pour a small amount of stripper into a plastic container; keep the main sup-ply capped. When possible, work on the piece horizontally. Strip one side or section at a time, or the dissolved finish may dry before you can remove it. Even if some finish remains on the first section, continue stripping the piece. Go back and attack stubborn sections later, using fresh remover and No. 2 steel wool. If the stripper drips onto a clean section, wipe it off with gum turpentine. After the piece dries slightly, inspect it carefully for glazed spots—a sign of unstripped finish—and remove them before applying the new finish. Lastly, make sure you clean off all stripper residue (p.82) before you begin applying the new finish.

Removing a finish

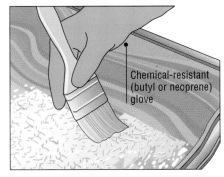

Apply a thick coat of stripper with a paint-brush (use a natural-bristle brush for a solvent-base stripper); spread it in one direction with a minimum of brushstrokes. Leave the stripper on for the recommended time. If using a solvent-base stripper, apply additional stripper if first coat dries too quickly.

Chemical-resistant (butyl or neoprene) glove

Remove bulk of stripper and dissolved finish from flat surfaces with flexible putty knife, working in direction of grain. Even if package directions recommend a water rinse to remove stripper, use a putty knife; water can weaken glue at joints. Remove remaining stripper with No. 2 steel wool; repeat process if necessary.

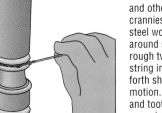

For molded edges and at intricately carved areas, use a brass-bristle brush (available at woodworker's supply outlets), an old toothbrush, or a vegetable brush to gently scrub off the stripper and dissolved finish.

Clean out crevices and other nooks and crannies with No. 2 steel wool wrapped around string or with rough twine. Move the string in a back-and-forth shoeshine-type motion. Cotton swabs and toothpicks also come in handy for removing stripper and finish from small, hard-to-reach areas.

Removing stripper residue

The wax and other chemical residues left behind by a furniture stripper can prevent a new finish from adhering to the surface; a wrinkled finish is a common sign of poor wax removal. If you used a solvent-base stripper, remove any residue with turpentine, denatured alcohol, or other solvent; use water or denatured alcohol for a water-base stripper. Because the products differ, always follow the instructions on the label of the stripper you buy.

Once the wood is dry, lightly sand it, paying particular attention to areas that retain tinges of color from the old finish. Finally, check the wood for defects and make necessary repairs; fill any scratches (p.80) and gouges (p.76).

1 Dip No. 00 steel wool in solvent or water; quickly and completely wet the surface of the wood, and scrub gently. Use a nylon-bristle brush for porous wood such as walnut, oak, or ash.

2 Wipe solvent off wood with a clean piece of cheesecloth (or other open-weave natural-fiber cloth). Let the wood surfaces dry before continuing to the next step.

3 To smooth wood fibers raised by the solvent, very lightly sand the piece with 280-grit garnet paper. Follow up by vacuuming, using a 2- or 3-in.-dia. brush attachment.

Bleaching

Once a surface has been stripped of finish, most water rings, ink spots, and other discolorations can be lightened with one or more applications of laundry bleach. You can also use bleach to unify or lighten the overall color of the wood. Treat oak, ash, maple, poplar, and beech with full-strength laundry bleach. For mahogany, cherry, chestnut, cedar, rosewood, and walnut, use a commercial two-step wood bleach. To avoid removing too much color, follow the package directions carefully.

To stop the bleaching process, apply a 50/50 solution of water and white vinegar to the surface; then rinse it with clear warm water and wipe with a cloth. After the wood dries, lightly sand it with 220-grit garnet paper; this smooths fibers raised by the bleach.

| White oak |
| Cherry |
| Mahogany |

Natural wood color (far left) can be substantially lightened (near left) with bleach. Leave bleach on surface until wood is slightly darker than desired color. As wood dries, it lightens in color. If color is still too dark, repeat.

To bleach a small stain, saturate the area with full-strength laundry bleach, using a cotton swab. Repeat application until desired lightness is achieved.

For a large area, apply bleach with a sponge or nylon-bristle brush; spread it liberally along grain, avoiding overlapping strokes. Follow with vinegar solution, then light sanding. **CAUTION:** Wear goggles and gloves when bleaching.

Masking tape

To bleach a section, protect the adjacent wood by covering it with strips of masking tape. In this example, you can bleach the apron of the table a lighter color but leave the leg and underside of the tabletop the darker color.

Metal wools

Steel wool, the most common of the metal wools, is cheap, easy to work with, and comes in several grades. It does, however, leave behind tiny filaments that can rust and stain the wood. If the work will be exposed to water, use bronze wool or copper wool, available at supermarkets.

When using steel wool, wear rubber gloves. Turn and fold the pad to expose fresh surfaces; discard it when clogged.

Steel wool	Uses
4 Extra-coarse	Remove tough paint and varnish
3 Coarse	Remove paint and other finishes
2 Medium-coarse	Remove scuff marks and old wax; strip off old finish
1 Medium	Smooth raised grain
0 Medium-fine	Clean copper and brass
00 Fine	Clean a finish; remove residues
000 Extra-fine	Polish or buff furniture
0000 Superfine	Buff and clean final finish

Abrasive powders

Pumice, emery, and rottenstone are soft abrasive powders that can be used to remove superficial scratches and water marks or other stains, and to polish a surface until it's glossy. Mix the powder with a lubricant, such as mineral oil (or in a pinch, vegetable oil), and rub it onto the surface with a clean cloth.

Powder	Uses
PUMICE	
Extra-coarse	Buff and polish wood
Coarse	Smooth surfaces, remove dust and specks in a finish
Medium	Buff and polish final finish
Fine	Same as medium
Extra-fine	For high luster on final finish
EMERY	Clean or buff metal
ROTTENSTONE	For high luster on final finish

Wood filler and sealer

Paste wood filler

When you want to create an extremely smooth surface finish, use paste wood filler to fill the pores of open-grain woods such as oak, mahogany, ash, and walnut. Close-grain woods, such as pine, birch, maple, and cherry, rarely need filling; nor do woods that will be finished with a natural look. Filler is sometimes used to highlight the wood grain. To do this, use a filler that contrasts with the wood's natural color: white or light-colored filler on dark wood, dark filler on light wood (p.88).

Applying filler. Filler is usually applied after staining (p.84), but it can be applied beforehand. Because alcohol-base stains can dissolve filler, always apply such stains first. When filling after staining, be careful to avoid damaging the stain as you remove the excess filler.

Pick a filler to match the stain you'll be using. If you can't find the shade premixed, tint a natural-color filler with an oil stain or japan color (p.84). Be sure to mix enough filler to finish the job.

To keep the pigment from settling, stir the filler before using it and often during use. The filler's consistency should be that of heavy cream. If necessary, thin the filler with turpentine, but first check the manufacturer's recommendations on the filler's label.

Before removing excess filler, make sure it has dried sufficiently; otherwise you might pull the filler out of the wood's pores. Let the wood dry overnight; then sand it lightly with 220- or 240-grit sandpaper, removing any streaks left by the filler. Wipe off the sanding residue before proceeding with the finishing process (p.85).

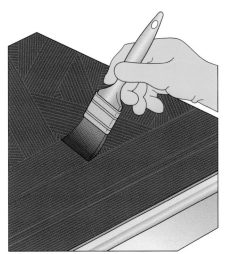

Brush on filler heavily and evenly, forcing it into the pores of the wood with a stiff brush. Brush diagonally in both directions, then along the grain. Work on one surface at a time—once hardened, filler is difficult to remove.

Scrape off excess filler after sheen dulls (in about 15 min.). On a large flat area, use a stiff putty knife held at a slight angle to the grain. (To avoid gouging wood, round off knife corners with file.) Clean filler from tool's blade after each pass.

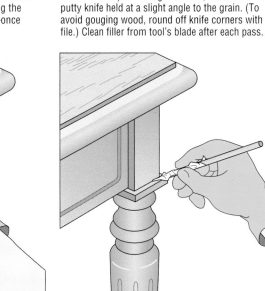

Remove excess filler from small areas by vigorously scrubbing across the grain with a piece of burlap. Scrub until filler is completely removed, turning rag often to expose fresh surfaces. Finish by lightly stroking a clean rag along the grain.

In tight spots, such as corners and crevices, remove excess filler by lightly scrubbing with a pointed wooden dowel; wrap the dowel in cloth to avoid damaging the wood. Change the cloth as it becomes clogged with filler.

Wood sealer

Basically a diluted finish (p.85), sealer is used as a primer over bare wood to control penetration of a succeeding coat of stain or finish. Without a sealer, softwoods absorb stains unevenly, resulting in blotches. Unsealed end grain absorbs more stain than the rest of the wood, resulting in a darker color. Sealer is also applied over a stain or filler to prevent bleeding between the top coat and undercoat and to improve adhesion between the two.

Types of sealers. Shellac, sold in orange or white flakes, is a good all-purpose sealer—unless you're using a polyurethane finish, in which case use another type of sealer, such as diluted varnish. White shellac can be hard to work with; use it only when it's critical to avoid darkening a light wood. To use shellac as a sealer, mix 1 pound of shellac flakes in about 4 litres of denatured alcohol. Or buy 1-pound-cut liquid shellac. (Use shellac within 6 months of mixing; check the date on premixed shellac.) To use a varnish as a sealer, dilute it with the recommended solvent until it's the consistency of milk. If the final finish will be lacquer, use a lacquer-base sealer under it. A penetrating or tung oil finish requires no sealer.

Applying the sealer. Stroke the sealer along the grain on dry and dust-free wood. If you're applying sealer over an alcohol- or water-base stain, use either a brush or a pad; if you're sealing an oil-base stain or filler, use only a brush—a natural-bristle brush for shellac and lacquer sealers, a synthetic brush for varnish. Once the sealer dries, smooth the wood with No. 000 steel wool.

If you prefer a wood's natural color, don't stain it. But if you want to change the appearance and color of a plain wood, accentuate the natural grain pattern of a beautiful wood, or unify the color of different woods within a furniture piece, staining becomes an important part of the finishing process.

Stains come in two basic types. Penetrating stains, such as aniline dyes and NGR (non-grain-raising) stains, are absorbed into the wood's fibers, resulting in deep, transparent colors that highlight the grain. Pigmented stains, such as wiping stains and stains made with japan colors, deposit a thin film of color on top of the wood, muting rather than accentuating the grain.

Containing dyes or pigments, gel stains combine the best qualities of both types of stain—the deep colors of penetrating stains and the easy, run-free application of pigmented stains. Combination products that stain and finish in one step may save time, but the final finish they produce is often inferior to that achieved by conventional staining and finishing.

Pigmented stains have traditionally been oil-base, but they now come in water-base formulations too. Penetrating, gel, and combination stains come in both forms. Water-base stains are nontoxic and easy to clean up, but they dry quickly, which means you must remove excess stain right away to avoid streaks. Oil-base products allow more drying time and are less streaky, but they release toxic fumes. Work in a well-ventilated area when applying oil-base products; wear rubber gloves and goggles when working with any stain.

The stain you use must be compatible with the finish that's going over it. Some stains will bleed into the finish unless they are first sealed (p.83). A water-base finish won't bind to an oil-base stain if it is not left to dry the recommended length of time.

When choosing a stain color, pick one that is slightly lighter than the desired shade—it's easier to darken a light stain than to lighten a dark one. To match an existing color, try the new stain and finish on a matching scrap of wood or on a hidden area of the furniture piece; the final color will depend on the wood and the finish. A stain may react differently to stripped wood than to unfinished wood. A water-base stain, for example, may blotch on previously finished wood. Because color also varies according to the manufacturer's formula, don't mix products.

A stripped furniture piece with surfaces mottled by patches of old stain requires a new stain with maximum coverage. Try either a full-strength pigmented wiping stain or a glazing stain (p.88) thinned to a workable consistency with gum turpentine. Spread the stain or glaze evenly over the piece with the tips of a brush, using decreasing pressure as the stain begins to dry.

Check the directions on the label for applying the stain. Working in small sections, stain the top of the piece first; continue to the bottom, moving from the back to the sides to the front. When possible, orient the piece so that you work on horizontal surfaces. Avoid splattering or dripping the stain on the work. Let the stain dry overnight before proceeding with the finishing process.

A guide to stains

TYPE OF STAIN	ADVANTAGES/DISADVANTAGES	APPLICATION
Aniline dye stain (powder)	Clear penetrating color accentuates grain. Fast drying (especially alcohol-base type) but can streak, blotch, or show overlaps. Water-base stain raises wood grain; may require several coats to achieve desired color.	Dissolve powder in hot water or alcohol. Mix in a non-metallic container. Brush on, following grain with long, even strokes, or spray on. Before using water-base stain, raise grain and sand (see Step 6, p.87).
NGR (non-grain-raising) stain (liquid)	Leaves bright, transparent penetrating color. Premixed stain won't raise wood grain, but color can be hard to control.	Thin, if necessary, with NGR liquid thinner. Spray on, or apply in long strokes with brush. When brushing, use NGR retarder to slow drying and prevent lap marks.
Pigmented wiping stain (oil-base)	Semi-opaque color can hide grain, especially useful for plain wood. Comes premixed. Easy to use—little chance of leaving streaks, blotches, or lap marks. Long drying time makes it ideal for covering large surfaces.	Stir stain often during use. Apply with foam pad or wipe on; first with grain, then diagonally in both directions, finally with grain. Leave stain on wood for length of time recommended by manufacturer; wipe off. To remove excess, rub immediately with rag soaked in paint thinner.
Pigmented wiping stain (water-base)	Same characteristics as the oil-base version but with less intense colors. Nontoxic, quick drying, and easy to clean with soap and water. May raise grain, and can show streaks, blotches, and overlaps.	Raise surface grain and sand before using. Apply with grain, using a water-moistened rag; then rub in a circular motion. Even out color by wiping with grain. Wipe off excess color immediately with a wet rag.
Gel stain	Combines both dyes and pigments for deep, uniform color. Extremely easy to apply. Excellent for touch-ups.	Rub along grain with cloth until color is even. Control color by varying pressure: rub hard for light color, lightly for a darker one. Repeat coats for darker color.
Japan colors	Pure pigment, available in many colors. Comes as varnishlike liquid. Can add to paint (except latex), varnish, lacquer, stain, or filler.	Apply with synthetic brush in long strokes along grain. To use Japan color for staining purposes, thin with turpentine or mineral spirits.

Staining and finishing tools

Chisel-end brush with flagged bristles (p.89) spreads stain or finish smoothly and efficiently.

Foam pad doesn't leave brush strokes, but it can leave ridges and dissolves in some thinners.

Cloth rag should be clean lint-free 100 percent cotton. Bed sheet or cheesecloth is ideal.

Wood finishes

Before choosing a finish, consider both its look and how you'll be using the finished piece. Built-up finishes (lacquer, polyurethane, shellac, and varnish) harden on top of wood, creating a film that resists stains and abrasions. Penetrating finishes (oils) soak into wood and harden in its fibers, imparting a soft sheen that's less protective than a built-up finish but easier to spot-repair.

Built-up finishes have either water- or solvent-bases; all penetrating finishes are solvent-base. Water-base finishes are nonflammable, but they can be difficult to apply and may raise the wood grain. They also won't work well with oil-base stains and fillers if they have not dried properly; before using finishing materials, make sure to check product labels for their compatibility.

Always spread a finish with the grain. Applying a penetrating finish is simple: Pour the finish on the work, spread it with a rag, and let it soak for 15 to 30 minutes before removing any excess. Brushing on a good built-up finish is trickier. First, avoid making bubbles in the finish by wiping the brush against the side of the can (not the rim). Brush from the center of the work to the ends. Instead of one thick coat, apply several thin ones. After each coat dries, sand it with fine-grit paper. To remove dust specks, wipe the surface with a tack cloth after each sanding.

Lacquer is hard to apply with a brush, and spraying equipment can be costly; think twice before using it.

Brushing on a finish

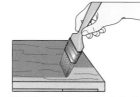
Hold brush at a 45° angle to the work as you brush with the grain. Don't overlap strokes.

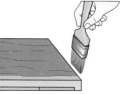
To prevent drips, lift the brush at the end of each stroke; don't let it drag over the end.

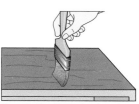
Smooth the finish by dragging an almost dry brush along the grain, holding it at a 90° angle.

On vertical surface, start 2 in. from top, brushing up; then spread finish, brushing down.

For interior surface, first coat vertical sections, working from the top down and back to front.

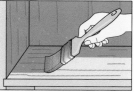
Then coat horizontal surfaces from back to front, brushing out drips from vertical sides.

A guide to finishes

FINISH TYPE	APPEARANCE	APPLICATION	SOLVENT	COMMENTS
Lacquer: synthetic- and water-base	Matte (flat) or gloss (shiny) built-up finish. Enhances grain. Darkens less than oil-base finishes. Synthetic-base type more likely to yellow than water-base type.	Synthetic-base: Spray on three coats with professional equipment. Water-base: Brush or spray on two coats, or wipe on three.	Synthetic-base: lacquer thinner. Water base: water	Provides more protection than oils, less than varnishes. Difficult to apply. Synthetic-base type is highly flammable. Water-base type is nonflammable, but may raise wood grain.
Polyurethane: synthetic- and water-base	Very durable matte (flat) or gloss (shiny) built-up finish. Looks plastic. Darkens wood slightly. Synthetic-base type may yellow; water-base type is nonyellowing.	Synthetic-base: Brush on liquid formula; wipe on gel type. Apply a minimum of two coats. Water-base: Brush on, following product label for recommended number of coats.	Synthetic-base: mineral spirits or turpentine. Water-base: water	Both synthetic- and water-base types are good for items subject to heavy use. Water-base polyurethane may raise wood grain; sand between coats to remove raised fibers.
Shellac	Orange shellac deepens wood color; enhances grain. White shellac dries clear; enhances grain slightly.	Preferably, brush or spray on several thin coats of 3-lb.-cut shellac; or apply with cheesecloth.	Denatured alcohol	Water and alcoholic beverages may damage finish. Pre-mixed shellac may have short shelf life; check can for date.
Varnish: alkyd- and water-base	Durable matte (flat) or gloss (shiny) built-up finish. Comes clear to dark brown. Alkyd type may darken wood. Water-base type won't darken wood as much.	Alkyd-base: Brush on liquid formula; wipe on gel type. Apply at least two coats; more for gel type. Water-base: Brush on, following product label for recommended number of coats.	Alkyd-base: mineral spirits or turpentine. Water-base: water	Alkyd-base: Provides general-purpose protection; some formulations good for outdoor furniture. Water-base: May raise wood grain. Dries quickly; try to avoid overlapping strokes. Generally less durable than alkyd-base type.
Varnish: tung oil	Most natural-looking durable varnish. Can darken wood slightly.	Brush or wipe on three coats.	Mineral spirits or turpentine	While it gives better protection than oils, it's less protective than other varnishes.
Tung oil	Natural-looking matte (flat) penetrating finish. Deepens wood color; enhances grain of wood.	Brush or wipe on unstained wood. Apply two to three coats; rub in vigorously.	Mineral spirits or turpentine	Suitable for all interior objects. Provides little protection against abrasion, but is easy to spot-repair.
Danish oil	Natural-looking matte (flat) penetrating finish; enhances grain. Clear and tinted types darken wood.	Wipe on unstained wood, wipe off. Apply three coats, four for heavily used items.	Mineral spirits or turpentine	Good for interior objects. Special types available for oily woods. Easy to spot-repair.

For best results, pick a cool day with low humidity to work on a refinishing project. Before you start, carefully plan the sequence. There are many ways to finish wood, and although the steps involved are similar, the particular sequence you use depends on the condition of the piece and the type of finish you desire. For example, if the piece has never been finished, the stripping sequence obviously isn't necessary; just lightly sand the piece with 180-grit paper before staining and/or finishing it. For a natural-looking penetrating oil finish, simply flood the piece with oil and wipe it off after a specified time. By contrast, a formal dark varnish finish calls for staining (p.84), filling (p.83), and sealing (p.83) before the application of several coats of a varnish (p.85).

Whatever type of finish you select, it will be only as good as the preparation of the wood surface under it. After stripping the old finish (p.81), repair all nicks, scratches, dents, nail holes, and any other imperfections (p.76). Smooth most woods with 220-grit sandpaper (p.77); use 280- or 320-grit paper for dense hardwoods such as maple and birch. Remove sanding dust with the brush attachment of a vacuum, or wipe down the work with a tack cloth. (To make a tack cloth, dampen a piece of cheesecloth with turpentine, then knead a little varnish into it.)

If you're changing the color of the wood, make sure the stain is compatible with your other finishing products. It's best to stick with products from one manufacturer's line. Before staining, seal the end grain of the wood to prevent overabsorption of stain; seal softwoods to ensure that the stain will be absorbed uniformly. If you are using a water-base stain, raise the grain by moistening the wood with a damp sponge; after it dries, remove the raised fibers with 180-grit paper, then vacuum with a brush attachment. If you are applying a filler, determine up front whether to apply it before or after staining.

Follow the manufacturer's directions for applying the finish. Once it is dry, you can polish the finish with an abrasive powder (p.82). Protect any type of finish with several thin coats of a high-quality furniture wax.

Before

The original finish on this table was murky, obscuring the wood's grain. The finish was also badly scratched.

After

After stripping the old finish and applying a new stain and finish, the natural mahogany wood grain shows through.

Stripping the work

1 To remove the old finish, wear goggles, a respirator, and chemical-resistant gloves or two pairs of rubber gloves. Apply the stripper with a brush, liberally coating the piece. Work from top to bottom, a section at a time. As necessary, reposition the furniture for easier access.

2 Scrape stripper off a large flat surface with a metal or plastic putty knife. (Using a file, round off the corners of a metal blade to avoid marring the wood.) If some of the finish remains, reapply the stripper and remove it with No. 2 steel wool.

For easier access, place work on a steady table

3 Continue stripping process, brushing stripper on vertical surfaces a section at a time. While it's still wet, remove stripper and dissolved finish from turned pieces and small surfaces with No. 2 steel wool. For best results, unravel steel wool from pad.

4 Examine work for missed spots. If necessary, work stripper into crevices with brush tip. To remove stripper from crevices, use a pointed implement, such as a tool for removing grout (shown). For other ways to remove stripper from tight spots, see page 81.

5 Remove stripper residue by scrubbing with No. 00 steel wool dipped in solvent. Then wipe with a clean cloth and vacuum with the brush attachment. Check wood surfaces for nicks, cracks, gouges, and other damage. Now is the best time to fill in or repair any damage.

Finishing the work

6 If the piece has never been finished, lightly sand it with 180-grit paper. If you're using water-base stain, raise grain with damp sponge. Let dry. Remove raised wood fibers by sanding. This is also the time to apply sealer to softwood and end grain to ensure even staining.

7 If you want to stain the work, apply the stain with a brush or cloth, following manufacturer's instructions. Proceed from top to bottom, working with the grain of the wood. Don't overlap strokes, particularly on a large flat surface.

8 To unify the stain on dense wood, such as birch, cherry, or maple, go over it with a dry brush, using light pressure. Make sure you work with the grain of the wood.

9 Use a clean lint-free cloth, such as cheesecloth, to apply the stain on turned and detailed sections. To avoid drips, don't overly saturate the cloth. Make sure the stain doesn't collect in crevices, corners, and other nooks and crannies.

10 To fill an open-pore wood, such as ash, mahogany, or oak, brush on paste wood filler after staining. (In some projects, filler is applied before staining or not at all.) Remove any excess filler with a putty knife or a piece of burlap (p.83).

11 Applying a sealer is the next step in many projects. Make sure the surfaces are dry and dust-free before applying the sealer. After it dries, smooth the work with No. 000 steel wool.

12 The finish may have to be applied in several coats; make sure the surfaces are dry and dust-free before each application. As with the stain, work from top to bottom, a section at a time. And remember to follow the grain of the wood.

13 Some types of finishes require sanding between coats. After each coat dries, sand work with 280-grit paper. Remove dust and debris by vacuuming or with a tack cloth. Let final coat dry for about 48 hr.; then go over work gently with No. 0000 steel wool.

14 Rub on furniture wax with lint-free cloth; wipe it off with a clean cloth. For a high-gloss shine, first sand work with 400-grit wet-or-dry paper, then with 600-grit paper. Use paper dry; or soak it in oil for shellac, in water or oil for other finishes. Rub work with abrasive powder; apply wax.

Furniture repair ▪ Special finishes

Antiquing, graining, and liming (also referred to as pickling) are special finishing techniques that can enhance the look of a bland surface. Antiquing artificially ages a piece, graining creates the illusion of an exotic wood grain, and liming gives wood a weathered look.

To antique a piece, apply a top coat of glaze over an enameled or painted base; then wipe, blot, or brush off most of the glaze. The glaze that stays in any scratches and crevices gives the appearance of wear. Buy an antiquing kit that contains all the materials you'll need, or make your own glaze by mixing 1 part glazing medium or clear varnish, 1 part paint, and 1 to 2 parts mineral spirits (for oil-base paint) or water (for water-base paint). Make the glaze coat darker than the base color, and use only compatible products.

Like antiquing, the graining process requires both a base and a glaze coat. You create the wood grain in the wet glaze using a graining tool, a graining comb, and a badger-hair brush. Buy supplies individually or in a kit.

Liming involves filling the pores of open-grained wood (such as oak, chestnut, and ash) with white paste wood filler or white paint to create a weathered appearance. Unusual effects can be created with pigmented filler in colors other than white. Read the labels of the products you buy to make sure the materials are compatible.

Before applying a special finish to a furniture piece, test the color and perfect your technique on scrap wood. Protect the surface of the finished piece by applying the finish recommended on the label of the glazing or filler product.

Antiquing

1 Clean surface to be finished. Brush on base coat with grain; let dry for 24 hr. If old finish is in good condition (p.80), paint over it; carefully sand and seal new wood before painting (p.77).

2 Working on one section at a time, liberally apply the top coat of glaze. For complete coverage, use the bristle tips to force the paint into any nooks and crannies.

3 Pounce off glaze on high spots with cheesecloth; leave some glaze in low spots. Use a stiff dry brush to remove glaze in detailed area. For speckled effect, spatter glaze with stiff brush.

Graining

Graining tool

1 Brush on base coat as for antiquing. Brush glaze over dry base. For a heartwood pattern, remove ringed surface of graining tool from handle. Pull it through wet glaze; tilt tool as you pull.

3 To make a knot, press thumb into wet glaze. Use a cotton swab or pencil eraser to remove some glaze from the center of knot and to draw grain lines around it.

Liming

1 Highlight wood grain by brushing paste wood filler first with the grain, then across it. Use a colored filler or paint if desired.

Graining comb

2 To make a straight grain pattern, pull a graining comb straight through glaze while it's still wet. Alter the path of the comb to create a curved grain pattern or to accommodate a knot.

Graining tool | Badger-hair brush

4 With glaze still wet, feather grain with toothed edge of graining tool. Then soften pattern by lightly brushing over it with a clean dry badger-hair brush. After 24 hr., apply a final coat of finish.

2 Scrub off excess filler or paint across the grain with a wad of burlap or jute; then scrub with the grain. After 24 hr., apply a final coat of finish.

Painting furniture

Paint can be used to camouflage ugly or poor-quality wood and to generally enhance the appearance of a furniture piece. Semigloss enamel is a good, long-lasting choice; other alternatives include a flat or satin latex or oil-base paint. (High-gloss paint does not cover well and must be deglossed, or sanded, between coats; think twice before using it.) Latex paint is quick-drying, nonflammable, and needs only water for cleanup, but it raises the wood grain and does not sand well. Oil-base paint, made with a synthetic resin called alkyd, is toxic and combustible, but it flows better than latex, leaves a smoother coating, and sands well.

A painted finish requires as much surface preparation as a clear one; any imperfections in the wood will show through the paint after it dries. Fill blemishes and seal dark knots on unfinished wood; fill open-pored woods with a paste wood filler. You can paint over an existing finish if it is sound, but first clean the piece thoroughly and sand it with 120-grit paper. Feather the edges of a chipped area into the surrounding surface by sanding with 120-grit paper. Remove all sanding dust; then prime the piece. Priming seals the wood and reduces the number of coats of paint needed to achieve opaqueness. Wood primers are either alkyd- or shellac-base. Make sure the primer is compatible with the paint you plan to use (check package labels). Sand the primer coat if recommended by the maker.

To apply an even coat of paint, see *Brushing technique,* below. Work in small areas at a time, slightly overlapping wet edges. If the work has detailed areas, such as a paneled cabinet door, work on the details before the flat areas. To paint a vertical surface, brush downward to prevent sags or runs. After the last coat has dried, remove brush marks and specks by wet-sanding the entire surface with 400-grit wet-or-dry paper. Wipe off the sanding debris; brush on a protective coat of clear gloss or semigloss finish (p.85). Let the finish dry completely before lightly rubbing it with 400-grit wet-or-dry paper, then 600-grit paper. For a high-sheen finish, see Step 14 on page 87.

The paintbrush

Choose a good-quality brush with thick bristles: natural for oil paints, synthetic for latex. Bristles should be tapered (bottom)—longer in the center—and should have flagged, or split, tips (inset).

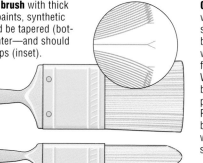

Clean brush with mineral spirits for oil-base paint, with water and soap for latex paint. When dry, store brush in brown paper wrapper. Protect bristles by folding wrapper as shown.

Loose-fitting rubber band

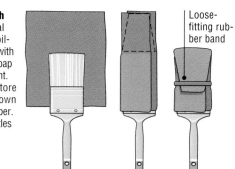

Brushing technique

1 Dip bristles 2 in. into paint; remove extra paint by pressing brush against inside of can.

2 For complete coverage, spread the paint by first brushing with the grain, then across the grain.

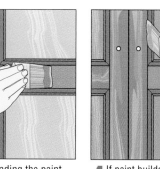

3 After spreading the paint, smooth it by lightly brushing with the grain.

4 If paint builds up in crevices or carvings, remove excess paint with a clean dry brush.

Stenciling

You can personalize a furniture piece by painting a design on top of an opaque coat of paint. To copy a pattern, use tracing paper, then wax-free transfer paper. For a repeat design, use a stencil. Protect the dried work with a coat of finish.

To make a stencil, draw the design on tracing paper. Tape the paper to acetate and place them on a cardboard backer. Cut pattern through the acetate with a craft knife.

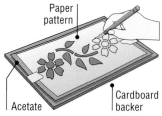

Paper pattern

Cardboard backer

Acetate

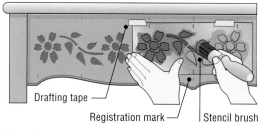

Drafting tape

Registration mark

Stencil brush

To position the stencil, make registration marks on the acetate and the work; use them for alignment. Tape stencil in place with drafting tape. Apply artist's acrylic paint with a stencil brush. If you use several colors, apply one at a time.

To tell whether a chair has been caned by hand, look for holes drilled into its frame. Chairs with a continuous groove around the seat opening have been caned with prewoven cane webbing (p.92). The material used for hand-weaving, called strand cane, is harvested from the outer bark of the rattan palm, a tree native to Southeast Asia. It's cut into 10- to 20-foot-long strips ranging in width from 1/16 to 3/16 inch. The width of the cane used depends on the size of the holes in the chair (see chart at far right). Available from craft stores or woodworking supply houses, strand cane comes in hanks of 1,000 feet; an average-size chair needs about 250 feet.

Traditional weave

Sold with each hank is a wider strand of cane, the binder, used to form a border around the weaving.

Reweaving a cane seat yourself is a large project, so it's best to break the job into several sessions. Before starting, examine the chair carefully and make any necessary repairs. Cut away the old cane and save it to use as a guide for the new seat. Remove any remaining cane and binder from the chair; use an awl to clear the caning holes. The tools required for caning are simple: scissors, caning pegs (or golf tees), an awl, a pail, a sponge, clothespins, and lacquer, Danish oil, or tung oil to seal the completed seat.

Cane is easier to weave if it is wet. To ensure that you always have damp cane on hand, gently pull several strands from the hank; coil each one and fasten it with a clothespin. Soak the coils in warm water for at least 15 minutes. As you remove one coil, replace it with another. Periodically moisten the weaving with a damp sponge.

Always weave with the glossy side of the cane facing up. Use pegs to secure both ends of each strand, leaving 4-inch tails for tying off; for some jobs you may need several strands to complete each step. Maintain uniform tension while weaving, but don't make the cane too tight. You should be able to depress the weaving 1/2 to 3/4 inch; as the strands dry, they shrink, resulting in a tight weave. After each step, make sure that the strands are not twisted or kinked and that the rows are parallel. When you're done, thoroughly dampen the seat and singe off any frayed cane with a moving match flame. Stain the seat, if desired; then seal both sides of the weaving.

Determining cane size

SIZE OF HOLE	SPACE BETWEEN HOLES	WIDTH OF CANE
1/8 inch	3/8 inch	Superfine
3/16 inch	1/2 inch	Fine fine
3/16 inch	5/8 inch	Fine
1/4 inch	3/4 inch	Medium
5/16 inch	7/8 inch	Common

The basic weaving pattern

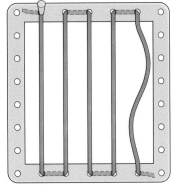

1 Starting from left rear corner, weave first layer of vertical strands from back to front. Push cane up first hole, leaving a tail; hold strand ends in place with pegs.

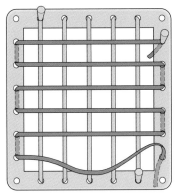

2 Pass cane from right to left over cane woven in previous step. Advance strands by passing them under frame and up through nearest hole.

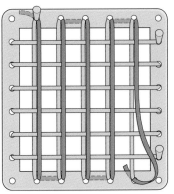

3 Weave second set of vertical strands through same holes as first set, but over the cross strands. Keep new cane to the right of strands installed in Step 1.

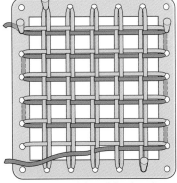

4 Moving from left to right, thread cane under strands placed in Step 1 and over those placed in Step 3. Moisten cane with wet sponge to make weaving easier.

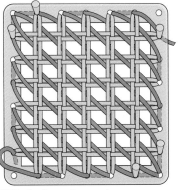

5 Begin diagonal weave from any corner. Weave under pairs of vertical strands and over horizontal pairs. Use an awl to help push cane through holes.

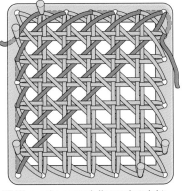

6 Weave the second diagonal at right angle to first. Pass cane over vertical strands and under horizontal strands. When done, check pattern and tie off ends.

Hand-caning a splayed seat

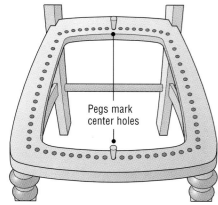

Pegs mark center holes

1 Locate center holes at both back and front of seat by counting in from each corner hole; mark with pegs. On chairs with round-back seats, count around from each front corner hole.

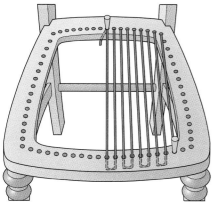

2 Start weaving from the center back. Push the strand up through back center hole and down through front center hole. Weave from the center of the seat out to the side.

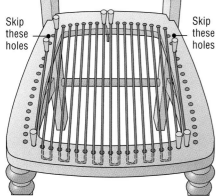

Skip these holes

Skip these holes

3 Repeat procedure on the opposite side of the seat. Keep rows parallel by skipping holes as necessary. Fill gussets by weaving in separate strands on the sides. Proceed to Step 2 of basic weaving pattern (facing page).

Tying off loose ends

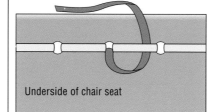

Underside of chair seat

Tie off strands underneath the frame with an overhand knot. First dampen cane; then pass the loose end under the weave.

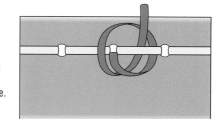

Bring cane back over weave. Tuck the end underneath the weave and then through the loop. Pull the end tight, and trim to 1 in.

Applying the binder

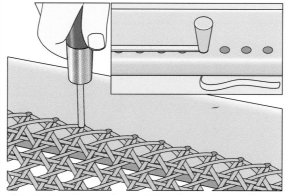

1 Cut binder a bit longer than seat circumference. Insert awl into holes to make room for binder. Peg binder in back center hole, leaving tail. Hold binder taut over holes in seat frame as you stitch.

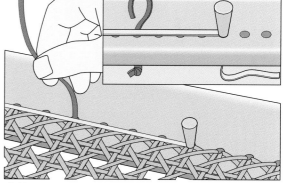

2 Knot one end of a length of cane and pull it up through fourth hole from peg. Loop cane over binder and push it down through the same hole.

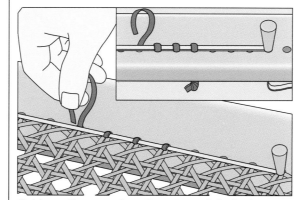

3 Advance the cane underneath seat to next hole. Continue stitching from hole to hole all along circumference of seat until you reach the back center peg.

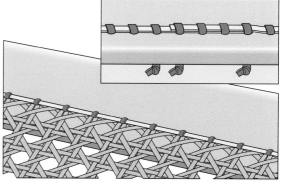

4 To finish, remove peg and lay the end of the binder over the starting point. Continue stitching until all holes have been completed. Trim the binder just beyond last stitch. Tie off ends.

Furniture repair ▪ Reseating chairs with prewoven cane

If the cane in a furniture piece is held in place with a spline, it has been woven by machine, not by hand. Machine-woven (or prewoven) cane is easier to replace than the hand-woven variety (p.90). Available in various patterns at craft stores or through woodworking supply catalogs, prewoven cane is sold by the running foot in sections 12 to 24 inches wide. To determine the amount you'll need, measure the length and width of the area to be recaned from the outer edges of the caning grooves, then add 2 inches to both dimensions.

If possible, match the new spline to a piece of the original. Otherwise, find the right size by measuring the width of the groove and subtracting ½₂ inch (to allow for the cane). If the seat is rounded, use one continuous strip of spline; use four individual pieces for square seats. In both cases, the total length of spline should be 6 inches longer than the entire length of the caning groove.

Other required supplies include yellow carpenter's glue, a utility knife, a chisel, a mallet, and a tung-oil

sealant or lacquer. You'll also need four wedges to hold the cane in place during caning and an additional wedge to push the cane into the groove. Buy wedges from your caning supplier.

Soak the cane in warm water for an hour prior to working; the cane will shrink as it dries, creating a taut surface. Don't bend dry cane; it may crack and break. Try working the spline dry, but if it's difficult to maneuver, dampen it until it's pliable. Don't soak it too long, or the wood won't absorb the glue.

Replacing prewoven cane

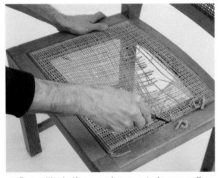

1 Run utility knife around groove to loosen spline; pry out spline with chisel. If needed, cut V-notch into spline; apply 50-50 solution of vinegar and water to soften glue. Remove cane; sand groove.

2 Place damp cane over opening, glossy side up. Align pattern. Place a wedge in center of back rail groove; then lightly stretch cane to center of front rail, and wedge. Repeat with sides.

3 Lightly tap the cane into the groove with a wedge and mallet. Insert the cane a little at a time. Alternate between opposite sides to maintain uniform tension.

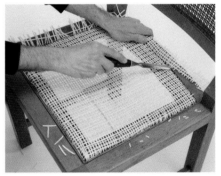

4 Remove wedges. Use a chisel to cut off protruding cane just below the top of the outer edge of the groove. Be careful not to pull cane out of the groove or to damage the wood.

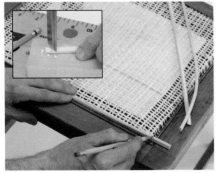

5 For square seats, use four pieces of spline. Measure spline against groove; mark ends with pencil. Use a chisel to cut the ends at a 45° angle. On rounded seats, use one length of spline.

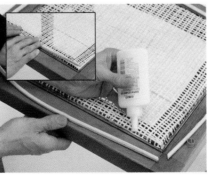

6 Try working spline dry, but if necessary, soak it until pliable; do not oversoak. Place a bead of yellow carpenter's glue into the groove and gently press the spline into place.

7 Using wedge and mallet, tap spline into place, making sure it is flush with seat surface. Take care not to distort spline shape or to damage wood of chair. Let cane and glue dry for 24 hr.

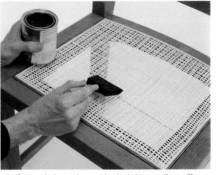

8 Smooth frayed cane by lightly sanding off loose fibers. Starting with the underside, seal both sides of the seat with tung-oil sealant or lacquer; let it dry thoroughly before use.

Repairing wicker

The term "wicker" refers to a type of woven construction based on basketry techniques, not to any one material. Wicker furniture can be made from a variety of materials, including cane and reed (both obtained from the rattan palm), willow, sea grass, natural rush, and fiber rush (machine-twisted paper). Since these materials can be hard to tell apart, especially if they've been painted or stained, buying replacement wicker is tricky. To ensure that the new material matches the old in size, shape, and composition, take a snippet of your wicker along when shopping, or send it to your mail-order supplier.

Only basic tools are required for the common repairs shown here: a hammer, ½- to ¾-inch nails, yellow carpenter's glue, and heavy-duty scissors or pruning shears. Needle-nose pliers are invaluable for pulling materials through the weave. If you are working with cane, reed, willow, or natural rush, you'll need a soaking container (work sea grass and fiber rush dry). Soak the material for only a few moments, just until it's pliable. Avoid oversoaking—the material will swell and fray, making it difficult to handle.

Before starting any repair, clean the piece with a damp sponge and check that the frame is sound. Damaged strands (horizontal pieces) and broken spokes (vertical supports) are the most common wicker problems. Another common repair is replacing the cane wrapping around the legs of a wicker piece; for this job, use binder cane, which is slightly wider than the cane used for other parts of wicker furniture.

Patching a single strand: Locking

Cut off damaged portion of strand from back of piece, if possible. Cut ends at an angle over nearest spokes (vertical supports). Cut new strand 1 in. longer than snipped-off section of strand.

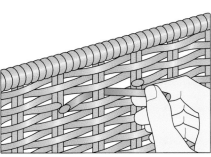

Weave in new strand from back, following existing pattern and keeping strand taut. Once new strand is in place, trim it to fit so that its ends butt against cut ends of old strand.

Larger patches: Under-and-over weave

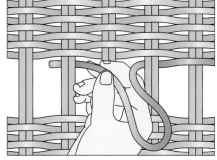

Remove old strands. Weave new strand in opposite direction of adjoining one. For instance, if the next intact strand starts by going under a spoke, new strand should start by going over the spoke.

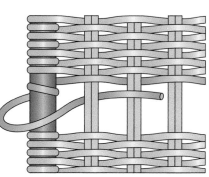

Loop strand around rail before weaving back toward opposite rail. When weaving is complete, nail down end of strand or tuck it under a neighboring one. Dab glue on ends of new strands.

Replacing a spoke

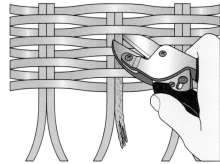

Snip off broken spoke near top, at least four or five rows into the horizontal weave. Repeat at bottom and pull out spoke. If necessary, use a screwdriver to pry out a stubborn spoke.

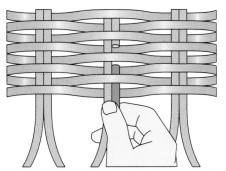

Dab glue on cut ends of old spoke. Insert one end of new spoke into horizontal weaving at bottom. Bend spoke to follow original pattern; slide top end of spoke into horizontal weaving at top.

Rewrapping a leg

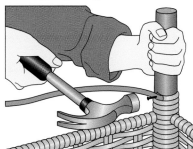

Remove any frayed or dirty binder cane. Nail loose end of old cane to inside of leg. Attach new (presoaked) cane over end of old cane, nailing it into place on inside of leg.

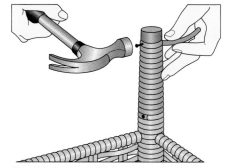

Wrap binder cane tightly around wood. Nail end to leg, leaving ½ in. of wood exposed at bottom. Trim off excess cane; then apply a drop of glue to both ends of newly attached cane.

Furniture repair ■ Working with rush

When a rush seat sags or breaks, there's no repairing it—the seat must be rewoven. You may choose either natural or imitation rush for the job. Natural rush, derived from the leaves of marshland plants, offers intriguing textures and colors, but it can be hard to find and difficult to work with. Imitation rush, or fiber rush, which consists of strands of twisted kraft paper, is easy to handle and is available from most craft stores or woodworking catalogs.

Select rush that is in proportion to the size of the seat: smaller-diameter rush for small seats, larger-diameter for bigger ones. An average chair will need 2 or 3 pounds of rush; a large armchair or rocker may take up to 5 pounds.

In addition to rush, you'll need a hammer, upholstery tacks (p.97), a utility knife, a smooth piece of wood or a yardstick (called an evener) to force the strands into parallel rows, and unprinted corrugated cardboard to stiffen the seat. To seal the weave, use tung, Danish, or boiled linseed oil for natural rush; shellac for fiber rush. If you use an oil sealer on fiber rush, apply a top coat of polyurethane over the oil (see *A guide to finishes,* p.85).

Start by cutting away the old rush with a utility knife. Remove any nails or tacks on the seat rails; if the rails have sharp edges, smooth them before installing the new seat or they will weaken the rush. Prepare the rush for weaving by dipping it into warm water until it's pliable; don't let fiber rush soak too long or it may disintegrate.

Weaving begins at the corners and progresses toward the middle. Attach new lengths of rush with a square knot.

Square seat frames are easy to weave, but if the frame is rectangular, the shorter side rails will be filled before the front and back rails, leaving an unfinished area in the center. Weave this open area last with a series of figure-8 loops that pass over the front and back rails. If the seat is splayed, fill in the corners first with short lengths of rush before starting the regular weaving. As you weave, straighten the rows with the evener. To finish weaving, tie the last strand to itself under the seat using several half hitches. Then seal both the top and the underside.

Basic weaving pattern

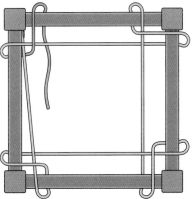

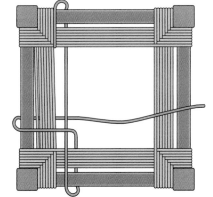

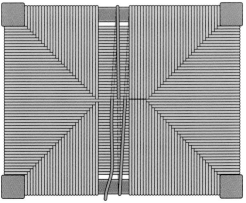

1 Tack rush to left rail near back post. Pass rush over and around front rail, then over and around left side rail. Continue to move around seat while repeating this pattern.

2 Continue weaving around all four corners consecutively. Use a square knot to tie on new lengths of rush as needed. Keep strands close together and maintain uniform tension.

Weave rectangular seat in same manner as square one until the side rails are covered. Close center gap with figure-8 loops; pass rush between center rows. Continue until front and back rails are filled; tie off rush.

Weaving pattern for a splayed seat

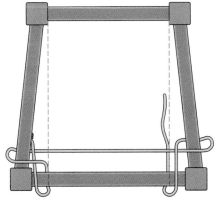

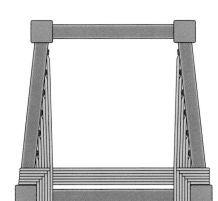

1 Measure back rail and mark its length on the front rail. Then tack a 3- to 4-ft. length of rush to the front of the left rail. Pass the rush around both front corners and tack it to right side rail.

2 Fill in front rail to marks with 3- to 4-ft. lengths of rush, tacking ends to side rails. Then tack a long length of rush to the back left corner of the side rail, and weave using basic pattern.

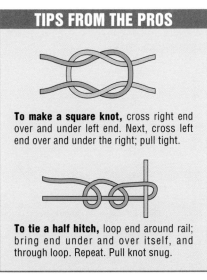

TIPS FROM THE PROS

To make a square knot, cross right end over and under left end. Next, cross left end over and under the right; pull tight.

To tie a half hitch, loop end around rail; bring end under and over itself, and through loop. Repeat. Pull knot snug.

Reweaving a rush seat

1 For splayed seat, fill in corners before starting regular weaving. To begin, tack a 3- to 4-ft. length of rush to the front of the left side rail. Loop rush around front rail, then around side rail.

2 Bring rush across seat to right front corner. Loop it over right side rail, then around front rail. Keep rush taut as you work, pulling it with uniform tension.

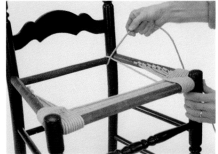

3 Tack rush to inside of right rail, directly across from tack on opposite rail. If necessary, untwist rush a bit to insert tack. Trim rush to meet tack. Repeat until corners are filled.

4 Begin regular weaving using a 15- to 20-ft. length of rush tacked to back of left rail. Weave around front corners and back right corner. Start with this step if seat is square.

5 Repeat pattern around left back corner to complete the first row of continuous weaving. Press rush tight against corner post, keeping the tension consistent.

6 Continue weaving around seat, adding new lengths of rush with square knots. Use evener to straighten rush every five to six rows so that strands lie close together and are parallel.

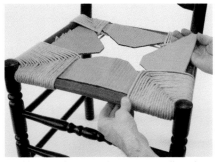

7 After weaving several rows, cut cardboard to fit corner diagonals and wedge it into front corners. Continue weaving and then pad the sides. The cardboard will be covered by weaving.

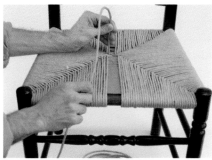

8 Side rails may be filled first, leaving a gap in center. Feed end of rush up through center of seat. To ensure you'll have enough rush to finish seat, tie on new length; keep knot under seat.

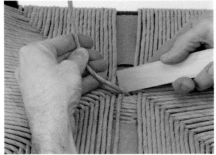

9 Fill open area by weaving a series of figure-8's over front and back rails, each time passing the rush through the narrow center opening. Align the loops with the evener.

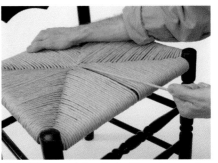

10 After completing the last loop, bring end of strand up through the center. Stretch it over front rail to the underside of seat, keeping the rush taut.

11 Turn chair over, and tie off rush with two or three half hitches. Pull the knots tight; then trim off excess rush. Conceal knots by pushing them down inside the weave.

12 Dress seat on both sides with evener. Rub flat surface of evener over the loops on the rails so that no strands protrude. Seal both sides of seat; two or three coats may be needed.

Traditionally, splint seats were woven with hand-split lengths of hickory, white oak, or ash. Wood splints are difficult to work with and hard to find today. Because of this, most splint seats are now woven with flat reed. Harvested from the rattan palm, flat reed is durable, easy to handle, and available from most woodworking and craft supply houses. While fiber splint, made from kraft paper, may also be used, it's less durable than reed and shouldn't be exposed to moisture.

You'll need about one hank of splint to reseat an average-size chair. Splint is commonly available in widths of ¼, ⅜, ½, and ⅝ inch—choose the size closest to the original material. You'll also need a utility knife, an unserrated kitchen knife, carpet tacks, a hammer, a stapler, and a sealant containing tung

oil. Flat reed is easier to work with if it's damp, so before weaving, soak the splints in warm water for 10 to 15 minutes, coiling them smooth side out. Find the smooth side by bending the splint; the smooth side won't have any splintery fibers at the crease.

Prior to weaving, cut away the old seat, saving it to use as a guide for the new weaving. Examine the chair carefully and make all necessary repairs. Remove any nails or tacks, and smooth any rough edges.

Splint seats are woven in two stages: the warp and the weft. The warps are the splints passed from the back of the seat to the front; the wefts are woven from side to side. Create diagonals by offsetting each successive weft one row. Square and splayed seats are woven in

the same way. Fill in the corners of a splayed seat last by tucking short strips of splint into the weave. Keep the warps perpendicular to the back rail; leave equal space between each side rail and the first and last warps.

To complete the project, trim off any splinters with a utility knife. Then protect the seat with several coats of a tung-oil sealant.

Diagonal weaving pattern

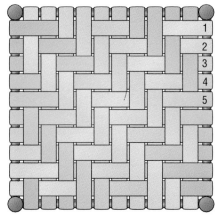

Weave wefts under and over alternating pairs of warps, but offset each successive weft one row as you move across seat. For example, start first splint over two warps, second splint over one. Pass the third under two, the fourth under one. Every fifth splint repeats the first.

The weaving process

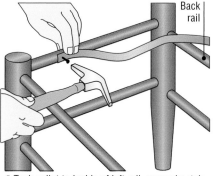

1 Tack splint to inside of left rail, approximately one-third of the way back from front rail. Wrap the splint over and around back rail at left corner, keep the smooth side facing outward.

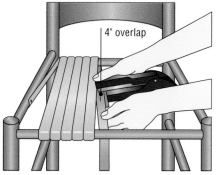

2 Wrap splint around front and back rails, adding new splint as needed. Attach new splint underneath chair. Overlap ends by 4 in. and staple twice. Use pliers to flatten staples.

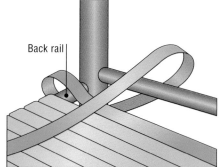

3 After reaching right corner post, wrap splint over and under rear rail. Pull it around the front of the corner post, and up over the right side rail. Splint is ready to be woven horizontally.

4 This step begins the weaving process. Pack rows close together; use kitchen knife to help push wefts along. At end of each row, turn chair over and weave back across on underside.

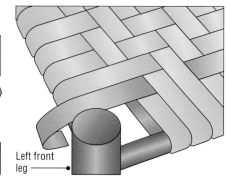

5 Secure the end of the last weft splint to seat by tucking it into the weave or by stapling it to the splint on the underside of the chair. Again, double-staple and flatten the prongs.

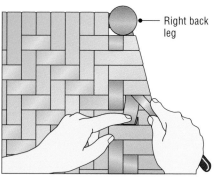

6 Fill in the corners of a splayed seat with short lengths of splint; secure them by tucking the ends into the weave. Allow seat to dry before coating it with a protective sealant.

Reupholstery basics

With care and patience, beginners can handle many upholstery projects, from re-covering a dining chair or a small occasional chair to reinforcing the supporting webbing of an easy chair. Those with more upholstery experience can tackle larger pieces.

The shape and softness of upholstered furniture is created by a combination of various types of padding, stuffing, and springs. The stuffing in older pieces may be fiber or loose animal hair. Newer stuffing materials include polyurethane foam, fiberfill, and cotton batting.

When reupholstering a piece, try to keep the existing springs and stuffing when possible. Fill any gaps in the stuffing with pieces of cotton batting; then cover the entire seat with a layer of foam and fiberfill. Never try to replace broken springs with stuffing; instead, tie new springs in place (p.99).

When selecting a cover fabric, balance sturdiness with workability. Heavy materials such as corduroy and the thicker upholstery blends can be difficult to work or to sew on a home sewing machine. Light fabrics, such as drapery cottons, are less sturdy but easier to stretch and pleat.

Professionals fasten fabric with a costly pneumatic staple gun. Other kinds of staplers are useful for softwood and plywood bases, and for holding underlayers in position. As a rule, such guns aren't powerful enough to penetrate deeply into the hardwood of large furniture pieces. For a hardwood chair, use a magnetic hammer and tacks.

Basic upholstery tools

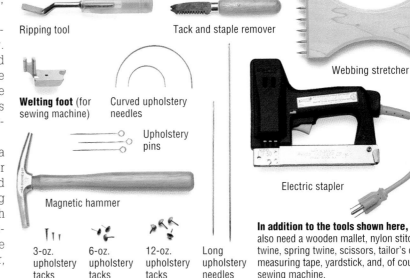

Ripping tool

Tack and staple remover

Webbing stretcher

Welting foot (for sewing machine)

Curved upholstery needles

Upholstery pins

Magnetic hammer

Electric stapler

3-oz. upholstery tacks

6-oz. upholstery tacks

12-oz. upholstery tacks

Long upholstery needles

In addition to the tools shown here, you'll also need a wooden mallet, nylon stitching twine, spring twine, scissors, tailor's chalk, measuring tape, yardstick, and, of course, a sewing machine.

Anatomy of coil-spring upholstery

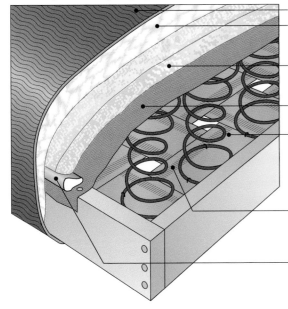

Cover: Top layer of upholstery.

Fiberfill: Holds stuffing and provides smooth foundation for final cover.

Stuffing: Foam or rubberized hair is built up to desired height; use cotton batting to fill gaps.

Burlap: Fabric is tacked to frame over springs to support padding.

Springs: Hourglass-shaped springs are stitched to webbing and then tied together with spring twine. Zigzag-type springs (p.101) are secured to frame with nails and metal clips.

Webbing: Strips of jute are stretched and tacked to underside of furniture frame to support springs or padding.

Fox edge: Burlap-covered padding is tacked along frame edges to give upholstery cover a smooth appearance.

Anatomy of slip or drop seat

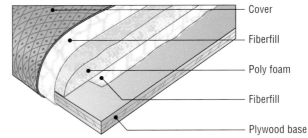

Cover

Fiberfill

Poly foam

Fiberfill

Plywood base

Removable drop seat has plywood base. To cover this seat type, center fiberfill on base, leaving 2 in. of plywood exposed at each edge. Glue foam layer to edge of plywood; then staple second fiberfill layer and cover fabric to underside of plywood base.

Anatomy of a fitted seat

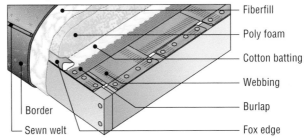

Fiberfill

Poly foam

Cotton batting

Webbing

Burlap

Border

Sewn welt

Fox edge

Nonremovable seat has a webbing and burlap base. Tack fox edge to edge of frame to contain stuffing. Shape seat in layers: cotton batting, poly foam, and fiberfill. If seat is to have box cushion shape, sew welt to border and top cover (p.102); attach cover.

Stripping a dining chair

A dining chair that is in good overall repair but has a worn seat cover usually needs just a new layer of fiberfill and a new cover. But if you need to get at the stuffing and springs, use a ripping tool to pull away the dust cover and the old fabric. Then pry the remaining staples or tacks from the frame with a remover tool (p.97). To avoid damaging the finish of an exposed wood frame, always work from the outside edge toward the inside. Reinforce the wood frame as necessary (pp.64–67).

Covering a chair seat: Basic operations

If a chair's stuffing is sagging or lumpy, add webbing as needed, stretching it taut enough to support the springs but not so taut that the webbing twists the frame. Retie any loose springs, fill gaps with cotton batting, and add a layer of poly foam and fiberfill. Position the cover fabric on the seat, centering any design. Gently but firmly tension the fabric over the seat so that there are no wrinkles. Fasten the fabric by baste-tacking or baste-stapling (see Step 2, below). Once the fabric is properly tensioned, do the final tacking.

Covering a fixed seat

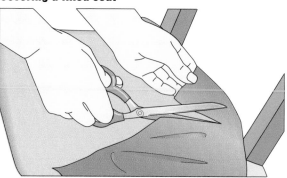

Measure seat top and depth. Cut cover fabric, allowing 1 in. on all sides for tacking under frame. Use chalk to mark center of front and back seat frame and of fabric front and back. Position fiberfill, baste-staple at center marks, then trim it. Position cover fabric. Fold back fabric at rear, and notch corners to fit posts as shown below.

Covering a slip seat

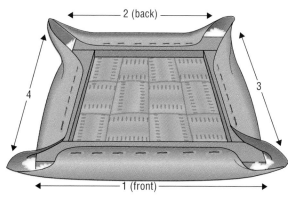

1 Place fiberfill on top of seat; trim it. Turn seat over. Mark center of seat at front and back with chalk. Cut cover, allowing extra fabric for stapling. Mark fabric center at front and back. Match centers; baste-staple fabric at center marks, holding gun just above surface.

2 Baste-staple cover, checking that fabric weave is square to the frame and avoiding wrinkles. Begin at center of front. Work outward in each direction, stopping 3 in. from corners. Baste-staple back edge and two sides similarly; then do final stapling.

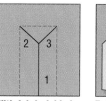

With fabric folded back (see above), cut notch 1, leaving 1-in. gap between end of cut and post. Make cuts 2 and 3.

Fold under fabric as shown. If necessary, extend the second and third cuts to accept the post width.

Slide cover into place around post; adjust folds as necessary. Tension and tack cover to underside of frame.

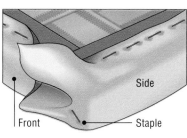

3 To make a neat corner, pull the cover fabric from the side of the frame toward the front, smoothing the fabric as you proceed. Staple this tensioned fabric to the front of the frame.

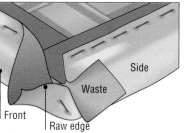

4 Cut away excess fabric. Turn under the raw edge of the fabric so that the front fabric will hide it. Tension the front fabric.

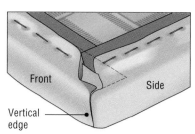

5 Align the vertical edge of the cover with the corner of the frame. Pull the front fold into place. The fabric at the corner should be free of wrinkles. Staple corner and trim the fabric.

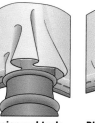

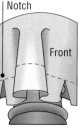

Fit front corners. First, notch fabric at either side of leg; then turn under raw edge around leg.

Tension and tack fabric to rail bottom. Pleat fabric at corner, stapling and folding as for slip seat (see left).

Blind-stitch (p.102) corner neatly, using curved needle. Vertical edge of fold should align with frame corner.

Reupholstering an occasional chair

Installing springs

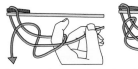

Secure twine to webbing by tying a slip knot after first stitch. To tie knot, hold one twine end in place. Crook finger and wrap other twine end around finger. Continue by wrapping this second end around twine loop two or three times counterclockwise. Slip end into hole created by finger. Pull knot taut.

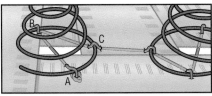

Sew springs to webbing at three points. At point A, draw twine up through webbing, around bottom coil, and back through webbing. Draw twine under webbing to B; sew last stitch near next spring at C.

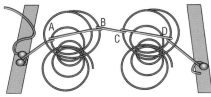

Tie each row of springs together. Tack double strand of twine to frame back. Tie strand 1 (red) to first spring at points A (second coil from top) and B (top coil) and to last spring at C (top coil) and D (second coil). Tie any intermediate springs at two points on top coil. Tack strand end to frame front.

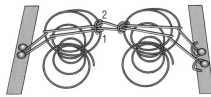

Loop strand 2 (green) to top coils only, as shown. Where strands 1 and 2 coincide, wrap strand 2 over strand 1, around coil, and through resulting loop. Tack strand 2 to front of chair frame.

1 Strip chair as far as needed. If frame requires repairs, put stuffing and springs safely aside for reuse. Make repairs and assemble materials such as webbing, fox edge, fiberfill, and foam padding. Finished chair is shown at right.

4 Place springs where webbing strips cross and near the center of seat. This provides good support where the weight will be concentrated. Sew bottom coils to webbing. To begin, tie twine to webbing with slip knot (see left).

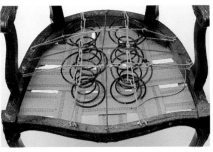

7 Reinforce newly installed lengths of twine by tacking a single strand from back to front and one from side to side, at right angles to each other (shown in red). Knot these strands to the double strands and to each other (not to the coils).

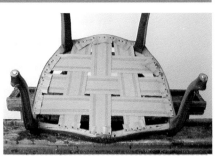

2 Install webbing with No. 12 tacks. Fold one end and tack it (raw end up) with seven tacks. Always stagger tacks. Hook webbing onto teeth of webbing stretcher. Brace the tool against frame and pull it down to stretch webbing taut.

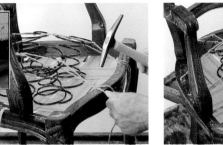

5 Tie springs together. Cut twine 3 times the distance to be covered. Tack to rear of frame at midpoint of each twine length (inset), placing strands in line with each row of springs. Tie both strands from back to front (see drawings at left).

8 Tack generous piece of burlap snugly over springs with No. 6 tacks. Starting at rear of chair, pull burlap forward to front and tack; tack sides. Make sure tension is even; then fold back burlap and tack down edges with No. 6 tacks.

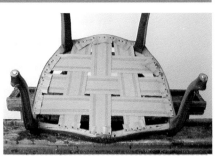

3 Fasten other end with three tacks. Trim webbing 2 in. overlong; then fold and fasten with four tacks. Work from back to front; then weave strips side to side. Strips should be equally taut and oriented toward center to support sitter's weight.

6 When back-to-front strands are tacked in place, tie side-to-side ones. As you work, check that springs are forming the desired (in this case, rounded) contour. Adjust strands as necessary.

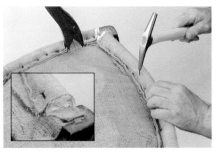

9 To give outside edge of chair a smooth line, cut lengths of fox edge with a sharp knife and fasten them with No. 12 tacks around frame on top of burlap. Angle nails slightly to hold fox edge upright (inset).

continued

10 If old stuffing is unusable, as is the case here, fill crevices with pieces of cotton batting torn with your fingers. Then add a full cotton layer over seat. If stuffing is usable, reposition old filling carefully and proceed to next step.

11 Cut foam and place it over cotton layer (or repositioned stuffing). Notch to fit it around chair posts. Position the foam layer, pulling it snugly over the seat. Staple it a few times to hold it in place. Trim the foam with scissors.

12 Cover foam layer with fiberfill. Notch fiberfill to fit around posts. Tuck edges of fiberfill down between posts and seat. Staple fiberfill in place like foam layer (Step 11); trim.

13 Rough-cut fabric to size. Make cuts for the posts as shown on page 98. Baste-tack, tensioning fabric; then do final tacking. Trim by pulling excess taut and away from fastened edge as you cut (inset); avoid marring finished wood.

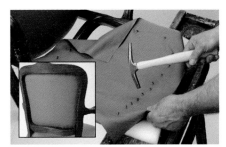

14 Tension and tack outside back cover to inside of frame. Fold over raw edges and tack; trim. (In some chairs, outside back cover fits over outside of frame; in that case, tack burlap to inside of frame; build up back on both sides of burlap.)

15 Add layer of fiberfill on the tacked cover fabric; then cover the fiberfill with a layer of burlap. First tack it to frame at bottom. Tension and tack top edge, then the sides. Fold over raw edges and tack; trim.

16 Build a slight curve in seat back by adding a layer of fiberfill in center of burlap. Then cut a layer of foam to fit (shown), and staple in place. Staple a second layer of fiberfill to chair frame.

17 Fasten inside back cover, beginning at bottom. Fold under raw edge of bottom; tack. Tension fabric and tack top edge. Check shape of curve, then tack sides. Wrinkles should disappear when last side is tacked. Trim close to tacks.

18 Cover arm panels. Reuse old stuffing or make new padding out of a layer of poly foam cut to size. Cover foam with a layer of fiberfill, stapling it in place; trim close to staples.

19 Tack arm cover, folding under first raw edge. Work from rear to front of arm, then tack sides; trim close to tacks. These and all exposed tacks will be covered with glued-on double welt (Step 21).

20 Cut cambric dust cover, allowing an extra inch all around. Baste-tack cover to underside of chair frame at center of each side. Cut to fit around legs. Fold under raw edge of cambric and tack down along inner edge of frame.

21 Hide all exposed tacks with double welt (p.102) or braid. Glue with white glue and baste-tack to chair. Form curves by holding welt in place at point of curve with tacks. Trim welt where ends meet (p.102); remove tacks when glue is dry.

Club and wing chairs

Choosing a project

A large upholstered furniture piece begins with a wood frame and is built up in layers much like those of a dining chair (pp.97–100). A club or wing chair, however, has several cover pieces that must fit together well, making it more challenging than a dining chair. Pick your project wisely: A small club chair with straight lines and a sound foundation is a good project for those with some experience in dining-chair upholstery. A wing chair with curved, or scrolled, arms or a curved back is more difficult to work on—cutting, fitting, and tensioning curves requires some expertise. The most difficult chair to cover, the tufted, or overstuffed, chair, is best left to a professional.

Repairing the frame and springs. Before you decide to reupholster a chair yourself, estimate the structural repairs that are needed. Check it for broken or loose frame pieces. Sagging or lumpy upholstery or a bulging dust cover often calls for major rebuilding, such as retying all the coil springs. If you do re-cover the chair, make all repairs to the frame and springs before you begin. For more on repairing chair frames, see pages 64–67.

You may be able to rescue coil springs simply by reinforcing the webbing underneath (p.99). Zigzag springs (right) span the chair frame and require no webbing. The ends hook into clips that are nailed on the chair frame and then nailed closed. Reattaching and replacing a zigzag spring is a fairly easy repair job.

Choosing an upholstery fabric. Remember that patterns that require little matching or centering are the easiest to handle. Beware of fabrics with strong vertical lines—a stripe that is even slightly misaligned will be obvious.

Installing zigzag springs

Nail clips to frame. Hook one end of spring in clip; nail clip closed. Holding other end firmly, stretch it to reach clip on second side; nail clip closed.

Helical coils connect sides of zigzag springs, allowing them to act as one unit. A typical pattern is to stagger the coils in diagonal rows.

The frame

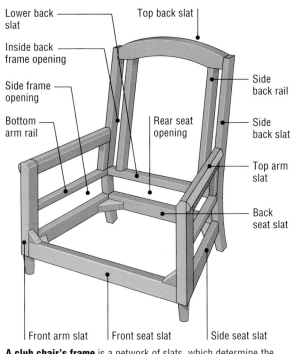

Lower back slat
Top back slat
Inside back frame opening
Side back rail
Side frame opening
Side back slat
Bottom arm rail
Rear seat opening
Top arm slat
Back seat slat
Front arm slat
Front seat slat
Side seat slat

A club chair's frame is a network of slats, which determine the shape of the chair, and rails, which strengthen the frame and provide more nailing and stapling surfaces for the upholstery layers.

The upholstery layers

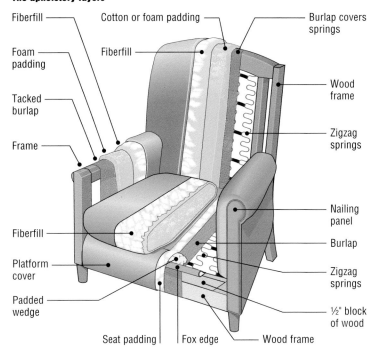

Fiberfill
Cotton or foam padding
Burlap covers springs
Foam padding
Fiberfill
Tacked burlap
Wood frame
Frame
Zigzag springs
Fiberfill
Nailing panel
Platform cover
Burlap
Padded wedge
Zigzag springs
½" block of wood
Seat padding
Fox edge
Wood frame

Padded wedge at seat front helps keep cushion in place. Springs are topped with burlap. The wedge is built up by nailing wood block to front seat slat and tacking fox edge. Pack wedge with padding. (To form wedge for spring-edge wire frame, see page 103.)

The cover pieces

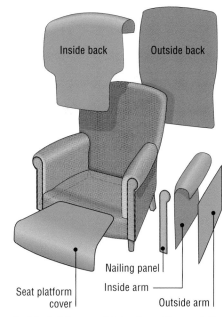

Inside back
Outside back
Nailing panel
Seat platform cover
Inside arm
Outside arm

A club chair's cover fabric pieces fit over stuffing and are tacked or sewn in place. Inside pieces and the seat platform cover are cut and notched to allow fabric to pass through openings between rails and slats to rear and side of chair.

Laying out the project

To estimate how much upholstery fabric you'll need, use a tape measure to measure each section of the chair from top to bottom and from side to side, at the longest and widest points of the section. Tuck the tape measure deep into the corners; follow all curves carefully. Add a few extra inches to all sides for a tacking allowance (left) and for centering and matching a design. If you are making your own welt—the fabric-covered cord that is used to hide seams and tacks—add ¾ yard to the estimate.

To measure out a 3-in. tacking allowance, grip tape measure at 3-in. mark as shown.

Upholstery fabric is often costly. To avoid waste and mismatched designs, make a full-size paper pattern using your measurements as a guide. To check the pattern pieces, chalk-mark the center of each rail or slat and the center of the edge of each pattern piece. Lay each piece on the chair and align the marks. Then arrange pattern pieces on the uncut fabric so that crosswise grain will be horizontal on the chair, lengthwise grain will be vertical, and stripes or designs will align across the parts of the chair. Once the pattern pieces are in place, cut the fabric.

Stripping the chair. To remove the old fabric pieces and inner upholstery layers, place the chair on a pair of upholsterer's sawhorses (right) or on a sheet of plywood supported by regular sawhorses. An easy way to keep track of how the pieces fit together is to remove the outside cover pieces first, then free only the bottom and sides of the inside pieces, tacking them up and out of the way. Re-cover the chair sections in this order: first the seat, then the inside arms, the inside back, the outside arms, and the outside back.

Working with welt

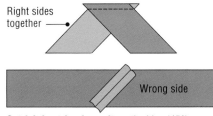

Right sides together

Wrong side

Cut fabric strips for welt on the bias (45°). Make strips 2 in. wide for single welt, 2½ in. wide for double welt. Seam strips together into one long piece; press seams open.

To make single welt, place No. 60–size cord in center of 2-in. strip. Fold one edge over cord, and machine-stitch close to cord (1). **To make double welt,** fold 2½ -in. strip over No. 60 cord and stitch closed (2). Wrap other edge around second cord (3), and stitch between two cords (4). Use a zipper foot or welting foot attachment to sew single welt; use only a welting foot for double welt.

Blind-stitching cover pieces

When you can't machine-sew two pieces together, blind-stitch them by hand. Cut the thread twice as long as the area to be sewn. With a curved needle, begin sewing on the wrong side, pulling the needle through the fabric.

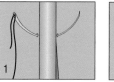

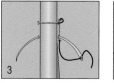

Sew close to welt so that welt hides stitches, as in the stitching sequence illustrated here. Keep stitches to about ½ in.; "back up" at each stitch, inserting the needle a few threads above where previous stitch ended. Draw seam tight; stitches will close completely.

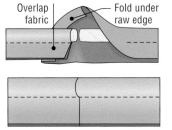

Overlap fabric — Fold under raw edge

To join single welt ends (as for a cushion), remove a few stitches; cut cord to butt. Trim welt fabric to ½ in.; fold under raw edge. Stitch ends.

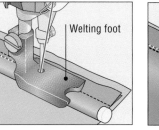

Welting foot

Sew welt to right side of fabric. Align welt to seam line, using fingers to hold it on line. Stitch close to cord, leaving a ½-in. seam allowance.

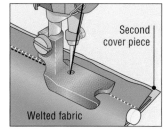

Second cover piece

Welted fabric

Stitch welted fabric to second cover piece with right sides together; sew through all thicknesses.

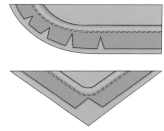

At corners and around curves, make small snips in seam allowance so that welt will be able to bend. Hold in position as you sew.

Reupholstering a club chair

Blind-tacking cover pieces

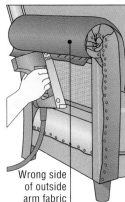

To attach cover fabric so that tack heads don't show, blind-tack it. Cut fabric, leaving 1-in. tack allowance on all sides. Place top edge of fabric, wrong side out, along slat to which it is to be attached. Baste-staple fabric into place.

Wrong side of outside arm fabric

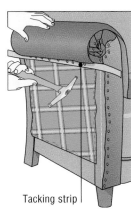

Staple scrap fabric over gap at arm frame. Position a thin cardboard tacking strip above baste staples; tack strip securely along top edge. Cardboard strip ensures a neat top edge when right side is revealed (below).

Tacking strip

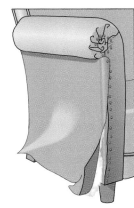

Staple thin layer of batting over scrap fabric. Pull cover fabric into position; baste-tack bottom edge to underside of slat. Tack both sides (Steps 23–25, p.105), or tack single welt to frame and blind-stitch sides closed (facing page).

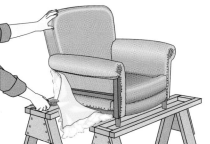

1 Support chair at comfortable working height on sturdy sawhorses. Remove nailing panel, skirt (if any), cambric dust cover, outside back, and outside arm covers. Cut fabric with scissors; pull off tacked fabric with pliers.

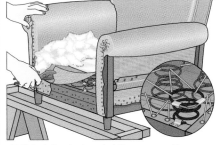

4 Detach front edge of platform cover. Remove cover, stuffing (often reusable), fox edge, and burlap to expose frame and, in some chairs, a spring-edge wire (inset) above frame. Make needed spring or frame repairs. Tack new burlap over seat.

Scrap strip

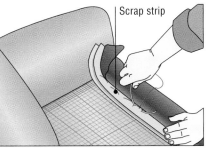

7 To attach platform cover to burlap-lined seat platform, first fold cover forward, wrong side out, at scrap strip seam. Fold back scrap strip as shown; sew through both thicknesses of scrap strip to burlap.

Seat platform cover

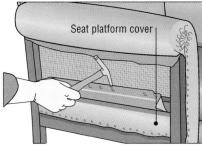

2 Begin removing seat platform cover. To access tacked edge of cover, free tacked lower edge of inside arm panel and tack it out of the way as shown. Repeat on other side.

Sewn-on fox edge

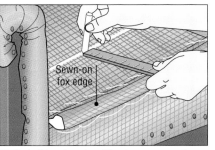

5 To build wedge at seat front, use a curved needle to sew fox edge to burlap-covered edge wire. If chair lacks edge wire, nail scrap wood and fox edge to frame (p.101). To mark inner edge of wedge, chalk a line 5 in. from front of fox edge.

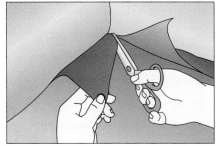

8 Replace old stuffing, if reusable, in rear of seat behind platform cover seam; or cut new poly foam to fit and add new fiberfill. Fold back rear portion of cover fabric over stuffing. Make diagonal cut for each rail at rear corners as shown.

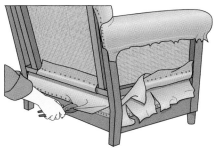

3 Free platform cover at sides. Free and tack lower edge of inside back cover to back seat slat. Detach back edge of platform cover; pull out all tacks (or staples) from chair frame. Detach exposed seat burlap from frame; pull out its tacks.

Scrap fabric

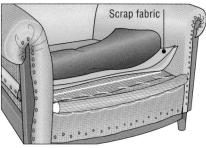

6 Align platform cover on chair. Mark a second chalk line on wrong side of cover fabric at inner edge of wedge (mirrors first chalk line). Cut and machine-seam a 2-in.-wide strip of sturdy scrap fabric, such as denim, to cover fabric at chalk line.

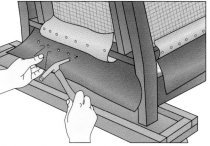

9 Push, then pull back of platform cover through rear seat and side frame openings; tension cover and tack it to back seat slat and side seat slats. Trim excess.

continued

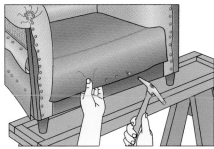

10 Pad front of seat with cotton and fiberfill. Pull and tension front part of platform cover over stuffing; tack cover to front and side slats. Since this chair has a deep frame, it requires a second piece of fabric to cover lower front (Step 11).

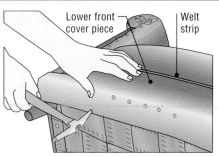

Lower front cover piece — Welt strip

11 Tack a welt strip to conceal tacks securing bottom edge of platform cover. Measure and cut lower front cover piece; blind-tack (p.103) it close to welt. Add fiberfill to frame, pull cover over fill, and tack it to underside of front seat slat.

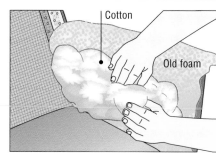

Cotton

Old foam

12 Strip off inside arm cover. (You may have to remove inside back to gain full access to the arm.) Fill holes with cotton and add a layer of poly foam on inside of arm, stapling it a few times to hold it in place.

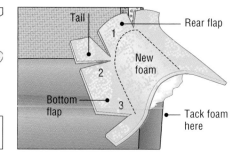

Tail — Rear flap

1

2

New foam

Bottom flap

3

Tack foam here

13 Make diagonal cuts 1 and 2; fit tail through rear seat opening. Make straight cuts 3 and 4. Fit bottom flap through side frame opening. Fit rear flap through lower inside back frame opening. Tack foam under curve of arm; trim excess.

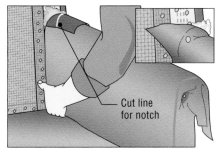

Cut line for notch

14 Cover inside arm with fiberfill. Baste-tack fabric; make cuts as in foam (Step 13); push tail through rear seat opening, flaps through lower inside back and side frame openings. To fit fabric at top of arm, notch and tack it (inset).

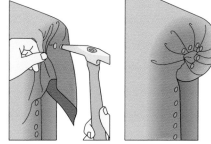

15 Smooth and pull front of inside arm cover into place; baste-tack straight edge of cover, working toward curve. Carefully hand-pleat fabric around curve and tack in place. Nailing panel (Step 29) will cover tacks and raw edge.

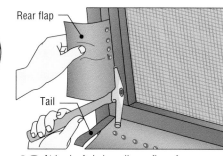

Rear flap

Tail

16 At back of chair, pull rear flap of arm cover through inside back opening; pull tail through rear seat opening. Tension and baste-tack both to inside of side back slat. Check fabric alignment, then final-tack. Trim excess material.

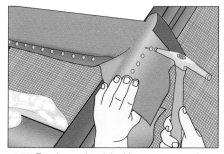

17 Tension and tack inside arm cover under top arm slat. Continue tacking fabric at side back slat. Then, tack bottom flap of inside arm cover to side seat slat. Cover other arm so that pattern mirrors that of first arm.

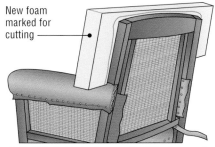

New foam marked for cutting

18 Strip inside back cover, if still in place, and old padding, if unusable. Tack burlap to back rails and slats. Rough-cut foam; cut to fit, using chair back as guide. (To reuse old padding, add cotton, thin foam layer, and fiberfill over padding.)

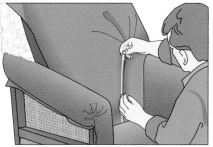

19 Cover new foam with fiberfill. To fit the inside back cover, place cover fabric over padding; chalk a line on fabric along sides and top of padding. Add seam allowance; cut. Sew welt to chalk line, leaving a welt tail at each bottom edge.

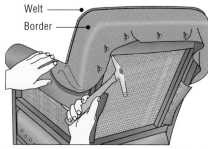

Welt

Border

20 To cut border panel, measure depth of back padding and frame; add seam allowance. Sew border to welted inside back; fit on chair. Tuck cotton into corners to fill. Baste-tack border all around, tensioning it so all sides are even.

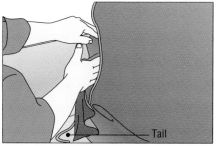

Tail

21 Make cuts in border at arm junction so bottom of border can be pushed through inside back frame opening (shown). Push welt tail through *side* frame opening. Push bottom of inside cover through rear seat opening.

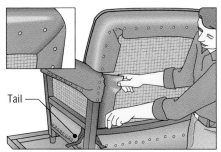

22 Baste-tack inside back cover and adjust fit. Then final-tack back edge all around. Tack top first, then sides, pleating corners (inset). Then tack bottom edge of inside back cover to back seat slat. Tack tail to side back slat. Trim.

Tail

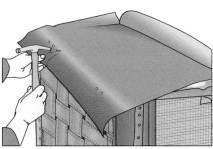

23 Blind-tack outside arm cover (see *Blind-tacking cover pieces*, p.103). Be sure that cover fabric is straight and pattern is centered. Then tension and tack bottom edge.

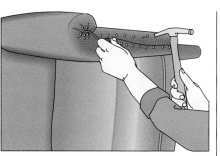

24 Beginning at top of front edge, tension and tack outside arm cover to front of arm. Make sure nailing panel (Step 29) will cover tacks. If not, adjust tack positions or cut new nailing panel from thin wood. Trim excess fabric.

Making a cushion

Because more padding is added to a chair during reupholstery, its old cushion often won't fit. To make a new one, cut a piece of foam to fit the seat. Wrap a layer of fiberfill around the foam, and secure the fiberfill with a long chain stitch.

To make the cover, cut the top, bottom, and side, or border, fabric pieces using the chair itself as a guide (below). Sew welt to the top and bottom pieces (p.102). Seam the ends of the border together and finish assembling it as shown below.

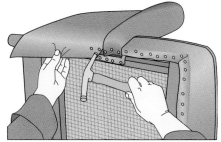

25 Finish outside arm cover by tacking its rear edge to side back slat. Trim excess fabric. Cover outside of other arm.

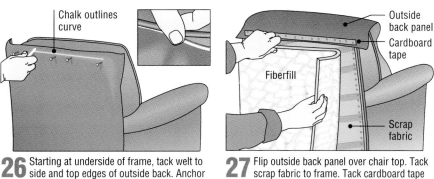

Chalk outlines curve

26 Starting at underside of frame, tack welt to side and top edges of outside back. Anchor back cover fabric. Chalk top welt line on cover. Add tacking allowance; trim. Turn under raw edge at chalk line; baste-tack through fold near welt (inset).

Outside back panel
Cardboard tape
Fiberfill
Scrap fabric

27 Flip outside back panel over chair top. Tack scrap fabric to frame. Tack cardboard tape to raw edge of back panel snug to welt, removing baste tacks as you go. Add fiberfill layer. Fold outside back panel back into place; baste-tack bottom.

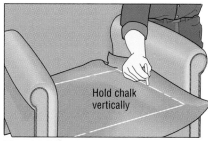

Hold chalk vertically

Place fabric on chair, matching pattern to inside back. Chalk cushion outline. Add seam allowance. Cut top and bottom pieces, marking rear and front edges. To find border length, measure chalk line. Cut pieces 4½ in. wide (finished side is 3½ in.).

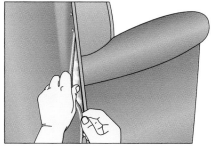

28 At side edge of back panel, mark fold line by chalking welt position on fabric. Trim, leaving ½-in. allowance. Turn under at fold line; baste-tack as in Step 26. Blind-stitch sides (p.102). Tack bottom edge to underside of chair.

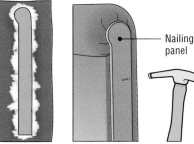

Nailing panel

29 Strip nailing panels; cover with fiberfill. Fasten fabric with ¼-in. staples to underside of panel; tack welt to panel edge. Attach to chair with a few thin headless brads inserted between threads. Gently pull fabric over brads with needle.

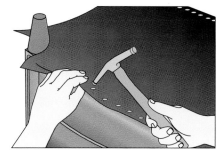

30 Cut cambric cover 2 to 3 in. wider and longer than bottom of chair. Fold raw edges under, notch corners to accommodate legs, and fasten to bottom of frame, stretching evenly. Tack rear cambric edge first, then front and side edges.

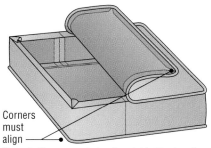

Corners must align

Seam bottom cover to border, right sides together. Position top, aligning front and back of top and bottom. Seam top to back and sides; leave an opening for stuffing cushion. Turn cover right side out; insert cushion. Fill corners with cotton; blind-stitch.

A wing chair is basically a club chair with a wing section fastened to the top arm slat and the top back slat. It may consist of joined wood pieces or, in finer chairs, a solid piece of shaped wood. To cover a wing chair, start with the seat platform and the inside arms. Then follow the steps at right.

Wing frame

Covering other styles of chairs

Finished wood-frame chair with separate seat cushion. Skill level: intermediate. Required amount of fabric: about 5 yards. Cover seat platform. Fit inside back and arms to chair in one piece; then tack to decorative frame. Fit outside back and sides as one piece; then tack. Cover arms (p.100). Disguise tack heads with glued-on strip of double welt. Sew cushion cover to fit (p.105).

Continuous-arm wing chair. Skill level: advanced. Required amount of fabric: about 7 yards. Cover seat platform. Cut inside and front border of wing-arm panels. Sew welt to inside wing-arm panels (p.102). Sew front borders to inside panels. Fit, then tack wing arms to the frame. Cover inside back. Glue welt to outside of frame. Chalk outside arm panels, add ½-inch. hem, and blind-stitch; repeat for outside back. Sew cushion cover.

Covering the wings on a wing chair

1 Cover inside of wings: Pad wing with cotton, poly foam, and fiberfill. Place cover, and chalk a line at bottom edge where wing cover meets arm top; sew single welt to line. Align welt to arm; anchor bottom edge of fabric to top arm slat.

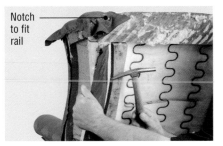

Notch to fit rail

2 Make double cut to notch fabric at top back slat. Pull fabric through inside back frame opening. Anchor side and top edges of fabric. Tack notch (see inset, Step 14, p.104). Baste-tack side and top edges of fabric, but not corner curve.

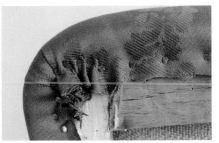

3 Final-tack top and side edges of wing cover, again omitting corner curve. Fold fabric at corner curve into pleats as shown and tack. Trim all extra fabric.

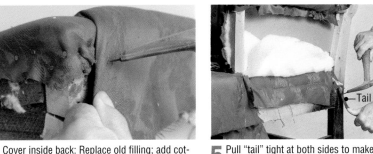

4 Cover inside back: Replace old filling; add cotton layer. Anchor fabric; cut notches for slats at top and "tails" at bottom corners. Baste-tack top to back rail; pull cover through side and seat openings. Fold under raw edge at top and tack as shown.

Tail

5 Pull "tail" tight at both sides to make a smooth line across the lower inside back cover. Baste-tack bottom, then sides, of cover. Adjust fabric, then final-tack top, bottom, and sides of cover. Pull "tail" tighter and tack down as shown.

6 Cover outside of wings: Staple scrap fabric over the frame; add layer of fiberfill. Align fabric, and outline shape of wing with chalk; trim. Fold under raw edge and tack top, side, and bottom edges. Double welt will cover tacks (Step 9).

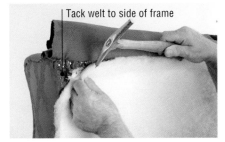

Tack welt to side of frame

7 Blind-tack outside arm covers (p.103). Then cover outside back: Anchor fabric at its top. Staple scrap fabric to outside back. Tack single welt down both side back slats, finishing underneath seat. Tack fiberfill layer to outside back.

8 Pull down outside back cover. Chalk outline of outside back at top and sides; trim. Fold under raw edge and tack top; baste-tack and blind-stitch sides (see Steps 26–28, p.105). Cut cover at leg. Fold under raw edge; tack bottom.

9 Cover all tacks: Glue strip of double welt long enough to cover outside edges of wings and top of back. Hold welt in place with tacks. Tack dust cover to underside of chair.

Plumbing

A breakdown in any part of a home's plumbing system is more than annoying. Some plumbing mishaps— leaking pipes and backed-up drains, for example— can cause serious damage if they aren't dealt with immediately. This section shows how, with the proper tools, you can handily fix a dripping faucet and stanch a leaking pipe. Steps for replacing a sink strainer, adjusting a tub stopper, changing a shower head, and diagnosing a malfunctioning toilet's problem are also spelled out. You will see how to locate a clog in the drainage system and choose the appropriate tool to clear the stoppage. You'll also find that working with plumbing pipe isn't difficult. You just have to choose the correct pipe and fittings for the job—and be sure the materials conform to local plumbing codes.

Plumbing ▪ Tools and supplies

A home tool kit (p.10) contains many of the tools needed for plumbing jobs—hammers, chisels, screwdrivers, pliers, a hacksaw, and various wrenches. Make sure you have an adjustable wrench; one of these is as good as a complete set of open-end wrenches for tightening or loosening plumbing fasteners and fittings of various sizes. A pair of pipe wrenches will let you unfasten most household drains, traps, and pipes. Locking pliers afford a nonslip grip on nuts and also serve as a clamp. A plunger, or plumber's friend, clears minor toilet and drain clogs by manipulating water and air pressure. The closet, or toilet, auger clears away more resistant blockages by slinking through curved pipes right into the obstruction as you turn the tool's crank handle.

If you don't already own the basic plumbing tools shown below, you may want to acquire some or all of them, but wait until the need arises before you buy or rent more specialized tools.

To cope with emergencies as well as with the occasional leaky faucet or toilet that won't stop running, it's a good idea to keep certain plumbing supplies on hand. These include all-temperature washers, diaphragms, and O-rings that fit your sink fixtures; clamps, tubing, pipe tape, and sealants for patching pipes; and penetrating oil for loosening frozen nuts. Tools for working with various kinds of plumbing pipe are described on page 120.

described on page 120.

TIPS FROM THE PROS

To protect the surface of chrome and other polished pipes, tape the jaws of the tool or wrap the pipe in a rag or a scrap of leather before applying the tool to the pipe.

Basic plumbing tools

Closet auger has a coiled steel spring that winds through sharp curves in waste pipes to break up clogs.

Adjustable wrench is a versatile tool for tightening and loosening nuts and bolts.

Pipe wrench grasps a pipe securely. Two are needed to tighten or loosen threaded fittings.

Groove-joint pliers have a wider range of settings than standard slip-joint pliers.

Spud wrench is used to turn fittings on sink strainers, drainpipes, and toilet connections.

Locking pliers can be used variously as a wrench, clamp, or pliers.

Bulb-type plunger unclogs toilets; with the rubber extension folded back, it can also be used to unstop sinks.

Special plumbing tools

Blow bag, affixed to a hose, is used to unclog drains.

Valve-seat dresser, sold with cutters of various sizes, refaces worn faucet valve seats.

Strap wrench grips plastic or polished metal pipes without marring them.

Deep socket and ratchet set may be needed to remove recessed fasteners.

Trap-and-drain auger, or snake, longer and more flexible than a closet auger, tackles clogs in long pipes and vents.

Valve-seat wrench unscrews worn faucet valve seats.

Chain wrench grips large-gauge waste pipes or pipes in awkward or inaccessible places.

Basin wrench, with adjustable jaws, is angled to reach connections under sinks.

Plumbing supplies

Pipe tape and wicking are both used to seal threaded pipe joints.

Penetrating oil loosens frozen nuts.

Rubber or plastic hose scraps, held in place by hose clamps, stop small leaks in pipes.

Replacement washer or O-ring is often all that's needed to fix a faucet leak.

Plumber's grease lubricates faucets without affecting water quality.

Pipe repair clamp kits are used to stop larger leaks.

Plumber's seal, a moldable two-part epoxy putty, is used to seal leaky pipe joints.

Plumber's putty creates a watertight seal on sink or tub drains and faucets.

Emergencies

When a plumbing pipe leaks, the first step is to cut off the water supply to the problem area. Make it a rule to know where the shutoff valves in your home are located. As an extra precaution, tag the main shutoff valve, usually located near an exterior wall close to the water meter or the well supply. (Typically, there are two main valves, one on either side of the water meter.) The valve controlling a house's total hot-water supply is usually on the outlet pipe at the top of the water heater. Cutoffs for each plumbing fixture and water-using appliance are normally in an adjacent cabinet, on the wall behind the fixture or appliance, or directly below it in the basement. If a leak is in a feeder line to a fixture or appliance, you will need to shut off a more distant water valve.

Once the water supply is cut off, drain the pipe by opening the nearest faucet. Wipe the leak area dry so that you can assess the problem. A temporary fix can be as easy as applying duct tape to a pinhole or clamping a section of hose over a crack. Permanent repairs may require replacing a piece of pipe (pp.120–122). Leaks often occur at joints. Simply tightening the fitting with two wrenches may stop the leak. But be careful: damaged or aged pipe can break under added pressure. Where the risk of a break exists, seal the joint with epoxy compound instead. This and other ways to seal damaged pipes are shown at right.

Never ignore even a minor leak; it will likely enlarge over time. Dripping water can damage walls and ceilings, create an electrical hazard, and even rot structural members of your house.

Finding shutoff valves

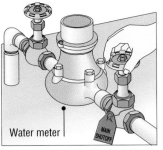

The main water shutoff should be identified and labeled. Closing it cuts off all water to the house.

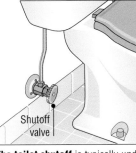

The toilet shutoff is typically under the flush tank. To close the valve, turn the knurled handle clockwise.

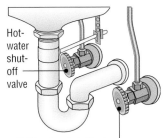

Sink valves separately shut off hot and cold water. To work on a single-lever faucet, turn both valves off.

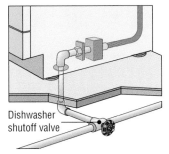

The dishwasher shutoff may be next to the kitchen sink shutoff or in the basement below appliance.

Fixing small pipe leaks

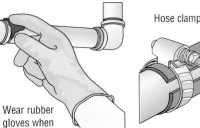

Seal a leaky joint with plumber's seal (moldable two-part epoxy). Prepare and apply the epoxy according to package directions.

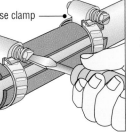

Stop a small leak by wrapping a section of rubber hose, split lengthwise, around the damaged area. Hold hose in place with two hose clamps.

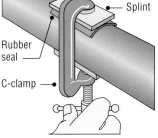

Pipe repair clamp stops larger leaks. Center clamp's rubber sleeve over damaged area; tighten clamp nuts.

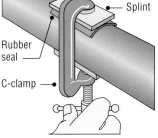

A C-clamp and wood splints temporarily hold a rubber seal over a small leak in a steel or brass pipe.

Frozen pipes

The combination of power outages and winter temperatures can result in frozen and cracked pipes. To safely thaw pipes, first turn off water to the affected area and open the nearest faucet. If heat is restored, let pipes thaw on their own. Otherwise, apply heat by moving a hair dryer over the pipe (right). Warm the pipe no hotter than your hand can tolerate. When the ice has thawed, turn the water supply back on and check for leaks. Prevent a recurrence by covering vulnerable pipes with an insulating jacket (far right).

When thawing a pipe with a hair dryer, keep the dryer moving to prevent a steam buildup in the pipe. Work from open end of pipe back toward the frozen area.

To keep any exposed plumbing pipes from freezing, cover them with an insulating sleeve or wrap them with rolled insulation.

Compression faucets

The various types of compression faucets all work basically as described below. Spout drips develop when the seat washer wears out or the valve seat is damaged. A leak at the handle signals that the O-ring, or in some models the packing, needs replacement.

Before you tackle a repair job, turn off the water supply to the fixture. With the shutoff valves closed, open the faucets to drain the line. Close the stopper to prevent loose screws and washers from falling down the waste pipe, and line the sink with a towel to protect it from scratches. As you disassemble the parts, lay them down on a work surface in the order that you removed them. Carefully examine each part, replacing those that look deformed or worn. Remove any corrosion and grit before reassembling the pieces.

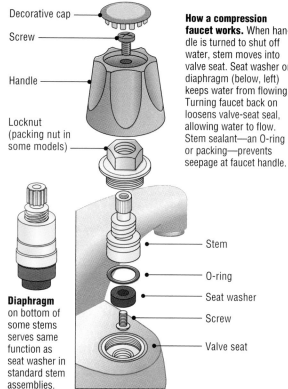

Decorative cap

Screw

Handle

Locknut (packing nut in some models)

How a compression faucet works. When handle is turned to shut off water, stem moves into valve seat. Seat washer or diaphragm (below, left) keeps water from flowing. Turning faucet back on loosens valve-seat seal, allowing water to flow. Stem sealant—an O-ring or packing—prevents seepage at faucet handle.

Stem

O-ring

Seat washer

Screw

Valve seat

Diaphragm on bottom of some stems serves same function as seat washer in standard stem assemblies.

Repairing spout drips and handle leaks

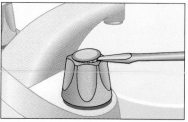

1 To gain access to the working parts of a faucet, pry off decorative cap with a screwdriver and remove screw that holds handle to stem. Lift off handle.

2 Remove lock- or packing nut by turning it counterclockwise with adjustable wrench. Pull up stem assembly by hand; gently turn it counterclockwise if needed.

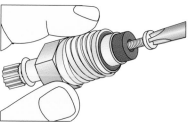

3 To fix a spout drip, remove worn seat washer by unscrewing brass screw that holds it in place. Replace with a new duplicate washer; retighten screw.

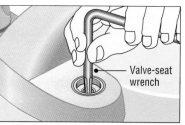

Valve-seat wrench

4 If spout still drips, valve seat may be rough. On some faucets, you can remove seat with valve-seat wrench and install a duplicate. If seat can't be replaced, reface it.

Dresser guide should fit snugly inside valve

5 To reface valve seat, fit seat dresser with right-size cutter. Screw dresser into faucet until cutter is flush against valve seat. Turn handle clockwise. Flush out grindings.

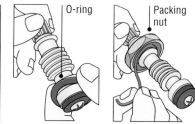

O-ring

Packing nut

To stop handle leak, tighten lock- or packing nut. If leak persists, pry off and replace worn O-ring (left) or wrap new packing around stem under packing nut (right).

Replacing a faucet

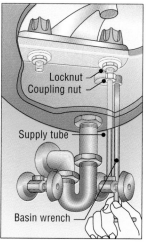

Locknut

Coupling nut

Supply tube

Basin wrench

1 Shut off water supply to faucet and drain it. Use a basin wrench to unscrew supply tube coupling nuts and locknuts holding faucet to sink. Apply penetrating oil to loosen rusted locknuts. In some sinks, you may also have to disconnect sink stopper under basin (p.114). Remove old faucet. Measure between centers of faucet holes; use this measure, called the *centerset,* to buy new faucet. When replacing faucet, consider replacing old supply tubes with new flexible tubes.

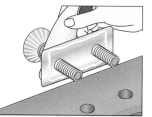

2 Use a putty knife to remove old plumber's putty from sink surface; clean and dry the surface. Apply putty to bottom of new faucet body. Insert new faucet through sink holes. Press faucet down to make sure putty forms a tight seal.

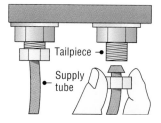

Tailpiece

Supply tube

3 Screw locknuts to tailpieces of new faucet over washers; tighten with groove-joint pliers or basin wrench. Connect supply tubes to tailpieces with coupling nuts; connect tubes to shutoff valves with compression fittings (p.121). Test for leaks; tighten nuts if needed.

Washerless faucets

All washerless faucets are based on the same principle: When you move the handle, a ball, a ceramic disc, or a cartridge shifts, opening a channel for water to flow. Moving the handle back closes the channel, stopping the water flow. Single-lever faucets combine volume and temperature control in one handle. Washerless doesn't mean dripless or leakless. O-rings, valve seats, and other parts wear out. Before starting a repair, shut off the water supply and open the faucet to drain it. Close the stopper to keep small parts from falling through; protect the sink with a towel. Disassemble the faucet, keeping the parts in order. Take worn parts to the hardware store for exact duplicates; a repair kit may be necessary for certain faucets.

Faucet attachments

To unclog aerator, disassemble it. Soak parts in vinegar; scrub with toothbrush. Reassemble in correct order. If water spurts from side of aerator, replace washer.

Washer
Perforated disc
Screen
Aerator housing

Faucet sprayer nipple
Diverter valve
Sprayer head
Hose

If a sprayer works slowly or not at all, suspect a clogged head, a kinked hose, or a bad faucet diverter valve. To clean head, disassemble it, if possible, and follow directions at left. If hose is kinked, use groove-joint pliers or basin wrench to unscrew old hose from faucet sprayer nipple; install a replacement sprayer set. If hose is OK and cleaning sprayer does not work, diverter valve is faulty. Remove faucet handle and spout sleeve. Pull out valve with needle-nose pliers. Clean valve; replace worn washers or O-rings. If problem persists, replace valve.

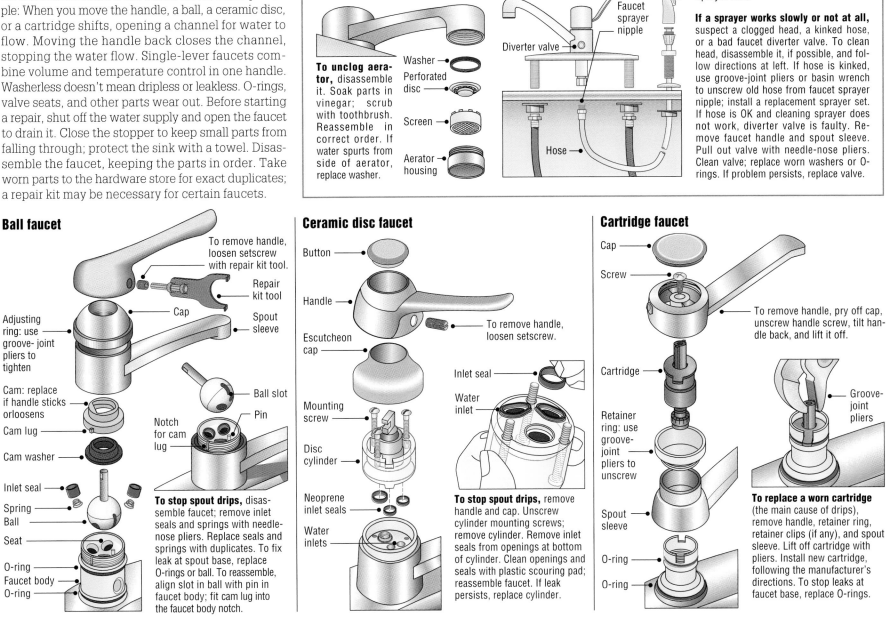

Ball faucet

To remove handle, loosen setscrew with repair kit tool.
Repair kit tool
Cap
Spout sleeve
Adjusting ring: use groove-joint pliers to tighten
Cam: replace if handle sticks or loosens
Cam lug
Cam washer
Ball slot
Notch for cam lug
Pin
Inlet seal
Spring
Ball
Seat
O-ring
Faucet body
O-ring

To stop spout drips, disassemble faucet; remove inlet seals and springs with needle-nose pliers. Replace seals and springs with duplicates. To fix leak at spout base, replace O-rings or ball. To reassemble, align slot in ball with pin in faucet body; fit cam lug into the faucet body notch.

Ceramic disc faucet

Button
Handle
Escutcheon cap
Mounting screw
Disc cylinder
Neoprene inlet seals
Water inlets

To remove handle, loosen setscrew.
Inlet seal
Water inlet

To stop spout drips, remove handle and cap. Unscrew cylinder mounting screws; remove cylinder. Remove inlet seals from openings at bottom of cylinder. Clean openings and seals with plastic scouring pad; reassemble faucet. If leak persists, replace cylinder.

Cartridge faucet

Cap
Screw
Cartridge
Retainer ring: use groove-joint pliers to unscrew
Spout sleeve
O-ring
O-ring

To remove handle, pry off cap, unscrew handle screw, tilt handle back, and lift it off.
Groove-joint pliers

To replace a worn cartridge (the main cause of drips), remove handle, retainer ring, retainer clips (if any), and spout sleeve. Lift off cartridge with pliers. Install new cartridge, following the manufacturer's directions. To stop leaks at faucet base, replace O-rings.

Tub-shower arrangements

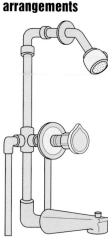

Tub-spout diverter works with single or dual handles.

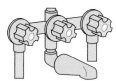

In three-handle systems, diverter valve in center works like a handle.

Dual-handle faucet features a push-pull diverter valve.

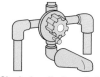

Single-handle faucet also has a push-pull diverter.

The basic parts of a tub faucet—whether it's a single-lever ball, disc, or cartridge faucet or a dual-handle compression faucet—are the same as those found in sink faucets. Repairs are similar too, but gaining access to the working parts can be a challenge; for example, you may have to remove wall tiles if there is no other access to the parts.

Modern shower faucets usually have anti-scalding safety devices, such as temperature-limiting valves and pressure-balancing controls. Digital thermostatic mixing valves allow you to adjust the temperature of the water; a battery backup powers the valves in case of a power failure. Test the battery every 6 months, following the manufacturer's directions. Before replacing a battery, turn off the power to the control (p.127).

Combination tub-shower arrangements have a diverter valve, which directs water to the shower head or the spout. If a spout drips when the shower is running, the diverter is faulty. Depending on the problem, a diverter may simply need cleaning and lubricating, or you may have to replace the diverter or a worn part. Some spouts are attached to adapters on copper tubing; remove the spout carefully or you may twist the tubing.

Compression tub faucet

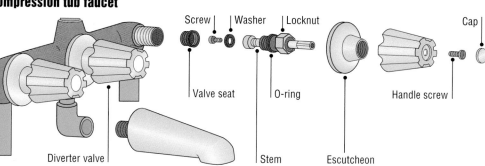

Screw | Washer | Locknut | Cap

Valve seat | O-ring | Handle screw

Diverter valve | Stem | Escutcheon

The parts of a compression tub faucet are arranged like those of a compression sink faucet (p.110). If the faucet leaks, clean or replace worn washers, O-rings, packing, or stem. If necessary, reface the valve seat (p.110). To reach some parts of the faucet, you may have to chip away tile to remove a recessed locknut (see right).

Washerless tub faucet

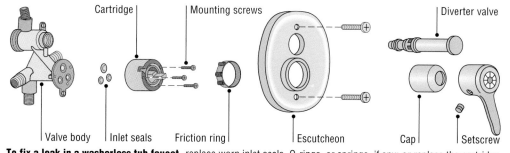

Cartridge | Mounting screws | Diverter valve

Valve body | Inlet seals | Friction ring | Escutcheon | Cap | Setscrew

To fix a leak in a washerless tub faucet, replace worn inlet seals, O-rings, or springs, if any; or replace the cartridge if necessary. You may have to unscrew the diverter valve before removing the escutcheon.

Removing a recessed locknut

To chip away ceramic tile and concrete that may block access to the locknut, use a ball-peen hammer and cold chisel. Wear safety goggles to protect your eyes.

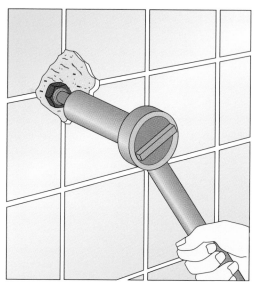

To dislodge the locknut, loosen it with a reversible ratchet wrench. Make sure the wrench has a socket deep enough to fit over the valve stem.

Repairing diverter valves

To fix leaky diverter in a threaded spout, use hammer handle to unscrew spout counterclockwise; apply pipe tape to threaded nipple. Thread spout back onto nipple and tighten by hand.

Diverter in nonthreaded spout can't be fixed. To replace spout, loosen setscrew with hex wrench; twist spout off pipe. Install new same-size spout, or add extension pipe to fit new spout.

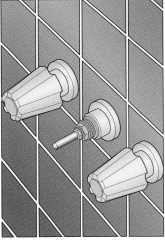

Remove handle-type diverter valve in the same way you would a faucet. Replace washers, O-rings, and packing. If the inside of the housing is worn, replace entire valve.

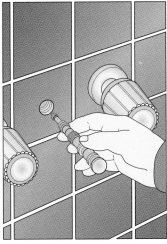

Remove a push-pull diverter in a dual-handle faucet with an adjustable wrench. Disassemble diverter by unscrewing its knob. Clean and lubricate spring; replace any O-rings.

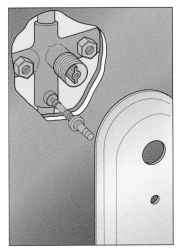

If diverter on a single-handle faucet doesn't work properly, remove handle, escutcheon, and diverter. Soak parts in vinegar; scrub with toothbrush. If water leaks at diverter, replace it.

Shower-head maintenance

Leaks are uncommon at shower heads because they are not subjected to high water pressure. Maintenance usually means unclogging holes blocked by mineral deposit buildup.

Some municipalities require shower heads that conserve water. Devices that restrict the water flow can be added to some shower heads. You may also buy a shower head with a built-in device that restricts the flow. Look for a model with other features, such as a pulsating water control, an antiscalding device, or an extension rod that holds the shower head at various heights. To turn the water off temporarily without changing the temperature setting, add a push-button shutoff valve to the shower head.

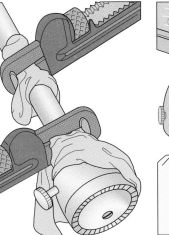

To remove shower head, hold arm with pipe wrench; exert pressure on second wrench. To protect finish, cover pipe with rags.

To clean a shower head, brush or soak parts in vinegar (keep track of assembly order); unclog holes with a toothpick.

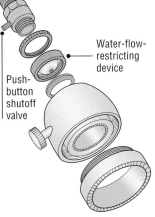

Reassemble shower head; if desired, add water-flow-restricting device, temporary shutoff valve, or antiscalding device (not shown).

To mount hand-held shower, install a wall bracket; attach nozzle to shower-head arm.

Kitchen sink drain assembly

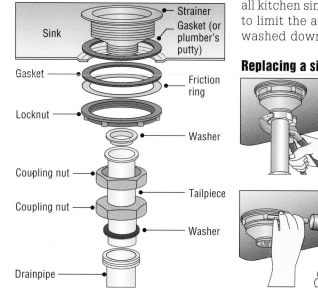

- Sink
- Strainer
- Gasket (or plumber's putty)
- Gasket
- Friction ring
- Locknut
- Washer
- Coupling nut
- Tailpiece
- Coupling nut
- Washer
- Drainpipe

Unless equipped with a disposal unit, all kitchen sink drains have a strainer to limit the amount of debris that is washed down the drain. A bad seal between the sink and the strainer body can cause a leak under the sink. Before dismantling the strainer assembly, try tightening the locknut that holds the assembly together. If the leak persists, take apart the sink drain assembly (below). Replace any worn gaskets and, if necessary, the strainer body.

Replacing a sink drain assembly

1 To remove existing strainer, use groove-joint pliers to loosen coupling nuts from ends of tailpiece (tape pliers' serrated teeth). Slide nuts clear of threads; remove tailpiece.

2 Undo locknut with a spud wrench. To loosen a stuck locknut, tap on one of the locknut's lugs with a dowel and hammer, as shown.

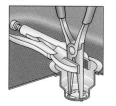

3 If strainer rotates when locknut is tapped, restrain it by inserting long-nose pliers. Hold them—and strainer—steady with locking pliers wedged into corner of sink.

4 Remove old strainer and scrape off any putty remaining on lip of drain opening. Be careful not to gouge sink surface.

5 To seal strainer to sink, use adhesive gasket that comes with some strainers or apply a bead of plumber's putty to lip of drain opening.

6 Place strainer in drain opening. From under sink, install gasket, friction ring, and locknut. Tighten locknut. Install tailpiece. Scrape off excess putty around drain opening.

Bathroom drain stoppers

The most common tub drain stoppers are pop-up stoppers and plunger-type stoppers, both controlled by lift mechanisms. A tub with a plunger stopper has a strainer instead of a stopper in the drain opening; a plunger in the overflow tube controls water flow. Push-in stoppers (not shown) are controlled by a spring instead of a lift mechanism and screw into the drain for easy replacement.

Most bathroom sink stoppers are removed by lifting them out or rotating them a quarter turn counterclockwise. The stopper shown below is secured to the lift mechanism by means of a pivot rod that threads through a loop at the stopper's base. To remove the stopper, close it, loosen the retaining nut that holds the rod in place beneath the sink, and pull the rod from the stopper.

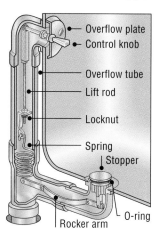

- Overflow plate
- Control knob
- Overflow tube
- Lift rod
- Locknut
- Spring
- Stopper
- Rocker arm
- O-ring

If a pop-up tub stopper leaks, pull out stopper and rocker arm and clean them with wire brush dipped in vinegar. Replace O-ring if worn. If tub still doesn't hold water or drains too slowly, adjust stopper height: Remove screws on overflow plate; pull out and clean lift assembly. Unscrew locknut on lift rod. If tub doesn't hold water, screw or slide lift rod up slightly. If tub drains too slowly, move rod down. Replace worn parts.

- Overflow plate
- Control knob
- Locknut
- Threaded lift rod
- Overflow tube
- Stopper, or plunger

In a plunger-type tub stopper, both the stopper and the lift assembly are located inside the overflow tube. To service and adjust the lift assembly, unscrew the overflow plate and pull out the assembly. Loosen the locknut on the threaded lift rod and raise the rod for better drainage or lower it for a better seal. Tighten the locknut.

- Control knob
- Set-screw
- Stopper
- Lift rod
- Pivot rod
- Retaining nut

If a pop-up sink stopper fails to keep water from seeping through drain, remove stopper and clean out hair and debris from drain. Use a wire brush to clean a metal stopper, a plastic scouring pad to clean a plastic stopper. Replace worn O-ring (if any) on stopper. If problem persists, adjust lift rod: Use pliers to loosen lift-rod setscrew under sink. Pull stopper control knob up, push stopper down, and retighten setscrew.

Dealing with clogs

The best way to handle drain stoppages is to prevent them. Don't pour fat or food scraps down the kitchen sink. When preparing food, always use the sink's removable strainer; because its holes are smaller than those of the built-in strainer, it catches more debris. Bathroom sink, tub, and shower drains get blocked by hair and soap scum. Regularly take out all bathroom strainers and stoppers and clean them.

Act promptly when you notice a drain emptying more slowly than usual.

A slightly clogged drain is much easier to clear than a totally blocked one. In many cases, flushing the drain with liberal doses of boiling water will restore free flow. (However, don't use this method on plastic pipes, as they are not made to withstand temperatures above 180°F/82°C). When a blockage does occur, try to clear it first with a plunger, then with a liquid drain opener. If both these methods fail, use an auger. If the auger doesn't work, the problem may be a blockage in the main drain (p.119).

Using a plunger

Dishwasher hose

To unclog a sink or tub drain with a plunger, first bail out most of the backed-up water. To increase pressure against clog, stuff wet rags in overflow drain and, in kitchen, clamp off dishwasher hose. Seat plunger firmly over drain and pump vigorously up and down for 1 or 2 min. Repeat if necessary.

Clearing a sink drain with an auger

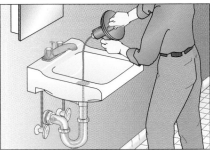

Insert auger cable into drain opening until it hits trap; then slowly crank auger handle clockwise to move end of cable past trap. If auger hook catches debris, carefully withdraw auger while still turning it.

If you can't get auger past trap, try entering pipe through cleanout opening. Before removing plug, place a bucket under trap to catch water. If there's no cleanout plug, remove trap (see below).

Turn auger handle to snake cable into cleanout opening, up through trap, and into drain line. Do not force auger. If you can't clear drain this way, you'll have to remove the trap.

Tackling bathtub blockages

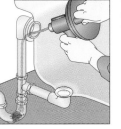

To clean a tub trap located near the drain hole, remove overflow plate and stopper assemby; thread auger through overflow opening into trap.

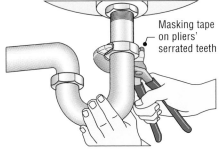

Masking tape on pliers' serrated teeth

To remove trap, unscrew first coupling nut with a wrench or taped groove-joint pliers while bracing trap with your other hand. You must also support trap as you remove second nut.

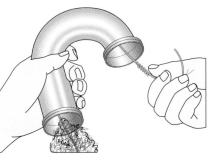

Clear the trap with a probe made from a straightened wire coat hanger. To clean out soap scum, scrub vigorously with a bottle brush dipped in detergent and hot water.

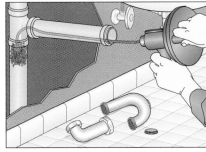

Feed auger cable directly into drain line, rotating it slowly until it hits blockage. Churn auger back and forth to break up clog. Wipe auger clean as you remove it.

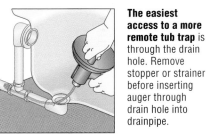

The easiest access to a more remote tub trap is through the drain hole. Remove stopper or strainer before inserting auger through drain hole into drainpipe.

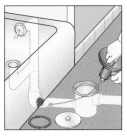

To clean a drum trap, often found in older homes, unscrew trap's top (sometimes found under a tile, but usually exposed) and insert auger through opening.

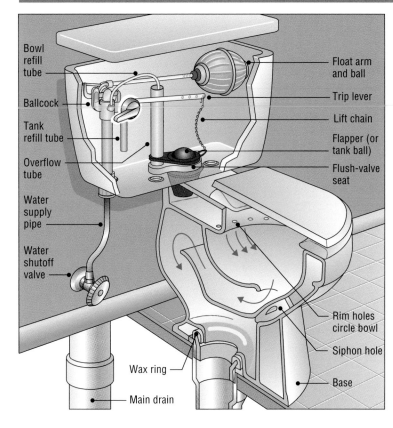

Bowl refill tube

Ballcock

Tank refill tube

Overflow tube

Water supply pipe

Water shutoff valve

Wax ring

Main drain

Float arm and ball

Trip lever

Lift chain

Flapper (or tank ball)

Flush-valve seat

Rim holes circle bowl

Siphon hole

Base

Most home toilets are the gravity-flush type shown at left. Its key parts are two control valves: a ballcock, or inlet valve, and a flush (outlet) valve, consisting of a rubber flapper (or a tank ball in older toilets) and a valve seat.

When the flush handle is depressed, the trip lever and lift chain (or wire) pull the flapper or ball out of its seat, releasing water into the bowl. As the tank empties, the flapper drops back into the valve seat, plugging the outlet, and the float ball drops, lowering the float arm and opening the inlet valve. Water from the supply pipe then flows through a pair of tubes to refill both the tank and the bowl. As the tank fills, the float ball rises, lifting the float arm until the inlet valve is closed.

Common variants: Ballcock assemblies. Traditional brass ballcocks control water flow by means of a plunger valve linked to the float arm and ball. Newer, more efficient plastic ballcocks are shown below. In a diaphragm ballcock, a rubber diaphragm takes the place of the traditional ballcock's washers and packing rings, thereby eliminating the cause of many inlet valve problems. In a floating-cup ballcock, a plastic cup controls the water

level. Floatless ballcocks have a built-in pressure sensing device to control the water level.

Solving toilet problems. Clogged toilets (p.118) are among the most common plumbing problems. Most other toilet defects involve the valves. If the inlet valve fails to close, either because it's defective or because the float is incorrectly adjusted, the result is a nonstop trickle of water into the tank and bowl. If the flapper (or ball, in older toilets) doesn't fit snugly in its seat, the tank won't refill, causing a continuous flow of water.

You can take care of many common toilet problems by making minor adjustments to the handle and lift chain (or lift wire) or by adjusting the water level in the tank (see below). Replacements for worn toilet parts are available at hardware and plumbing supply stores and home centers, as are ballcock assembly and flush-valve replacement kits. Instead of replacing worn washers and packing on an old-fashioned plunger-valve ballcock, consider replacing the entire assembly with a more efficient floating-cup or floatless ballcock. Similarly, replace a worn or cracked tank ball with a rubber flapper (facing page).

Adjusting the water level

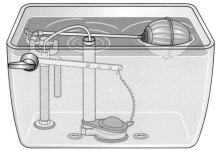

Water level in a full tank should be about 1 in. below rim of overflow tube. If it's lower, float ball may not rise high enough to close ballcock. If level is too high, water will flow continuously through overflow pipe into bowl.

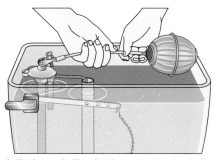

A diaphragm ballcock (shown here) and a traditional plunger-valve ballcock (left) are both linked to a float arm and ball. To raise water level, gently bend float arm upward from center. To lower water level, bend arm downward slightly.

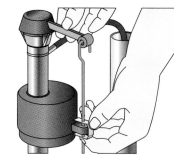

In a floating-cup ballcock, the position of the float cup on the ballcock shank controls water level in tank. To lower water level, pinch clip on side of float cup and slide cup down ballcock shank; slide cup up to raise level.

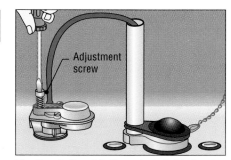

Adjustment screw

Floatless ballcock is the easiest of all ballcock assemblies to adjust. Simply turn the unit's adjustment screw counterclockwise in ½-in. intervals to lower water level; turn screw clockwise to raise water level.

Troubleshooting

Problem	CAUSE? / Solution
Toilet won't flush	WATER SUPPLY SHUT OFF? Turn on water supply. ◇
	TANK HANDLE LOOSE OR DISCONNECTED? Adjust handle (see right). ◇
	LIFT CHAIN (OR LIFT WIRE) DISENGAGED OR BROKEN? Adjust or replace the lift chain or wire (see right). ◇
Toilet does not flush completely	WATER LEVEL TOO LOW? Adjust water level (see facing page). ◇
	LIFT CHAIN TOO LONG? Shorten lift chain (see right). ◇
Toilet drains sluggishly	TOILET CLOGGED? Unclog toilet (p.118). ◆
	WATER LEVEL TOO LOW? Adjust water level (see facing page). ◇
	BLOCKED FLUSH HOLES OR SIPHON HOLE? Unblock holes (p.118). ◆
Toilet runs continuously	TANK HANDLE STUCK? Loosen tank handle (see right). ◇
	LIFT CHAIN TOO SHORT OR LIFT WIRE BENT? Adjust or replace chain; adjust wire (see right). ◇
	FLOAT BALL LEAKS OR RUBS AGAINST TANK? Unscrew float ball; replace it if water has leaked into it. If ball rubs against tank, adjust float arm to correct (see facing page). ◇
	DEFECTIVE BALLCOCK? Repair or replace ballcock (see right). ◆
Noisy toilet	LEAKY FLUSH VALVE? Clean valve (see right). ◇
	DEFECTIVE BALLCOCK? Repair or replace ballcock (see right). ◇
	BADLY POSITIONED REFILL TUBE? Adjust tube so that it empties into overflow tube. ◇
Bowl overflows	TOILET CLOGGED? Unclog toilet (p.118). ◆
Toilet tank or bowl leaks	LOOSE NUTS? Tighten nuts on water supply line. Tighten nuts on bolts connecting tank to bowl. ◆
	SWEATING TANK? Insulate tank (p.118). ◆
	FAULTY WAX RING? Have a new wax ring installed. ◆
	CRACK IN BOWL OR TANK? Have replacement parts installed. ◆

Degree of difficulty: Simple ◇   Average ◆   Complex ◆

Adjusting the tank handle

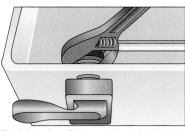

To tighten handle, turn locknut inside tank counterclockwise (handle-mounting nut has reversed threads). To loosen, turn nut clockwise (apply penetrating oil if needed). Clean handle parts with vinegar and water.

Replacing the ballcock assembly

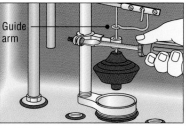

Coupling nut

1 Shut off water; flush toilet. Sponge-dry tank bottom. Undo supply line coupling nut and ballcock locknut under tank (use locking pliers inside tank to keep ballcock from turning as you undo locknut).

Servicing the flush valve

Guide arm

Tank ball should fit tightly in valve seat. If it doesn't, shut off water and flush toilet. Loosen and realign guide arm. If tank ball is cracked, worn, or no longer pliable, unscrew it from lift wire and replace it.

Adjusting the lift chain

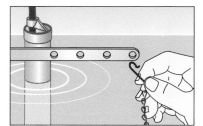

Lift chain should hang straight from trip lever with about ½ in. slack. To adjust chain length, move it to another hole in lever or remove links with needle-nose pliers. Replace a too-short chain.

Cone washer

2 Remove ballcock. Replace it with one of the same type or with a floating-cup or floatless ballcock (see facing page). Fit cone washer on new ballcock tailpiece. Insert tailpiece into tank opening.

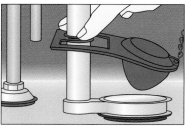

A valve seat caked with mineral deposits and sediment can keep tank ball or flapper from sealing tank. Scour brass valve seat with fine steel wool; use a plastic scouring pad for a plastic valve seat.

Repairing a plunger ballcock

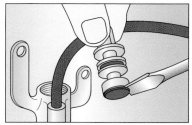

To replace plunger washers, shut off water; flush toilet. Undo ballcock wing nuts; slide out float arm. Lift off plunger. Pry off and replace washers. Clean inside of ballcock with steel wool and reassemble.

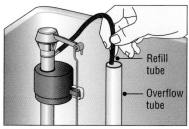

Refill tube

Overflow tube

3 Follow package directions for installing ballcock. Make sure refill tube is inside overflow tube. Reconnect supply line (don't overtighten nuts). Turn on water; check for leaks. Adjust water level.

To replace tank ball with flapper, move refill tube aside; remove ball assembly. Slide flapper collar over overflow tube (or hook flapper ears to lugs on tube). Fasten lift chain to trip lever; reposition refill tube.

Most toilet clogs are caused by accumulations of paper products in the bowl's narrow trap or by miscellaneous items that accidentally fall into the toilet and get stuck in the trap. A complete blockage can cause a toilet to overflow; a partial clog can result in sluggish flushing. Toilet blockages are usually easy to clear up with a plunger or a closet auger (right).

If the water in a toilet bowl begins to rise above its normal level after you flush, suspect a clog. To prevent an overflow, remove the top of the tank and close the flush valve by hand—putting either the flapper stopper or the ball stopper back in the closed position.

To deal with the stoppage, bail out the excess water in the bowl (leave enough to cover a plunger's cup), and then apply a plunger. If that doesn't work, use a closet auger. In a pinch, you can try to snag the obstruction with a hook made out of a straightened wire hanger, but never use a chemical drain cleaner to unclog a toilet. Such products are harmful to pipes and to people, and they are not effective in penetrating toilet clogs. If you cannot unclog the toilet with a plunger or an auger, the problem may be a blockage somewhere else in the drainage system, possibly in the main drain or the vent stack. (To clear up such blockages, see the facing page.)

Sluggish flushing may also be caused by mineral deposits clogging the flush holes located under the rim of the toilet bowl (a problem common in areas with hard water) and by waste blocking the siphon hole, located opposite the toilet's drain opening.

Unclogging a toilet

To unclog a toilet with a plunger, bail out excess water, leaving enough to cover plunger cup. If possible, use a flanged plunger. Place plunger cup snugly over drain opening. Standing directly over plunger, pump up and down vigorously 10 times. On last stroke, yank up on plunger with a strong pull. Repeat if necessary.

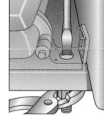

Use a closet auger if plunger fails to unclog toilet. Place auger bend in bottom of toilet drain opening; push auger cable into trap. Crank auger handle clockwise to get cable past trap. If auger becomes hard to turn, pull it back a little and try again. When auger tip hits clog, move auger from side to side to break up clog.

Finding and clearing small clogs

1 To find out if rim flush holes are fully open, hold a mirror under the toilet bowl rim at an angle that allows you to see the holes.

2 To unblock rim flush holes, cut a short section of wire from a coat hanger. Insert wire into each hole, with care to protect porcelain. Turn wire to loosen built-up mineral deposits.

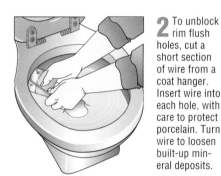

A blocked siphon hole may house bacteria. To clear the blockage, insert a wire probe into hole and twist it in and out to remove waste buildup.

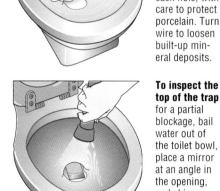

To inspect the top of the trap for a partial blockage, bail water out of the toilet bowl, place a mirror at an angle in the opening, and shine a flashlight on the mirror.

How to replace a toilet seat

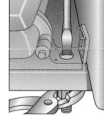

Lower the seat and cover. Open tabs covering bolts that hold seat to bowl. To remove a bolt, steady it with a screwdriver as you undo its nut with a wrench.

To loosen a corroded bolt, apply penetrating oil and wait overnight. If it's necessary, saw through the bolt with a hacksaw. (Protect bowl with duct tape.)

Remove the old seat. Clean off stains from rim; install matching-size seat. Turn fasteners finger-tight; tighten a half-turn with wrench. Don't overtighten.

Insulating a toilet tank

To keep tank from dripping moisture in a heated bathroom, empty and dry tank, then insulate it with plastic foam liner, sold in kits. Follow kit directions; take care not to block flush-valve assembly.

Branch and main drain clogs

Your home's water supply system delivers water under pressure to fixtures and appliances. The drain-waste-vent (DWV) system relies on gravity to carry liquid and solid wastes to the main house drain, which slopes down to a sewer line or a septic tank. The P- or S-shaped trap under most plumbing fixtures holds water that acts as a seal to keep sewer gases from entering the house. Beyond the traps, gravity pulls waste along branch drains to the soil stack, a large vertical pipe that conducts waste to the main house drain. Main and branch vent pipes extend from the soil stack and fixture drains up through the roof, providing the air circulation required for the safe and effective operation of the DWV system.

Locating clogs. If you can't unclog a sink or toilet with a plunger or auger, or if several fixtures are backed up, suspect a clog in the branch drain below the affected fixture(s). If running an auger through the drain doesn't clear it, the soil stack or the main drain may be clogged. The former is often easier to clear through the roof vent. The main drain is accessed through the main cleanout, a Y-shaped fitting at the bottom of the soil stack, usually in the basement or crawl space. (The main drain in older homes may also have a house trap, a U-shaped fitting with two floor-level cleanouts near where the main drain exits the house.) Most main drain clogs can be cleared with a hand auger or a garden hose fitted with an expansion nozzle. For major clogs, such as those caused by tree roots, you may need to rent a power auger or, preferably, hire a sewer cleaning service.

Clearing a branch drain

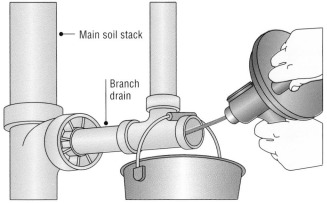

Main soil stack

Branch drain

Locate cleanout fitting at end of branch drain and hang a bucket under opening to catch backed-up waste water. Stand away from the opening as you slowly loosen cleanout plug. Once all standing water has drained into bucket, push end of auger cable into drain; crank handle until auger reaches obstruction. Keep cranking handle to retrieve or break up obstruction.

Clearing the main drain

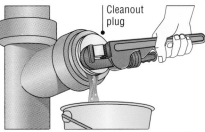

Cleanout plug

Locate main cleanout; place bucket under it. Shut main water supply or make sure no one in house uses water. Loosen cleanout plug enough to release backed-up water. When bucket fills, retighten plug; empty bucket. Repeat until water flow stops.

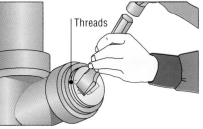

Threads

To loosen rusted plug, apply penetrating oil to threads; wait overnight. If wrench won't move plug, tap it loose with hammer and cold chisel. Replace with a plastic or rubber plug. (Apply auto grease to plug threads to prevent future opening problems.)

Slowly feed drain auger into cleanout until you feel it hit clog. Crank auger while moving it back and forth to break up clog. Withdraw auger. If you're reusing old plug, clean its threads with wire brush; coat with auto grease to prevent rust.

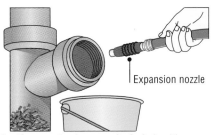

Expansion nozzle

Another way to clear a main drain is with a garden hose equipped with an expansion nozzle that will fit 3- to 6-in. drainpipe. Screw nozzle onto garden hose attached to basement water valve or fed through window. Push nozzle into cleanout.

Inflate nozzle by running water into hose. When nozzle expands to maximum size, it automatically shoots pressurized water against blockage. Repeat procedure as needed to clear obstruction. Let nozzle deflate before removing it.

Soil and vent stack obstructions

Clear clogs in main vent and soil stack by running a long, flat sewer snake through roof vent into stack. **CAUTION:** Working on a roof can be dangerous. Unless you're experienced, this job is best left to a professional.

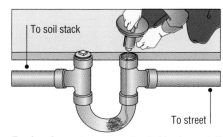

To soil stack

To street

To clear house trap, open street-side cleanout. If water flows, clog is beyond trap toward sewer. If there's no seepage, use drain auger to clear trap. If trap isn't clogged, undo inside plug; use auger to probe main drain between trap and soil stack.

Plumbing ▪ Working with pipe

Household plumbing once relied exclusively on heavy cast-iron pipe. Today's options include brass, copper, galvanized steel, and plastic (see table below). Fittings are available to handle almost any pipe connection. Copper pipes are soldered together or joined with easily removed compression or flare fittings. Plastic pipes are joined with plastic fittings or solvent cement. Transition fittings can be used to join plastic and metal pipes, but not different types of plastic.

CAUTION: Check local plumbing codes for pipes allowed in your area and for required permits and inspections. Shut off the water supply to the relevant pipes and drain them (p.109) before starting a plumbing project. When soldering, wear goggles, sturdy gloves, and a long-sleeved shirt. Keep a fire extinguisher handy. When soldering pipes near studs or other flammable building materials, place fireproof cloth (sold at hardware stores) between the fitting and the material.

Tools for cutting and joining pipes

Pipe cutter cuts metal or plastic tubing; includes built-in reamer

Plastic pipe cutter easily snips through flexible plastic pipe

Pipe brush for cleaning interiors of pipe fittings before making a joint

Flaring tool spreads ends of copper tubing for flare fitting

Propane torch (lit by a striker) for soldering copper pipe

Lead-free solid-core solder and **paste flux** for joining copper pipes

Solvent cement for joining rigid plastic pipe

Hacksaw, used with a miter box, cuts both metal and plastic pipes

Miter box holds saw at specific angles

Joints, fittings, plugs, and caps

Turns and branches. Elbows (left and center) create a curve with two rigid pipes of the same material. T-fitting (right) joins three pipes of the same material.

In-line fittings. Union (left) and nipple (center) join same-size metal pipes. (Joint made with a union can be taken apart.) Reducer (right) joins pipes of different sizes.

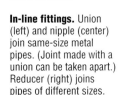

Plugs and caps. Plug (left) screws into a pipe or fitting to seal it. (Drain cleanouts have plugs.) Copper and brass caps (center and right) close open pipes.

Transition fittings

To connect pipes of different metals, use a dielectric fitting, like this copper-to-steel fitting. A plastic spacer in the dielectric fitting prevents the electrochemical reaction between two different types of metals that results in corrosion.

A plastic-to-steel connector features a plastic sleeve that is solvent-welded to a pipe of the same plastic (left) and a threaded nut to grip a threaded steel pipe (right).

Copper and plastic pipes can be joined with the copper-to-plastic connector shown on page 122 or with the grip fitting shown here. Each side has a grip ring and a plastic sealing cone to create the seal.

Pipe characteristics

PIPE MATERIAL	FORMS	USES	CUTTING METHODS	JOINING METHODS
Brass	Rigid, natural or chrome plated	Water supply, sink and tub waste	Hacksaw, metal-pipe cutter	Threaded or compression fitting
Cast iron	Rigid	Drain-waste-vent (DWV)	Reciprocating saw w/cast-iron-cutting blade	Neoprene coupling, cold caulking
Copper	Rigid and flexible	Water supply	Hacksaw, metal-pipe cutter	Solder; compression or flare fitting (flexible only)
Galvanized steel	Rigid	Water supply, DWV	Hacksaw, metal-pipe cutter	Threaded or compression fitting
ABS (acrylonitrile butadiene styrene)	Rigid, black	DWV, sewer	Hacksaw w/miter box, plastic-pipe cutter	Solvent welding, flare or grip fitting
CPVC (chlorinated polyvinyl chloride)	Rigid, beige	Water supply	Hacksaw w/miter box, plastic-pipe cutter	Solvent welding, flare or grip fitting
PB (polybutylene)	Flexible, beige	Water supply	Hacksaw w/miter box, plastic-pipe cutter	Flare or grip fitting
PVC (polyvinyl chloride)	Rigid, white or beige	DWV, cold-water supply, sewer	Hacksaw w/miter box, plastic-pipe cutter	Solvent welding, flare or grip fitting

Cutting rigid copper

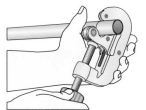

Slide pipe cutter onto copper pipe; tighten cutting wheel until it lightly scores the surface. (Tightening too much may bend the pipe wall, causing a leak later.) After scoring once, tighten the cutter and revolve again. Repeat until pipe is cut.

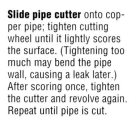

A hacksaw and miter box can also be used to cut copper pipe. Hold pipe securely in miter box with thumb, as shown. Place blade in 90° slot and make cut, keeping blade vertical.

Use a reamer to remove metal burrs left inside cut pipe. (Burrs can cause leaks when pipe is joined to a fitting.) Rotate reamer inside lip until it feels clean. Smooth rough spots inside and out with emery cloth.

RULES OF THUMB

Measuring pipe. To determine a pipe's actual, or *end-to-end,* length, which includes a screw-in allowance at both ends, measure between bottom of fitting sockets. A pipe's *face-to-face* length is the distance between two fittings. *Center-to-center* is the distance between the centers of two parallel pipes. Pipe diameters are measured from inside rim to inside rim, circumferences around the outside.

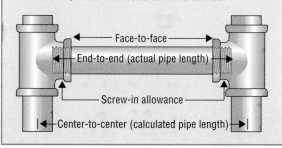

Face-to-face
End-to-end (actual pipe length)
Screw-in allowance
Center-to-center (calculated pipe length)

Sweat soldering copper

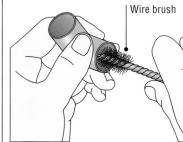
Wire brush

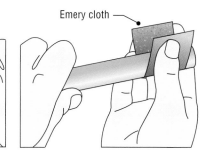
Emery cloth

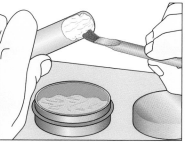

1 Clean the inside of the pipe fitting with a small wire brush or with emery cloth just until it shines.

2 Clean the outside of the pipe the same way as the fitting. Avoid touching cleaned surfaces.

3 Immediately apply paste flux. Brush a thin coat inside the fitting and outside the end of the pipe.

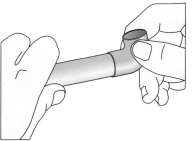

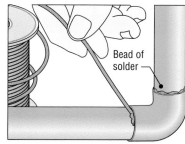

Bead of solder

4 Insert the pipe end in the fitting; give the joint a half turn to spread the flux. Wipe off any excess flux.

5 Heat the pipe joint evenly with a propane torch set for soft flame. When the pipe gets hot enough to melt solder, turn off the torch.

6 Touch solder to joint and move it around until a thin bead of solder forms around the entire joint rim. Don't apply too much solder. Wipe off excess.

Connecting flexible copper tubing

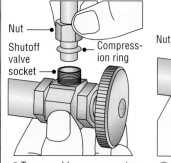
Nut
Shutoff valve socket
Compression ring

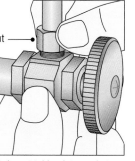
Nut

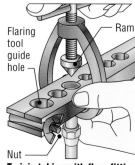
Flaring tool guide hole
Ram
Nut

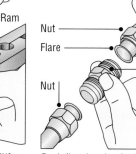
Nut
Flare
Nut
Flare fitting

1 To assemble a compression fitting (shown here on a shutoff valve), first slide nut and ring over tubing.

2 Insert tubing into socket. Slide compression ring and nut down to threads; tighten nut over threads with a wrench.

To join tubing with flare fitting, slide flare nuts over tubing ends. Clamp each end into flaring tool. Screw ram into tubing.

Push flared ends of tubing onto flare fitting; then screw flare nuts onto fitting. Tighten nuts with two wrenches.

Plumbing ▪ Working with pipe

Joining plastic pipe

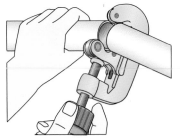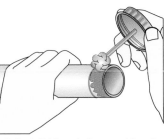

1 If you are cutting plastic pipe that is in position, use a pipe cutter as shown; cut loose pipe in a miter box with a hacksaw. For pipe cutting techniques, see page 121.

2 Remove any burrs from inside of pipe with a utility knife. Bevel outside edge of pipe to improve solvent take-up.

3 Insert pipe in fitting. Use felt-tip marker to draw guideline across joint; draw a line on pipe to mark depth of fitting socket.

4 Apply thick coat of appropriate solvent cement to outside of pipe end and thick coat to inside of fitting. If using PVC or CPVC pipe, apply primer first; wait 15 sec.; then apply cement.

5 Working quickly, push pipe into fitting so that guides are ½ in. apart. Twist pipe to align guides and spread cement. Wipe off excess; let dry for time specified on cement label.

Replacing a leaking threaded pipe

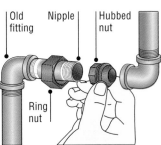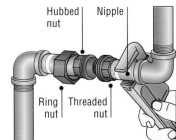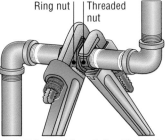

Old pipe

Replacement nipples

Ring nut Hubbed nut Threaded nut

Center union

1 Shut off water to pipe and drain it. Cut through damaged pipe with hacksaw. Unscrew cut sections from fittings, using two wrenches as shown.

2 Replace old pipe with two nipples joined by center union. When all joints are tightened, the assembly must equal length of old pipe.

3 Apply pipe tape to nipple threads. Screw one nipple into fitting; tighten with wrench. Slide ring nut over nipple. Screw hubbed nut onto nipple.

4 Screw threaded nut onto second nipple; screw nipple into second fitting. Tighten nipple and nut. Apply pipe tape to threaded nut.

5 Butt faces of threaded and hubbed union nuts. Slide ring nut to center of union. Screw ring nut to threaded union nut. Tighten with two wrenches.

Patching rigid copper pipe with plastic pipe

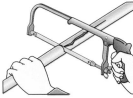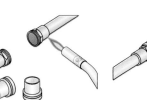

1 Shut off water supply to damaged pipe; open faucet to drain pipe. Cut out damaged pipe section with pipe cutter or hacksaw. Deburr remaining ends of pipe.

2 Measure gap between pipe ends. Cut rigid plastic pipe of same diameter as copper pipe to fit gap, allowing for transition fittings. Deburr and bevel ends of plastic pipe.

3 Sweat solder (p.121) copper section of copper-to-plastic fittings to two ends of copper pipe. Screw brass and plastic sections of fittings to copper sections.

4 Test-fit the plastic patch without solvent cement. Disassemble; apply appropriate solvent to inside of fittings and to outside of pipe ends; reinstall the patch.

FOR YOUR SAFETY

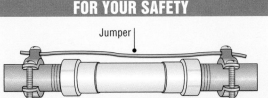

Jumper

If your home electrical system is grounded through its metal water pipes, make sure you don't break the ground connection when you install a plastic pipe patch. Attach ground clamps to bare metal pipes on either side of the repair, and connect the clamps with jumper wire as shown.

122

Appliance repair basics

Large and small appliances accomplish a great deal by putting a few basic electrical and mechanical concepts to work. You can begin to understand how most appliances operate if you master those concepts—they're explained on the following pages. The *General troubleshooting* pages concluding this section describe common problems that most electrical and mechanical devices fall prey to.

Electrical repairs are a large part of appliance servicing, so be sure to review the basics of working with wires, plugs, and motors. You'll find that an inexpensive device called a volt-ohm meter is an invaluable tool for troubleshooting. Even minor electrical repairs can be hazardous if not made correctly, however: *For your safety* boxes are found throughout this book, and those on the following pages are particularly important.

Many of the tools required for electrical work and appliance repair, including screwdrivers, wrenches, pliers, and a utility knife or jackknife, are probably already part of your home tool kit (p.10). In addition, you will need special tools for working with wire and for soldering. These tools, as well as the electrical testers shown on the facing page and the supplies described at right, are readily available at most hardware stores and home centers.

Buying tools. To minimize costs, purchase special tools only as needed. (An exception is the volt-ohm meter, an invaluable and moderately priced device that will quickly repay your investment.) A quality tool may cost more, but it will last longer and be safer to work with. Tools used for electrical and appliance repairs should have fully insulated handles in good condition to minimize shock hazard if you accidentally touch a live circuit with the tool.

Rubber grips (shown on the screwdrivers below) help you hold a tool more securely and comfortably.

TIPS FROM THE PROS

Make a screwdriver more useful by running a magnet along its shank several times in one direction. A magnetized screwdriver will help you to start small screws and to retrieve screws that fall inside the appliance as you work.

Basic supplies

Contact cleaner is a solvent that removes corrosion and dirt. Unlike other solvents, however, it will not damage plastic. Use with adequate ventilation, avoid skin contact, and use a nozzle extension to aim the spray where it's needed.

Lubricant will keep an appliance running smoothly. White grease is used on small-appliance gears. Electric motors may require 20-weight oil. An extended-spout oiler will help you reach tight places.

Plastic electrical tape is waterproof and safe at temperatures up to 180°F (82°C). Use it to insulate wiring repairs and to secure wire connectors.

Solder for joining metallic surfaces. Rosin-core solder contains rosin flux to help the solder bind to metal parts. For more on soldering, see page 136.

Twist-on wire connectors are used to join wires. For more on wiring connections, see page 135.

Crimp-on terminals often replace soldered connections in appliances. Important types to have on hand include ring, spade, and U-shaped quick-connect.

Tools for appliance repairs

Hex keys (also called Allen wrenches) for turning setscrews.

Nut drivers come in several sizes for removing nuts, bolts, and hex-head machine screws.

Torx drivers for removing special fasteners found within small appliances.

Soldering iron for melting solder to make electrical connections (p.136). Soldering guns and soldering pens can often do the same job.

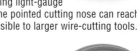 Standard tip

 Phillips tip

Screwdrivers. Standard-tip models should have nonflared blades (called cabinet or electrician's screwdrivers) for reaching recessed screws. You'll need several sizes of Phillips-tip drivers.

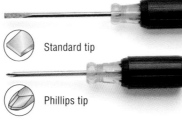

Multipurpose tool for crimping terminals, cutting and stripping wire, and cleaning bolt threads.

Wire stripper for removing wire insulation.

Automotive-point file with tungsten cutting edges for cleaning electrical contacts.

Side-cutting pliers (also called lineman's pliers) for gripping, twisting, and cutting wire.

Diagonal pliers for cutting light-gauge wire. The pointed cutting nose can reach places inaccessible to larger wire-cutting tools.

Long-nose pliers for maneuvering wire and small terminals into place. They can also be used to cut light-gauge wire.

Utility knife for general use and for splitting and stripping wire. A jackknife can do the same jobs.

Electrical testers

A volt-ohm meter (VOM) is the most important and versatile electrical tester you can own. (A full description of the meter is given on pages 130–131.)

A neon test light and a voltage probe (or power pen) are inexpensive tools that tell you at a glance whether or not you've turned off the power to a circuit. You must have this critical information before you make *any* electrical repair. **CAUTION:** Never work on a circuit or an appliance unless you know for sure that the power has been disconnected.

A continuity tester is used to find open and short circuits. Such tests often require the use of jumper wire, which you can buy at a hardware store or make yourself (see bottom right).

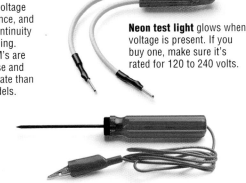

Volt-ohm meter measures voltage and resistance, and tests for continuity and grounding. Digital VOM's are easier to use and more accurate than analog models.

Neon test light glows when voltage is present. If you buy one, make sure it's rated for 120 to 240 volts.

Continuity tester is a small flashlight that lights up when its probe and clip are connected to make a complete circuit. Use this tester only with the power off.

Voltage probe does the same job as a neon test light (top right) but is safer and more convenient to use.

Plug-in outlet analyzer can diagnose reverse polarity, a bad grounding connection, and other wiring faults.

Canadian Standards Association (CSA) is Canada's oldest and largest integrated standards-development, certification, testing and inspection organization. It is a non-profit, non-governmental organization with regional offices and laboratories across Canada and affiliation with other testing and inspection agencies around the world. Its standards reflect a national consensus of producers, users and regulatory authorities in more than 35 technologies and business fields.

Using voltage testers

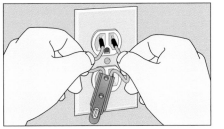

Using a neon test light to verify that power to a receptacle is off requires caution. Keeping fingers away from probe tips, insert tester probes into both slots of an outlet. If power is off, tester won't light up. Be sure to test *both* outlets.

A voltage probe need not be inserted into a receptacle. Simply hold the probe close to each slot. If voltage is present in receptacle, probe will light up and/or emit an audible tone. The probe can also detect voltage within appliances.

Using a continuity tester

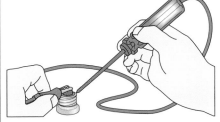

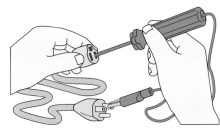

To test a plug-type fuse, attach tester clip to fuse contact; touch probe to fuse threads. To test a cartridge fuse, touch tester clip to one end of fuse and tester probe to the other end. In both cases, tester light will glow if fuse is good.

To test an extension cord, attach tester clip to one flat prong on the plug, and insert the probe in the corresponding hole as shown. Tester light will not glow if there are breaks in the conductor. Repeat the procedure on the other prong.

How to make a jumper wire

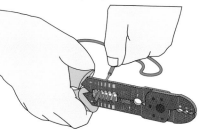

1 Jumper wire can be purchased in a hardware store, but it's also easy to make. Take a 2- to 3-ft. length of insulated No.18 wire (p.134) and strip ½ in. of insulation from both ends.

2 Slip insulating sleeves past the ends of the wire, crimp alligator clips to the bare wires, and slide sleeves over the clips. Make sure that sleeves completely cover bare wire.

Appliance repair basics ▪ Understanding electricity

The flow of electricity through a wire is often compared to the flow of water through a pipe. Although the analogy is hardly precise, it's useful in describing a force that intimidates many people. Electricity is basically the flow of subatomic particles called electrons through a conductor (a material whose resistance to electrical flow is low; copper wire is one example). Materials, such as plastic or rubber, that offer high resistance to electrical flow are called insulators. Electricity can be described by its rate of flow, or current, measured in amperes; by the pressure that forces it to move through a conductor, measured in volts; and by its power, or ability to do work, measured in watts. Resistance to electrical flow is measured in ohms.

AC/DC. Household electricity is produced by power plants as alternating current (AC), which reverses direction 120 times per second (60 "cycles" per second) as it flows through circuits. Batteries supply direct current (DC), which flows in one direction only. AC power must be converted into DC power in order to charge batteries.

In North America, electric current is delivered to homes and offices at 120 and 240 volts. Light fixtures and small appliances operate on 120 volts; heavy-duty electrical appliances use 240 volts. (In other countries, standard voltages may differ.) The wattage of any electrical device—the amount of power it uses—is determined by multiplying volts by amperes (see box below). For example, an air conditioner that draws 5 amps at 120 volts consumes 600 watts of electricity (5 x 120 = 600). If you run the air conditioner for an hour, it will consume 600 watt-hours worth of electricity. If you use 1,000 watts for an hour, you've consumed 1,000 watt-hours (1 kilowatt-hour). Your electric bill is based on kilowatt-hours, determined by the total wattage of all your lights and appliances and the length of time they are in use.

Electric circuits. To light a bulb or run a washer, electricity must flow in a circuit, a closed loop formed by conductors that lead from a power source to a "load" (a power-using device) and back to the source. An on-off switch may be located between the source and the

---

QUICK FORMULAS

AMPS	=	volts ÷ ohms
VOLTS	=	watts ÷ amps
WATTS	=	volts × amps
OHMS	=	volts ÷ amps

---

load. The power cable for a typical residential electric circuit contains three conductors—usually copper wire—wrapped in plastic or rubber insulation. One or two hot conductors, usually sheathed in black or red insulation, each carry current at 120 volts from the main service panel to a load. A white-coded neutral conductor carries current at zero volts from the load back to the service panel. A bare or green-coded grounding or bonding wire provides a safe path to earth for abnormal current flow (p.128) anywhere along the circuit.

Grounding. In a properly grounded electrical system, an uninterrupted grounding path links all receptacles, switches, and metal outlet boxes to the ground/neutral bus bar in the main service panel. The main ground wire connects the bus bar to a plumbing pipe and to a metal rod driven into the ground just outside the house. Because current follows the path of least resistance and copper wire offers less resistance than your body does, grounding ensures that abnormal current will flow into the ground, not through you.

FOR YOUR SAFETY

Most electrical accidents are caused by carelessness or ignorance. If you combine a basic knowledge of electricity, a healthy respect for it, and a dose of common sense, you can safely tackle many household electrical repairs. Here are some basic guidelines for working with electricity:

Before working on a circuit, go to the main service panel and remove the fuse or trip the breaker that controls that circuit (see facing page). Tape a sign to the panel warning others to leave the circuit alone while you work.

Before touching any wire, use a voltage tester (p.125) to make sure it's not live.

Whenever you check for voltage in a receptacle, check both outlets—each may be controlled by a separate wiring circuit.

Never stand on a wet or damp floor when working around electricity. Cover the floor with rubber mats or dry boards.

When replacing fuses, turn off the main power first. Make sure your hands and feet are dry, and place one hand behind your back to prevent electricity from making a complete circuit through your chest. Touch a plug fuse only by its insulated rim. Remove cartridge fuses with a fuse puller.

Use tools with insulated handles and ladders made of wood or fiberglass.

To protect children, place safety covers over any unused outlets.

When unplugging a power tool or appliance, pull on the plug, not on the power cord.

Improperly used extension cords are a leading cause of electrical fires. They are for temporary use only—do not use them to extend a circuit permanently.

Keep dry-chemical fire extinguishers in the kitchen, basement, and workshop.

Never disable grounding devices. Make sure that all appliances requiring grounding are properly grounded, and that the electrical system itself is properly grounded.

Meet or exceed all electrical code requirements that cover the work you are doing.

Always work with enough light to see what you are doing; it's easy to make mistakes when you're working in dim light.

When in doubt about the safety of any electrical repair or test, call in a professional.

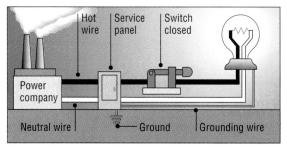

An electric circuit is a continuous path from a power source to a power-using appliance, then back to the source. With the switch closed (power on), excess electrons in the hot wire flow toward fewer electrons in the neutral wire, creating an electrical current that powers a light or an appliance. With the switch open (power off), current flow ceases.

Electricity in the home

Electricity enters the home through the main service panel, where it is divided into branch circuits, each protected by a fuse (in old houses) or circuit breaker (in newer ones). Each branch circuit extends from the service panel to a particular area of the house, supplying power to lights and receptacles. The amperage rating of a fuse or breaker is matched to that of the circuit it protects. If a circuit draws more current than it can handle, its circuit breaker trips or a metal strip in its fuse melts and breaks, thereby cutting off current flow and preventing a fire. Unlike circuit breakers, which can be reset after they trip, a blown fuse must be replaced. Never replace a blown fuse (or

Electrical codes

Your home's electrical system should meet or surpass the minimum safety standards set in the Canadian Electrical Code (CEC). Published and updated every 4 years by the Canadian Standards Association, the CEC serves as the model for provincial and local codes. Before repairing or adding to a home electrical system, call your local electrical inspector for up-to-date code information. Make sure you adhere to local electrical codes, which may be more stringent than the CEC.

a defective breaker) with one rated for higher amperage, and never reactivate a circuit until you've identified and corrected the cause of the problem.

There are three types of branch cir-

cuits. Lighting circuits are 120-volt, 15-amp circuits that power all light fixtures and most receptacles in a house. Small-appliance circuits are 120-volt, 15-amp circuits that supply receptacles in the kitchen, laundry, and home workshop (more amperage accommodates the many electrical devices used in these areas). Individual appliance circuits supply ranges, dryers, and other major appliances. They can be either 120- or 240-volt and range from 20 to 50 amps. How much current a circuit can handle depends on its wire gauge. Most 120-volt circuits contain 14- or 12-gauge solid copper wire. Most 240-volt circuits use 12- or 10-gauge wire. For more on wire gauges, see page 134.

Turning off the power

To cut power throughout the house, trip the main breaker at the service panel; if you have a fuse box instead of a breaker panel, remove the main pullout block or turn the lever switch to *Off*. To cut power to a circuit, trip the breaker or remove the fuse that controls it (see *For your safety*, facing page).

Correcting circuit overloads

Overloaded circuits are the most common cause of blown fuses or tripped breakers. The easiest way to eliminate an overload is to reduce the number of appliances on the circuit. But to do so you need to find out which fixtures and receptacles are involved. First turn off the affected breaker (or remove the fuse). Then walk through the house, flipping switches and checking receptacles with a voltage tester (p.125) or with a lamp that you know works. Fixtures and receptacles on the problem circuit are the ones that are inactive. (Remember that circuits may extend into adjoining rooms and other floors.) Next add up the wattages of all the lights and appliances on the circuit. (If an appliance is rated in amperes only, multiply the rating by 120 volts to get its wattage.) If the total wattage on a 15-amp circuit exceeds 1,800, the circuit is overloaded; the limit for a 20-amp circuit is 2,400 watts.

Move some appliances to another circuit and restore power to the inactivated circuit. If the circuit still fails, the cause may be a faulty breaker or a short circuit in a lamp, appliance, or the house wiring. For more on short circuits and other circuit faults, see page 128.

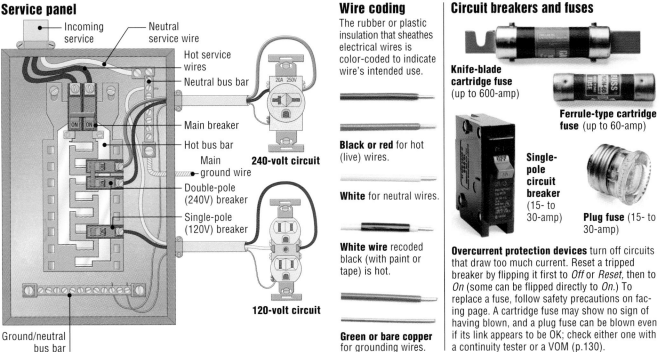

Service panel

- Incoming service
- Neutral service wire
- Hot service wires
- Neutral bus bar
- Main breaker
- Hot bus bar
- Main ground wire
- **240-volt circuit**
- Double-pole (240V) breaker
- Single-pole (120V) breaker
- **120-volt circuit**

Ground/neutral bus bar

Wire coding

The rubber or plastic insulation that sheathes electrical wires is color-coded to indicate wire's intended use.

Black or red for hot (live) wires.

White for neutral wires.

White wire recoded black (with paint or tape) is hot.

Green or bare copper for grounding wires.

Circuit breakers and fuses

Knife-blade cartridge fuse (up to 600-amp)

Ferrule-type cartridge fuse (up to 60-amp)

Single-pole circuit breaker (15- to 30-amp)

Plug fuse (15- to 30-amp)

Overcurrent protection devices turn off circuits that draw too much current. Reset a tripped breaker by flipping it first to *Off* or *Reset*, then to *On* (some can be flipped directly to *On*.) To replace a fuse, follow safety precautions on facing page. A cartridge fuse may show no sign of having blown, and a plug fuse can be blown even if its link appears to be OK; check either one with a continuity tester or a VOM (p.130).

Appliance repair basics ▪ Circuit faults

Short circuits

If a circuit that is not overloaded (p.127) fails repeatedly, the problem is probably a short circuit in the house wiring or in a lamp or appliance plugged into the circuit. A short occurs when a hot wire whose insulation has worn down touches a bare patch on a neutral wire or (in the case of 240-volt circuits) on another hot wire. A short may also occur in the windings of a motor. When a worn hot wire touches the metal cabinet of a grounded appliance (i.e., one with a three-prong plug), the condition is called a short to ground. Either way, the result is the creation of an

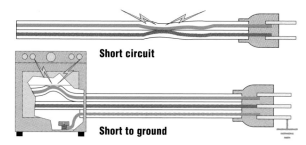

Short circuit

Short to ground

abnormal low-resistance path for a large amount of current. Although the current surge will quickly trip a breaker or blow a fuse, it can also create sparks and start a fire—which is why it's crucial that you locate and cure a short before restoring power to the circuit.

To determine whether a short is in the house wiring or in an appliance or fixture, unplug all electrical devices from the affected circuit and look for damaged plugs or cords—a common cause of shorts—and repair or replace them (p.144). With the devices still unplugged, restore power to the circuit. If it fails right away, the short is in the house wiring; call in an electrician. If the circuit fails only when you plug in and turn on a lamp or appliance, the short is in that device; repair it or replace it.

Ground faults

A ground fault is an abnormal electric current that's large enough to be felt but not large enough to trip a circuit breaker or blow a fuse. Such faults usually

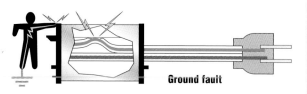

Ground fault

occur when a loose or worn hot wire touches an ungrounded metal outlet box or the metal housing of an ungrounded appliance. Because the metal isn't connected to ground, very little current flows—until you touch it and provide the missing ground connection. The resulting current surge may not be large enough to trip a breaker or blow a fuse, but it can be fatal. To protect against ground faults, install a ground fault circuit interrupter wherever water and electricity could come together (see *For your safety,* right).

Open and partial circuits

If an appliance fails to work when you plug it into a live receptacle (see *General troubleshooting,* p.144), suspect an open circuit—a broken wire or connection—in the power cord or in the plug. To do its work, electricity must travel in an uninterrupted circuit. If

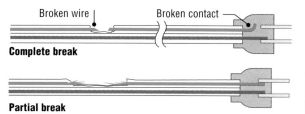

Broken wire | Broken contact

Complete break

Partial break

there is a break (a lack of continuity) anywhere along the circuit, current flow stops. Because a power cord is subject to wear, it's not unusual for one of its wires to break or come loose from a terminal, creating an open circuit. To test for continuity, see page 131.

A nicked or partially severed wire won't stop current flow but will impede it, causing a light to flicker or an appliance to run poorly. The increased resistance can overheat a wire and melt its insulation; that can lead to a short circuit or ground fault.

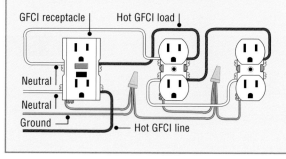

Receptacles and switches

The 120-volt receptacle

A standard 120-volt, 15- or 20-amp duplex receptacle, which can take two plugs at the same time, has two silver-colored screw terminals, to which neutral wires attach, two brass-colored terminals, to which hot wires attach, and a green grounding screw (newer receptacles may have neutral and hot push-in terminals as well). Break-off tabs between the sockets allow you to wire a receptacle so that one socket is always live while the other is switch-controlled.

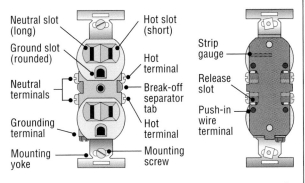

Neutral slot (long)
Hot slot (short)
Ground slot (rounded)
Hot terminal
Neutral terminals
Break-off separator tab
Grounding terminal
Hot terminal
Mounting yoke
Mounting screw
Strip gauge
Release slot
Push-in wire terminal

Receptacles don't often fail, but cases can crack, dirty slots can prevent contact between receptacle and plug, and an appliance short can burn out a receptacle. Whatever the problem, always replace a defective receptacle with one of the same amperage and voltage rating. Replace ungrounded two-slot receptacles with grounded three-slot models—but only if the outlet box is grounded or if the house wiring includes a separate grounding wire.

Special-purpose receptacles

Appliances that use 240-volt service require special outlets and mating plugs to prevent other appliances from being plugged into that circuit. Three of the most common configurations are shown below.

Electric stove
120V/240V, 50A

Air conditioner
240V, 30A

Clothes dryer
120V/240V, 30A

Replacing a receptacle

Before working on a receptacle, cut off power to it at the service panel (p.127), then use a neon test light or a power pen (p.125) to make sure the receptacle is not live. Remove the cover plate and loosen the mounting screws. Pull out and remove the old receptacle. Connect circuit wires to the new receptacle: hot wires (black) to brass screws, neutral wires (white) to silver screws, and the ground wire to the green screw.

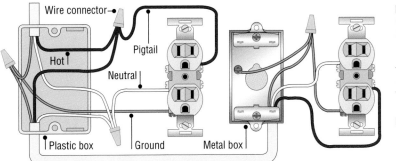

Wire connector
Pigtail
Hot
Neutral
Plastic box
Ground
Metal box

Mid-circuit receptacle is connected to incoming and outgoing circuit wires (far left). Some codes require that mid-circuit receptacles be joined to circuit wires by means of short lengths of wires called pigtails. A wire connector joins the pigtail to incoming and outgoing circuit wires. This way, a problem in one receptacle won't interrupt continuity in the rest of the circuit.

End-of-circuit receptacle at left is connected directly to incoming circuit wires. For more on wiring connections, see page 134.

Testing and replacing wall switches

The common single-pole switch controls a light or receptacle from one location. It has two brass-colored terminals, to which only hot wires attach, and On/Off settings are marked on its toggle (newer models may also have push-in terminals and a grounding screw). Three-way switches, with two brass and one dark terminal, control a light from two locations. A 4-way switch, with four brass terminals, is used with two 3-way switches to control a light from three locations. (Three- and 4-way switch toggles are not marked On/Off.) A simple continuity test (Step 2, below) can tell you if a single-pole switch is defective. Always replace a switch with one of the same type and of the same voltage and amperage ratings as the original.

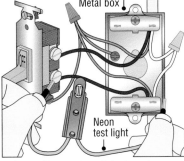
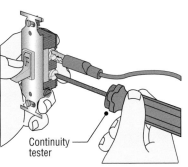
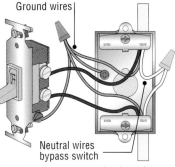

Metal box
Neon test light

Continuity tester

Ground wires
Neutral wires bypass switch

1 Turn off power to switch at service panel (p.127). Remove cover plate, and use a neon test light or power pen (p.125) to make sure power is off. Place a probe on metal box (or on bare grounding wire if box is plastic); touch each switch terminal with second probe. Tester shouldn't light at all.

2 Once you're sure circuit is dead, disconnect old switch and test it for continuity. Set clip of continuity tester (p.125) on one terminal; touch probe to the other terminal. Flip switch on and off. Tester should light only when switch is on. If the switch is faulty, replace it.

3 Switches are connected to hot wires, never to neutral. A mid-circuit switch (shown) is connected to two black wires. In a switch loop, in which only one cable enters box, switch is connected to a black wire and to a white wire recoded black (p.127); in this case, white wire is also hot.

129

Digital VOM

Display. A digital readout panel displays reading and, in many models, the selected function and range. Some models also have a beeper or buzzer to make continuity test results audible.

Meter body or housing should be sturdy and shock-resistant.

On-off switch activates the meter. Many meters have an "auto-off" feature to save batteries.

Selector switch determines the function to be measured. Autoranging models like the one shown here automatically set proper range. On other VOM's range must be set manually.

Jacks connect each test probe to the meter. Normally the red probe is plugged into the "+" jack and the black probe is plugged into the "-" jack.

Metal probes on test leads are used to touch various components in a circuit. Insulating sleeves keep user from contacting a live electrical circuit.

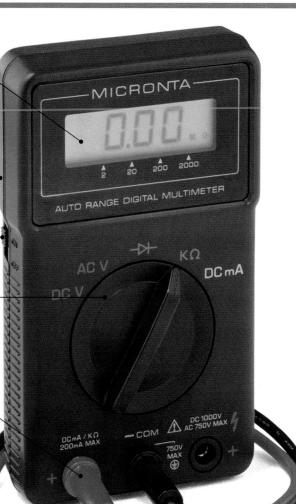

A multitester, or volt-ohm meter (VOM), is a simple, inexpensive electrical tester that is well worth acquiring if you plan to do appliance or other electrical repairs. In addition to testing a circuit for continuity, the VOM measures the actual amount of resistance in a circuit (ohms) and the strength of the electrical force passing through a circuit (volts); some models also measure the amount of current (in milliamps) passing through a circuit.

How it works. When you touch its probes to a circuit, the VOM samples resistance, voltage, or current and displays its findings on a digital readout or an analog scale. Knobs or buttons on the meter allow you to select the specific test you wish to make as well as the proper range for the item you're testing. For ohms readings, a battery inside the VOM passes a tiny current through the component being tested to gauge the amount of resistance in the circuit. Because the current is battery-supplied, ohms tests are done on unplugged appliances. Voltage tests, either AC or DC, involve live circuits and must be done very carefully (see *For your safety*, facing page).

Buying a VOM. Electrical and radio supply stores carry a wide variety of volt-ohm meters. The cost of a VOM is usually in direct proportion to its accuracy. Digital meters are generally more expensive than analog, but they are also more accurate and easier to use. Autoranging meters automatically establish the proper range. Buy a meter that has a fuse or circuit breaker to protect itself against electrical surges or improper hookup.

The tests on the facing page feature an autoranging digital VOM; other VOM's may differ. Read the manual that comes with your VOM, and practice the test procedures. To test electronic components, see page 148.

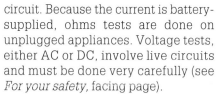

Alligator clips attached to VOM probes grip component being tested so you can adjust meter or manipulate wires in ohms tests. Clips also keep hands away from live connections in voltage tests.

Analog VOM

Display. To read VOM, note needle's position on selected function scale.

Calibration screw adjusts needle to compensate for inaccuracy caused by temperature changes or shock.

Zero ohms dial must be adjusted before an ohms test. To "zero" a VOM, select desired range. Touch probes together and turn dial until needle hits zero exactly.

Selector switch may have more range settings than digital version.

Testing for continuity

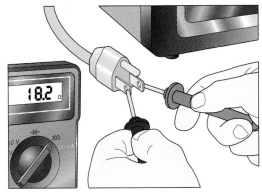

A continuity test determines if a complete circuit exists within an appliance. Select the ohms function and lowest range, usually RX1, on the VOM. ("Zero" an analog meter as described on facing page.) With the appliance unplugged but its switch turned on, touch meter probes to the flat prongs of a grounded plug (or to both prongs of an ungrounded plug). Meter will read near zero ohms if circuit is complete. A high reading indicates that the circuit is open and must be repaired.

Testing for resistance

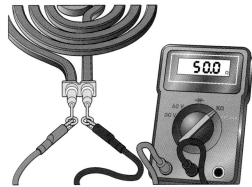

A resistance test is a good way to check whether a heating element, for example, is bad. A resistance test can be done only when at least one of the leads to a component is disconnected. Set meter as for continuity test at left. Unplug appliance and disconnect element. Touch meter probes to both terminals and compare reading to appliance specifications. In general, if an analog meter's needle sweeps toward zero or if a digital meter's reading is low (below 120 ohms for a standard range element), element is OK. A reading of infinity indicates an open circuit.

Testing for AC voltage

A volt-ohm meter not only detects the presence of AC voltage but, unlike a neon test light or voltage probe (p.125), it quantifies the reading. This is especially useful when you suspect low voltage. To test for voltage, first select the AC voltage function on the VOM, and then pick a range just above the receptacle's voltage (choose the highest range when testing unknown voltage). *Holding VOM test leads by their insulating sleeves,* carefully insert probes into receptacle. Reading should be within 10 percent of the receptacle's rated voltage (either 120 volts or 240 volts).

Testing AC circuit loading

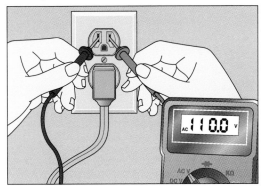

To test a house circuit's capacity, and to find out whether it can handle a new appliance, test a receptacle on that circuit for voltage as described at left. Once you've obtained a reading, remove VOM probes, plug appliance into receptacle, and turn appliance on. *Holding VOM test leads by their insulating sleeves,* carefully insert probes into free socket. If voltage drops 10 volts or more from first reading, circuit capacity is not sufficient for that appliance. Try the appliance on another circuit or consult an electrician.

Testing for DC voltage

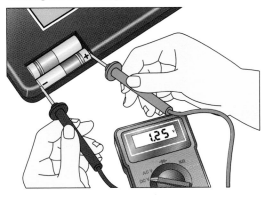

To measure battery voltage, select DC voltage function and appropriate range on VOM. Touch red probe to positive (+) side of circuit and black probe to negative (-) side. Reading should be within 20 percent of rating on appliance or battery. For a more accurate reading, try to check batteries under load, but only if it's possible to run the appliance safely while you conduct the test.

FOR YOUR SAFETY

A volt-ohm meter is an invaluable diagnostic tool for anyone attempting appliance or other electrical repairs. But if not used correctly, a VOM can be dangerous. Be sure you know what you want to test (ohms, volts, or current) before touching tester probes to a voltage source. Any tests on the ohms (resistance) scale must be done on an unplugged appliance or dead circuit. If the meter is set on the ohms scale and the probes come into contact with voltage, the meter can sustain internal damage.

Voltage tests involve even greater risk since you're probing potentially deadly voltage. Always hold VOM test leads by their insulating sleeves and exercise great care when touching the metal probes to a live receptacle or other voltage source. Never touch the metal probes when they're in contact with a voltage source.

Although there is no alternative to a volt-ohm meter if you need to determine actual voltages, a voltage probe (p.125) is a much safer alternative when all you need to know is whether or not a particular circuit is live.

The first step in appliance repair is simple: check the warranty. Most manufacturers provide free service on their products for a year or more—a benefit you may forfeit if you undertake a repair yourself. If a broken appliance is still under warranty, let the manufacturer repair it. Some companies also offer extended service contracts. Although a service contract can be expensive, it's an option to consider if the appliance is used heavily and you would rather not tackle major repairs.

If you have neither a warranty nor a service contract, try fixing the appliance yourself. Many repairs are simple enough that a layperson with a little patience can do them. Most appliance problems are caused by a single component or connection. In addition, the guts of many appliances are very similar. Once you've fixed your vacuum cleaner motor, for example, you'll have the know-how necessary to repair a blender or mixer motor.

Understanding the ratings plate

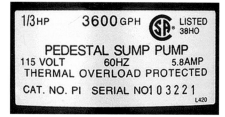

1/3 HP   3600 GPH   CSA LISTED 38HO

PEDESTAL SUMP PUMP
115 VOLT   60HZ   5.8AMP
THERMAL OVERLOAD PROTECTED

CAT. NO. PI   SERIAL NO1 0 3 2 2 1   L420

An appliance ratings plate lists, at the very least, the device's model (or catalog) number and a serial number—information you'll probably need to order parts. The plate may also rate the appliance for watts, volts, amps, or RPM—information that can help you decide whether the appliance is overloading the circuit it's plugged into (p.127). The plate shown here also gives the pump's capacity: 3,600 GPM (gallons per minute).

What to repair. Large appliances such as washers and dryers can sometimes be the simplest to fix; they are designed to be taken apart, and the most serviceable components are usually accessible. Inexpensive small appliances, however, are sometimes designed to be discarded rather than repaired. Manufacturers may discourage repairs on such appliances by sealing the housing or by assembling it with fasteners that require special tools for removal.

Not all appliances with serviceable parts can or should be repaired by their owners. Some manufacturers place a label on the appliance warning that repairs should be undertaken only by an authorized service center. Even though you may be able to open the appliance, you might not be able to buy the parts to repair it.

Many new appliances come with some type of electronic control, such as a digital timing clock. These components are durable but are not readily serviceable if they go bad; generally the entire component must be replaced.

Avoid needless repairs. Don't take the appliance apart unless you have to. Start by looking for the obvious: Is the machine unplugged? Is the circuit breaker off or the fuse blown? Are you using the appliance improperly? Problems such as these generate more than a third of all service calls. Then check the owner's manual for maintenance and troubleshooting tips. A little effort—putting a few drops of oil on a fan bearing or cleaning the filter on a vacuum cleaner—might be all it takes to get an uncooperative appliance running like new again.

The next step is to check the power cord and plug for fraying and breaks (see *General troubleshooting*, p.144). If you must disassemble the appliance, remove as few parts as possible. If you do remove a part, mark connecting wires with tape or sketch their alignment. Do not tamper with calibrated devices such as thermostats, particularly if their adjusting screws are secured with a drop of plastic as a reminder to leave them alone.

Getting parts. Parts lists are sometimes included in the service manual (a good reason to keep the manual). Check the list for the name and number of the part you're looking for, and check the appliance rating plate (see below, left) for the make, model number, and serial number. With this information you can order the part from the manufacturer or from one of its authorized service centers (they're listed in the Yellow Pages of your phone book).

Reading wiring diagrams

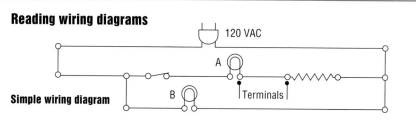

120 VAC

Simple wiring diagram

A   B   Terminals

A wiring diagram is a guide to the inner workings of an appliance. On a typical diagram, straight lines represent conductors and a variety of symbols represent individual electrical components such as switches, fuses, and motors. Some of the more common wiring diagram symbols are shown below, but there are many others.

The diagram for any appliance may seem daunting at first glance, but reading it isn't difficult. To get your bearings, start at the point where electricity enters the appliance; then trace the flow as it passes through various components and back to the power supply. In the diagram above, for example, light B is energized whenever the appliance is plugged in; light A and the heating element are controlled by the switch. If you already know where the problem may be, focus on the components leading to and from it.

The owner's manual may contain a wiring diagram; if not, try ordering one from the manufacturer. On some large appliances, the diagram is on the back of a cabinet panel.

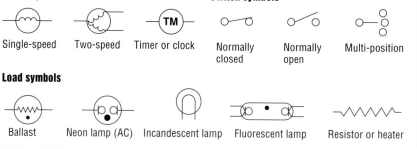

Motor symbols

Single-speed   Two-speed   Timer or clock (TM)

Switch symbols

Normally closed   Normally open   Multi-position

Load symbols

Ballast   Neon lamp (AC)   Incandescent lamp   Fluorescent lamp   Resistor or heater

Disassembly

Before working on an appliance, *make sure it is unplugged.* Check its manual to identify potential hazards. Certain microwave components, for example, should be fixed only by professionals. The sealed parts of appliances that are used or washed in water should also be left to professionals; such parts are nearly impossible to reseal properly.

Your next step is to find the fasteners that hold the case of the appliance together. As the drawings below indicate, they may be hard to locate.

Because reassembly is generally the reverse of disassembly, pay close attention to the exact sequence in which you remove parts. It's a good idea to make a sketch of the assembled parts or to take a Polaroid picture of them. Making a light scribe mark across the junction of mating components is also helpful. Another trick is to arrange small parts on a strip of masking tape as you remove them. At the very least, group small parts and fasteners together in saucers. Note how parts are oriented—which end of a control shaft is up, or which side of a bearing faces forward.

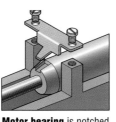

Motor bearing is notched to prevent rotation.

A dot of paint will help you keep track of orientation. Pay particular attention to the location and position of washers. Most appliances are carefully engineered—every marking, part, tab, and notch has its purpose. A notch, for example, may be used to keep a motor bearing from rotating. The following techniques will make appliance disassembly much easier:

- To loosen a metal part that's force-fitted into plastic, try warming the plastic with a hair dryer.
- To remove a tight-fitting control knob, slip a rag behind it, then pull evenly on the rag.
- Remember that nuts and bolts on rotating parts may have left-hand threads. Forcing them out the wrong way can strip the threads.
- When replacing an electrical part, remove the leads from the old part and attach them to the new part one by one.
- Don't remove dials or control cams unless absolutely necessary; they can be difficult to replace.
- Wrap the jaws of pliers with tape to protect finishes.
- To loosen rusted screws, use penetrating oil and patience, not force.
- Work on a clean uncluttered surface; keep parts out of a child's reach.

Special-purpose fasteners. Many new appliances are assembled with metric fasteners and Torx or square-drive screws. Metric wrenches and Torx and other special drivers are sold at many hardware stores and home centers. To discourage owner servicing, manufacturers sometimes seal appliances with unusual fasteners that may be difficult or impossible to remove.

FOR YOUR SAFETY

Before testing or repairing an appliance, unplug it. If you can't unplug it, turn off the power at the main service panel (p.127).

Do not use metal instruments to probe the interior of appliances, especially open-coil heating appliances such as toasters. You could short-circuit the appliance and receive a shock.

If you receive a shock when touching any appliance, disconnect the power immediately.

Never light a match near a malfunctioning combustion appliance, such as a gas dryer, stove, or furnace. If you smell gas, don't turn on the lights—a small spark in an outlet box could trigger an explosion. Instead, shut off the gas, open the windows, and call the gas company from a neighbor's house.

Never move an appliance connected to a gas or water line without first disconnecting it.

Get help when moving heavy appliances.

Never circumvent built-in safety devices.

Remember to discharge capacitors (p.146) before starting a repair job.

Buy only electrical components listed by Canadian Standards Association (p.125).

Beware of sharp metal edges when removing service panels or reaching inside an appliance.

Don't run an appliance with the access panel removed unless absolutely necessary. Avoid moving parts; don't touch electrical terminals.

After servicing an appliance, check it for ground faults (p.147) before plugging it in.

Hidden fasteners and trick connections

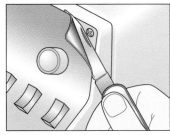

Press decorative facings with finger to find hidden screws. Use knife to lift facing after softening glue with hair dryer. Use contact cement to reglue facing.

A dial cap (or the dial itself) may hide a fastener. Use a knife to gently pry off a cap. Remove a dial only if necessary; mark its position with tape first.

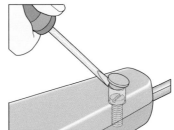

Remove plastic screw caps with a screwdriver or other strong, sharp instrument. Minor surface marring is probably inevitable.

The flexibility of plastic allows plastic parts to be connected by tab-and-notch arrangements that are easy to pry apart if you work slowly and carefully.

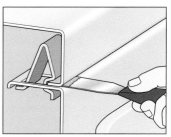

To loosen hidden spring clips, such as those securing a dryer top, slip a stiff tape-wrapped putty knife under appliance top and push knife against clip.

Appliance repair basics ▪ Wires, cords, and plugs

Wires and cords

Electrical wires are usually made of solid or stranded copper, sheathed in rubber, plastic, or heat-resistant insulation. Wire sizes are designated by American Wire Gauge (AWG) numbers: the higher the number, the smaller the wire and the lower its amperage rating. The wiring within small appliances is typically small-gauge stranded wire insulated in a variety of colors. Most wires found in household lighting and small-appliance circuits (AWG Nos. 10, 12, and 14) are solid. The cable used in household wiring consists of two or more insulated wires enclosed in a thermoplastic covering. Power cords are two or more insulated wires joined to bring power to a lamp or appliance. On flat lamp and small-appliance cords, the neutral conductor can usually be identified by a molded ridge on its insulation.

A replacement wire or cord, available at electrical parts suppliers or hardware stores, must be of the same gauge and type as the original. (Gauge, type, and other information are marked on the insulation.) A power cord's amperage rating should match that of the appliance it's connected to. All heating appliance wiring must have heat-resistant insulation. If you're unsure of the type of wire required, show a sample of the wire you are replacing to the supplier.

Small-gauge appliance wire connects internal components of small appliances.

Zip cord is a two-wire 12- or 14-gauge cord used mostly on lamps.

Two-wire 14- or 16-gauge cord is used on small appliances with two-prong plugs.

Heater cord has heat-resistant insulation for appliances such as irons, toasters, and portable space heaters.

Three-wire 12- or 14-gauge cord is used on 120-volt appliances that have grounded three-prong plugs.

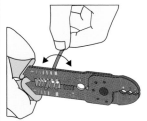

Three-wire 6- or 8-gauge cord delivers power to ranges, large air conditioners, and other heavy-duty 240-volt appliances.

How to strip wire

Most appliance repairs call for stripping insulation from a wire. When doing so, be careful not to cut into the wire. Nicked wires are weaker, carry less current, and are more likely to overheat or break. If you use a knife to strip wire, take care not to cut yourself; a multipurpose tool or wire stripper (p.124) is safer.

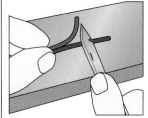

1 With wire pressed against a board, use a jackknife to shave off a strip of insulation on one side of wire.

2 Peel back remaining insulation. With stranded wire, make sure no strands remain with insulation.

3 Slice off loose insulation. Cut cleanly so no loose strands of insulation remain.

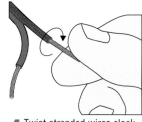

4 Twist stranded wires clockwise. For better connections, tin ends of stranded wire with solder (p.136).

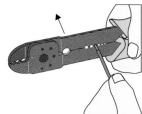

To strip wire with a multipurpose tool, feed wire into hole of correct gauge. Close and rotate tool to cut insulation.

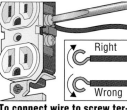

Squeeze handle and push tool away from you to remove cut insulation. Tool leaves tapered cut on remaining insulation.

Making connections: Wire to terminal

Whether you're connecting wire to a wall switch, a receptacle, or a terminal inside an appliance, make sure all connections are tight and neat, with no frayed ends or loose strands. It's good practice to tin the ends of stranded wires (p.136) before attaching them to a screw terminal or inserting them in a push-in terminal. Most wiring connections inside a power tool or appliance are soldered or involve terminals that are crimped onto wire ends. The most common terminal is

Wire ends should fit completely beneath screw terminal.

Always loop wire clockwise around screw terminal.

the spade lug that slides onto a plate terminal. Round or U-shaped crimp-on terminals (p.124) attach to screw terminals. The color of the insulation on crimp-on terminals indicates the size wire they fit.

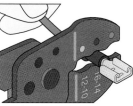

To install spade lug, cut ½ in. of insulation from wire, insert wire into lug sleeve, and crimp with a multipurpose tool.

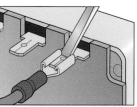

To disengage spade lug, push lug off plate terminal with a screwdriver. If you pull on the wire itself, you may damage it.

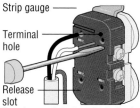

Strip gauge
Terminal hole
Release slot

To connect wire to screw terminal, strip ½ in. of insulation from wire end; bend wire into a loop with long-nose pliers. Hook wire clockwise around screw shaft. Tighten screw.

To wire push-in terminal, feed solid or tinned stranded wire into holes (gauge shows how much insulation to strip). To release wire, turn off power; push screwdriver tip into slot.

Right
Wrong

Making connections: Wire to wire

The easiest way to join wires is with a screw-on wire connector or, for a more secure connection, a crimp-on wire cap (the latter is particularly useful for joining wires in appliances that vibrate). Be sure to use the right size connector for the type and number of wires you're joining (the package usually includes a sizing chart). Strip off only enough insulation so that no bare wire is exposed once the connector is in place. To make sure that wires joined with a wire connector don't come loose, wrap the splice with electrical tape. Wires can also be soldered together. For a discussion of soldering, see page 136.

Pigtails. Never connect more than a single wire directly to a single terminal. To join two hot wires to a switch terminal, for example, first turn off power to the circuit (p.127). Use a wire connector to join the two wires to a short length of wire called a pigtail; then connect the pigtail to the switch terminal.

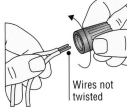

Solid wires. Hold stripped wires together and twist the connector on clockwise. Do not overtighten or you could break the wire.

Stranded wires. First twist each stripped wire clockwise; then twist them together and twist on the wire connector.

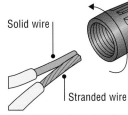

Solid to stranded wire. Twist stranded wire clockwise. Holding solid and stranded wires together, screw on connector.

To join wires with crimp-on cap, twist bare wire ends together, cap the wires, and crimp with multipurpose tool.

Plugs

Faulty plugs are a leading cause of appliance failure. Replace any plug that is cracked, burnt, or has loose prongs. A round-cord plug whose insulating disc is broken or missing must also be replaced. In general, replace a plug with one of the same type. The most common type is the flat-cord plug, which connects to zip cord by means of terminal screws. You can replace a flat-cord plug with a quick-connect plug, but only if it won't be subject to repeated insertion and removal. Some lamps and many appliances use round cords and round-cord plugs.

A polarized plug, in which one prong is wider than the other, fits into a polarized receptacle only one way. A safety feature designed to keep hot and neutral sides consistent throughout a circuit, polarity works only if the receptacle (p.129) and plug are properly wired. When installing a polarized plug, connect the cord's neutral (ridged) wire to the wider prong.

Flat-cord plugs are found on lamps and light-duty appliances.

Quick-connect plugs are easy to attach but lack durability.

Molded plugs form a single sealed unit with their cord.

Round-cord plugs come in standard and heavy-duty versions. The latter may feature a prong configuration specific to a particular large appliance.

Twist-lock plugs cannot be removed inadvertently; they require matching receptacle.

Heater plugs connect detachable cords to fryers and other heating appliances.

How to replace plugs

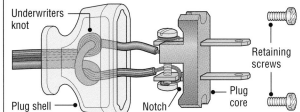

Underwriters knot · Plug shell · Notch · Retaining screws · Plug core

Flat-cord plug. Unplug appliance. Remove old plug by cutting cord with cutting pliers. Unscrew core of new plug from shell (or, depending on plug type, separate shell halves or remove insulating disc). Separate wires at cord's end. Strip ¾ in. of insulation from each wire. Feed wires into shell (if there's room in shell, tie Underwriters knot as shown below). Loop each wire over notch (if any) in terminal; then connect wire to terminal screw. Reassemble plug.

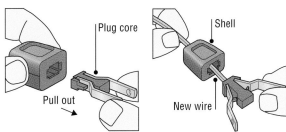

Plug core · Pull out · Shell · New wire

Quick-connect plug. Remove old plug as described above. Do not separate or strip wire ends. Pinch prongs of new plug and pull out plug core.

Feed cord through rear of shell. Spread prongs apart and insert cord into plug core. Squeeze prongs together to pierce cord; slide core back into shell.

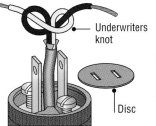

Underwriters knot · Disc

Round-cord plug. Cut off old plug. Pry off insulating disc from new plug or remove plug core from shell. Cut 1½ in. off cord jacket and ¾ in. off wire insulation. Feed cord into plug. Tie Underwriters knot as shown. Connect wires to plug terminals. In three-prong plug (right), tie Underwriters knot in black and white wires; hook white wire to silver screw, black to brass, and green to green. Reassemble plug; tighten cord clamp, if any.

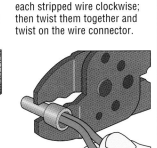

Soldering is the technique of joining wires or other metallic surfaces with molten metal. Although twist-on wire connectors and crimp-on caps (p.135) are commonly used to join appliance wires, soldering still plays an important role in repair work, especially to fasten wires to non-crimp-on terminals and in situations where vibration might loosen other connectors.

Soldering tools. To solder the fine wires found in small appliances, use a 25- to 50-watt soldering pen. Higher-wattage soldering guns and irons are more suitable for the heavier wiring of large appliances (some guns, however, feature high and low heat settings and can be fitted with special tips for intricate work). The tip of any soldering tool must be kept tinned—coated with solder—to improve heat transfer and prevent pitting and tarnishing.

Solders and flux. The strongest solder for electrical work, and the easiest to use, is a mixture of 60 percent tin and 40 percent lead. (The high melting points of lead-free and silver solders make them inappropriate for most appliance repairs.) Before a joint is soldered, it must be coated with flux, a paste that removes tarnish and helps the solder penetrate the joint. Of the two kinds of flux available, use only rosin flux on wiring; acid flux corrodes copper. The best solder for most wiring jobs is rosin-core solder, a hollow wire of solder filled with rosin flux, which eliminates the need for a separate application of flux.

Applying and removing solder. Since solder always flows toward a heat source, it will penetrate a joint more effectively if you touch the iron to one side of the joint and the solder to the other. Before soldering, clean dirt or corrosion from the wires with fine-grit sandpaper or emery cloth. Twist or crimp the wires together to create a strong mechanical connection. If you need help holding the parts, place the iron in a soldering stand or the work in a soldering clamp (see *Tips from the pros,* above right). To avoid inhaling fumes, solder only in a well-ventilated area.

When removing large deposits of solder, use a desoldering pump. Small amounts of solder can be removed with desoldering braid.

Preparing a soldering iron

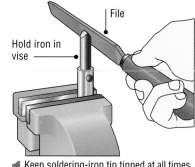

Hold iron in vise — File

1 Keep soldering-iron tip tinned at all times. To tin the tip, unplug iron; file, scrape, or sand tip until bare metal shows through.

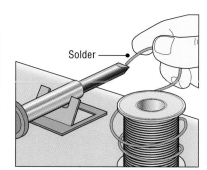

Solder

2 Plug in iron and turn it to medium heat. Hold solder to tip until tip is coated. Wipe off excess solder with a damp sponge.

Soldering and tinning techniques

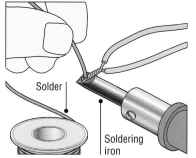

Solder — Soldering iron

To solder wires, clean them with sandpaper, then twist together. Hold tip of iron to underside of joint; touch solder to wires from above.

Soldering iron

Stranded wire — Solder

To tin a stranded wire, melt just enough solder to coat the strands evenly. Snip off any untinned strands of wire.

Terminal

Solder — Wire

To solder a wire to a terminal, use just enough heat to melt the solder without causing it to sputter.

How to desolder

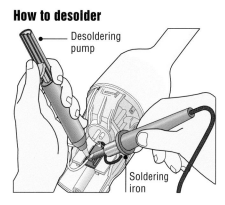

Desoldering pump

Soldering iron

To desolder large areas, melt solder with a soldering iron (don't overheat the work—you could damage parts). Press plunger of desoldering pump to suck up molten solder. Clean pump after use.

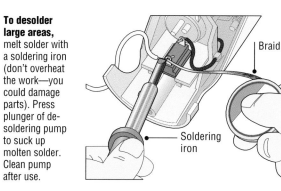

Braid

Soldering iron

To remove small solder deposits, place desoldering braid between iron and solder: braid absorbs solder as it's heated. Clean up flux residue with a foam swab soaked in denatured alcohol.

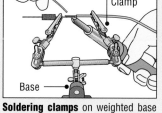

Cleaning and lubrication

Cleaning contacts and terminals

Dirt, corrosion, and paint on electrical contacts and terminals inhibit conduction and are a major cause of appliance problems. Use an automotive-point file or emery paper to clean contacts and terminals. After cleaning, be sure to flush away any trace of dust or filings with electrical contact cleaner, an antistatic solvent that removes dirt and corrosion without dam-

aging plastic. As with any solvent, avoid skin contact and do not spray on hot surfaces. Some contact cleaners contain a light lubricant; do not use them to clean wires prior to soldering.

Some switch contacts are made of soft silver for better conductivity. You can clean such contacts by sliding a piece of paper back and forth between them.

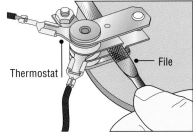

Faces of contacts on switch or thermostat should meet fully. Lightly file or sand clean; flush away residue with contact cleaner.

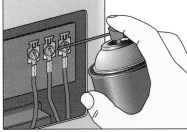

Clean hard-to-reach connections with electrical contact cleaner from a can equipped with an extension nozzle.

Use steel wool to polish *external* contacts only; the loose particles and oily residue it leaves behind can damage internal parts.

Lubricants and lubricating

Periodic lubrication will keep an appliance running smoothly and can solve many problems. When lubricating an appliance, carefully follow the directions in the service manual. Keep on hand a supply of commonly used lubricants such as SAE 20-weight nondetergent oil (for motors and bearings), lightweight machine oil (for everything from sewing machines to

fishing reels), powdered graphite spray (for locks), penetrating oil (to loosen rusty fittings), and white lithium grease (for gears, hinges, and sprocket-and-chain mechanisms). Use only plastic-compatible lubricants on plastic parts. Most jobs require only a few drops of oil or a light coat of grease—too much lubricant can damage parts and attract dust and dirt.

Most gears need a light coat of grease on the top edges and around the teeth. Be careful not to coat nearby parts.

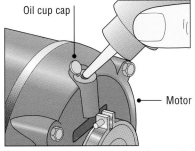

Some motors have a small oil cup (or a port covered with a plastic plug) for adding oil. Look for one on both ends of motor.

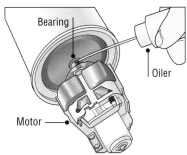

A telescoping-spout oiler makes it easy to reach hidden parts. Gently squeeze bottle to dispense oil. *Don't oil electrical connections.*

Repairing plastic parts

A cracked housing or control knob can make it risky to operate an appliance, so be sure to repair damaged appliances without delay. Most nonmetallic appliance parts are made of ABS or polystyrene thermoplastic, for which epoxy is the best general-duty repair adhesive. For good results, parts should fit together tightly.

Light scratches can be polished out with white toothpaste (not gel). To polish deeper scratches and smooth mended cracks, rub the area lightly with fine sandpaper; then remove the sandpaper marks with fine steel wool.

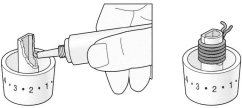

Broken control-knob shafts can be mended if the break is clean and the parts fit closely. Apply epoxy; then assemble the pieces. Wrap the shaft tightly with nylon thread; then coat the windings with glue. The thread reinforces the repair.

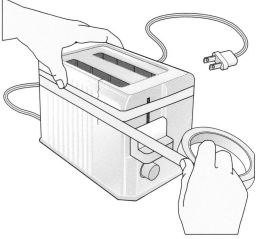

To repair large parts, coat one broken edge with epoxy and squeeze the parts together for 1 min. Then "bandage" the part at a right angle to the crack (pull the tape tight as you go). Let the part sit overnight before removing the tape.

Appliance repair basics ■ How motors work

In an electric motor, electricity flowing through bare wires called windings is used to generate magnetism, which in turn is used to rotate the motor shaft.

The magnetic field generated in this way is called electromagnetism. It has the same properties as ordinary magnetism—like poles repel each other and opposite poles attract—except that the poles can be reversed simply by reversing the direction of the electricity flowing through the windings.

The universal motor, so called because it will work on either alternating or direct current (p.126), is the most common type of motor in small appliances. All electric motors, however, have two features in common: a magnetized stationary component (called a stator or a field) and a rotating component (called a rotor or an armature). The rotor is also magnetized, either by direct application of current or by induction, a process in which current is created by the movement of the rotor within the stator's magnetic field. Continually reversing the current generat-

Inside a universal motor

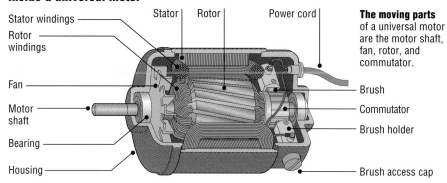

Stator windings
Rotor windings
Fan
Motor shaft
Bearing
Housing

Stator | Rotor | Power cord

Brush
Commutator
Brush holder

Brush access cap

The moving parts of a universal motor are the motor shaft, fan, rotor, and commutator.

ing one or both of these magnetic fields turns the rotor and thus the motor shaft.

A distinguishing feature of universal motors is that both the stator and the rotor have windings (often called coils). In contrast, DC motors have rotor windings but usually no stator windings, and induction motors have stator windings but no rotor windings (see *Types of motors*, facing page). Universal motors also

have two brushes and a commutator. The commutator is simply a series of brass bars insulated from each other; each bar is wired to the rotor windings. Brushes, mounted on the motor frame, press against the commutator, conducting current to the rotor windings. As each winding is activated, it sets up a magnetic field that interacts with the stator's magnetic field to produce rotation.

QUICK FORMULAS

Horsepower is the unit commonly used to describe a motor's power.

$$\text{Horsepower} = \frac{\text{amps} \times \text{volts}}{746}$$

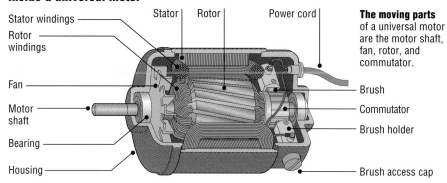

FOR YOUR SAFETY

If you suspect that a motor is faulty, shut it off before touching it or the appliance that houses it. If it has no plug, or if touching the plug may bring you in contact with water, turn off power to the circuit by tripping the circuit breaker or removing the fuse that controls it.

Disconnect any motor from its power source before servicing it. Never work on a motor in a damp or wet location. When performing tests requiring electricity, place the motor on a dry insulating surface such as a wood or rubber mat.

Discharge capacitors (p.146) before servicing the motor. Capacitors store electricity and can deliver a shock even if the motor is unplugged.

Dry a wet electric motor before servicing or operating it. To dry a motor, place it in an oven set at the lowest temperature (no more than 150°F/65.5°C); leave it with the door open until the motor stops steaming.

When reinstalling a motor, make sure the grounding wire is connected before restoring power.

Before starting a motor, be sure belts and pulleys are fully secured. Keep hands, hair, clothing, and tools out of the way.

Understanding a basic motor

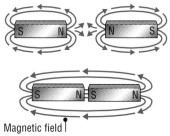

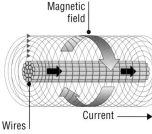

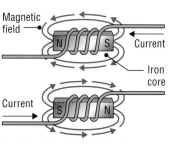

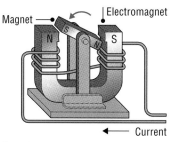

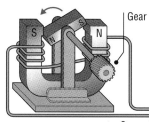

Magnetism. When suspended freely, magnets naturally align along the Earth's magnetic north-south axis. Similar ends, or poles, of magnets repel each other; opposite poles attract.

Electromagnetism. Any electricity flowing through a wire creates a magnetic field around it. Wires placed close together strengthen the effect as each field overlaps adjoining fields.

Applying the concepts. An electromagnet can be created by wrapping current-carrying wire around an iron core. Reversing the direction of current reverses the location of the poles.

Household electricity (60-cycle alternating current) reverses direction 120 times per second. An electromagnet's poles will therefore change just as often once current begins to flow.

As the current changes direction, the bar magnet will spin constantly as its poles try to align with the constantly changing poles of the electromagnet. A gear harnesses this motion.

Types of motors

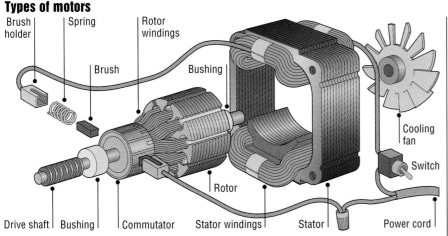

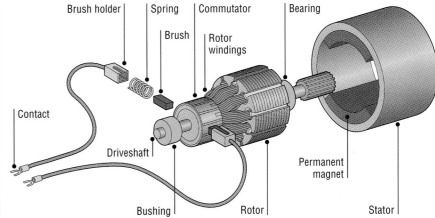

Universal motor is found in many small appliances and power tools. Commutator has parallel brass bars, each wired to a separate rotor winding. As rotor turns, brushes carrying current press against commutator, individually energizing bars and corresponding rotor windings. Magnetic field at each winding interacts with magnetic field of stator to rotate shaft. *Advantages:* efficient; high torque (turning force) at low speeds; easy speed control. *Disadvantages:* rapid wear of parts, especially brushes.

DC motor of the permanent-magnet (PM) type shown here often powers battery-operated appliances, tools, and toys. Design of a PM motor is similar to universal motor except that the stator consists of a permanent magnet instead of electrified windings. Current is supplied to the rotor only, via brushes. Some DC motors include a fan. *Advantages:* high power-to-size ratio and high torque at low speed. *Disadvantages:* poor performance at subfreezing temperatures; tendency to overheat under heavy load.

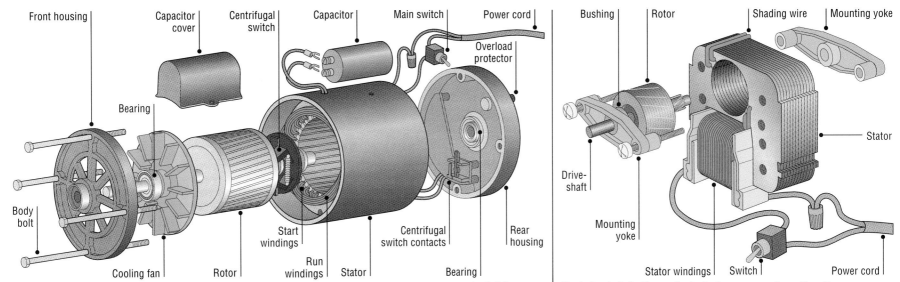

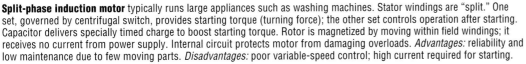

Split-phase induction motor typically runs large appliances such as washing machines. Stator windings are "split." One set, governed by centrifugal switch, provides starting torque (turning force); the other set controls operation after starting. Capacitor delivers specially timed charge to boost starting torque. Rotor is magnetized by moving within field windings; it receives no current from power supply. Internal circuit protects motor from damaging overloads. *Advantages:* reliability and low maintenance due to few moving parts. *Disadvantages:* poor variable-speed control; high current required for starting.

Shaded-pole induction motor typically powers such small appliances as can openers and hair dryers. Windings magnetize iron stator. Copper shading wire creates electrical imbalance that provides torque needed for starting. *Advantages:* low cost, small size, and extreme reliability. *Disadvantages:* low power and inability to reverse direction unless specially modified.

Starting a motor

Universal and DC motors lack starting mechanisms because in both cases the stator and the rotor are magnetized as soon as the power supply is turned on. The resulting interaction between mag- netic fields causes the rotor to spin. (In a universal motor, current magnetizes both stator windings and rotor wind- ings. In a DC motor, current magnetizes rotor windings only; the stator itself is a permanent magnet.) Lacking rotor windings, induction motors require start windings or other devices to give the rotor an initial spin so that it becomes magnetized by induction.

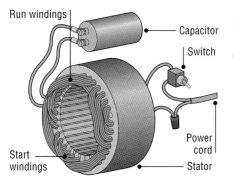

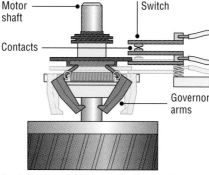

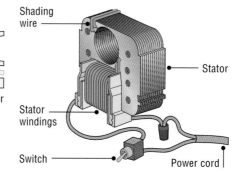

A split-phase induction motor has two sets of stator windings—start windings and run wind- ings—that are magnetized at different instants. These interacting magnetic fields give the rotor a starting spin. A capacitor connected to the start windings strengthens its field, helping to start the motor under load. *Always discharge a capac- itor before handling it* (p.146).

Centrifugal switch on a split-phase motor pre- vents start windings from burning out by cutting power to them when motor approaches top speed. Arms on a governor attached to the motor shaft swing outward as the shaft spins faster, eventually causing switch contacts to open, thereby cutting power to start windings. Switches may be outside the motor for easy servicing.

On a shaded-pole induction motor, shading wire delays rate at which parts of the stator are mag- netized by the stator windings. The delay is just enough to get rotor to move. Once in motion (and depending on load and voltage), rotor quickly gains speed. Because a typical shaded-pole motor lacks a capacitor, starting torque (turning force) is low; if overloaded, motor won't start.

Controlling a motor's speed

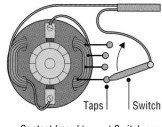

Tapped field speed control is used to vary speeds in appliances that have several leads (taps) coming from the stator windings. Multi- speed switch allows power to be applied to any tap. Motor speeds are lowest when current flows through entire winding, highest when it flows through smallest segment.

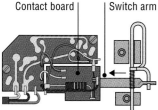

Solid-state control is an electronic version of a governor. Key part is a silicon-controlled rectifier (SCR) that allows current to pass accord- ing to factory-set voltage. Speed is controlled as SCR "clips" a portion of each cycle; the greater the clip, the slower the speed. Control is less prone than rheostat to heat buildup.

Governor is similar to a centrifugal switch. In type shown here, weighted scissorlike device is linked to motor shaft. When shaft spins, centrifugal force pulls weights outward, causing actuator pin to push against contact arm. At high speed, pin opens con- tacts, cutting power to motor. When motor slows, power is restored.

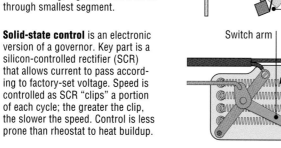

Rheostat may control speed in older tools or appliances. It is basically a wire coil that can be tapped at any point by means of a sliding contact. When wired into a motor circuit, a rheostat's sliding contact provides a means of varying resistance. If resis- tance is high, current drops and so does motor speed.

Before pulling out a volt-ohm meter to test a faulty motor, repair professionals generally gather information from a more immediate source: their own senses. You can do the same simply by paying atten- tion to what the motor is trying to "tell" you as it operates.

If you can **see** the motor and drive mechanisms while the appliance is running, look for gears and motor shafts that wobble, if only slightly. Worn bearings are the likely culprit, but a wobble could also indicate a misalignment of the moving parts. In either case, the problem will strain the motor and make the appliance noisy.

You can usually **smell** a faulty motor before serious damage is done. A mild odor of hot oil, metal, or plastic usually means that the motor is overheating, a problem often caused by overheated winding insu- lation or by friction in the motor bearings or drive components. Prompt lubrication may be all it takes to save the motor. But if the windings burn and short internally, the charred plastic insulation will emit a pungent acrid odor—a sure sign that the windings have to be replaced.

A motor too hot to **touch** is in trouble (a properly running motor will get warm but not hot). The air intakes may be clogged with lint or other debris, prevent- ing the fan from drawing cool air over the windings. Excess heat also indicates an overworked motor—check to see if the gears are clogged, a belt is too tight, or the bearings are dry.

If you **hear** a grinding noise, suspect a worn-out bearing. A squealing noise, often intermit- tent, means it's time for lubri- cation. It's normal to hear the "snap" of a centrifugal switch closing in a split-phase motor, but if the switch is bad (or if the motor overheats) you'll hear the overload protector "click" as it shuts off the motor.

Drive mechanisms

Drive belts and gear assemblies put a motor's power to work but also create much of the stress placed on the motor during operation. As a result, it is sometimes these parts, not the motor, that cause problems in an appliance. Drive parts must be properly lubricated, adjusted, and aligned. Before disassembling, note their arrangement to ensure correct reassembly.

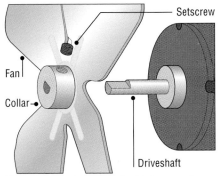

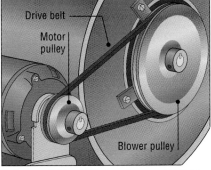

Direct-drive parts such as fan blades mount directly on the motor's driveshaft, often by means of a collar that mates with a flattened portion of the shaft. Noisiness or vibration may indicate that the collar is loose. Tighten the setscrew with a hex key (p.124) or screwdriver, but do not overtighten. Do not start motor until guard or shield is reinstalled around moving parts.

Pulleys and drive belts transfer power in large appliances such as washing machines and furnace blowers. Pulleys usually mount to motor and component shafts with pins (keys) and setscrews. If belts are too tight, they can damage motor; if too loose, they can slip or fly off. Replace worn belts promptly. Do not get oil on belts when lubricating motor or other parts.

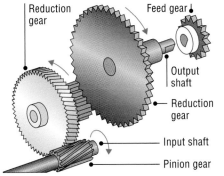

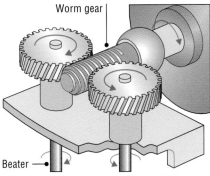

Reduction gears, commonly found in electric tools and in appliances such as can openers, reduce the speed of a driveshaft to a speed below that of the motor itself, while increasing torque. Gears may come in pairs, and may have straight- or helical-cut teeth. Examine gears for tooth damage and wear; replace them if necessary.

Worm gears change the direction in which driveshaft power is applied. Such gearing can also be used to create multiple driveshafts, as in the mixer shown above (note that the paired shafts rotate in opposing directions). One or more gears may be plastic to reduce noise; check them for damage or wear, and replace if necessary.

Motor disassembly

Taking apart a small electric motor is fairly easy. Be sure, however, to note *exactly* how it comes apart so that you can readily put it back together again. **CAUTION:** Disconnect the power source and discharge the capacitor (p.146) before starting to disassemble a motor.

Start by removing anything attached to the motor shaft, including collars, pulleys, and fans (left). Carefully examine each part as you remove it, and look for distinguishing features that will serve as landmarks during reassembly. Use masking tape to label each part.

Most motor cases can be opened as shown at right. Once the case is open, however, what you will find depends on the type of motor. Usually the motor shaft and rotor (see *Types of motors*, p.139) can be pulled free after you remove the rear housing. In split-phase motors, part of the centrifugal switch will come out at the same time.

Keep a rag on hand to remove any grease or oil that may get on your fingers; these materials shouldn't get on electrical connections, including the rotor and coils. Tag wires as you unfasten them, and be careful not to dislodge the brushes, which may spring loose before you can study their proper position. With the rotor removed, you can easily check the bearings for signs of wear. (Don't remove any fibrous packing around the bearings—it serves as an oil reservoir near lubrication points.)

When you're reassembling a motor, tighten body bolts evenly (a bit at a time) to prevent the shaft from binding. Turn the shaft periodically by hand to make sure that it moves freely.

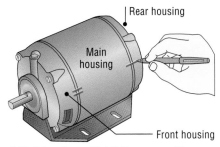

1 Mark housings with felt-tip pen or awl to ensure precise reassembly. Make two sets of marks on one end, one set on the other, to avoid reinstalling center housing backward. All marks must straddle seams.

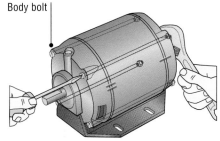

2 Use screwdriver and a wrench or nut driver to unfasten body bolts holding end housings in place. Most motors have four long bolts. Some have cover plates over one or both housings that must be removed to access body bolts.

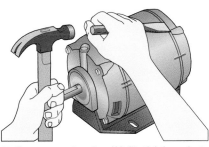

3 Remove rear housing. If it fits tightly against main housing, tap lightly at several points around circumference with a hammer and cold chisel (not a woodworking chisel) or wood block. With housing off, internal parts will be accessible.

Thanks to improved battery technology and the advent of powerful lightweight motors, a wide range of power tools, appliances, and electronic devices are now available in cordless models, the best of which *nearly* match the power and performance of their corded counterparts. Three features distinguish cordless appliances from corded models: a direct-current (DC) motor, rechargeable batteries, and a battery recharging unit.

Unlike corded appliances, which must be plugged into 120-volt alternating current (AC), cordless models go where they're needed. Periodically, depending on the type and design of the appliance and how long it has been used, either the appliance or its detachable battery pack must be returned to the charger.

Cordless appliances and tools are subject to most of the same problems as their corded counterparts. If a problem is not due to a defect in the appliance or tool itself, the culprit is usually worn batteries or a defective charging unit. Techniques for testing and troubleshooting batteries and chargers are described on the facing page.

Rechargeable batteries. Many cordless appliances operate on nickel-cadmium batteries (nicads), either individual cells or a battery pack consisting of as many as 20 cells. Each cell provides direct current at about 1.2 volts, approximately the same as an AA penlight battery. Battery packs slip directly into the appliance or tool or have snap-on terminals. The wire leads of some battery packs (like those in cordless phones) are soldered to the appliance circuitry. Don't try to solder individual cells; overheating will damage them.

Nicad battery

Battery pack

Although nicads can be recharged up to 1,000 times before they wear out, undercharging them shortens their life. Read the package directions carefully before using a new cordless appliance, and make sure to charge nicads fully.

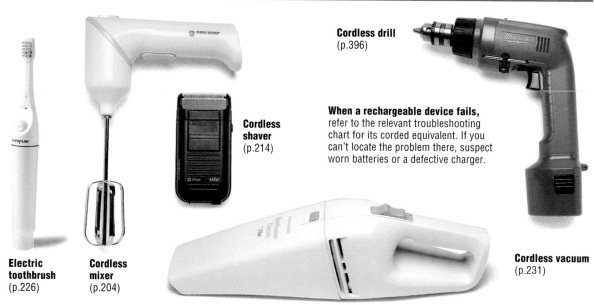

Cordless drill
(p.396)

Cordless shaver
(p.214)

When a rechargeable device fails, refer to the relevant troubleshooting chart for its corded equivalent. If you can't locate the problem there, suspect worn batteries or a defective charger.

Cordless vacuum
(p.231)

Electric toothbrush
(p.226)

Cordless mixer
(p.204)

Recharging units

Recharging a battery involves two items: a transformer and a diode rectifier. The transformer steps voltage down from 120-volt household current to the much lower voltages required by rechargeable batteries. The ratings plate on the charger lists both input and output voltages. The rectifier, located either in the charger or in the appliance itself, converts AC current to the DC current that batteries use. During the charging process some electricity is lost as heat, which is why chargers get warm as they operate.

How long it takes to recharge batteries depends both on their condition and on the amperage supplied by the charger. "Trickle" chargers, working at very low amperage, may take 14 to 16 hours to fully recharge a battery pack. Fast chargers, using much higher amperage, can do the job in as little as 15 minutes. To keep the batteries from overheating or even exploding, fast chargers include special sensing circuitry that prevents overheating. Always make sure that the charger you use is compatible with the appliance or battery pack.

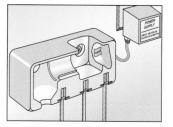

Stand-type chargers connect directly to the appliance during charging. Electricity flows into the seated appliance through metal contacts or via an electromagnetic field that induces an electric charge (see facing page).

Battery-pack chargers turn tools and appliances into steady performers. While one battery pack is at work in the tool, a second or third can be charging so you never have to wait for fresh batteries. This is the preferred system for charging cordless power tools.

Recharging tips

Use the proper charger. The charger supplied with a tool or appliance is the only one you should use to charge its batteries, even if the batteries fit other chargers. This ensures that the voltage and charging rate are correct for the batteries.

Don't overcharge. Don't store a battery pack or appliance in the charger base all the time unless the manufacturer's instructions specifically recommend it.

Avoid short memory syndrome. If you recharge a nicad before it's fully discharged, it may start retaining its charge for shorter and shorter periods. Before discarding a battery pack afflicted with short memory syndrome, try to restore its memory: Operate the device until the battery is completely exhausted. Then recharge the battery pack fully. Repeat this drain/charge cycle at least three times. If the battery pack still doesn't return to full power, test the charger and battery (see right). New types of rechargeable batteries, more potent than nicads and therefore not subject to short memory syndrome, are increasingly being used in cordless equipment.

Testing charger units and batteries

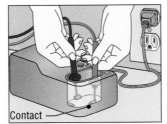

DC output charger (transformer and rectifier). Set a VOM on 25 DCV scale. Plug in charger and touch VOM probes to charger contacts. If meter reads zero, reverse the probes. Charger is OK if either reading is approximately 1 volt above the charger's rated output.

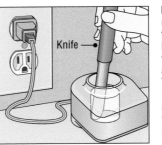

Induction charger, the type usually used with electric toothbrushes and other oral hygiene devices, works without metal contacts to appliance or battery pack. To test, plug in power cord. Hold a steel knife blade against interior of charging well. Blade will vibrate if charger is working properly.

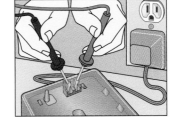

AC output charger (transformer only). Set a VOM on 25 ACV scale (be certain charger output is less than 25 volts before connecting to VOM). Touch probes to contacts. If no reading is obtained, the transformer is faulty. Do not test chargers rated higher than 25 volts.

Battery pack. Pack should be fully charged for test. Set a VOM on the DCV range just above pack's rated output. Touch red VOM probe to the pack's "+" terminal and the black probe to the "–" terminal. If reading is more than 1 volt below rated output, pack is bad and should be replaced.

Troubleshooting batteries and chargers

Problem	CAUSE? / Solution
Cordless appliance or tool doesn't run, lacks power, or does not run long enough	POWER OFF AT OUTLET? See *General troubleshooting,* p.144. Also make sure that the outlet is not wired into a wall switch that has been turned off. The charger must be on continuously in order to keep the batteries fully charged. ◇
	POOR ELECTRICAL CONTACT? With the charger unplugged, clean the contacts between the power handle and the charger with an automotive-point file or emery paper. If the contacts are difficult to reach, try spraying them with electrical contact cleaner (p.124). To improve contact, rotate and slide the power unit in and out of the charger well several times. ◇
	DEFECTIVE CHARGER? Test the power cord (see *General troubleshooting,* pp.144–145) and the charger (see tests above). Replace the power cord if it is defective. If the charger test reveals a defect, take the charger to an authorized service center for repair or replace it. Most newer chargers cannot be repaired or are not worth repairing. ◆ ▪
	WORN OUT OR DEFECTIVE BATTERIES? If a cordless tool or appliance runs for shorter and shorter periods between rechargings, the nicad batteries are probably worn out. Do a visual check of the batteries or battery pack. Look for corroded terminals or a sticky substance (electrolyte) leaking from the battery. If you find electrolyte leaking, replace the battery pack (be sure to avoid skin contact with leaking electrolyte). If there is no leakage visible, test the battery pack (see above) and replace it if necessary. To avoid battery "memory" problems in the first place, see *Recharging tips,* above. ◇ ▪

Degree of difficulty: Simple ◇   Average ◆   Complex ◆

Volt-ohm meter required: ▪

ENVIRONMENTAL HINTS

Recycling batteries

Cadmium and other heavy metals used to make rechargeable batteries can pose a serious health hazard if released into groundwater or air. Long-term exposure to these metals may be linked to higher incidences of kidney disease, birth defects, and cancer.

Concern about the number of rechargeable batteries being sold has led many provincial and local governments to organize battery recycling programs. In some provinces it is unlawful to dispose of rechargeable batteries in household trash. Instead, residents must recycle their rechargeable batteries through an established collection network. Selected retail outlets that sell cordless appliances and rechargeable batteries sometimes serve as drop-off points. Manufacturers may also accept batteries for recycling.

All rechargeable batteries should carry a logo like the one above. Below the logo will be a designation for the type of battery ("Ni-Cd" for nickel cadmium or "Pb" for lead).

If there's no recycling program in your area, see if local tool and small-appliance retailers will accept rechargeables for recycling, or hold on to the batteries until a community recycling program has been established.

Appliance repair basics ▪ General troubleshooting

Described here and on the next three pages are the most common problems that afflict appliances—the appliance does not work, it repeatedly trips a circuit breaker, or it shocks the user—as well as possible causes and solutions. This section has been designed to work with the appliance troubleshooting charts that appear in the rest of the book. In addition, the information in these pages will help you diagnose the common problems of nearly any appliance, even those that are not covered in this book.

First steps. Before you begin troubleshooting an appliance, check the owner's manual to make sure you are using the device properly. Don't overlook the obvious. Is the appliance plugged in and turned on? Is it plugged into a switched receptacle whose switch is turned off? Have you been maintaining the appliance properly? Often, a few drops of oil in the right place is all it takes to restore a balky appliance. Once you've determined that an appliance is defective, check its warranty (p.132). If the appliance is still under warranty, let the

manufacturer or an authorized service center do the repair. If you decide to handle a repair yourself, read this chapter carefully first; pay special attention to the pages entitled *Getting started* (p.132), *Disassembly* (p.133), and *Wires, cords, and plugs* (pp.134–135). Then turn to the section of the book devoted to the appliance in question. If you are new to appliance repair, bear in mind that even the most complicated procedure can be broken down into a logical sequence of simpler steps.

Finding problems. Most appliance repairs fall into two broad categories: mechanical and electrical. Jammed gears, a broken drive belt, and other mechanical problems are relatively easy to locate with your eyes or ears. (For more on troubleshooting with your senses, see *Tips from the pros,* p.140.) While some electrical problems, such as dirty switch contacts, may be visible, most are not. Tracking them down often requires a volt-ohm meter (pp.130–131). If you don't own a VOM, buy one and learn how to use it before tackling an appliance repair.

APPLIANCE DOES NOT WORK

Power off at outlet?

1 Test receptacle with a lamp you know works. If lamp doesn't light, receptacle may be faulty (see *Replacing a receptacle,* p.129); more likely, appliance has tripped a breaker or blown a fuse.

2 Check service panel for tripped breaker or blown fuse; reset or replace as needed. If breaker keeps tripping or fuses keep blowing, turn to *Appliance trips breaker,* p.147.

Faulty power cord?

⚡ A defective cord or plug— often the result of pulling on the cord rather than on the plug—can cause an appliance to fail and can create a shock hazard. With the device unplugged, check the cord and plug for damage; try to locate and eliminate the cause of cord wear. To replace a plug, see page 135. To test and replace a cord, see the facing page.

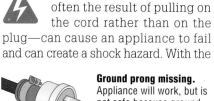

Ground prong missing. Appliance will work, but is not safe because grounding circuit isn't complete. Replace plug.

Bent prongs make it hard to insert plug. They can usually be straightened with pliers, but if prongs are loose, replace plug.

Damaged housing creates a serious shock hazard. Check housing for cracks, chips, or missing insulator. Replace defective plug.

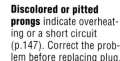

Discolored or pitted prongs indicate overheating or a short circuit (p.147). Correct the problem before replacing plug.

Loose wire may have pulled from terminal. Cut plug off, strip cord to new wire, and reinstall plug.

Frayed cord can expose conductors, usually near plug. Cut off damaged section of cord; reinstall plug.

Worn insulation may expose conductors anywhere along the cord. Replace cord.

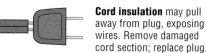

Cord insulation may pull away from plug, exposing wires. Remove damaged cord section; replace plug.

Nicked or cut insulation can be seen by bending cord. Replace cord before conductors are exposed.

APPLIANCE DOES NOT WORK

Servicing 120-volt power cords

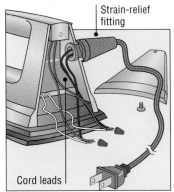

Strain-relief fitting

Cord leads

1 To test cord for continuity, unplug appliance and disassemble it just enough to access cord terminals. Free cord leads by removing wire connectors, by removing leads from screw or plate terminals (see *Making connections*, p.134), or by desoldering (p.136). You may also have to remove a strain-relief fitting (p.170).

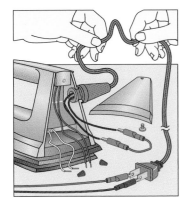

2 Set VOM on RX1 scale. Clip meter probes to plug prongs; clip jumper wire across cord leads. Bend and pull on entire cord. A steady zero-ohms reading means cord is OK. A high or fluctuating reading means cord is faulty and should be replaced with a duplicate. Connect new cord leads to appliance leads (using wire connectors) or to appliance terminals.

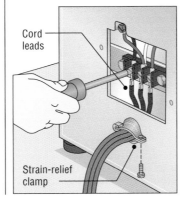

Jumper wire

Female plug

To check heater cord (removable type) for continuity, unplug appliance. Set VOM on RX1 scale. Insert VOM probes into female plug; clip jumper wire across male plug. Bend and pull cord along its entire length. If meter reads zero ohms, cord is good. A high or fluctuating reading indicates an open circuit; replace cord and/or plug.

Servicing 240-volt power cords

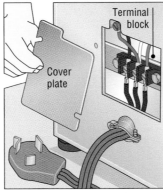

Terminal block

Cover plate

The power cord in 240-volt appliances usually connects to a terminal block at rear of unit. To access terminal block, unplug appliance, then unscrew and remove terminal block cover plate. Check terminals for discoloration, corrosion, and charring. If there are any signs of damage, replace the block. If the block is OK, test the power cord.

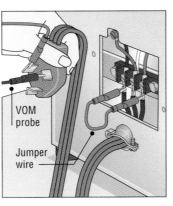

VOM probe

Jumper wire

To test a 240-volt cord for continuity, clip jumper wire across outer cord terminals. Set VOM on RX1 scale; clip meter probes to plug's outer prongs. Bend and pull cord. Repeat test with jumper clipped across middle and one outer terminal; clip VOM to corresponding prongs. Look for steady zero-ohms readings. If readings fluctuate, cord is bad.

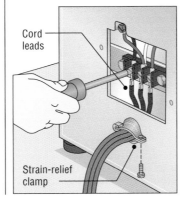

Cord leads

Strain-relief clamp

To replace a 240-volt cord, remove its strain-relief fitting (unscrew a metal clamp-type fitting; use pliers to slightly compress and pull out a plastic fitting that is molded to the cord). Loosen screws that hold cord leads in place, or push out spade lugs from plate terminals (p.134). Remove cord; replace with one having same rating and plug type.

Faulty switch?

Appliance switches vary in complexity and functions. A simple on-off switch is easy to test with a VOM, but more complex switches, like a blender's multiple-position switch, can be trickier to test. A visual check, however, is often enough to detect a fault. Unplug the appliance and disassemble it just enough to access the switch components. Look for and repair any loose or broken wire connections. Clean dirty or pitted contacts. When the switch is closed, the contacts should make a firm connection.

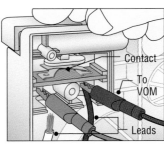

Contact

To VOM

Leads

To test on-off switch, unplug device, access switch, and disconnect one lead from switch. Set VOM on RX1 scale. Clip probes to switch terminals or leads; turn switch on. Zero ohms means switch is OK. High or fluctuating ohms means switch is broken or dirty.

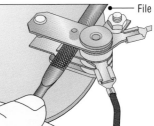

File

Clean switch contacts with an automotive-point file (p.124). Flush away any residue with electrical contact cleaner. Contacts should make firm contact when switch is on. If they don't, it is usually best to replace switch rather than attempting repair.

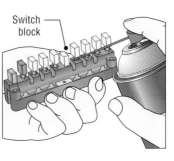

Switch block

Use electrical contact cleaner to clean less accessible switch contacts. In order to work cleaner into switch, operate control buttons as you spray cleaner into apertures.

APPLIANCE DOES NOT WORK

Faulty universal motor?

The power cord (p.145), brushes, commutator, and field coil (stator windings) are the likeliest sources of electrical problems in a universal motor. You can test the field coil and commutator with a volt-ohm meter, but a visual check can also provide many repair clues. (For more on sensory detection of mechanical prob-lems, such as worn bearings and misaligned parts, see *Tips from the pros*, p.140.) Before working on a motor, unplug the appliance. Replace a defective part with a new one from the manufacturer. In the case of an open-circuited field coil or commutator, replace the entire motor or the appliance itself.

Lubricate moving parts following manu-facturer's directions. A drop or two of SAE 10- or 20-weight nondetergent motor oil on end of motor shaft will lubricate bearings. Fill oil cups if motor has them.

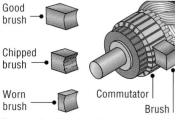

Remove brushes from housing and look for damage or wear. In general, replace brushes when they're shorter than they're wide. Always replace both brushes.

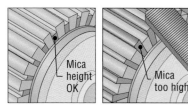

Commutator bars are divided by mica insula-tion. If insulation sticks out, use a small file to flatten it; then use hacksaw blade to grind it below level of bar surface.

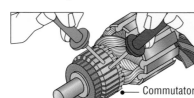

Bar-to-bar commutator check. Set VOM on RX1. Touch probes to adjacent bars all around commutator. All readings should be similar. An unusually high ohms reading sig-nals an open circuit; zero indicates a short.

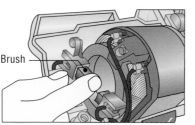

Brush should move freely in housing; spring should press brush firmly against your finger. Replace weak springs; clean housing and brush with contact cleaner.

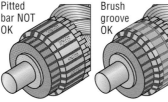

Pitting, discoloration, or rough spots on commutator bars indicate short or open cir-cuit in rotor windings. Wear caused by brush contact is OK, as long as bars aren't pitted.

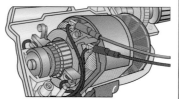

Field coil check. Set VOM on RX1 scale. Clip probes to field coil leads. High ohms or infinity indicates open circuit. The motor in multispeed appliances will have several field coil leads.

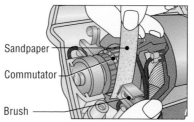

Fitting brushes. If new brushes aren't pre-curved, place 600-grit sandpaper between brush and commutator; apply pressure to brush while turning commutator.

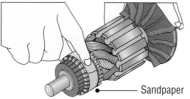

To polish a rough commutator, hold fine sandpaper around it and turn it. Then bur-nish bars with hardwood stick. Replace brushes too (they're a cause of roughness).

Faulty split-phase motor?

Most split-phase motor problems are similar to those in universal motors: worn bearings, a faulty power cord, open-circuited windings. Starting circuitry, how-ever, can create special problems. If the motor hums but won't turn, suspect an open-circuited capacitor (p.139) or a faulty centrifugal switch (p.140). A capac-itor that's shorted can cause a motor to start weakly. If the motor stops after long use or won't start after stalling, suspect a tripped overload protector (p.141).

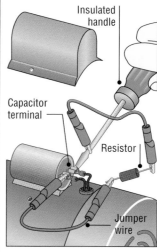

⚡ **Discharging the capacitor** is a criti-cal safety measure before working on a motor. To make a discharging tool, clip a jumper to each lead of a 20,000-ohm, 2-watt *wire-wound* resistor (sold at elec-tronics stores). Clip free end of one jumper to blade of an insulated screwdriver. To dis-charge capacitor, unplug device. Clip free end of sec-ond jumper to one capacitor terminal; touch screwdriver blade to other terminal. If there are three terminals, dis-charge across outer terminals as well as across center and each outer terminal in turn.

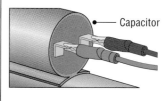

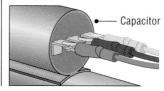

Check discharged capacitor for bulges or leaks; replace if found. Test with VOM on RX100 scale. Clip probes to terminals. Reading should jump toward zero ohms, then drift to high. Reverse probes and test again; look for same reading. Steady zero ohms indicates a short; steady high ohms, an open circuit. If capacitor has three termi-nals, test with one probe touching center terminal and second probe touching each outer terminal in turn.

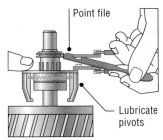

Centrifugal switch (p.140) can stick in open position (motor won't turn) or closed position (motor shuts down soon after starting). Look for dirty contacts or stuck mechanism. Clean contacts with automotive-point file and contact cleaner. Lightly oil pivot points. Replace switch that has burnt terminals.

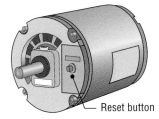

Manual overload protector has a reset button that lets you start a stalled motor (check first for binding parts). If overload protector is internal, turn off appliance, let motor cool (this may take several hours), then restart appliance.

Faulty shaded-pole motor?

Shaded-pole motors seldom break down in normal use, and when they do, it's usually best to replace the entire motor or the appliance itself.

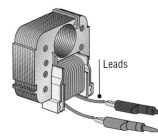

To test a shaded-pole motor for continuity, unplug appliance and disassemble. Set VOM on RX1; clip meter probes to both leads from field coil. Reading of infinity means motor is defective and should be replaced.

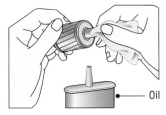

To service a shaded-pole motor, remove rotor from field. Clean dirt and corrosion with electrical contact cleaner. Lubricate shaft with oil and remove excess.

APPLIANCE TRIPS BREAKER

Circuit overloaded?

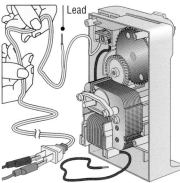

When an appliance trips a breaker or blows a fuse, the circuit is probably overloaded. Trace circuit (see *Correcting circuit overloads,* p.127) and reduce the number of appliances on it. If problem persists, suspect a shorted cord or motor.

Short circuit?

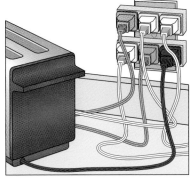

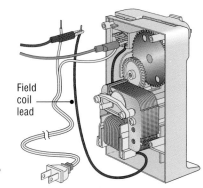

To test cord, unplug appliance and disassemble sufficiently to access cord terminals. Disconnect one cord lead. Set VOM on RX1 scale. Clip VOM to plug prongs. Bend cord. Zero or fluctuating ohms indicates short. Steady high ohms means cord is OK.

To test motor, unplug appliance and disassemble. Set VOM on RX1 scale. Clip VOM probes to each field coil lead. Motor is shorted if meter reads zero ohms. Steady high ohms means motor is OK.

APPLIANCE SHOCKS USER

Ground fault?

A frayed power cord or an electrically live component that touches a metal appliance part can deliver a serious shock. If handling a power cord gives you a shock, the cord is defective; replace it without delay (p.145). A breakdown of wiring insulation can cause a live conductor to touch the metal frame of an appliance. If the appliance is grounded, the resulting short to ground will trip a circuit breaker or blow a fuse. If the device is not grounded, ground-fault, or leakage, current will charge the frame and shock anyone touching the appliance.

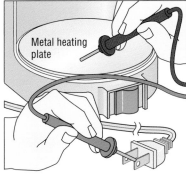

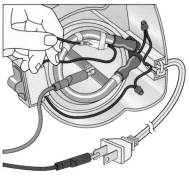

To test for a ground fault, unplug appliance. Set VOM on highest ohms scale (usually RX1000). Touch one VOM probe to metal frame or part; touch second probe first to one plug prong, then to the other. Meter should show infinite resistance. A lower reading indicates a ground fault.

To locate cause of ground fault, unplug and disassemble device; check internal wires for bare spots. Clip a VOM probe to a metal part; clip other probe to plug. Turn switch to *On* or *High;* bend and pull wires. If reading jumps as a wire moves, that wire is grounded; replace it. If you can't find the fault, have appliance professionally serviced.

Solid-state electronic components are often used to monitor or control the operation of an appliance or power tool. When troubleshooting an appliance with electronic components, first eliminate mechanical or electrical parts as the cause of the trouble. If these parts are OK, you can assume that an electronic component is probably at fault.

Digital readouts. Liquid-crystal displays (LCD's) or light-emitting diodes (LED's) are sometimes used to indicate a knob setting or show the time. Check non-working readouts for loose or dirty connections first. Readouts that are easily removed can be replaced if faulty, but it is often more practical to replace the entire circuit board containing the readout.

Diodes, resistors, and capacitors. A diode allows current to flow in one direction only, while resistors limit the amount of current flowing through a circuit. Capacitors store electrical energy, releasing it on demand to provide a momentary burst of extra current (see *For your safety,* p.144). These components are often found on or near switches and motors.

How to test a diode

To test a diode for continuity, unplug the appliance; disconnect one end of the diode. Set a VOM on the RX1 scale (or on the diode function, if any; consult your owner's manual). Probe both ends of the diode; then reverse the probes. If one reading is low and the other infinity, the diode is OK. The same reading in both directions indicates damage. To make sure current flows properly, install a new diode so that its identifying band is on the same end as the original's.

With VOM on RX1, touch probes to both ends of diode.

Reverse probes. One reading should be low, the other infinity.

How to test a resistor

Unplug the appliance; disconnect one end of the resistor. Electronic components are usually soldered in place, so you may have to desolder the connection (p.136). Set a VOM on the RX1 scale (or the next highest scale above the resistor's rating); touch its probes to the resistor's leads. The meter reading should be within 10 percent of the resistor's rating. The reading may rise or fall slowly within this range during the test.

Resistor

Compare meter reading to resistor's rating.

How to test a capacitor

 A capacitor stores electricity after the device to which it is connected has been turned off. Even if the capacitor is a small one, such as those found within some electronic devices, you *must* discharge it before working on the circuit. To discharge a capacitor, see *General troubleshooting,* p.146. To test the capacitor in an electronic device, desolder one end (p.136). Set the VOM on the lowest resistance scale; touch its probes to the capacitor's terminals. The meter should show low resistance, then resistance gradually increasing toward infinity. Reverse the probes; the results should be the same. If the results differ, the capacitor is defective and should be replaced.

Capacitor

Terminal

Discharge and disconnect capacitor; attach VOM probes to terminals.

Reverse probes. Readings on both tests should start low, then rise slowly to infinity.

Reading diodes and resistors

One end of a diode is usually marked with a band indicating the direction of current flow; electricity should enter on the unbanded end. To read a resistor's color code, the bands closest together must be on your left. The first three bands identify the resistor's capacity in ohms: The first two represent single digits; the third indicates the number of zeros that follow the first two numbers (see below). Band four represents an accuracy tolerance: gold indicates +/-5%; silver, +/-10%; no band, +/-20%. A fifth band is sometimes included to indicate the estimated failure rate of the resistor.

Color	Number it represents
Black	0
Brown	1
Red	2
Orange	3
Yellow	4
Green	5
Blue	6
Violet	7
Gray	8
White	9

8 6 00 +/-5%

Resistor

The color bands above indicate a capacity of 8,600 ohms and a tolerance of +/-5%. The lack of a fifth band means that the resistor does not have a failure rating.

Electronic touch-pad controls

Touch pads are sealed switch assemblies. If the entire pad does not work, check the circuit board or pad wiring for faulty connections. If a single button does not work, clean its contacts (if accessible) by rubbing them gently with a pencil eraser and then wiping with a foam swab dipped in alcohol. If the pad still does not work, replace the entire assembly.

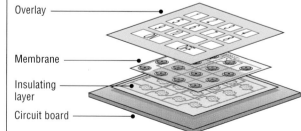

Overlay

Membrane

Insulating layer

Circuit board

Electronic touch pads, such as those found on microwave ovens, are layered assemblies that usually cannot be repaired.

Small appliances

One of the best reasons for repairing a small appliance is the sense of satisfaction you'll gain from seeing it roar back to life. Though it's possible to revive many faulty appliances, not all of them *should* be repaired by their owner. Some are so inexpensive that repair is hardly worth the effort, while others require professional attention.

The appliances on the following pages represent commonly available models with the most popular features. Each troubleshooting chart is keyed to detailed repair sequences, as well as to the *General troubleshooting* section that starts on page 144. Your safety is paramount when working on any electrical appliance. Be sure to follow the safety tips here, as well as those in your owner's manual.

Small appliances ▪ Air cleaners

Poor ventilation can lead to high levels of indoor air pollution, especially in houses that are well sealed to reduce energy loss. If the source of a pollutant such as tobacco smoke or animal dander can't be eliminated, or if a house can't be adequately ventilated, air cleaners can reduce the level of harmful pollutants—primarily smaller airborne particles. No cleaner, however, will remove all pollutants from the air.

There are two main kinds of air cleaners: the mechanical type shown here and the electronic type featured on page 152. Both come in small-room and whole-house models.

In a typical mechanical air cleaner, a blade fan or a squirrel-cage fan draws air through a series of filters, including a prefilter (to remove the largest particles), one or more activated carbon or charcoal filters (to remove smaller odor-causing particles), and/or a type of HEPA (high-efficiency particulate-arresting) filter. Some mechanical units include an ion generator to charge remaining dirt particles, causing them to adhere to room surfaces.

Mechanical air cleaner

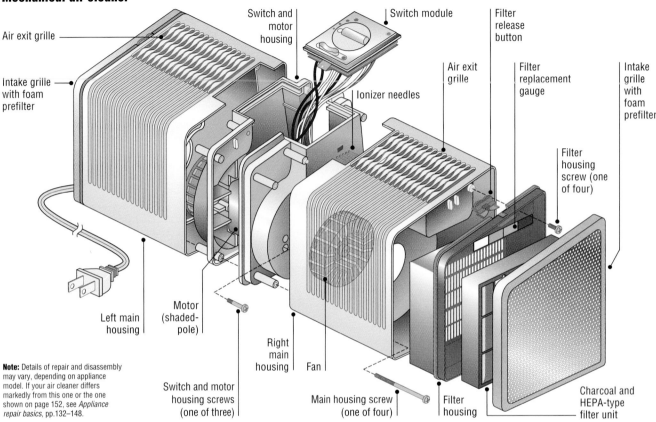

Note: Details of repair and disassembly may vary, depending on appliance model. If your air cleaner differs markedly from this one or the one shown on page 152, see *Appliance repair basics*, pp.132–148.

Disassembly

HEPA-type filter

Foam prefilter

1 Turn off air cleaner and unplug it. Press release buttons to remove intake grilles containing foam prefilters (there's a grille on both sides of cleaner). Pull out successive filters.

Filter housing

2 Remove screws holding filter housing in place. To access fan, remove long screws holding main housing together. Separate halves of main housing.

3 Remove fan by prying or twisting locking ring from end of motor shaft (wear safety goggles). Be careful not to bend ring as you remove it.

4 Remove screws holding switch and motor housing together; pull housing apart to expose motor; switch module will now slide out from channels in switch and motor housing.

Troubleshooting

Problem	CAUSE? / Solution
Air cleaner does not run or runs sluggishly	POWER OFF AT OUTLET? See *General troubleshooting*, p.144.
	FAULTY POWER CORD? See *General troubleshooting*, p.144.
	FAULTY SHADED-POLE MOTOR? See *General troubleshooting*, p.147.
	FILTERS INSERTED INCORRECTLY? Some electronic air cleaners (p.152) have interlock switches that prevent operation unless filters are correctly positioned. Remove filters and reinstall properly. ◇
	FAULTY SWITCH? Inspect and service switch (right). ◆
	FAN LOOSE? Check for a broken fan hub or a loose setscrew on the fan; either one would allow the fan blades to spin freely on the motor shaft. Replace a fan with a broken hub; tighten a setscrew. ◆
	MOTOR SHAFT FROZEN? Attempt to turn fan blades by hand. If motor shaft sticks, lubricate motor bearings (see *Lubricants and lubricating*, p.137). ◆
Air cleaner is noisy	PRECIPITATING CELL DIRTY? If an electronic air cleaner hisses, crackles, or pops excessively (some noise is normal), remove and clean cell (p.152). ◇
	DRY MOTOR BEARINGS? Lubricate bearings (follow manufacturer's directions). ◆
	FAN LOOSE OR OBSTRUCTED? Access fan (*Disassembly*, Step 2) and tighten fan on motor shaft. Remove any obstructions that might be hitting blades. ◇
Air cleaner fails to clean air	UNIT INCORRECTLY SIZED? Check owner's manual for air cleaner capacity, and compare it with room volume. Replace cleaner if necessary. ◇
	CLOGGED OR DIRTY FILTERS? Replace charcoal and HEPA-type filters. Clean foam prefilters (right). To clean precipitating cells, see page 152. ◇
	BLOCKED OR CLOGGED AIR INTAKES? Position inlet and outflow sides of unit away from obstructions like walls, drapes, and large furniture. Vacuum dust and lint from filter covers and air passages. ◇
	BENT COLLECTOR PLATES? *(Electronic cleaners only)* Remove cell and examine plates; they should be flat and uniformly spaced. Have plates repaired professionally, or install new cell (p.152). ◆
	SHORT IN PRECIPITATING CELL? *(Electronic cleaners only)* Test cell (p.152); replace if necessary. ◆ ▪
	BROKEN IONIZER WIRES? *(Electronic cleaners only)* Replace wires (p.152). ◆
Unpleasant odor of ozone in room	AIR CLEANER NEW? Electronic cleaners (p.152) produce small amounts of ozone, especially when new. Level should drop in a few weeks. If odor persists, look for defective collector plate or ionizer wire (see *Air cleaner fails to clean air*, above). Make sure you've removed the plastic cover that the carbon postfilter came in. If problem still persists, have unit professionally serviced. ◇
Air cleaner trips breaker or shocks user	See *General troubleshooting*, p.147.

Degree of difficulty: Simple ◇   Average ◆   Complex ◆   Volt-ohm meter required: ▪

Servicing the switch

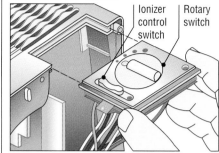

Ionizer control switch   Rotary switch

1 Disassemble cleaner just enough to reach switch module (see facing page); gently pull module from its channels in appliance housing.

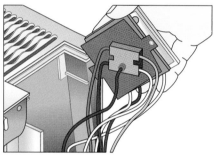

2 Check back of switch module for any loose, broken, or burned wires. Repair or replace as needed (see *Making connections,* pp.134–135). If module looks OK, spray electrical contact cleaner where wires enter rear of rotary switch.

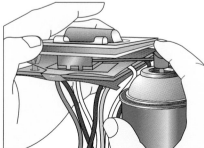

3 Turn module to expose base of ionizer control switch. Spray contact cleaner into openings in base; operate switch several times to work fluid in. Replace entire module if switch is still faulty.

Cleaning the filter

To clean foam-type prefilter, remove intake grille from air cleaner and use a crevice tool to gently vacuum the filter through the grille.

Electronic air cleaners

Unlike mechanical air cleaners, which rely on filters to remove pollutants from the air, electronic air cleaners electrify pollutants to collect them in various ways.

In the electrostatic air cleaner featured on this page, the fan draws air through a prefilter, which removes large particles, and into a pull-out chamber called a precipitating cell. Ionizer wires in the front of the cell create a high-voltage field that gives incoming particles a positive charge; the positively charged particles adhere to negatively charged collector plates at the back of the cell. Once past the cell, the air flows through a carbon postfilter and out of the unit.

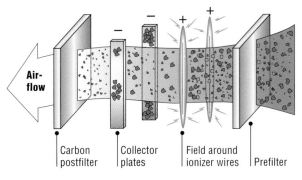

Air-flow

Carbon postfilter | Collector plates | Field around ionizer wires | Prefilter

Servicing the precipitating cell. A dirty or defective cell is a common cause of problems in electronic air cleaners (see *Troubleshooting*, p.151). Clean the cell regularly, following the manufacturer's instructions. To clean the cell shown here, turn off and unplug the air cleaner, remove the top, and pull out the cell. Soak it in a tub of hot soapy water; then rinse it well and let it dry thoroughly. To replace a broken ionizer wire or to test the cell for a short circuit, see far right.

Other electronic cleaners. In an electret air cleaner, a special filter—the electret—is charged with static electricity, causing particles entering the cleaner to cling to the filter. In a negative-ionizing cleaner, charged needles or wires ionize dirt particles. A fan blows these particles into the room, where they are attracted to positively charged surfaces such as walls and furniture (which may become soiled over time).

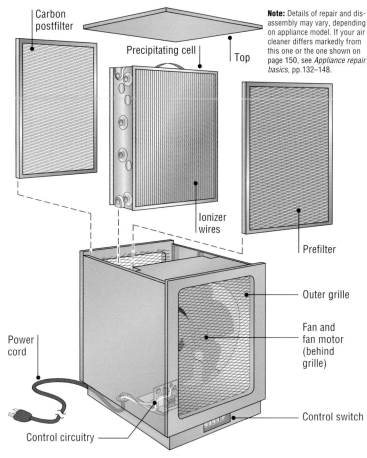

Carbon postfilter

Precipitating cell

Top

Ionizer wires

Prefilter

Outer grille

Fan and fan motor (behind grille)

Power cord

Control circuitry

Control switch

Note: Details of repair and disassembly may vary, depending on appliance model. If your air cleaner differs markedly from this one or the one shown on page 150, see *Appliance repair basics*, pp.132–148.

FOR YOUR SAFETY

Do not operate an electronic air cleaner, or a mechanical cleaner equipped with ionizer needles (p.150), in a room containing oxygen equipment or where combustible gases are present.

Always unplug the power cord before removing air cleaner parts or cleaning the interior surfaces of the cabinet; high-voltage current is present.

Handle a precipitating cell carefully; it contains sharp metal edges and delicate parts. Be particularly careful when handling collector plates and working near the ionizer wires.

To protect yourself from puncture wounds when working on air cleaners that have ion-emitter needles, tape a cardboard "tent" over the needles.

Replacing ionizer wires

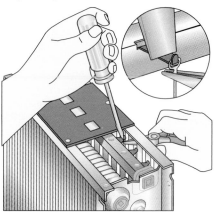

Broken ionizer wire can interfere with unit's operation. To replace wire, unplug unit; pull out precipitating cell. Use needle-nose pliers to unhook wire from spring connector at each end of cell (if necessary, depress connector with screwdriver to free wire). Reverse procedure to install new wire. Use only exact replacement wire from manufacturer.

Testing the cell for a short

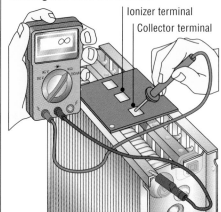

Ionizer terminal

Collector terminal

Remove cell from air cleaner; set VOM on RX1. Clip one VOM probe to cell frame; touch the other probe first to the ionizer terminal (in the middle), then to each of the two outer collector terminals in turn. Infinity readings indicate cell is OK. A lower ohms reading indicates a short circuit; replace the cell.

Blenders

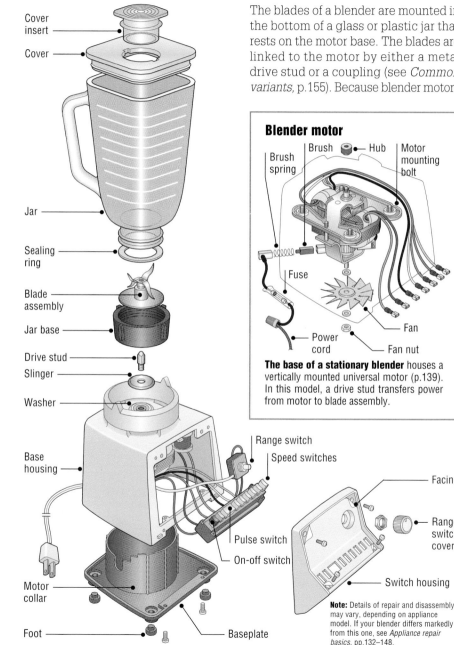

- Cover insert
- Cover
- Jar
- Sealing ring
- Blade assembly
- Jar base
- Drive stud
- Slinger
- Washer
- Base housing
- Motor collar
- Foot
- Range switch
- Speed switches
- Pulse switch
- On-off switch
- Baseplate
- Facing
- Range switch cover
- Switch housing

The blades of a blender are mounted in the bottom of a glass or plastic jar that rests on the motor base. The blades are linked to the motor by either a metal drive stud or a coupling (see *Common variants*, p.155). Because blender motors are designed primarily for speed, not power, they are easily overloaded.

Switches are another trouble spot. Blenders usually have an on-off switch, a row of multispeed switches, a high-low range switch that doubles the number of speeds, and a pulse switch that allows you to run the blender only as long as you press the switch. To avoid blender problems, keep the appliance and its switches clean (see *Use and care*, p.154) and don't overload it.

Blender motor

- Brush
- Brush spring
- Hub
- Motor mounting bolt
- Fuse
- Power cord
- Fan
- Fan nut

The base of a stationary blender houses a vertically mounted universal motor (p.139). In this model, a drive stud transfers power from motor to blade assembly.

Note: Details of repair and disassembly may vary, depending on appliance model. If your blender differs markedly from this one, see *Appliance repair basics*, pp.132–148.

Disassembly

1 Unplug blender; remove jar. Undo screws securing baseplate; then separate baseplate and attached motor collar from base housing.

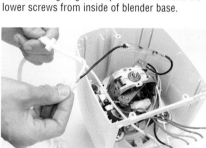

2 To remove switch housing, peel back decorative facing to get at top screws. Remove the lower screws from inside of blender base.

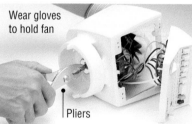

Wear gloves to hold fan

Pliers

3 Hold fan to keep motor shaft from turning as you unscrew drive stud. Remove shield and any washers. Unscrew fan nut to remove fan.

4 Disengage strain relief-fitting (p.170) from housing. Remove wire connector joining the power cord and the lead to the brush housing.

5 Label and disconnect leads from switch block (p.155). Remove motor mounting bolts, and lift out motor if necessary.

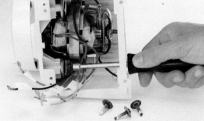

6 To free brushes, remove leads attached to brush housing. Use screwdriver to press lead terminal through slot in housing. Brush spring may pop out.

Small appliances ■ Blenders

Troubleshooting

Problem	CAUSE? / Solution
Motor does not run or runs sluggishly	POWER OFF AT OUTLET? See *General troubleshooting,* p.144.
	FAULTY POWER CORD? See *General troubleshooting,* p.144.
	INTERNAL FUSE BLOWN? Disassemble blender enough to access fuse (*Disassembly,* Step 4, p.153). Test fuse with VOM (facing page) or continuity tester, and replace if defective. ◆
	BLENDER JAMMED? Run blender with and without empty jar in place. If motor runs fast without jar but slows down noticeably when jar is in place, blade assembly may be jammed. Take apart assembly, if possible (see *Common variants,* facing page); clean parts. ◇
	FAULTY MULTISPEED SWITCH? Test and service switch block (facing page); replace if necessary. ◆ ▤
	FAULTY UNIVERSAL MOTOR? See *General troubleshooting,* p.146.
Motor runs but blades do not turn	LOOSE COUPLING? If blender has couplings instead of a drive stud (see *Common variants,* facing page), unplug blender; turn jar and motor couplings by hand. If either one spins freely, its threads may be stripped. Remove coupling and replace. ◇
Motor hums but blades do not turn **CAUTION:** Turn off appliance immediately to avoid damaging motor.	OVERLOADED BLENDER JAR? If you are trying to process large or heavy chunks of food, try a lighter load or a higher speed, or add liquid. ◇
	RESIDUE BUILDUP AROUND BLADE SHAFT? Unplug blender and remove blade assembly. Clean shaft with liquid dishwashing detergent and water (be sure not to leave soapy residue in bearing assembly). ◇
	POOR BRUSH CONTACT? Unplug blender, access motor (*Disassembly,* Step 6, p.153), and service brushes (see *General troubleshooting,* p.146). ◆
Blender operates at some speeds but not at others	FAULTY MULTISPEED SWITCH? Test and service switch block (facing page); replace if necessary. ◆ ▤
	FAULTY PULSE SWITCH? Service along with other switches in main switch block (facing page). Also examine spring that is attached to pulse switch and replace if broken. ◆ ▤
	FAULTY ON-OFF OR HIGH-LOW RANGE SWITCH? If switch is not part of main switch block, access switch opening and terminal posts, if possible, and spray with electrical contact cleaner. ◆
	DEFECTIVE SWITCH WIRING? Unplug blender; remove switch housing from blender base (*Disassembly,* Step 2, p.153). Look for worn or burned switch wires. Cut out damaged section and join ends together with wire connector; if damage is next to terminal, cut off damaged section including terminal and crimp on a new terminal (see *Making connections,* p.134). ◆

Problem	CAUSE? / Solution
Blender makes excessive noise or vibrates excessively	LOOSE OR BENT BLADE ASSEMBLY? Run blender at several speeds without jar. If noise goes away, problem is with the blade assembly. Replace damaged blades and/or tighten loose parts. ◇
	BASE COMPONENTS BROKEN OR LOOSE? Unplug blender and tighten all knobs and screws on exterior of base. If noise persists, remove lower panel of base, tighten all internal fasteners, and lubricate motor bearings (see *Cleaning and lubrication,* p.137). If fan blades are bent, replace them. ◇
	BASE OFF-BALANCE? Restore any missing feet on bottom of blender. ◇
	DRIVE STUD WORN? Remove jar and inspect stud. If its edges are rounded rather than square, it may slip in the drive socket and make noise, particularly when the blender is heavily loaded. Remove stud (*Disassembly,* Step 3, p.153) and replace it. You may have to replace mating socket beneath jar as well. On some blenders you may have to replace the entire blade assembly. ◆
	WORN COUPLINGS? If the blender has rubber couplings instead of a drive stud, check them for wear or damage and replace if necessary (facing page). ◇
Blender leaks	POOR SEAL BETWEEN JAR AND JAR BASE? Remove blade assembly and examine jar and jar base for chips; inspect sealing ring for splits and cracks. Replace jar, jar base, or sealing ring as needed. ◇
	LOOSE BLADE SHAFT? If jar and sealing ring are OK, then blade shaft and/or its bearing is probably worn. Replace the entire blade assembly. ◇
	CRACKED JAR? Fill jar with water to check for leaks; replace faulty jar. ◇
Blender trips breaker or shocks user	See *General troubleshooting,* p.147.

Degree of difficulty: Simple ◇ Average ◆ Complex ◆ Volt-ohm meter required: ▤

USE AND CARE

Place blender on dry, clean surface during use to keep foreign material from being drawn into the motor.

Rest hand on jar cover when using the blender to keep the jar firmly seated.

Clean jar after each use. Fill jar half full with warm water, add liquid detergent, cover, and blend at low speed for 5 seconds. Run blender with clean water to rinse; then run it empty to dry blades. After washing, take out blades and wipe with a cloth to remove residue. *(Be careful—blades are sharp.)*

Clean base with damp sponge. Never immerse base in water or rinse under faucet.

Don't let power cord touch hot surfaces or hang over edge of countertop. Running the blender with a damaged cord is dangerous.

Never store the jar on the blender without seating it properly; accidental starting of the blender could cause severe injury.

Never lift jar until motor has fully stopped; drive stud may be damaged otherwise.

Keep fingers and utensils out of jar while blender is operating.

Servicing the multispeed switch

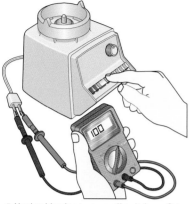

1 Unplug blender; turn on-off switch on. Set VOM on RX1 scale; clip VOM probes to plug prongs. Press one switch at a time and note each reading: low ohms indicates switch is good; reading of infinity indicates a dirty or defective switch.

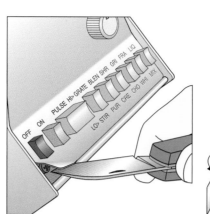

2 Remove switch housing from base housing (*Disassembly*, Step 2, p.153). To remove switch block from switch housing, carefully lift lower corners of decal or facing that surrounds the push buttons; remove lower screws.

3 Spray electrical contact cleaner into push-button slots and into openings and terminals in back of switch block (see *General troubleshooting*, p.145). If cleaning fails, replace switch with a duplicate. Mark wires; use screwdriver to pry wires off.

Testing the fuse

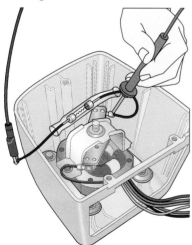

To access fuse, unplug blender and disassemble it enough to remove wire connector joining power cord and lead containing fuse (*Disassembly*, Step 4, p.153). Set VOM on RX1 scale; clip probes to both ends of lead. Replace fuse with duplicate if reading is high.

Common variants: Blade assemblies

In the type of blender featured on page 153, the motor is linked to the blade assembly by means of a drive stud. Such blade assemblies are frequently riveted together and cannot be disassembled. In the type of blender featured at right, the blade assembly can be taken apart. A toothed rubber or metal coupling under the jar engages a rubber or plastic coupling attached to the motor shaft. Inspect the couplings periodically; if their "teeth" are rounded over or broken, the couplings should be replaced—they cannot be repaired. A worn gasket should also be replaced.

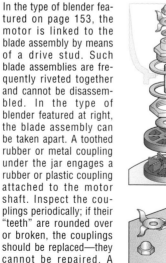

- Cap nut
- Blade
- Spring washer
- Bearing
- Blade shaft
- Gasket
- Jar coupling
- Motor coupling

To remove the jar coupling, hold cap nut with taped pliers, then turn coupling clockwise. To remove motor coupling, hold motor shaft with pliers and unscrew coupling.

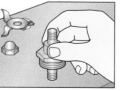

To unjam the blade shaft, disassemble the drive as far as you can; strike shaft against wood block. Lubricate parts with white grease.

Hand-held blenders

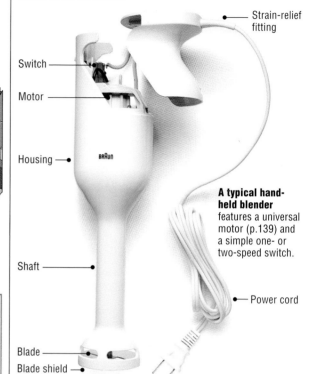

- Strain-relief fitting
- Switch
- Motor
- Housing
- Shaft
- Blade
- Blade shield
- Power cord

A typical hand-held blender features a universal motor (p.139) and a simple one- or two-speed switch.

Hand-held blenders are convenient for blending liquids and soft vegetables, but they lack the power of stationary blenders. Most models can operate only while their on-off switch is pressed, but it is still possible to touch the moving blades accidentally. Use hand-held blenders with care, and keep them out of children's reach.

Avoid standing a hand-held blender upside down during use, even if it has a flat base for the purpose. Liquid running down the motor shaft can enter the housing and damage the motor. Instead, place the blender flat or hang it upright.

To clean the blender, place its shaft in a pan of hot soapy water, run the blender at top speed, then rinse it off. Unplug the blender and wipe the base with a damp cloth. Never immerse or rinse the base in water.

Small appliances ▪ Can openers

Common variants

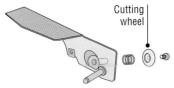

Cutting wheel

A can opener's cutter assembly may include a cutting blade (see right) or a cutting wheel, above. To replace a worn cutting wheel, unplug opener; remove cutter assembly (*Disassembly,* Step 1). Unscrew cutting wheel screw; carefully pull wheel off shaft. Install new wheel with slanted side facing opener. Unlike a wheel, a cutting blade is meant to be dull. Don't sharpen it.

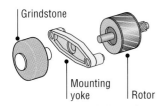

Grindstone

Mounting yoke

Rotor

A knife-sharpening grindstone is a feature of many can openers. A dirty or wobbly stone won't produce sharp edges. To replace a stone, disassemble opener. Unscrew yoke, lift out stone and rotor, and pull them apart. In some models, a C-clip secures stone to rotor shaft.

Disassembly

Note: Details of repair and disassembly may vary, depending on appliance model. If your can opener differs markedly from this one, see *Appliance repair basics,* pp.132–148.

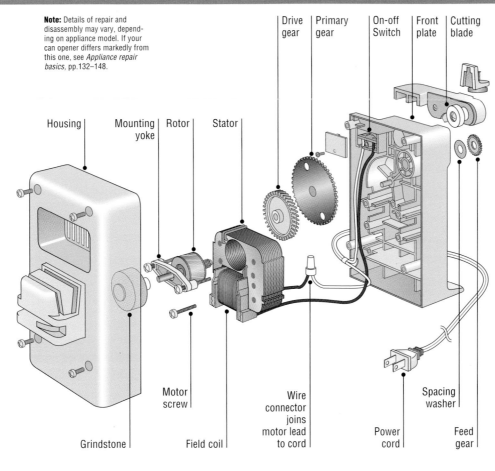

Housing

Mounting yoke

Rotor

Stator

Drive gear

Primary gear

On-off Switch

Front plate

Cutting blade

Grindstone

Motor screw

Field coil

Wire connector joins motor lead to cord

Power cord

Spacing washer

Feed gear

The standard electric can opener has a blade or wheel-type cutter and operates automatically. Unlike nonautomatic electric can openers, whose levers have to be held down to intitiate and maintain the cutting action, automatic openers allow hands-off operation. Once the cutting action begins, an automatic opener keeps on running until the lid is removed, then shuts itself off. In a typical design, the sideways

Lever holds switch closed as can is cut.

Lever rises when cutting is done.

pressure from the can against the cutter locks the cutter assembly lever in the down position, pressing the halves of a leaf switch together and activating a shaded-pole motor. Drive gears linked to the motor turn a toothed feed gear on the outside of the opener. Once the lid is cut all around, the sideways pressure drops, allowing the spring action of the leaf contact to open the switch and shut the motor off.

In addition to countertop models, electric can openers come in under-the-counter and cordless models. Troubleshooting procedures are virtually the same for all electric can openers. The parts most likely to need servicing or replacement are the cutting wheel and the feed gear. Internal gears, often made of plastic to reduce noise, are also prone to wear.

1 Unplug opener. Depending on model, lift or slide off cutter assembly. Unscrew housing screws; remove housing from front plate.

2 Holding grindstone to keep motor from turning, unscrew feed gear with pliers. (Wrap plier jaws with tape to protect gear.)

3 Remove the motor screws with screwdriver or socket wrench, depending on type of screw; then gently lift out motor.

4 With feed gear and motor taken out, internal gears are easy to lift off. In some models, you may have to pry off C-clip securing drive gear.

Troubleshooting

Problem	CAUSE? / Solution
Opener does not run	POWER OFF AT OUTLET? See *General troubleshooting*, p.144.
	OVERLOAD PROTECTOR TRIPPED? If the motor stops after extended knife sharpening or if it won't start again after it has stalled, the motor's internal overload protector has probably tripped. Wait about 10 minutes for the motor to cool, then try starting it again. ◇
	FAULTY POWER CORD? See *General troubleshooting*, p.144.
	FAULTY SWITCH? Test switch (see *General troubleshooting*, p.145) and service it (right) or replace it as needed. ◆ ▣
	FAULTY SHADED-POLE MOTOR? Test the motor (see *General troubleshooting*, p.147). If the motor is defective, replace the opener. ◆ ▣
Opener runs sluggishly	MOTOR, WHEELS, OR GRINDING WHEEL JAMMED? Remove any obstructions in internal gears or field coil (right). ◆
Opener runs but does not cut can	WORN CUTTING WHEEL? If the cutting wheel rotates but does not cut properly, replace it (facing page). Do not attempt to resharpen a worn cutting wheel. And remember that a cutting blade is meant to be dull; don't sharpen it. ◆
	WORN OR DIRTY FEED GEAR? If the feed gear rotates but fails to turn can, its teeth are clogged or worn. Scrape off packed-in residue with a knife or stiff brush. If the problem persists, remove the feed gear (*Disassembly*, Step 2) and replace it. ◇
	TOO MUCH SPACE BETWEEN CUTTER AND FEED GEAR? The cutting blade or wheel should bite cleanly into a can's lid. If the can falls off or rides up while the opener is running, or if the opener stops, shim the feed gear (right). ◆
	WORN OR STRIPPED INTERNAL GEARS? If the motor runs but the feed gear does not turn, one of the internal gears is worn or stripped. Defective internal gears may also make the can opener noisy. Open the appliance and examine the gears for worn teeth and other signs of wear. If either gear is defective, replace both (*Disassembly*, Step 4). Lubricate new parts (p.137). ◆
Opener trips breaker or shocks user	See *General troubleshooting*, p.147.

Degree of difficulty: Simple ◇ Average ◆ Complex ◆
Volt-ohm meter required: ▣

Removing obstructions

An opener that runs sluggishly or hums without turning is probably jammed. Unplug the power cord and remove the housing. Examine the gears and sharpener guides for objects jammed in them. The motor shaft and the primary gear should turn freely. Remove the gears, if necessary, to clean them. Pull out the rotor and clean both ends of the rotor shaft with silver polish or automobile polishing compound (see *General troubleshooting*, p.147). Wipe dirt from the bearings and gears with a clean lint-free cloth. Remove any polish residue, and lubricate the gears, bearings, and motor shaft (p.137) before reassembly.

Servicing the switch

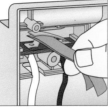

1 Unplug power cord and remove housing (*Disassembly*, Step 1). Unscrew switch cover, if any. Polish switch contacts with an automotive-point file or very fine sandpaper; remove sanding residue with electrical contact cleaner (p.137).

2 Bend leaf contacts of switch with a pair of needle-nose pliers so that firm contact is made between leaves only when switch is pressed.

Replacing the cord

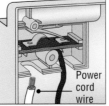

Power cord wire

One power cord wire is soldered to switch's leaf contact; the other (not shown) is joined by wire connector to a lead from the motor. To replace cord, desolder wire attached to leaf contact (p.136) and disconnect wire joined to motor lead.

Shimming the feed gear

Proper spacing between a can opener's cutter and the feed gear ensures that the can will not fall out of the opener or ride up on the feed gear. If either problem

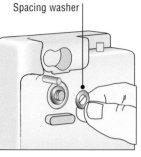

Spacing washer

occurs, try shimming the feed gear. First, unplug the power cord and remove the cutter assembly and housing. Hold the motor shaft steady and unscrew the gear (*Disassembly*, Step 2). Add spacing washers (sold by parts suppliers) to the feed gear shaft one at a time. Replace the feed gear; test the opener after each addition to see if it operates properly.

Small appliances ▪ Clocks

The synchronous motor of an electric clock relies on the 60-cycle-per-second alternations of household current to ensure accurate timekeeping (see *Understanding electricity*, p.126). The motor drives a gear train, which in turn moves the clock's hands. Older clocks may have metal gears, but the gears of new clocks are generally made of plastic to reduce operating noise. Many electric clocks have a lighted dial.

Although electric clocks are relatively trouble-free, occasionally the hands work loose or the gear teeth wear down or break. A loose hand can usually be tightened—simply squeeze its

hub with pliers. If the gears are broken or worn, however, replace the clock. Synchronous motors are dependable, although a power surge can damage their fine windings. Another potential problem: Even a small dent in the rotor cover can jam the rotor itself or allow dust into the mechanism; pry off the cover, if possible, to repair the dent.

Digital clocks. Instead of using gears and levers, digital clocks rely on electronic circuitry that is quite reliable. If a component fails, however, it will probably have to be replaced; most are difficult or impossible to repair (see *Electronic components,* p.148).

Note: Details of repair and disassembly may vary, depending on appliance model. If your clock differs markedly from this one, see *Appliance repair basics,* pp.132–148.

The alarm mechanism

A faulty alarm may sound at the wrong time or not at all. To solve the first problem, pull the alarm lever out and turn the clock hands until the alarm goes off. Unplug the clock, pry off the crystal, and move the alarm hand until it agrees with the time the alarm sounds.

If the alarm doesn't ring or has a poor tone, access the alarm mechanism; spray it with electrical contact cleaner. Make sure the vibrator arm is clean; try bending the arm to adjust the gap between it and the field frame.

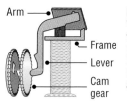

How an alarm works. When an alarm is first set, cam gear presses against lever, which in turn holds vibrator arm above field frame.

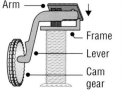

At preset time, cam gear moves outward, allowing vibrator arm to contact field frame. Alarm buzzes as arm vibrates against field frame.

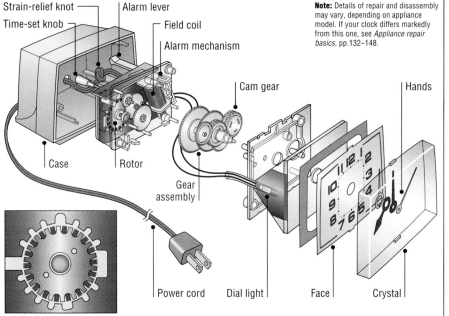

Synchronous motor rotor

Disassembling a clock. Most electric clocks are easy to disassemble. To reach the hands, unplug the clock and pry off the crystal with the blade of a knife. To reach the gears and motor, remove the screws from the case and slide the motor and gears out. If necessary, desolder the power cord leads from the field coil terminals to remove the cord (see *Soldering and desoldering*, p.136).

Troubleshooting

Problem	CAUSE? / Solution
Clock does not run or keeps time poorly	POWER OFF AT OUTLET? See *General troubleshooting*, p.144.
	FAULTY POWER CORD? See *General troubleshooting*, p.144.
	FIELD COIL FAULTY? Unplug clock. To test coil, set VOM on RX100 scale; touch probes to motor terminals. If meter reads between 500 and 1,000 ohms, motor is OK. Higher reading means coil is bad. Replace motor or entire clock. ◆ ▪
	ROTOR OBSTRUCTED OR BROKEN? Unplug clock. Access motor and remove any dirt or lint obstructing rotor. Check rotor cover for dents and proper alignment. If no obstructions are evident, remove motor and set it on an insulated surface with the small pinion gear facing up. Plug in clock. If pinion gear turns slowly, unit is OK. If gear does not turn, replace motor or clock. **CAUTION:** Do not touch motor while clock is plugged in. ◆
	DAMAGED OR BROKEN GEARS? Unplug and disassemble clock to access gears (left). Examine mechanism closely for bent, worn, or broken gears. Although you may be able to straighten bent metal gears with needle-nose pliers, replace clock if gears are worn or broken. If gears look OK, turn time-set knob at rear of clock; clock hands and gears should move freely. If they don't, spray gears with electrical contact cleaner and turn time-set shaft to help cleaner penetrate. Lubricate rotor shaft and gears with light machine oil before reassembling. ◇
Clock is noisy	LOOSE PARTS? Secure a rattling crystal with a drop of clear silicone adhesive. If movement is noisy, unplug clock and tighten motor mounting screws. ◇
	ROTOR SHAFT DRY? Often, a noisy rotor unit can be silenced by applying a drop of light oil at the point where the rotor shaft exits the housing. ◆
Clock trips breaker or shocks user	See *General troubleshooting*, p.147.

Degree of difficulty: Simple ◇   Average ◆   Complex ◆   Volt-ohm meter required: ▪

Coffeemakers / drip

Drip coffeemakers work by passing hot water through ground coffee beans contained in a disposable paper filter or a reusable mesh filter. In a pump-type drip coffeemaker—by far the most common kind—water heated in the base is forced to the top of the appliance, where it is spread over the coffee grounds. Displacement and gravity-feed drip coffeemakers work somewhat differently (p.160).

The heating element in most newer coffeemakers also automatically keeps the brewed coffee hot. Older coffeemakers may have a separate keep-warm element that must be switched on manually.

The most common problem with drip coffeemakers is the accumulation of mineral deposits in the water passages. These deposits interfere with proper operation and can affect the coffee's taste. Regular cleaning (p.161) will extend the useful life of the appliance.

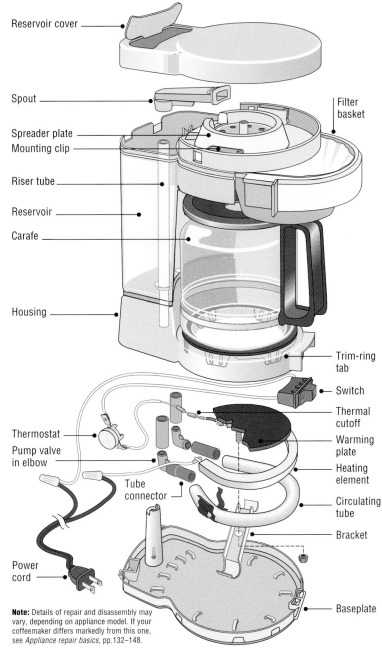

Reservoir cover
Spout
Spreader plate
Mounting clip
Riser tube
Reservoir
Carafe
Housing
Filter basket
Trim-ring tab
Switch
Thermal cutoff
Warming plate
Heating element
Circulating tube
Bracket
Baseplate
Thermostat
Pump valve in elbow
Tube connector
Power cord

Note: Details of repair and disassembly may vary, depending on appliance model. If your coffeemaker differs markedly from this one, see *Appliance repair basics*, pp.132–148.

Disassembly

1 Unplug coffeemaker; remove carafe and filter basket. Unscrew baseplate, and gently pry it away from housing with a flat-bladed screwdriver.

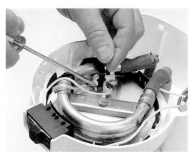

2 Pull thermostat away from heating element by prying up mounting bracket with screwdriver. Remove thermostat leads only when removing or testing faulty thermostat.

3 Pull tube connectors from ends of circulating tube. Do not remove them from elbows unless replacement is called for.

4 Remove leads from heating element; lift switch out of housing. To remove heating assembly (warming plate, element, and circulating tube), squeeze trim-ring tabs inward and down with both hands.

Small appliances ▪ Coffeemakers / drip

Troubleshooting

Problem	CAUSE? / Solution
Hot water does not flow from drip tube	POWER OFF AT OUTLET? See *General troubleshooting*, p.144.
	FAULTY POWER CORD? See *General troubleshooting*, p.144.
	WATER PASSAGES CLOGGED? Clogging is usually the result of mineral accumulation and is most common in regions with hard water. Clean coffeemaker frequently (see *Use and care*, facing page). ◇
	TIMER DEFECTIVE? Some coffeemakers incorporate an analog or digital clock that turns the coffeemaker on at a preset time. To see if an analog clock is working properly, remove it from the coffeemaker and refer to *Clocks*, p.158; for information about digital clocks, see *Electronic components*, p.148. ◆ ▨
	THERMOSTAT FAULTY? Open thermostat prevents brewing. Test thermostat (facing page); replace if faulty. ◆ ▨
	PUMP VALVE JAMMED OR BROKEN? In pump-type coffeemakers, water will not rise through the fill tube if the pump valve is broken or stuck. Unplug coffeemaker and access pump (*Disassembly*, p.159). If the pump is sealed, as it is in newer models (p.159), replace it. If the pump valve is accessible, try cleaning it (facing page). ◆
	THERMAL CUTOFF TRIPPED? If coffeemaker overheats, cutoff will open circuit. Test with VOM (facing page). Locate cause of overheating and repair it; then replace cutoff (if unit has two cutoffs, test and replace both). ◆ ▨
	BREWING SWITCH BROKEN? If coffeemaker has a main brewing switch, unplug and disassemble coffeemaker and test switch with VOM (facing page). Replace faulty switch. (Coffeemaker switches are sometimes sealed units that cannot be serviced. Check with manufacturer for availablity of replacement switch.) ◆ ▨
	HEATING ASSEMBLY FAULTY? Unplug and disassemble coffeemaker. Test heating element with VOM (facing page). On some models a faulty element can be replaced separately, but in most cases you'll have to replace the entire heating assembly, which also includes the circulating tube and warming plate. ◆ ▨
Brewed coffee does not keep warm	AUTO SHUTOFF ENGAGED? Some coffeemakers contain a safety circuit that automatically cuts power to the keep-warm element after about 2 hr. Check owner's manual for advice on how to reset the circuit. ◆
	KEEP-WARM SWITCH FAULTY? If coffeemaker has a keep-warm switch, unplug and disassemble coffeemaker; test the switch with VOM (facing page). If switch is faulty, replace it. ◆ ▨
	KEEP-WARM ELEMENT FAULTY? Disassemble coffeemaker and test element with VOM (facing page). Replace element or entire heating assembly if faulty. ◆ ▨
Coffeemaker sputters, leaks, or steams	LEAK IN TUBE CONNECTORS OR SEALS? Leaks in pump-type coffeemakers are often due to faulty tube connectors. Unplug appliance, remove baseplate (*Disassembly*, Step 1, p.159), and fill reservoir with water. If water leaks from an elbow, clean mating surfaces before replacing it. If water leaks from a tube connector, replace tube *and* mating elbow to ensure a good fit. Under-cabinet coffeemakers may leak around reservoir seals; replace if necessary. ◆
	WATER PASSAGES CLOGGED? Clean coffeemaker (see *Use and care*, facing page). ◆
Coffee not to taste	SPREADER PLATE DAMAGED OR CLOGGED? Most coffeemakers have a plastic plate above the basket which prevents the water from dripping over coffee grounds at only one point. A damaged or clogged plate can result in weak coffee. Unclog plate with toothpick (facing page) or replace it (it usually unscrews or snaps out). A loose spreader plate can also cause coffee basket to overflow, especially with displacement-type coffeemakers. ◇
Unit trips breaker or shocks user	See *General troubleshooting*, p.147.

Degree of difficulty: Simple ◇   Average ◆   Complex ◆ Volt-ohm meter required: ▨

Other drip coffeemakers

The first drip coffeemakers were simple units that relied on gravity to drip heated water over ground coffee. Although they're no longer widely sold, many of these gravity-feed coffeemakers are still in service. Like other drip coffeemakers, gravity-feed units require regular cleaning to prevent minerals from clogging the water passages.

Displacement-type coffeemakers for home use are small versions of drip coffeemakers often found in restaurants. To clean the unit, scrape the spreader plate and water inlet tube with a special tool supplied by the manufacturer.

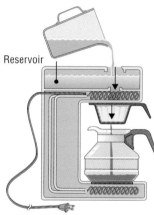

Gravity-feed coffeemaker heats cold water in reservoir located above carafe. When heated, the water drips through a container holding a filter and ground coffee. This type of coffeemaker has the same basic components as the pump type; its keep-warm element, however, is always separate from the main element. Disassembly (p.159) is similar.

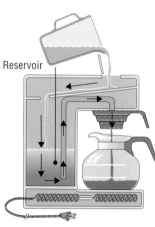

Displacement coffeemaker maintains heated water at all times in a reservoir. Cold water poured into the coffeemaker from above displaces the hot water, pushing it up a tube and over the ground coffee. While this is happening, the newly added cold water is heated and held until needed. The appliance must be left on all the time.

Servicing the main brewing switch

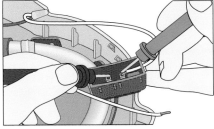

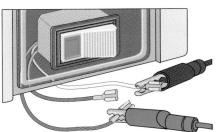

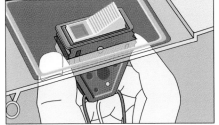

To test switch, unplug coffeemaker; remove baseplate (*Disassembly,* Step 1, p.159). Disconnect one switch lead; set VOM on RX1 scale. Turn on switch; touch VOM probes to both leads. Zero ohms reading means switch is OK.

Lighted brewing switch found on many coffeemakers has three or four leads instead of two. Test as you would an unlighted switch, touching VOM probes to two leads at a time. Zero ohms reading for one pair of leads means switch is OK.

Switch case on some coffeemakers may be locked into place behind the coffeemaker's housing. To remove, compress spring clamps with your fingers and push switch through opening.

Testing the heating element

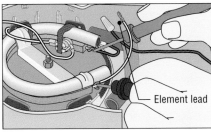

Element lead

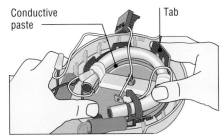

Conductive paste — Tab

Access heating element (*Disassembly,* Step 1, p.159); disconnect one element lead. Set VOM on RX1 scale and touch probes to element terminals. Element is OK if meter reads 100 to 300 ohms.

To replace a faulty element, remove entire heating assembly (*Disassembly,* Step 4, p.159). Conductive paste between element and plate will be on replacement unit as well.

Testing the thermostat

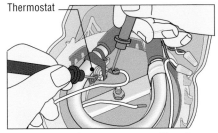

Thermostat

Thermostat regulates temperature of brewing water. To test it, remove one lead, set VOM on RX1, and touch probes to both terminals. Reading of zero ohms means thermostat is OK.

Testing a thermal cutoff

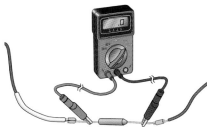

A thermal cutoff (also called a cutout or link) opens a circuit if it senses excessive temperature. To test, remove protective sleeve; set VOM on RX1 scale, and place probes as shown. If meter reads zero, cutoff is OK; replace a tripped or faulty cutoff.

Testing the keep-warm system

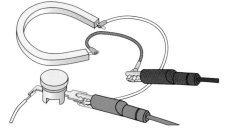

If coffeemaker has keep-warm switch and element, test switch as you would main brewing switch (above). To test element, disconnect a terminal. Set VOM on RX1 scale; touch probes to both terminals. VOM should read 100 to 300 ohms.

Cleaning the spreader plate

A clogged spreader plate causes water to drip over coffee grounds unevenly, resulting in weak coffee. Upend coffeemaker and unclog plate with a toothpick. If that doesn't work, replace plate.

Cleaning a pump valve

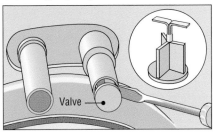

Valve

If stuck valve on older pump-type coffeemaker keeps water from flowing, carefully pry it from tube; clean it thoroughly (see *Use and care,* above). Valve should move easily when pushed up and down. If valve still sticks after cleaning, replace it.

Small appliances ▪ Coffeemakers / percolator

In a percolator, cold water heated in the bottom of the pot rises up the pump tube and out over a spreader plate. From there the water drips over the coffee grounds and back into the pot. As the cycle is repeated, the brew eventually reaches the desired strength. A thermostat then turns off the main heating element and turns on a warming element to keep the coffee heated.

Standard percolators are easily repaired (as are percolator urns used to brew large quantities of coffee), but don't try to fix the inner workings of an immersible percolator—its electrical components are sealed in a watertight base assembly that cannot be opened without damaging the seals. Other problems, such as a leaky handle, can be fixed the same way in both immersible and standard percolators.

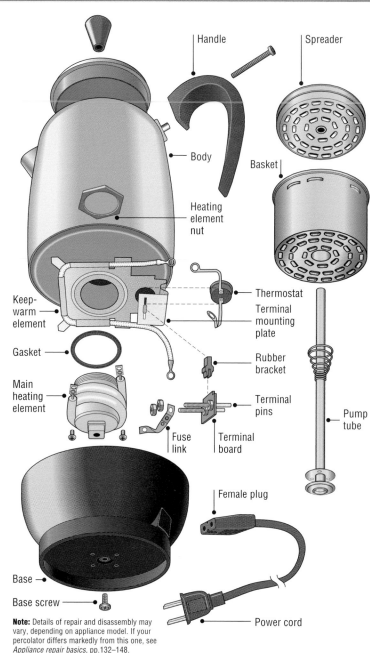

Handle

Spreader

Body

Basket

Heating element nut

Keep-warm element

Gasket

Main heating element

Thermostat

Terminal mounting plate

Rubber bracket

Terminal pins

Fuse link

Terminal board

Pump tube

Base

Base screw

Female plug

Power cord

Note: Details of repair and disassembly may vary, depending on appliance model. If your percolator differs markedly from this one, see *Appliance repair basics*, pp.132–148.

Disassembly

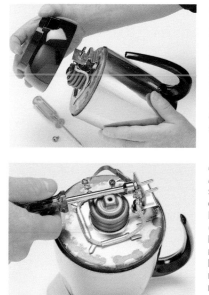

1 Unplug percolator; remove basket assembly; then remove screw in center of base. Pull base away from pot. Some models have a two-piece base rather than the one-piece assembly shown.

2 Remove nuts holding thermostat, keep-warm element, and fuse link to terminal pins (don't remove nuts holding pins to terminal board). Lift board away from rubber bracket; remove bracket.

3 To free keep-warm element and thermostat, remove screw from main heating element terminal. Lift off thermostat. To remove keep-warm element, pry up tabs holding it in place and slide it around heating element.

4 Large nut inside pot holds heating element in place. Use pliers or socket wrench to remove nut (keep element from turning with a second wrench). When reassembling, make sure the gasket is in place and the nut is tight.

Troubleshooting

Problem	CAUSE? / Solution
Coffeemaker does not heat	POWER OFF AT OUTLET? See *General troubleshooting*, p.144.
	FAULTY POWER CORD? See *General troubleshooting*, p.144.
	FUSE LINK BROKEN? If the percolator overheats, a solder connection on the fuse link will melt, breaking the circuit. A broken fuse link is readily visible, and should be replaced. ◆
	THERMOSTAT FAULTY? Unplug percolator and remove base. Be sure bottom of thermostat is touching body of percolator; then check for open circuit (far right). If the percolator has a brew selector, set it on *Strong* before making test. Replace a faulty thermostat with an exact duplicate. ◆ ▣
	MAIN HEATING ELEMENT BROKEN? Unplug percolator and remove base. Check element for open circuit (far right). Replace faulty element. (*Note:* A percolator heating element should be tightly screwed in place and can be difficult to remove; if you can't remove the element, have an authorized service center replace it.) ◆ ▣
Water heats but does not percolate	PUMP TUBE CLOGGED? If the pump tube is OK, its washer will rattle when you shake the tube. If it doesn't rattle, clean the pump tube (right) or replace it. The pump-tube flanges can also become pitted. To fix moderate pitting, rotate flanges and washer against medium-grit sandpaper (to clean facing sides of washer and bottom flange, insert sandpaper between them, then rotate pump tube). ◇
Coffee is too weak	WARM WATER USED TO FILL PERCOLATOR? Percolators should be filled with cold water (between 40°F/4°C and 50°F/10°C) to work properly. Test the temperature of your water with a kitchen thermometer. ◇
	TOO MUCH COFFEE? If basket contains an excess of grounds, water won't pass through them properly. Check owner's manual for right amount of grounds to use. ◇
	BASKET CLOGGED? Hold basket up to light. If holes are clogged, clean them (right) and rinse basket before operating percolator again. ◇
	PUMP TUBE PARTIALLY CLOGGED? Clean or replace it (right). ◇
	THERMOSTAT OUT OF ADJUSTMENT? If the percolator won't brew to your taste even after you adjust the brew selector (if any), the thermostat is out of adjustment and should be replaced. A percolator thermostat cannot be readjusted. ◆
Coffee is too strong	PERCOLATION LASTS TOO LONG? If brewing takes an unusually long time, the thermostat is broken or out of adjustment and should be replaced. ◆
	COFFEEMAKER REPERCOLATES? If percolating stops as it should but begins again a few minutes later, the keep-warm element is probably faulty. Unplug percolator, remove base, and take out keep-warm element (*Disassembly*, Step 3). Install new element and test percolator. ◆
Coffeemaker trips breaker or shocks user	See *General troubleshooting*, p.147.

Degree of difficulty: Simple ◇   Average ◆   Complex ◆   Volt-ohm meter required: ▣

Cleaning the pump tube and basket

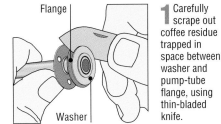

Flange
Washer

1 Carefully scrape out coffee residue trapped in space between washer and pump-tube flange, using thin-bladed knife.

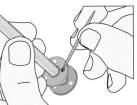

2 Remove debris from holes in pump-tube flanges with a needle or toothpick.

Unclog holes in basket by poking out residue with a needle or toothpick.

Cleaning terminals

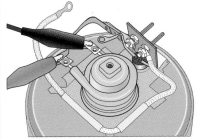

Terminal pins

Clean internal terminals with emery cloth, and spray with electrical contact cleaner (p.124). Tighten and loosen screws several times to work cleaner in. Clean terminal pins with emery cloth.

Testing for open circuits

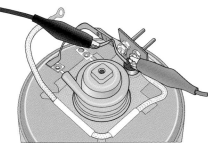

To test thermostat, disconnect one thermostat terminal. Set brew selector, if any, to *Strong;* set VOM on RX1 scale. Touch probes to both terminals. If reading is zero, thermostat is OK.

To test main heating element, move probes to element terminals after testing thermostat. Set VOM on RX1 scale; if element is OK, meter will read 10 to 35 ohms. Replace faulty element.

Common variant: Handles

The handles on some percolators are attached with one or two bolts that run through the pot. If percolator leaks near handle, remove nuts and replace gasket beneath each.

163

Espresso is made by forcing hot water under high pressure through finely ground coffee. The mark of well-brewed espresso is a layer of brownish foam, called *crema,* floating on top of the coffee itself. Crema consists mainly of delicate coffee oils and forms only

under ideal brewing conditions that not all household espresso makers can achieve. Models with pumps generally do the best job but are costly. Models that operate by steam pressure, like the one featured here, perform reasonably well and are moderately priced.

Many espresso makers include a steam nozzle or a more elaborate frother for making cappuccino and caffè latte. Cappuccino is espresso topped with steam-frothed milk; latte is made by mixing steam-heated milk with espresso.

How it works. An electric steam-pressure espresso maker heats water in a small boiler controlled by a thermostat. When steam forms, a brew-steam switch is opened manually to direct pressurized water through coffee grounds contained in the filter basket. The same switch also conducts steam through the steam nozzle (or frother) and into a frothing pitcher.

Because espresso makers operate under pressure, they should not be disassembled completely except by a professional. Be sure to check for a warning label beneath the appliance (see *For your safety,* p.159) before opening the case to check the electrical sytem. **CAUTION:** To avoid burns, don't touch metal parts, especially the filter basket assembly and the steam tube, for at least 15 minutes after turning off an espresso maker. To avoid steam burns, never open the boiler lid or remove the filter basket assembly while the appliance is still warm.

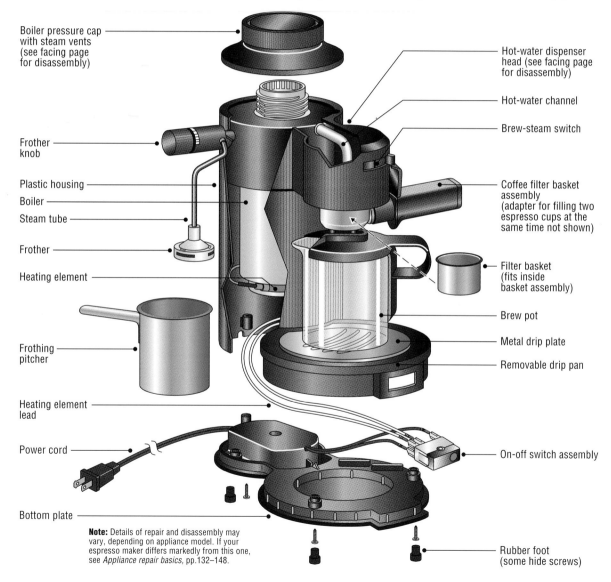

Boiler pressure cap with steam vents (see facing page for disassembly)

Frother knob

Plastic housing
Boiler
Steam tube

Frother

Heating element

Frothing pitcher

Heating element lead

Power cord

Bottom plate

Note: Details of repair and disassembly may vary, depending on appliance model. If your espresso maker differs markedly from this one, see *Appliance repair basics,* pp.132–148.

Hot-water dispenser head (see facing page for disassembly)

Hot-water channel

Brew-steam switch

Coffee filter basket assembly (adapter for filling two espresso cups at the same time not shown)

Filter basket (fits inside basket assembly)

Brew pot

Metal drip plate

Removable drip pan

On-off switch assembly

Rubber foot (some hide screws)

USE AND CARE

Clean espresso maker after each use by rinsing or washing filter basket parts and steam nozzle. To clean frother assembly, allow steam to escape into a water-filled frothing pitcher for a few seconds after use, then wipe tube and frother with damp cloth to remove milk film before it hardens. Never immerse the appliance in water.

Remove mineral deposits from inner channels if coffee is made with hard water. Remove filter screen from hot-water dispenser head; fill boiler with equal parts distilled water and white vinegar (or as specified in your owner's manual), then brew. Collect solution in brew pot or pitcher. Repeat two or three times with plain distilled water to flush. Reinstall the screen.

Prolong gasket life by removing filter basket assembly and loosening boiler cap when espresso maker is not in use.

Use proper coffee grind, about the texture of table salt, for best results. If grind is too coarse, brew will be thin and weak; if grind is too fine, coffee will taste bitter or burned.

Troubleshooting

Problem	CAUSE? / Solution
Espresso maker does not work	POWER OFF AT OUTLET? See *General troubleshooting*, p.144.
	FAULTY POWER CORD? See *General troubleshooting*, p.144.
	FAULTY SWITCH, HEATING ELEMENT, THERMOSTAT, OR FUSE? See *Checking the electrical system*, right. ◆ ▩
No coffee drips from filter cup	NO WATER IN BOILER? Unplug unit; allow it to cool *completely*. Remove cap; add water to boiler. ◇
	GROUNDS TOO FINE OR TAMPED TOO HARD? Use proper grind (see *Use and care*, facing page). Tamp grounds once, gently. ◇
Coffee comes out quickly and is weak	GROUNDS TOO COARSE? Use proper grind (see *Use and care*, facing page). ◇
	COFFEE OVEREXTRACTED? Use correct amount of water (¼ cup per 2 tbsp. coffee). ◇
Coffee spurts from around filter cup	COFFEE GROUNDS ON FILTER CUP RIM? Turn off unit; allow to cool. Inspect and clean filter cup. ◇
	FILTER BASKET ASSEMBLY SEATED INCORRECTLY? Turn off unit; allow it to cool. Loosen and refasten filter basket assembly firmly in locking ring; it should seat completely. ◇
	TOO MUCH COFFEE, OR COFFEE GROUND TOO FINE OR TAMPED TOO HARD? Use the correct amount of espresso-grind coffee (2 tbsp. per ¼ cup of water). Avoid overfilling filter cup; tamp coffee only once, gently. ◇
	DISPENSER-HEAD GASKET DAMAGED? Remove gasket; replace if necessary (right). ◇
Steam escapes from beneath pressure cap	CAP LOOSE? Minor steam escaping is normal on some units. With others, unplug unit; allow it to cool. Remove cap; clean threads; inspect for damage. Retighten cap firmly by hand. ◇
	PRESSURE-CAP GASKET DAMAGED, OR SAFETY PLUG OPEN? Inspect gasket and plug (right), especially if steam escapes despite tightening cap. Replace gasket if hardened or worn; replace cap if safety plug has loosened or popped out. ◇
Coffee not hot	HEATING ELEMENT OR THERMOSTAT FAULTY? See *Checking the electrical system* (right). Professional repair may be required. ◆ ▩
Unit makes little or no steam	STEAM TUBE OR FROTHER CLOGGED? Turn unit off and let cool. Disassemble and clean frother (right). Clean steam tube with care, using pipe cleaner. ◇
Unit trips breaker or shocks user	See *General troubleshooting*, p.147.

Degree of difficulty: Simple ◇ Average ◆ Complex ◆
Volt-ohm meter required: ▩

Checking the electrical system

Systems vary, but all espresso makers have an on-off switch, a heating element, a thermostat, and a fuse. Most wiring is accessible when the appliance baseplate is removed (see *For your safety*, p.159). If the main electrical components test OK yet problems persist, other wiring may be at fault; have the appliance checked by an authorized service center.

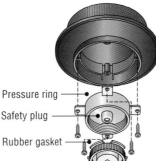

Boiler — Heating element — On-off switch

Thermostat — Fuse — Power lead

To test the on-off switch (usually lighted), the heating element, and the thermostat, see page 161. Test the fuse just as you would a thermal cutoff (p.161).

Servicing the pressure cap

A pressure cap must seal perfectly to contain steam pressure inside the boiler. Inspect the gasket often, and replace it if it is worn or hardened. If the safety plug has "popped" due to excess pressure, replace the cap.

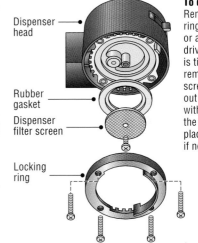

Pressure ring

Safety plug

Rubber gasket

To disassemble: Gently pry gasket out with flat-bladed screwdriver; then remove screws from pressure ring. With ring out, inspect cap for cracks; replace it if any are found.

Servicing the hot-water dispenser head

Pressurized hot water flows through the dispenser head, usually keeping the parts clean. The gasket, however, should be checked periodically; replace it with a new one if it is hard, worn, or damaged.

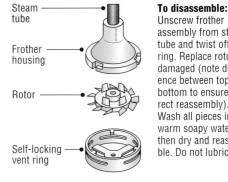

Dispenser head

Rubber gasket

Dispenser filter screen

Locking ring

To disassemble: Remove locking ring with stubby or angled screwdriver (clearance is tight); then remove the filter screen and pry out the gasket with care. Wash the parts; replace the gasket if necessary.

Servicing the frother

Some espresso makers have only a simple steam tube with no moving parts; others have elaborate frothers with rotors that spin under steam pressure. Clean either type after each use by running it briefly in a container of water.

Steam tube

Frother housing

Rotor

Self-locking vent ring

To disassemble: Unscrew frother assembly from steam tube and twist off vent ring. Replace rotor if damaged (note difference between top and bottom to ensure correct reassembly). Wash all pieces in warm soapy water; then dry and reassemble. Do not lubricate.

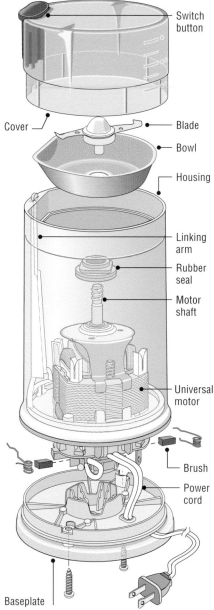

Switch
button

Cover

Blade

Bowl

Housing

Linking
arm

Rubber
seal

Motor
shaft

Universal
motor

Brush

Power
cord

Baseplate

Note: Details of repair and disassembly may vary, depending on appliance model. If your grinder differs markedly from this one, see *Appliance repair basics*, pp.132–148.

Unlike a coffee mill, which pulverizes coffee beans between grinding wheels, a coffee grinder actually chops the beans with a spinning blade. The appliance can also chop nuts, herbs, and spices, although frequent grinding of unusually hard spices may cause the grinder to wear out prematurely. If you store coffee beans in the freezer, let them warm to room temperature before grinding; they will grind more evenly and with less stress to the motor.

Grinders typically have a single-speed switch that can easily become clogged by coffee grounds. Dull blades, also common, may cause you to grind beans too long and overheat the motor. Blades cannot be resharpened, but on many models they can be replaced.

For safety, the on-off switch works only with the grinder's cover in place. Pushing the switch button depresses a plastic linking arm, which then closes switch contacts inside the grinder.

Troubleshooting

Problem	CAUSE? / Solution
Grinder does not run	POWER OFF AT OUTLET? See *General troubleshooting*, p.144.
	FAULTY POWER CORD? See *General troubleshooting*, p.144.
	BRUSHES WORN? Disconnect grinder, remove motor, and replace brushes if worn or damaged (see *General troubleshooting*, p.146). ◆
	THERMAL LIMITER BURNED OUT? The circuitry of some grinders includes a thermal limiter, which acts like a fuse to protect the motor from overheating. The limiter is usually connected to wiring near the motor and is housed in a flexible plastic sleeve. If the limiter burns out, replace it. Desolder or disconnect limiter, then take it to a service center to ensure correct replacement; limiters are temperature rated and must be replaced with exact duplicates. ◆
	MOTOR SHAFT FROZEN? Unplug and disassemble grinder. Clean shaft and lubricate with 1 or 2 drops of lightweight machine oil at each bearing point; rotate shaft several times by hand to distribute oil. ◆
Grinder runs intermittently or doesn't stop	SWITCH CLOGGED OR DAMAGED? Unplug grinder and brush grounds from switch. Depress switch several times with toothpick. If problem persists, disassemble grinder and inspect linkage for breaks; replace if necessary. If linking arm has slipped out of its mounting, reposition it. If grounds are found inside the grinder, seal may be faulty; replace it. ◆
Grinder vibrates	BLADE BENT? Inspect blade; replace if damaged or dull. ◇
	MOTOR BEARING WORN? Unplug grinder and remove access plate. Bearing is bad if motor shaft moves when pushed back and forth; replace grinder. ◇
Grinder trips breaker or shocks user	See *General troubleshooting*, p.147.

Degree of difficulty: Simple ◇   Average ◆   Complex ◆   Volt-ohm meter required: ◼

Disassembly

1 Unplug grinder. Remove screws underneath to free baseplate. Remove blade by gripping it with a towel while turning end of motor shaft counterclockwise with a screwdriver.

Strain
relief

2 The linking arm fits between motor and housing. Release small clip holding arm to lip of housing by pushing clip through its slot with a screwdriver; then pull motor out.

USE AND CARE

Unplug power cord and wait for blade to come to a complete stop before reaching into bowl for any reason.

Wipe blade and bowl after each use (be careful; blade is sharp). Do not immerse body of grinder in water.

Never run grinder when bowl is empty; the blade may spin too fast and damage the motor.

Do not operate grinder for more than 30 seconds at a time, or motor may overheat. Total running time for a 5-minute period should not exceed 1 minute.

Use pulse action to process beans. To pulse, release control switch every few seconds and press again immediately.

Convection ovens

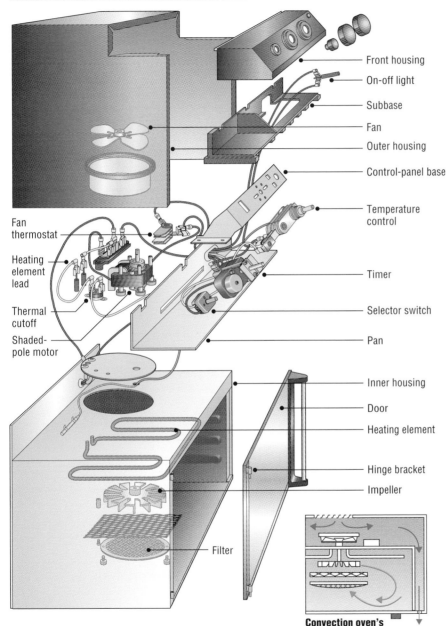

Front housing
On-off light
Subbase
Fan
Outer housing
Control-panel base
Temperature control
Timer
Selector switch
Pan
Inner housing
Door
Heating element
Hinge bracket
Impeller
Filter

Fan thermostat
Heating element lead
Thermal cutoff
Shaded-pole motor

Convection oven's fan cools housing; its impeller circulates air around food.

Note: Details of repair and disassembly may vary, depending on appliance model. If your convection oven differs markedly from this one, see *Appliance repair basics*, pp.132–148.

A convection oven works like a conventional electric oven but includes a fan that circulates hot air around the food. This feature allows convection ovens to cook food faster than conventional ovens and more evenly than microwaves. (Hybrid ovens combine the advantages of a convection oven and a microwave.) The fan (or fan and impeller, as in the model shown here) is driven by a shaded-pole motor (p.139) mounted between the unit's inner and outer housings. Typically, a timer controls the fan and the heating element. The timer, selector switch, and temperature control are located behind the front control panel. The thermal cutoff, which shuts off power to the heating element if the oven overheats, and the fan thermostat are accessible once the outer housing is removed.

Convection ovens require considerable current. Operating another appliance on the same circuit while the oven is on may trip the circuit breaker or blow the fuse governing the circuit.

Disassembly

1 Unplug oven. Remove door and shelves; pull off control knobs. Remove screws behind timer knob and around edges of front housing; then lift off control-panel housing. Disconnect on-off light before removing housing completely.

2 To remove selector switch, loosen screw near spindle and disengage metal tab holding control to panel base. To remove timer, loosen screws securing it. To remove temperature control, unscrew locking ring around spindle.

Tab

3 Slide plastic subbase forward to free its tabs from slots in oven's pan; then lift it carefully past control-panel base and wiring. This exposes screws in pan that secure outer housing.

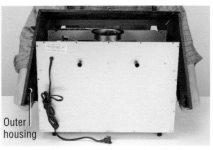

Outer housing

4 Remove screws holding outer housing to pan and frame (some models have a great many screws). To free housing, grasp sides from beneath and pull outward while lifting upward.

Troubleshooting

Problem	CAUSE? / Solution
Oven doesn't heat; on-off light doesn't work	POWER OFF AT OUTLET? See *General troubleshooting,* p.144.
	FAULTY POWER CORD? See *General troubleshooting,* p.144.
	TIMER FAULTY? Unplug oven; remove control panel-housing (*Disassembly,* Step 1, p.167). Test timer (right); replace if faulty. ◆ ▣
	THERMAL CUTOFF OPEN? Test cutoff (far right); replace if necessary. ◆ ▣
	SELECTOR SWITCH FAULTY? Remove control-panel housing (*Disassembly,* Step 1, p.167). Test switch (right) and replace if faulty. ◆ ▣
Oven doesn't heat; on-off light works	TEMPERATURE CONTROL FAULTY? Access temperature control (*Disassembly,* Step 2, p.167). Remove dirt or obstructions between bimetal arms of temperature control thermostat. Test control (right) and replace if faulty. ◆ ▣
	FAULTY SHADED-POLE MOTOR? See *General troubleshooting,* p.147. Replace motor if servicing doesn't work. ◆ ▣
	HEATING ELEMENT FAULTY? Test element (far right); replace if faulty. ◆ ▣
Oven heats; fan doesn't work	FAULTY SHADED-POLE MOTOR? See *General troubleshooting,* p.147. ◆ ▣
	FAN OR IMPELLER BLOCKED? Debris reaching motor through vents in housing can block fan; remove housing and clear debris. Cooking grease can impair impeller and clog filter. Remove and clean filter; inspect and clean impeller. ◆
Oven burns food or overheats	FAN THERMOSTAT FAULTY? Fan thermostat turns fan on when oven reaches proper temperature for convection cooking. Test (far right); replace if faulty. ◆ ▣
	THERMAL CUTOFF FAULTY? If cutoff trips, it should reset itself when oven cools. Test cutoff (far right); replace if faulty. ◆ ▣
Oven won't shut off	TEMPERATURE CONTROL FAULTY? See *Oven doesn't heat; on-off light works,* above. ◆ ▣
	TIMER FAULTY? See *Oven doesn't heat; on-off light doesn't work,* above. ◆ ▣
Oven trips breaker or shocks user	See *General troubleshooting,* p.147.

Degree of difficulty: Simple ◇   Average ◆   Complex ◆   Volt-ohm meter required: ▣

USE AND CARE

Allow an inch of space around food inside the oven so that air can circulate.

Turn all controls off before connecting or disconnecting oven from wall outlet. Unplug oven before cleaning it.

Wash fan filter often with grease-cutting cleaner. Clean interior of oven with nonabrasive spray cleanser and damp sponge.

Convection ovens reduce cooking times and heat requirements. Adapt recipes accordingly.

Testing oven switches

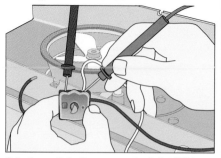

Selector switch. Remove one lead. Set VOM on RX1 scale; touch probes to terminals. Meter should read high ohms with switch on *Broil,* zero on *Convection.* Replace switch if faulty.

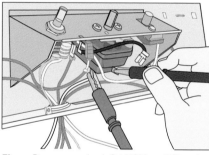

Timer. Remove one lead. Set VOM on RX1 and clip probes to terminals. With timer in *Off* position, VOM should indicate high ohms. With timer in any on position, VOM should read zero ohms.

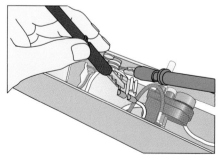

Temperature control. Disconnect leads from one terminal, set VOM on RX1, and clip probes to terminals. Meter should read high ohms with control off, zero ohms with control on highest setting.

Testing internal components

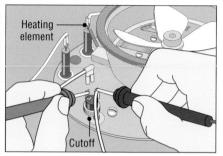

Heating element

Cutoff

Thermal cutoff. Remove one lead from cutoff. Set VOM on RX1; touch probes to terminals. Meter should read zero ohms. Replace cutoff if meter reads high ohms.

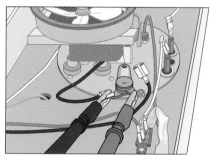

Fan thermostat. Disconnect one lead. Set VOM on RX1; touch probes to terminals. On cool oven, meter should show high ohms. Heat bimetal arm with hair dryer; reading should move to zero.

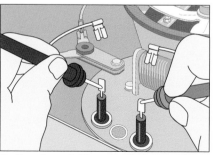

Heating element. Disconnect both leads. With VOM on RX1, touch probes to terminals. If meter reads low ohms, element is OK. A reading of infinity indicates an open circuit; replace element.

Corn poppers

Corn poppers come in two basic types. Hot-air poppers have a fanlike impeller that agitates the kernels with a turbulent stream of hot air in the popping chamber. Oil poppers employ a rotating rod to stir the kernels in a small amount of heated cooking oil. As with waffle irons and slow cookers, the heat in both styles of popper is generated by an element in the base, activated by a simple on-off switch and controlled by a thermostat. The element can be either a horseshoe-shaped solid rod or a springlike resistance coil.

Common problems with poppers, such as scorched or unpopped corn and protracted popping time, usually indicate a faulty thermostat or thermal cutoff. Corn popper motors and other components can be replaced, but since these appliances (particularly air poppers) are inexpensive, you may prefer to buy a new popper instead.

Air popper

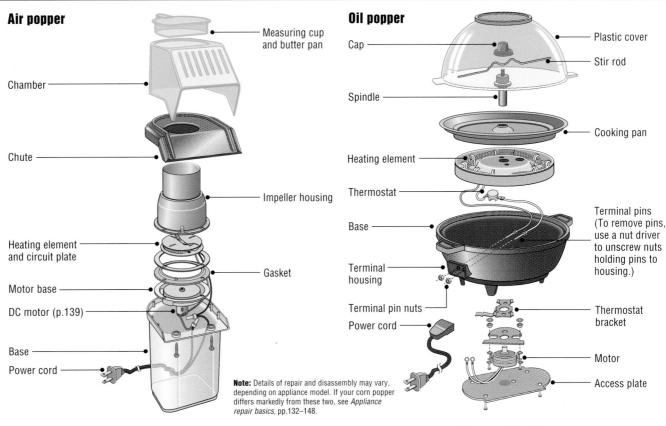

- Measuring cup and butter pan
- Chamber
- Chute
- Impeller housing
- Heating element and circuit plate
- Gasket
- Motor base
- DC motor (p.139)
- Base
- Power cord

Oil popper

- Cap
- Plastic cover
- Stir rod
- Spindle
- Cooking pan
- Heating element
- Thermostat
- Base
- Terminal pins (To remove pins, use a nut driver to unscrew nuts holding pins to housing.)
- Terminal housing
- Terminal pin nuts
- Thermostat bracket
- Power cord
- Motor
- Access plate

Note: Details of repair and disassembly may vary, depending on appliance model. If your corn popper differs markedly from these two, see *Appliance repair basics*, pp.132–148.

Disassembly: Air poppers

- Base
- Chute

1 Unplug popper; turn it upside down. Remove screws holding chute to base; pull chute away. Remove strain-relief fitting (p.170), and guide cord through base as you lift motor out.

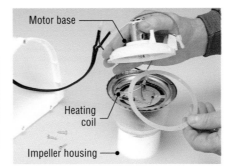

- Motor base
- Heating coil
- Impeller housing

2 Remove screws holding motor base and impeller housing together; separate the units (be careful not to damage gasket between them). This exposes heating coil and all circuitry.

Disassembly: Oil poppers

- Access plate
- Nut driver

To access motor and circuitry, unplug popper and turn it over. Remove screws securing access plate; all serviceable components are beneath plate. Note orientation of motor before lifting it out.

Testing air-popper circuits

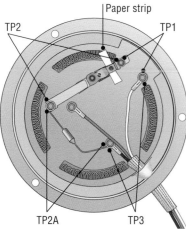

Paper strip

TP2 TP1

TP2A TP3

Circuit tests. Unplug popper; access circuit plate (*Disassembly*, p.169). Separate thermostat contacts with paper strip. To test motor, set VOM on RX100. Touch probes to test points (TP) 1; reading should be relatively high (about 700 ohms). To test thermostat (TP2) or thermal cutoff (TP2A), remove paper strip; touch probes to respective test points. Reading should be zero ohms. To test element, set VOM on RX1. Touch probes to TP3; reading should be low ohms.

Diode test. Four diodes atop motor form a circuit called a bridge rectifier, which converts incoming AC current to DC for popper's motor. Free one end of each diode (see *Soldering and desoldering*, p.136); use a VOM to test diodes one by one (p.148). Replace each faulty diode with exact duplicate.

Removing a clamshell-type strain-relief fitting

The small plastic fitting that keeps a power cord from being pulled away from internal connections is called a strain-relief fitting. To remove a clamshell-type fitting, squeeze it and pull it out; then pull the halves apart. To reach other types of strain-relief fittings, you may have to disassemble the appliance.

Testing oil-popper circuits

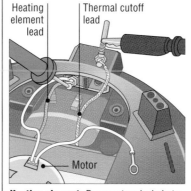

Heating element lead | Thermal cutoff lead

Motor

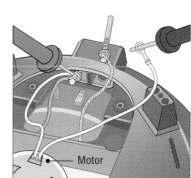

Motor

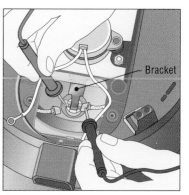

Bracket

Heating element. Remove terminal pin to which thermal cutoff lead is soldered (p.169). Disengage motor lead from freed pin. Set VOM on RX1 scale. Clip VOM probe to freed pin; touch other probe to element lead. Meter should read low ohms.

Motor. Set VOM on RX100 scale. With one motor lead disengaged from terminal pin, touch probes to both motor leads. VOM should read relatively high ohms.

Thermal cutoff. Remove a lead from cutoff (see *Soldering and desoldering*, p.136). Set VOM on RX1; touch probes to terminals. Look for zero ohms reading. If meter reads high ohms, carefully pry cutoff away from retaining bracket. Replace with a duplicate.

Troubleshooting

Problem	CAUSE? / Solution
Popper doesn't work at all	POWER OFF AT OUTLET? See *General troubleshooting*, p.144.
	FAULTY POWER CORD? See *General troubleshooting*, p.144.
	FAULTY SWITCH? Many corn poppers are turned on and off by plugging and unplugging them. If your popper has an on-off switch, see *General troubleshooting*, p.145. ◇
	FAULTY THERMAL CUTOFF? Test cutoff for continuity (see left for air poppers, above for oil poppers). Replace cutoff if faulty. ◆ ▣
Unit doesn't heat	HEATING ELEMENT OR COIL FAULTY? On oil popper, test element (see above) and replace popper if element is faulty; it cannot be replaced. On air popper, check coil for breaks; if found, replace popper. ◆ ▣
Corn doesn't pop but popper is OK	DEFECTIVE CORN? If the moisture content of popcorn is too low, it will not pop or will pop only partially. Try a different brand, and be sure to keep popcorn in an airtight container to prevent moisture loss. ◇
Stirring rod doesn't turn (*Oil poppers*)	MOTOR FAULTY? Check motor with VOM (above). Replace the motor (or the whole appliance) if the motor tests faulty. ◆ ▣
Fan doesn't work (*Air poppers only*)	IMPELLER BLOCKED? On an air popper, a fanlike impeller draws air past the heating coil. Disassemble popper and clear any debris keeping the impeller from spinning. ◇
	BRIDGE RECTIFIER FAULTY? Check diodes for continuity (left) and replace if faulty. ◆ ▣
Popper trips breaker or shocks user	See *General troubleshooting*, p.147.

Degree of difficulty: Simple ◇   Average ◆   Complex ◆   Volt-ohm meter required: ▣

Fans / box and oscillating

A box fan is simply a set of fan blades attached directly to the shaft of a small motor. Box fans are best used for exhausting hot or stale air from a room. In contrast, an oscillating fan (p.172) includes a gear assembly that swivels the fan, making it the better choice for circulating air within a room. An oscillating fan can also be set to exhaust air, but it usually can't move the great volume of air a box fan does.

Both types of fans are run by either a shaded-pole or a split-phase motor (p.139) controlled by a multispeed switch. A split-phase motor may have a capacitor to give it a starting boost. **CAUTION:** Always discharge the capacitor before servicing the motor (see *Discharging a capacitor,* p.146).

A problem common to both types of fans is excessive noise, which can be caused by, among other things, misaligned blades. To align fan blades, see bottom right. For other fan problems and solutions, consult the *Troubleshooting* chart on page 173.

Box fan

Note: Details of repair and disassembly may vary, depending on appliance model. If your box fan differs markedly from this one, see *Appliance repair basics,* pp.132–148.

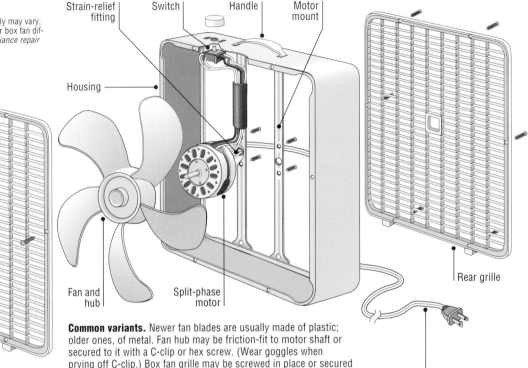

Strain-relief fitting · Switch · Handle · Motor mount · Housing · Fan and hub · Split-phase motor · Rear grille · Power cord · Front grille

Common variants. Newer fan blades are usually made of plastic; older ones, of metal. Fan hub may be friction-fit to motor shaft or secured to it with a C-clip or hex screw. (Wear goggles when prying off C-clip.) Box fan grille may be screwed in place or secured with plastic clips; pry clips off with screwdriver to remove grille.

Disassembly

1 Unplug fan and remove screws holding front grille. To remove blades, place fan on a flat surface. If hub is friction-fit, grasp it from below and lift it up slowly but firmly.

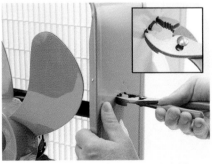

2 Pull off switch knob. Switch body is held to housing with tabs; compress tabs with pliers and push shaft through housing.

Aligning metal blades

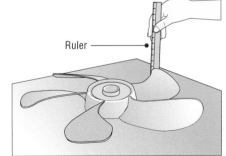

Ruler

Unplug fan; remove blade hub. Place hub on flat surface. Each blade should touch surface. Measure height of each blade. If heights vary by more than ¼ in., bend blades to align or replace assembly.

Oscillating fans

Common trouble spots in an oscillating fan are the switches, pivot assembly, and in fans that have one, the fuse (see *Common variants,* below right). Noise is often a problem in both oscillating and box fans (p.171). To silence rattling blade guards, try wedging a piece of cardboard between their edges. If the cap on the front guard is noisy, secure it with a drop of silicone sealant.

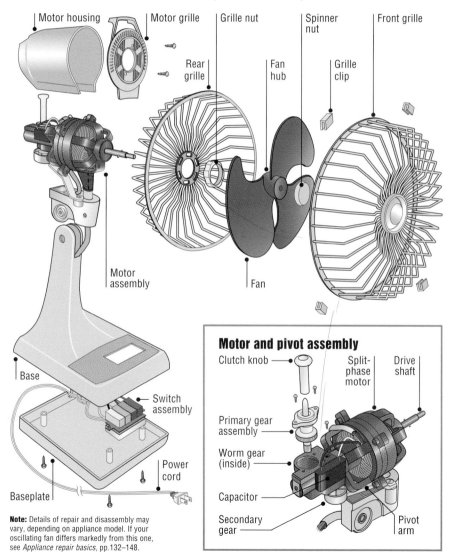

Motor housing — Motor grille — Grille nut — Spinner nut — Front grille

Rear grille — Fan hub — Grille clip

Motor assembly

Fan

Base

Switch assembly

Power cord

Baseplate

Note: Details of repair and disassembly may vary, depending on appliance model. If your oscillating fan differs markedly from this one, see *Appliance repair basics,* pp.132–148.

Motor and pivot assembly

Clutch knob — Split-phase motor — Drive shaft

Primary gear assembly

Worm gear (inside)

Capacitor

Secondary gear

Pivot arm

Disassembly

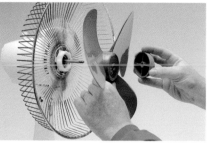

1 Unplug fan. Pry off clips to remove front blade guard. Unscrew spinner nut *clockwise;* then pull fan hub from motor shaft. Unscrew plastic grille nut to free rear blade guard.

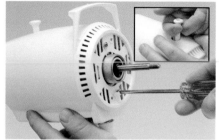

2 Remove screws holding motor grille in place; then remove grille to expose motor shaft and front of motor. Pull off or unscrew clutch knob (inset); it may release with difficulty.

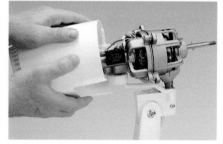

3 Remove bolt on rear of motor housing. Tilt housing up and slide it off to expose remainder of motor and all of pivot assembly. **CAUTION:** Discharge capacitor, if any (p.146).

4 Unscrew baseplate screws and remove plate to access switch assembly. Lift switch assembly away from base. Gently pry switch housing away from switch module to expose terminals.

Common variants

As with box fans, older oscillating fans may have metal blades secured to the motor shaft with a setscrew located at the back of the fan hub. To realign metal blades, see page 171. Plastic blades can't be repaired, but in some fans the blades are attached to metal brackets that can be bent to bring them into proper alignment.

Fuses. The motor in some fans may be protected from overheating by a fuse connected to a motor lead near the field coil. The connection may be made with crimp-on connectors (p.135) or by soldering (p.136). To test the fuse, unplug the fan and disassemble it sufficiently to access the motor. Pull back the fuse's protective sleeve, and test it for continuity with a VOM (p.155); the meter should read zero ohms. Replace a defective fuse with a duplicate.

Clutch control knobs. On some oscillating fans, the control knob is beneath the housing. To access the gears, remove the rear housing; unscrew the gearbox and pull it away from the fan.

Troubleshooting

Problem	CAUSE? / Solution
Fan does not run, or runs intermittently	POWER OFF AT OUTLET? See *General troubleshooting*, p.144.
	FAULTY POWER CORD? See *General troubleshooting*, p.144.
	FAULTY SWITCH? *Box fan:* Access switch (*Disassembly*, Step 2, p.171) and test it (right). *Oscillating fan:* Access switch (*Disassembly*, Step 4, facing page) and test it (right). In either case, try cleaning switch with electrical contact cleaner (see *General troubleshooting*, p.145). If this doesn't help, replace switch. ◆ ▣
	INTERNAL FUSE BLOWN? Test and replace fuse on models having one (see *Common variants*, facing page). ◆ ▣
	FAULTY MOTOR? If motor is shaded-pole type, see *General Troubleshooting*, p.147. For the split-phase motor of an oscillating fan, see *General Troubleshooting*, p.146. Replace motor if faulty. ◆ ▣
Fan does not run; motor hums	CAPACITOR FAULTY? Discharge and test capacitor (see *General Troubleshooting*, p.146). ◆ ▣
	FAULTY MOTOR? See *Fan does not run, or runs intermittently*, above. ◆ ▣
Fan operates sluggishly or starts slowly	MOTOR BEARINGS DRY? Lubricate motor (see right). ◇
	PIVOT MECHANISM DIRTY? *(Oscillating fans only)* Clean and lubricate gear assembly and pivot arm; repair or replace damaged parts (right). ◆
	CAPACITOR FAULTY? See *Fan does not run; motor hums*, above. ◆ ▣
Fan operates only on some speeds	FAULTY SWITCH? See *Fan does not run, or runs intermittently*, above. ◆ ▣
	FAULTY MOTOR? See *Fan does not run, or runs intermittently*, above. ◆ ▣
	CAPACITOR FAULTY? See *Fan does not run; motor hums*, above. ◆ ▣
Oscillating fan does not swivel, or swivels erratically	PIVOT ARM ASSEMBLY WORN? *(Oscillating fans only)* Disassemble fan enough to access pivot assembly (*Disassembly*, Step 3). Service pivot mechanism (right). Replace damaged or worn parts. ◆
Fan is noisy or vibrates excessively	MOTOR BEARINGS DRY? Lubricate motor (see right). ◇
	FAN BLADES LOOSE OR DAMAGED? Inspect plastic blades for cracks, metal blades for damage; repair or replace as needed. Tighten fan hub to shaft by tightening spinner nut or setscrew (on some older fans). If hub loosens repeatedly, secure with 1 drop of thread-locking compound. ◇
	PARTS LOOSE? Inspect fan guards, decorative emblems, and housing for looseness. Tighten part; use tape or adhesive only as needed. If rattling persists, disassemble fan and check for loose internal fasteners. ◇
	FAN POORLY SUPPORTED? Replace pads missing from base. If fan runs quietly on cushioned surface, rattle may be due to surface fan normally rests on. ◇
	FAN BLADES OUT OF ALIGNMENT? Test blades for alignment (p.171); replace them if they cannot be adjusted. ◇
Fan trips breaker or shocks user	See *General troubleshooting*, p.147.

Degree of difficulty: Simple ◇   Average ◆   Complex ◆   Volt-ohm meter required: ▣

Lubricating the motor

Unless the owner's manual advises you not to, lubricate the motor of an oscillating fan at least once a year. Use SAE 20 nondetergent oil, and apply no more than 2 drops to each oil port. If a motor without ports runs sluggishly, carefully spray the shaft near the housing with lightweight spray lubricant.

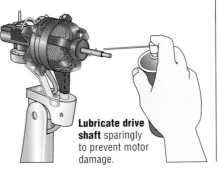

Lubricate drive shaft sparingly to prevent motor damage.

Servicing the pivot mechanism

In oscillating fans, a primary gear assembly meshes with a worm gear on the motor shaft, transferring power to a secondary gear, which operates the pivot arm. Stripped gears are a common malady. The primary gear assembly is easily removed for repair or replacement, but a worn or damaged worm gear (and sometimes the secondary gear) must be professionally serviced.

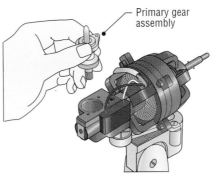

Primary gear assembly

Remove screws, then lift out primary gear assembly and inspect gear teeth. Clean and lubricate with lithium grease; replace assembly if damaged.

Inspect pivot arm and secondary gear. Remove gear for cleaning if possible; otherwise clean with toothpick and relubricate with lithium grease. Tighten pivot arm screw if loose.

Pivot arm

Testing the switch

Oscillating fan. Set VOM on RX1 scale. Clip one probe to common lead on switch. Touch other probe to each switch terminal in turn, pushing corresponding button as you do so. All readings should be zero ohms.

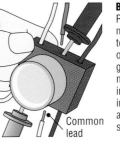

Box fan. Set VOM on RX1. Remove common lead from its terminal; insert probe of similar or smaller gauge. Remove remaining leads and insert second probe in terminals, one at a time. All readings should be zero ohms.

Common lead

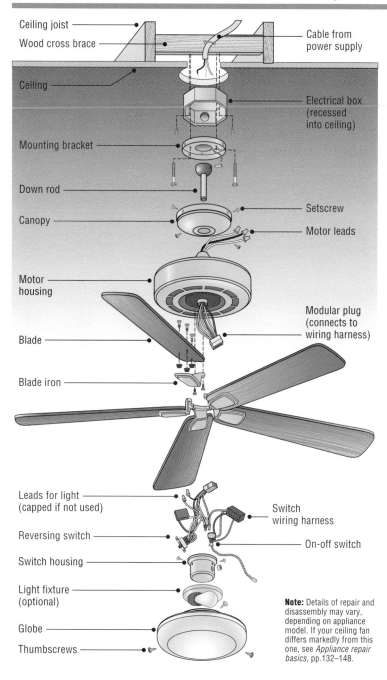

Ceiling joist

Wood cross brace

Cable from power supply

Ceiling

Electrical box (recessed into ceiling)

Mounting bracket

Down rod

Setscrew

Canopy

Motor leads

Motor housing

Modular plug (connects to wiring harness)

Blade

Blade iron

Leads for light (capped if not used)

Switch wiring harness

Reversing switch

On-off switch

Switch housing

Light fixture (optional)

Globe

Thumbscrews

Note: Details of repair and disassembly may vary, depending on appliance model. If your ceiling fan differs markedly from this one, see *Appliance repair basics*, pp.132–148.

In summer, a ceiling fan creates a cooling indoor breeze that can reduce or eliminate the need for air conditioning. In winter, the reversing switch found on many ceiling fans allows you to reverse the rotation of the fan and force rising warm air to circulate through the room. (Bear in mind, however, that the cooling effect of increased air movement may counteract any warming effect. Experiment to see if wintertime use of your ceiling fan actually does improve your comfort.)

Ceiling fans come in a wide variety of styles, and most can be fitted with a light or with various types of switches. A fan of good quality is durable and rarely needs attention beyond periodic cleaning with a soft brush or lint-free cloth (do not use water). Check the owner's manual, or call the manufacturer, to see if the motor on your fan requires occasional oiling; in some models the motor bearings are permanently lubricated. Ceiling fan repairs usually involve faulty switches or wobbling blades. Since ceiling fan motors tend to have lengthy warranties, have the manufacturer deal with a faulty motor rather than attempting to repair it yourself.

FOR YOUR SAFETY

Before servicing a ceiling fan, turn off the power to its circuit at the service panel (p.127).

If you are installing a ceiling fan, be sure to comply with national and local electrical and building codes. Use only an electrical outlet box that has been approved for use with ceiling fans. The box must be securely mounted to a ceiling joist or to a cross brace fitted between joists and be capable of supporting the fan's weight. Fan blades must be at least 7 feet above the floor and 1 foot below the ceiling.

When installing or servicing the fan, use a ladder of adequate strength and height. Ask a helper to steady the ladder as you work on the fan.

Disassembly

1 Turn off power to fan. Remove screws holding switch housing to main housing. Detach switch wiring harness from fan by disconnecting it from modular plug leading to motor (or, on some fans, remove wire connectors).

Blade iron

2 To remove a fan blade, support the blade while you unscrew blade iron from motor. Separate blade from iron by removing all screws and washers connecting them.

3 To remove on-off switch from switch housing, unscrew knurled knob protruding from housing. Push switch through housing; then reach in and pull switch free.

4 Remove the reversing switch from the switch housing by removing the two screws that hold it in place. To free the switch, push it through the housing.

Troubleshooting

Problem	CAUSE? / Solution
Fan does not move	POWER OFF AT OUTLET? See *General troubleshooting*, p.144.
	LOOSE WIRING? Cut power to the fan and check wiring connections inside the switch housing; tighten any that are loose. ◇
	INCORRECT WIRING? Check to see if house wiring is properly connected to fan (see *Wiring to a wall switch*, right). ◆
	REVERSING SWITCH NOT SET? Push switch firmly to one side or the other; it should not be in the middle of its throw. ◇
	FAULTY ON-OFF SWITCH? Check to see if switch is on. If fan still does not operate, service switch (see right). ◆
	DEFECTIVE MOTOR? Check all other possible causes first. If you still suspect the motor, contact manufacturer; most ceiling fan motors are covered by lengthy warranty. ◇
Fan is noisy	LOOSE FASTENERS? Check the motor housing, switch housing, blades, and blade irons for loose screws. Check wiring connectors (p.135) to be sure that they aren't rattling against each other or against switch housing. ◇
	LOOSE LIGHT FIXTURE? Thumbscrews holding globe in place can work loose over time. Stretch a wide, flat rubber band around neck of globe to prevent them from loosening. ◇
	BLADE DAMAGED? Inspect blades for warping and cracks. Remove damaged blade (*Disassembly*, Step 2) and replace it; repair is probably impossible, and may compromise safety. ◇
	DRY BEARINGS? Lubricate only according to owner's manual; some motors have sealed bearings that can't be lubricated. ◇
Fan wobbles (some movement is normal)	BLADES OR IRONS LOOSE? Tighten blade and iron screws. ◇
	BLADE IRON BENT OR CRACKED? Tip of each blade should be equidistant from ceiling. If they are not, remove irons, detach blades, and stack irons atop one another: all should be equally angled. Replace a cracked or improperly angled iron. ◇
	BLADES OUT OF BALANCE? Clean tops of blades with soft cloth or vacuum; if this doesn't help, see *Balancing blades*, right. ◇
	FAN NOT LEVEL? Check by placing small level atop motor housing. Make sure canopy and mounting bracket are tight. ◇
	FAN IMPROPERLY MOUNTED? Consult owner's manual. Fan's electrical box should be secured directly to a joist, a wood cross brace, or an approved metal bracket mounted between joists. ◆
Fan trips breaker or shocks user	See *General troubleshooting*, p.147. Also make sure fan is properly wired (see *Wiring to a wall switch*, right.) ◇

Degree of difficulty: Simple ◇ Average ◆ Complex ◆
Volt-ohm meter required ▣

Balancing the blades

Wobbling blades will reduce your fan's efficiency and create noise. Some fans come with a balancing kit that includes self-adhering weight strips. Even without a kit, you can balance the blades by the simple trial-and-error procedure described below.

Switch adjacent blades

1 Before adding weights, try switching the position of adjacent fan blades to see if that diminishes or eliminates the wobble. Check the fan at several speeds. If switching blades doesn't work, proceed to Step 2.

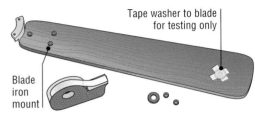

Tape washer to blade for testing only

Blade iron mount

2 Tape small washers to a blade; run fan at several speeds. Repeat test until you find blade which, when weighted, produces least wobble. Permanently fasten washer(s) to blade by placing beneath a blade mount.

Servicing the switches

Cleaning the switch contacts may restore a faulty switch, but if not, fan switches are easily replaced. Never use an ordinary lamp switch, however, even if it looks identical.

On-off switch. Remove switch from housing (*Disassembly*, Step 3); spray contact cleaner into it. Pull chain a few times to work cleaner across the face of contacts. If cleaning doesn't work, replace the switch.

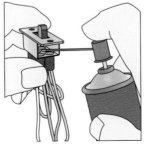

Reversing switch. Remove switch from housing (*Disassembly*, Step 4); use a flashlight to check contacts. If they're broken or corroded, replace switch. If not, spray switch with contact cleaner; flip toggle back and forth to work cleaner into switch.

Wiring to a wall switch

The speed control and optional light on a ceiling fan are often controlled by pull chains on the fan itself. For greater convenience, however, the fan and/or the light can be controlled from a wall switch, as shown below. Be sure to use a speed control and a light dimmer that are CSA approved (p.125).

If there is no ceiling box near where you wish to mount the fan, you may be able to plug the fan's wiring into an existing wall outlet. Special wiring kits that include swag chain are available for this purpose.

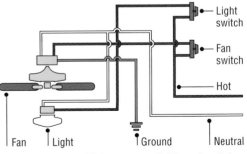

Both ceiling fan and light are controlled by wall switches in this schematic. For other wiring possibilities, consult your owner's manual or a licensed electrician.

Food processors employ removable metal discs or curved blades to chop, slice, shred, and mix foods. Most newer full-size and compact processors, like the one shown here, are belt-driven: the motor and mixing bowl are arranged side by side; the blade assembly fits over a spindle linked to the motor by a drive belt and a reduction gear, which increases the motor's torque. (See also *Common variant*, right.)

All food processors include a safety interlock switch to keep the motor from running when the bowl is not in place. Some may include a pulse switch or touch-pad switches (p.148). Some full-size processors have an internal fuse that keeps the motor from overheating. Unless it is faulty, the fuse will usually reset itself when the motor cools.

CAUTION: Older units may contain a capacitor, which must be discharged before you service the appliance (see *Discharging the capacitor*, p.146).

USE AND CARE

Keep hands and utensils away from moving blades or discs. Always use the pusher to guide food into the feed tube, and let gravity do most of the work.

If the processor stops working, unplug it; look for and remove any food lodged beneath the blades.

Unplug processor when cleaning it, changing blades, or when it's not in use.

Clean parts, including spindle, after each use. Use care when handling blades.

Close cover securely and make sure it's locked before starting food processor.

Add food in small quantities. Foods *not recommended* for processing include ice, coffee beans, raw grains, and dried fruits.

Base

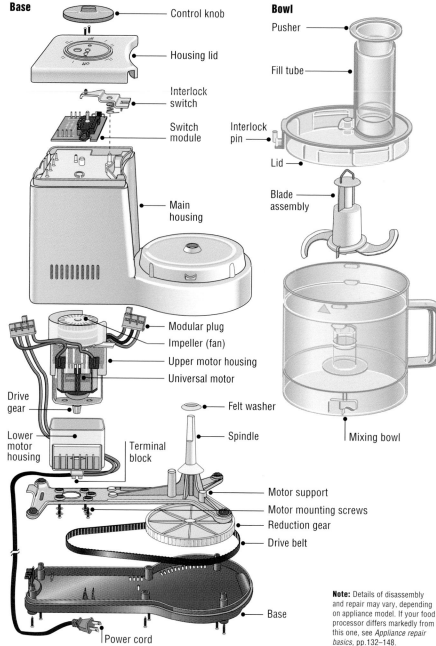

- Control knob
- Housing lid
- Interlock switch
- Switch module
- Main housing
- Modular plug
- Impeller (fan)
- Upper motor housing
- Universal motor
- Drive gear
- Lower motor housing
- Terminal block
- Motor support
- Motor mounting screws
- Reduction gear
- Drive belt
- Base
- Power cord

Bowl

- Pusher
- Fill tube
- Interlock pin
- Lid
- Blade assembly
- Felt washer
- Spindle
- Mixing bowl

Note: Details of disassembly and repair may vary, depending on appliance model. If your food processor differs markedly from this one, see *Appliance repair basics*, pp.132–148.

Common variant: Direct-drive motor

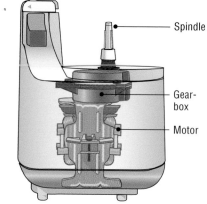

- Spindle
- Gearbox
- Motor

In a direct-drive food processor, the mixing bowl sits on top of the motor and gear assembly; the spindle is connected directly to the motor (p.179) or to gears driven directly by the motor, as shown here. Some full-size and compact processors, as well as most mini-processors and food choppers (p.179), are direct-driven.

Servicing the blades

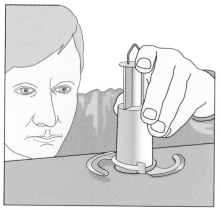

To check for bent blades, lift blade assembly out of appliance and place upright on a flat surface. Sight across blades; both should be parallel to surface. If either blade is bent, replace entire blade assembly; blades are not replaceable separately and cannot be repaired safely. Be careful when handling blade assembly as blades are extremely sharp.

Disassembly

1 Pry up control knob (or loosen setscrew). Remove two screws beneath knob; then lift or pry off housing lid.

2 Pull modular plugs from circuit board; then lift off interlock switch and spring. Lift off board and main switch case.

3 Turn processor upside down. Pry off feet. Remove screws and base to expose belt, gears, and motor support.

4 Slide drive belt off drive gear. Lift support at center to remove it, along with spindle, reduction gear, and motor.

5 Free motor from support by loosening cord's strain-relief fitting; remove motor mounting screws.

6 Pull off lower half of motor housing to expose bottom of motor. Pry off fan blade to remove upper motor housing.

Troubleshooting

Problem	CAUSE? / Solution
Processor does not run	POWER OFF AT OUTLET? See *General troubleshooting*, p.144.
	FAULTY POWER CORD? See *General troubleshooting*, p.144, and *Testing the power cord*, p.178.
	INTERLOCK SWITCH NOT ENGAGED? Bowl cover must be locked in place; check pin on cover for damage. ◇
	INTERLOCK SWITCH JAMMED? Remove obstructions and clean (pp.178 and 179); replace if cleaning fails. ◆
	INTERNAL BREAKER TRIPPED? Most newer processors have an internal circuit breaker. Wait 15 min. for motor to cool; then restart it. If breaker trips again and you're not overloading motor with hard-to-process foods, have appliance serviced. If appliance has a fuse instead of a breaker, check it with VOM (see *Testing the fuse*, p.155); replace if faulty. If processor has a thermal limiter instead of a fuse, repair could be difficult; have appliance serviced. ◇ ▣
	MODULAR PLUG LOOSE? Disassemble appliance to access switches. Pull modular plugs from terminals and spray electrical contact cleaner into each plug. Straighten bent terminals (p.178); then push plugs back into place. ◆
	FAULTY MOTOR? Most units have a universal motor, though some older ones may have a split-phase motor. In either case, see *General troubleshooting*, p.146, for servicing of faulty motor. ◆
Processor does not operate on all speeds	SPEED CONTROL OR PULSE SWITCH FAULTY? If spraying with electrical contact cleaner does not solve problem (p.178), replace switch. ◆ ▣
	WORN BRUSHES? On food processors with universal motors, access the motor and examine brushes (p.179). Replace brushes if worn or damaged (see *General troubleshooting*, p.146). ◆
Motor runs but blades don't turn	DRIVE BELT SLIPPED OR BROKEN? Disassemble food processor; examine belt for wear and damage. Remount belt that's in good condition. Test belt tension (p.178) and adjust if necessary. Replace belt if broken or damaged. ◆
	WORN OR STRIPPED DRIVE GEAR? Remove base of food processor and examine gear; replace worn or damaged gear if possible. If gear cannot be removed from drive shaft, you may have to replace entire spindle assembly. ◆
	SPINDLE BROKEN? Disassemble appliance and examine base of spindle. Tighten spindle locknut or speed nut on appliances having one; otherwise replace spindle or entire spindle assembly (p.178). ◆
Bowl leaks	BOWL TOO FULL? Do not fill mixing bowl more than recommended in owner's manual. ◇
	CONTENTS TOO LIQUID? Food processors cannot accommodate pure liquid; always add liquid last. ◇
	MIXING BOWL CRACKED? Fill bowl to rim with water and examine for leaks. Cracked bowl must be replaced. ◇
Processor is noisy or vibrates excessively	BLADES BENT? Carefully check blades (facing page); replace blade assembly if either blade is bent. ◇
	DRY OR WORN MOTOR BEARINGS? Lubricate bearings with 2 or 3 drops of SAE 20-weight nondetergent oil. ◆
	RUBBER FEET MISSING? Examine base and replace missing or damaged feet. ◇
	DAMAGED DRIVE BELT? Remove base and examine belt. Replace damaged belt; then check tension (p.178). ◆
	BROKEN OR BENT SPINDLE? Disassemble appliance and examine base of spindle shaft. Tighten shaft locknut or speed nut if possible. Otherwise, replace spindle (p.178) or entire spindle assembly, depending on model. ◆
	COUPLINGS OR REDUCTION GEARS PARTIALLY STRIPPED? Disassemble appliance and examine couplings (food choppers) or gears (full-size units). Replace couplings (p.179) or gears if worn or damaged. ◆
	DRIVE TRAIN BINDING? Disassemble appliance and remove any obstructions. Lubricate spindle base with SAE 20-weight nondetergent oil. If drive train still binds when you try to turn spindle by hand, have appliance serviced. ◆
Processor trips breaker or shocks user	See *General troubleshooting*, p.147.

Degree of difficulty: Simple ◇   Average ◆   Complex ◆   Volt-ohm meter required: ▣

Small appliances ▪ Food processors and choppers

Switches and modular plugs

The main switch on full-size food processors may be electronic. Such switches are durable, but when they do fail, they can't be repaired. If cleaning doesn't solve the problem, replace the switch module.

Modular plugs are used on some processors, in part to resist the vibration that might loosen them. If you suspect that a plug is faulty, clean it (see below). If this doesn't help, have the unit serviced. To access the switch and plugs, see *Disassembly,* Step 2, p.177.

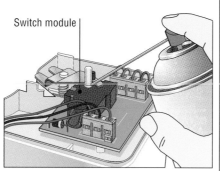

If main switch is part of circuit board, it cannot be repaired. Try to clean shaft base with contact cleaner; replace switch module if problems persist.

Switch module

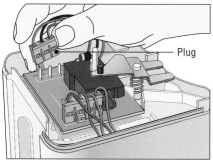

Plug

To remove modular plug, gently rock it end to end as you lift it up (don't bend terminals). Spray plug contacts with contact cleaner to clean.

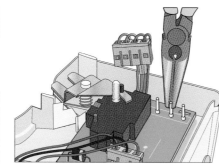

Sight along plug terminals to see if they are straight. Straighten terminals *carefully* if bent, using needle-nose pliers.

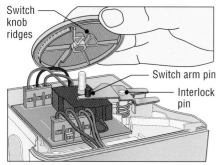

Switch knob ridges

Switch arm pin

Interlock pin

How interlock switch works. When interlock pin slides into place, switch arm pivots, disengaging another pin from ridges beneath knob. Once knob is "unlocked," device can be switched on safely.

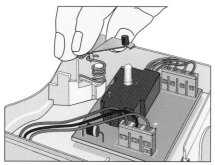

To service interlock switch, lift arm and spring off post; replace spring if damaged. Arm must not bind against housing lid after reassembly. Also check interlock pin for dirt or damage.

Servicing the drive belt

Erratic operation or failure of the spindle to turn when the motor is running signals a drive belt problem. To access the belt, see *Disassembly,* Step 3, p.177. Some models have an adjustable bearing, or idler, that allows you to tension the drive belt; on processors that lack this feature, adjust the belt by loosening the motor mounting screws and repositioning the motor. When correctly tensioned, the belt should fit snugly and move smoothly when the gears are turned by hand.

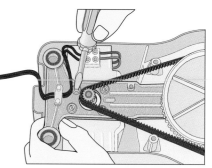

To adjust drive belt, loosen screws securing motor to support. Slide motor to a point where belt tension is correct, then retighten screws.

Replacing the spindle

Excessive vibration is one sign of a bent or damaged spindle; contact between the blade or cutting disc and the bowl is another. On the food processor featured on page 176, the spindle is part of the reduction gear assembly and cannot be replaced separately. On some models, the spindle is secured to the reduction gear by a locknut or a special washer called a speed nut. To remove a locknut, simply unscrew it (some spindles have left-handed threads; turn them clockwise to loosen). To remove a speed nut, carefully pry it off with a small screwdriver. On other models, the spindle or the drive shaft is covered by a plastic sheath. You can pry off the sheath with a screwdriver, but be careful not to mar the plastic when doing so.

Sheath

To remove spindle sheath on some processors, pry it off with a screwdriver.

Testing the power cord

If the power cord or plug breaks or shows signs of wear, replace the entire cord and plug as a unit. In processors like the one featured here, the cord ends at a special terminal block that links it to the wires leading through the rest of the appliance. To release the cord leads from the terminal block, use a small screwdriver to loosen each screw on the cord side of the block, then pull the wires free. Retighten the screws when replacing the cord.

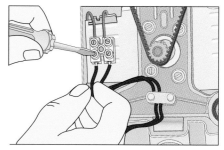

To test cord, set VOM on RX1. Loosen screws on terminal block to remove leads; then proceed as shown in *Servicing 120-volt power cords,* p.145.

Food choppers

Food choppers come in two basic types: one, featured here, looks like a coffee grinder; the other type resembles a miniature food processor. Food choppers chop, grind, and puree food in small quantities. They lack the power of larger processors as well as the ability to slice or shred food.

Most choppers are run by a direct-drive universal motor, whose brushes may wear out over time (see *Troubleshooting*, p.177, and *General troubleshooting*, p.146). If you access the motor to replace the brushes, dust the motor with a dry paintbrush, wipe out the housing, and check the wiring for breaks before reassembling the appliance. As you do so, take care not to pinch any wires between parts of the food chopper.

Examine the jar and base couplings periodically. If either one is damaged or worn, replace both of them. To keep its motor from overheating, don't overload a food chopper. Choppers are designed for "pulse" use; don't operate one continuously for more than a few seconds.

Base

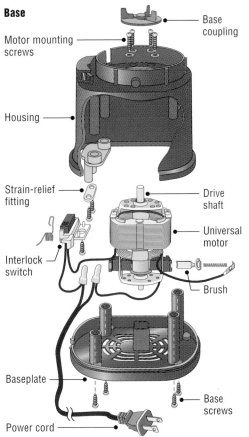

- Motor mounting screws
- Base coupling
- Housing
- Strain-relief fitting
- Drive shaft
- Universal motor
- Interlock switch
- Brush
- Baseplate
- Base screws
- Power cord

Bowl

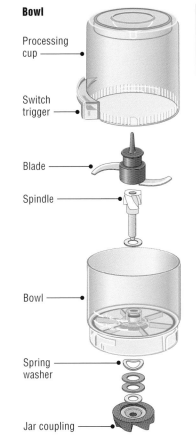

- Processing cup
- Switch trigger
- Blade
- Spindle
- Bowl
- Spring washer
- Jar coupling

Servicing the interlock switch

Most food choppers have only a simple interlock switch. Mini food processors may have on-off, high-low, or pulse switches like those of larger units.

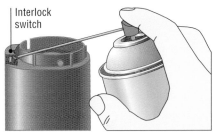

- Interlock switch

Clean interlock switch often to remove debris. If switch sticks occasionally, spray it with electrical contact cleaner; do not use spray lubricants.

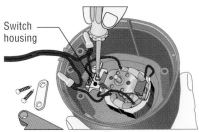

- Switch housing

If sticking persists, unplug chopper and remove baseplate and switch mounting screw. Pull out and disconnect switch. Replace with a duplicate.

Removing the couplings

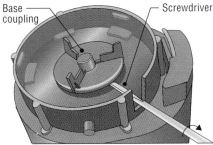

- Base coupling
- Screwdriver

To remove base coupling, insert screwdriver blade and twist screwdriver slightly. Pry evenly around coupling to avoid jamming it on shaft.

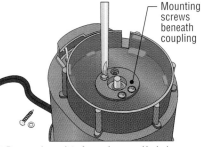

- Jar coupling
- Tape

Unscrew jar coupling (usually clockwise) while gripping spindle with taped pliers. *Note:* Concave side of spring washer points toward housing.

Replacing the brushes

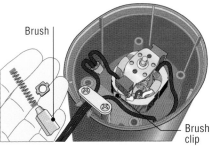

- Mounting screws beneath coupling
- Brush
- Brush clip

1 Remove baseplate from chopper. Undo base coupling (left), and loosen mounting screws to free motor. Slide motor from housing.

2 Pry each brush clip loose with screwdriver, being careful not to let spring and square washer pop out. Remove and replace brushes.

179

Despite differences in appearance, electric frying pans, griddles, skillets, and woks all work in much the same way. Most models feature a detachable heat control, a device that distinguishes this family of appliances from grills, sandwich makers, and waffle irons (p.182). When in use, the control's temperature probe is in direct contact with the pan, cycling the heating element on and off to maintain a precise temperature. The fact that the control is removable means that the appliance usually can be immersed in water (never immerse the control). Problems with the heat control are often due to food spills and are usually solved with a good cleaning.

The sheathed heating element on frying pans and related appliances (see *Types of heating elements,* p.182) can't always be repaired. Some models, however, have a detachable element that can be replaced.

Frying pan with detachable control

Wok with detachable control

The heat control

- Temperature control dial
- Upper housing
- On-off light
- Power cord
- Thermostat contacts
- Female terminal
- Lower housing

- Temperature control shaft
- Female terminal
- Temperature probe

Control probe schematic

- Bimetal strip
- Thermostat contacts

Note: Details of repair and disassembly may vary, depending on appliance model. If your frying pan, griddle, etc., differs markedly from those described here, see *Appliance repair basics,* pp.132–148.

USE AND CARE

Never immerse control, cord, or plug in water.

Check owner's manual for cleaning instructions; some appliances can't be immersed in water even if they have detachable heat controls.

Unplug cord after each use to prevent accidental heating of pan. Avoid using extension cords.

Do not use these appliances outdoors, nor warm them over a gas or electric burner (or in oven).

Be careful when moving a hot pan. Never move a pan that contains hot oil or hot water.

Recondition nonstick coatings with cooking oil; check owner's manual for frequency.

Troubleshooting

Problem	CAUSE? / Solution
Frying pan, griddle, etc., does not heat	POWER OFF AT OUTLET? See *General troubleshooting,* p.144.
	FAULTY POWER CORD? See *General troubleshooting,* p.144. Cord must be replaced with high-temperature cord of equal capacity. In some cases it is best to replace entire heat control unit along with the cord. ◆
	HEATING ELEMENT FAULTY? Test element (facing page). Replace a faulty element if possible; otherwise replace appliance. ◇ ▨
	TERMINALS DIRTY OR DAMAGED? Inspect terminal pins on heating element, as well as both female terminals on the heat control. Clean if necessary (facing page). If female terminals can't be cleaned or repaired, replace entire heat control along with cord; terminals cannot be replaced separately. ◇
	THERMOSTAT FAULTY? Test and service as needed (see *Servicing the heat control,* facing page). ◆ ▨
	BROKEN CONNECTIONS IN HEAT CONTROL? Unit is often dropped. Disassemble and check for loose or broken connections. To repair, see *Servicing the heat control,* facing page. ◆ ▨
Pan doesn't cook at proper temperature	HEAT CONTROL IMPROPERLY ADJUSTED? Heat 1½ in. of water in pan; set control to 212°F (100°C) and insert probe. When water reaches boiling point, control should shut off. Adjust control as needed (facing page). ◇
	THERMOSTAT CONTACTS FAULTY? If appliance *overheats,* check for sticking contacts. If appliance *underheats,* check for burned contacts making intermittent connection. Service as necessary (see *Servicing the heat control,* facing page). ◆
Pan trips breaker or shocks user	See *General troubleshooting,* p.147.

Degree of difficulty: Simple ◇   Average ◆   Complex ◆

Volt-ohm meter required ▨

Testing the heating element

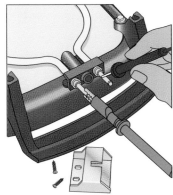

Check for continuity with VOM set on RX1. Touch or clip probes to each terminal pin; a reading of 10 to 30 ohms is typical if element is OK. A reading of infinity means element is faulty. If the element is removable, replace it. If it is cast in place, replace the entire appliance.

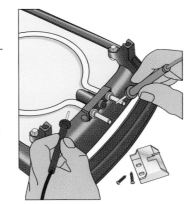

Test for ground fault with VOM on RX1000. Hold one probe firmly against metal part of pan while touching the other probe to each terminal pin in turn. Meter should read infinity each time. If reading moves toward zero ohms, element is grounded and appliance must be replaced.

Cleaning terminals

1 Renew burned or pitted heating element terminal pins by cleaning with sandpaper or an automotive-point file. Use brush with brass bristles to remove corrosion. Spray pins with contact cleaner to remove sanding dust or metal filings.

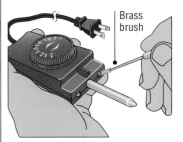

Brass brush

2 Clean female terminals by swabbing with a small round brass brush sprayed with contact cleaner; a rolled cylinder of fine sandpaper may also work. Make certain terminals have not lost their tension for firm contact.

Servicing the heat control

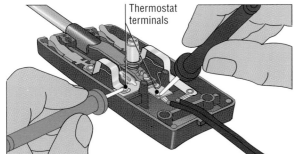

Thermostat terminals

Probe

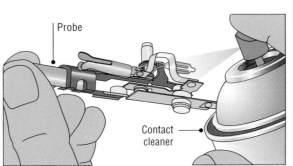

Contact cleaner

Unplug control and open housing. Set VOM on RX1 and probe thermostat terminals. Meter should read near zero ohms with control in *On* position, infinity with control off.

Sand probe lightly to remove corrosion; then polish with steel wool and wipe clean. Food residue can foul terminals. Lift control out; clear buildup by spraying all components with contact cleaner.

Adjusting a heat control

Some controls can be adjusted by prying up knob and repositioning it at a slightly different setting. Recheck temperature afterward (see *Heat control improperly adjusted?* in *Troubleshooting* chart, facing page). Don't force knob; it might be held in place by a small screw.

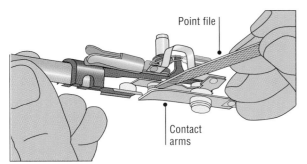

Point file

Contact arms

Clean burned or pitted contacts with a point file (see *General troubleshooting*, p.145); burnish with a strip of white bond paper. Use only the pressure of contact arms to hold contacts against file.

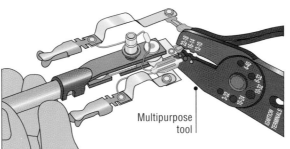

Multipurpose tool

To make repairs inside control, use only crimp connectors, solder, and wiring rated for high temperatures. All connections must be tight, or high current flow within control will cause them to fail.

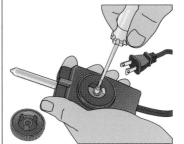

Heat control may have temperature-adjusting screw in center of shaft or beneath label. Turn screw counterclockwise (usually) to lower heat, clockwise to raise it. Recheck temperature afterward (see *Heat control improperly adjusted?* in *Troubleshooting* chart, facing page).

Small appliances ▪ Grills, sandwich makers, and waffle irons

A basic distinction between this family of cooking appliances and the frying pan group (p.180) is the lack of a removable heat control. Simple grills (exploded view not shown) have one element and no thermostat. Sandwich makers and waffle irons have two cooking surfaces heated by a pair of resistance elements, whose temperature is regulated by a built-in thermostat. Typically none of these devices are immersible; some have parts that can be removed for cleaning.

Types of heating elements. The element in most waffle irons and some sandwich makers is an exposed spring-like coil of Nichrome wire. The replaceable coil, called an open element, is suspended between ceramic insulating supports. In contrast, most sandwich makers, some waffle irons, and all grills have a sheathed heating element—a Nichrome coil wrapped in an insulating material (usually manganese) and an outer jacket of steel. Depending on the appliance type and model, sheathed elements may or may not be replaceable.

Sandwich maker with sheathed heating element

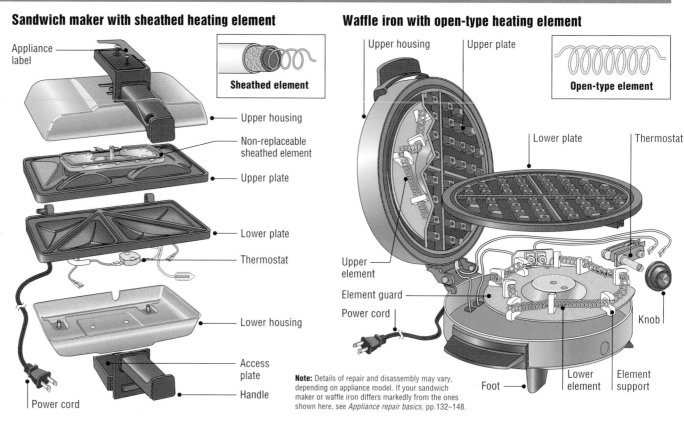

Appliance label

Sheathed element

- Upper housing
- Non-replaceable sheathed element
- Upper plate
- Lower plate
- Thermostat
- Lower housing
- Access plate
- Handle

Power cord

Waffle iron with open-type heating element

Upper housing | Upper plate

Open-type element

- Lower plate
- Thermostat
- Upper element
- Element guard
- Power cord
- Knob
- Foot
- Lower element
- Element support

Note: Details of repair and disassembly may vary, depending on appliance model. If your sandwich maker or waffle iron differs markedly from the ones shown here, see *Appliance repair basics*, pp.132–148.

Disassembly

Label

Sandwich maker. To reach upper element, pry off metal label and remove screw holding housing in place. To reach cord and lower element, remove bottom access plate.

Plate

Housing

Waffle iron. To remove lower cooking plate, remove screw in underside of housing; pull control knob off; then lift plate up. Take care not to damage or scratch nonstick finish on plate.

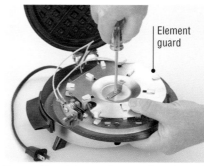

Element guard

Turn cooking plate over. Remove element guard by removing screws at center of guard and/or around perimeter. Older models of waffle irons may not have element guard.

Adjusting thermostats

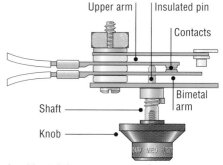

Upper arm | Insulated pin

Contacts

Shaft

Knob

Bimetal arm

DARK MED LIGHT

In a bimetal thermostat, an insulated pin pushes against upper arm, regulating temperature range. In some models, an adjustment screw in the shaft allows you to adjust range.

Troubleshooting

Problem	CAUSE? / Solution

Appliance does not heat

POWER OFF AT OUTLET? See *General troubleshooting*, p.144.

FAULTY POWER CORD? See *General troubleshooting*, p.144.

HEATING ELEMENT OPEN? Test for continuity (right). Problems with open elements are often visible as breaks in the coil. Elements in grills, waffle irons, and sandwich makers are usually replaceable unless they form part of the plate. ◆ ▣

FAULTY TERMINAL PINS? Inspect terminal pins on appliances that have removable cords. Clean pins with automotive-point file or sandpaper if pitted, or with brass brush if corroded; then spray with contact cleaner. Replacements for removable cords can often be found at a hardware store. Be sure new cord has capacity equal to old one. ◇

OPEN THERMOSTAT? When the appliance is cool, contacts should be closed in any position other than *Off*. With one thermostat lead removed, set VOM on RX1 and clip probes to terminals. Meter should read zero ohms with thermostat control turned on and infinity with control on *Off*. Thermostat problems are often caused by residue from food splatters. Use contact cleaner and brush to remove residue. ◆ ▣

Appliance heats on only one side

ONE ELEMENT OPEN? When checking for continuity, always test elements in both sides of a waffle iron or sandwich maker (right). The heating elements are wired in parallel, so that one will operate even if the other one is defective. Replace the faulty element. ◆ ▣

FAULTY INTERNAL WIRING? Disassemble appliance and look for broken wiring and loose connections. In particular, check any wiring near the hinge between upper and lower sections of appliance. Frequent flexing of wire passing through this area often leads to broken conductors. Replace appliance if wiring cannot be repaired. ◆

Appliance does not heat to proper temperature

THERMOSTAT CONTACTS FAULTY? If appliance overheats or doesn't heat at all, disassemble it and check for contacts that may be stuck in fully closed or fully open position. If appliance does not heat enough, check for burned contacts making intermittent connection. If thermostat cannot be cleaned successfully with contact cleaner or an automotive-point file (see *Cleaning contacts and terminals*, p.137), replace it. ◆

LINKAGE LOOSE OR POORLY ADJUSTED? The temperature of some waffle irons can be adjusted by moving a front-mounted sliding control called a linkage. Check linkage for loose or bent parts. Repair linkage if possible; otherwise replace it. ◆

Appliance trips breaker

See *General troubleshooting*, p.147.

Appliance shocks user

GROUND FAULT IN ELEMENT? Test sheathed or open element for ground (right). Make sure open element is not sagging. If meter reading moves toward zero ohms, element is grounded and should be replaced. ◆ ▣

GROUND FAULT IN THERMOSTAT? Set VOM on highest resistance scale (usually RX1000) and remove element leads. Touch one test probe to metal housing of appliance, the other to each thermostat contact in turn. If meter reading moves toward zero ohms, thermostat or internal wiring is grounded. Open and inspect for broken wires or damaged components. Do not use appliance until fault is located and repaired. ◆ ▣

Degree of difficulty: Simple ◇   Average ◆   Complex ◆   Volt-ohm meter required: ▣

Testing heating elements

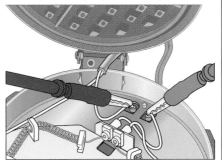

To test open or sheathed element for continuity, set VOM on RX1. Clip probes to each terminal; element is OK if meter reads about 15 ohms.

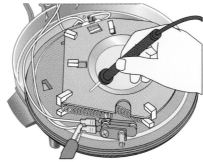

To test open element for ground, set meter on RX1000. Touch probe to various parts of metal housing; clip other probe to each element lead in turn. Meter should read infinity in both cases.

Sheathed element in a simple grill

Test sheathed element for ground with meter on RX1000. Hold one probe on sheathing; clip other probe to each terminal. Meter should read infinity.

Replacing an open element

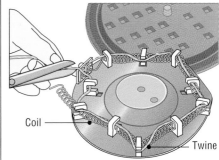

Coil

Twine

1 To measure coil, route twine through element supports in same pattern as damaged coil, then measure length of twine.

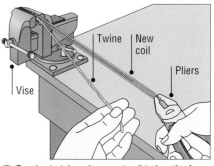

Twine | New coil | Pliers | Vise

2 Evenly stretch replacement coil to length of twine as shown.
CAUTION: Wear eye protection and do not stand directly behind stretched element.

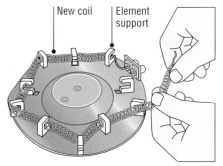

New coil | Element support

3 Install stretched element by carefully looping coil through element supports. Be certain that connections to terminals are clean.

Electric hair curlers and curling irons (facing page) contain the same basic components: a heating element, usually controlled by a thermostat, and a thermal cutoff or fuse that prevents burnouts due to overheating. In a set of curlers, a solid metal plate called a heat sink transfers heat from the element to the warming posts on which the rollers are placed. In contrast, the barrel of a curling iron is heated by an element located inside the barrel.

Curlers and curling irons are easy to disassemble and troubleshoot. Whenever either device doesn't heat, a faulty power cord is the most likely culprit. Replacement parts for curlers and curling irons, however, may be hard to obtain, even from the manufacturer. Don't attempt repairs without first contacting the manufacturer or a local service center to find out if you can get the necessary replacement parts. Bear in mind, too, that these appliances, curling irons in particular, are often so inexpensive that replacement may be more cost-effective than repair.

Hair curlers

Note: Details of repair and disassembly may vary, depending on appliance model. If your hair curler or curling iron differs markedly from those shown here and on the facing page, see *Appliance repair basics*, pp.132–148.

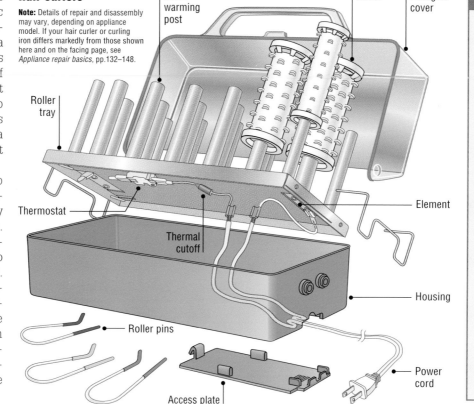

Roller warming post

Roller tray

Thermostat

Thermal cutoff

Roller pins

Access plate

Roller

Plexiglas cover

Element

Housing

Power cord

FOR YOUR SAFETY

Never use a curler or curling iron while bathing, standing in water, or while your hands are wet. If the device falls into water, shut off power at the service panel (p.127), then unplug curler or iron before retrieving. Have appliance professionally inspected.

Never leave a curler or iron unattended when plugged in. Even with the switch off, an electrical appliance can cause a shock if it's still connected to a power source.

Place appliances only on hard surfaces when in use; soft surfaces present a fire hazard. Inspect air intake grilles frequently; remove hair or lint that could reduce air circulation and lead to overheating and subsequent fire.

Always use the counter rest to support a hot curling iron. Barrel can damage many countertop surfaces.

Apply hair spray only after curling. Do not operate appliance while using aerosols.

Allow appliances to cool before storing. Keep out of reach of children.

To prevent cord damage, don't wrap it tightly around curling iron to store it. Loop cord loosely and fasten with plastic tie, or slip loops through empty toilet tissue roll.

Disassembly

1 Unplug hair curler; remove cover and rollers. Use a small screwdriver to pry open catch on access plate. On some models, remove screws from base instead.

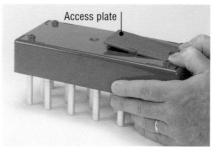

Access plate

2 Rest curler on flat surface and grasp housing firmly with both hands; slide plate forward and upward with thumbs to expose inner parts.

3 Loosen one end of roller tray by prying metal clips from mounts on housing. Free power cord; then loosen other end of tray by prying second set of metal clips from mounts.

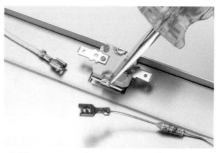

4 Disconnect push-on connectors linking thermostat to heating element. Remove thermostat by prying up metal tabs securing it to underside of roller tray.

Troubleshooting

Problem	CAUSE? / Solution
Appliance does not heat	POWER OFF AT OUTLET? Check and reset outlet GFCI (p.128), if any. If power is still off, see *General troubleshooting*, p.144.
	FAULTY POWER CORD? For curlers, see *General troubleshooting*, p.144. For curling irons, see *Servicing swivel cords*, right. ◇
	INTERNAL WIRING FAULTY? Disassemble appliance and look for wires disconnected from terminals. Reattach if possible; otherwise replace appliance. ◆
	SWIVEL CONTACTS DIRTY OR CORRODED? *(Curling iron only)* Test cord (see *Servicing swivel cords*, right). Replace cord if contacts are damaged. ◆ ▨
	FAULTY HEATING ELEMENT? *(Curler set only.)* Access heating element leads (*Disassembly*, Step 3) and test element (below). If faulty, replace entire appliance (element itself is usually not replaceable). ◆ ▨
	THERMAL CUTOFF FAULTY? Test cutoff (below) and replace if part is available; otherwise replace entire appliance. ◆ ▨
	FAULTY SWITCH? Some curlers and irons (including the curler shown here) do not have a switch; current is supplied when the appliance is plugged in. When there is a switch, however, it will be a very simple one. Spray contacts and moving parts with electrical contact cleaner to flush away debris. If this doesn't help, test switch with VOM (see *General troubleshooting*, p.145); replace if necessary. ◆
Appliance shocks user or trips breaker	See *General troubleshooting*, p.147.

Degree of difficulty: Simple ◇   Average ◆   Complex ◆   Volt-ohm meter required: ▨

Servicing hair curlers

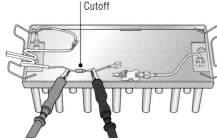

Cutoff

Test thermal cutoff with VOM set on RX1 scale. Disconnect one lead and clip probes as shown; meter should show zero ohms. Replace faulty cutoff if part is available.

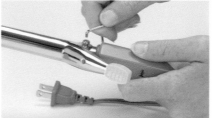

Plate | Heating element (beneath plate)

Test heating element with VOM set on RX1 scale. Disconnect one terminal; clip probes to both terminals. Meter should move toward zero but show moderate (100 to 200 ohms) resistance.

Curling iron

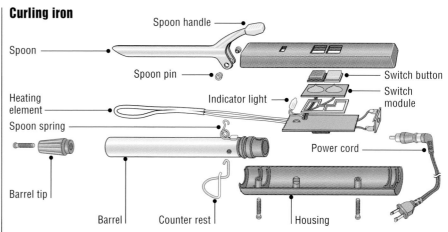

Spoon handle — Spoon — Spoon pin — Switch button — Switch module — Heating element — Indicator light — Spoon spring — Power cord — Barrel tip — Barrel — Counter rest — Housing

Disassembly

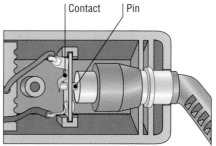

1 Remove counter rest by pulling apart legs. Shake out pins securing spoon, or else remove them with pliers. Set spoon aside.

2 Loosen screws joining halves of housing; then separate halves gently. Note positions of parts before lifting them out.

Servicing swivel cords

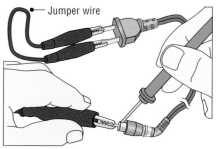

Contact | Pin

Check contacts for burned or broken wire connections; repair if possible. Clean contacts by sanding and then spraying with electrical cleaner; both contacts must touch swivel cord leads.

Jumper wire

Test cord for continuity, using jumper wire and VOM set on RX1 scale. Clip jumper to plug; touch VOM probes as shown. Bend and pull cord; meter should show zero ohms at all times.

The hair dryers shown here and on page 188 all share the same basic components: a fan, powered by a small motor, that blows air across an open-coil heating element (see *Types of heating elements*, p.182). In addition to on-off and heat control switches, some hand-held dryers also have a button that momentarily cuts power to the element, resulting in a flow of unheated air that can help hair to set.

Newer dryers feature a safety plug (see *For your safety*, below) to reduce shock hazards. Some safety plugs cut off power when an internal sensor detects moisture; others contain conventional ground-fault circuit interrupters (p.128). Sensor-type plugs lack a reset button; once the sensor has been activated, the dryer must be returned to the manufacturer for servicing. Dryers with GFCI plugs can be reset, but they should be professionally serviced before use if the appliance has been immersed in water.

Dryers designed for overseas use have a switch that allows them to operate on 250-volt current (standard in many countries). When you travel, determine the local voltage before using any appliance. The wrong voltage could damage the appliance. In the U.S. and Canada, keep a dryer on the 125-volt setting.

FOR YOUR SAFETY

If a dryer falls into water, turn off power at the service panel (p.127); then unplug the dryer from the wall outlet before retrieving it.

If dryer plug is equipped with a GFCI safety plug (see exploded view, right), test it on a regular basis (p.128).

Never leave a dryer within reach of children while it is plugged in; unplug a dryer when not using it.

Avoid blocking a dryer's air openings; never place it on a soft surface like a bed or couch. The dryer can overheat and cause a fire. Keep openings free of hair and lint.

Always let a dryer cool down completely before storing it.

Don't use a dryer in the presence of aerosols. Motor sparks can cause an explosion; apply hair spray *after* drying.

CAUTION: A hair dryer made before 1980 may contain asbestos in its heating assembly. Do not disassemble.

Pro-style dryer

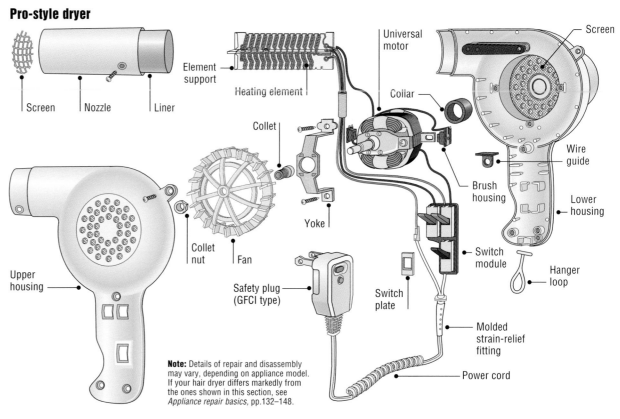

Screen | Nozzle | Liner

Element support | Heating element | Collar | Universal motor | Screen

Collet | Wire guide | Brush housing | Lower housing

Collet nut | Fan | Yoke | Switch module | Hanger loop

Upper housing | Safety plug (GFCI type) | Switch plate | Molded strain-relief fitting | Power cord

Note: Details of repair and disassembly may vary, depending on appliance model. If your hair dryer differs markedly from the ones shown in this section, see *Appliance repair basics*, pp.132–148.

Disassembly

1 Unplug dryer and remove nozzle. Remove screws fastening halves of housing; then carefully separate halves.

Wire guide

2 To gain access to the switch module, free plastic wire guide from its post and lift module from lower housing.

3 Remove collet nut (or C-clip in some models). Lift fan; then remove collet from motor shaft with fingers.

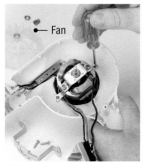

Fan

4 Free motor by unscrewing yoke and motor mounting screws. Note orientation of wires for correct reassembly.

Euro-style dryer

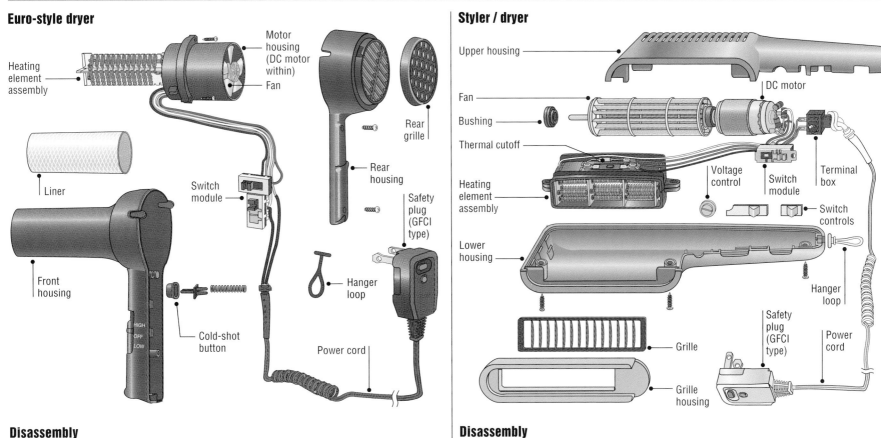

Heating element assembly

Motor housing (DC motor within)

Fan

Rear grille

Rear housing

Liner

Switch module

Safety plug (GFCI type)

Front housing

Cold-shot button

Hanger loop

Power cord

HIGH OFF LOW

Styler / dryer

Upper housing

Fan

Bushing

Thermal cutoff

Heating element assembly

Lower housing

DC motor

Voltage control

Switch module

Terminal box

Switch controls

Hanger loop

Power cord

Safety plug (GFCI type)

Grille

Grille housing

Disassembly

Safety plug

1 Unplug dryer. Twist off rear grille for cleaning and to expose intake screen.

2 Remove screws holding housing together. Separate halves carefully—switch modules may drop out.

3 Remove screws from motor housing. Pull housing from case, together with fan, motor, and heating element.

Disassembly

1 Unplug dryer. Remove screws holding housing together, and gently pull halves apart (switches may be loose).

2 To remove power cord, lift terminal box containing leads from lower case. Remove cover plate to expose leads.

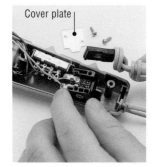

Cover plate

3 Lift cord away from leads. Note that sharp prongs inside terminal box pierce cord when plate is tightened fully.

Bonnet type

Heated air flows through hollow support arm and into hood, where it exits through vent holes. In "shower cap" bonnet dryer, air flows through flexible tube into flexible hood.

Vent holes

Hood

Support arm

Knob

Housing

Power cord

Yoke

Switch

Shaded-pole motor

Rotor

Yoke

Mounting plate

Grille

Impeller

Heating element assembly

C-clip

Base

Disassembly

1 Unplug dryer; turn it upside down. Remove base screws and pry base from housing.

2 Pull off switch knob; then squeeze switch tabs as you push switch through housing.

Grille

3 Remove screws in mounting plate and grille. Pry off C-clip to free impeller (p.189).

Nut driver

4 Remove yoke to free motor. Yoke contains fibrous wick; add 2 or 3 drops of oil to it.

Troubleshooting (all types of hair dryers)

Problem	CAUSE? / Solution
Motor does not run	POWER OFF AT OUTLET? See *General troubleshooting*, p.144.
	FAULTY POWER CORD? See *General troubleshooting*, p.144.
	SAFETY PLUG GFCI TRIPPED? Press reset button on GFCI. If GFCI trips again, replace dryer or have it professionally serviced. ◇
	FAULTY SWITCH? Open dryer housing to access switch. Clean switch and repair connections (facing page). Replace switch or dryer if appliance still fails to work. ◆
	MOTOR JAMMED? Disassemble dryer. Clean and lubricate motor (facing page). ◆
	FAULTY MOTOR? If dryer has a universal or shaded-pole motor, see *General troubleshooting*, pp.146–147; if dryer has a DC motor, lubricate it (facing page) and test diodes (p.170). ◆ ▣
Motor runs but dryer does not heat at one or more settings	THERMAL CUTOFF FAULTY? Access heating element and test cutoff (facing page). Replace cutoff if available separately; otherwise replace entire element assembly. ◆
	FAULTY SWITCH? See *Motor does not run*, above. ◆ ▣
	HEATING ELEMENT FAULTY? Test element (facing page). Replace if faulty (see *Caution*, p.186). Repair of coil is not advised. ◆ ▣
	FILTERS CLOGGED? Clean intake filters (facing page) and/or grilles. Some disassembly may be required, depending on type of dryer. ◇
	HOSE PUNCTURED? *(Bonnet-type dryers with "shower cap" hoods only)* Inspect flexible hose for holes and tears. Repair (facing page) if possible; replace if hose is old and brittle. ◇
Dryer heats but motor runs poorly	FAN JAMMED? Inspect fan; it should turn freely. Clean fan to remove dust and lint; look especially for hair wrapped around ends of shaft. Lubricate each bushing supporting shaft with 1 to 3 drops of lightweight machine or household oil. ◆
Dryer is noisy	IMPELLER OBSTRUCTED? *(Bonnet-type dryers only)* Access dryer impeller (*Disassembly*, Step 3, left). Remove obstructions and lubricate shaded-pole motor (facing page). ◆
	DRY BEARINGS? Lubricate motor (facing page). ◆
	FOREIGN OBJECT IN FAN? Problem is most likely to occur in bonnet-type fan because objects can fall through vent grille. Access fan and remove object. ◆
Dryer shocks user or trips circuit breaker	SHORT IN WIRING? Dryers are typically used in damp environments and are particularly susceptible to circuit faults that will trip a GFCI. If GFCI or safety plug trips repeatedly, disassemble dryer and check for shorted wiring (see *General troubleshooting*, p.147). Dry internal parts thoroughly to remove any moisture that may contribute to problem. If problem persists, replace dryer. ◆

Degree of difficulty: Simple ◇   Average ◆   Complex ◆   Volt-ohm meter required: ▣

Servicing hair dryers

Faulty cords and clogged filters are the most common causes of hair dryer problems. If a dryer with toggle switches runs poorly, first make sure the switches are correctly set (check the manual).

A dryer motor is small, so be careful when lubricating it; getting oil on switches or adding too much oil can ruin the appliance. When reassembling any hair dryer after removing the motor, apply thread-

locking compound to the motor mounting screws to keep them from vibrating loose. To prevent premature failure of the power cord, don't wrap it around the appliance during storage.

Lubricating the motor

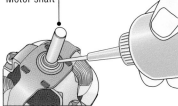

Motor shaft

Universal motor. Apply 1 drop of lightweight (SAE 20) household or machine oil to the bushing at each end of the motor.

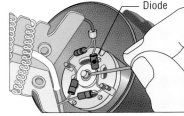

Diode

DC motor. Dip straight pin into lightweight machine oil; dab oil on end of motor shaft and on bushing. Do not get oil on diodes.

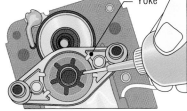

Yoke

Shaded-pole motor. Remove yoke. Apply 2 or 3 drops of lightweight machine oil to fibrous wick on underside of yoke.

Cleaning the intake filter

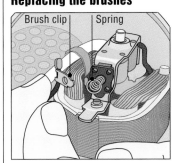

Vacuum cleaner

Brush or vacuum grille and filter screen (if there is one) to remove hair, lint, and dust. In severe cases, disassemble hair dryer to remove hair from fan, motor shaft, and other internal parts. To loosen any material hardened by hair spray, spray it with electrical contact cleaner and pry loose.

Servicing the heater assembly

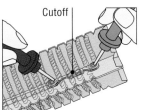

Brush away dust. Repair wiring break if near terminals; otherwise replace element assembly.

Lead

Probe element terminals with VOM on RX1. Reading should be 15 to 50 ohms with switch off.

Cutoff

Probe thermal cutoff leads with VOM on RX1; reading should be zero ohms. Replace if faulty.

Fit leads of new cutoff around terminal posts; clip off excess. Secure with silver solder.

Replacing the brushes

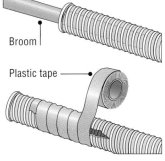

Brush clip   Spring

Universal motors may need new brushes to replace worn originals. Remove motor to access brush holders. Pry brush clips loose, and remove brush and spring. Replace brushes as needed (see also *General troubleshooting*, p.146).

Servicing the switches

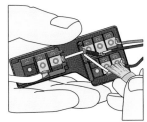

Access switches. Resolder broken connections. Brush switches to remove dust or lint.

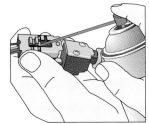

Spray switches with electrical contact cleaner. Check slide-type switches for obstructions.

TIPS FROM THE PROS

C-clips are tiny fasteners often found in hair dryers and other small appliances. To remove the type shown here, insert a small flat-bladed screwdriver between clip and shaft, then twist the screwdriver slowly; the clip will slide out. Hold one hand over the clip in case it pops loose suddenly.
CAUTION: Wear safety goggles.

Screwdriver

Repairing the hose

Broom

Plastic tape

Use plastic tape to mend flexible hose found on bonnet-type hair dryers that have "shower cap" hoods. Insert broom handle in hose to maintain hose shape; tightly wrap tape parallel to hose spring spirals. An old, brittle hose probably cannot be repaired; replace it instead.

Small appliances ▪ Heaters

A convenient source of supplemental heat, portable space heaters come in two basic types. In convective heaters, air heated by one or more heating elements is blown into the room by a fan. In radiative heaters, the elements heat a liquid (such as diathermic oil) or reflect heat off a metal pan; either way, the heat radiates into the room rather than being blown into it. Radiative heaters are generally more effective than convective heaters in large open rooms.

Radiative heater

A heater's basic components are the control switches, elements, and (in convective heaters) fan. Heaters may also have a thermostat. Common safety features found in all types of space heaters include a tip-over switch, which shuts off the heater if it's knocked over, and a thermal cutoff, which shuts off an overheating unit. Some cutoffs reset after the heater has cooled down; others must be replaced if they trip. The parts most likely to need service, however, are the switches, thermostats (if any), and heating elements. Most heaters have sheathed or coil-type elements (see *Types of heating elements*, p.182); some have ceramic elements (see *Ceramic-type heaters*, p.193).

Convective heater

Space heaters may draw up to 13 amps of power. Because most homes have 15-amp breakers or fuses, heaters are a main cause of tripped breakers or blown fuses. If a heater causes circuit failure, turn off other appliances on the same circuit or move the heater to another circuit (see *Correcting circuit overloads*, p.127). Never install a higher-rated fuse or breaker to accommodate a heater; the result could be a fire.

Heaters are sometimes identified by their output, measured in British thermal units (BTU's). More often, they are rated by how much current they consume, measured in watts. Heaters designed to run on household current are usually rated at 1,500 watts or less. A 1,500-watt heater typically has two elements, one rated 900 watts, the other 600 watts, connected by a common terminal. You can select either or both elements to provide various levels of warmth; the more watts you use, the higher the heat output will be–and the higher your heating cost.

Kerosene space heaters. Unvented kerosene heaters can poison indoor air and have been banned for indoor use in many provinces. For indoor heating, use only a vented kerosene heater.

Troubleshooting

Problem	CAUSE? / Solution
Heater doesn't heat	POWER OFF AT OUTLET? *See General troubleshooting*, p.144.
	FAULTY POWER CORD? *See General troubleshooting*, p.144.
	HEATING ELEMENT BROKEN OR FAULTY? Inspect for damage; then test with VOM (see facing page for sheathed elements, p.192 for coil-type elements, p.193 for ceramic elements). Repair or replace element if faulty. ◆ ▣
	FAULTY SWITCH? See *General troubleshooting*, p.145.
	THERMAL CUTOFF TRIPPED? See *Testing a thermal cutoff*, p.161. ◆ ▣
	TIP-OVER SWITCH ACTIVATED? If heater equipped with internal gravity switch has tipped over, switch will reset after heater has been righted. Be sure heater is on level surface, however, or switch may not reset. ◇
	WIRING BURNED? Burned wiring is a fairly common problem with all types of heaters. Remove control housing; examine wires and terminals for signs of damage. Replace any suspect wiring. ◆
	THERMOSTAT FAULTY? If unit has a thermostat, test it for continuity (see *Testing the thermostat*, p.194). File contacts with automotive-point file; flush with contact cleaner. Replace thermostat if still faulty. ◆ ▣
Heater warms but fan does not run (Convective heaters only)	LOOSE OR JAMMED FAN BLADE? Disassemble heater far enough to reach fan. Inspect for debris that might obstruct blade. Spin blade by hand to see if it hits surrounding parts; metal blades can sometimes be bent back into position. Check hub of fan; tighten setscrew if loose (on some heaters, hub is replaceable if damaged). ◇
	MOTOR SHAFT FROZEN? Loosen shaft with spray solvent-type lubricant. Use oiler with an extension spout to lubricate bearings with SAE 20-weight nondetergent oil (see *Servicing the motor*, p.192.) ◆
	MOTOR FAULTY? Test for continuity (see *General troubleshooting*, p.146, for universal and split-phase motors; p.147 for shaded-pole motors, the most common type found in heaters). Replace faulty motor if possible. ◆ ▣
Heater leaks (Oil-filled heaters only)	GASKET OR TANK DAMAGED? Remove element (see *Servicing a sheathed element*, facing page) and inspect gasket for cracks or crumbling edges; replace damaged gasket. Also check surface of mounting collar; lightly scrape away any residue remaining from the old gasket. Have a leaking tank professionally serviced. ◆
Heater provides insufficient heat, or cycles on and off frequently	BLOCKED AIR VENTS? Use vacuum cleaner to remove lint and dust from air intake vents. Clean air filter, if any (look for filter at rear of heater). Move heater away from draperies or furniture that might block intake vents. ◇
	DIRTY REFLECTOR? *(Radiative heaters only)* Some heaters have a shiny metal pan behind elements to reflect heat into room. Unplug heater and disassemble just enough to reach pan. Remove dust; polish with dry lint-free cloth. ◇
	HEATING ELEMENT FAULTY? In units with coil- or ribbon-type elements, one element can be bad without affecting the other. Check elements for damage; then test (see *Heater doesn't heat*, above). Repair or replace faulty element. ◆ ▣
	MOTOR FAULTY? If motor runs too slowly, heater may overheat and trip thermal cutoff. Test motor (see *Heater warms but fan does not run*, above) and replace if faulty. ◆ ▣
	THERMOSTAT FAULTY? See *Heater doesn't heat*, above. ◆ ▣
Heater trips breaker or shocks user	See *General troubleshooting*, p.147.

Degree of difficulty: Simple ◇   Average ◆   Complex ◆   Volt-ohm meter required: ▣

Radiative heater (liquid-filled)

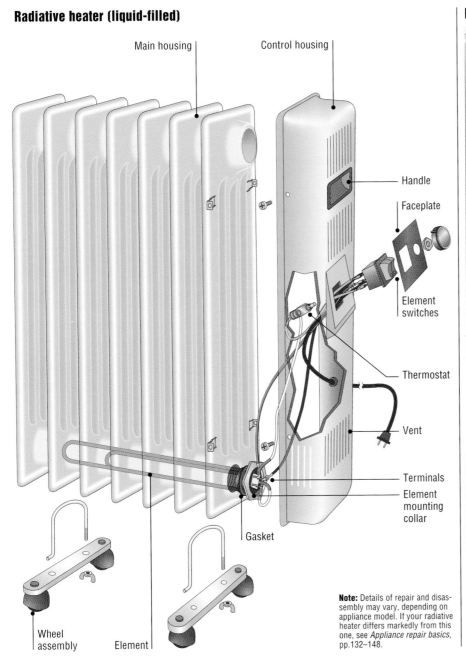

Main housing

Control housing

Handle

Faceplate

Element switches

Thermostat

Vent

Terminals

Element mounting collar

Gasket

Wheel assembly

Element

Note: Details of repair and disassembly may vary, depending on appliance model. If your radiative heater differs markedly from this one, see *Appliance repair basics,* pp.132–148.

Disassembly

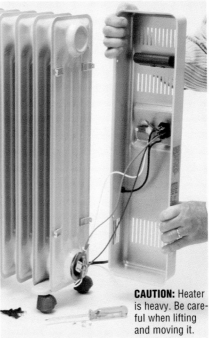

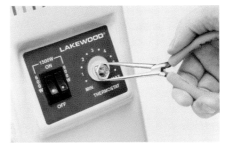

CAUTION: Heater is heavy. Be careful when lifting and moving it.

1 Unplug heater and let it cool completely. To open the control housing, remove screws holding it in place at the edges and lift it away; all wiring is now accessible.

2 To remove thermostat, pull off knob, then mark and remove leads. Use long-nose pliers to remove recessed nut from thermostat shaft; then push shaft through mounting hole.

3 To remove switch, label and disconnect leads. Switch is secured by clips on top and bottom; squeeze clips together and push switch through mounting hole.

Servicing a sheathed element

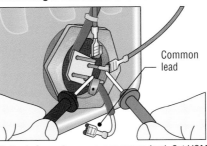

Common lead

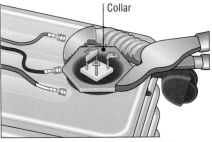

Collar

To test elements, remove common lead. Set VOM on RX1 scale. Touch probe to common terminal, other probe to each remaining terminal. Meter should read 12 to 17 ohms for 900-watt element, 20 to 24 ohms for 600-watt element.

To remove faulty elements, mark and disconnect leads from element terminals. Put heater on an old towel. Upend heater (collar facing up), and unscrew collar with groove-joint pliers. Remove gasket and lift out elements.

Convective heater

Note: Details of repair and disassembly may vary, depending on appliance model. If your convective heater differs markedly from this one, see *Appliance repair basics,* pp.132–148.

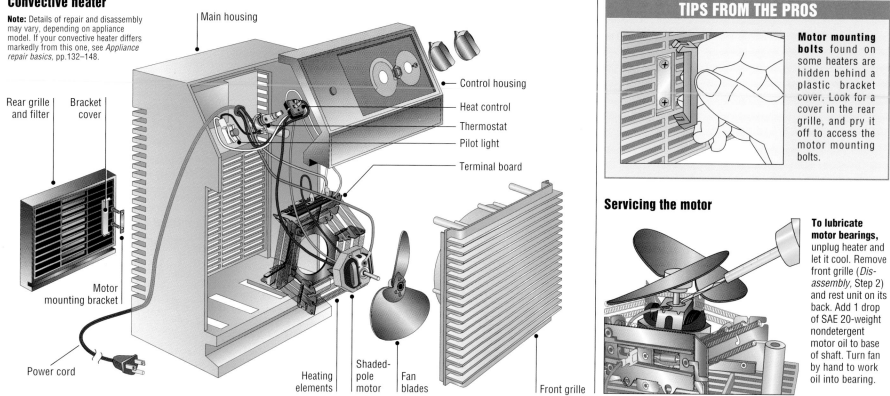

Main housing

Control housing

Heat control

Thermostat

Pilot light

Terminal board

Rear grille and filter

Bracket cover

Motor mounting bracket

Power cord

Heating elements

Shaded-pole motor

Fan blades

Front grille

TIPS FROM THE PROS

Motor mounting bolts found on some heaters are hidden behind a plastic bracket cover. Look for a cover in the rear grille, and pry it off to access the motor mounting bolts.

Servicing the motor

To lubricate motor bearings, unplug heater and let it cool. Remove front grille (*Disassembly,* Step 2) and rest unit on its back. Add 1 drop of SAE 20-weight nondetergent motor oil to base of shaft. Turn fan by hand to work oil into bearing.

Disassembly

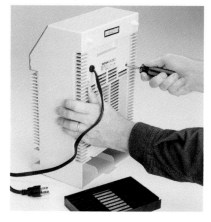

1 Unplug heater; wait until it cools. Remove rear grille; then label and pull off control knobs. Release front grille by removing screws on back of housing (these may be Torx screws).

2 To remove front grille, lift control housing slightly, then pull front grille toward you; motor, fan, and elements are now accessible. To reach controls, lift off control housing entirely. (When reassembling, keep wiring clear of screw mounts.)

3 Remove thermostat from control housing by unscrewing recessed retaining nut with long-nose pliers. Disconnect wires. To remove heat control, remove mounting screw, disengage tab holding control to housing, then disconnect wires.

Testing two-part elements

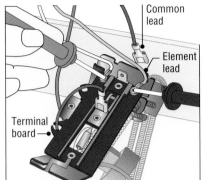

Common lead

Element lead

Terminal board

Elements

Trace element leads from heat control switch to terminal board. Set VOM on RX1. To test both elements, turn switch off, disconnect common lead, and probe element lead terminals. For a 1,500-watt heater, reading of 30 to 40 ohms means elements are OK.

To identify faulty element, probe common terminal and each element terminal in turn (with VOM still on RX1). Look for reading of 12 to 24 ohms for each element. Depending on model, you may be able to replace the one bad element. If not, replace both.

FOR YOUR SAFETY

Never connect a heater to any household extension cord.

Always place a heater on a hard, flat, dry surface. Keep it at least 3 feet from combustible materials such as drapes and bed linens.

Never use a heater near combustible liquids, such as kerosene or polyurethane. Such liquids and their fumes can be ignited by the unit's heating element or by the arcing of components within the heater.

Wait for a heater to cool down before moving it, and use the handle. The housing can get hot enough to burn you.

Supervise children and invalids when a heater is near.

Clean a heater with a vacuum or by dusting with a lint-free cloth. Accumulated dust and lint can ignite; blocked vents can cause the unit to overheat.

Ceramic heaters

Like other convective heaters, ceramic heaters employ a fan to move air past a series of elements. What distinguishes these heaters, however, is the element itself. The extra surface area of a ceramic element allows the heater to be operated at lower temperatures, making it somewhat safer than convective heaters that rely on conventional elements.

Another feature that distinguishes ceramic heaters from other types is their diminutive size. Often small enough to fit on a desktop, the units still manage to pack a full array of features inside, including a *Power on* light, a fan speed control, various types of air filters, and a thermostat. For safety reasons, the units also include an internal tip-over switch.

The fact that ceramic heaters pack so many features into such a small package makes them difficult for novices to service. Wires and other parts are tightly packed, so pay particular attention during disassembly. Internal housings, for example, may be held together by a series of spring-loaded clips that can be difficult to reposition. If the heater includes a circuit board as part of its control system, servicing is complicated even further.

Ceramic heater

Servicing ceramic elements

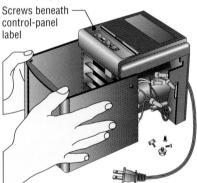

Screws beneath control-panel label

1 Heater housing may have several interlocking parts. Look for hidden fasteners behind labels, and try to slide parts away from each other as each group of fasteners is removed.

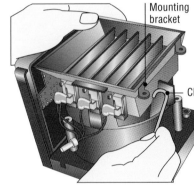

Mounting bracket

Clip

2 Internal portions of heater may be held together with spring-loaded clips. To remove, lift clips from mounting brackets while holding heater together with other hand. Use long-nose pliers if clips are difficult to reach.

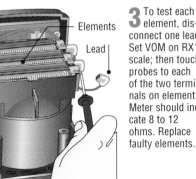

Elements

Lead

3 To test each element, disconnect one lead. Set VOM on RX1 scale; then touch probes to each of the two terminals on element. Meter should indicate 8 to 12 ohms. Replace faulty elements.

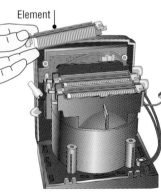

Element

4 To replace an element, disconnect terminal lead on each side, then lift element out of housing. Note position of element to facilitate replacement.

The main parts of a hot plate are one or two heating elements and one or more devices to regulate the heat. In some units, a thermostat calibrated for limited heat settings is paired with an on-off switch. In other units, thermostats (sometimes called cycling switches) provide a wide range of temperatures.

A common problem afflicting hot plates is a burned-out heating element. If the element is good but the appliance still doesn't work properly, suspect the power cord or a switch. Replace or repair any defective parts promptly. Make sure any repairs can stand up to the heat generated by this appliance.

To disassemble a hot plate, remove bolts in drip pans; pry housings apart.

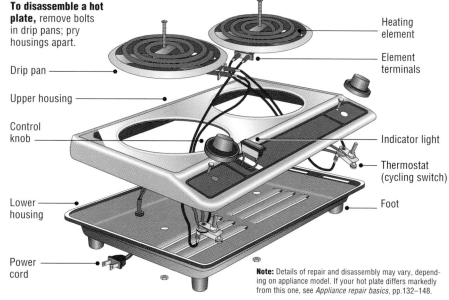

Heating element

Element terminals

Drip pan

Upper housing

Control knob

Indicator light

Thermostat (cycling switch)

Lower housing

Foot

Power cord

Note: Details of repair and disassembly may vary, depending on appliance model. If your hot plate differs markedly from this one, see *Appliance repair basics,* pp.132–148.

Troubleshooting

Problem	CAUSE? / Solution
Burner doesn't heat	POWER OFF AT OUTLET? See *General troubleshooting,* p.144.
	FAULTY POWER CORD? See *General troubleshooting,* p.144.
	INTERNAL WIRING DAMAGED? Examine internal wiring for damage or wear; problems spots *may* look burned. Replace damaged wires and connectors. ◆
	THERMOSTAT FAULTY? Check each thermostat for continuity (see below). Clean electrical contacts if possible; replace switch if not. ◆ ▣
	ELEMENT FAULTY? Test elements for ground (below) and resistance (p.131). Replace element if faulty. ◆ ▣
	THERMAL CUTOFF TRIPPED? If appliance has a thermal cutoff, check it for continuity (see *Testing internal components,* p.168). Replace cutoff if defective. Check wiring for damage or wear to locate cause of overload that tripped cutoff. ◆ ▣
Hot plate is not level or tips when used	FEET DAMAGED? Check feet for damage. Repair broken part if possible (see *Repairing plastic parts,* p.137), or replace foot. **CAUTION:** An unsteady hot plate is a safety hazard; hot foods and liquids may spill. ◇
	LEVELING LEG IMPROPERLY SET? On most hot plates, one leg can be adjusted to account for slight variations in countertop surface. Adjust leg as needed to level appliance, or move appliance to another surface. ◇
Hot plate doesn't shut off or heats whenever it's plugged in	CONTACTS FUSED? Examine thermostat contacts. If you cannot push them apart with finger pressure, they are fused and cannot be serviced. Replace thermostat. ◆
Hot plate trips breaker or shocks user	See *General troubleshooting,* p.147.

Degree of difficulty: Simple ◇   Average ◆   Complex ◆   Volt-ohm meter required: ▣

Testing an element for ground

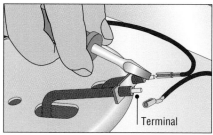

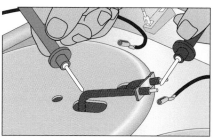

Terminal

1 Unplug the appliance and access the element terminals (this might require opening the appliance housing). Detach leads by gently prying them off with a flat-bladed screwdriver.

2 Set VOM on highest ohms scale; probe element sheathing and each terminal in turn. Both readings should be infinity. If either one moves toward zero ohms, element has a ground fault; replace it.

Testing the thermostat

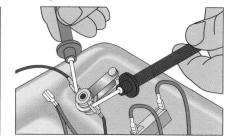

Disconnect one thermostat lead. Turn thermostat knob to high setting, set VOM on RX1, and touch probes to terminals. VOM should read zero ohms. If it does not, replace thermostat.

Ice-cream makers

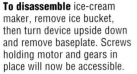

To disassemble ice-cream maker, remove ice bucket, then turn device upside down and remove baseplate. Screws holding motor and gears in place will now be accessible.

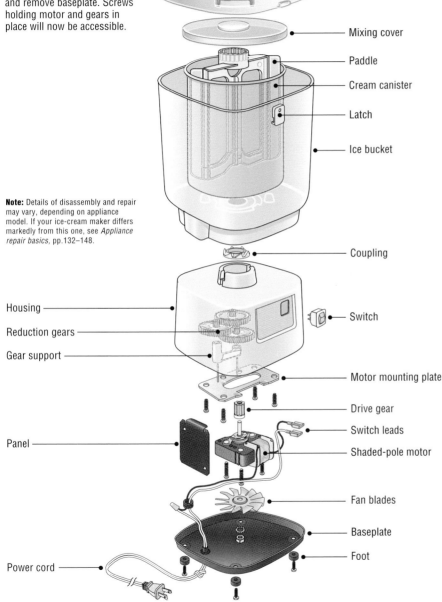

Ice bucket cover

Mixing cover

Paddle

Cream canister

Latch

Ice bucket

Note: Details of disassembly and repair may vary, depending on appliance model. If your ice-cream maker differs markedly from this one, see *Appliance repair basics*, pp.132–148.

Coupling

Housing

Reduction gears

Gear support

Switch

Motor mounting plate

Drive gear

Switch leads

Shaded-pole motor

Panel

Fan blades

Baseplate

Foot

Power cord

Ice cream is still made the traditional way: by packing layers of salt and ice around a metal canister. These days, however, a small electric motor (mounted above or below the canister) drives gears that do the work of a hand crank. Although tabletop ice-cream makers are fairly durable machines, the motor and gears can be damaged if you mix overly large batches of ice cream or if you neglect a jammed mixing paddle.

Clean the canister after each use to remove any salt residue. Also, be sure your hands are dry before touching a chilled canister; wet fingers can stick to its icy surface, injuring your skin.

Servicing the gears

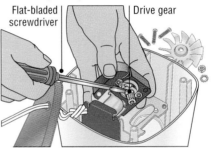

Flat-bladed screwdriver | Drive gear

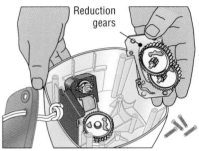

Reduction gears

1 Unplug appliance. Turn housing upside down and remove baseplate. Remove fan blades, then motor mounting screws; lift out motor. Pry drive gear off motor shaft if worn or damaged.

2 Remove motor mounting plate (reduction gears might come out with it). Wipe away grease, examine each gear for wear and damage, and relubricate or replace gears as necessary.

Troubleshooting

Problem	CAUSE? / Solution
Motor doesn't work	POWER OFF AT OUTLET? See *General troubleshooting*, p.144.
	FAULTY POWER CORD? See *General troubleshooting*, p.144.
	MOTOR BEARINGS DRY? Lubricate carefully with lightweight machine oil. ◇
	FAULTY SHADED-POLE MOTOR? See *General troubleshooting*, p.147.
Motor runs; paddle doesn't turn	GEARS WORN OR DAMAGED? Replace worn or damaged gears (above). Lubricate new plastic gears with 1 tbsp. plastic-compatible grease. ◆
Ice-cream maker is unusually noisy	GEARS WORN OR DAMAGED? See *Motor runs; paddle doesn't turn*, above. If gears are OK but unit is still noisy, lubrication might solve problem. ◆
Ingredients don't mix properly	IMPROPER INGREDIENTS? Check recipe and owner's manual. ◇
	PADDLE DAMAGED? Inspect paddle and replace if damaged. ◇
	GEARS WORN OR DAMAGED? See *Motor runs; paddle doesn't turn*, above. ◆
Appliance trips breaker or shocks user	See *General troubleshooting*, p.147.

Degree of difficulty: Simple ◇   Average ◆   Complex ◆   Volt-ohm meter required: ◼

Whether it's a basic "no-frills" iron, a cordless model, a compact travel iron, or an electronic iron loaded with features, all steam irons work in the same way. They press out wrinkles in fabric using moisture, pressure, and heat. The iron's working surface, the soleplate, may be plain metal or coated with an easy-to-clean nonstick material.

Among the more useful features found on higher-end irons are an automatic shutoff, which turns off the iron if you haven't moved it within a specified period of time; a burst-of-steam mode, which blasts badly wrinkled or hard-to-iron fabric with extra steam; a spray mechanism for moistening fabric; self-cleaning vents to help keep the soleplate free of mineral deposits; and dual-voltage capacity and a plug adapter, which allow you to use the iron in other countries. Bear in mind, however, that the more features an iron has, the more difficult it may be to repair.

Because even a basic steam iron has many parts that fit together exactly, repairing an iron can be tricky. Disassemble an iron slowly and carefully—small components have a tendency to pop out of place before you note their positions. To make reassembly easier, take an instant photograph at each stage of disassembly and lay out the parts in order as you remove them.

Common steam iron problems include a blocked water system, a gummed-up soleplate, and a frayed or shorted power cord, all of which are fairly simple to remedy. Any problems with an iron's electronic components should be dealt with by an authorized service center.

Electronic spray/steam iron

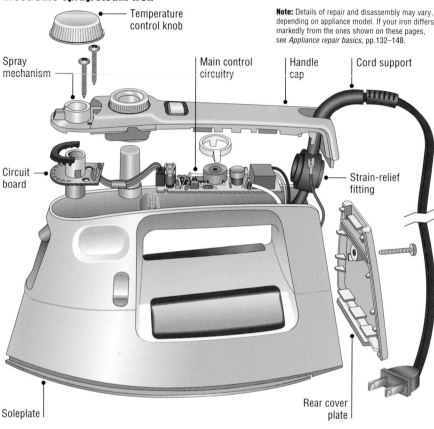

Temperature control knob

Spray mechanism

Main control circuitry

Handle cap

Cord support

Circuit board

Strain-relief fitting

Soleplate

Rear cover plate

Note: Details of repair and disassembly may vary, depending on appliance model. If your iron differs markedly from the ones shown on these pages, see *Appliance repair basics*, pp.132–148.

How a steam iron works

Valve

Chamber

When steam valve is closed (left), iron operates dry. Open valve (right) allows water to drip into heated steam chamber, where it exits vents in soleplate as steam.

FOR YOUR SAFETY

Don't use iron on a circuit with other high-wattage devices—it could trip a circuit breaker. With switch on *Off*, plug iron into a wall outlet, never into an extension cord.

Unplug iron before refilling water tank.

When not in use, keep the iron on a heel rest with the steam button set on *Off*.

If you leave the ironing area, turn off the iron and unplug it before walking away.

Before storing iron in a cabinet, make sure iron is completely cool.

Disassembly

1 Unplug iron. Unscrew and remove rear cover plate to access wiring connections. Some plates may be fastened with specialty screws (p.201).

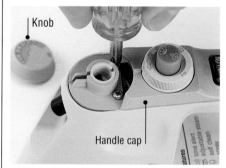

Knob

Handle cap

2 Carefully pry up temperature control knob with taped screwdriver. Remove screws under knob to loosen handle cap.

3 Feed part of cord through strain-relief fitting; then lift off handle cap. Steam and spray mechanisms are under circuit board at front of iron.

Non-electronic steam iron

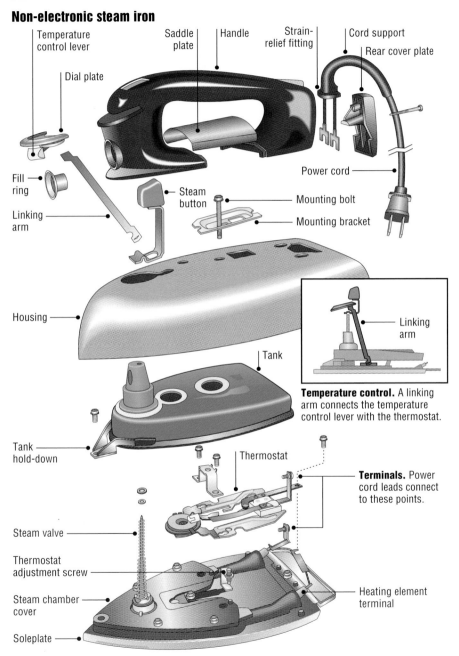

- Temperature control lever
- Dial plate
- Fill ring
- Linking arm
- Housing
- Tank hold-down
- Steam valve
- Thermostat adjustment screw
- Steam chamber cover
- Soleplate
- Saddle plate
- Handle
- Steam button
- Tank
- Thermostat
- Strain-relief fitting
- Cord support
- Rear cover plate
- Power cord
- Mounting bolt
- Mounting bracket
- Heating element terminal

Linking arm

Temperature control. A linking arm connects the temperature control lever with the thermostat.

Terminals. Power cord leads connect to these points.

Disassembly

1 Unplug iron and let cool. Remove rear cover plate. To remove cord, disconnect leads from terminals; slide cord support out of handle.

2 To expose the thermostat adjustment screw, gently pry the saddle plate from the housing with a flat-bladed screwdriver.

Box wrench

3 Unbolt the mounting bracket and remove it. When reassembling parts, align square hole in bracket with corresponding hole in iron.

4 Pry out fill ring with screwdriver. The aluminum ring is easily damaged during disassembly, so plan on replacing this part.

Lever

5 Lift off handle. Linking arm hooked to underside of lever will be loose. To avoid incorrect reassembly, be sure to note lever's position.

6 Lift housing off tank. Unbolt tank with nut driver. Lift tank and bracket straight up, trying not to lose tiny washers atop steam valve.

Small appliances ▪ Irons

Troubleshooting

Problem	CAUSE? / Solution
Iron doesn't heat	**TEMPERATURE SELECTOR OFF?** Turn the selector to the desired setting. ◇
	POWER OFF AT OUTLET? See *General troubleshooting*, p.144.
	FAULTY POWER CORD? See *General troubleshooting*, p.144. Damaged cord support may lead to premature cord failure; replace damaged support. ◇
	FAULTY OR OBSTRUCTED THERMOSTAT? Disassemble iron (pp.196–197); clean lint from thermostat. Test thermostat (facing page). Replace if necessary. ◆ ▦
	DEFECTIVE HEATING ELEMENT? Test element (facing page). Replace iron if element is faulty. ◆ ▦
	CIRCUIT BOARD FAULTY? *(Electronic irons only)* Disassemble iron (p.196); remove leads from board. Set VOM on RX1 and connect probes to lead terminals. Reading should be near zero; if not, have iron professionally serviced. ◆ ▦
Iron heats but steams improperly	**CONTROLS SET IMPROPERLY?** Make sure steam setting is set to *On*. Turn temperature selector to a higher setting if necessary. ◇
	NO WATER IN TANK? Check water level; fill tank as needed. ◇
	STEAM VENTS CLOGGED? Inspect soleplate and clean vents (below). ◇
	CLOGGED STEAM CHAMBER? Flush out sediment (below). ◇
	CLOGGED OR BROKEN STEAM VALVE? Disassemble iron. Valve should move freely when pushed down. Clean valve; replace if necessary (facing page). ◆
Iron produces too little heat	**FAULTY POWER CORD?** See *General troubleshooting*, p.144.
	THERMOSTAT NOT CALIBRATED CORRECTLY? Check and adjust calibration (facing page). **CAUTION:** Use pot holders to handle hot test pieces. ◆
	FAULTY THERMOSTAT? Test thermostat (facing page); replace if faulty. ◆ ▦
	CIRCUIT BOARD FAULTY? See *Iron doesn't heat*, above. ◆ ▦

Problem	CAUSE? / Solution
Iron gets too hot	**THERMOSTAT NOT CALIBRATED CORRECTLY?** Check and adjust calibration (facing page). CAUTION: Use pot holders to protect hands during test. ◆
	THERMOSTAT BROKEN? Replace thermostat. ◆
Iron does not spray properly	**SPRAY NOZZLE CLOGGED?** Inspect and clean nozzle (facing page). ◇
	FAULTY SPRAY MECHANISM? Clean or replace mechanism (facing page). ◆
Iron leaks or spits	**WATER TANK OVERFILLED?** Drain excess water. ◇
	WRONG TEMPERATURE SETTING? Check manual for guide to correct temperature. If knob indicates correct setting but problem persists, check thermostat calibration (facing page). ◆
	BROKEN STEAM VALVE? Replace defective parts. ◆
	STEAM CHAMBER CRACKED? Replace iron. ◇
	WATER TANK CRACKED? A crack indicates that iron was dropped, most likely damaging other parts as well. Replace iron. ◇
	STEAM VENTS, NOZZLE, OR TANK CLOGGED? Clean iron (below). ◇
Iron sticks to fabric	**INCORRECT TEMPERATURE?** Adjust temperature to proper setting. ◇
	SOLEPLATE DIRTY OR SCRATCHED? Clean or repair soleplate (facing page). ◇
Iron stains fabric	**SOLEPLATE DIRTY?** Clean soleplate (facing page). ◇
	WATER TANK DIRTY? Clean tank with a commercial cleaner (below). ◇
	WATER TOO HARD? Use distilled water in water tank. ◇
Iron trips breaker or shocks user	See *General troubleshooting*, p.147.

Degree of difficulty: Simple ◇   Average ◆   Complex ◆   Volt-ohm meter required: ▦

Cleaning an iron

As tap water evaporates inside a steam iron, it leaves behind mineral deposits that can clog the iron's steam and spray mechanisms. To keep a steam iron in good condition, clean it often. If you have a self-cleaning iron that blasts out sediment at the touch of a button, use this feature after each ironing session. If your iron doesn't have this feature, at the first sign of mineral buildup clean the iron with a commercial steam iron cleaner. For an older iron or one without cleaning instructions, flush the tank with a 50/50 solution of white vinegar and water. If your iron needs frequent cleaning, always use distilled water to fill the tank.

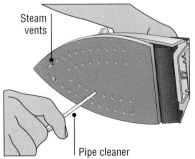

Remove buildup in steam vents by gently poking them with a toothpick or pipe cleaner. Tip the iron so debris won't fall into the vents. Vents may be easier to clean if you heat iron first, but don't touch soleplate until it's sufficiently cool.

Steam vents

Pipe cleaner

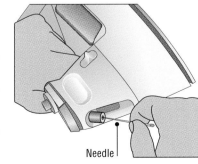

Clean spray nozzle of mineral deposits with a very fine sewing needle. Work carefully—pushing the needle forcefully into the nozzle hole will enlarge opening, causing a leak.

Needle

To flush sediment from iron, pour solution into water tank, place iron on rack over broiling pan, and set iron to steam until tank runs dry. Repeat if necessary. Turn off the iron. Flush out solution by repeating process with clear water.

Cleaning solution

198

Servicing the steam and spray mechanism

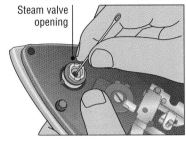

Steam valve opening

Unclog steam valve of basic iron by pulling out valve assembly and poking deposits out of opening with fine sewing needle or straight pin. Check valve spring; if it's broken or has lost tension, replace it.

Spray pump on some irons is not easily serviceable. If pump is accessible, remove it and check for leaks. Place spray tube in water and squirt pump; clean pump (below) if blocked. Replace a leaky pump.

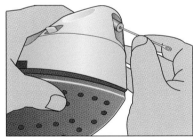

Check spray nozzle again. Make sure any debris loosened earlier is cleaned away. If spray still fails to function, soak pump assembly in white vinegar for 30 min. Retest. If needed, replace spray assembly.

Calibrating the thermostat

While it's easy to adjust the calibration of a standard steam iron's thermostat, have a service center adjust an electronic iron's thermostat. In operation, the heat-ing element in either type of iron cycles on and off; the iron's temperature will fluctuate about 20 Fahrenheit degrees (11 Celsius degrees) between cycles.

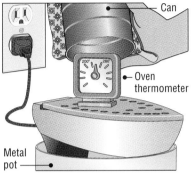

Can

Oven thermometer

Metal pot

1 To check temperature, set iron to start of steam range. Brace iron in a pot and plug in. Rest oven thermometer on soleplate; cover with can. After 5 min., remove can (use a pot holder). Thermometer should read between 220° and 280°F (104° and 138°C).

2 Unplug iron and let cool. Reset thermostat by turning adjustment screw, a quarter turn at a time, with a thin screwdriver. Counterclockwise rotation usually increases the heat, but some irons may differ. Recheck temperature after each adjustment.

Adjustment screw

Testing the thermostat

Wood or plastic stick

Disassemble iron (pp.196–197). Set VOM on RX1 scale. Clip probes to thermostat terminals; open and close thermostat contacts with stick. When contact is closed, VOM should jump from high to zero ohms. Replace thermostat if defective.

Testing the heating element

Terminal

To test element, unplug iron. Set VOM on RX1 scale; then touch probes to exposed heating element terminals. If element is OK, meter will read 10 to 25 ohms. A high reading indicates a faulty element; replace iron.

Cleaning a metal soleplate

A clean, shiny soleplate glides over fabric; a dirty, rough one will drag over fabric or snag it. Regularly inspect the iron's soleplate for scratches and burnt-on starch or other debris; remove them as needed. A badly scratched soleplate can sometimes be resurfaced at a service center, but get an estimate first.

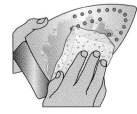

Wipe off dirt buildup on soleplate with a sponge and a commercial soleplate cleaner, mild detergent, or baking soda and water; work around steam vents. Rinse well with water and dry. Never immerse iron in water or use cleaners with harsh abrasives.

Remove scratches and burrs by stroking soleplate lengthwise in one direction with very fine steel wool (not a soap pad) or emery cloth. Wipe off remaining steel wool fibers and debris. Never use abrasives on a nonstick surface.

Juice extractors shred fruits and vegetables and separate the juice from the pulp. While most extractors (including the one featured here) rely on a combination of centrifugal force, generated by a permanent-magnet DC motor (p.139), and a perforated filter basket to extract the juice, some models press the pulp to force the juice out. Like food processors, many extractors have an interlock switch that keeps the unit from working if it's not fully assembled.

Because the filter basket in a juice extractor rotates as fast as 6,000 rpm, an accidental jam can easily bend a motor shaft or other part. If the motor coupling doesn't turn easily by hand when the appliance is disassembled, look carefully for bent or broken parts.

Juicers. Designed to process citrus fruits (a job extractors don't do well), juicers employ a shaded-pole motor and gear assembly to drive a spring-loaded shaft capped by a reamer. Pressing half a citrus fruit against the reamer activates an internal switch that starts the motor. The turning reamer scrapes the fruit, releasing juice into a container. For servicing information, see page 202.

For servicing information, see page 202.

USE AND CARE

Wash removable parts with a soft brush in hot soapy water (check owner's manual to see if any parts can be cleaned in dishwasher). To remove stubborn stains, make a paste of baking soda and water. Rinse stained parts with water; rub paste on stained area with soft damp cloth; rinse and dry before reusing appliance.

Do not use a damaged or bent filter basket; replace it immediately to avoid risk to you or damage to the appliance.

Juice extractor

Note: Details of disassembly and repair may vary, depending on appliance model. If your juice extractor differs markedly from this one, see *Appliance repair basics*, pp.132–148.

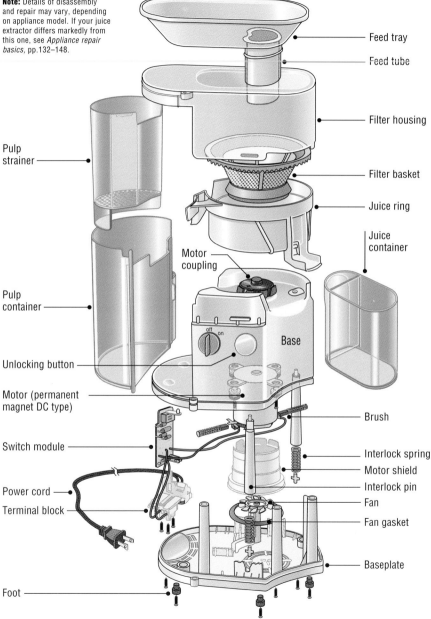

- Feed tray
- Feed tube
- Filter housing
- Pulp strainer
- Filter basket
- Juice ring
- Juice container
- Motor coupling
- Pulp container
- Base
- Unlocking button
- Motor (permanent magnet DC type)
- Switch module
- Brush
- Interlock spring
- Motor shield
- Interlock pin
- Fan
- Fan gasket
- Power cord
- Terminal block
- Baseplate
- Foot

Disassembly

- Baseplate

1 Unplug extractor; remove strainer and pulp assemblies. Upend unit, remove baseplate screws (they may be under feet), and remove plate.

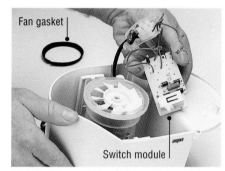

- Fan gasket
- Switch module

2 Lift off fan gasket and slide switch module out of slots in base. Remove motor coupling (see p.201); then pull wire leads from motor.

Keep grease away from electrical parts

3 Remove motor mounting screws and lift motor out of base. Interlock mechanism is now readily accessible.

Troubleshooting

Problem	CAUSE? / Solution
Extractor or juicer doesn't work	POWER OFF AT OUTLET? See *General troubleshooting*, p.144.
	FAULTY POWER CORD? See *General troubleshooting*, p.144.
	INTERNAL WIRING FAULTY? Look for broken wires or corroded connections. On a juicer, also test internal switch (p.202). ◆ ▨
	INTERLOCK SWITCH JAMMED? *(Extractors only)* Make sure unit is assembled properly. Clean interlock pins if clogged with debris. ◆
	WORN BRUSHES? *(Extractors only)* Replace brushes (below). ◆
	FAULTY MOTOR? To test an extractor's DC motor, see right. For a juicer's split-phase motor, see *General troubleshooting*, p.146. ◆ ▨
Motor stops or slows during use	INTERNAL FUSE TRIPPED? *(Extractors only)* If extractor has internal fuse, press reset button or let motor cool for at least 10 min. before restarting. ◇
	MOTOR OVERLOADED? *Extractors:* Cut food into smaller pieces and feed more slowly. Replace filter basket if shredding edges dull. Make sure fruit is ripe, not hard. *Juicers:* Use less force to press fruit against reamer. ◇
	PULP BUILDUP AROUND SHAFT? *(Juicers only)* Unplug appliance, remove reamer, and clear away pulp with moist (not wet) sponge. ◇
Motor runs but reamer does not turn (Juicers only)	SPINDLE OR REAMER DAMAGED? Disassemble juicer (p.202) and inspect spindle and coupling. Replace broken or cracked parts if possible. If reamer is cracked or portion that fits over spindle is worn, replace it. ◆
	DRIVE GEARS STRIPPED? Disassemble appliance and clean gears. Inspect gears for worn or damaged teeth (p.202). Replace gears as a set. ◆
Food jams in food tube	FOOD PIECES TOO LARGE? *(Extractors only)* Unplug appliance and clear jam. Cut fruits and vegetables into smaller pieces. ◇
Device is noisy	FOOD CHUNKS IN BASKET? *(Extractors only)* Pieces of solid food may disturb balance of fast-spinning basket. Unplug extractor; remove chunks of food. ◇
Device trips breaker or shocks user	See *General troubleshooting*, p.147.

Degree of difficulty: Simple ◇   Average ◆   Complex ◆   Volt-ohm meter required: ▨

Replacing the brushes

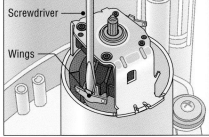

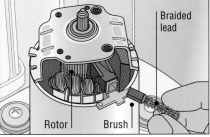

1 Brushes and springs in this permanent-magnet DC motor are held in place by flexible metal terminals. To remove brushes, gently pry terminal "wings" outward with screwdriver.

2 A braided lead within each brush spring links the brushes to the terminals. Spray rotor and brush housing with contact cleaner; replace brush assembly if brushes are worn.

Testing a DC motor (PM-type)

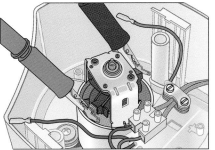

1 To test a permanent-magnet DC motor, access motor and remove leads from brush housings. Set VOM on RX1; clip probes to brush terminals.

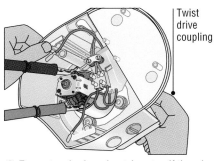

2 Turn rotor slowly and watch meter. If there is no reading, brushes are bad. If reading fluctuates briefly, rotor windings are bad. If readings are steady, motor is OK. Replace faulty motor.

Specialty screws

To discourage repairs by anyone but authorized service centers, some appliance makers use specialty screws that require a removal tool not readily available. If you encounter such a fastener and still want to proceed, check with a well-stocked hardware or specialty tool store to see if they have the needed removal tool (take the appliance with you). If that fails, you may be tempted to improvise, but be aware that you're voiding any warranty and that *you* are proceeding *at your own risk.*

Removing friction-fit parts

Some plastic parts, such as the motor couplings in some extractors, are friction-fit to a shaft and may be hard to remove. If you force such parts off, you may mar or break the plastic. Instead, try to coax the part off using one of the methods below; if that fails, have the appliance serviced professionally.

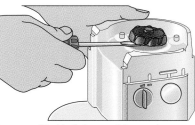

Insert a wide-bladed screwdriver under coupling and *gently* twist it to lift coupling upward. Work around part to avoid jamming it on shaft.

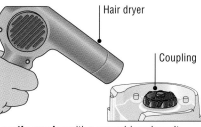

If gentle coaxing with a screwdriver doesn't work, heat coupling slightly. Heated part may expand just enough so you can pull it from shaft.

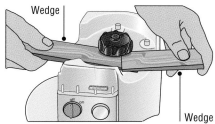

If other methods fail, slip a pair of thin wood wedges beneath coupling. Push wedges toward each other to lift the coupling evenly.

Small appliances ▪ Juice extractors and juicers

Juicer

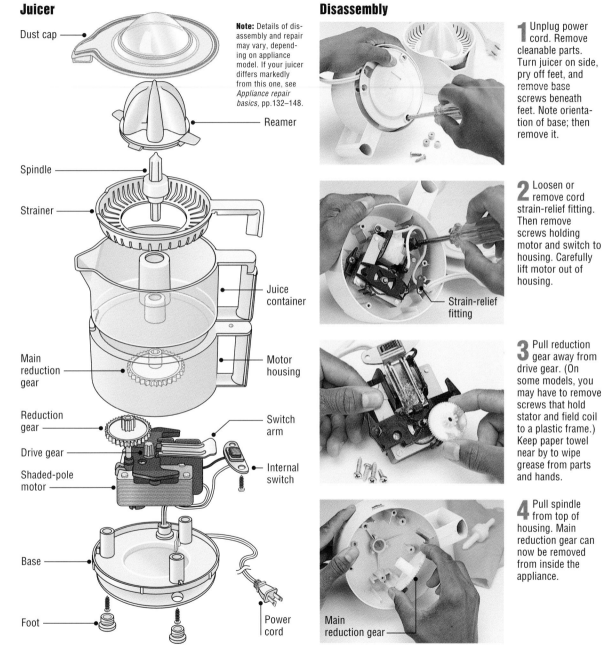

Dust cap

Reamer

Spindle

Strainer

Juice container

Main reduction gear

Motor housing

Reduction gear

Switch arm

Drive gear

Shaded-pole motor

Internal switch

Base

Foot

Power cord

Note: Details of disassembly and repair may vary, depending on appliance model. If your juicer differs markedly from this one, see *Appliance repair basics,* pp.132–148.

Disassembly

1 Unplug power cord. Remove cleanable parts. Turn juicer on side, pry off feet, and remove base screws beneath feet. Note orientation of base; then remove it.

2 Loosen or remove cord strain-relief fitting. Then remove screws holding motor and switch to housing. Carefully lift motor out of housing.

Strain-relief fitting

3 Pull reduction gear away from drive gear. (On some models, you may have to remove screws that hold stator and field coil to a plastic frame.) Keep paper towel near by to wipe grease from parts and hands.

4 Pull spindle from top of housing. Main reduction gear can now be removed from inside the appliance.

Main reduction gear

Servicing the drive system

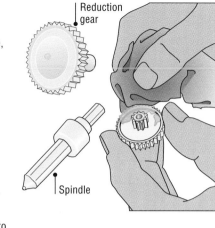

Reduction gear

Spindle

Access gears (*Disassembly,* Step 2). Remove gears and spindle. Wipe off grease; check gears for worn teeth, spindle for rounded edges. During reassembly, apply a thick coat of plastic-compatible grease over gear edges. Keep grease away from electrical connections.

Servicing the switch

1 Remove switch (Disassembly, Step 2) and lift out switch. Clear away any debris beneath switch or switch arm. Clean switch by spraying electrical contact cleaner into switch housing.

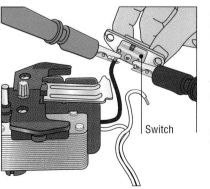

2 To test switch for continuity, desolder one lead, set VOM on RX1, and clip probes to switch terminals. Press switch on and off; meter should read zero with switch on, infinity with switch off.

Switch

Knives / electric

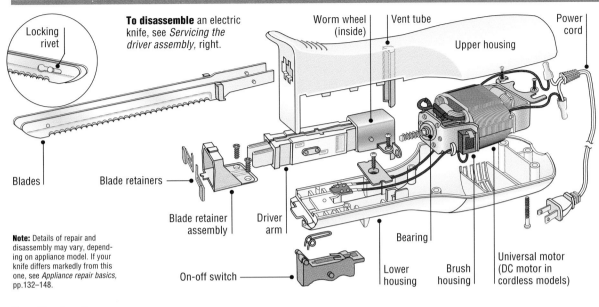

Locking rivet

Blades

Blade retainers

Blade retainer assembly

Driver arm

On-off switch

Note: Details of repair and disassembly may vary, depending on appliance model. If your knife differs markedly from this one, see *Appliance repair basics*, pp.132–148.

To disassemble an electric knife, see *Servicing the driver assembly*, right.

Worm wheel (inside)

Vent tube

Upper housing

Power cord

Bearing

Lower housing

Brush housing

Universal motor (DC motor in cordless models)

An electric knife's gear-and-pinion assembly converts the motor's rotary motion into a reciprocating action. The assembly is linked to a driver arm that moves a pair of serrated blades, pushing one forward as it pulls the other one back.

Most electric knife problems are the result of dull blades or misuse (the knife is forced down during use, for example, or is operated in a sawing fashion). Bad switches and worn gears can also cause problems. If you have to disassemble the knife in order to make repairs, check the brushes and the switch while they're accessible; worn brushes should be replaced.

Servicing the driver assembly

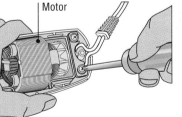

Trigger switch

1 With the knife unplugged and blades removed, remove screws at back of housing. Carefully pull housing apart. Knife's blade retainers will be loose and may fall out as you open housing.

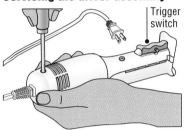

Motor

2 Remove screws holding driver assembly and motor to housing. Then lift motor and driver assembly; slide them over the vent tube and out of the housing. They may come out as two separate assemblies.

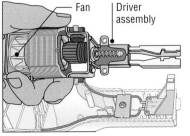

Fan

Driver assembly

3 Inspect parts for wear. Turn fan by hand. If there's more than slight resistance, clean and lubricate driver assembly with lightweight grease. Add a drop of light machine oil to each bearing; then reassemble parts.

Troubleshooting

Problem	CAUSE? / Solution
Motor fails to run or runs poorly	POWER OFF AT OUTLET? See *General troubleshooting*, p.144.
	FAULTY POWER CORD? See *General troubleshooting*, p.144.
	INTERNAL WIRING DAMAGED? Knives are easily dropped, which may jar internal connections loose. Open housing and look for loose wires and damaged wire insulation. Reconnect wires if possible. ◆
	FAULTY OR DIRTY SWITCH? Spray electrical contact cleaner into switch area to clean. If problem persists, remove switch and clean off any corrosion. To test switch, see *General troubleshooting*, p.145; replace faulty switch. ◆
	BRUSHES WORN OR DAMAGED? Replace as needed (see *General troubleshooting*, p.146). ◆
	BEARINGS DRY? Put 1 drop of very light machine oil on each motor bearing; turn rotor to distribute oil. ◆
	BATTERIES NOT CHARGED? *(Cordless models only)* See *Cordless tools and appliances*, p.142. ◇
Knife slices poorly	BLADES NOT LOCKED? Push the blades into the handle until they click. Check by tugging on the guards. ◇
	BLADES DULL? If motor runs but knife cuts poorly, replace worn blades; they cannot be resharpened. ◇
	BLADES MISALIGNED? To repair a bent blade, carefully press it against a flat tabletop (wear leather work gloves to protect your hands). If this fails, replace both blades. Don't try to match blades from different pairs. ◇
	LOCKING RIVET WORN? With the back of the blade resting on a metal surface, gently peen the rivet with a ball-peen hammer. If this fails, replace the blades. ◇
	DRIVE GEARS FAULTY? Faulty gears are noisy. As they get worse, the knife will slow down until it stops functioning. See *Servicing the driver assembly*, right. ◆
Blades won't stay in place	BLADE RETAINER ASSEMBLY DAMAGED? The blade retainers lock the blades to the knife. Open knife housing and check retainers for worn or cracked parts and damaged springs. Replace entire assembly if damaged. ◆
Knife trips breaker or shocks user	See *General troubleshooting*, p.147.

Degree of difficulty: Simple ◇   Average ◆   Complex ◆   Volt-ohm meter required: ▨

Types of motors 139
Drive mechanisms 141
Cordless tools and appliances 142

Small appliances ▪ Mixers

With their smaller motors and more compact housings, portable hand-held mixers (right) are lighter in weight than stand, or pedestal, mixers (p.206). While hand-held mixers are fine for light mixing, only the sturdiest models have sufficient muscle to mix heavy doughs; a stand mixer is generally the better choice for that job.

The beaters of a hand-held mixer are spun by two drive gears (often nylon) turning in opposite directions. These gears connect to a metal worm gear that is driven by a universal motor. The drive gears are seated so as to prevent the beaters from colliding as they spin past each other—when reassembling a mixer, be sure to align any timing marks or arrows on the gears (they should point toward each other).

Some stand mixers are built with the same type of gearing as hand-held mixers; many models have a planetary gear system (p.206). In this type of mixer, drive gears spin a single beater while planetary gears move it around inside the bowl.

Speed controls. Mixer speed is usually regulated by either a tapped field speed control or a governor (see *Controlling a motor's speed,* p.140). If your mixer has numerous wires running between the motor and a multispeed switch (as on the mixer shown here), and "clicks" when the speed is changed, it has a tapped field speed control; otherwise, a governor or (in electronic mixers) a circuit board regulates the speed.

Cordless hand mixers are portable but are less powerful than their plug-in counterparts. See pages 142–143 for more on cordless appliances.

Note: Details of repair and disassembly may vary, depending on appliance model. If your hand-held mixer differs markedly from this one, see *Appliance repair basics,* pp.132–148.

Hand-held mixer

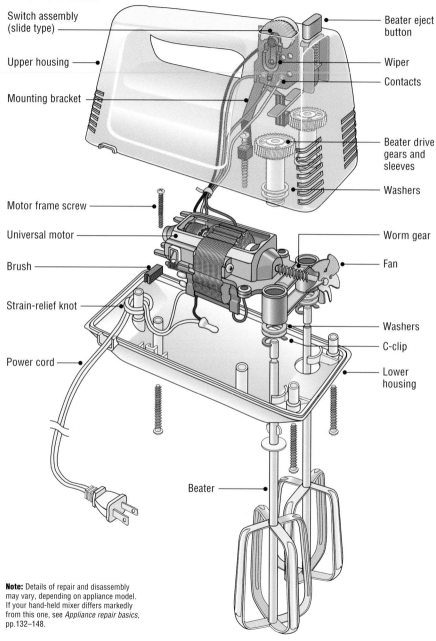

- Switch assembly (slide type)
- Upper housing
- Mounting bracket
- Motor frame screw
- Universal motor
- Brush
- Strain-relief knot
- Power cord
- Beater eject button
- Wiper
- Contacts
- Beater drive gears and sleeves
- Washers
- Worm gear
- Fan
- Washers
- C-clip
- Lower housing
- Beater

Disassembly

1 Unplug mixer. Remove screws from lower housing; then carefully pull housings apart to reveal the motor, gears, and switch assembly.

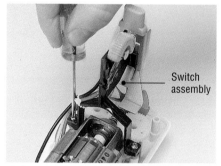

Switch assembly

2 Remove screws holding switch assembly in place; then lift off assembly. Note position of mounting bracket for correct reassembly.

Screw

3 Loosen screw holding back of motor frame to the mixer housing. Carefully lift motor and worm gear away from housing.

Troubleshooting

Problem	CAUSE? / Solution
Motor doesn't run	POWER OFF AT OUTLET? See *General troubleshooting*, p.144.
	FAULTY POWER CORD? See *General troubleshooting*, p.144.
	SPEED CONTROL FAULTY? *(Stand mixers only)* Adjust the control (p.207). ◆
	FAULTY UNIVERSAL MOTOR? See *General troubleshooting*, p.146.
Mixer runs sluggishly	FOOD MIXTURE TOO THICK? With either type of mixer, add liquid to mixture. With stand mixer, use different beater attachments if available. ◇
	DAMAGED OR WORN GEARS? Check gears (for hand mixer, see right; for stand mixer, see page 207). Replace gears as necessary and relubricate. ◆
	FAULTY BRUSHES? See *Faulty universal motor?*, p.146. ◆
	SPEED CONTROL FAULTY? *(Stand mixers only)* See *Motor doesn't run*, above. ◆
Motor runs but beaters don't turn	BEATERS NOT INSERTED PROPERLY? Remove beaters and reinsert correctly. Beaters should snap audibly into place. ◇
	DAMAGED OR WORN GEARS? See *Motor runs sluggishly*, above. ◆
Bowl doesn't rotate *(Stand mixers only)*	BEATER HEIGHT INCORRECT? Beaters with nylon button on bottom should just touch bowl; beaters without button should clear bowl by 1⁄16 in. (see *Adjusting beater clearance*, p.207). ◇
	TURNTABLE JAMMED? Non-planetary mixers may have a rotating base mounted on bearings. Remove and clean base and bearings. Some mixers have gear- or belt-driven bowls; check turning mechanism for wear or damage; lubricate according to manufacturer's instructions, and replace belt as needed. ◇
Mixer vibrates or makes excessive noise	MISALIGNED OR DAMAGED BEATERS? Remove beaters and inspect for damaged tines; straighten if possible, otherwise replace. Reinsert properly. ◇
	DAMAGED OR WORN GEARS? See *Motor runs sluggishly*, above. ◆
	BEATERS HITTING BOWL? *(Stand mixers only)* Realign beaters or bowl. ◇
	LOOSE PARTS? Tighten screws. Replace missing feet on a stand mixer. ◇
Motor runs only at high speed	FAULTY CONTROLS? On hand mixer, service rotary slide switch (right) or replace it. On stand mixer, adjust speed control (see *Adjusting the speed control*, p.207). Have mixers with electronic controls professionally serviced. ◆ ▪
	CAPACITOR SHORTED? *(Stand mixers only)* See *Faulty split-phase motor?*, p.146. **CAUTION:** Always discharge a capacitor before working near it. ◆ ▪
Motor overheats	FOOD MIXTURE TOO THICK? See *Motor runs sluggishly*, above. ◇
	FAULTY UNIVERSAL MOTOR? See *General troubleshooting*, p.146.
	DAMAGED OR WORN GEARS? See *Motor runs sluggishly*, above. ◆
	AIR INTAKE CLOGGED? Vacuum intake vents or clean with pipe cleaner. ◇
	SPEED CONTROL FAULTY? *(Stand mixer only)* See *Motor doesn't run*, above. ◆
Beaters difficult to remove	BEATER SLEEVES DIRTY? Unplug mixer; clean debris from sleeve. If problem persists, remove gears, clean in sudsy water, then relubricate and replace. ◇
Mixer trips breaker or shocks user	See *General troubleshooting*, p.147.
Cordless mixer does not recharge fully	CHARGER FAULTY? Check for poor electrical contact or faulty power cord. If problem persists, test batteries and replace if faulty (pp.142–143). ◇ ▪

Degree of difficulty: Simple ◇   Average ◆   Complex ◆   Volt-ohm meter required: ▪

Servicing hand-mixer drive gears

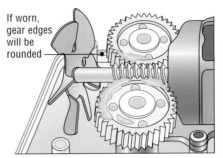

If worn, gear edges will be rounded

1 Access gear area (*Disassembly*, Step 1, facing page). Wipe grease off gears; check for wear or damage. Replace both gears if one is defective.

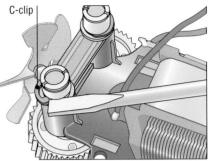

C-clip

2 To free gears, pry C-clip retainer off each gear shaft with small flat-bladed screwdriver. *Retainers can fly off—protect your eyes.*

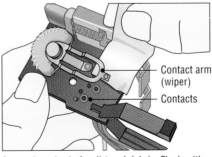

C-clip

Washers

3 Lift off thin washers under each C-clip. Pull out drive gears; then remove additional washers from each gear shaft (grease may hide them).

4 Align timing marks, if any, on gears. Lubricate gear edges with recommended lubricant or with high-temperature multipurpose grease.

Servicing a hand mixer's rotary slide switch

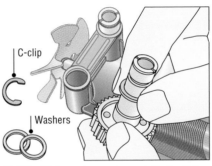

Contact arm (wiper)

Contacts

Inspect contacts for dirt and debris. Flush with electrical contact cleaner; then slide clean paper beneath arm to burnish contact on underside.

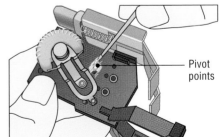

Pivot points

Carefully lubricate pivot points of contact arm with tiny dab of white grease applied with toothpick. Do not get grease on contacts.

Stand mixer with planetary gearing

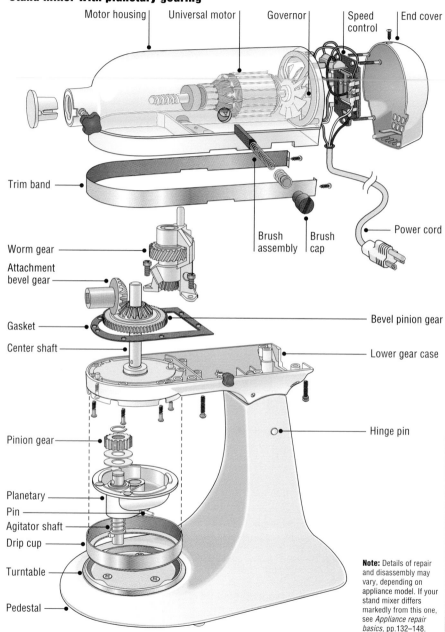

Motor housing
Universal motor
Governor
Speed control
End cover
Trim band
Worm gear
Attachment bevel gear
Gasket
Center shaft
Brush assembly
Brush cap
Power cord
Bevel pinion gear
Lower gear case
Hinge pin
Pinion gear
Planetary
Pin
Agitator shaft
Drip cup
Turntable
Pedestal

Note: Details of repair and disassembly may vary, depending on appliance model. If your stand mixer differs markedly from this one, see *Appliance repair basics,* pp.132–148.

Disassembly

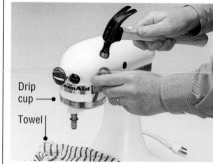

Drip cup
Towel

1 Unplug mixer; remove bowl and any attachments. Carefully tap off drip cup at its upper edge with blade of screwdriver.

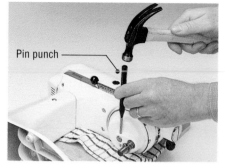

Pin punch

2 To remove pin holding planetary gear housing to gear shaft, tap it out with a pin punch and hammer. If you don't have a punch, use a nail.

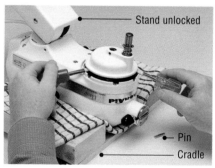

Stand unlocked
Pin
Cradle

3 Pry planetary gear housing off with two flat-bladed screwdrivers. To support mixer, build a simple cradle out of 2 x 4 and plywood scraps.

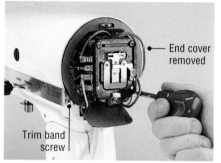

End cover removed
Trim band screw

4 Remove screw from top of end cover, tilt cover backward, then lift up to release. Screws holding trim band can now be removed.

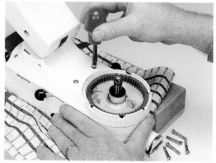

5 Remove trim band; then remove screws from around planetary gear and those holding lower and upper housings together.

6 With pedestal in locked position, gently tap it upward with heel of hand; halves of housing will separate, revealing internal gears.

Adjusting the speed control

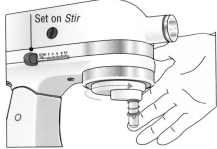

Set on *Stir*

1 Test speed at *Stir* setting. Hold finger at planetary, turn on mixer, and let shaft brush against finger; it should touch about once per second.

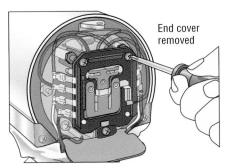

End cover removed

2 Unplug mixer. Turn screws at top of speed control to adjust *Stir* speed; retest as above. When correct, tighten nuts behind both screws.

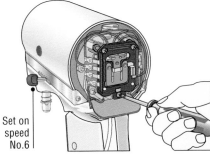

Set on speed No.6

3 To test other speeds, move switch lever to speed No. 6. Test as above; planetary should turn 3 times per second. Adjust by turning bottom screw. Other speeds are automatically set correctly when *Stir* and No. 6 speed are correct.

Servicing the gears

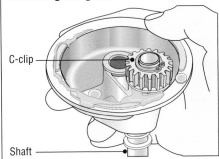

C-clip

Shaft

1 Remove planetary (*Disassembly*, Step 3). Check for play in shaft; check gear for wear. Remove C-clip to replace damaged parts.

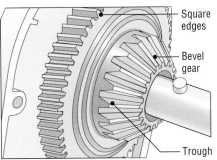

Square edges

Bevel gear

Trough

3 Inspect gears, including bevel gear, for damage or wear; edges and troughs should not look rounded over. Replace gears as necessary.

Reassembling a stand mixer

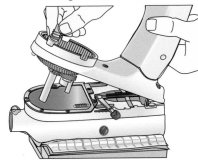

To reassemble mixer, lock pedestal and start main shaft into its bearing. Line up housing locator pins and lower housing into place; *do not force fit.*

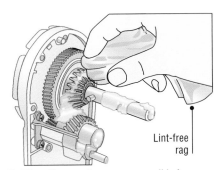

Lint-free rag

2 Wipe off as much grease as possible from main gears; then spray with electrical contact cleaner to dissolve the remainder. Wipe clean.

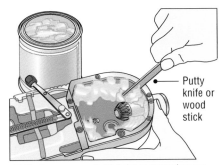

Putty knife or wood stick

4 Pack recommended lubricant around gears during reassembly. Appliance shown here requires approximately 6 oz. of grease.

Adjusting beater clearance

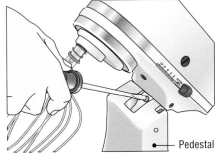

Pedestal

Beater tip should clear bottom of bowl by 1/16 in. (a dime's thickness). Raise or lower beater by turning adjustment screw beneath motor housing.

Stand-mixer attachments

Most stand mixers come with dough hooks and a whisk as well as beaters. Some may also accept a wide variety of specialty attachments, including shredders, slicers, and grinders. If an attachment doesn't work, disconnect the mixer and see if the attachment is mounted properly; then look for any moving parts that might be binding. Also check the owner's manual for lubrication instructions, particularly when the attachment contains gears.

On non-planetary-type stand mixers, hooks and beaters aren't interchangeable: each must be inserted into its designated socket. A beater should snap easily into its socket—never try to force it into place. If you feel resistance, pull out the beater, give it a quarter turn, and reinsert it.

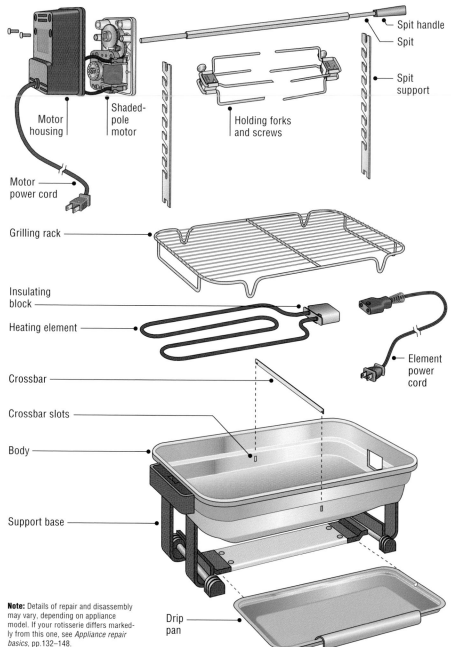

Spit handle

Spit

Spit support

Motor housing

Shaded-pole motor

Holding forks and screws

Motor power cord

Grilling rack

Insulating block

Heating element

Crossbar

Crossbar slots

Body

Support base

Element power cord

Drip pan

Note: Details of repair and disassembly may vary, depending on appliance model. If your rotisserie differs markedly from this one, see *Appliance repair basics*, pp.132–148.

An open rotisserie consists of a sheathed heating element, a wire grilling rack, and a roasting spit that is turned by a shaded-pole motor. The rotisserie lets air circulate freely around food, sealing in the natural juices, and allows unwanted fat to drain away. The position of the element and the drip pan helps to eliminate smoke and splatter. Because motor and element have separate power cords, you can use the appliance as a standard electric grill.

Troubleshooting

Problem	CAUSE? / Solution
Rotisserie doesn't heat	POWER OFF AT OUTLET? See *General troubleshooting*, p.144.
	FAULTY POWER CORD? See *General troubleshooting*, p.144, for motor power cord; facing page for element power cord. ◇ ▣
	FAULTY HEATING ELEMENT? Test element (facing page); replace if faulty. ◆ ▣
	TIMER FAULTY? If rotisserie has a timer, check for damaged leads and test timer for continuity (p.168). If cleaning with electrical contact cleaner fails, replace timer. ◆ ▣
	FAULTY SWITCH? If rotisserie has separate on-off switch, test switch for continuity (see *General troubleshooting*, p.145). Service or replace switch as necessary. ◆ ▣
Rotisserie is noisy	SPIT BINDING IN SUPPORTS? Repair bent support (facing page); lubricate. ◇
	MOTOR GEARS DAMAGED? Check gears (facing page) and replace if necessary. ◆
Rotisserie heats; spit doesn't turn	FAULTY SHADED-POLE MOTOR? Test motor (facing page). If motor is faulty, replace entire motor assembly. ◆ ▣
Rotisserie heats poorly	TIMER FAULTY? See *Rotisserie doesn't heat*, above. ◆
	THERMOSTAT FAULTY? If element is controlled by a thermostat, adjust it if possible (p.182). Otherwise, test and replace it (see *Testing the thermostats*, p.194). ◆ ▣
Rotisserie trips breaker or shocks user	See *General troubleshooting*, p.147.

Degree of difficulty: Simple ◇   Average ◆   Complex ◆   Volt-ohm meter required: ▣

Disassembly

Motor

Sheathed element

1 Unplug motor and lift it from the motor support. Remove screws holding the motor case together. Separate halves of case.

2 Unplug element power cord and let appliance cool down. Remove spit, supports, and grilling rack. Detach element by pulling insulating block.

Servicing the motor and gears

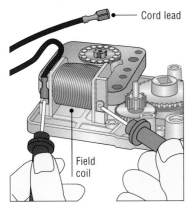

Cord lead

Field coil

1 Unplug motor and open case (*Disassembly,* Step 1). To check field coil for open circuit, remove cord leads from terminals. Set VOM on RX1 and touch probes to coil terminals. If coil is good, meter will read 40 to 100 ohms. If meter reads high ohms, replace entire motor assembly, including cord.

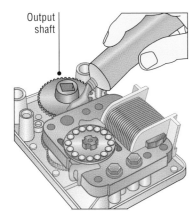

Rotor

2 If motor tests OK, turn gears by hand; the rotor should turn rapidly and the output shaft (which turns the spit) should turn very slowly. If they don't, a gear may be stripped or the rotor may be jammed. Lift out rotor and inspect gears beneath.

Output shaft

3 Remove plastic drive gear beneath rotor. Clean grease from all gears and examine parts for damage and wear; replace parts as needed. Lubricate metal gears and output shaft lightly with white lithium grease before reinserting. Lubricate plastic gears with silicone-base grease.

Testing the element

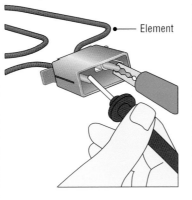

Element

When element cord is plugged into wall outlet, element should glow cherry-red in approximately 2 min. Dark spots on element *may* indicate trouble. Unplug and remove cord. Let element cool; then examine it. Replace element if cracked. If element is OK, set VOM on RX1 and probe terminal pins. Meter should read 10 to 20 ohms.

Testing the element power cord

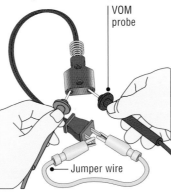

VOM probe

Jumper wire

Remove cord and clip jumper wire to plug. Set VOM on RX1 and touch probes to female terminals. Bend and pull power cord. If cord is OK, meter will read zero ohms; if cord is faulty, reading will fluctuate or show steady high ohms. Replace a faulty cord with an exact duplicate.

Repairing supports

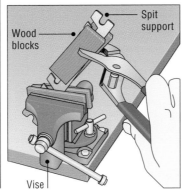

Spit support

Wood blocks

Vise

To straighten a bent spit support, clamp it in a bench vise and bend it back into shape between two blocks of wood held with a pair of groove-joint pliers. If the spit squeaks as it turns in the support, lubricate support with small amount of high-temperature grease.

Enclosed rotisseries

An enclosed cabinet-type rotisserie features two sheathed heating elements, one each at the top and bottom of the cabinet. This arrangement allows the appliance to double as a broiler oven. Troubleshoot it as you would an open unit or a toaster oven (p.223), except that you may have to remove all or part of the housing to reach most parts. The unit may include a timer (see *Testing and replacing a timer,* p.224), thermostat (see *Testing the thermostat,* p.194), and various other controls.

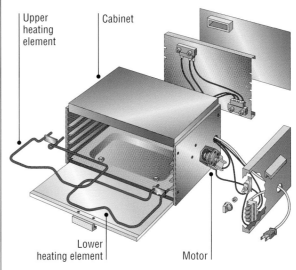

Upper heating element

Cabinet

Lower heating element

Motor

USE AND CARE

Unplug power cords and let appliance cool before cleaning it.

Do not immerse the motor or heating element in water. Wipe other parts clean with damp sponge.

Do not use metal scouring pads or abrasive cleaners, as these can scratch the rotisserie. The bottom surface of the oven should shine to reflect heat upward. If necessary for heavy-duty cleaning, use a plastic mesh pad or nonabrasive stainless steel cleaner.

 Do not use an electric rotisserie outdoors; its cords are not rated for use where moisture may be present and could be a shock hazard.

Small appliances ▪ Sewing machines

Lubrication points. Apply 1 drop of high-quality sewing machine oil to any place where metal rubs against metal. Pay particular attention to hook area and take-up lever assembly.
Needle. A bent, broken, loose, or unsuitable needle causes many sewing machine problems. Always check the needle *before* considering other troubleshooting steps.

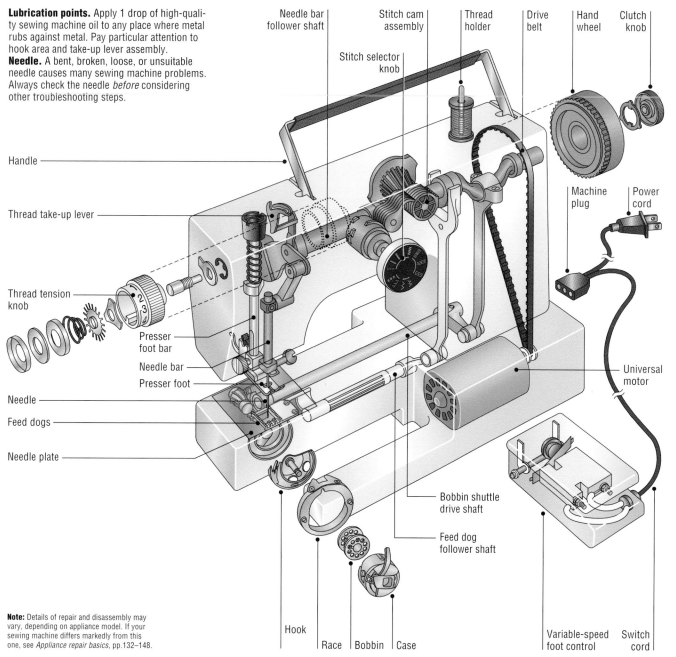

Handle

Thread take-up lever

Thread tension knob

Presser foot bar

Needle bar

Presser foot

Needle

Feed dogs

Needle plate

Needle bar follower shaft

Stitch selector knob

Stitch cam assembly

Thread holder

Drive belt

Hand wheel

Clutch knob

Machine plug

Power cord

Universal motor

Bobbin shuttle drive shaft

Feed dog follower shaft

Hook

Race   Bobbin   Case

Variable-speed foot control

Switch cord

Note: Details of repair and disassembly may vary, depending on appliance model. If your sewing machine differs markedly from this one, see *Appliance repair basics*, pp.132–148.

All sewing machines, whether mechanical, electronic, or computerized, form a stitch by looping the needle thread around a separate thread that comes from the bobbin; the fabric is advanced with little tugs from the feed dogs (toothed ridges that rise and fall in tandem with the needle). A foot control modulates the speed of the machine and may also serve as an on-off switch.

In mechanical models (such as the one at left), an AC motor drives a series of wheels, shafts, and levers; they in turn move the needle. Stitch width, length, and tension are set manually with dials. Electronic models are similar but incorporate a circuit board that makes more features possible, such as steady power at all speeds and a greater range of patterned stitches. Computerized models are driven by a DC step motor and are governed by advanced electronic circuitry that can automatically execute particular stitch patterns. As with a personal computer, however, a sewing machine's electronic circuitry is vulnerable to power surges (p.320) that can erase stored data.

Typical problems. Sewing machine problems are most often due to operator error or poor maintenance, not mechanical failure. Careful attention to the manufacturer's usage guidelines and regular maintenance keeps these machines humming along reliably for years. If parts do fail—in computerized machines the motor and circuit board are common culprits—take your machine to an authorized repair shop. The parts of any sewing machine are meticulously synchronized, and major repairs are best left to a specialist.

Troubleshooting

Problem	CAUSE? / Solution
Machine doesn't work	POWER OFF AT OUTLET OR FAULTY POWER CORD? See *General troubleshooting*, p.144.
	FAULTY SWITCH? If machine has on-off switch, see *General troubleshooting*, p.145.
	FOOT CONTROL FAULTY? See *Servicing motor and electrical system*, p.213. To make sure control is securely attached, remove machine plug and reinsert firmly into sewing machine. ◆ ▣
Motor runs or hums but machine does not sew	BOBBIN OR TAKE-UP LEVER JAMMED? Use tweezers, brush, or wooden toothpick to clear lint and thread from bobbin assembly (see *Servicing mechanical parts*, p.212) and take-up lever. ◆
	MACHINE NEEDS LUBRICATION? See lubrication points indicated on facing page. ◇
	HAND WHEEL SLIPPING? Tighten clutch knob by turning screw on hand wheel clockwise. ◇
	DRIVE BELT FAULTY OR LOOSE? See *Servicing the drive belt*, p.213. ◆
Needle thread breaks	MACHINE THREADED INCORRECTLY? See *Needle and stitch formation problems*, p.212. ◇
	THREAD TENSION TOO HIGH? Adjust tension dial; clean lint from tension assembly (p.212). ◇
	THREAD GUIDES OR HOOK ROUGH? Smooth burred edges and remove corrosion with fine emery cloth. Replace affected parts if roughness cannot be removed. ◆
Bobbin thread breaks	BOBBIN INSERTED IMPROPERLY? Remove bobbin and reinsert; index arm should point up. ◇
	BOBBIN OR BOBBIN CASE DAMAGED? Bobbin case should be very smooth, but can be scratched by bent needle. Replace damaged parts. ◇
	BURRED EDGES ON NEEDLE PLATE? Smooth edges with very fine emery cloth or replace plate. ◇
	BOBBIN CASE CLOGGED? Clean out lint and thread (see *Servicing mechanical parts*, p.212). ◇
	BOBBIN THREAD TENSION TOO HIGH? Adjust (see *Thread tension adjustments*, p.212). ◇
	BURRS OR ROUGH EDGES ON PARTS? Check bobbin case, bobbin, hook, and bobbin tension spring. Remove burrs and corrosion with very fine emery cloth; otherwise replace parts. ◇
	WRONG BOBBIN? Replace with bobbin that fits machine exactly. ◇
	WRONG THREAD FOR FABRIC? Replace with better quality or properly rated thread. ◇
Needle breaks	BOBBIN CASE INSERTED INCORRECTLY? See *Bobbin thread breaks*, above. ◇
Thread loops or bunches	THREAD TENSION SET INCORRECTLY? Adjust needle thread tension first. If problem persists, adjust bobbin thread tension. See *Thread tension adjustments*, p.212. ◇
	MACHINE THREADED INCORRECTLY? See *Needle and stitch formation problems*, p.212. ◇
	LINT CLOGGING THREAD PATH? Clean lint away from needle thread tension assembly and bobbin area (see *Servicing mechanical parts*, p.212). ◇
	HOOK BURRED? Remove burrs if possible with emery cloth; otherwise replace hook. ◇
	TIMING OFF? Hook and needle must be professionally synchronized by service center.
Fabric feeds poorly	PRESSER FOOT UP? Be sure presser foot is lowered so that it rests against fabric. Adjust foot as needed (see *Servicing mechanical parts*, p.212). ◇
	STITCH LENGTH SET AT ZERO? Adjust stitch length setting on front of machine. ◇
	FEED DOG CLOGGED? Clear lint from feed dogs (see *Servicing mechanical parts*, p.212). ◇
Bobbin winds unevenly	MACHINE THREADED INCORRECTLY? See *Needle and stitch formation problems*, p.212. ◇
	BOBBIN THREAD GUIDE INCORRECTLY POSITIONED? Adjust bobbin thread tension guide. ◇
Motor sputters or arcs	JAMMED OR DAMAGED MOTOR BRUSHES? Access motor and replace brushes. Make sure they slide freely in brush housing (see *Servicing the motor and electrical system*, p.213). ◆
	OIL ON MOTOR? Avoid over-oiling machine; wipe off spills promptly. ◆
Device trips breaker or shocks user	See *General troubleshooting*, p.147.

Degree of difficulty: Simple ◇   Average ◆   Complex ◆   Volt-ohm meter required: ▣

Disassembly

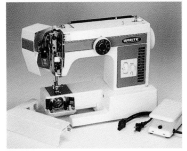

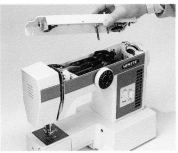

1 Unplug unit. Remove power cord assembly and extension table; then disengage and remove thread. Pivot open shuttle cover and face cover if necessary.

2 Remove screws in top cover; then lift off cover and set aside. Main workings of machine, along with some lubrication points, are now accessible.

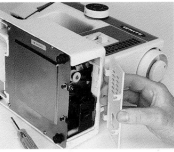

3 Raise presser foot; remove needle. Remove screws in needle plate and remove plate. (If plate is magnetized, pry up with small flat-bladed screwdriver.)

4 To remove belt access panel, gently tip machine on its side. Loosen (do not remove) screws on bottom of machine; then slide access panel off.

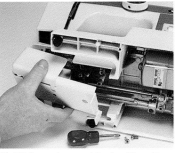

5 Remove remaining screws in motor access plate; then lift plate away. Motor and motor mounting screws are now accessible.

6 While sewing machine is still on its side, remove screws holding panel beneath sewing arm. This will expose underside of feed dog mechanism.

Small appliances ▪ Sewing machines

Needle and stitch formation problems

Because the interactions of needle, feed dogs, and shuttle hook are so precisely orchestrated, small variances can create big problems. Repeated thread breakage may be due to a bent, dull, or burred needle; always check the needle as your first troubleshooting step.

If the fabric feeds unevenly, the feed dogs are probably at fault. Check for lint buildup between them; then check their alignment by placing a needle, flat side down, next to them. Turn the hand wheel until the feed dogs rise. If their teeth are higher than the needle, have the machine professionally serviced.

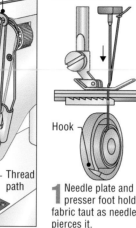

Take-up lever

Hook

Thread path

How a stitch is formed

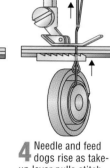
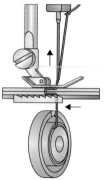

1 Needle plate and presser foot hold fabric taut as needle pierces it.

2 Feed dogs drop at same time needle carries upper thread through fabric.

3 Hook grabs needle thread and pulls it around bobbin thread. Dogs move forward.

4 Needle and feed dogs rise as take-up lever pulls stitch taut, forming stitch

5 Feed dogs move back, pulling fabric into position for next stitch. Cycle repeats.

Thread tension adjustments

To correct problems, adjust the needle thread tension first. If thread loops appear on the backside of fabric, the tension is too loose; if fabric puckers on the front side, tension is too tight. Cleaning the thread tension assembly (below) may also help. Problems can also occur if bobbin thread tension is improperly set.

Thread tension dial

Adjust needle thread tension with machine threaded and presser foot down. Turn thread tension dial as needed: high numbers increase tension; low ones decrease it.

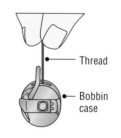

Thread

Bobbin case

To test bobbin thread tension, wind bobbin and suspend (with case) from thread. Case should drop 2-4 in.. If it drops farther, thread is too loose; if it drops less, it's too tight.

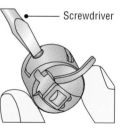

Screwdriver

Adjust bobbin thread tension by turning screw on bobbin case. Only tiny adjustments are usually needed. Turn screw clockwise to increase tension, opposite way to decrease it.

Servicing mechanical parts

Frequent thread jams or breakage not caused by improper threading suggests a problem in the needle or bobbin thread assemblies. Keep these parts free of lint and dust. Check parts (including the foot's edges and underside) for nicks, burrs, or rust; replace worn or damaged parts as needed.

If the fabric moves unevenly, the feed dog teeth may be dull (see *Needle and stitch formation problems,* above). Also, the presser foot may be out of alignment; open the face cover and adjust it (below). If you have a manual for the machine, check it for other servicing procedures.

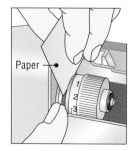

Paper

Thread tension assembly consists of discs on a spindle; a knob and spring regulate disc pressure on thread. To clean, slide paper or toothpick between discs to remove tangles of thread.

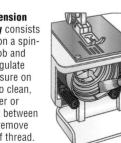

Bobbin thread tension assembly. Sand off burrs or rust with very fine emery cloth (keep sanding dust out of assembly). Brush out lint. Replace dented or damaged parts.

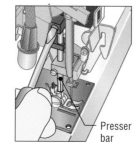

Presser bar

Presser foot. If foot is misaligned, turn presser bar screw until foot is straight. If this alters pressure exerted on the fabric, have the machine serviced. Replace scratched or damaged foot.

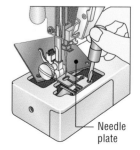

Needle plate

Feed dog assembly. Raise presser foot; remove needle and needle plate. Remove screws holding feed dogs in place and lift them out; then clear out lint and debris with tweezers.

Servicing motor and electrical system

A sewing machine's electrical system is fairly simple. It includes the light bulb, a universal motor, switches, and the foot pedal (the pedal is actually a rheostat that regulates the amount of voltage flowing to the machine). Electrical problems such as broken wires, loose connections (p.134), worn brushes (p.146), and dirty or corroded contacts (p.137), especially in the foot pedal, are usually easy to fix.

Sewing machine cords are prone to damage because they run along the floor.

CAUTION: A faulty sewing machine cord is particularly hazardous: accumulations of lint and fabric scraps are highly flammable. Replace a faulty cord without delay.

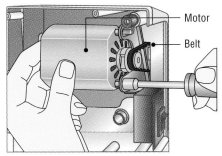

To access motor brushes, unplug machine; disassemble it enough to reach motor (*Disassembly,* Steps 4–5, p.211). Remove motor mounting bolts with nut driver. Slip belt off pulley; lift motor free.

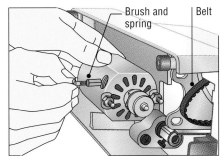

Unscrew protective caps to reach brushes. Replace brushes if worn to less than ¼ inch. If brush binds in housing, grind it down with fine sandpaper until it moves freely.

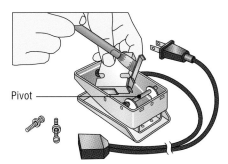

To service foot pedal, disconnect power cord and open the housing. Brush or blow away accumulated lint and dirt, particularly from around contact areas. Lubricate pivot with dab of grease.

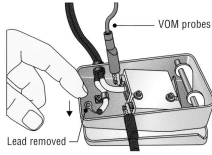

To test rheostat windings, disconnect a lead. Set VOM on RX1, clip probes to terminals, and push down on pedal. Meter should read zero ohms; if it doesn't, replace entire foot pedal unit and cord set.

Servicing the drive belt

Sewing machines are driven by a rubber belt that connects a pulley on the motor shaft to the hand wheel. Do not lubricate the belt, pulley, or wheel, or else the belt will slip. Remove oil or grease drips by wiping the belt with a cloth moistened with electrical contact cleaner. Dispose of the cloth properly.

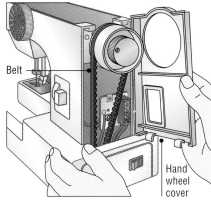

1 Unplug sewing machine. Remove top cover (*Disassembly,* Step 2, p.211); then remove screws holding hand wheel cover. To remove belt, stretch it over lower pulley; then lift off.

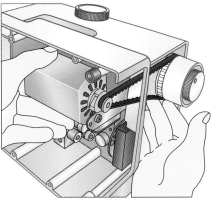

2 Replace damaged or worn belt. If belt is loose, move motor slightly, then retighten motor mounting bolts. Test tension by pushing on side of belt; it should move only slightly.

USE AND CARE

Most sewing machines require regular lubrication (some are permanently lubricated). Experts advise oiling after 4 to 5 hours of sewing; check your manual for specific recommendations. Remove lint before oiling.

You can identify lubrication points with nail polish. Mark each one with a dab of color: use one color for grease, another for oil.

Use only sewing machine-grade oil. Add it sparingly—too much is as bad as too little. After oiling the machine, sew a few rows of stitches in a scrap of fabric. This will circulate the new oil and catch any overflow.

If you sew infrequently, run the machine for a few minutes every 2 or 3 months. This will help to keep the parts lubricated.

Check needles for scratches, rust, burrs, or bending. Discard if damaged. Match needle size and type, and thread weight, to the fabric you are using. Incompatible supplies can throw off the machine's timing; correcting this problem calls for professional servicing.

A popping noise as the needle pierces the fabric or sluggish operation indicates a dull needle; replace the needle. If a new needle is not available, try piercing the emery bag on a pincushion to restore the needle's sharpness.

A finished stitch can't be undone by machine; pick it out by hand. Never turn a hand wheel backwards; you might jam the mechanism.

If thread breaks repeatedly, it may be old. Use different thread.

Remove lint and dust from the thread tension discs, feed dogs, and bobbin area after 4 or 5 hours of sewing.

Keep the machine covered when not in use. Use a vacuum cleaner frequently to clear lint and dust from your machine. Set the vacuum on low power.

A magnetized screwdriver is essential when working inside a sewing machine. Screws are difficult to manipulate and if dropped, almost impossible to recover.

Small appliances ▪ Shavers

Electric shavers come in two basic types: foil and rotary. A foil shaver (right) captures hairs in the tiny holes of its screen, or foil, and then cuts them with a series of blades mounted on a cutter block. Most foil shavers are equipped with a vibrator-type motor, which is essentially an electromagnet that causes a shaft to move the cutter block back and forth. A rotary shaver (far right) traps hairs in much the same way as a foil shaver, but with an assembly of combs and cutters that shear the hairs off. Rotary cutters, powered by a DC motor, all spin in the same direction.

There isn't any mechanical difference between men's and women's shavers of the same basic type. The internal parts of shavers intended for use in the shower, however, are protected with O-ring seals and should be serviced only by a professional.

You can avoid the need for many repairs by cleaning your shaver after every use and following the manufacturer's maintenance guide. In addition, periodically check to see that the cutters aren't dull or nicked; replace them as needed. Most men's electric shavers are equipped with a pop-up trimmer for trimming longer hair such as beards and sideburns—service the trimmer at the first sign of dullness or damage.

Most shavers sold today are either entirely cordless or offer both cordless and plug-in options. If a cordless shaver fails to operate, suspect either a faulty charger (see *Cordless tools and appliances*, p.142) or batteries (cells) in need of charging. Older cordless shavers may have a separate charger; newer ones have internal charging systems.

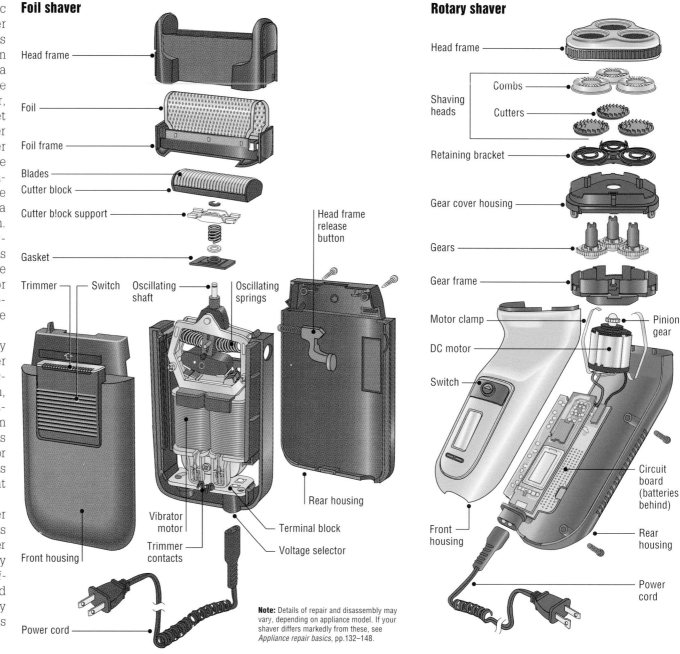

Foil shaver

Head frame

Foil

Foil frame

Blades

Cutter block

Cutter block support

Gasket

Trimmer — Switch — Oscillating shaft — Oscillating springs

Head frame release button

Rear housing

Vibrator motor

Terminal block

Trimmer contacts

Voltage selector

Front housing

Power cord

Note: Details of repair and disassembly may vary, depending on appliance model. If your shaver differs markedly from these, see *Appliance repair basics*, pp.132–148.

Rotary shaver

Head frame

Shaving heads — Combs — Cutters

Retaining bracket

Gear cover housing

Gears

Gear frame

Motor clamp — Pinion gear

DC motor

Switch

Circuit board (batteries behind)

Front housing

Rear housing

Power cord

Troubleshooting

Problem	CAUSE? / Solution
Shaver doesn't work	POWER OFF AT OUTLET? See *General troubleshooting*, p.144. With cordless shavers, be sure battery charger works and batteries are charged (p.143).
	FAULTY POWER CORD? See *General troubleshooting*, p.144. Check cord leading to charger of a cordless shaver.
	FAULTY SWITCH? See *General troubleshooting*, p.144.
	PARTS JAMMED? Debris may jam cutters, head, or gears (depending on shaver type). Disassemble, clean, and lubricate shaver; replace damaged parts. ◇
	FAULTY MOTOR? Fine motor coil wires in older rotary (and many foil) shavers can break if shaver is dropped. Crimp or solder wires if possible (see *Servicing the gears and motor*, p.216); otherwise replace motor or entire shaver. ◆
	HEAD NICKED? *(Rotary shaver only)* If nicks prevent a cutter from turning, replace all three heads as a set. ◇
	BRUSHES FAULTY? If motor has brushes, see *General troubleshooting*, p.146.
Shaver operates sluggishly	HEAD CLOGGED? Clean heads (see right for foil shavers; see *Servicing the shaving heads*, p.216, for rotary shavers). ◇
	SHAVER SET TO WRONG VOLTAGE ? Set voltage switch to 110-volt position. ◇
	FOIL OR HEAD DRY? Spray foil of foil shaver (see *Cleaning and lubricating a foil shaver*, right). Spray heads of rotary shaver in similar fashion. ◇
	BATTERIES LOW? *(Cordless shavers only)* Charge or replace batteries. ◇
Cordless shaver doesn't charge	CHARGER OR BATTERIES FAULTY? On older units, check voltage regulator switch; for newer units, see *Troubleshooting batteries and chargers*, p.143. ◇ ▪
Shaver cuts poorly or is unusually noisy	DULL OR DAMAGED CUTTING EDGES? Disassemble shaver. Inspect cutter block (foil shaver) or cutters (rotary shaver). Replace if dull or damaged. ◇
	HEAD CLOGGED? See *Shaver operates sluggishly*, above. ◇
	DAMAGED FOIL OR HEAD? Inspect foil (foil shaver) or heads (rotary shaver) for dents or other damage, and replace as needed. ◇
	GEARS FAULTY? *(Rotary shavers only)* Inspect and clean gears (p.216); replace if damaged or worn. Inspect pinion gear at same time; replace as needed. ◆
	BEARINGS DRY? Lubricate lightly (see *Servicing the gears and motor*, p.216). ◆
Motor works but shaver won't cut	CUTTER BLOCK LOOSE? *(Foil shavers only)* Remove shaver head; push cutter back onto cutter block support. Replace support if worn. ◇
	GEARS FAULTY? See *Shaver cuts poorly or is unusually noisy*, above. ◆
	CUTTING EDGES CLOGGED? Remove cutter block (foil shaver) or cutters (rotary shaver). Clean in special solvent (see *Servicing the shaving heads*, p.216). ◇
Shaver works intermittently	FAULTY MOTOR? See *Shaver doesn't work*, above. Check all internal wires, particularly at connections. Resolder (p.136) or crimp as needed. ◆ ▪
	CONTACTS FOULED? If shaver contains contacts, inspect and clean them (see *Cleaning and lubricating a foil shaver*, right). ◆
	FAULTY POWER CORD? See *Shaver doesn't work*, above. ◇ ▪
	CIRCUIT BOARD FAULTY? If shaver contains electronic control circuitry and problem persists, have shaver professionally serviced.
Shaver trips breaker or shocks user	See *General troubleshooting*, p.147.

Degree of difficulty: Simple ◇   Average ◆   Complex ◆   Volt-ohm meter required: ▪

Disassembling a foil shaver

1 Unplug and remove cord. Press release button on side of shaver and lift off shaver head. Separate foil frame and head frame.

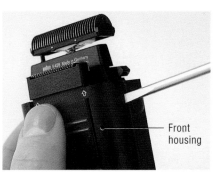

Front housing

2 Remove housing screws; then pull off front housing. If necessary, coax housing off with screwdriver blade (above).

3 Gently pry off rear housing, using taped screwdriver blade if needed. Work slowly to keep small parts from dropping out.

Cleaning and lubricating a foil shaver

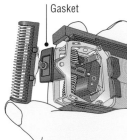

Gasket

Inspect rubber gasket beneath cutter block for cracks; gasket prevents debris from entering motor area. To remove damaged gasket, unclip cutter block (below).

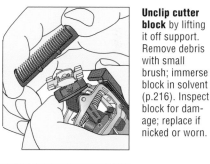

Unclip cutter block by lifting it off support. Remove debris with small brush; immerse block in solvent (p.216). Inspect block for damage; replace if nicked or worn.

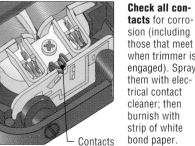

Contacts

Check all contacts for corrosion (including those that meet when trimmer is engaged). Spray them with electrical contact cleaner; then burnish with strip of white bond paper.

Reassemble shaver; then turn it on. Spray foil lightly with shaver-head lubricant to reduce friction between blades and foil. Spray again before each shave.

Disassembling a rotary shaver

Trimmer

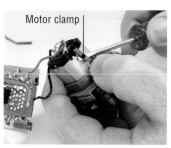
Motor

Motor clamp

1 Remove power cord and lift off head. Note orientation for reassembly later. (To disassemble head, see *Servicing the shaving heads,* below.)

2 Remove screws from back of housing (you may have to lift trimmer to access some screws). Close trimmer; *carefully* pry off back of housing.

3 Lift battery assembly away from case, noting position of wires leading to motor. Remove screws and pull motor assembly loose (above).

4 Squeeze metal motor clamps (spring clips) holding motor to gear frame as you pry ends of clips away from motor with screwdriver.

5 Lift up gear cover housing after prying it away from holding tabs on frame. With the gears now exposed, you can lift them out for servicing.

Servicing the gears and motor

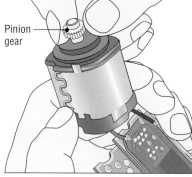
Pinion gear

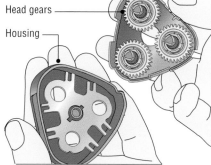
Head gears
Housing

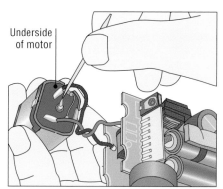
Underside of motor

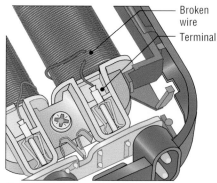
Broken wire
Terminal

Access motor (see above, Step 4) and inspect pinion gear for broken or worn teeth. Replace gear or motor if necessary.

Examine head gears for damaged teeth; replace gears as needed. Lubricate gears with lightweight grease or with recommended lubricant.

Turn pinion gear by hand to make sure shaft rotates freely; then use a toothpick or pin to apply 1 drop of lightweight machine oil to bearings.

Check for broken motor coil wires, especially near terminals. Crimp or solder wires to reconnect (see *Tips from the pros,* below; see also p.136).

Servicing the shaving heads

Locking wheel

Lift off heads. Push down on locking wheel; then turn wheel slightly to free bracket holding combs and cutters. Loosen debris with small brush and blow it away.

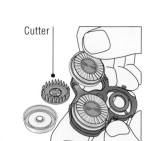
Jar top

Immerse heads and retaining bracket in liquid shaving-head cleaner (buy where shavers are sold). Soak for 10 min.; let dry for 5 min.; then reassemble shaver.

Cutter

To replace heads, carefully slide each one out from retaining bracket. Sometimes sold in sets of three, replacement heads contain new cutters.

Slicers

Intended for speedy, repetitive slicing of cheeses, breads, and meats, a food slicer employs a universal motor to spin a serrated circular blade. Food held in a sliding tray is sliced as it is pushed past the spinning blade. The stainless-steel blade is easily removed for cleaning, but it cannot be sharpened; replace it if it becomes dull or is damaged.

A dull blade or a buildup of food residue is usually the culprit behind most slicer problems. Excessive noise may signal a damaged blade gear or idler gear. The slicer's motor is permanently lubricated and normally requires little attention. Gears require lubrication only when they are being replaced.

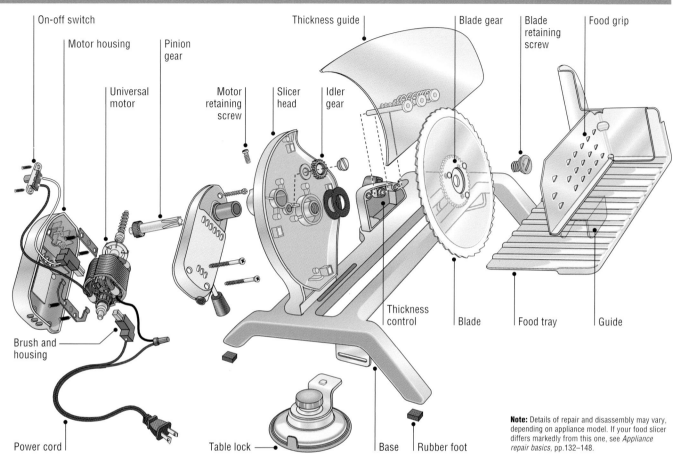

Note: Details of repair and disassembly may vary, depending on appliance model. If your food slicer differs markedly from this one, see *Appliance repair basics,* pp.132–148.

Disassembly

1 Unplug slicer, loosen blade retaining screw, and tap blade lightly from behind to loosen it. Remove screw and lift blade away with care.

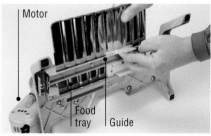

2 The food tray rides on a plastic guide in the base. To remove tray, tip slicer over onto its motor and gently pry tray guide off rails.

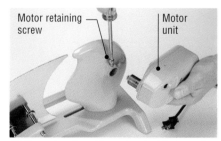

3 Support motor with one hand while loosening motor retaining screw. Slide motor away from the slicer head.

4 Remove screws (note differing sizes) to separate halves of motor housing. This exposes pinion gear, motor, and on-off switch.

Troubleshooting

Problem	CAUSE? / Solution
Slicer doesn't work	POWER OFF AT OUTLET? See *General troubleshooting*, p.144.
	FAULTY POWER CORD? See *General troubleshooting*, p.144.
	SWITCH FAULTY? Test for continuity (right); replace if faulty. ◆ ▨
	MOTOR FAULTY? Replace brushes if needed (right; see also *General troubleshooting*, p.146). If motor still fails to work, have it serviced. ◆
Slicer slips during use	RUBBER FEET DIRTY? Wipe with grease-removing cleaner such as alcohol or glass spray. Remove feet if necessary to clean thoroughly. ◇
	TABLE LOCK DIRTY? Some slicers are held to countertop with a suction cup. Clean cup with grease-removing cleaner such as glass spray. ◇
Slicer makes excessive noise	GEARS WORN OR DAMAGED? Access gears and examine for wear or damage (below). A dull blade can damage gears by overloading the motor. ◆
	RUBBER FOOT MISSING OR WORN? Replace foot to prevent rocking. ◇
Food tray doesn't slide smoothly	TRAY GUIDES DIRTY? Clean with sponge dipped in soapy water. Lubricate guides with a few drops of salad oil. ◇
	SLICER JAMMED? Remove food scraps around tray and blade; clean both with soapy water. **CAUTION:** Wear gloves and use care when handling blade. ◇
Excessive pressure required for slicing	BLADE CLOGGED WITH FOOD RESIDUE? Remove blade and clean with soapy water. **CAUTION:** Wear gloves and use care when handling blade. ◇
	BLADE LOOSE? Tighten blade retaining screw with coin or screwdriver. ◇
	BLADE DULL? A dull slicer blade cannot be sharpened; replace it. ◇
	THICKNESS GUIDE DIRTY? Remove guide (right), and wash it in hot soapy water or in top rack of dishwasher. Lubricate as needed. ◇
	THICKNESS GUIDE IMPROPERLY ADJUSTED? Adjust guide to cut thinner pieces. Also, remove any pieces of food jammed in the guide; they can push guide out of alignment. ◇
Slicer trips breaker or shocks user	See *General troubleshooting*, p.147.

Degree of difficulty: Simple ◇   Average ◆   Complex ◆   Volt-ohm meter required: ▨

Testing the switch

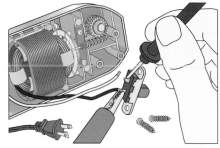

Unplug slicer and access switch (*Disassembly*, Step 4, p.217). Disconnect one switch lead. Turn switch on and probe both leads with VOM on RX1 scale. Reading of zero ohms means switch is OK.

Servicing the thickness guide

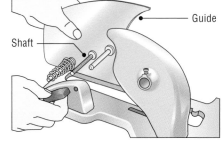

Loosen control knob until guide's threaded shaft pulls free. Wash and dry guide. Lubricate shaft with petroleum jelly; reinstall guide.

Replacing the brushes

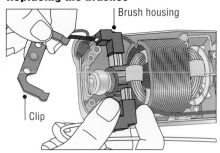

Open motor housing (*Disassembly*, Step 4, p.217). Remove brush retaining clip, lift out brush housings, and remove brushes to inspect for wear (p.146); replace in pairs as needed.

Servicing the slicer gears

Any appliance with moving parts that come into contact with food has special lubrication needs. Never use standard grease or machine oil on a slicer's blade gear, idler gear, or thickness gauge. Lubricate these moving parts with petroleum jelly or other suitable lubricant. Gears inside the motor housing, however, can be greased with standard products intended for that use. Consult the owner's manual for lubrication advice.

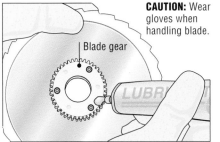

Blade gear. Remove blade (*Disassembly*, Step 1, p.217) and lubricate blade gear. If gear is damaged, blade and gear must be replaced.

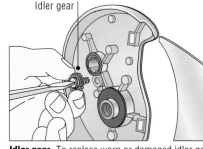

Idler gear. To replace worn or damaged idler gear, remove retaining screw with screwdriver. Install new gear and lubricate it.

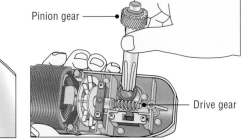

Drive gear. Lift out pinion gear. Check it and drive gear for wear or damage. Pinion gear can be replaced; replace motor if drive gear is faulty.

Slow cookers

To disassemble slow cooker and access heating elements and switch leads, see *Testing the cord and elements*, Step 1, below.

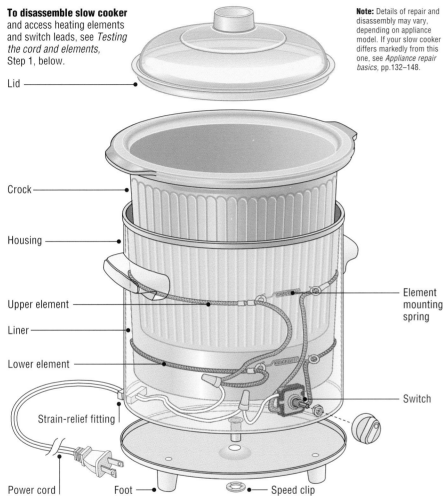

Lid

Crock

Housing

Upper element

Liner

Lower element

Strain-relief fitting

Power cord

Foot

Speed clip

Element mounting spring

Switch

Note: Details of repair and disassembly may vary, depending on appliance model. If your slow cooker differs markedly from this one, see *Appliance repair basics*, pp.132–148.

Troubleshooting

Problem	CAUSE? / Solution
Cooker doesn't heat	POWER OFF AT OUTLET? See *General troubleshooting*, p.144.
	FAULTY POWER CORD? See *General troubleshooting*, p.144.
	THERMOSTAT FAULTY? If cooker has a thermostat, service as you would a switch (see *General troubleshooting*, p.145). Replace if faulty. ◆
	HEATING ELEMENT FAULTY? Test and replace as needed (below). ◆ ▪
Cooker heats on one temperature only	FAULTY SWITCH? See *General troubleshooting*, p.145.
	HEATING ELEMENT FAULTY? Test and replace as needed (below). ◆ ▪
	THERMOSTAT FAULTY? See *Cooker doesn't heat*, above. ◆
Cooker overheats	THERMOSTAT FAULTY? See *Cooker doesn't heat*, above. ◆
Cooker leaks	CROCK CRACKED? Replace crock, or cooker if crock not removable. ◇
Appliance trips breaker or shocks user	See *General troubleshooting*, p.147.

Degree of difficulty: Simple ◇   Average ◆   Complex ◆   Volt-ohm meter required: ▪

Testing the cord and elements

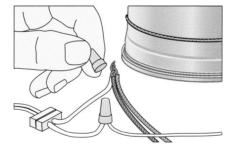

1 Unplug cooker; remove crock. Upend cooker; then remove speed clip, baseplate, and housing. Remove wire connectors and test cord (p.145).

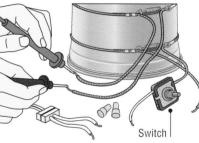

Switch

2 With liner still upside down, disconnect leads of lower element; probe with VOM set on RX1. Reading should be about 180 ohms.

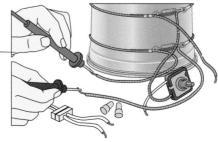

3 If lower element tests OK, probe leads of upper element as above. Reading should be about 100 ohms. Replace faulty elements.

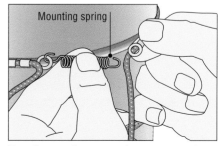

Mounting spring

To replace an element, gently remove mounting spring. Lift element out of guide slot. If element is open type, stretch new one to fit (p.183).

Slow cookers cook food and keep it warm for up to 18 hours. The combination of a tight lid and a low, steady temperature reduces evaporation and promotes thorough cooking. Most models have a ceramic crock that can be lifted out for cleaning.

A slow cooker's Nichrome wire elements encircle a metal liner; the liner, in turn, transfers heat to the crock. The elements may be sheathed with a flexible insulating material.

Problems in a slow cooker are limited because the appliance is so simple, and replacing the whole unit may be more cost-effective than repairing it. If the ceramic crock cracks, however, it can be replaced easily with a new one.

An electric steamer is designed primarily for steaming vegetables. A rice cooker is a type of steamer designed specifically for cooking rice.

All steamers contain sheathed heating elements; some include a thermostat. Simple steamers have a rotary timer that turns the elements off after a specified length of time. Other units, such as the rice cooker shown here, contain a sealed device that senses when the water has boiled off in the rice pan. At that point the cooker automatically switches to a lower heat setting which can keep the food warm for hours until the unit is unplugged.

USE AND CARE

Clean a steamer thoroughly after every use. Soak the rice pan in warm soapy water, then wipe it clean with a sponge (don't use abrasive cleansers or pads).

To prevent moisture damage to upper kitchen cabinets, don't operate a steamer directly beneath them.

Disassembly

Unplug cooker. Remove cover and rice pan. Upend outer pot and remove access plate (check beneath feet for hidden screws). All internal parts, including contacts, are now accessible.

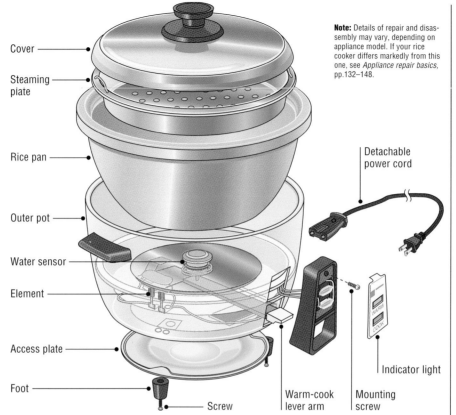

Cover
Steaming plate
Rice pan
Outer pot
Water sensor
Element
Access plate
Foot
Screw
Warm-cook lever arm
Mounting screw
Indicator light
Detachable power cord

Note: Details of repair and disassembly may vary, depending on appliance model. If your rice cooker differs markedly from this one, see *Appliance repair basics*, pp.132–148.

Troubleshooting

Problem	CAUSE? / Solution
Steamer doesn't heat properly	POWER OFF AT OUTLET? See *General troubleshooting*, p.144.
	FAULTY POWER CORD? See *General troubleshooting*, p.144. Steamers often have a removable 120-volt power cord that is easily replaced.
	ELEMENT FAULTY? Test element (right). If faulty, replace appliance; these elements cannot be repaired or replaced. ◆ ◼
	RESISTOR FAULTY? During warming cycle, current is routed through a rectangular circuit called a voltage-drop resistor. Its purpose is to reduce current reaching the element, thereby reducing its temperature. Test the resistor (right), and replace it if faulty. Also check for disconnected wires. ◆ ◼
	SWITCH CONTACTS DIRTY? Access contacts; clean if necessary (right). ◆
Unit trips breaker or shocks user	See *General troubleshooting*, p.147.

Degree of difficulty: Simple ◇   Average ◆   Complex ◆   Volt-ohm meter required: ◼

Servicing the heating components

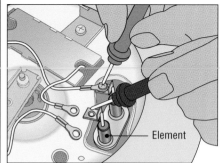

Element

To test element, disconnect wires from one terminal. Set VOM on RX1; touch probes to terminals. Element is OK if meter reads about 20 ohms.

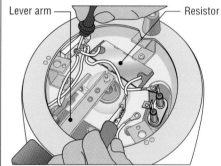

Lever arm
Resistor

To test resistor, remove lead to element. Set VOM on RX1; touch probes to both resistor leads. Resistor is OK if meter reads near zero ohms.

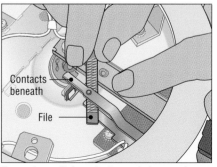

Contacts beneath
File

To service switch contacts, push down on lever arm to see if contacts meet fully. File contacts as needed with point file; spray with contact cleaner.

Toasters

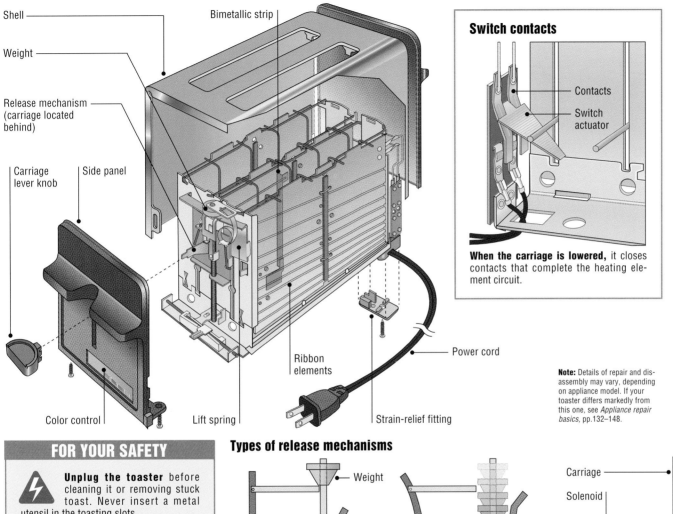

Shell

Weight

Release mechanism
(carriage located
behind)

Carriage
lever knob

Side panel

Color control

Lift spring

Bimetallic strip

Ribbon
elements

Power cord

Strain-relief fitting

Switch contacts

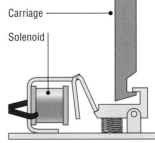

Contacts

Switch
actuator

When the carriage is lowered, it closes contacts that complete the heating element circuit.

Note: Details of repair and disassembly may vary, depending on appliance model. If your toaster differs markedly from this one, see *Appliance repair basics,* pp.132–148.

Despite its apparent simplicity, a common toaster holds an ingenious array of interdependent parts. When you lower a toaster's spring-loaded carriage, contacts close to complete the heating circuit. The thermostat—a bimetallic strip—gradually bends with the heat, triggering a chain of events that eventually causes the carriage to pop up and the elements to turn off (see *Types of release mechanisms,* below).

Because the parts in a toaster are so closely integrated, the entire carriage assembly may have to be replaced if any single part is beyond repair; in such a case, consider replacing the toaster because a carriage may cost nearly as much. Luckily, simple cleaning can solve some toaster problems, like a jammed keeper or a balky carriage. When you disassemble a toaster, use the opportunity to lubricate its moving parts with graphite. Before servicing the unit, however, bear in mind that slight differences in the way breads brown may be due to the bread itself, not the toaster.

FOR YOUR SAFETY

Unplug the toaster before cleaning it or removing stuck toast. Never insert a metal utensil in the toasting slots.

Never use a metal scouring pad to clean a toaster; small pieces of the pad might fall inside, short-circuiting the elements and creating a shock hazard.

Check a metal-shell toaster for a ground fault after each repair (p.147).

Never immerse a toaster in water to clean it. Instead, dislodge crumbs with a soft brush and shake crumbs out of toaster.

Types of release mechanisms

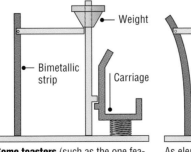

Weight

Bimetallic
strip

Carriage

Carriage

Solenoid

Keeper

Keeper
release

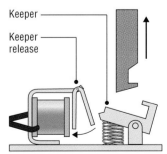

Some toasters (such as the one featured above) rely on a bimetallic strip and a weight to trigger the release of the spring-loaded carriage.

As elements heat the toast (and the bimetallic strip), the strip bends, releasing the weight that trips the carriage. Carriage and toast pop up.

In other toasters, the carriage is held down by a keeper mechanism and a solenoid (a type of electromagnet).

When toasting is done, the solenoid is energized, pulling the keeper release away from the keeper, which in turn releases the carriage.

221

Disassembly

1 Unplug toaster, turn it over, and remove screws from base, including those holding strain-relief fitting. Release cord from fitting.

2 Remove carriage lever knob. Pull toaster's side panels outward to release metal shell; lift each panel away.

End cap

3 Mark shell and chassis to aid in reassembly (especially on toasters with a one-slice slot); then separate them.

Troubleshooting

Problem	CAUSE? / Solution
Toaster doesn't work	POWER OFF AT OUTLET? See *General troubleshooting*, p.144.
	FAULTY POWER CORD? See *General troubleshooting*, p.144.
	SWITCH ACTUATOR FAULTY? When the carriage is down, the switch actuator (a mica plate) closes the contact arms, completing a circuit that delivers current to the elements (see exploded view and inset, p.221). If actuator is cracked or out of position, contact arms won't close. Remove toaster shell and reposition (or replace) actuator. ◆
Carriage does not stay down	CARRIAGE OBSTRUCTED? Clean crumbs and dirt from moving parts with a soft brush. ◇
	TRIP ROD DISLODGED? When the bimetal strip bends in response to heat (see *Release mechanisms*, p.221), it pulls the trip rod, releasing the carriage. If the rod slips out of its mounting hole, the carriage won't stay down. Unplug the toaster; use needle-nose pliers to guide the rod back into its mounting hole. ◆
	WORN OR DEFECTIVE KEEPER OR LATCH? If edges are rounded over by wear, file latch so that it securely grabs keeper. Straighten bent parts with needle-nose pliers. ◆
Toast is ejected from toaster	FAULTY PISTON? In some toasters, a damper called a dashpot piston slows the carriage as it rises. If the piston is faulty, the carriage pops up with enough force to eject the toast. If cleaning the piston slide rod does not solve the problem, replace the toaster; the piston assembly cannot be replaced separately from the chassis. ◆
Carriage stays down, but toaster does not heat	SWITCH ACTUATOR FAULTY? See *Toaster doesn't work*, above. ◆
	SWITCH CONTACTS FAULTY? See *Servicing cords and switches*, right. ◆ ▣
	FAULTY POWER CORD? See *General troubleshooting*, p.144.
Bread does not toast to desired color	INTERIOR SURFACE OF SHELL STAINED? A stained or dirty shell can vary the amount of heat reflected to the toast. Remove shell and clean inside surface with mixture of baking soda and water. ◆
	HEATING ELEMENT FAULTY? See *Checking the elements*, right. ◆ ▣
Toast burns or does not pop up	BIMETAL STRIP BLOCKED? Brush away obstructions. If strip is bent, straighten with needle-nose pliers. ◆
	RELEASE LATCH BROKEN? Replace the toaster. ◇
	LIFT SPRING BROKEN? Before replacing spring, make sure that spring has not simply slipped from its seat. If toaster has a dashpot piston (see *Toast is ejected from toaster*, above), clean slide rod. ◆
	COLOR CONTROL FAULTY? Remove shell of toaster and reseat slide control if it has slipped out of position. ◆
	KEEPER RELEASE SOLENOID FAULTY? If toaster has magnetic release (see *Release mechanisms*, p.221), test with VOM set on RX 100 scale. If meter reads close to zero ohms, the magnet is OK. If not, replace magnet. ◆ ▣
Toaster trips breaker or shocks user	See *General troubleshooting*, p.147.

Degree of difficulty: Simple ◇   Average ◆   Complex ◆   Volt-ohm meter required: ▣

Servicing cords and switches

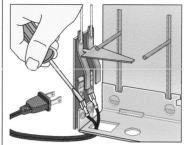

If elements don't heat, the problem may be a break in the power cord. Access chassis (*Disassembly*, Step 2). Pry terminal leads from toaster and remove the cord. Test cord for continuity (p.145), and replace it if faulty.

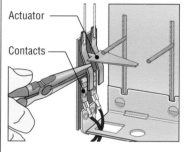

Actuator

Contacts

If cord is OK, depress carriage to see if the switch contacts meet. If not, check switch actuator and replace if damaged. Reposition the contact arms using needle-nose pliers. Clean burned or pitted contacts with automotive-point file (p.145).

Checking the elements

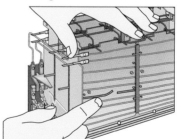

Heating elements in most toasters are a series of flat Nichrome ribbons wrapped around mica panels. To examine elements for obvious breaks or damage, unplug toaster and remove chassis (*Disassembly*, Step 3).

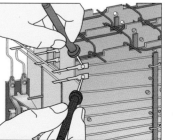

To verify that elements are intact, probe their terminals VOM set on RX1. Look for a reading of 14 to 20 ohms. Patch an isolated break with a soldering lug; otherwise replace chassis (replacing the entire toaster may be more economical).

Toaster ovens

Unlike a toaster, which simply browns bread, a toaster oven can also heat food, using one or both sets of its heating elements. Most models have two upper elements for broiling and two lower elements for baking; the pairs are controlled separately. The elements are usually sheathed, although coil-type elements are also found. The baking temperature is typically maintained by a thermostat; toasting is typically controlled by a timer. The controls are usually grouped on one side of the appliance and are easily reached.

Most toaster oven problems can be traced to either the heating elements, the thermostat, the power cord, or the switch contacts.

CAUTION: Once you complete a repair, check the oven for a ground fault before using it (see *General troubleshooting*, p.147). This is a good practice after repairing any appliance, but particularly those with a metal housing, such as a toaster or toaster oven.

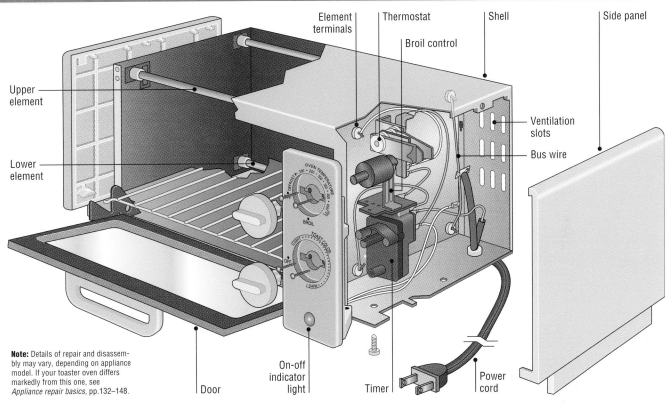

Note: Details of repair and disassembly may vary, depending on appliance model. If your toaster oven differs markedly from this one, see *Appliance repair basics*, pp.132–148.

Labels: Element terminals · Thermostat · Shell · Side panel · Broil control · Upper element · Lower element · Ventilation slots · Bus wire · Door · On-off indicator light · Timer · Power cord

Disassembly

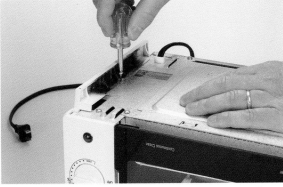

1 Unplug the oven, and if it's warm, let it cool completely. Most serviceable parts are behind the side panels. To open the panels, turn the oven upside down and remove the retaining screws.

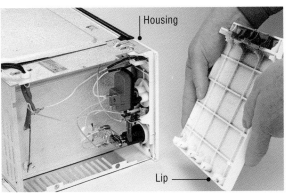

Housing · Lip

2 Pull the side panels away from the toaster oven; internal wiring or controls may be mounted on them. To reassemble, slide panels into place; lips on panel edges fit over edge of metal housing.

Small appliances ▪ Toaster ovens

Troubleshooting

Problem	CAUSE? / Solution
Oven does not heat or overheats	POWER OFF AT OUTLET? See *General troubleshooting*, p.144.
	FAULTY POWER CORD? See *General troubleshooting*, p.144.
	ELEMENTS FAULTY? Inspect both sets of elements for damage and corrosion; clean dirty or corroded terminals. Test each element independently with VOM (right). Elements are typically connected in series; to test one, disconnect it from the others. Replace faulty elements as needed. ◆ ▧
	THERMOSTAT FAULTY? Inspect thermostat for corrosion, and clean as needed (below right). If contacts are fused shut, replace thermostat. If thermostat looks OK, test it and service contacts if needed (p.194). Some thermostats can be recalibrated if the temperature range is out of adjustment (p.182). ◆ ▧
	OVEN TIMER FAULTY? If your toaster oven is controlled by a timer that shuts off heating elements after a certain length of time, check it for continuity (right). If timer is faulty, replace it. ◆ ▧
Oven does not broil	ELEMENT FAULTY? When broiling, top elements should be at maximum output and bottom elements at partial or zero output. If food is warm but top is not browned, or if top is browned but food is cold, test elements with VOM (right); replace as needed. ◆ ▧
Bread does not toast to desired color	TOAST TIMER FAULTY? When toasting, the upper and lower elements are controlled by a timer that serves much like the color control of a toaster. Check timer for continuity (right) and replace it if faulty. ◆ ▧
	INTERIOR DIRTY? Most newer toaster ovens are continuous-cleaning, but older units with a shiny metal interior won't toast properly if metal is dirty or covered with crumbs. Unplug oven and clean it (facing page). Wipe interior with damp sponge. ◇
	ELEMENT FAULTY? When toasting, upper and lower elements should be at maximum output. If one element is faulty, only one side of bread will toast properly. Inspect and test elements (see *Oven does not heat,* above). Replace faulty element. ◆ ▧
	BREAD PLACEMENT WRONG? Arrange bread on racks so that it will be evenly toasted by elements. ◇
Toast burns	TOAST TIMER FAULTY? See *Bread does not toast to desired color,* above. ◆ ▧
	BREAD TOO CLOSE TO ELEMENTS? Reposition bread. ◇
Broiling rack slides poorly	RACK OR OVEN WALLS DIRTY? Clean oven (facing page). Some ovens link a rack with the door, so that rack slides forward when door is opened. Follow manufacturer's recommendations concerning lubrication of this mechanism. ◇
Oven trips breaker or shocks user	See *General troubleshooting,* p.147.

Degree of difficulty: Simple ◇   Average ◆   Complex ◆
Volt-ohm meter required: ▧

Testing and replacing the elements

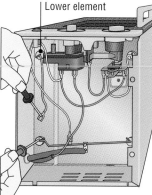

Lower element

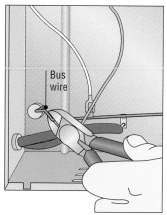

Bus wire

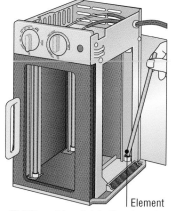

Element

1 Unplug oven; access element terminals (*Disassembly,* Step 2, p.223). Remove lower element lead; test element with VOM on RX1. Meter should read 10 to 18 ohms. Test both sets of elements separately.

2 To replace a defective element, use diagonal pliers (p.124) to clip off bus wire attached to each end of element. Clip wire as close as possible to element terminal to facilitate reassembly.

3 Lift or slide out defective element and replace with identical part. To connect new element, solder its ends to the bus bar using high-temperature (silver) solder, or crimp if recommended by manufacturer.

Testing and replacing a timer

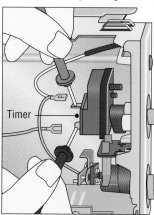

Timer

1 Access timer (*Disassembly,* Step 2, p.223). Remove leads; clean timer terminals as needed with contact cleaner. Turn timer off to test. Set VOM on RX1 and touch probes to timer terminals. Look for infinity reading with timer off, zero ohms reading with timer on any setting except *Off.*

2 Some timers can be repaired, but replacement is usually the better course. To replace timer, pull knob from front of control panel. Remove screws holding timer in place, and pull timer from oven. Replace timer with an identical model.

Servicing the thermostat

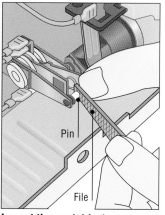

Pin

File

Inspect thermostat for loose connections or damaged contacts. Clean dirty or corroded contacts with emery paper or automotive-point file (slip file past pin to reach contacts). If problems persist, test for resistance with VOM (p.194). Replace thermostat if faulty.

Servicing the broil control

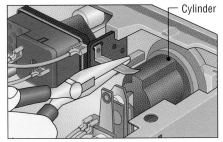

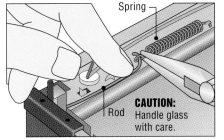

Cylinder

1 Remove side panel (*Disassembly,* Step 2, p.223) and inspect broil control mechanism for physical damage. Gently straighten a bent contact arm with needle-nose pliers. Arm should rest against temperature control cylinder so that broil contacts open and close as cylinder is turned.

2 Inspect broil contacts for dirt, pitting, or corrosion. Clean contacts (located beneath contact arm) with automotive-point file, and remove filings by spraying contacts with electrical contact cleaner.

Replacing the door

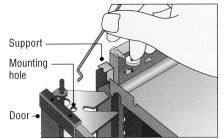

Spring

Support

Mounting hole

Door

CAUTION: Handle glass with care.

Rod

1 If the glass door of a toaster oven breaks, remove racks and pan from oven. Remove side panel on hinge side of oven. To release damaged door, hold connecting rod while unhooking tension spring with needle-nose pliers.

2 Lift old door off supports. To install new door, insert end of connecting rod through mounting hole and place door on supports. Hook one end of tension spring over tab in toaster housing, the other over hooked end of rod.

USE AND CARE

With a new oven, monitor cooking times carefully until you know your oven's behavior. Oven temperatures may not match the dial settings exactly, and they may differ somewhat from the settings on your full-size kitchen oven.

Make sure cooking containers are an appropriate size and material for the oven. Containers and lids must not touch any heating element.

A toaster oven is best used for reheating; broiling; long slow baking of small items such as potatoes or chicken parts; cooking frozen dinners or small casseroles; and warming breads, rolls, or pastries. It is not a substitute for a full-sized oven.

Remove crumbs or spatters inside the oven after each use—the residue and debris are a serious fire hazard.

Wash racks and trays in hot sudsy water; never clean them by placing in the oven of a self-cleaning range.

The continuous-cleaning surfaces of many ovens can be badly damaged by scouring.

Some manufacturers recommend leaving the oven unplugged when not in use. This will prevent it from being activated accidentally.

To clean a toaster oven's interior, unplug oven and let it cool. Remove racks and trays, then shake out crumbs (use soft brush to loosen crumbs if necessary). Wipe crumb tray with a damp cloth.

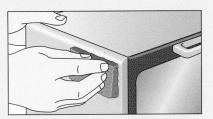

To clean exterior, wipe off smudges with a damp sponge or nylon scrubbing pad moistened with liquid dishwashing detergent (metal scouring pads or abrasive cleansers will damage finish). Polish with a clean dry cloth.

Common variants

As an extra safety feature, many ovens have an on-off switch that's connected to an interlock mechanism (a set of contacts on the door and housing that separate when the door is opened). If the oven does not operate, check to make sure the interlock contacts are meeting properly; clean them if they're dirty.

Some ovens use a solenoid as part of the color control circuitry (see *Release mechanisms,* p.221). If you notice a burnt wiring smell and the toaster lever won't stay down, check the solenoid's coils for signs of overheating; replace the solenoid if it's damaged or if the plunger won't operate properly.

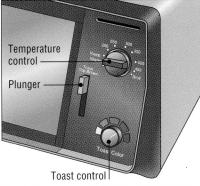

Temperature control

Plunger

Toast control

Check the owner's manual for proper use of control dials. With units that have multiple dials, you may need to turn all controls off to deactivate the oven. Setting controls improperly is a common source of problems.

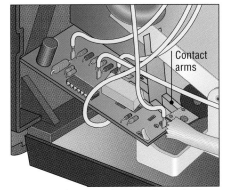

Contact arms

If the controls are regulated by electronic circuitry, servicing is best left to professionals. Check first, however, for switch contacts that may be mounted on circuit board; cleaning them may restore the appliance to working order.

Electric toothbrush

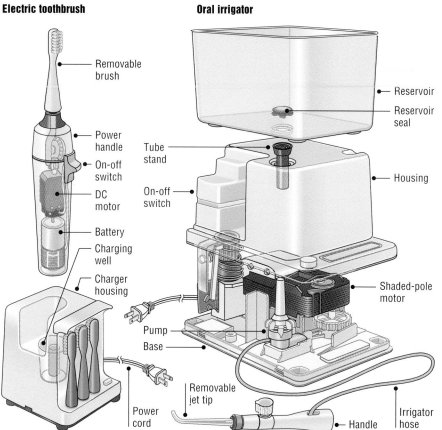

- Removable brush
- Power handle
- On-off switch
- DC motor
- Battery
- Charging well
- Charger housing
- Power cord

Oral irrigator

- Reservoir
- Reservoir seal
- Tube stand
- On-off switch
- Housing
- Shaded-pole motor
- Pump
- Base
- Removable jet tip
- Handle
- Irrigator hose

Troubleshooting

Problem	CAUSE? / Solution
Appliance doesn't work	POWER OFF AT OUTLET? See *General troubleshooting*, p.144.
	FAULTY POWER CORD? See *General troubleshooting*, p.144. On cordless models, a faulty power cord on charger will prevent battery from charging.
	FAULTY SWITCH? *(Irrigator only)* Flush out debris fouling contacts (below). ◇
	BATTERY OR CHARGER FAULTY? *(Toothbrush or plaque remover only)* Clean charger post (bottom). See also *Cordless tools and appliances*, p.142. ◇
Appliance leaks	HOSE OR FITTINGS FAULTY? *(Irrigator only)* Look for holes in hose; check hose connections (below). Replace damaged or brittle hose. Make sure reservoir seal and tube stand are properly seated; replace seal if hardened. ◆
Appliance trips breaker or shocks user	See *General troubleshooting*, p.147. Sealed assemblies such as those in toothbrushes and some plaque removers are unlikely to cause problems, but if a charger shocks user, have it professionally serviced.

Degree of difficulty: Simple ◇   Average ◆   Complex ◆

Servicing an oral irrigator

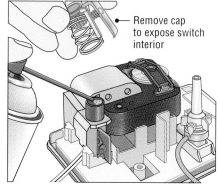

Remove cap to expose switch interior

Remove screws under base, then pry upper housing away from tabs in base. Spray switch with electrical contact cleaner to clean.

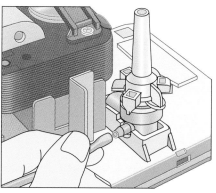

Check hose connection on pump. If hose is stiff or damaged, replace it. Lubricate plastic gears with silicone-base grease approved for plastics.

Cleaning a charger post

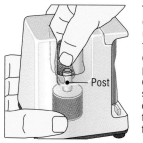

Post

The metal post of a charging unit can become fouled with debris. Wipe post with fine emery cloth; spray it with electrical contact cleaner; then wipe clean.

Cleaning a brush head

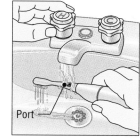

Port

If the brush head on a plaque remover or toothbrush has a cleaning port, turn appliance on and run warm water through the port to flush out debris.

A cordless electric toothbrush employs a small DC motor (p.139) to move the toothbrush shaft from side to side or back and forth, depending on the model. A plaque remover is similar, except that its internal gearing causes individual tufts of the brush to move in a circular pattern. Problems with either unit may involve the brush heads, which are easily replaced if worn or faulty, or the induction-type charger (see *Cordless tools and appliances*, pp.142–143). The power handles of both appliances are typically sealed to prevent shock hazard. A sealed handle should simply be replaced if faulty.

An oral irrigator draws water from a reservoir on top of the appliance, then sprays it under pressure through the jet tip. The unit's shaded-pole motor (p.139) is relatively trouble-free, but the hose and the seal beneath the reservoir can leak. Another leakage point is the tube stand. Be sure the stand is firmly seated on the pump (it is easily dislodged).

Vacuum cleaners

There are two basic types of vacuum cleaner: upright and canister. Both operate on a similar principle: a universal motor drives a fan that draws dirt into a filter bag.

On uprights, the motor also drives a built-in brush roller that loosens dirt from carpets. Most uprights employ a direct (dirty-air) draft system: the stream of dirty air passes over the fan before entering the filter bag. This filtration path leaves the fan and motor vulnerable to damage. Bypass uprights (p.232) overcome this problem. A "tools on board" upright can divert the suction to an accessory hose.

Canister vacuums (p.228) employ a bypass (clean-air) system: dirty air is drawn through the filter bag first; relatively clean air is then exhausted over the motor. Canisters are usually more reliable than uprights because the fan never comes in contact with the dirt, but they aren't as powerful because the motor is farther away from the carpet. Newer models may include a power-driven brush roller and other attachments.

Upright vacuum cleaner

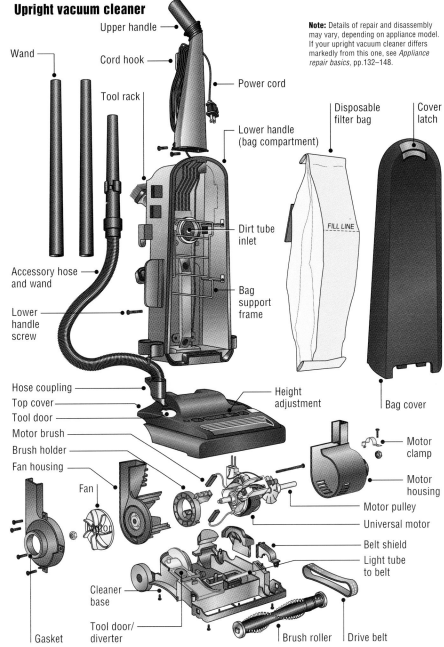

Wand · Upper handle · Cord hook · Power cord · Tool rack · Lower handle (bag compartment) · Disposable filter bag · Cover latch · FILL LINE · Dirt tube inlet · Bag support frame · Accessory hose and wand · Lower handle screw · Hose coupling · Top cover · Tool door · Motor brush · Brush holder · Fan housing · Fan · Motor · Gasket · Cleaner base · Tool door/diverter · Gasket · Brush roller · Drive belt · Height adjustment · Bag cover · Motor clamp · Motor housing · Motor pulley · Universal motor · Belt shield · Light tube to belt

Note: Details of repair and disassembly may vary, depending on appliance model. If your upright vacuum cleaner differs markedly from this one, see *Appliance repair basics*, pp.132–148.

Disassembly

1 Unplug vacuum and allow its parts to cool. Remove lower handle screw and handle (left); unscrew accessory hose and lift it off (above).

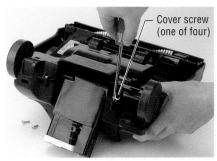

Cover screw (one of four)

2 To remove top cover, turn vacuum over and remove top cover screws. Turn the unit right side up, slide the height adjustment to the left, and lift off the cover.

Motor · Gasket · Motor clamp

3 To remove motor, take out brush roller and drive belt (p.229). Remove screw securing motor clamp. Be careful not to damage gasket at other end of the motor during reinstallation.

Canister vacuum cleaner

- Filter bag compartment cover
- Motor compartment cover
- Bag-full indicator
- Brush assembly
- Switch assembly
- Motor cover plate
- Motor (see below)
- Power cord
- Secondary filter
- Filter/dust bag compartment
- Disposable filter/dust bag
- Hose with integral wiring
- Accessory power cord
- Wand
- Top cover
- Housing
- Accessory motor
- Drive belt
- Motor brush
- Brush roller
- Power brush accessory (base)

Note: Details of repair and disassembly may vary, depending on appliance model. If your vacuum cleaner differs markedly from this one, see *Appliance repair basics*, pp.132–148.

Exploded view of canister motor

- Brush assembly
- Foam gasket
- Fan assembly
- Motor housing
- Universal motor
- Motor housing
- Fan housing

Disassembly

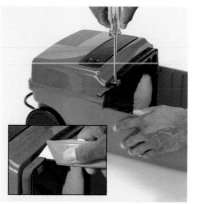

1 Unplug vacuum; remove hoses, dust bag, and filter. Remove cover screws (left), then lift off cover. (On unit shown here, a self-stick gasket covers screws; cut it and peel it back to reach screws.) Canister motor and electrical components are now accessible.

2 To service motor brushes or canister motor itself, remove screws that secure motor cover plate and lift out motor. Keep track of parts and pieces for proper reinstallation. Refit gaskets to maintain a tight seal.

3 To access serviceable parts of the brush roller, turn power nozzle over and clean out dust and debris. Then remove screws securing top cover. (Don't remove motor mounting screws, usually identified by arrows or other symbols.) Turn unit right side up and lift off top cover.

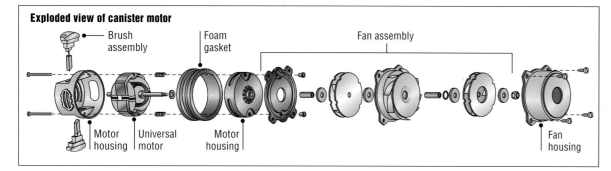

Troubleshooting

Problem	CAUSE? / Solution
Motor does not run	POWER OFF AT OUTLET? See *General troubleshooting*, p.144.
	FAULTY UNIVERSAL MOTOR? See *Servicing a motor*, p.230. Canister vacuum cleaners contain two motors. ◆
	FAULTY POWER CORD? See *Replacing the cord*, p.231. ◇
	FAULTY SWITCH? See *Servicing a switch*, p.231. ◇ ▣
Sluggish motor	FAN JAMMED? Look for and remove debris, caked dirt, or other obstructions. Replace fan if damaged (p.231). ◇
	WORN BRUSHES? Replace brushes (p.230). ◆
	DRY OR WORN MOTOR BEARINGS? Apply oil or light grease (see *Lubricants and lubricating*, p.137); otherwise replace. ◆
Motor stops and starts	FAULTY POWER CORD? See *Motor does not run,* above.
	FAULTY SWITCH? See *Motor does not run,* above.
	FAULTY MOTOR BRUSH? Replace brushes (p.230). Also check brush springs, and replace them if damaged or weak. ◆
	DRY OR WORN MOTOR BEARINGS? See *Sluggish motor,* above. Also check for debris that might be affecting bearings.
	FAN JAMMED? See *Sluggish motor,* above.
Motor is noisy	MOTOR DIRTY? Open vacuum housing; clean out dirt and debris. Clean or replace filters (right). ◇
	FAULTY DRIVE BELT? Remove belt (right) and replace. ◇
	FAN LOOSE OR DAMAGED? Inspect for chips, dents, warping, and other damage; replace if needed (p.231). If loose, tighten connection to motor shaft. ◆
Vacuum works poorly (reduced suction)	DUST BAG FULL OR CLOGGED? Empty or replace bag. ◇
	BLOCKED ATTACHMENT? Locate and remove obstruction. ◇
	CLOGGED HOSE? Clear hose (p.230). ◇
	CLOGGED FILTER? Clean or replace filter (right). ◇
	FAN JAMMED? See *Sluggish motor,* above.
Brush leaves lint on carpet	WORN OR DAMAGED DRIVE BELT OR ROLLER? See *Motor is noisy,* above. Also inspect roller brushes (right) and clean, adjust, or replace them. ◇
	CLOG BLOCKING AIRFLOW? Clean air passages inside cleaner and hoses. ◇. In central systems (p.232), clean tubing. ◆
Vacuum trips breaker or shocks user	See *General troubleshooting*, p.147.
Cordless vacuum does not run	See *Troubleshooting batteries and chargers*, p.143

Degree of difficulty: Simple ◇   Average ◆   Complex ◆
Volt-ohm meter required: ▣

Servicing the brush roller and drive belt

Vacuum-cleaner problems are commonly caused by worn or clogged roller brushes or a damaged drive belt. Use a comb to remove lint, pet hair, and other debris from the brush roller after every vacuuming. More thorough cleaning may require removal of the roller. Brush roller bristles should be long enough to touch a straightedge held across the plate.

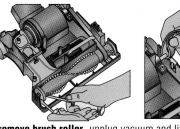

— End cap

To remove brush roller, unplug vacuum and lift off cover (*Disassembly,* Step 2, p.227, for uprights; *Disassembly,* Step 3, facing page, for canisters). Pry roller out with screwdriver (left). Remove belt to check for wear (right).

To clean a brush roller's end fittings, to access bearings, or to change replaceable-type bristles (inset), first remove end caps from roller. Some twist off as shown; others are simply pulled off.

Brush roller bearings on newer models are often sealed; replace if stiff. Bearings in older vacuum cleaners should be sparingly lubricated with oil or light grease.

End cap

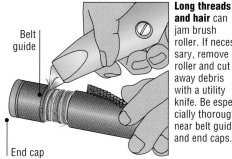

Belt guide

Long threads and hair can jam brush roller. If necessary, remove roller and cut away debris with a utility knife. Be especially thorough near belt guide and end caps.

Replacing or cleaning filters and bags

Replace a disposable dust bag, or empty and clean a cloth dust bag, as directed in the owner's manual—usually when it is no more than three-quarters full. On some models disposable secondary filters screen the motor or clean exhausted air. Replace them when they become dirty (clogged filters reduce suction and stress the motor) or if they are torn.

An exhaust filter removes fine dust that otherwise would be blown into the room. Replace it every five to six dust-bag changes.

A disposable filter protects this canister motor from dust that might get past the dust bag (the primary filter). Replace it when it looks dirty.

Clearing clogged hoses

Hoses are vulnerable to clogs (as well as tears and punctures) caused by vacuuming up sharp objects. A toothpick, for example can lodge inside and collect debris.

To clear a clog, attach hose to exhaust and nozzle into intake using rag to seal it (left); turn vacuum on. If exhaust air does not propel debris into dust bag, disconnect hose. Carefully feed a garden hose (right) or similar item through hose to jar clog loose.

Repairing non-electric hoses

Most cleaner hoses are made of plastic reinforced with a spiral metal wire. Have a damaged electric hose professionally repaired but you can replace or cut off the damaged end of non-electric hoses. The simplest type just snaps on its fittings. Other types, including a threaded one that's a popular replacement hose, are shown below.

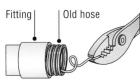

To begin repair on a glued type of hose, cut it near fitting using knife and wire cutter. Twist and pull out remaining wire and hose and scrape out any glue.

If hose is the type that glues into fitting, brush rubber cement onto the end of the hose and inside the fitting; then press the hose into the fitting.

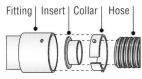

If hose has a pegged collar, press pegs and pull to release hose from fitting. Glue hose to insert, cover it with collar and insert into fitting to engage pegs.

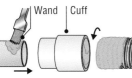

If replacing an entire hose, you can use a special reverse-threaded hose and a universal cuff that glues over your wand or machine-end fitting.

Servicing a motor

Corded vacuums are powered by universal motors. If a vacuum fails to run and the switch or cord is not at fault, the motor may need servicing (p.146) that may involve nothing more than cleaning or lubricating. Canister and bypass upright vacuum motors are less exposed to dirt, but clean a motor whenever disassembly is necessary. Use compressed air or a brush; and a damp cloth on plastic parts. Use electrical contact cleaner to remove dirt or corrosion from electrical parts. You may have to disassemble a motor to replace carbon brushes. The motor of an inexpensive vacuum may be sealed, however, and can't be serviced. You may have to replace the vacuum instead. **CAUTION:** Unplug any vacuum before disassembing it.

Disassembling motors

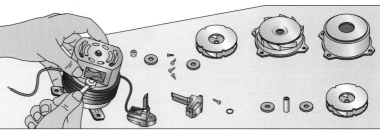

In a stacked motor and fan, parts are held together with screws or bolts. To disassemble this complex assembly for servicing or cleaning, remove fasteners and carefully lay out every part in the order it was removed.

A motor in a clamshell housing is much easier to disassemble: just unscrew top cover and remove it.

Replacing the motor brushes

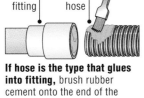

Brush assembly

1 Unscrew brush assemblies and inspect brushes for wear or damage (p.146). You may have to remove motor to reach carbon brushes (*Disassembly*, p.228, for canisters; p.227 for uprights).

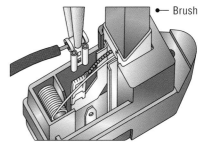

Brush

2 Replace both brushes if either is damaged or is worn shorter than it is wide. Mark or label brush wires to ease reinstallation. Use long-nose pliers to disconnect each brush end from its terminal.

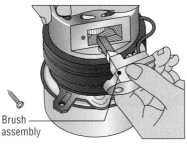

Awl

In some vacuums, motor brushes may be held in place by a spring clip. Use awl to lift spring clip gently and hold it while you pull out the brush for inspection or replacement.

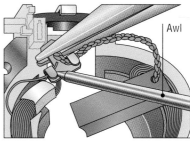

Awl

Brush wires may be crimped or soldered in place. Pry open crimped connections with an awl; see page 136 for desoldering instructions. Some new brushes come with spring clips attached.

Servicing the fan

1 Grasp fan (or insert screwdriver or hex wrench in shaft end) to keep it from turning while removing nut (usually reverse threaded) with a wrench.

2 Wiggle fan free; loosen it first, if necessary, by tapping the motor shaft lightly with the handle of a screwdriver or mallet.

3 Lift off fan and clean. Replace fan if partially melted or badly chipped; this causes excessive vibration that can damage motor.

Servicing a switch

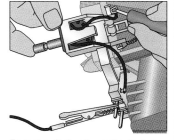

To access a handle switch, unplug vacuum; remove one or two screws. To access a foot switch, remove the unit's cover and motor housing (*Disassembly,* p.227).

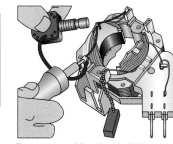

Switch
Plug

To replace switch, disconnect leads. The switch shown here has a simple plug-in connector that can be pulled out by hand or with long-nose pliers.

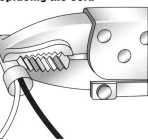

To test switch, clip continuity tester (p.125) on one terminal; probe other terminal while operating switch. The tester should light only when switch is turned on.

To remove soldered switch leads, heat connections with soldering gun; use solder pump or braid to absorb excess solder (see *How to desolder,* p.136).

Replacing the cord

Unplug vacuum and disassemble to access cord connections (see drawings, p.227 or p.228). Use locking pliers to open crimped connectors (above) or cut them off.

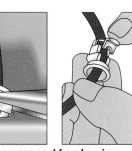

To disengage cord from housing, grasp strain-relief fitting with long-nose pliers, squeeze, and with a twisting/pulling motion pull it out. Reuse fitting on replacement cord.

Cordless vacuums

A cordless vacuum cleaner has a direct-current (DC) motor (p.139), a rechargeable battery pack, and a battery recharging unit consisting of a transformer and a diode. Problems with cordless vacuums are usually due to a charger defect or batteries that no longer hold a charge (see *Troubleshooting batteries and chargers,* p.143). Replace a faulty charger.

Like corded vacuum cleaners, cordless models require proper maintenance. Shake dust from the filter after each use, and wash cloth filters periodically in warm soapy water (let the filter dry thoroughly before reusing it). Replace a filter if it's damaged, or if its gasket seal is nicked or stiff.

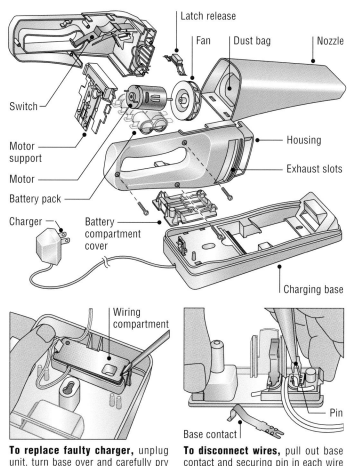

To replace faulty charger, unplug unit, turn base over and carefully pry open wiring compartment.

To disconnect wires, pull out base contact and securing pin in each wire using long-nose pliers.

Tank vacuums

Except for the orientation of its parts (the motor and fan are mounted behind the dust bag rather than above it), a tank vacuum cleaner is very similar to a canister vacuum. Because tank vacuums are also considerably more compact than canisters, however, their internal components are more difficult to reach.

A sensor on some models shuts down the unit and pops open the filter bag compartment when the bag is full. Replace the exhaust port filter (p.229) after every six dust-bag changes, or sooner if it's dirty.

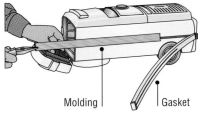

To gain access to the type of tank vacuum shown here, pull gasket off side seam and slide molding from groove. Other models have access screws.

Molding | Gasket

Cord reel

If cord is faulty, reel can usually be replaced. Turn vacuum over. Open housing enough to pull out reel. Label and disconnect wires; then remove reel.

Mini-vacuums

More powerful than a standard cordless vacuum, mini-vacs are useful for vacuuming stair carpets and for other small jobs. Because the mini-vac employs a dirty-air system (p.227), try not to pick up objects, such as coins, that might damage the fan.

Dust bag

Maintenance and repair procedures for mini-vacs are similar to those for uprights. Change dust bags often; clean rollers and change worn belts (p.229) as needed.

Shop vacuum

A shop vac is a high-powered, high-capacity machine designed to collect the chunky debris that would hobble a household vacuum. Some will suck up water as well as dirt. In such "wet/dry" vacs, the electrical components are housed in a separate chamber suspended at the top of the collection tank. The motor has its own cooling fan and is protected from the dirty air that flows through the main chamber. Use flat paper or foam filters for wet pick up; switch to pleated paper filters for dry vacuuming.

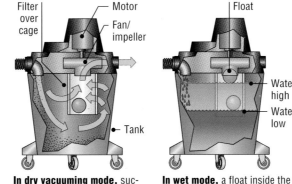

Filter over cage | Motor | Fan/impeller | Tank | Float | Water high | Water low

In dry vacuuming mode, suction draws dirt into the collection tank. Debris falls to the bottom of the tank and fine dust is filtered at the fan.

In wet mode, a float inside the collection tank rises with the water to block suction when the tank is full. That prevents water from infiltrating the motor.

Bypass vacuum

This type of vacuum is not quite as powerful as other uprights (the motor is relatively far from the carpet), but because its motor and fan are protected, a bypass vacuum offers greater reliability.

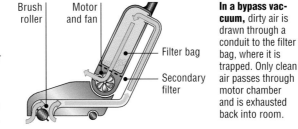

Brush roller | Motor and fan | Filter bag | Secondary filter

In a bypass vacuum, dirty air is drawn through a conduit to the filter bag, where it is trapped. Only clean air passes through motor chamber and is exhausted back into room.

Stick vacuum (electric broom)

Essentially a mini-upright without a brush roller, stick vacuums are powered by a universal motor and have a detachable dust cup. Repairable problems include cord and switch failure and a faulty impeller fan.

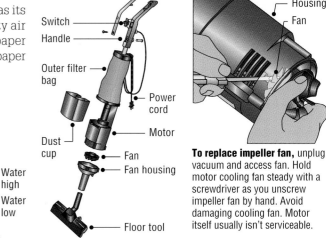

Switch | Handle | Outer filter bag | Power cord | Motor | Dust cup | Fan | Fan housing | Floor tool | Housing | Fan

To replace impeller fan, unplug vacuum and access fan. Hold motor cooling fan steady with a screwdriver as you unscrew impeller fan by hand. Avoid damaging cooling fan. Motor itself usually isn't serviceable.

Central vacuum systems

Quiet, convenient and reliable, central vacs consist of a collection unit, PVC tubing, conveniently located hose fittings, hose, power brush and accessories. To clear clogged tubing, cut it with a hacksaw where it is exposed above or below the outlet. Fish out the clog with a snake and repair the tube with coupling.

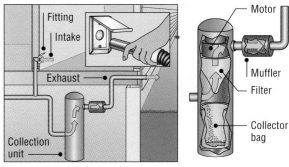

Fitting | Intake | Exhaust | Collection unit | Motor | Muffler | Filter | Collector bag

Central vacuum tubing is run inside walls from collection unit in basement, attic or garage to fittings in rooms throughout house.

Large appliances

Despite their size, most large appliances are relatively simple machines. On average, they are only slightly more complex—and slightly more difficult to fix—than small appliances. If you consider the cost of a service call or the cost of replacing a large appliance, fixing one yourself is usually well worth the effort.

Repairing a large appliance rarely requires special tools. Only screwdrivers, nut drivers, or wrenches are usually needed for disassembly—although a socket wrench will speed the process and help loosen stubborn fasteners. A volt-ohm meter (VOM) is the only special item you may need; for simple tests, you can often use an inexpensive continuity tester instead.

Most of the large appliances shown on the following pages are typical freestanding models. In most cases, the repair procedures shown here can be easily adapted to built-ins and other models.

The tests and repairs on these two pages are common to many large appliances. Familiarize yourself with this section and with *Appliance repair basics* (pp.123–148) before tackling any large-appliance repair.

When fixing a large appliance, it's often helpful to refer to the wiring diagram; it is usually located inside the unit—glued to a back panel, folded and tucked under a chassis strut, or sealed inside the door panel. If you can't find it, call the manufacturer and refer to your appliance model number. Wiring diagrams are fairly easy to read (p.132). Even if you can't follow one fully, it can be useful for identifying wires by color and tracing them to break down a circuit into its simplest components. It also shows if a switch is normally open or normally closed, or whether a motor is single or multiple speed. It includes charts that help you test selector switches and timers (below), and may include the VOM reading to look for when testing a component.

Cosmetic repairs for a cabinet

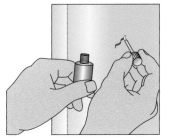

To fix a scratch, use appliance touch-up paint in a matching color (sold by appliance dealers and repair stores). Apply a tiny amount of paint with the bottle's brush. Fill a deep nick in layers; let each dry before applying the next. Smooth with fine auto-finish rubbing compound.

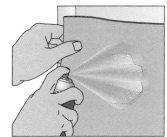

To spray-paint large area, use matching appliance spray paint. Cut an irregular hole in cardboard slightly larger than the damage. Hold spray can about 12 in. from surface with cardboard midway between, and make several quick passes over hole to feather edges. Don't let paint build up and drip.

Replacing a hose

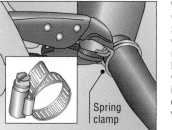

When removing a hose, wear safety goggles. Squeeze the spring clamp with locking pliers, slide it up the hose, then pull the hose off. Slit a stuck hose with a utility knife and peel it off. Replace a loose or corroded clamp with a worm-drive clamp (inset).

Spring clamp

Testing a selector switch

A multiposition push-button or rotary switch lets you select a fan speed, water or air temperature, cooking mode, or long or short cycle. Before testing a malfunctioning switch, check for loose wires or burnt terminals. Try spraying the switch with electrical contact cleaner. To test the switch, find the chart on the wiring diagram that shows the switch terminal designations (letters, numbers, or wire colors) and the switch positions for each switch setting.

Testing a timer

A timer energizes inlet valves, motors, and other parts at the proper times. If a timer is dead, test its motor if the motor's leads are accessible (right). If a timer malfunctions, check first for loose wires or burnt terminals. To check it more fully, use the chart on the wiring diagram that shows its terminals designated by letters, numbers, or wire colors. Some charts look complex, but they can be deciphered with a little study. The (partial) chart below is for a dryer .

Testing a timer motor

Motor

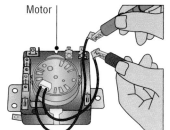

To test timer motor, trace and free motor leads and probe them with VOM on RX10. Look for a relatively high reading (usually 2,000 to 3,000 ohms), indicating continuity. If reading is infinity, replace motor (if possible) or entire timer mechanism.

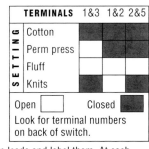

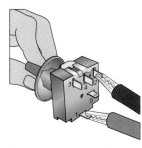

TERMINALS	1&3	1&2	2&5
Cotton			
Perm press			
Fluff			
Knits			

Open ☐   Closed ■

Look for terminal numbers on back of switch.

To test selector switch, remove leads and label them. At each switch position, use a VOM set on RX1 to probe all terminal combinations in the switch chart for the appliance. Look for a zero reading when the chart shows closed contacts and infinity otherwise. Replace a switch that deviates from results noted in chart.

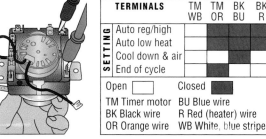

TERMINALS	TM WB	TM OR	BK BU	BK R
Auto reg/high				
Auto low heat				
Cool down & air				
End of cycle				

Open ☐   Closed ■

TM Timer motor   BU Blue wire
BK Black wire   R Red (heater) wire
OR Orange wire   WB White, blue stripe

To test timer, check timer chart and note which contacts should close during part of cycle that isn't working. Set timer knob to that part of cycle; then disconnect and label leads for terminals that should close. With VOM on RX1, probe each terminal pair. Look for a zero reading on each; replace timer if reading is infinity or high ohms.

Testing a thermal cutoff or disc thermostat

A thermal cutoff is a safety thermostat that turns off an appliance before it overheats. Like a thermal cutoff, a disc thermostat opens or closes a circuit at a set temperature; it is used to regulate the operation of appliances such as dishwashers and dryers. Both devices have an internal disc made of two metals that expand at different rates. At a set temperature (stamped on the unit's metal flange with an F after it), the disc flexes, closing or opening the contacts.

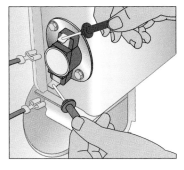

1 To test a thermal cutoff that turns off a circuit at a high temperature, set VOM on RX1 and remove a lead. At room temperature, probe both terminals; look for a reading of zero. If cutoff fails this test, replace it. If it passes, go to Step 2.

Testing an adjustable thermostat

The temperature control on air conditioners, refrigerators, and ranges is usually an adjustable capillary thermostat. It has a long sensing tube filled with liquid (or gas) that expands when heated, closing electrical contacts. When you raise the setting, the distance between the contacts increases so that the liquid has to get hotter and expand more to close

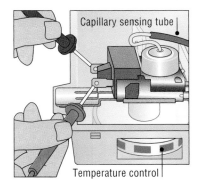

Capillary sensing tube

Temperature control

1 To test a thermostat for a cooling appliance, set it on its coldest setting and test it at room temperature. With VOM on RX1, remove leads and probe both terminals. Look for a reading of zero. If the thermostat fails this test, replace it. If it passes the test, proceed to Step 2.

Most of these nonadjustable thermostats turn *off* a circuit at a high temperature (to prevent overheating or to turn off a heating element when the water is hot enough); they are tested as shown below. A disc thermostat that turns *on* a circuit at a high temperature (to start the motor when the water is at the right temperature) is tested the same way, but should give opposite results: infinity at room temperature and zero when heated.

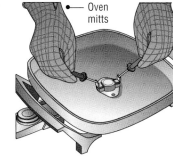

Oven mitts

2 Remove the cutoff and put it in a electric skillet or a heated oven, or hold it next to a hot light. Heat the cutoff to a temperature higher than the one stamped on its metal flange. After you hear a click, probe again; look for a reading of infinity. Replace the cutoff if it fails this test.

them. Lowering the setting does just the opposite.

The test below is for an air conditioner or refrigerator thermostat. A range thermostat should read zero at room temperature when set on its highest setting. The best way to test it at a high temperature is to turn on the oven for 15 minutes and compare the thermostat's setting against an oven thermometer.

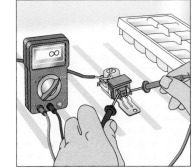

2 Remove the thermostat, set it on its hottest setting, and put it in a working freezer (or immerse it in an ice bath). After 15 min., probe again; look for a reading of infinity. Replace thermostat if it fails this test.

Testing a motor

Most large appliances are run by a split-phase motor (p.139). Before testing this usually reliable motor, check its starting components—the capacitor (p.140), if any, which provides an extra power surge to start the motor, and the centrifugal switch (pp.140,147) or the start relay (p.257), which disengages the motor's start windings once it approaches full speed. Only a pro can test a motor fully, but you can test the motor's windings for continuity. If a winding does test faulty, it's usually more cost-effective to replace the motor. **CAUTION:** Always discharge the capacitor (p.146) before testing a motor.

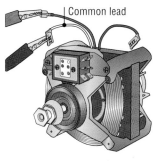

Common lead

To test motor, trace and disconnect leads. Set VOM on RX1. Clip one probe to common lead (usually white); probe other leads in turn. (There's one lead for start winding and one for each motor speed.) Look for low to moderate ohms reading, indicating continuity with some resistance. A reading of infinity or near-zero ohms indicates a faulty winding.

Testing solenoids

A solenoid is an electromagnetic coil with a central plunger that pulls in when the coil is energized and drops out when the current goes off. This allows it to perform such functions as opening water inlet valves, releasing detergent dispensers, and locking doors.

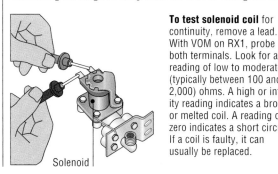

Solenoid

To test solenoid coil for continuity, remove a lead. With VOM on RX1, probe both terminals. Look for a reading of low to moderate (typically between 100 and 2,000) ohms. A high or infinity reading indicates a broken or melted coil. A reading of zero indicates a short circuit. If a coil is faulty, it can usually be replaced.

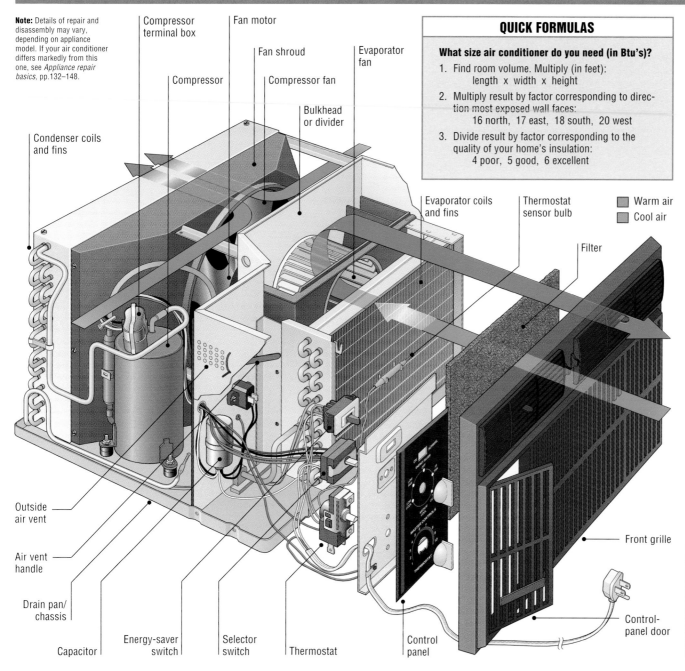

Note: Details of repair and disassembly may vary, depending on appliance model. If your air conditioner differs markedly from this one, see *Appliance repair basics*, pp.132–148.

Compressor terminal box

Fan motor

Fan shroud

Evaporator fan

Compressor

Compressor fan

Bulkhead or divider

Condenser coils and fins

Evaporator coils and fins

Thermostat sensor bulb

■ Warm air
□ Cool air

Filter

Outside air vent

Air vent handle

Drain pan/ chassis

Capacitor

Energy-saver switch

Selector switch

Thermostat

Control panel

Front grille

Control-panel door

QUICK FORMULAS

What size air conditioner do you need (in Btu's)?

1. Find room volume. Multiply (in feet):
   length x width x height
2. Multiply result by factor corresponding to direction most exposed wall faces:
   16 north, 17 east, 18 south, 20 west
3. Divide result by factor corresponding to the quality of your home's insulation:
   4 poor, 5 good, 6 excellent

An air conditioner circulates refrigerant in a continuous loop through two sets of coils. In the unit's indoor half, the refrigerant flows through the evaporator coils as a heat-absorbing gas. In the condenser coils outdoors, the gas is compressed and changed into a liquid, causing it to give off heat. Fins on the coils and fans maximize the heat transfer. A thermostat controls the operation.

Air-conditioner capacity is measured in Btu's (British thermal units) per hour. The capacity should match the room size (see *Quick formulas,* left). A unit that's too small cools poorly and runs too long, which may damage it. A unit that's too large cools quickly without removing enough humidity.

If a unit smells bad, unclog the drain hole, if any, and pour in 1 teaspoon of household ammonia. Clean the evaporator fins with automotive degreaser or refrigeration coil cleaner; make sure the product is marked safe for use on aluminum. Wash the drain pan with disinfectant. If the odor persists, have the unit steam-cleaned at an auto repair shop.

To prevent indoor dripping, slope a unit toward the outside by a reading of a quarter bubble on a spirit level.

FOR YOUR SAFETY

⚠ **Unplug an air conditioner** before opening the control panel or removing the cabinet.

Discharge the capacitor (p.146) before working on any of the parts inside an air conditioner.

Test for adequate voltage (p.131) before plugging in an air conditioner. If a unit's compressor doesn't work or cuts on and off, the outlet voltage may be too low.

Troubleshooting

SYMPTOM	POSSIBLE CAUSE	SOLUTION
Won't run	Power off at outlet or faulty power cord	See *General troubleshooting*, p.144.
	Faulty selector switch	Test and replace (p.239). ◆ ▣
Doesn't cool; fan runs	Dust-clogged filter or evaporator fins	Clean (p.239). ◇
	Faulty thermostat or selector switch	Test and replace (p.239). ◆ ▣
	Faulty compressor overload protector	Test and replace (p.238). ◆ ▣
	Faulty capacitor	Test and replace (p.146). ◆ ▣
	Dust-clogged condenser fins	Clean (p.239). ◇
	Faulty compressor	Test and have serviced (p.238). ◆ ▣
Fan doesn't run	Faulty selector switch	Test and replace (p.239). ◆ ▣
	Faulty capacitor	Test and replace (p.146). ◆ ▣
	Motor hums: loose or obstructed fan	Tighten or remove obstruction (p.238). ◇
	Motor hums: binding motor shaft or bearing	Oil motor (p.239). ◇
	No motor hum: faulty fan motor	Test and replace (p.238). ◆ ▣
Cools poorly	Outdoor air leaking into room	Seal air gaps around air conditioner. ◇
	Dust-clogged filter or evaporator fins	Clean (p.239). ◇
	Clogged or blocked condenser	Clean or clear obstruction. ◇
	Ventilator stuck open or broken	Spray lubricant on sticking parts; replace broken ones. ◇
	Loss of refrigerant	Have serviced. ◇
Cycles on and off often	Thermostat too high	Lower setting. ◇
	Overload protector activated	Shut off unit; wait 20 min. before restarting. ◇
	Clogged or blocked condenser	Clean or clear obstruction. ◇
	Thermostat sensor bulb touching coils	Put bulb back in supports. ◇
	Faulty capacitor	Test and replace (p.146). ◆ ▣
Noisy	Clicking sound: fan hitting housing or tubes	Reposition unit slightly; gently shift tubes. ◆
	Knocking at shutoff: faulty compressor spring	Seldom serious; ignore or have compressor replaced. ◇
	Vibrating screws or trim	Tighten screws; shim loose trim. ◇
	Tubes hitting cabinet	Gently shift tubes. ◇
	Loose fan	Tighten (p.238). ◇
	Pinging sound: condensate hitting condenser	Ignore; this is how unit evaporates condensate.
	Whistling sound: bent evaporator fins	Straighten (p.239). ◇
Frosts up	Low outdoor temperature	Don't run unit when it's below 60°F outside. ◇
	Dust-clogged filter or evaporator fins	Clean (p.239). ◇
	Loose or binding fan; slow motor	Check fans; test motor (p.238). ◆ ▣

Degree of difficulty: Simple ◇   Average ◆   Complex ◆   Volt-ohm meter required: ▣

Gaining access

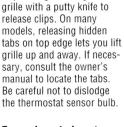

To remove grille, unplug unit; remove grille screws or press against edges of grille with a putty knife to release clips. On many models, releasing hidden tabs on top edge lets you lift grille up and away. If necessary, consult the owner's manual to locate the tabs. Be careful not to dislodge the thermostat sensor bulb.

To reach controls and power cord on many models, remove panel beneath switch knobs. First unplug the unit; then remove the grille and gently pry or pull the knobs from their shafts. Lift off faceplate and unscrew the panel.
CAUTION: Discharge the capacitor (p.146) before testing or working on controls.

To open a large unit, unplug the power cord, remove the front grille, pull the chassis forward, and place a support under the front edge. Most interior parts can be reached with chassis only partly removed from cabinet. To remove the chassis completely, get a helper; two people are needed to carry it safely.

To open a small unit, unplug the power cord and lift unit from the window. Grasp sides securely while a helper raises sash; otherwise air conditioner may fall. Set unit on a work surface and remove the grille. Then remove the screws along the lower edges and lift off the cabinet.

Fans and fan motor

To reach the fans or fan motor, unplug the air conditioner and open the cabinet (*Gaining access*, p.237). Rotate the fan until you see the screw that secures it to the motor shaft. On a plastic fan, the screw is on a clamp around the fan's hub; it's on the hub itself on a metal fan.

If a fan is hard to turn, the motor may need oil (facing page). Or it may have vibrated out of position: Temporarily loosen the motor's mounting nuts and reposition it until the fan rotates freely.

If the motor runs poorly or not at all, trace its leads back to the control panel. Label each lead and remove it from its terminal. With a VOM on RX1, clip one probe to the common (often white) lead and probe each of the other leads in turn. Look for a low ohms reading at each test. If a reading is high, replace the motor or test it more fully (see *Faulty split-phase motor*, p.146).

CAUTION: Before testing or removing the motor, discharge the capacitor (p.146).

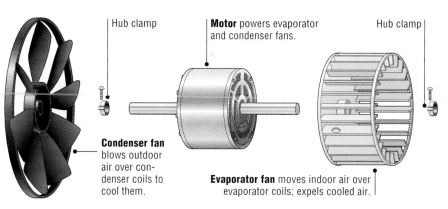

Hub clamp

Motor powers evaporator and condenser fans.

Hub clamp

Condenser fan blows outdoor air over condenser coils to cool them.

Evaporator fan moves indoor air over evaporator coils; expels cooled air.

To secure condenser fan blades, tighten screw on metal clamp around hub; there's usually an access hole. (On metal blades, use hex key to tighten setscrew against shaft's flat side.)

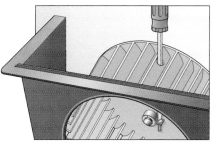

Tighten evaporator blower fan by inserting long screwdriver into access hole or gap in blades to reach screw on metal clamp. (On metal blades, use long hex key to tighten setscrew.)

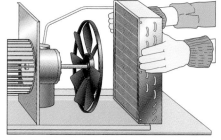

To replace a motor, carefully unscrew and shift condenser coils out of the way. Remove fan shroud and both fans. Trace motor leads to terminals on control panel, note locations, and disconnect them.

Unscrew mounting bolts and pull out motor. If motor leads follow an intricate path, tie strings to the ends and pull the strings through the unit as a guide for rethreading new leads.

Compressor

If the compressor doesn't work, the unit won't cool. Open the terminal box on the compressor and test its motor terminals and the overload protector (usually located inside the box). If the motor and protector are OK, check for a defective thermostat (facing page) or capacitor (p.146). Suspect a shorted capacitor if the compressor operates briefly after a long interruption, then stops.

CAUTION: Before testing a compressor, unplug the unit; make sure that 20 minutes have passed since you last ran it. Discharge the capacitor (p.146).

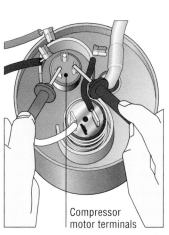

Compressor motor terminals

To test compressor motor, pry off clamp holding terminal box cover, and take off leads from motor terminals. With VOM on RX1, test all possible pairings of the three terminals for continuity. Look for a reading of low ohms on each pair. Then test for a ground fault: With VOM on RX100, touch one probe to bare metal on compressor or its refrigerant line; touch second probe to each terminal in turn. Reading should not waver from infinity. If motor fails any test, have compressor replaced.

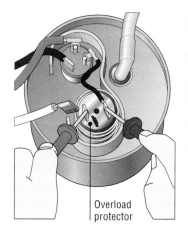

Overload protector

Check overload protector, and replace it if it has a cracked housing or burned terminals. To test it, detach the lead and set VOM on RX1. Check for continuity by probing both terminals. Look for a zero reading; replace if reading is high or infinity. If the overload protector is internal, you won't be able to inspect or test it. Suspect a faulty internal protector if a test of the motor terminals (left) results in an infinity or high ohms reading.

Switch and thermostat

The selector switch controls the compressor and fan speeds. It's also linked to the thermostat, which monitors room temperature with its sensor bulb on the evaporator coils. Before testing a troublesome rotary or push-button selector switch, try spraying it with electrical contact cleaner; the spray alone may clear up the problem. Electronic touch-pad controls are difficult to test and, if faulty, usually require replacement. Unplug the unit before opening the control panel.

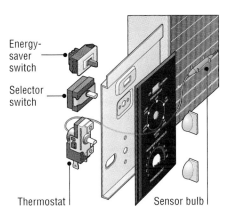

Energy-saver switch

Selector switch

Thermostat

Sensor bulb

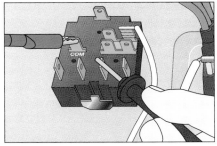

Test a rotary selector switch with VOM on RX1. Clip a probe to COM terminal. Setting knob in one position at a time, probe other terminals in turn as shown in *Testing a selector switch* (p.234).

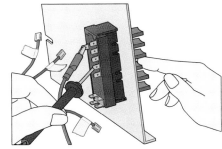

Test a push-button switch with VOM on RX1. Clip one probe to COM terminal. Pressing one button at a time, probe each of the other terminals as shown in *Testing a selector switch* (p.234).

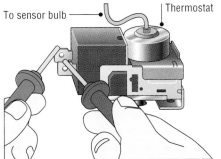

To sensor bulb

Thermostat

Test thermostat at room temperature with control switch on coldest setting. Remove leads and set VOM on RX1. Probe terminals. Look for reading of zero; replace if reading is infinity or high ohms.

When replacing faulty thermostat, thread tube along the same path as the original. Mount bulb in same position, using original clips or plastic tube or new mounts supplied with replacement.

USE AND CARE

Clean filter at least once a month during cooling season. Wash foam and metal mesh filters in soapy water. Rinse, let dry; reinstall. Replace disposable filters with same type.

Fin comb

Vacuum evaporator fins when changing filter. To clean clogged evaporator or condenser fins, spray with coil cleaner; flush with water. Straighten bent fins with fin comb.

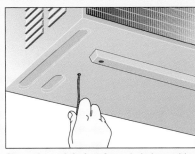

Clear clogged drain tube or hole in partition with wire. To kill organisms that cause sludge, pour in (or drip in with old medicine dropper) 1 tsp. of household ammonia.

Lubricate fan motor every 6 mo. if motor has oil ports—they're usually plugged with screws or caps (p.137). Put no more than 5 drops of SAE 20 nondetergent motor oil in a port.

Here are some more tips on keeping your air conditioner running efficiently and safely:

Keep potential obstructions like curtains, furniture, and houseplants 2 feet away from the unit. Frosted coils also block airflow; don't run a unit when it's below 60°F outside.

On very hot days, turn on the unit early in the morning for maximum efficiency, and let it run continuously. Water dripping from the drain pan of an air conditioner during periods of high humidity is normal.

Cover air conditioner before winter unless you can remove and store it. It's also a good time to clean and straighten condenser fins and repair rust on cabinet and drain pan.

After turning off an air conditioner, wait 5 minutes before restarting it, to lessen strain on the compressor. Turn off a unit immediately if the fan motor doesn't run.

Large appliances ▪ Central air conditioners

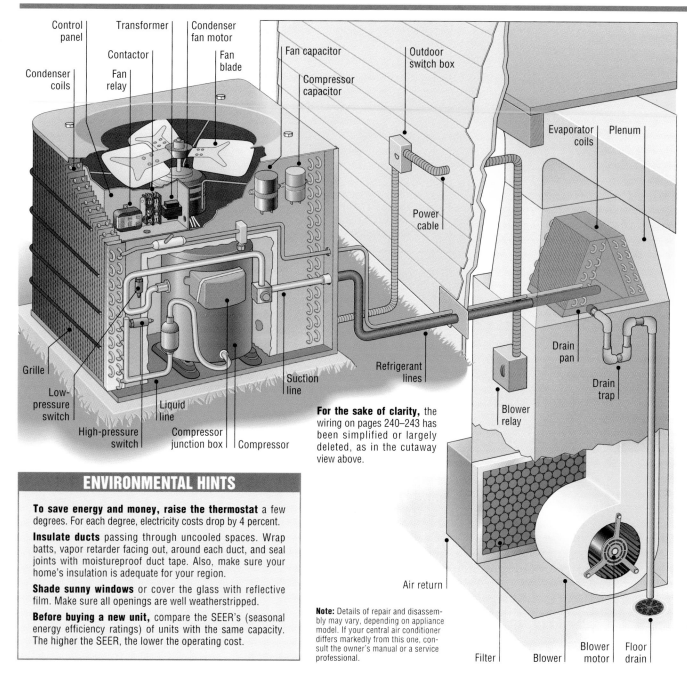

Control panel
Transformer
Condenser fan motor
Contactor
Fan blade
Fan capacitor
Outdoor switch box
Condenser coils
Fan relay
Compressor capacitor
Evaporator coils
Plenum
Power cable
Grille
Suction line
Refrigerant lines
Drain pan
Low-pressure switch
Drain trap
Liquid line
Blower relay
High-pressure switch
Compressor junction box
Compressor
Air return
Filter
Blower
Blower motor
Floor drain

For the sake of clarity, the wiring on pages 240–243 has been simplified or largely deleted, as in the cutaway view above.

Note: Details of repair and disassembly may vary, depending on appliance model. If your central air conditioner differs markedly from this one, consult the owner's manual or a service professional.

ENVIRONMENTAL HINTS

To save energy and money, raise the thermostat a few degrees. For each degree, electricity costs drop by 4 percent.

Insulate ducts passing through uncooled spaces. Wrap batts, vapor retarder facing out, around each duct, and seal joints with moistureproof duct tape. Also, make sure your home's insulation is adequate for your region.

Shade sunny windows or cover the glass with reflective film. Make sure all openings are well weatherstripped.

Before buying a new unit, compare the SEER's (seasonal energy efficiency ratings) of units with the same capacity. The higher the SEER, the lower the operating cost.

A typical central air conditioner works like a room unit (p.236), except that the condenser coils, condenser fan, and compressor are outdoors while the evaporator coils and blower are indoors. Insulated tubing carries the refrigerant between the two parts.

Indoors, cool air circulates through ducts, most often the ducts of a forced-air heating system. The evaporator coils are usually inside the main supply duct, or plenum, directly above the furnace's blower, which circulates the air. This arrangement is called a split or remote system (as opposed to a "package" unit, which is basically an extra-large room unit connected to ducts).

The compressor and condenser fan generally operate on a 240-volt circuit and the blower on a separate 120- or 240-volt circuit with the furnace. A thermostat (p.249) controls the system.

A central air conditioner's cooling capacity is rated in Btu's per hour. As a rule, you need 12,000 Btu's for 1,000 square feet of well-insulated space or 400 square feet of poorly insulated space. But structure, climate, and other factors also affect a house's cooling needs. Have the best system size determined by a contractor using a standard such as the Heating, Refrigerating and Air-Conditioning Institute of Canada's *Heat Loss/Heat Gain Manual*.

For even cooling, balance the ducts (p.246) for cooling as well as heating. Seasonal needs vary. A kitchen, for example, may need little heat in winter but extra cooling in summer. Make sure the ducts can carry as much air as the system supplies. Inadequate return ducts are a major cause of poor cooling.

Balancing a forced-air system 246
Testing a blower relay 246
Thermostats 249

Troubleshooting

SYMPTOM	POSSIBLE CAUSE	SOLUTION
Won't start	Power off at service panel or at switch	See *General troubleshooting*, p.144; check outdoor switch. ◇
	Tripped high- or low-pressure safety switch	Press reset button (p.243); wait 5 min. before restarting unit. ◇
	Faulty high- or low-pressure safety switch	Test and have replaced (p.242). ◆ ▨
	Faulty transformer	Test and replace (p.247). ◆ ▨
	Faulty compressor	Test and have serviced (p.242). ◆ ▨
	Faulty capacitor	Test and replace (pp.146, 148). ◆ ▨
	Faulty contactor	Test and replace (p.243). ◆ ▨
	Faulty thermostat	Test; repair or replace (p.249). ◆ ▨
Starts but stops	Faulty condenser fan motor	Test; repair or replace (p.242). ◆ ▨
Cools poorly	Dirty filter or blower	Clean or replace filter (p.243). ◇ Vacuum blower (p.245). ◇
	Clogged or frosted evaporator coils	Have dirty coils serviced. See *Frosted evaporator coils*, below.
	Clogged condenser coils	Clean (p.243). ◆
	Loose or broken blower fan belt	Tighten or replace (p.245). ◆
	Faulty blower motor or relay	Repair or replace motor (p.146); test and replace relay (p.246). ◆ ▨
	Insufficient return-air flow	Open or unblock return registers. ◇ Or have return system enlarged.
	Compressor runs: faulty condenser fan motor	Test; repair or replace (p.242). ◆ ▨
	Condenser fan runs: faulty compressor	Test and have serviced (p.242). ◆ ▨
	Low refrigerant level	Check for oily spots on or below refrigerant lines and have serviced. ◇
Compressor runs nonstop	Faulty thermostat	Test; repair or replace (p.249). ◆ ▨
	Dirty filter	Clean or replace (p.243). ◇
	Clogged evaporator coils	Have serviced. See also *Frosted evaporator coils*, below.
	Clogged condenser coils	Clean (p.243). ◆
	Low refrigerant level	Check for oily spots on or below refrigerant lines and have serviced. ◇
	Faulty contactor	Test and replace (p.243). ◆ ▨
Cycles on and off often	Faulty thermostat	Test; repair or replace (p.249). ◆ ▨
	Clogged condenser coils	Clean (p.243). ◆
	Faulty condenser fan motor	Test; repair or replace (p.242). ◆ ▨
Frosted evaporator coils	Dirty filter	Clean or replace (p.243). ◇
	Clogged evaporator coils	Have serviced.
	Loose or broken blower fan belt	Tighten or replace (p.245). ◆
	Faulty blower motor or relay	Test and repair (p.246). ◆ ▨ Run blower alone to melt frost. ◇
	Low refrigerant level	Check for oily spots on or below refrigerant lines and have serviced. ◇
	Insufficient return-air flow	Open or unblock return registers. ◇ Or have return system enlarged.
Wet furnace	Clogged evaporator drainpipe	Clear (p.243). ◆
Noisy outdoor unit	Fan hitting obstruction	Remove obstruction. ◇
	Loose fan blades	Tighten (p.242). ◆
	Loose screws in housing	Tighten. ◇
	Unoiled fan motor	Oil motor bearings (p.243). ◆
	Faulty fan motor	Test; repair or replace (p.242). ◆ ▨

Degree of difficulty: Simple ◇   Average ◆   Complex ◆   Volt-ohm meter required: ▨

Gaining access

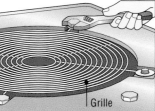

To remove fan grille on outdoor unit, loosen and take out cap nuts securing the grille to the top panel. Then lift off the grille. **CAUTION:** Turn off the power to the outdoor unit and the indoor blower before opening the unit.

Grille

To remove coil guard wrapped around many models, unscrew bolts or screws around base. Lift off guard, being careful not to strike fan or delicate condenser fins.

Other housings are removed by loosening screws in top and removing screws on sides. Be careful not to remove the wrong screws. Wearing heavy gloves, lift up top slightly while freeing base.

To reach controls, loosen screws holding access panel in place. Inside are the capacitor, contactor, and high- and low-pressure safety switches. On some units controls are in a small box with a removable cover.

To open compressor junction box, pry away clip with screwdriver; lift off cover. Inside are compressor motor terminals. Some models, like the one shown here, also contain an overload protector.

Compressor

Large appliances ▪ Central air conditioners

Condenser fan and fan motor

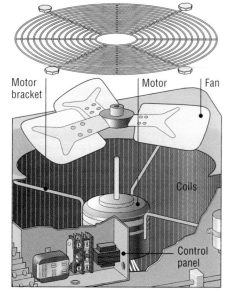

Motor bracket | Motor | Fan

Coils

Control panel

The condenser fan dispels heat from the compressor and condenser coils. If it slows down or stops working, the system will cool poorly and the compressor may overheat and shut down. A fan needs attention if a clicking or grating noise indicates that the blades are striking an obstruction or some part. If a blade becomes bent, replace the entire blade unit. A straightened blade may become unbalanced and can loosen the fan motor or hit the condenser coil.

Fan motors, usually split-phase, run on the 240-volt circuit that powers the compressor. To service a faulty motor, see *General troubleshooting*, p.146.
CAUTION: Before testing, discharge the fan and compressor capacitors (p.146).

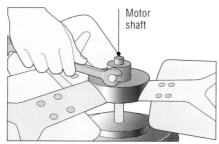

Motor shaft

Tighten loose fan blades, using a wrench for bolts or a hex key for setscrews. Make sure fan rotates freely and doesn't wobble. If fan loosens often, apply a drop of thread-locking compound.

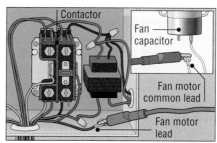

Contactor

Fan capacitor

Fan motor common lead

Fan motor lead

Test fan motor with VOM on RX1. Free and label motor leads at control panel contactor and capacitor. Probe common lead and other motor lead(s) in turn. Look for reading of low ohms on all.

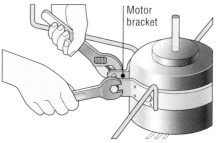

Motor bracket

To replace motor, record positions of motor lead connections; unfasten leads and any clips holding them. Remove fan; loosen motor bracket with wrenches. Lift motor free, pulling leads behind it.

Compressor and refrigerant lines

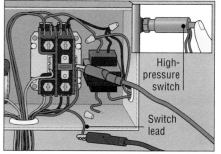

Low-pressure switch

Compressor

High-pressure switch | Compressor junction box

A central air-conditioning compressor is a larger version of the one in a room unit (p.238). Some have a heater that runs constantly or on cold days to keep the compressor oil flowing freely. The heater also keeps the refrigerant from mixing with the oil in the compressor when the unit is off for a long time.

In addition to the compressor motor terminals, the compressor junction box may also contain an overload protector; to test it, see page 238. If you find a refrigerant leak, have the compressor professionally recharged. If your system has a high- or low-pressure safety switch and it tests faulty, have a pro replace it.
CAUTION: Before testing, discharge the compressor and fan capacitors (p.146).

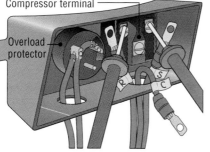

Compressor terminal

Overload protector

To test compressor motor for continuity, label and disconnect its leads. Set VOM on RX1; touch probes to all possible pairs of compressor motor terminals. All readings should be low ohms.

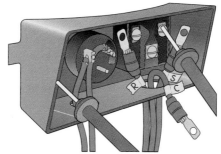

Test motor for ground fault with leads disconnected. Set VOM on RX100. Touch one probe to bare metal on compressor, the other to each terminal in turn. Look for a reading of infinity on all.

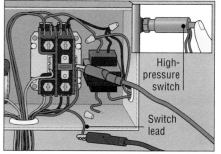

High-pressure switch

Switch lead

To test high- or low-pressure switch, let compressor cool. Push switch reset button; disconnect one switch lead. With VOM on RX1, probe both switch leads. Look for zero ohms reading.

Testing the contactor

The contactor starts the compressor and the condenser fan. Before testing it, turn off the power to both the indoor and outdoor units, and discharge the capacitor (p.146). Then open the control panel (p.241), and label the wires by tracing them to their sources (this may require removing the fan grille and coil guard). Check for loose or corroded connections first. Clean any corrosion from the terminals with an automotive-point file. Clean the switch contacts with electrical contact cleaner.

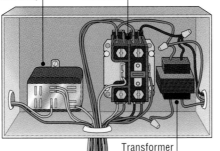

Fan relay   Contactor

Transformer

Control panel on an outdoor unit typically contains the contactor, fan relay, and transformer.

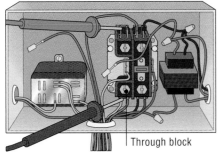

Through block

1 Test contactor through terminals. Set VOM on RX1. Remove leads from one terminal and touch probes to both terminals. Look for a reading of zero ohms, indicating continuity.

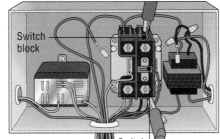

Switch block

Switch

2 Test contactor switch terminals with switch contacts open. Remove leads from one terminal. With VOM on RX1, clip probes to both terminals. Look for a reading of infinity.

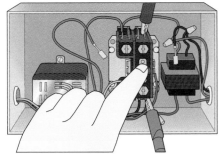

3 Leaving the VOM clipped to the contactor switch terminals, test them again while pressing button to close switch contacts. Look for a steady reading of zero ohms.

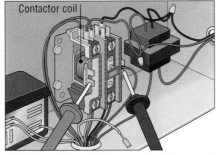

Contactor coil

4 Test contactor coil. Remove a lead from a coil terminal. Set VOM on RX100 and probe both coil terminals. Look for a low reading approaching zero. If contactor fails any test, replace it.

Evaporator drainage

Warm indoor air contacting the evaporator coil condenses, causing moisture to collect and drip. In most units, a plastic pipe carries the water outdoors or to a floor drain. Algae and bacteria growth can clog the pipe. When this happens, backed-up water can puddle, causing rust or shorting the blower.

To check the evaporator drain, look for water dripping from the lower end when the air conditioner is running. Also inspect beneath the coil, if possible, to detect puddling.

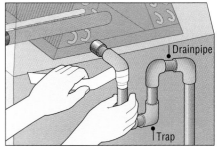

Drainpipe

Trap

To clear evaporator drain, remove plastic tape holding trap to elbow. (If necessary, saw through pipe at elbow.) Flush trap with hose; pour in 1 tbsp. chlorine bleach. Reattach with new tape.

USE AND CARE

Clean or replace air filter every month during cooling season. Don't run the unit with the filter removed. Let a filter you've washed dry completely before reinstalling it.

Before restarting unit in the spring or after a long shutdown, restore power to the air conditioner for 24 hours first. This produces the heat needed to separate the oil from the refrigerant in the compressor.

Before restarting after a brief interruption, turn the thermostat off for at least 5 minutes.

To avoid damaging the compressor, don't operate the unit when it's below 60° F outside.

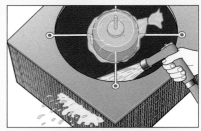

Clean condenser coils before cooling season. Shut off power; uncover coils and gently brush dirty side. Then hose from inside unit, using plastic bags to protect other parts.

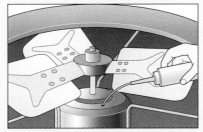

Lubricate fan motor yearly if it has oil ports (they're usually plugged with rubber or metal caps). Use nondetergent lightweight SAE 20 oil; add no more than 10 drops per port.

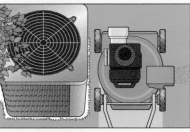

Prune vegetation away from outdoor unit by 2 ft. on each side and above. Spray grass clippings away from unit when mowing lawn. During fall, keep fan grille free of leaves.

Large appliances ▪ Central heating systems

Central heating systems in most modern homes have a forced-air distribution system like the one shown at right. Typically, a gas or oil furnace heats air, and the blower propels it into supply ducts that carry it throughout the house. Return ducts carry the air back to the heat source. To heat a house evenly, a forced-air system may need to be balanced (p.246) by adjusting the dampers inside the supply ducts that control air distribution. A dirty filter, poorly adjusted dampers, and obstructed registers are the usual causes of inefficient heating by a forced-air system.

Most other central heating systems use pipes to carry hot water or steam to convectors or radiators throughout the house. Easily solved problems, such as trapped air or insufficient boiler water (p.248), are the most common causes of complaints.

Adjusting and fixing a gas furnace is relatively easy (p.246). Except for changing oil and air filters and restarting the unit in an emergency (p.248), oil furnace repairs are best left to a professional.

One or more thermostats control a central heating system. You can clean and adjust a troublesome mechanical thermostat; replace an electronic model that tests faulty (p.249).

For safety, keep the area around a furnace clear of combustible materials. Cut off both fuel and electricity to a furnace whenever you shut it down for repairs. Don't try to remove the asbestos coating found on some older ducts or pipes; that's a job for an asbestos-abatement contractor (listed in the Yellow Pages).

ENVIRONMENTAL HINTS

Turning down the thermostat 10°F (5.5°C) at night and when you leave the house for longer than 6 hours can cut 15 percent or more off your fuel bill. The catch is remembering to do it. To make these adjustments routine, install a programmable thermostat. On a digital model, you can punch in a week's schedule. For example, you can lower the daytime heat on workdays but not weekends and have the nighttime setback occur later on nights that you stay up late. The program can be overridden manually on nontypical days. Such a thermostat may pay for itself in a season.

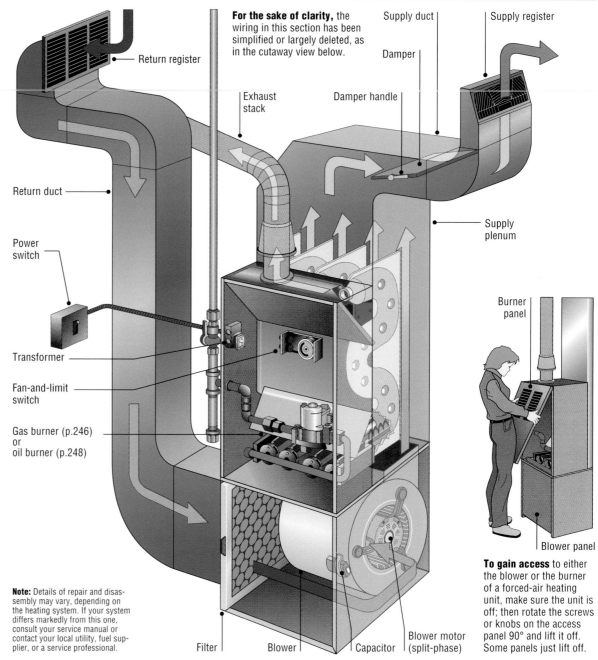

For the sake of clarity, the wiring in this section has been simplified or largely deleted, as in the cutaway view below.

Return register

Return duct

Power switch

Transformer

Fan-and-limit switch

Gas burner (p.246) or oil burner (p.248)

Exhaust stack

Supply duct

Damper

Damper handle

Supply register

Supply plenum

Burner panel

Filter

Blower

Capacitor

Blower motor (split-phase)

Blower panel

To gain access to either the blower or the burner of a forced-air heating unit, make sure the unit is off; then rotate the screws or knobs on the access panel 90° and lift it off. Some panels just lift off.

Note: Details of repair and disassembly may vary, depending on the heating system. If your system differs markedly from this one, consult your service manual or contact your local utility, fuel supplier, or a service professional.

Troubleshooting

SYMPTOM	POSSIBLE CAUSE	SOLUTION
ANY SYSTEM: **Won't run**	Power off at service panel or at switch	See *General troubleshooting*, p.144; check switches (p.248). ◇
	Thermostat too low	Set to above room temperature. ◇
	Faulty thermostat	Test and adjust or replace (p.249). ◇ ▣
	Pilot out or faulty thermocouple *(gas burner)*	Relight pilot or test and replace thermocouple (p.247). ◇
	Faulty electric ignition *(gas burner)*	Have serviced.
	Tripped reset *(oil burner)*	Reset once (p.248). ◇
	No fuel *(oil burner)*	Measure fuel (p.248); call supplier if needed. ◇
	Clogged filter *(oil burner)*	Replace cartridge (see owner's manual). ◇
	Clogged nozzle *(oil burner)*	Have serviced.
FORCED-AIR UNIT: **Poor or no heat;** **furnace on**	Blocked supply or return registers	Clear obstructions. Open supply registers fully. ◇
	Closed or poorly adjusted dampers	Open or adjust dampers (p.246). ◇
	Dirty filter or blower	Clean or replace (right). ◇
	Loose or broken blower belt	Tighten or replace (right). ◆
	Faulty fan-and-limit switch	Test and replace (p.246). ◆ ▣
	Faulty blower relay	Test and replace (p.246). ◆ ▣
	Faulty blower motor (split-phase)	See *General troubleshooting*, p.146. ◆ ▣ Or have serviced.
Blower squeals **or rumbles**	Loose blower belt	Tighten (right). ◆
	Motor or blower needs oil	Oil motor (right). ◇ Or oil blower (see owner's manual). ◇
	Foreign object in blower	Remove object. ◇
	Bad blower or motor bearings	Have serviced.
HOT-WATER UNIT: **No heat;** **furnace on**	Faulty circulator motor (split-phase)	See *General troubleshooting*, p.146. ◆ ▣ Or have serviced.
	Faulty pump	Have serviced.
	Faulty aquastat	Have serviced.
Poor or uneven **heating**	Air trapped in radiators or convectors	Bleed (p.248). ◇
	Waterlogged expansion tank	Drain (p.248). ◇ Or recharge (p.248). ◆
	Faulty pump	Have serviced.
	Faulty pressure gauge or reducing valve	Have serviced.
Runs nonstop	Faulty aquastat	Have serviced.
Gurgling noise	Air trapped in radiator or convector	Bleed (p.248). ◇
STEAM UNIT: **Furnace won't run**	Low water in boiler	Refill boiler (p.248). ◇
No heat; furnace on	Air trapped in radiators	Bleed (p.248). ◇
Banging pipes	Return water blocking steam	Slope radiator (p.248). ◆
Hissing radiator	Clogged air vent	Replace vent (p.248). ◆

Degree of difficulty: Simple ◇   Average ◆   Complex ◆   Volt-ohm meter required: ▣

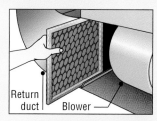

Clean or change filter monthly during heating season or as directed by owner's manual. Don't remove filter while unit is operating. For more on cleaning filters, see page 151.

Return duct   Blower

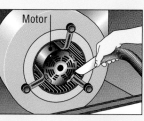

Vacuum blower every year or more often if dusty. Clean blower blades with brush. Lubricate motor and bearings with 3 to 5 drops SAE 20 oil if oil ports are present. Avoid overfilling.

Motor

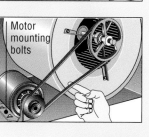

Check blower belt alignment yearly or if blower is noisy. Make sure belt is perpendicular to motor shaft and that motor and blower pulleys line up. Loosen setscrew to move motor pulley.

Motor pulley

Check blower belt tension yearly. Belt should deflect ½ to ¾ in. To tighten belt, loosen motor mounting bolts and move motor back. Replace frayed, cracked, or shiny worn belt.

Motor mounting bolts

Check for loose ducts yearly. Refasten flanges with sheet-metal screws; seal joints with duct tape. Wrap supply ducts in unconditioned spaces with foil-faced batts rated R-11, foil out.

Testing a fan-and-limit switch

Forced-air systems usually have a combined fan-and-limit switch mounted on the supply plenum or on the furnace near the plenum. The switch reacts to the furnace temperature, turning the blower on and off and shutting down the furnace before it overheats. If a fur-

nace blower short-cycles—turns on and off often—adjust the switch's fan control to widen the spread between the blower's start and stop temperatures. But don't set temperatures too low. Below 90°F (32°C) or so, the blower may turn on on a hot summer day.

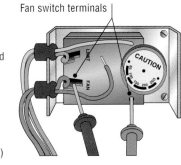

Limit switch terminals

1 Turn off power to furnace and remove cover. Test limit switch with VOM on RX1. Release a switch lead and probe switch terminals. Look for zero reading when setting is low. Move cam to above 200°F (93°C); look for infinity reading. (Some limit switches share one terminal with fan switch.)

Fan switch terminals

2 To test fan switch, release a fan lead. With VOM on RX1, probe fan terminals. Look for infinity reading when temperature setting is low. Gently move cam higher and look for zero reading. Replace entire switch unit if either fan or limit switch tests faulty.

Balancing a forced-air system

A forced-air system is balanced when each room is as warm or cool as you want it to be. Balancing involves partly closing some ducts' dampers while leaving others open; the results are gauged with thermometers. A trial-and-error process, balancing may take a day or so. When you finish, mark each damper handle's position. If the system also cools, balance it separately for the cooling season.

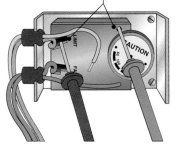

1 Distribute thermometers throughout the house, putting one in the center of each room at table level. Use identical thermometers or ones that all read the same when side by side.

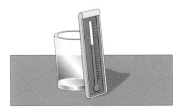

2 Open all registers and dampers. Set thermostat at 68°F (20°C); start furnace. After 30 min., partly close dampers for warmest rooms. Readjust dampers until each room is at desired temperature.

Handle, Open damper, Closed damper

Common variant: Blower relay

Forced-air systems that both heat and cool may have a multispeed blower governed by a relay. When the furnace is on, current from the fan-and-limit switch to the relay energizes the blower's low-speed windings. When the system is cooling, current from the thermostat to the relay energizes the high-speed windings. If the thermostat circuit tests faulty, check for a faulty transformer, wiring, or thermostat (p.249).

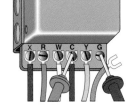

To test thermostat circuit, turn off power to system. Set VOM on ACV scale, 50-volt range; clip probes to relay terminal (G) and common terminal (C). *Without touching probes,* restore power and set thermostat for cooling. Blower should go on; VOM should read about 24 volts.

Test relay coil for continuity with power to heating system off and wire to either G or C terminal disconnected. Set VOM on RX1 and touch probes to G and C terminals. Look for a low ohms reading. If reading is infinity, replace relay.

Gas furnaces

Whether it uses natural gas or liquefied petroleum (LP), a gas furnace works in a simple, straightforward manner. Gas enters by way of a thermostatically controlled valve and goes to burners, which are ignited by a constantly burning pilot flame or by an electric spark that lights a pilot or the burners directly. For safety, a device called a thermocouple senses heat from the ignition system and allows gas to flow only when enough heat is present for combustion.

Gas furnace troubles usually stem from ignition problems and clogged burners. Clean the burners on an older furnace yearly. Burners on newer units require cleaning only every few years. Have the furnace inspected once a year by a gas service technician.

CAUTION: If you smell gas, turn off the gas at the main shutoff valve. Extinguish any open flame; do not operate electrical switches or the phone. Evacuate the house. Call the gas company from a neighbor's house.

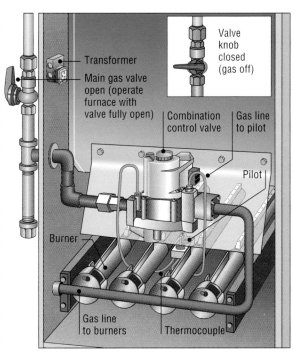

Valve knob closed (gas off)

Transformer

Main gas valve open (operate furnace with valve fully open)

Combination control valve

Gas line to pilot

Pilot

Burner

Gas line to burners

Thermocouple

Adjusting the pilot and burner flames

If a pilot won't stay relighted or keeps going out, make sure that the flame is lapping over the end of the thermocouple. If not, adjust it, and if necessary, clean the pilot opening. A defective thermocouple or dead transformer may also result in no pilot light. Too much yellow in a pilot flame may indicate an air or fuel-line obstruction; call a gas service technician. Have a malfunctioning electric igniter serviced also. To burn efficiently, burners may occasionally need their air intake adjusted, usually by moving a plate or sleeve on a shutter. Have burners with fixed shutters or without shutters serviced. The flame colors shown below are for natural gas; LP flames may differ.

CAUTION: When adjusting a pilot flame, never remove the adjusting screw. Always replace the screw's cap.

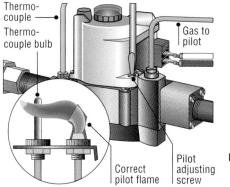

To adjust pilot flame, remove any cap covering the pilot adjusting screw on a combination control and turn screw counterclockwise to increase flame or clockwise to decrease it. Flame should envelop thermocouple bulb by ½ in. and be dark blue with slight bit of yellow at tip.

Clean pilot opening with a toothpick if flame flickers or won't stay lit (also test thermocouple, below). Some models require removing pilot gas line to access opening.

To adjust burner flame, loosen any lock screw and open air shutter until flame lifts from tube, then close shutter until it settles back and is correct color (right). Retighten screw.

Correct burner flame reflects the right proportion of gas and air. Adjust air shutter (left) until flames on burner resemble the "right" flame, above.

WRONG
Not enough air; yellow tip, lazy inner flame

WRONG
Too much air; sharp, blue, hard inner flame

RIGHT
Distinct blue-green cone in softer blue flame

Relighting a gas furnace

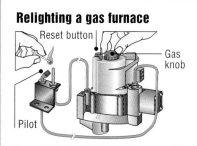

To relight the pilot on a furnace with a combination control, turn gas knob and main electric switch to *Off;* lower thermostat. Let gas dissipate; then turn gas knob to *Pilot.* Depress and hold in reset button (or gas knob) and light pilot. Release button after 1 minute. If pilot goes out, repeat, holding in longer, before calling for service. If pilot stays lit, turn gas knob to *On.* Turn on current and raise thermostat.

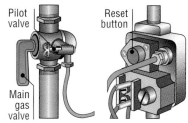

On older furnace, lower thermostat and close main and pilot gas supply valves. Wait 5 minutes for gas to dissipate; then open pilot gas valve only. Depress and hold in thermocouple reset switch and light pilot. Release switch after 1 minute. If pilot goes out, repeat, holding knob in longer, before calling for service. If pilot stays lit, open main gas supply valve and raise thermostat.

Cleaning the burner tubes

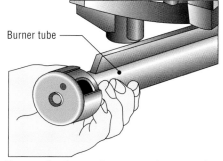

Burner tubes in most furnaces can be removed for cleaning. Shut off gas and power. Unscrew tubes from supporting bracket (some tubes are not screwed on); then gently twist and lift tubes free. Brush or vacuum tubes to clean them; avoid damaging burner ports. Carefully clear any clogged ports with a stiff wire.

Testing the thermocouple

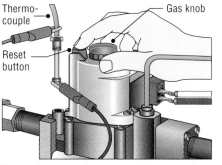

To test thermocouple, unscrew it from control valve. With VOM on DCV scale, lowest setting, clip one probe to thermocouple's unscrewed tip below insulation and clip other probe to its housing. Press and hold in reset button (or gas control knob on some models) and light pilot. Any reading above zero means thermocouple is OK.

Testing the transformer

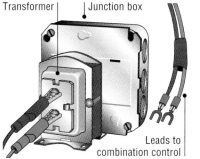

To test transformer, turn off power to furnace. Remove leads going to combination control. Set VOM on ACV scale, 50-volt range. Clip probes to terminals. *Without touching probes,* restore power. Look for a reading of 24 volts. If reading is zero, turn off power, open junction box, and replace transformer (p.26).

Oil furnaces: Restarting in an emergency

If raising the thermostat doesn't start an oil furnace, check for blown fuses or tripped circuit breakers at the service panel. Then follow the steps below.

CAUTION: Never press a reset button repeatedly. Excess fuel oil pumped into the furnace could explode.

1 Make sure the emergency switch is on. There may be two switches, one on the furnace and another on a nearby wall or at the head of the stairs.

2 Check the fuel oil level in storage tank. If tank has no gauge, put a clean 8-ft.-long dipstick into the filler pipe to check for the presence of oil.

3 Look on the burner motor for a thermal overload button. If you find one, press it once.

Overload button

Reset button

4 Press the reset button on the primary control once. If furnace doesn't start, turn off power and call for service.

Steam heaters

Most steam systems are one-pipe systems. Steam enters a radiator, condenses to water as it cools, and returns to the boiler through the same pipe. If a radiator develops a noisy knock, it's usually the result of a water buildup that is blocking the steam; in this case, the radiator needs to be angled so that the water drains. If the noise is in the pipes, check for a sagging pipe that needs to be resecured. If you have no heat, check the boiler water level. If it's not halfway up the glass gauge (see below, right), add water. If the water level is all right, sediment may be blocking the low-water cutoff and should be removed.

CAUTION: Turn off the system, let it cool, and let the pressure drop to zero before making any repair.

Air vent

To replace drippy air vent, unscrew it and screw in one of the same size. Also replace a vent that spits or that fails to hiss as radiator heats.

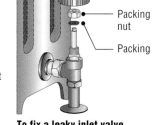

Packing nut

Packing

To fix a leaky inlet valve, tighten packing nut on valve. If leak persists, close inlet valve, remove knob and nut, and replace packing (p.110).

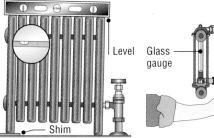

Level   Glass gauge

Shim

To stop knocking, tilt radiator toward the inlet valve so that water won't block incoming steam. Always open inlet valve fully when turning radiator on.

To remove sediment, open boiler's low-water cutoff valve and let water run until clear. Then refill boiler until glass gauge is half to two-thirds full.

Hot-water systems

Convectors and radiators heat poorly when air is trapped inside them. Bleed them yearly or when the heat is poor or uneven. An expansion tank above the boiler provides an air cushion that lets the hot water expand safely, but it can fill with water. If water drips from the boiler's safety relief valve and the expansion tank feels hot all over, the tank is probably waterlogged. Drain an older expansion tank. If a diaphragm tank has an air valve, try recharging it. If it doesn't have an air valve or can't be recharged to the correct pressure, replace it. Because the tank is filled with water and heavy, replacement is a two-person job.

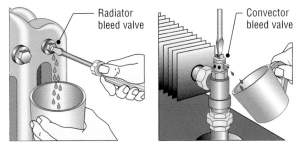

Radiator bleed valve

Convector bleed valve

Bleed radiators and convectors to purge internal air when furnace is on. Starting on top floor, *slowly and carefully* open the bleed valve on one unit at a time until hot water flows without sputtering. Capture the water in a cup or thick towel. Bleed valves usually require a screwdriver. Some radiator valves can be turned by hand.

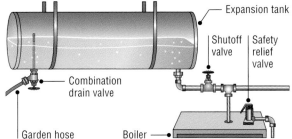

Expansion tank

Shutoff valve   Safety relief valve

Combination drain valve

Garden hose   Boiler

To drain old-style expansion tank, *turn off system and let tank cool.* Close the shutoff valve on pipe from boiler. Connect hose to the combination drain valve and open it. A combination valve lets air into tank as water drains out. After tank drains, close drain valve and reopen shutoff valve. Bleed radiators or convectors (left).

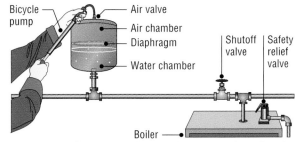

Bicycle pump

Air valve

Air chamber

Diaphragm

Water chamber

Shutoff valve   Safety relief valve

Boiler

To recharge a diaphragm tank, *turn off system and let tank cool.* Close shutoff valve on pipe from boiler. Use tire air-pressure gauge to take a reading on the air valve. If it's less than 12 psi (pounds per square inch), add air with bicycle pump. If you can't get correct pressure, unscrew tank from pipe and replace it.

Central heating systems / thermostats

A thermostat is basically a switch that turns a furnace (or central air conditioner) on or off at a preset temperature. Try cleaning and adjusting a mechanical thermostat before replacing it. An electronic thermostat has fewer moving parts to cause trouble.

Replace the backup batteries with new alkaline ones when the low-battery indicator goes on.

If an electronic thermostat tests faulty, replace it with an identical model. Replace a defective mechanical thermostat with an electronic model for greater furnace efficiency. This may require having an isolation transformer or relay (or both) installed.

Most thermostats have extra switches for selecting fan operation and for choosing heating, cooling, or *Off* settings. Such switches operate on 24-volt current.

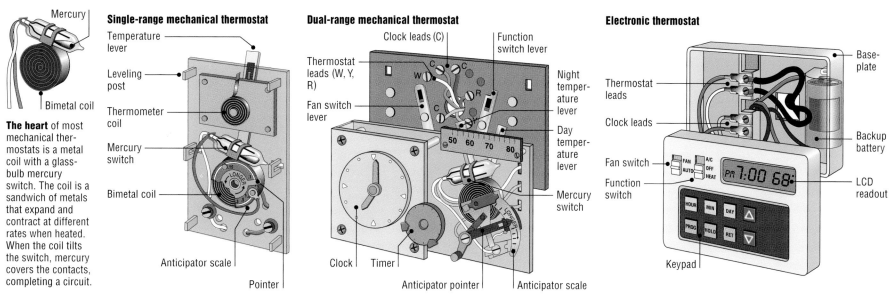

Single-range mechanical thermostat

Mercury

Bimetal coil

The heart of most mechanical thermostats is a metal coil with a glass-bulb mercury switch. The coil is a sandwich of metals that expand and contract at different rates when heated. When the coil tilts the switch, mercury covers the contacts, completing a circuit.

Temperature lever

Leveling post

Thermometer coil

Mercury switch

Bimetal coil

Anticipator scale

Pointer

Dual-range mechanical thermostat

Clock leads (C)

Function switch lever

Thermostat leads (W, Y, R)

Fan switch lever

Night temperature lever

Day temperature lever

Mercury switch

Clock   Timer

Anticipator pointer   Anticipator scale

Electronic thermostat

Thermostat leads

Clock leads

Fan switch

Function switch

Keypad

Baseplate

Backup battery

LCD readout

Cleaning and adjusting a mechanical thermostat

Take off the thermostat cover by gently pulling on it. Remove the front assembly and check that the wall plate is level; if not, loosen the mounting screws and level it. Reattach the front assembly and clean all the parts with a small soft brush. Clean the switch contacts. If necessary, adjust the thermometer reading and the anticipator, which prompts the thermostat to cut the furnace off early to allow for residual heat.

Testing a thermostat

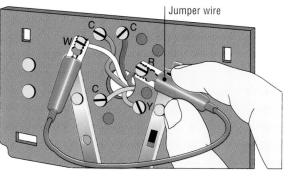

Jumper wire

To test thermostat, remove the thermostat body and clip an insulated jumper wire (p.125) to the R and W terminals on the baseplate. If the furnace goes on, the thermostat is faulty. Replace an electronic model; try cleaning and adjusting a mechanical one (left) before replacing it. If the furnace doesn't go on, the problem is with the furnace relay, the furnace itself, or the transformer.

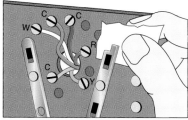

Clean contacts with coarse paper such as bond typing paper (never use sandpaper). Slip paper under each lever and clean by moving lever and sliding paper around.

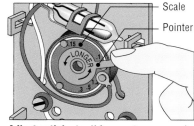

Adjust anticipator if furnace turns on and off too often or too seldom. If too often, move pointer a bit toward longer setting. If too seldom, move pointer the other way.

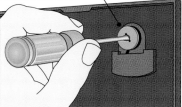

Scale

Pointer

Thermometer coil

Set thermometer reading to match an accurate room thermometer, using a small screwdriver or hex key. The thermometer is often a bimetal coil in the thermostat cover.

Large appliances ▪ Dehumidifiers

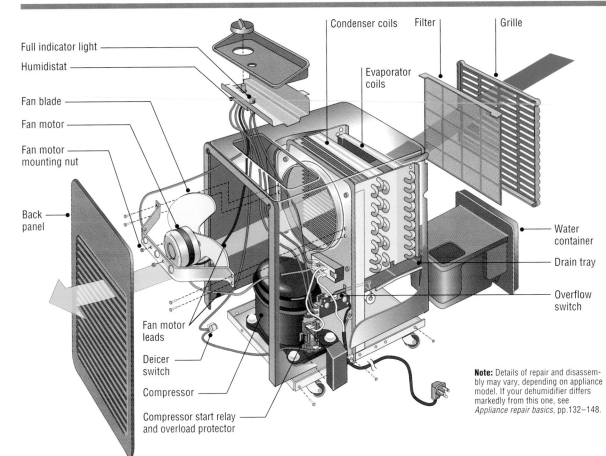

Full indicator light

Humidistat

Fan blade

Fan motor

Fan motor mounting nut

Back panel

Fan motor leads

Deicer switch

Compressor

Compressor start relay and overload protector

Condenser coils

Filter

Grille

Evaporator coils

Water container

Drain tray

Overflow switch

Note: Details of repair and disassembly may vary, depending on appliance model. If your dehumidifier differs markedly from this one, see *Appliance repair basics,* pp.132–148.

A dehumidifier is essentially a scaled-down air conditioner that doesn't cool. It has the same basic components as an air conditioner—compressor, fan, and coils—and uses a standard refrigeration cycle (p.236). An adjustable humidistat turns on the fan and compressor when the moisture in the air reaches the point set on the humidistat. The fan draws in moist room air and pushes it across cold evaporator coils. As water condenses on the coils, it's collected in a water container. Unlike an air conditioner's condenser, which expels heat outdoors, a dehumidifier's built-in condenser coils return the heat to the room.

Dehumidifier problems sometimes stem from extremes of humidity. A unit may run continuously when the air is very moist or not start at all when it's very dry. Because a dehumidifier closely resembles an air conditioner, many air-conditioner repairs (pp.236–239) can be adapted to a dehumidifier.

USE AND CARE

Vacuum the evaporator coils every 6 to 12 months, using a brush attachment. Be careful not to damage the coils' fins. Remove grime or mildew with a mild household cleanser and an old toothbrush, or use an auto degreaser that's safe for use on aluminum. Spray with water to rinse off all of the degreaser.

Empty the water container daily, or more often on humid days when water collects quickly. Don't let water stagnate in the container. Once a month, clean the container with a sponge and mild detergent and let it dry completely.

Wash or replace the air filter once a month as you would on an air conditioner.

Oil the fan motor if it requires lubrication. Check your owner's manual, or look for oil ports on the motor. Oil as recommended each season; a fan motor typically requires only 1 or 2 drops of SAE 20 oil in each port.

Gaining access

1 To access components in back of dehumidifier, unplug unit, then unscrew or unsnap back panel and remove it. Unscrew controls or switches attached to cabinet if you can reach them. If not, access them from the front.

Drain tray

2 To open front of unit, take out water container and filter; then snap out grille and remove it. Take out screws securing cabinet to base and drain tray; then remove drain tray, and lift off the cabinet.

Fan and compressor

To check these parts, unplug the unit and open the cabinet. *Without touching any wires,* plug in and turn on the unit. If the fan doesn't run, unplug the unit, disconnect the fan motor leads, and probe them with a VOM on RX1. Look for a reading between 25 and 75 ohms; if it's infinity, replace the motor. To do this, remove the fan blade (p.238), then the motor mounting nuts or screws. If the fan does run, feel the compressor for vibration. If there is none, check the deicer (far right), the start relay (right), and the overload protector (p.238), which is mounted on the start relay and is removed by pulling the relay off the compressor pins. If these parts test OK, the compressor has likely failed.

Testing the compressor start relay

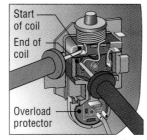

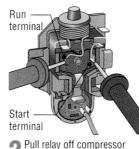

1 Remove leads and set VOM on RX1. First test coil by probing terminals at both ends of coil. Look for a reading of zero or very low ohms.

2 Pull relay off compressor pins. Probe run terminal and start terminal; look for infinity reading. Invert relay and repeat test; look for zero ohms reading.

Humidistat, overflow switch, and deicer

A humidistat senses the air's moisture and turns the dehumidifier on or off at the set point. Test it when the humidity is low. If there's a separate on-off switch, test it too (p.145). An overflow switch shuts off the unit before the water container spills. On some models, this switch is activated by a float; on others, it has a diaphragm activated by water rising in a tube, like the water-level switch on a washer (p.290). The deicer is a bimetal switch that turns off the compressor before the evaporator coils frost but lets the fan keep running. *Unplug the unit before testing a switch.*

Troubleshooting

SYMPTOM	POSSIBLE CAUSE	SOLUTION
Won't run	Power off at outlet or faulty power cord	See *General troubleshooting,* p.144.
	Faulty overflow switch or humidistat	Test and replace (right). ◆ ▪
Dehumidifies poorly	Dust-clogged evaporator coils or bent fins	Vacuum coils (facing page). ◇ Or straighten fins (p.239). ◇
	Bent, broken, or loose fan blade	Replace or tighten (p.238). ◇
	Faulty deicer switch	Test and replace (right). ◇ ▪
	Faulty fan motor or dry motor bearings	Test fan motor (above). ◆ ▪ Or oil bearings (facing page). ◇
	Faulty compressor start relay	Test and replace (above). ◆ ▪
	Faulty compressor overload protector	Test and replace (above; p.238). ◆ ▪
	Faulty compressor motor	Test for continuity (p.238). ◆ ▪ Have serviced if needed.
	Low refrigerant level (coils frost)	Have serviced.
Noisy	Loose screws on trim or exterior panels	Tighten. ◇
	Loose fan blade or motor mounts	Tighten. ◇
	Fan striking something	Remove obstruction. ◇
	Tubing rubbing together or against other part	Gently bend tubing in place. ◇
Evaporator coils frost up	Air temperature too low	Don't run unit when it's below 65° F. ◇
	Air circulation blocked or coils clogged	Move unit away from wall. ◇ Vacuum coils (facing page). ◇
	Faulty deicer switch	Test and replace (right). ◇ ▪
	Low refrigerant level	Have serviced.
Leaks water	Faulty overflow switch	Test and replace (right). ◆ ▪
Bad odor	Stagnant water in base or dirty coils	WIpe up water; wash base. ◇ Wash coils (facing page). ◇

Degree of difficulty: Simple ◇   Average ◆   Complex ◆   Volt-ohm meter required: ▪

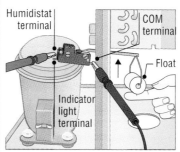

Test humidistat with VOM on RX1. Remove leads, and clip probes to terminals. Turn knob; look for reading to jump from zero to infinity (or vice versa) when you hear a click. A partial or continuous reading indicates a fault (unless humidity is very low or high).

Test overflow switch with VOM on RX1. Take off leads; clip probes to COM and humidistat terminals. Look for zero ohms. Lift float (or lower tube into water on diaphragm type); look for infinity. Repeat test with COM and indicator light terminals; look for opposite results.

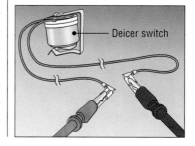

To test deicer, disconnect its leads and dismount it. With VOM on RX1, clip probes to leads. Look for a reading of zero. Then put deicer in a freezer for 10 min., and test it again. Look for reading of infinity. If deicer fails either test, replace it.

Large appliances ▪ Dishwashers

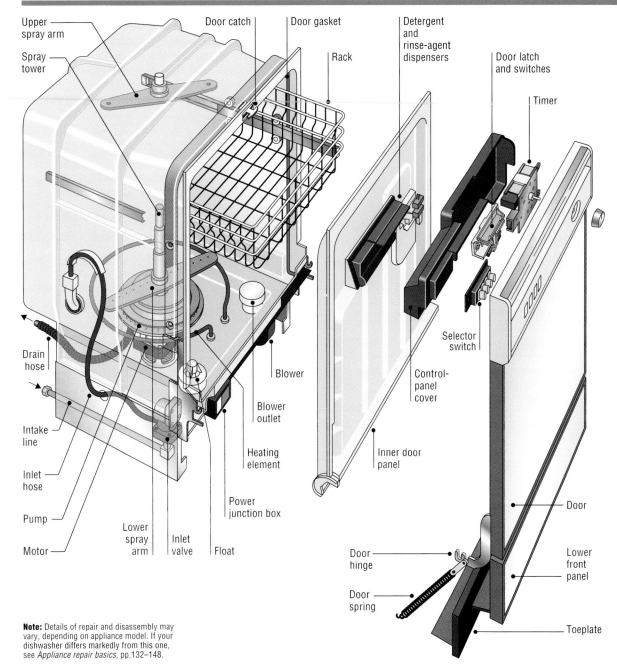

Upper spray arm
Spray tower
Door catch
Door gasket
Rack
Detergent and rinse-agent dispensers
Door latch and switches
Timer
Selector switch
Control-panel cover
Inner door panel
Blower
Blower outlet
Heating element
Power junction box
Drain hose
Intake line
Inlet hose
Pump
Motor
Lower spray arm
Inlet valve
Float
Door hinge
Door spring
Door
Lower front panel
Toeplate

Note: Details of repair and disassembly may vary, depending on appliance model. If your dishwasher differs markedly from this one, see *Appliance repair basics*, pp.132–148.

When you turn on a dishwasher, about 7.5 litres of hot water enters the tub, mixes with detergent delivered by the dispenser, and is pumped through the rotating spray assembly onto the dishes. The tub then empties and refills with fresh water that is sprayed to rinse the dishes. Most machines repeat this wash-and-rinse cycle at least once. A heating element keeps the water at 140° to 160°F (60° to 71°C), the temperature needed to dissolve grease. After the tub finally empties, the heating element, or an energy-saving combination of an element and a blower, dries the dishes. A timer controls the process.

Most dishwasher problems stem from improper loading, stale detergent, minor blockages, and low water temperature or pressure. To test your home's water temperature, run very hot water into a glass in the kitchen sink, and insert a meat thermometer. If it reads below 140°F (60°C), insulate the pipes between the water heater and the dishwasher. If needed, raise the water heater setting, but *not* if there are children or others in the house who might scald themselves.

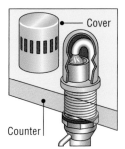

Cover

Counter

Air gap on drain line, required by some codes, keeps dirty water from reentering dishwasher. Clear an air gap regularly to prevent overflows.

FOR YOUR SAFETY

Shut off power to a dishwasher at the service panel before disassembling or working on it. If a unit leaks or sparks, don't touch it until you're sure the power is off. Let the unit cool before touching internal parts, especially the heating element.

Shut off the water supply to a dishwasher before disassembling or making repairs. Keep electrical parts dry; water on them can create shock and fire hazards and cause parts to short-circuit when you turn on power to the unit.

Place sharp utensils like knives so that the points face down. Keep them away from the door seal; one might puncture it and cause the door to leak.

Troubleshooting

SYMPTOM	POSSIBLE CAUSE	SOLUTION
Won't start	Power off at service panel	See *General troubleshooting*, p.144.
	Door not latching or faulty door switch	Adjust latch (p.254). ◇ Replace switch (p.254). ◈ ▣
	Faulty timer	Test and replace (p.255). ◆ ▣
	Faulty motor	Test; repair or replace (p.257). ◆ ▣
Hums but won't run	Clogged inlet valve	Disassemble and clean (p.255). ◈
	Clogged pump	Disassemble and clean (p.257). ◈
	Pump seals binding	Disassemble pump and replace seals (p.257). ◆
	Faulty motor start relay	Test; repair or replace (p.257). ◆ ▣
	Faulty motor	Test; repair or replace (p.257). ◆ ▣
Doesn't fill	Float switch faulty or stuck open	Check and repair (p.256). ◇ ▣
	Faulty or clogged inlet valve	Test and repair (p.255). ◈ ▣ Or clean (p.255). ◈
Drains during fill	Faulty drain valve *(some models)*	Test; repair or replace (p.256). ◈
Overfills	Inlet valve not closing	Disassemble and clean (p.255). ◈
	Faulty timer	Test and replace (p.255). ◆ ▣
Drains poorly or not at all	Clogged strainer	Clean (p.254). ◇
	Clogged or kinked drain hose	Remove and clean; or replace (p.234). ◇
	Clogged pump	Disassemble and clean (p.257). ◈
	Faulty motor	Test; repair or replace (p.257). ◆ ▣
	Faulty drain valve *(some models)*	Test; repair or replace (p.256). ◈
Leaks around door	Loose or misaligned door catch	Adjust (p.254). ◇
	Dirty, cracked, or hardened door gasket	Replace (p.254). ◈
Leaks underneath	Loose or cracked hose	Replace hose clamp or hose (p.234). ◇
	Loose heating element gaskets	Tighten or replace (p.256). ◇
	Rust-perforated tub	Repair, using epoxy patch kit as directed. ◈
	Deteriorated pump seals	Replace (p.257). ◆
Noisy	Improperly loaded dishes	Load correctly (p.255). ◇
	Foreign object in pump	Disassemble pump and remove (p.257). ◆
Dirty or spotted dishes	Improperly loaded dishes; stale detergent	Load correctly; use fresh detergent (p.255). ◇
	Water not hot enough	Check household water temperature (facing page). ◇
	Faulty detergent or rinse-agent dispenser	Test; repair or replace (p.254). ◈ ▣
	High mineral content in water	Have water softener installed on house water supply.
	Faulty heating element	Test and replace (p.256). ◈ ▣
	Faulty selector switch	Test and replace (p.255). ◈ ▣
	Faulty timer	Test and replace (p.255). ◆ ▣
	Dirty or faulty pump	Disassemble; clean or repair (p.257). ◆

Degree of difficulty: Simple ◇   Average ◈   Complex ◆   Volt-ohm meter required: ▣

Gaining access

To remove dish racks, unsnap and take off caps on front end of tracks. Other racks are held by pins that you pull out, and some racks simply slide out.

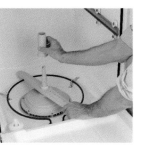

To remove spray arm, unscrew spray tower clockwise (it may be tight). Then lift off spray arm; on some models, remove plastic cap or nut to free it first.

To open inner door panel, take out screws on door's inside rim; lift up panel. On some models, outer panel opens after you remove inside screws or trim.

To access controls, open door panel (left); snap off control-panel cover. On other units, outer panel opens once knobs and inside screws are removed.

To remove lower front panel and toeplate, take out retaining screws. Some models have a single panel that you pull out and lift off hooks.

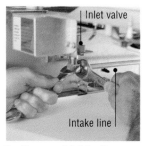

Inlet valve

Intake line

To disconnect intake line, shut off water at cutoff (p.109). Using one wrench to grip elbow under inlet valve, loosen nut on the line with a second wrench.

Door problems

Examine and adjust the door if it leaks or is hard to close. If adjusting doesn't stop the leak, suspect a bad door gasket. If a detergent or rinse-agent dispenser malfunctions, open the door panel and check for a stuck lever, broken spring, or other mechanical problem. Some dispensers are triggered by a lever on the timer, others by a solenoid or a bimetal arm. The test below for a solenoid is also valid for a bimetal arm.

A dishwasher door contains one or two switches in the latch assembly that prevent the unit from starting unless the door is latched. If the unit won't start and the door latches firmly, suspect these switches.

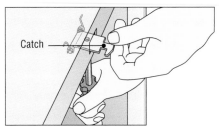

If door won't latch, reposition door catch (or strike plate). Loosen screw, slide catch mechanism inward or out; retighten firmly. Door should close tightly when latched, compressing gasket.

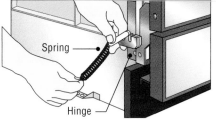

If door falls open, check the springs. Rehook a disconnected spring; replace a broken one. To tighten tension, hook spring in a new slot or hole. Keep tension on both springs the same.

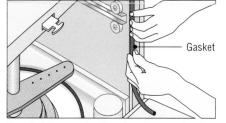

If gasket is worn, hardened, or torn, replace it. Unclip, unscrew, or pry off old gasket. If necessary, soak new one in warm water to remove kinks. Attach top, then sides and bottom.

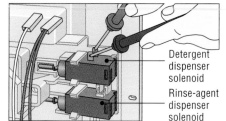

To test dispenser solenoid, take off leads. With VOM on RX100, probe terminals. Look for moderate resistance (about 2,500 ohms). Look for resistance approaching zero on a bimetal arm.

Testing and replacing door switches

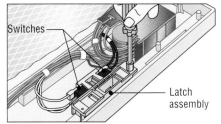

1 Free the latch assembly by taking out the screws that hold it to the door. Lift the assembly and press down on the latch mechanism to see if it operates the switches properly.

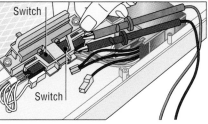

2 To test each door switch, remove leads and set VOM on RX1. Probe terminals. Look for zero reading when you press latch mechanism down to closed position, infinity when you release it.

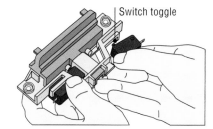

3 To replace a defective door switch, unclip it and slide it out of the latch assembly. If necessary, hold down the toggle to get switch out. Switch models vary; some are single rather than double.

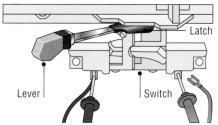

To test lever latch switch, open door's access panel. Remove a lead; set VOM on RX1. With door open, probe terminals; look for reading of infinity. Latch door and repeat; reading should be zero.

Sprayer, strainer, and racks

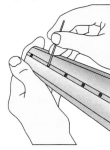

To unclog spray arm, gently probe holes with toothpick, awl, opened coat hanger, or other thin wire. Shake and rinse under hard spray to remove particles inside. To remove hard-water mineral deposits, scrub with hot vinegar.

Clean strainer in base of tub if there is one. On some models, also clean the raised guard that prevents food particles from recirculating onto dishes. Most strainers and guards lift out; some are secured with screws.

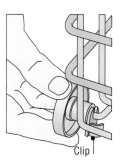

To repair chipped rack, remove it from machine, scour away rust with steel wool, then apply epoxy or plastic rack repair compound, or rubber caps—all sold at appliance parts stores. Be sure material is FDA-approved for contact with food.

Replace rollers if broken. Most can be pulled easily from prongs on racks but may need to be unclipped first. If a roller won't turn, scrub it with a brush and detergent.

Control panel

Remove the control-panel cover (p.253) to reach the timer and selector switch. The timer distributes power to other parts of the dishwasher at set intervals. Timers have a small electric motor, which can often be replaced if it tests faulty. Selector switches control special functions such as water preheating, air versus heat drying, or an extra pots-and-pans cycle. Most are simple on-off devices that can be tested as shown below. Solid-state timers and switches can't be repaired; replace one if it malfunctions.

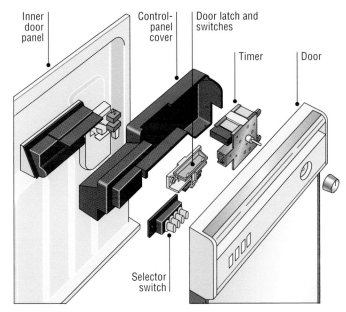

Inner door panel

Control-panel cover

Door latch and switches

Timer

Door

Selector switch

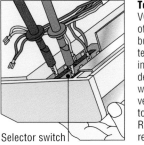

Selector switch

Test selector switch with VOM on RX1. Take leads off terminals for first push button, and clip probes to terminals. Look for a reading of zero when you depress button, infinity when button is out (vice versa for air-drying button). Reconnect leads. Repeat test for each remaining push button.

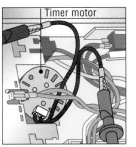

Timer motor

To test timer motor, disconnect motor leads from timer. With VOM on RX100, clip probes to leads. Look for a reading indicating moderate resistance. If reading is very high or infinity, replace motor. (To test timer itself, see page 234.)

Water inlet valve

When activated by current from the timer, the inlet valve's electromagnetic solenoid moves a metal plunger that opens the valve. When the current goes off, the plunger shifts back, closing the valve.

If a dishwasher doesn't fill fully, check for a stuck float (p.256) before testing the inlet valve. To test the inlet valve, shut off both the power and the water supply to the machine and open the lower front panel and toeplate (p.253). Test the valve solenoid first. If it's OK, take out the valve and check for a clogged intake filter. When the valve won't cut off, it's usually due to a rust or sand particle in the diaphragm bleed hole; disassemble the valve and wash it out.

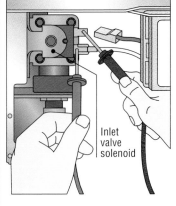

Inlet valve solenoid

Test inlet valve solenoid with VOM on RX100. Disconnect a lead and touch probes to both valve terminals; look for a reading showing moderate resistance (500 to 2,000 ohms). If reading is very high or infinity, dismount the valve (see below), detach the solenoid, and replace it.

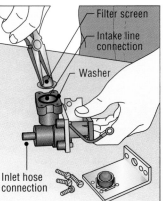

Filter screen

Intake line connection

Washer

Inlet hose connection

To clean intake filter, disconnect hose, pipe, and wires from valve, and take out its mounting screws. Pull filter from valve with long-nose pliers or pry out with small screwdriver. Clean under running water with an old toothbrush. If needed, take out screws holding valve together and clean valve. Check for damaged washer. When replacing washer, make sure its beveled side faces out.

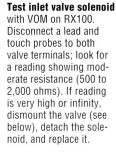

USE AND CARE

Load dishes so they are separated and face the center of the dishwasher. Put glasses between prongs, not over them.

Don't block the spray arm or spray tower or the flow of water to the detergent dispenser with large dishes, pots, or pans.

Use dishwasher detergent, never soap, laundry detergent, or dishwashing liquid. Use only fresh detergent; store it in a cool, dry place. Follow manufacturer's directions for amount. Less is needed if water is soft, more if it's hard.

Use a rinse agent to speed drying if you have hard water. But don't use it if your water is soft or artificially softened.

Avoid washing unenameled cast iron or ungalvanized tinware; pewter; fragile, antique, or gold-plated china and glassware; and plastics not labeled dishwasher-safe. The coating on disposable aluminum pans also degrades in a dishwasher.

To ensure the correct water temperature, run hot water at kitchen sink until it feels hot before turning on dishwasher.

To conserve water and energy, run a dishwasher fully loaded at night or during off-peak lower-cost utility hours. In hot weather, run it at night to keep cooling costs down.

Don't prerinse normally soiled dishes. Just scrape off food.

Use the hold-and-rinse cycle only when dishes must be left overnight and odors may result.

Use the lightest washing cycle for dishes that aren't very dirty. This cycle uses less hot water and energy than others.

Air-dry dishes to save energy when rapid drying is not needed. Don't warm plates in a dishwasher. Using its drying cycle as a plate-warmer wastes power. Use the oven instead.

Large appliances ▪ Dishwashers

Heating element, blower, and thermostats

A bad heating element or blower can cause poor drying; a faulty thermostat can keep the unit from running at all. When testing the element (below), check for a ground fault as well: With the VOM on RX100, probe the outer metal surface of the element and each terminal in turn. Both readings should be infinity.

The temperature-sensing thermostat keeps the unit off while the element heats the water during the sanitizing cycle. The limiting thermostat turns off the element if the unit gets too hot; test it as you would a temperature-sensing thermostat (below), but look for opposite results. *Turn off power to the unit before working on any of these parts.*

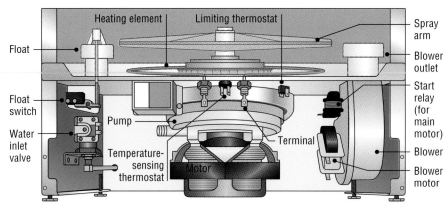

Opening the lower front panel and removing the toeplate (see *Gaining access,* p.253) allows you to reach the heating element terminals, the thermostats associated with the element, and the blower, if any. Opening the lower front panel also lets you access and test the float switch (bottom, left) and the motor and its start relay (facing page).

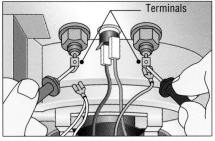

To test element, set VOM on RX1. Take off a lead and probe terminals. Look for reading of 15 to 30 ohms. If significantly higher, element is faulty. If OK, test for ground fault (see text above).

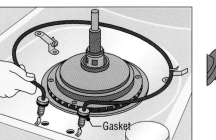

To replace element, disconnect both leads; from below, unscrew retaining nuts from terminals. Then lift element free from above. Install new element, using new gaskets.

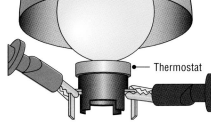

To test temperature-sensing thermostat, unclip it and remove leads. With VOM on RX1, clip probes to terminals; look for infinity reading. Hold thermostat next to a hot light; reading should be zero.

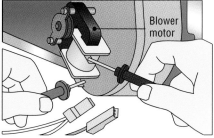

To test blower motor, disconnect leads from terminals. Set VOM on RX1, and probe terminals. Look for a reading between 20 and 100 ohms; replace motor if reading is infinity.

Float switch

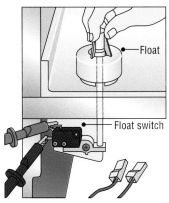

To test float switch, which prevents overflows, first check that float in tub moves freely and is not blocked by caked detergent or debris. Then remove leads from switch terminals. With VOM on RX1, clip probes to switch terminals; look for a reading of zero. Raise float; reading should change to infinity. If switch fails tests, replace it.

Common variant: Drain valve

A dishwasher with a nonreversible motor (see *Testing the motor,* facing page) contains a drain valve that enables the appliance to drain by shutting off water to the spray assembly while at the same time opening the drain hose. The drain valve may be located on the pump or linked to it by a short flexible hose.

Like an inlet valve (p.255), a drain valve is actuated by a solenoid. To check the valve, make sure that all exposed moving parts move freely. (Many valves have two springs, which must be intact.) After testing the solenoid (right), remove the valve and check it for clogs, taking it apart if necessary. You'll also have to disassemble it if you suspect a faulty seal.

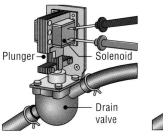

Test drain valve solenoid with VOM on RX1. Disconnect wires and probe both terminals. Look for reading of moderate to low ohms. Replace solenoid if reading is high ohms or infinity.

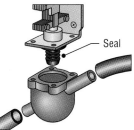

To remove drain valve, disconnect wires and hoses; unscrew valve from frame. Flush with water to clean. Remove obstructions with long-nose pliers. If necessary, disassemble valve.

Vertical pump and reversible motor assembly

Most pumps are mounted vertically above the motor, which in this configuration is usually reversible. If the motor malfunctions, try turning the lower spray arm, which is mounted on the motor shaft. If it moves freely, the problem is most likely electrical—a stuck relay or centrifugal switch (p.147) or a faulty field coil (see *Testing the motor,* right). If the spray arm doesn't turn, suspect a clogged pump or a binding pump seal. To repair the pump, *turn off power to the dishwasher* and remove the entire pump and motor assembly (below). Disassemble and clean the pump; then reassemble it, using replacement seals softened in hot water and coated sparingly with the recommended grease.

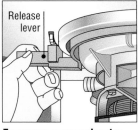

To remove pump and motor, disconnect hoses and motor leads. Then pull lever that releases assembly (or unbolt assembly from supports).

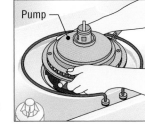

Remove spray assembly in tub, and lift out entire pump and motor assembly from above. On some models, motor comes out from below.

Common variant: Horizontal pump assembly

In some dishwashers, the pump and motor assembly is mounted horizontally. The motor is usually nonreversible and used with a drain valve (facing page); the pump has a single impeller instead of the two found in a reversible motor's pump. To access the assembly, remove the dishwasher's lower front panel. If the assembly is mounted front-to-back instead of side-to-side, disconnect the water intake line, pull the dishwasher forward, and tilt it up to reach the parts. To repair either pump or motor, remove the entire assembly from the dishwasher. If the motor hums but doesn't turn, check the pump as described for a vertically mounted assembly (above).

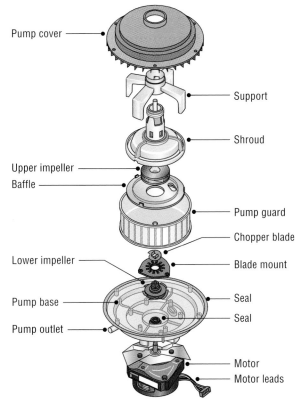

Pump cover
Support
Shroud
Upper impeller
Baffle
Pump guard
Chopper blade
Lower impeller
Blade mount
Pump base
Seal
Pump outlet
Seal
Motor
Motor leads

Testing the motor

Dishwasher motors are split-phase (p.139) and usually equipped with a start relay. A motor with four leads is reversible for draining. One with fewer leads is nonreversible and runs only to wash; a drain valve (facing page) expels the water. To test a motor's field coil and start relay (below), first identify the common lead (usually the white wire) or check the unit's wiring diagram. When testing the motor, make sure to do a ground-fault check as well: Set the VOM on RX100, and probe the motor's metal surface and each lead in turn. Look for a reading of infinity each time.

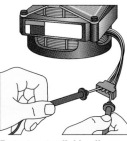
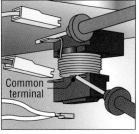

To test motor field coil, set VOM on RX1. Probe common lead (check wiring diagram, if needed) and each other lead in turn. In all cases, look for low resistance (3 to 15 ohms), indicating significant continuity.

To test start relay, remove leads. Probe common terminal and other two terminals in turn. Look for low ohms on one, infinity on other. Take off relay, turn it upside down, and repeat. Look for the reverse results.

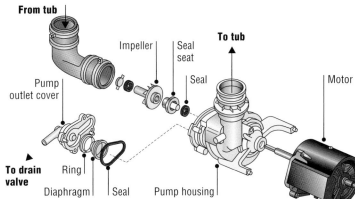

From tub
To tub
Impeller
Seal seat
Pump outlet cover
Seal
Motor
To drain valve
Ring
Diaphragm
Seal
Pump housing

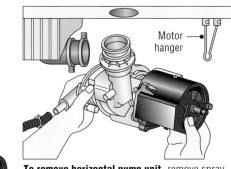

Motor hanger

To remove horizontal pump unit, remove spray arm (p.253). Disconnect hoses, motor leads, pump clamps, and motor hanger. Pull out.

A clothes dryer circulates heated air through wet clothing in order to evaporate the moisture. Its main components are a drum to hold and tumble the clothing, a heat source, a blower to circulate the hot air, an electric motor to turn the drum and the fan, and operating controls. The heat source in an electric dryer consists of heating coils. A gas dryer contains a burner.

Poor drying is often caused by lint buildup in the screen or in the exhaust system, although heater parts, the fan, or faulty seals around the drum or dryer door also may be to blame. Another common problem is a broken drum belt, which prevents the drum from turning.

FOR YOUR SAFETY

 Turn off power to a dryer before fixing it. Unplug a gas dryer; trip breakers or remove fuses that control an electric one (most electric dryers are wired to a 240-volt circuit controlled by double circuit breakers or two cartridge fuses in the service panel). An electric dryer cabinet should be grounded to the neutral line at the terminal block or to a metal cold-water pipe. A gas dryer is grounded through the power cord's grounding conductor.

Internal dryer wiring is heat-resistant. Never substitute ordinary wiring.

Shut off the gas supply to a gas dryer by turning valve to *Off* position (handle perpendicular to supply tube). If you disconnect gas line, test for leaks after you reconnect: Mix equal parts of cold water and dishwashing liquid and apply to joint; tighten fitting if bubbles appear.

If you smell gas, open windows. Put out any flames. Don't touch electrical switches or use the phone. Evacuate the house. Call the gas company from a neighbor's house.

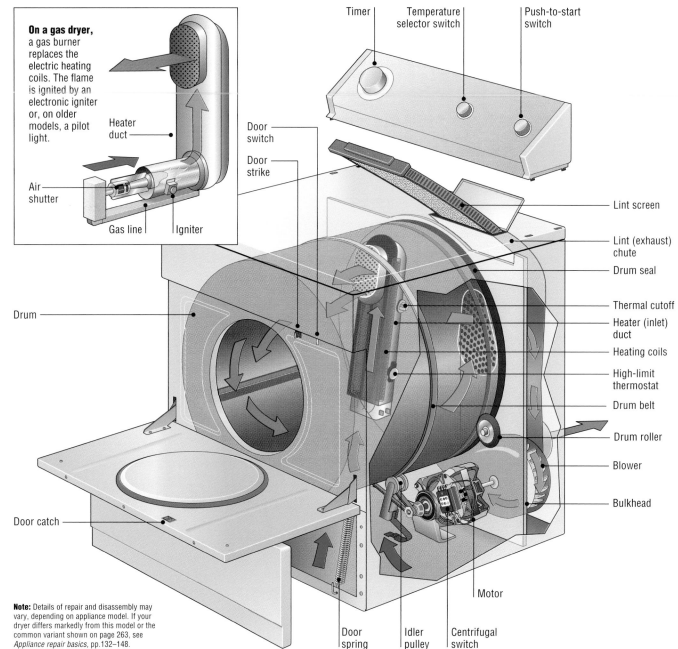

On a gas dryer, a gas burner replaces the electric heating coils. The flame is ignited by an electronic igniter or, on older models, a pilot light.

Heater duct

Air shutter

Gas line

Igniter

Timer

Temperature selector switch

Push-to-start switch

Door switch

Door strike

Drum

Door catch

Lint screen

Lint (exhaust) chute

Drum seal

Thermal cutoff

Heater (inlet) duct

Heating coils

High-limit thermostat

Drum belt

Drum roller

Blower

Bulkhead

Door spring

Idler pulley

Centrifugal switch

Motor

Note: Details of repair and disassembly may vary, depending on appliance model. If your dryer differs markedly from this model or the common variant shown on page 263, see *Appliance repair basics,* pp.132–148.

Troubleshooting

SYMPTOM	POSSIBLE CAUSE	SOLUTION
Won't run	Power off at outlet or faulty power cord	See *General troubleshooting*, p.144.
	Motor overload protector activated	Wait 15 min.; then restart. ◇
	Faulty terminal block *(electric dryer)*	Check and repair or replace (p.270). ◆
	Faulty door switch	Test and replace (p.260). ◆ ▣
	Faulty start switch	Test and replace (p.260). ◆ ▣
	Faulty timer	Test and replace (p.260). ◆ ▣
	Faulty operating thermostat	Test and replace (p.262). ◆ ▣
	Faulty motor or centrifugal switch	Test and replace (p.261). ◆ ▣
Drum won't turn; motor runs	Loose or broken drum belt	Replace (p.261). ◆
	Idler pulley or tension spring faulty	Repair or replace (p.261). ◆
	Drum binding	Remove obstruction (p.261). ◇
	Defective support roller	Repair or replace (p.261). ◆
	Loose or broken motor pulley	Tighten pulley (p.261). ◆ Or have motor serviced.
No heat; drum turns	One fuse blown *(electric dryer)*	Replace fuse. ◇
	Faulty temperature selector switch	Test and replace (p.260). ◆ ▣
	Faulty operating or high-limit thermostat	Test and replace (p.262). ◆ ▣
	Faulty timer	Test and replace (p.260). ◆ ▣
	Faulty heating coils *(electric dryer)*	Test and replace (p.262). ◆ ▣
	Faulty centrifugal switch	Test and replace (p.261). ◆ ▣
	Faulty burner or controls *(gas dryer)*	Adjust air shutter (p.262). ◇ Or have serviced.
Runs with door open	Faulty door switch	Test and replace (p.260). ◆ ▣
Dries too slowly	Clogged lint screen or exhaust vent	Clean (p.262). ◇
	Dryer overloaded	Divide load into smaller parts. ◇
	Leaking door seal	Check and replace (p.260). ◆
	Faulty drum seal	Check and replace (p.261). ◆
	Clothes too wet	Problem is likely with washing machine (p.288).
	Loose blower	Repair or replace (p.261). ◆
	Faulty operating thermostat	Test and replace (p.262). ◆ ▣
	Faulty heating coils *(electric dryer)*	Test and replace (p.262). ◆ ▣
	Faulty burner or controls *(gas dryer)*	Adjust air shutter (p.262). ◇ Or have serviced.
Gets too hot	Clogged outdoor exhaust vent	Clear vent (p.262). ◇
	Incorrectly installed exhaust duct	Check owner's manual for correct length and layout. ◇
	Faulty operating thermostat	Test and replace (p.262). ◆ ▣
	Faulty burner or controls *(gas dryer)*	Adjust air shutter (p.262). ◇ Or have serviced.
	Grounded heating coils *(electric dryer)*	Test and replace (p.262). ◆ ▣
Noisy	Foreign object in drum seal	Locate and remove (p.261). ◇
	Loose parts or fasteners vibrating	Tighten; make sure unit is level, with solid footing. ◇
	Worn drum belt	Replace (p.261). ◆
	Worn support rollers or drum bearing	Repair or replace (p.261). ◆
	Worn or broken idler pulley	Replace (p.261). ◆
	Loose blower	Repair or replace (p.261). ◆
	High-pitched whine: worn motor bearings	Have motor serviced.

Degree of difficulty: Simple ◇   Average ◆   Complex ◆   Volt-ohm meter required: ▣

Gaining access

Screw location

To open control panel, take out screws at ends; tilt panel forward and remove rear plate. **CAUTION:** Unplug dryer or turn off power to it before fixing it.

To lift top, remove lint screen and any top screws. Wrap putty knife with masking tape; insert it under top about 2 in. from each corner to release clips.

To remove rear panel, take off exhaust vent and loosen screws around edges with a nut driver. *On a gas dryer,* be sure to shut off gas supply first.

Free toeplate by pressing with stiff putty knife against spring clips located above ends of panel. On some models, take out screws at ends instead.

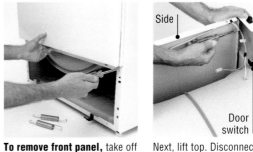

Side | Front |

Door switch |

To remove front panel, take off toeplate and take out screws just under front edge of panel on either side. Unhook and remove door springs.

Next, lift top. Disconnect and unhook door switch wires, loosen inside screws, and lift off panel. Put wood blocks under drum to support it.

Control panel

A dryer's control panel usually contains the push-to-start switch, the temperature selector switch, and the timer. On most dryers, the temperature selector controls one or more thermostats that regulate the temperature, but on some, this switch is an adjustable thermostat with a capillary sensing tube and is tested like the one on an electric range (p.274). Test a temperature switch with two selections as shown below. To test one with more options or to test a timer more fully, see page 234.

Some machines have other control-panel switches that govern an extra-care cycle or an end-of-cycle signal; test them like a simple on-off switch (p.145) or a selector switch (p.234).

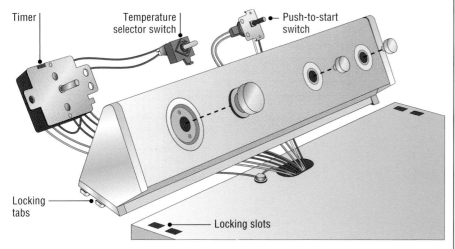

Timer
Temperature selector switch
Push-to-start switch
Locking tabs
Locking slots

Door problems

Dryer doors have a seal to keep hot air in and room air out. To check the seal, hold a piece of tissue near the edge of the door while the dryer is running. If the tissue is drawn in, examine the seal for looseness and replace it if it is worn, damaged, or has hardened. Install an identical new door seal. Dip it in warm soapy water to make it pliable; let it dry well. Use the special heat-resistant RTV silicone adhesive that comes with the seal (or is available from the same supplier). Avoid twisting the seal or pressing too hard. If the dryer door is loose, replace the catch, strike, or both.

All dryers have a door switch that cuts off the motor when the door is opened, preventing the drum from turning unless the door is closed. The door switch on most dryers is reached by lifting the top panel. On some models, it's attached to one of the door's hinges.

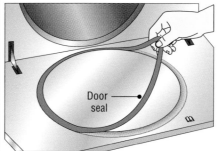

Door seal

To replace door seal, pull or pry off old seal and remove old adhesive with mineral spirits. Press on new seal with putty knife, using special heat-resistant RTV silicone adhesive sold with seal.

Door catch
Door strike

To replace door catch (left), take off front of door. Then use needle-nose pliers to squeeze catch and any tabs on it; push catch out. To remove strike (right), squeeze it and pull out.

Testing the switches and timer

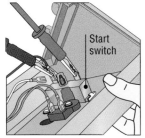

Start switch

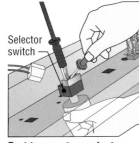

Selector switch

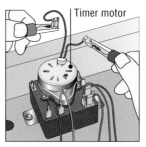

Timer motor

Test start switch with VOM on RX1. Remove one lead from switch; clip probes to both terminals. Look for infinity reading. Then press *Start* button; reading should change to zero.

Test temperature selector switch with VOM set on RX1. Remove leads and touch probes to terminals. Turn switch. Reading should change from zero to infinity or vice versa.

To test timer motor, disconnect both leads. Set VOM on RX100; clip probes on leads. Look for moderate resistance; if reading is very high or infinity, replace timer motor.

Testing and replacing the door switch

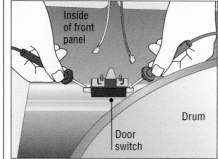

Inside of front panel
Drum
Door switch

1 Disconnect leads. With VOM on RX1, probe terminals. Look for reading of zero with door closed, infinity when open. If switch is wired to a light, look for reverse readings on light terminals.

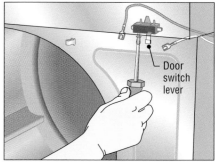

Door switch lever

2 To replace a defective switch, remove screws from front, then lift switch out from inside dryer. On some models, you must pry switch free with screwdriver, as on a refrigerator (p.280).

Drum and drum belt

Most drums are supported on rollers and turned by a belt that wraps around the drum. A steady rumbling or squealing often means worn rollers or a bad idler pulley bearing; a thumping sound, a worn belt. If the belt or idler pulley is broken, the motor will run but the drum won't turn. A screeching sound can signal an object stuck in the drum seal. To clear the seal, insert a putty knife in the edge and turn the drum one full turn. The seal should fully cover the ridge on the rear panel.

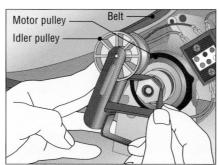

To remove worn drum belt, push idler pulley toward motor to loosen belt tension. Then pull belt off motor pulley. Slide belt off drum.

Motor and blower

Dryer motors are split-phase and operate on 120-volt current. Except for testing and replacing the centrifugal switch, most newer motors are not repairable and must be replaced if they test faulty.

The centrifugal switch (p.140) governs the motor's start and run windings and allows power to reach the heater or burner only after the motor is up to speed. Testing it may require the aid of a wiring diagram (p.132) to determine which leads come from the motor.

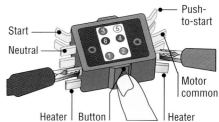

To test centrifugal switch, take off leads and set VOM on RX1. With button out, probe both heater terminals (often marked H1 and H2 or coded red); then probe push-to-start and neutral terminals. Look for zero reading on both tests. Next, probe push-to-start and start terminals; look for infinity. With button in, all readings should be reversed.

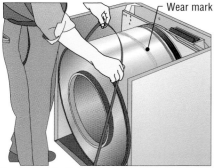

Install new belt around drum over mark left by old belt. At bottom, form loop with belt and route it under idler pulley and over motor pulley.

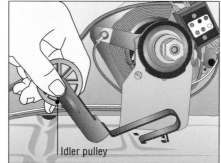

To remove a defective idler pulley, unhook bracket from dryer floor (or remove spring and mounting screw or clip). Replace entire pulley unit.

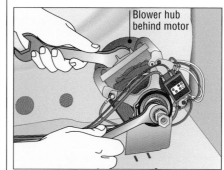

To remove blower, grip blower hub (which has left-hand threads) with a wrench; then use a second wrench to turn motor shaft clockwise.

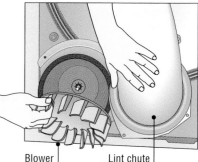

At back, unscrew lint chute and push it aside. Remove blower from motor shaft. Check blower for cracks and damaged threads and fins.

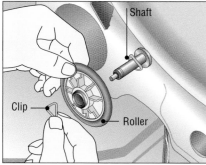

To replace worn roller, remove drum. Unscrew roller support bracket if necessary, and pry retaining clip from shaft to free roller.

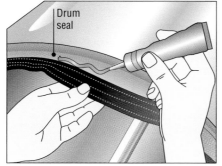

Install new drum seal with stitched side up and center fold against drum edge. Lift edge of seal and apply heat-resistant RTV silicone adhesive.

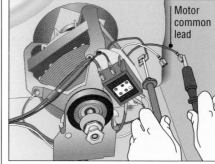

Test motor with VOM on RX1. Take motor leads off centrifugal switch. Probe common lead (here, blue) and other leads in turn; look for low ohms.

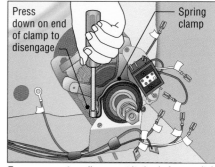

To remove motor, disconnect its leads from switch and remove blower (above). Release motor by disengaging spring clamps (some clamps unscrew).

Large appliances ▪ Dryers

Electric heater and thermostats

If a dryer doesn't heat, look for a tripped circuit breaker or blown fuse (p. 144), then test the dryer's thermostats, thermal fuse, thermal cutoff, and heating coils. Make sure the coil terminals are clean and tight. Also check the coils for a ground fault: With the VOM on RX100, probe the heater duct and each terminal in turn; look for an infinity reading.

If a thermostat has a second set of terminals, they go to an internal heater that activates the thermostat early when the heat setting is *Low*. If a dryer gets too hot on *Low*, test these terminals with a VOM on RX1; look for continuity with moderate resistance.

Opening a dryer's back panel gives you access to the heater duct that contains the heating coils. It also lets you reach the operating thermostat and thermal fuse on the blower housing and the high-limit thermostat and thermal cutoff on the heater duct. Some dryers have three operating thermostats; all are tested as shown at right. Still other dryers have a capillary thermostat with a sensing tube and an adjustable control; test it as you would the similar device on an electric range (p. 274).

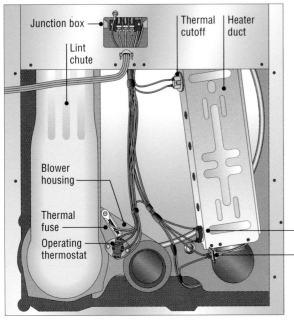

Junction box
Thermal cutoff
Heater duct
Lint chute
Blower housing
Thermal fuse
Operating thermostat
High-limit thermostat
Heating coil terminals

Testing thermostats, thermal fuse, and thermal cutoff

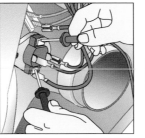
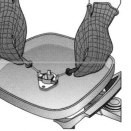
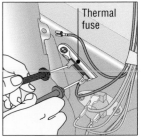

Thermal fuse

To test a thermostat, set VOM on RX1, remove a lead, and probe terminals (outer two terminals if there are more than two). Look for a reading of zero.

Remove thermostat; put it in an electric skillet heated to temperature higher than that stamped on device's metal flange. Test again. Look for infinity reading.

To test thermal fuse (or thermal cutoff), set VOM on RX1, take off a lead, and probe both terminals. Look for zero reading; replace if high or infinity.

Testing and replacing heating coils

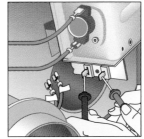
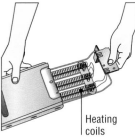

Stubby screwdriver

Heater duct

Heating coils

1 Test heater for open circuit. Remove leads, set VOM on RX1, and probe terminals. Look for reading of 5 to 25 ohms. If reading is zero, replace coils.

2 Disconnect thermal cutoff and thermostat from duct. Then open top and remove screw holding duct. Lift duct off brackets and pull out back.

3 Remove screws holding coils in duct; gently slide coils free. If coils are stretched and bent, look for obstruction blocking airflow.

Gas burners

Gas dryers generally suffer fewer problems than electric models. Have a faulty burner or ignition professionally serviced. If the burner has an air shutter, however, you can adjust it to admit more or less air. A yellow burner flame indicates too little air. A roaring sound (or popping when the burner shuts off) signals too much air—a common problem in dryers using bottled gas, but it can occur with natural gas as well.

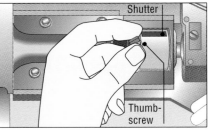

Shutter

Thumb-screw

Adjust air shutter by loosening thumbscrew and rotating shutter until burner flame appears light blue but does not roar. Retighten screw.

USE AND CARE

Clean the lint screen after each load. Remove the lint with your fingers; don't rinse or wash the screen. When reinstalling the screen, make sure it's seated fully.

Vacuum lint from the heater area, lint chute, blower housing, and exhaust duct connection at least once a year, and any time you service the dryer. Avoid damaging the wires.

Clear the outdoor vent hood with a soft wire.

Avoid vent duct sags and turns of 90° or more; they can trap water and lint. It's safest to use 4-inch-diameter rigid metal duct whenever possible. Limit flexible ducts to short runs.

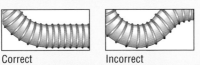

Correct   Incorrect

Common variant: Front blower and circular heating coils

In the popular dryer model featured on this page, the blower inlet is in front under the drum and is visible when you open the door. Its heating coils are attached to the rear panel in a circular pattern (or enclosed in a cylinder under the drum). The drum is supported by a rear bearing shaft.

Most tests and repairs require removing the drum (see right). If the drum won't lift out easily after you open the cabinet and release the drive belt, you may need to remove slides that hold the drum to the front bulkhead. Also, the drum's rear shaft may be held by a retaining ring, reached through a small access panel on the back.

Always replace both heating coils even if only one is faulty. To heat properly, new coils must be stretched uniformly and be the same length as the originals. Don't overstretch a coil.

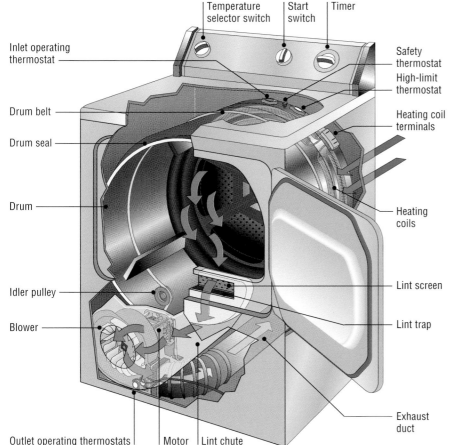

Temperature selector switch — Start switch — Timer

Inlet operating thermostat

Safety thermostat

High-limit thermostat

Drum belt

Heating coil terminals

Drum seal

Drum

Heating coils

Idler pulley

Lint screen

Blower

Lint trap

Exhaust duct

Outlet operating thermostats | Motor | Lint chute

Gaining access

1 Open top by removing the screws under the front edge that secure the top to the front panel. Then lift the top and tilt it to the rear.

2 To remove front panel, disconnect and unhook wires to door switch and light. Then take out screws that join panel to cabinet.

3 Pull panel forward to disengage door frame and lint chute on panel from drum. Then lift it up to free it from legs and hook-on connections.

Idler pulley

Motor pulley

4 To release drum belt, reach though lower back opening. Push idler pulley toward motor to relax belt tension while you slip belt off motor pulley.

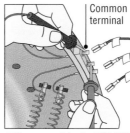

5 Remove any bolt or retaining clip on drum's rear shaft through rear access panel. Then lift drum, slide it out, and slip the belt off.

6 To remove motor, pry off bracket over its back end, unscrew blower blades in front, and then unscrew clamp connecting motor to blower.

Testing and replacing circular heating coils

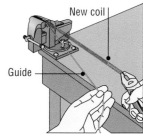

Common terminal

1 Remove coil leads. With VOM on RX1, probe common terminal and other two terminals in turn. Look for low ohms reading. Also test for ground (p.262).

Terminal block

2 To replace coils, use pliers to flatten small tabs on terminals; then pull terminals through terminal block. (Some coils are bolted to terminals.)

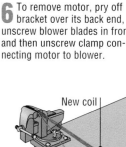

New coil

Guide

3 If new coils need stretching, use old coil or cord threaded along path as guide. Wearing safety goggles, grip coil in vise and pull evenly with pliers.

Large appliances ▪ Garbage disposers

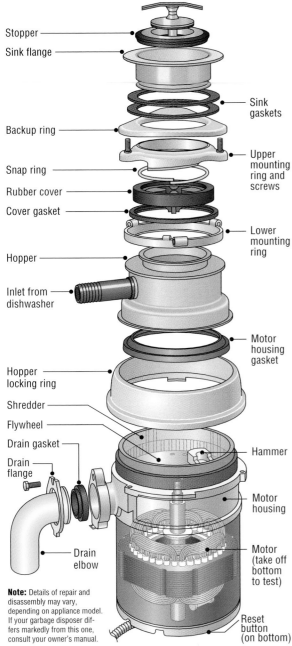

- Stopper
- Sink flange
- Backup ring
- Snap ring
- Rubber cover
- Cover gasket
- Hopper
- Inlet from dishwasher
- Hopper locking ring
- Shredder
- Flywheel
- Drain gasket
- Drain flange
- Drain elbow

- Sink gaskets
- Upper mounting ring and screws
- Lower mounting ring
- Motor housing gasket
- Hammer
- Motor housing
- Motor (take off bottom to test)
- Reset button (on bottom)

Note: Details of repair and disassembly may vary, depending on appliance model. If your garbage disposer differs markedly from this one, consult your owner's manual.

A garbage disposer's motor powers a flywheel that flings waste food against a shredder. The resulting biodegradable pulp is easily flushed down the waste line. Most units are of the continuous-feed type: a wall switch controls the unit and lets you scrape in waste while the motor runs. A batch-feed garbage disposer must be loaded before it can be turned on; the switch, located in the unit's sink mounting bracket, is activated by inserting and turning the stopper. Except for the switch, batch-feed disposer repairs are the same as those for the continuous-feed model featured here. If you suspect a switch problem in a batch-feed unit, test the switch as you would an on-off switch (see *General troubleshooting*, p.145).

To prevent jamming, avoid packing a disposer tightly. Don't grind bottle tops, clamshells, glass shards, or other hard waste, although grinding bones is OK and even helps prevent buildups inside the unit. Keep the cold-water faucet fully open when running a disposer. Cold water helps congeal grease, aiding its removal. After turning off a disposer, let the water run for about a minute to clear the drain line. Never use chemical drain cleaner; it can damage internal parts.

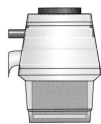

To cut noise, most disposers are covered by plastic foam in a hard shell.

Troubleshooting

SYMPTOM	POSSIBLE CAUSE	SOLUTION
Won't run	No power	See *General troubleshooting*, p.144.
	Overload protector tripped	Wait 15 min., then press reset button (facing page). ◇
	Faulty wall switch	Test and replace (p.129). ◆
	Faulty split-phase motor	See *General troubleshooting*, p.146. Replace unit if faulty.
Won't run; motor hums	Jammed flywheel	Clear jam (facing page). ◇
	Faulty split-phase motor or centrifugal switch	See *General troubleshooting*, p.146. Replace unit if faulty.
Drains poorly	Insufficient water flow	Open cold-water faucet fully. ◇
	Clogged drainpipe	Clear (p.115). ◇
	Dull shredder ring or damaged flywheel	Replace (facing page). ◆
Leaks	Loose drain gasket flange	Tighten gasket screws (facing page). ◆
	Poor seal at sink gasket	Tighten screws or apply sealant (facing page). ◆
	Defective motor housing gasket	Replace (facing page). ◆
Grinds slowly	Insufficient water flow	Open cold-water faucet fully. ◇
	Improper hard waste in disposer	Remove with tongs. ◇
	Dull shredder or damaged flywheel	Replace (facing page). ◆
Noisy	Foreign object in disposer	Remove with tongs. ◇
	Loose mounting screws	Tighten screws (facing page). ◆
	Broken flywheel	Replace (facing page). ◆
	Faulty split-phase motor	See *General troubleshooting*, p.146. Replace unit if faulty.
Won't stop	Faulty wall switch	Test and replace (p.129). ◆

Degree of difficulty: Simple ◇   Average ◆   Complex ◆   Volt-ohm meter required: ◼

Gaining access

Dishwasher drain hose

1 Shut off power to unit at service panel. Unclamp dishwasher drain hose and pull it off. Loosen slip nuts on drainpipe and disconnect trap.

Lower mounting ring

2 Supporting unit from below, rotate the lower mounting ring a quarter turn to free disposer. On some models, you need to take out screws first.

3 Remove cover plate from underside of disposer. Label wires; then unscrew wire connectors from power cord and pull cord free.

4 Unscrew and take off disposer outer shell; then lift off sound-insulating plastic foam. On some models, just unclip and unwrap insulation.

5 To open hopper, use a heavy hammer with protective wood block to rotate hopper locking ring and unlock the tabs. This requires extra force.

Clearing a jam

To unjam disposer, shut off power to disposer and move flywheel back and forth by pushing broom handle against hammer. This will release any problem-causing object, such as silverware. Then lift out object with tongs.
CAUTION: *Never* put your hand into the disposer.

On unit with hex-key opening on base, use hex key to turn motor shaft and flywheel. Rotate them in both directions to make sure they're fully free before removing any foreign object or using the disposer. You can use the hex key alone or in conjunction with broom handle (above).

If disposer won't start after unjamming, wait 15 min. for motor to cool fully, then press reset button—if there is one—on underside of unit and try again. (Make sure power has been restored.) After unjamming, drop in several ice cubes and grind them to help remove any remaining residue.

Stopping leaks

Most disposer leaks are caused by loose screws or damaged gaskets at the sink, the drainpipe, or between the hopper and the motor housing. Check all three sites if you see water dripping from the unit.

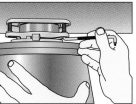

To stop leak at drainpipe, tighten the drain gasket screw with screwdriver, nut driver, or socket wrench. If leaking persists, take off trap (*Gaining access,* Step 1, above) and drainpipe, and replace gasket.

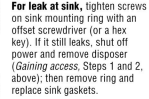

For leak at sink, tighten screws on sink mounting ring with an offset screwdriver (or a hex key). If it still leaks, shut off power and remove disposer (*Gaining access,* Steps 1 and 2, above); then remove ring and replace sink gaskets.

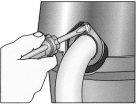

If leak is between hopper and motor housing, replace motor housing gasket. Shut off power, remove and disassemble disposer (*Gaining access,* above). Lift off gasket. Coat top of new gasket lightly with silicone sealant before reassembling unit.

Replacing the flywheel and shredder

Before you can free the flywheel on many disposers, the shredder must be pried out, as shown below. Install a new seal when you replace the shredder. Replace a stretched motor housing gasket.

Shredder

Flywheel

1 Disassemble disposer (*Gaining access,* above). Pry out any plastic cover over flywheel bolt. Immobilize flywheel by jamming wood between one of its hammers and the shredder. Use a socket wrench to loosen bolt; don't remove it.

2 Remove shredder: Place a socket from a socket wrench over flywheel bolt and use it as a pivot with a small pry bar and rubber mallet to pry off shredder. Work carefully around the shredder, prying it loose a bit at a time until it comes off.

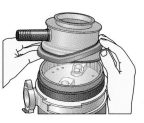

3 Take out the flywheel bolt and lift off the flywheel. Reverse steps to replace flywheel and shredder. Replace the seal on the lower edge of the shredder, and use a rubber mallet to gently tap shredder in place.

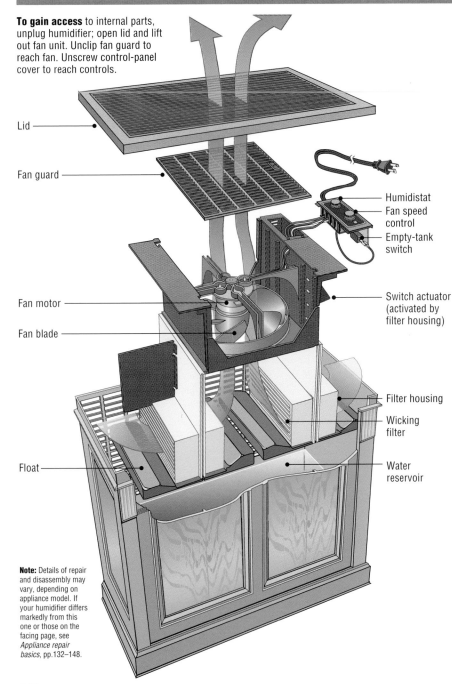

To gain access to internal parts, unplug humidifier; open lid and lift out fan unit. Unclip fan guard to reach fan. Unscrew control-panel cover to reach controls.

Lid

Fan guard

Humidistat
Fan speed control
Empty-tank switch

Switch actuator (activated by filter housing)

Fan motor

Fan blade

Filter housing

Wicking filter

Float

Water reservoir

Note: Details of repair and disassembly may vary, depending on appliance model. If your humidifier differs markedly from this one or those on the facing page, see *Appliance repair basics,* pp.132–148.

A humidifier helps ease skin and nasal irritations and can prevent dry-house problems, such as shrinking wood joints. But a humidifier can create health hazards (see *Environmental hints,* facing page). One of the safest types is the wicking-filter evaporative unit shown at left. It has disposable floating filters kept wet by wicking water and a fan that distributes the vapor evaporating off them. The humidifiers on the facing page use other moisture-delivery methods.

Most humidifier problems result from dirty or damaged evaporative foam or filters. Problems may also involve the fan, the fan speed switch, the empty-tank switch, which turns off the unit when the tank is empty, and the humidistat, which senses humidity and turns the unit on or off at the set point. All are easy to test and fix or replace. **CAUTION:** Unplug a humidifier and empty any water before testing or repairing it.

Fan and fan motor

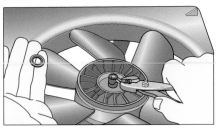

To remove fan blade, pry off grommet; then, wearing safety goggles, use pliers to release spring clamp. On some units, loosen setscrew.

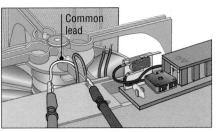

Common lead

To test fan motor, detach its leads from control. With VOM on RX1, probe common lead and other leads in turn. Look for moderate resistance.

Testing control switches

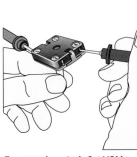

Humidistat. Free one humidistat lead, set VOM on RX1, and clip probes to terminals. Turn knob; look for VOM to jump from zero to infinity or vice versa when you hear a click. Partial or steady reading signals a fault (unless air is too humid or too dry).

Fan speed control. Set VOM on RX1. Unmount switch. Insert a probe in *L* terminal; touch other terminals in turn. With control in *Off* position, look for infinity reading at each terminal. In each other control position, reading at one terminal should be zero.

Empty-tank switch. Detach switch leads, set VOM on RX1, and clip probes to terminals. VOM should read zero ohms when you hold switch lever down, infinity when you release lever (as actuator does when water level drops).

Troubleshooting

SYMPTOM	POSSIBLE CAUSE	SOLUTION
Won't run	Power off at outlet or faulty power cord	See *General troubleshooting*, p.144.
	Humidistat set too low	Set higher. ◇
	Faulty lid switch *(some evaporative units)*	Test and replace like on-off switch (see *General troubleshooting*, p.145). ◆ ▣
	Faulty empty-tank switch	Test and replace (facing page). ◆ ▣
	Faulty fan speed control switch	Test and replace (facing page). ◆ ▣
	Faulty humidistat	Test and replace (facing page). ◆ ▣
	Faulty fan motor	Test and replace (facing page). ◆ ▣
Runs but doesn't humidify	Too little water in reservoir	Refill. ◇
	Clogged drive belt *(drum evaporative unit)*	Clean (below). ◇ Or replace belt. ◇
	Faulty shaded-pole belt motor *(belt evaporative unit)*	Test and replace (below; see also *General troubleshooting*, p.147). ◆ ▣
	Faulty drive train *(belt evaporative unit)*	Fix loose gear (below). ◆
Noisy	Loose fan blade	Tighten (facing page). ◇
	Faulty fan motor or foreign object in motor	Test and replace (facing page). ◆ ▣ Or remove object. ◇
	Clogged drive belt *(drum evaporative unit)*	Clean (below). ◇ Or replace belt. ◇
	Fan motor bearings dry	Put 2 or 3 drops of nondetergent SAE 20 oil in oil hole. ◇

Degree of difficulty: Simple ◇   Average ◆   Complex ◆   Volt-ohm meter required: ▣

Other common types of humidifiers

Humidifiers vary widely in appearance and in how they deliver moisture. But most have humidistats, and many have fans, fan speed controls, and empty-tank (or float) switches, which can be tested like similar parts in the model shown on the facing page. Problems specific to each humidifier type are described below. Clean a drum or belt evaporative model, or an ultrasonic unit, often; use an antibacterial solution. See *Environmental Hints,* above.

Drum evaporative humidifier rotates sponge-covered drum through water as fan draws air over it. Clean clogged drive belt with 1:1 white vinegar–water mix. Replace clogged sponge.

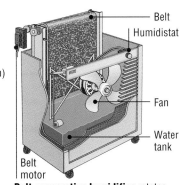

Belt evaporative humidifier rotates a sponge belt through water as fan blows air through it. Test a nonworking belt motor (p.146). Secure a loose gear on belt drive train with epoxy.

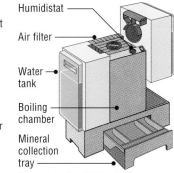

Warm-mist humidifier boils water and mixes the steam with air to cool it. Mineral deposits tend to build up in the boiling chamber. Clean it with soft brush and 1:1 vinegar-water mix.

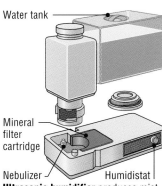

Ultrasonic humidifier produces mist with a high-frequency vibration. The nebulizer (vibrator) is a common trouble spot; clean it weekly. Also replace mineral filter, if any, regularly.

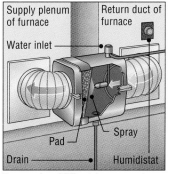

Furnace humidifier takes some air from return duct, adds moisture to it, and mixes it with hot air in plenum. If unit falters, test humidistat. On many models, also test fan and float switch.

Large appliances ▪ Microwave ovens

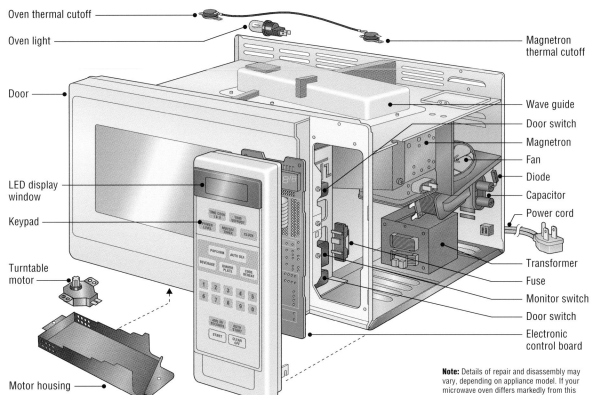

Oven thermal cutoff
Oven light
Door
LED display window
Keypad
Turntable motor
Motor housing

Magnetron thermal cutoff
Wave guide
Door switch
Magnetron
Fan
Diode
Capacitor
Power cord
Transformer
Fuse
Monitor switch
Door switch
Electronic control board

TIME COOK 1 & 2 **TIME DEFROST**
POWER LEVEL **MIN/SEC TIMER** **CLOCK**
POPCORN **AUTO DEF.**
BEVERAGE **DINNER PLATE** **COOK REHEAT**
1 2 3
6 7 4
8 9 5
0
ADD 30 SECONDS **AUTO START**
START **CLEAR OFF**

Note: Details of repair and disassembly may vary, depending on appliance model. If your microwave oven differs markedly from this one, see *Appliance repair basics,* pp.132–148.

A microwave oven bombards food with electromagnetic energy. This causes the food molecules to vibrate, generating internal heat from friction.

If a unit won't work or performs erratically, check its safety devices. These typically include a fuse that blows if there's a power surge or overload, a thermal cutoff that opens if the oven gets too hot, and a cutoff that opens if the microwave-generating magnetron overheats. To keep the oven from running with an open door, most units have two door switches and a monitor switch that blows the fuse if they fail. If one device is defective, test all the others also. The fan, turntable, capacitor, and diode are also serviceable. The capacitor, which stores high voltage, is potentially dangerous. Discharge it before touching any internal parts (p.146). Try testing a mechanical timer (p.234); have an electronic control board serviced by a pro. Also have a pro fix the magnetron and (because of possible microwave leaks) the door.

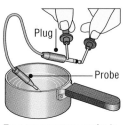

Plug
Probe

Test temperature probe in boiling-hot water. Set VOM on RX10; touch shaft and tip of plug. Look for moderate resistance, moving to infinity as water cools.

Gaining access

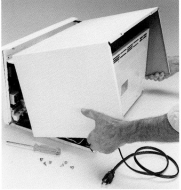

To remove cabinet, unplug oven. Remove screws securing cabinet to back and bottom. Then slide cabinet toward back while lifting up the rear. If cabinet is hard to remove, check for screws under plugs on the top or sides. **CAUTION:** Discharge capacitor (p.146) before touching any internal parts.

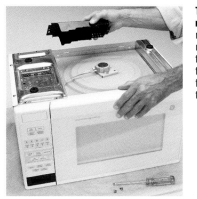

To reach turntable motor, turn the microwave oven upside down on a towel, then unscrew the motor housing from the bottom of the oven and lift it off.

Troubleshooting

SYMPTOM	POSSIBLE CAUSE	SOLUTION
Won't run	Power off at outlet or faulty power cord	See *General troubleshooting*, p.144.
	Blown appliance fuse	Test and replace (right). ◆ ▧
	Faulty door interlock switch	Test and replace (right). ◆ ▧
	Faulty fan motor	Test and replace (below). ◆ ▧
	Faulty mechanical timer	Test and replace (p.234). ◆ ▧
	Faulty door latch spring or control board	Have serviced.
Runs but doesn't cook	Faulty capacitor or diode	Test and replace (below). ◆ ▧
	Faulty thermal cutoff	Test and replace (right). ◆ ▧
	Faulty transformer or magnetron	Have serviced.
Keeps blowing fuses	Faulty door interlock or monitor switch	Test and replace (right). ◆ ▧
	Faulty capacitor or diode	Test and replace (below). ◆ ▧
	Faulty magnetron	Have serviced.
Cooks intermittently	Faulty door interlock switch	Test and replace (right). ◆ ▧
	Misaligned door or door seal	Have serviced.
	Loose or faulty wiring connection	Check and repair. ◆
	Faulty mechanical timer	Test and replace (p.234). ◆ ▧
	Faulty magnetron or control board	Have serviced.
Cooks slowly	Low voltage at wall outlet	Remove other appliances from circuit. ◇
	Faulty magnetron	Have serviced.
Cooks unevenly	Faulty turntable motor	Test and replace (below). ◆ ▧
	Loose or damaged wave guide	Have serviced.

Degree of difficulty: Simple ◇   Average ◆   Complex ◆   Volt-ohm meter required: ▧

Fuses, cutoffs, and safety switches

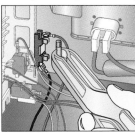 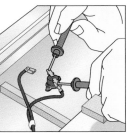

Remove fuse with fuse puller, or gently pry out with screwdriver. To test fuse, set VOM on RX1 and probe each end. Replace if reading is not zero.

Test thermal cutoff for oven or magnetron with VOM on RX1. Remove a lead and probe both terminals. Replace if reading is not zero.

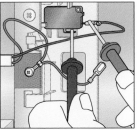 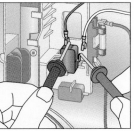

Test each door switch with VOM on RX1. Remove a lead and probe both terminals. Look for infinity reading when door is open, zero when closed.

Test monitor switch with VOM on RX1. Remove one lead and probe both terminals. Look for zero with door open, infinity when closed.

Fan and turntable motors

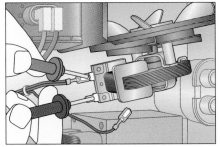 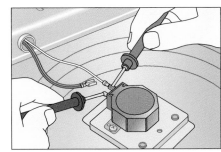

Test fan motor with VOM on RX1 (or RX100 for some small motors). Remove leads and probe both terminals. Look for reading of moderate ohms. Replace motor if reading is infinity.

Test turntable motor with VOM on RX1 (or RX100 for some small motors). Remove a lead and probe both terminals. Look for moderate ohms. Replace if reading is infinity.

Capacitor and diode

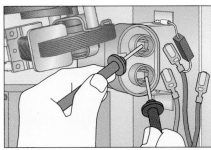 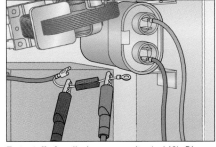

To test capacitor, *first discharge it* (p.146). Take off leads. With VOM on RX100, probe terminals. Look for low ohms increasing toward infinity. Reverse probes; look for same results.

To test diode, *discharge capacitor* (p.146). Disconnect diode from capacitor and cabinet. With VOM on RX100, probe wires; then reverse probes. One reading should be infinity; the other, low ohms.

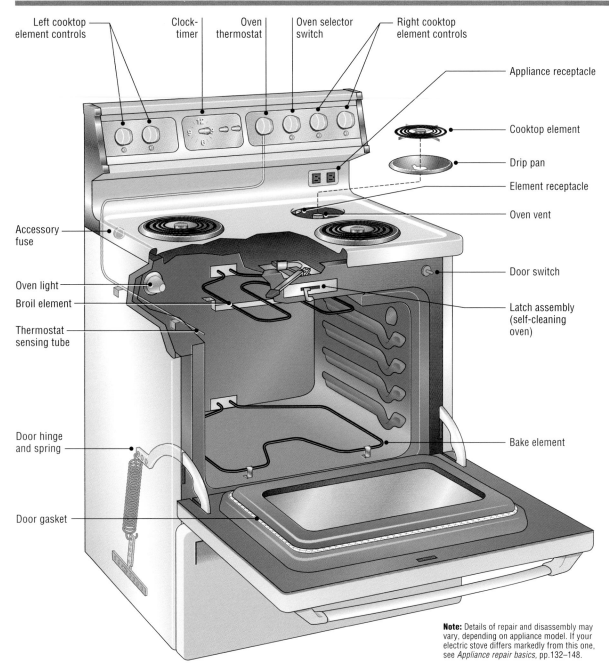

Left cooktop element controls

Clock-timer

Oven thermostat

Oven selector switch

Right cooktop element controls

Appliance receptacle

Cooktop element

Drip pan

Element receptacle

Oven vent

Door switch

Latch assembly (self-cleaning oven)

Accessory fuse

Oven light

Broil element

Thermostat sensing tube

Door hinge and spring

Bake element

Door gasket

In an electric stove, the flow of current through the heating elements is controlled by switches, a thermostat, and a timer. If your stove malfunctions, check the owner's manual to make sure you've been using it correctly. Some stove problems can be identified by sight, sound, or smell. Damaged wiring or parts often appear burned and emit a burning plastic odor; loose connections may buzz or hiss and give off a metallic smell.

Before investigating a problem, shut off power to the stove (see *For your safety*, below). A stove uses 240-volt power for heating and 120-volt power for the clock and lights, and is controlled by two circuit breakers or fuses at the service panel.

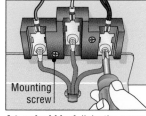

Self-cleaning ovens use high heat (900°F/ 480°C) to burn off residues. Special controls keep the oven door from opening during the cleaning and cool-down periods. Continuous-cleaning ovens have a catalytic coating that burns off spills as you use the oven. Never scrub this coating or clean it with a conventional oven cleaner. Instead, wipe up spills as soon as the oven cools; burn off baked-on deposits at 400°F (200°C) with the oven empty.

A terminal block links the power cord to internal wiring. To test cord (p.145), unscrew it from the block as shown. To replace a burned block, unscrew all wires and take out mounting screws.

Mounting screw

FOR YOUR SAFETY

 Before making a repair, turn off power to the stove at the service panel by tripping the circuit breakers or pulling the fuses. Don't unplug a stove before turning off the power; if a wire is loose, you can be shocked severely by just moving the stove to pull the plug.

Make sure a heating element is cool by carefully passing your hand near it before cleaning or removing it.

Don't try to open a self-cleaning oven until the cleaning cycle is finished and the stove has cooled for at least half an hour longer. Opening the oven for even an instant can cause severe burns.

Note: Details of repair and disassembly may vary, depending on appliance model. If your electric stove differs markedly from this one, see *Appliance repair basics*, pp.132–148.

Troubleshooting

SYMPTOM	POSSIBLE CAUSE	SOLUTION
No top or oven elements heat; no light	Power off at outlet or faulty power cord	See *General troubleshooting*, p.144.
	Burned terminal block	Inspect and replace (facing page). ◈
Single cooktop element won't heat	Faulty element or element receptacle	Clean contacts; test and replace (p.273). ◈ ▣
	Faulty control switch	Test and replace (p.273). ◈ ▣
Oven element doesn't heat	Improperly set timer	Reset. ◇
	Faulty element	Test and replace (p.273). ◈ ▣
	Faulty thermostat	Test and replace (p.274). ◈ ▣
	Faulty selector switch	Test and replace (p.274). ◈ ▣
	Faulty timer	Test and replace (p.272). ◈ ▣
	Faulty wiring or connector	Check for bad wires and loose connections. ◈ ▣
Oven temperature incorrect or uneven	Thermostat not calibrated properly	Adjust (p.274). ◈
	Misaligned oven door	Check and repair (p.272). ◇
	Worn or damaged oven gasket	Check and repair (pp.272, 274). ◈
	Clogged oven vent	Clean vent (p.272). ◇
	Faulty thermostat, or sensing tube touching oven wall	Test and replace (p.274). ◈ ▣ Reposition tube. ◇
Condensation in oven	Clogged oven vent	Clean vent (p.272). ◇
Oven door won't close tightly	Faulty hinge spring or misaligned oven door	Check and repair (p.272). ◈
	Worn or damaged oven gasket	Check and replace (pp.272, 274). ◈
Self-cleaning oven door won't latch or won't open	Faulty safety switch	Test and replace (p.274). ◈ ▣
	Faulty door latch	Check; repair or replace (p.274). ◆
	Faulty selector switch	Test and replace (p.274). ◆ ▣
	Oven too hot	Let cool for 30 min. ◇
Self-cleaning oven won't clean	Oven door not latched	Latch. ◇
	Faulty element	Test and replace (p.273). ◈ ▣
	Faulty timer	Test and replace (p.272). ◈ ▣
	Faulty thermostat	Test and replace (p.274). ◆ ▣ Or have serviced.
	Faulty selector switch	Test and replace (p.274). ◆ ▣
	Faulty door latch	Check; repair or replace (p.274). ◆
Oven vent smokes during self-cleaning	Faulty smoke eliminator	Replace (p.274). ◈
Oven light out	Burned-out bulb	Replace (p.272). ◇
	Faulty switch	Test and replace (p.272). ◈ ▣
	Faulty socket	Check and replace (p.272). ◈
Clock or timer doesn't work	Blown appliance fuse	Replace (p.272). ◇
	One fuse or one circuit breaker tripped	Replace fuse or reset breaker at service panel. ◇
	Faulty clock-timer	Test and replace (p.272). ◈ ▣
Receptacle doesn't work	Blown appliance fuse	Replace (p.272).
	One fuse or one circuit breaker tripped	Replace fuse or reset breaker at service panel. ◇
	Faulty receptacle	Check and replace (p.272). ◈
Indicator light out	Burned-out bulb	Replace bulb unit (p.272). ◈

Degree of difficulty: Simple ◇   Average ◈   Complex ◆   Volt-ohm meter required: ▣

Gaining access

To open control panel, remove screws and brackets from sides, then pivot panel forward onto a towel. If easy to reach, open back instead.
CAUTION: Turn off power to stove at service panel before opening any part.

To open back, move stove away from wall. Wearing work gloves, remove screws from around edges of the access panel or panels. On most stoves, this gives access to controls as well as to most wiring.

Open hinged cooktop by lifting at front corners. On some models, you have to push top toward rear before lifting. If the top doesn't have pop-in-place braces, support it in raised position with hinged rod located against side panel.

To remove oven door, open it partway and pull it up and off hinge arms. (On older models, remove screws holding hinges, being careful not to let hinges fly up and chip range.)

To reach front-mounted controls, raise cooktop and take out screws holding cover plate on top of them. (On other models, remove screws at sides of the front panel, then lift entire front panel up and off spring clips.)

Control-panel accessories

Accessories can be reached by either opening the control panel or removing the back panel (p.271), depending on the model and the back's accessibility. **CAUTION:** Cut power to the stove at the service panel before fixing accessories.

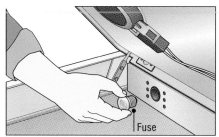

To change fuse governing clock-timer, receptacle, and other accessories, raise cooktop (p.271). Unscrew fuse; screw in same-amp replacement.

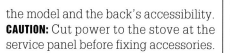
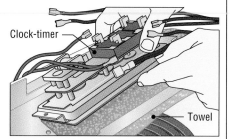

To replace broken or burned clock-timer, take off leads, unscrew timer from panel, and lift off. (Or depress side clips and pull through front.)

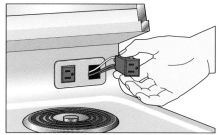

To replace faulty receptacle, depress clips at sides in back and pull through front of panel. Remove leads. Install an identical replacement.

Replace burned-out indicator light from rear. Pull it down and off peglike plastic mount. Replace entire light unit if bulb is burned out.

Oven light socket and door switch

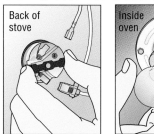

To replace oven light socket, remove bulb cover inside oven. Open back panel and remove socket leads. Depress socket clips (left); push socket partway into oven; then pull out from inside oven (right).

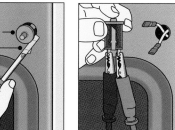

To test door switch, pry it out (left) and take off leads. With VOM on RX1, clip probes to switch terminals (right). Look for infinity reading when you push plunger in, zero when you release it.

Oven door and vent

A loose oven door or a bad gasket may cause low or uneven heating. If an oven overheats, make sure its vent is clear.

Don't cover the vent, oven floor, or a rack with foil. Heating problems may also be caused by the thermostat (p.274).

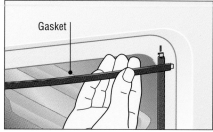

To replace oven door gasket on many older non-self-cleaning models, simply unhook ends from holes on front of oven. Install identical new gasket by hooking ends in holes.

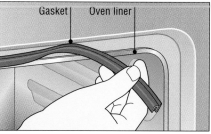

To replace gasket clamped between cabinet and oven liner, remove side screws (or nuts in rear of liner) and pull liner forward slightly. Fit new gasket over liner; slide liner in and reinstall screws.

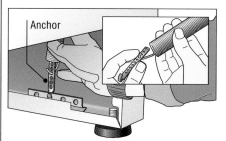

To adjust frame-attached springs, remove storage drawer. *Wearing gloves and goggles,* move anchor to new hole, or rehook spring in new hole on anchor. Keep tension equal on both springs.

To adjust springs inside door, remove door and take off its inner panel. Grasp each spring with locking pliers to unhook and reposition it. Wear safety goggles in case spring slips loose.

Adjust door warp by loosening screws holding inner panel. Push down on door while twisting it from side to side; then carefully retighten screws. Check by closing door and looking for gaps.

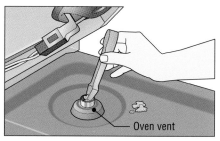

Inspect oven vent, usually located beneath rear cooktop element. Raise cooktop (or remove element and drip pan). Then unscrew and lift off any vent duct. Remove debris with tongs.

Testing cooktop elements

If an element doesn't work, first check that it is securely plugged in. (Make sure that the element is cool before touching it.) When testing an element for continuity, always test it for a ground fault too. If the element is OK, remove its receptacle and check it for damage. If necessary, check the element's temperature-control switch (far right) and the wiring between them.

To avoid problems, keep elements and drip pans clean and don't line drip pans with foil; use flat-bottom cookware.

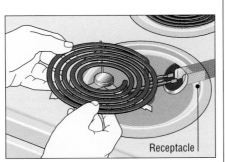

To remove element, lift it up and pull it out of receptacle. (Some elements are wired directly, with screw terminals inside a ceramic or glass case held closed by easily removed clips.)

Receptacle

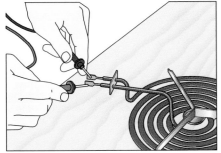

Test single-coil element for continuity with VOM on RX1. Touch probes to both terminals; meter should show partial resistance, typically between 10 and 70 ohms.

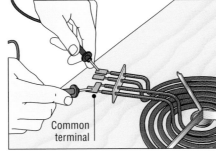

Test double-coil element with VOM on RX1. Touch one probe to terminals joined by bar (common terminal); probe each remaining terminal in turn. Look for partial resistance on both.

Common terminal

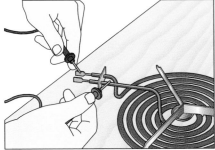

Test element for ground fault with VOM on RX100. Touch one probe to sheathing of element, the other to each terminal in turn. Look for constant infinity reading (no continuity).

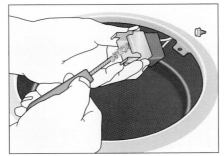

To check element receptacle, remove drip pan and take out mounting screw. Pry off any cardboard insulator. Clean dirty contacts with a wire brush or by scraping. Replace a damaged unit.

Testing cooktop switches

When diagnosing a cooktop switch, *cut power to the stove at the service panel,* open the back panel, and look for obvious faults like burned or loose wires. To test the switch (Step 1 below), simply compare the readings it gives to those of a switch that works. If the readings differ, replace the faulty switch.

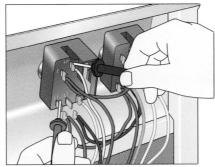

1 On a working switch, remove leads from L1 and L2 terminals. With VOM on RX1, probe all pairings of terminals at each heat setting; note readings. Compare with suspect switch readings.

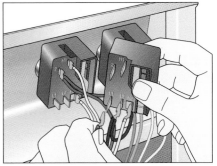

2 To replace switch, hold an identical new unit next to old one and transfer leads to corresponding terminals one at a time. Then detach old unit and attach new one.

Testing and replacing oven elements

Bake and broil elements are controlled by a selector switch, a thermostat (p.274), and often a clock-timer (facing page). A visible sign of a faulty element is pitting caused by internal grounding.

Poor heating can result if an element has a loose or bent support. To prolong the life of elements, protect them with foil when using oven cleaner and never use the oven as a room heater.

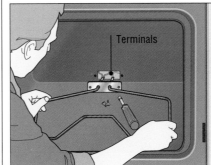

Terminals

1 To remove a cool bake or broil element, lift off door, take out screws holding element to back of oven, disengage any brackets, and pull forward. Then unscrew wires from element terminals.

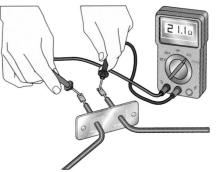

2 Test element with VOM on RX1. Touch probes to both terminals; meter should show some resistance (roughly 10 to 40 ohms). Also test the element for a ground fault (far left).

Oven controls

The oven selector switch governs whether current flows to the stove's bake, broil, timed-bake, or (if present) self-clean circuit. A thermostat controls the temperature, usually with a liquid-filled sensing tube in the oven cavity. Oven thermostats should be accurate to within 25°F (14°C); if an oven thermometer shows a thermostat is off by 25° to 50°F (14° to 28°C), adjust it by one of the methods below. Replace a thermostat that's off by more than 50°F (28°C).

The clock-timer controls the timed-bake and self-clean circuits. If an oven with a timed-bake circuit doesn't heat, be sure the timer is correctly set before testing the controls. Any control with an electronic circuit board should be serviced by a professional.

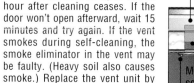

Terminals	1&3	2&4	8&9	8&10
Bake	■	□	■	□
Broil	■	□	□	■
Time bake	□	■	■	□
Clean	□	■	□	■

Open □   Closed ■

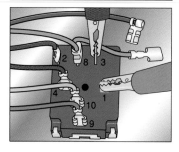

If thermostat adjustment is in knob, loosen screws holding disc; then turn disc toward *Raise* or *Lower* setting. Each mark on scale (or notch on disc) represents a set number of degrees. Retighten screws; test results with an oven thermometer.

Adjustment disc

MOVE POINTER
RAISE · · · LOWER
10° PER NOTCH

Test selector switch with VOM on RX1. Consult chart on stove's wiring diagram for pairs of terminals to test (a typical chart is shown). With switch in each position, remove one wire from each pair and probe both terminals. Look for zero reading when chart indicates closed contacts, infinity when it indicates open ones. (For more on testing selector switches, see page 235.)

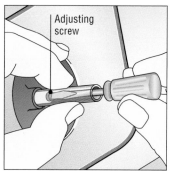

Adjusting screw

If thermostat adjustment is in shaft, insert thin screwdriver into adjusting screw at base. Holding shaft steady, turn screw clockwise to raise temperature, counterclockwise to decrease it on most stoves. A one-eighth turn equals about 25°F (14°C). If results are opposite those expected, turn screw in the other direction.

Self-cleaning ovens

These ovens have a safety switch that locks the door for up to half an hour after cleaning ceases. If the door won't open afterward, wait 15 minutes and try again. If the vent smokes during self-cleaning, the smoke eliminator in the vent may be faulty. (Heavy soil also causes smoke.) Replace the vent unit by taking out the mounting screws.

Vent
Eliminator
Mounting screws

Gasket

To replace gasket on door of self-cleaning oven, remove screws holding inner window panel on door and lift it off. Take off old gasket; insert a duplicate. (In some models, inner and outer door panels must be taken apart and door handle removed to reach screws holding inner window panel.)

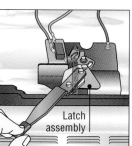

Latch assembly

To check latch, remove tray under cooktop by taking out screws around perimeter. Replace broken spring or switch (below); if another part is faulty, replace entire assembly. To remove latch, take out screws holding it in place inside oven.

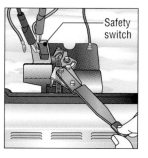

Safety switch

Test safety switch with VOM on RX1. Remove one lead from switch; clip probes to both terminals. Look for zero ohms reading with latch open, infinity with latch closed.

Testing and replacing the thermostat

Thermostat

Sensing tube

1 Set VOM on RX1. If a thermostat has two terminals, disconnect wires and clip probes to terminals. With thermostat control knob on *Off*, look for infinity reading; on 300°F (150°C), look for zero reading. Otherwise, replace thermostat. If a thermostat has more than two terminals, consult chart on stove's wiring diagram and test as you would a selector switch (above, center).

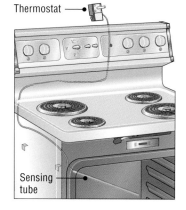

Thermostat

Sensing tube

2 Replace thermostat and sensing tube as single unit. Unclip and handle tube gently to avoid breaking; liquid in tube on self-cleaning ovens is caustic and can burn skin. On some stoves, tube follows complicated path. When replacing, tape string to end of original before pulling it out. Transfer string to new tube; then guide new tube into oven, pulling it with the string.

Stoves / gas

Gas stoves have few moving parts and are generally easy to repair. In older models that lack electrical parts, the burners are ignited by a continuously burning pilot flame. In newer models, the surface burners are lighted by electronic igniters that spark or heat a metal coil; the oven burners are lighted by igniters or electrically heated ceramic bars called glowbars.

For maximum efficiency, the burners must be clean and the flames must contain gas and air in the correct proportion. A proper flame burns steadily and quietly, and displays sharply defined blue cones about ½ to ¾ inch in height. Too much air produces a noisy, unsteady flame that may not completely encircle the burner and can result in erratic ignition. Too little air results in a weak, sooty flame with no blue cones.

Gas stoves must be adjusted for either liquid propane (LP) or natural gas. If you want to change the type of gas your stove uses, call the gas company.

Call the gas company also for any repairs involving the gas supply line or burner gas-control valves. Incorrect repairs to these parts can create hazardous gas leaks. Repairing accessories like a clock or an appliance receptacle, and purely mechanical parts such as oven door hinges and gaskets, is the same as for an electric stove.

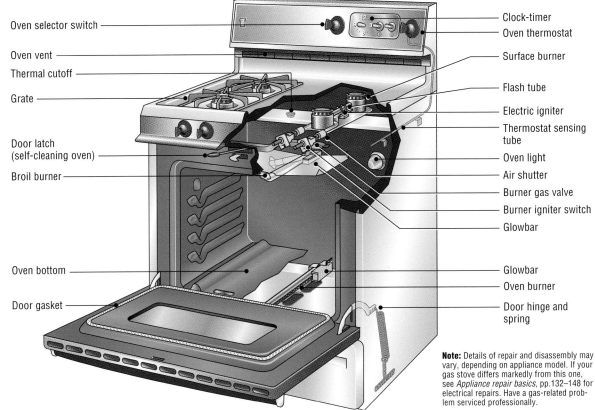

Oven selector switch —
Oven vent —
Thermal cutoff —
Grate —
Door latch (self-cleaning oven) —
Broil burner —
Oven bottom —
Door gasket —

— Clock-timer
— Oven thermostat
— Surface burner
— Flash tube
— Electric igniter
— Thermostat sensing tube
— Oven light
— Air shutter
— Burner gas valve
— Burner igniter switch
— Glowbar
— Glowbar
— Oven burner
— Door hinge and spring

Note: Details of repair and disassembly may vary, depending on appliance model. If your gas stove differs markedly from this one, see *Appliance repair basics,* pp.132–148 for electrical repairs. Have a gas-related problem serviced professionally.

FOR YOUR SAFETY

Shut off the gas supply before working on a stove. The gas supply valve, usually located behind the stove, is off when the valve handle is perpendicular to the pipe. Don't move a stove with a rigid gas supply pipe. Call the gas company or a professional.

Unplug the power cord before working on the electric ignition or other electrical parts of a gas stove.

If you smell a faint gas odor, check for a surface or oven pilot flame that's out or a burner that's on and unlighted. Air out the room, wait 5 minutes, and relight the pilot. If this fails, have the gas company check the supply line.

If there's a strong gas odor, open windows and doors, and evacuate everyone. Don't light a fire, flip a switch, or use a phone. Call the gas company from a neighbor's house.

Gaining access

To remove surface burners, lift cooktop (p.271). Pull burners up and off valve. Burner configurations vary greatly.

To reach lower oven burner, remove oven door (p.271). Release rear clips and lift out oven bottom and any burner cover.

To reach rear accessories and controls, take out top and bottom screws in ends of control panel; roll panel onto a towel.

To open front control panel, open cooktop (p.271). Pull off knobs, remove top and bottom screws, and lift off front.

Troubleshooting

SYMPTOM	POSSIBLE CAUSE	SOLUTION
Gas odor	Burner control on	Turn off. ◇
	Pilot flame out *(pilot-ignited models)*	Ventilate room; relight pilot. ◇
	Clogged oven burner	Clean (facing page). ◆
	Faulty or leaky gas supply line or fitting	Turn off gas supply valve, ventilate room, and call gas company. ◇
Cooktop pilot keeps going out	Pilot opening blocked *(pilot-ignited models)*	Clean (right). ◇
	Pilot light too low *(pilot-ignited models)*	Adjust flame (right). ◇
	Excessive air to burner blowing out pilot	Adjust burner air shutter (right). ◇
Cooktop burner won't light	Power off at outlet or faulty power cord	See *General troubleshooting,* p.144.
	Clogged burner	Clean (right). ◇
	Flash tube out of position	Reposition. ◇
	Faulty electronic igniter, switch, or module	Test and replace (facing page). ◆ ■
	Excessive air to burner	Adjust air shutter (right). ◇
	Insufficient gas to burner	Have serviced.
	Pilot light out *(pilot-ignited models)*	Clean and adjust pilot (right). ◇ If problem persists, have serviced.
	Gas supply off	Make sure gas valve is open before having serviced. ◇
Flame low, uneven, yellow, or sooty	Clogged burner	Clean (right, facing page). ◇
	Cooktop burner out of position	Reposition. ◇
	Insufficient air to burner	Adjust air shutter (right, for cooktop; facing page, for oven burner). ◇
	Insufficient gas to burner	Have serviced.
	Clogged oven vent	Clean vent cover. ◇
Flame noisy, uneven, too high	Excessive air to burner	Adjust air shutter (right, for cooktop; facing page, for oven burner). ◇
	Excessive gas to burner	Have serviced.
Oven pilot keeps going out	Pilot light too low *(pilot-ignited models)*	Adjust (facing page). ◆
	Pilot opening blocked *(pilot-ignited models)*	Clean (right). ◇
	Faulty safety valve *(pilot-ignited models)*	Have serviced.
Oven burner won't light	Incorrectly set clock-timer	Consult owner's manual for correct setting procedure. ◇
	Power off at outlet or faulty power cord	See *General troubleshooting,* p.144.
	Faulty glowbar igniter	Repair or replace (facing page). ◆ ■
	Faulty thermal cutoff	Test and replace (facing page). ◆ ■
	Faulty thermostat or selector switch	Have serviced.
	Pilot light out *(pilot-ignited models)*	Relight pilot (facing page). ◇
	Pilot light too low *(pilot-ignited models)*	Adjust (facing page). ◇
	Faulty safety valve *(pilot-ignited models)*	Have serviced.
	Clogged oven vent	Clean vent cover. ◇
	Gas supply off	Make sure gas valve is open before having serviced. ◇
Oven temperature incorrect or uneven	Thermostat not calibrated properly or faulty	Adjust (p.274). ◇ Or have serviced.
	Misaligned door or damaged gasket	Realign (p.272). ◆ Or replace gasket (pp.272, 274). ◆
	Clogged burner	Clean (facing page). ◆
	Clogged oven vent	Clean vent cover. ◇

Degree of difficulty: Simple ◇   Average ◆   Complex ◆   Volt-ohm meter required: ■

Adjusting and cleaning cooktop burners

Air shutters on the burner tubes regulate the gas-air mixture. Adjusting them and cleaning the burners will fix most burner problems. If a burner won't light, check the pilot (below) or electronic ignition (facing page). *Be careful working around open flames.*

To adjust air shutter, lift cooktop and loosen shutter adjusting screw. Turn burner on *High* and open shutter until flame is noisy and unsteady. Then close shutter slowly to produce steady flame with sharp blue cones. Retighten screw.

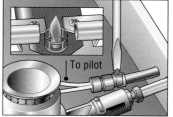

To clean burners, lift cooktop and remove burner unit. Open clogged flame openings with a toothpick; flash tube ports with a fine wire. Wash in hot soapy water with soft brush; rinse. Swab inside of flash tube. Let dry.

Adjusting and cleaning cooktop pilots

Adjust pilot flame by turning adjustment screw on pilot gas supply line. Turn the screw counterclockwise on most stoves to increase the flame. Correct flame is a sharp blue cone, 1/4 to 3/8 in. high.

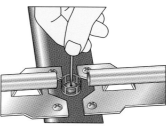

Clean pilot orifice if it's plugged. Remove shield, if any, around orifice and wipe orifice with dry lint-free cloth. Clean opening with pin or toothpick, taking care not to enlarge or deform opening.

Replacing electronic spark igniters and controls

Each igniter serves two burners. If a burner doesn't light, try the companion burner. If it works, the first burner's switch is likely faulty. If neither burner works, clean the electrode with a soft cloth. Check for loose connections on the ignition control module on the back of the stove. If no igniters work, suspect a faulty module. The switches for all the burners are usually wired together; replacements are sold as a unit. **CAUTION:** Unplug the stove before testing or fixing electronic ignition parts.

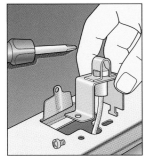

To replace igniter, unscrew bracket and clip off electrode and bracket. Tape end of new igniter wire securely to old wire, and pull new wire to control module on back of stove.

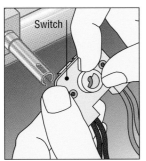

To test igniter switch, slip it off gas valve. Note how to set the switch on *Lite* and on *Off.* Then trace its leads to the harness plug and control module on back of stove.

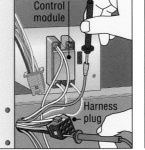

On back of stove, remove switch lead from module and disconnect harness plug. With VOM on RX1, probe lead and terminal in plug. Look for zero reading with switch on *Lite,* infinity on *Off.*

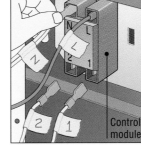

Replace control module on back of stove if no igniters work. Label and disconnect igniter wires; remove module from mounting bracket. Install identical new module.

Testing and replacing oven glowbars

On many stoves, the oven burners are lighted by electrically heated glowbars. Some glowbars snap into position, but many have a wire that goes to a plug on the rear of the stove. The plug for the bake burner's glowbar may be behind a small access panel.

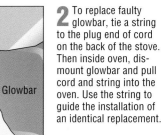

1 Trace glowbar's leads to harness plug on back of stove, and disconnect plug. With VOM on RX1, probe terminals in plug. Look for moderate resistance, indicating significant continuity. **CAUTION:** Unplug stove before testing glowbars. Use only the special heat-resistant wiring supplied with a replacement.

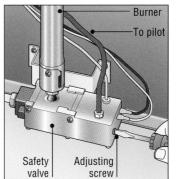

2 To replace faulty glowbar, tie a string to the plug end of cord on the back of stove. Then inside oven, dismount glowbar and pull cord and string into the oven. Use the string to guide the installation of an identical replacement.

Oven burners and thermal cutoff

A clogged oven burner produces an uneven flame that can affect baking and cause a gas odor when you turn it on. High hissing flames indicate an air-gas mix with too much air; yellowish flames, too little. Suspect a faulty thermal cutoff if the burners go off after the oven has been on for a long time at a high setting. **CAUTION:** Never clean or adjust an oven burner while it is on. After you fix it, turn it on to check the results.

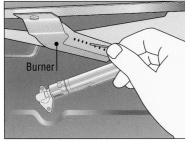

Clean clogged burner ports with a toothpick or a wire. If ports are rusty or grease-caked, go over them with a soft-bristle wire brush. Or remove burners and spray ports with auto degreaser; then rinse well.

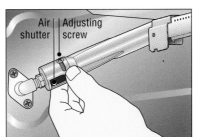

To adjust oven air shutter, loosen screw on shutter and open or close it to obtain steady blue flames 1 in. long with distinct inner cones. Make adjustments with burner off; light oven to check results.

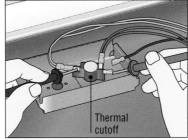

To test thermal cutoff, open cooktop. Lift out burners; unscrew metal shield beneath. Remove a lead from cutoff. Probe both terminals with VOM on RX1. Look for zero reading. If reading is infinity, replace cutoff.

Adjusting oven pilots

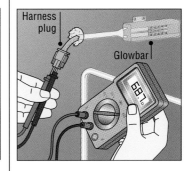

To adjust oven pilot, remove oven bottom. Slowly turn adjusting screw on safety valve to produce a steady blue flame with a yellow tip (or distinct inner core) about ¼ in. high. (On some models, adjusting screw is under thermostat knob.) A pilot flame should increase in size when burner goes on. If it doesn't or if pilot keeps going out, call for service.

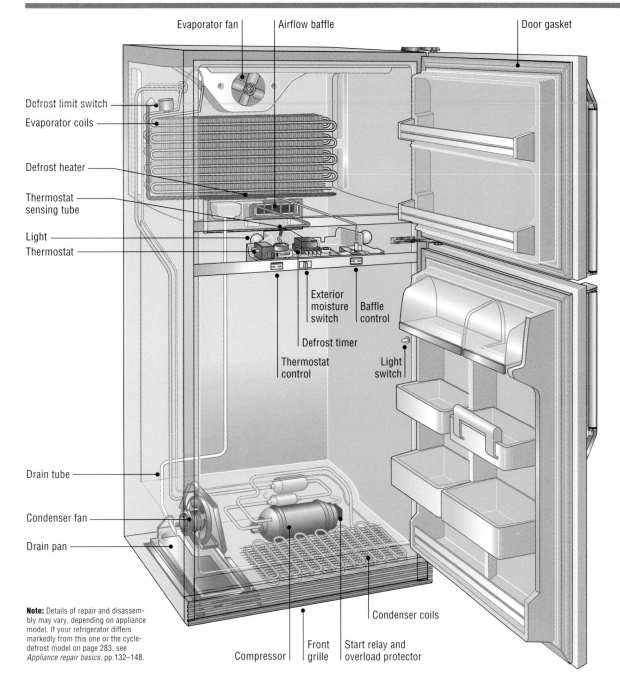

Evaporator fan | Airflow baffle | Door gasket

Defrost limit switch
Evaporator coils
Defrost heater
Thermostat sensing tube
Light
Thermostat
Exterior moisture switch
Baffle control
Defrost timer
Thermostat control
Light switch
Drain tube
Condenser fan
Drain pan
Compressor | Front grille | Start relay and overload protector
Condenser coils

Note: Details of repair and disassembly may vary, depending on appliance model. If your refrigerator differs markedly from this one or the cycle-defrost model on page 283, see *Appliance repair basics,* pp.132–148.

Like an air conditioner (p.236), a refrigerator operates on a standard refrigeration cycle. A compressor forces refrigerant through two connected sets of coils. In the low-pressure area of the evaporator coils inside the unit, the refrigerant becomes a gas and absorbs heat. In the high-pressure condenser coils outside, the gas becomes liquid and loses heat to the room air.

Frost buildup is a major obstacle to efficient refrigerator operation. Most models use either an automatic frost-free or a semiautomatic cycle-defrost system to melt the frost. On frost-free models (left), a timer turns on a defrost heater about twice a day to warm the evaporator coils—the place where frost collects. The coils are encased in the back or floor of the freezer along with a fan that circulates air over the coils and into the food compartments. A cycle-defrost system (p.283) keeps only the refrigerator free of frost; the freezer must be defrosted manually. On both types of defrost systems, the melted frost drains into a pan under the unit and evaporates.

Repairs to the sealed refrigeration system—the compressor, condenser coils, and evaporator coils—are best left to a professional. But repairs to most other parts are relatively easy. A common problem is lint- and dust-clogged condenser coils; with airflow across the coils blocked, the unit may stop running or run continuously. Vacuuming the coils regularly will extend the refrigerator's life and reduce running costs.

ENVIRONMENTAL HINTS

Ozone-destroying refrigerants

If you have work done on the refrigeration system of your refrigerator or air conditioner, there may be a charge for capturing the old refrigerant. It is illegal to release ozone-depleting chlorofluorocarbons (CFC's or Freon) and hydrochlorofluorocarbons (HCFC's) into the atmosphere. If you discard an appliance, you may also have to arrange for a licensed technician to capture the refrigerant. (Ask to see his Ozone Depletion Prevention card as proof of compliance with the regulations.) Restrictions on making CFC's began in 1995. Recycled CFC's are being used to recharge existing units; most new refrigerators use less-damaging substances.

Troubleshooting

SYMPTOM	POSSIBLE CAUSE	SOLUTION
Won't run; light off	No power or faulty power cord	See *General troubleshooting*, p.144.
Won't run; light on	Thermostat off	Turn thermostat on. ◇
	Overheated compressor	Vacuum condenser coils (p.282). ◇
	Obstructed or faulty condenser fan	Remove obstruction. ◇ Or test and replace (p.280). ◆ ▪
	Faulty thermostat	Test and replace (p.281). ◆ ▪
	Faulty defrost timer	Test and replace (p.281). ◆ ▪
	Faulty start relay or overload protector	Test and replace (p.281). ◆ ▪
	Faulty compressor	Test and have serviced (p.281). ◆ ▪
Cycles on and off often	Dirty condenser coils	Vacuum coils (p.282). ◇
	Obstructed or faulty condenser fan	Remove obstruction. ◇ Or test and replace (p.280). ◆ ▪
	Mispositioned thermostat sensing tube	Reposition (pp.281, 283). ◆
	Faulty start relay or overload protector	Test and replace (p.281). ◆ ▪
	Faulty compressor	Test and have serviced (p.281). ◆ ▪
Runs all the time or cools poorly	Thermostat too high or too low	Put on colder or warmer setting. ◇
	Frost buildup	See *Doesn't defrost*, below. Defrost cycle-defrost model. ◇
	Dust-clogged condenser coils	Vacuum coils (p.282). ◇
	Obstructed condenser fan	Remove obstruction. ◇
	Frosted evaporator plate *(cycle-defrost unit)*	Wash with dishwasher detergent; rinse well (p.283). ◇
	Door not closing by itself	Level refrigerator (p.280). ◇
	Warped door or damaged door gasket	Check and realign door (p.280). ◆ Or replace gasket (p.280). ◆
	Lights stay on when door is closed	Test and replace door switch (p.280). ◇ ▪
	Faulty defrost timer	Test and replace (p.281). ◆ ▪
	Faulty condenser fan	Test and replace (p.280). ◆ ▪
	Faulty thermostat	Test and replace (p.281). ◆ ▪
	Faulty evaporator fan	Test and replace (p.282). ◆ ▪
	Loss of refrigerant	Have appliance serviced.
Gets too cold	Thermostat too low	Put on warmer setting. ◇
	Faulty thermostat	Test and replace (p.281). ◆ ▪
Doesn't defrost	Faulty defrost heater or defrost limit switch	Test and replace (p.282). ◆ ▪
	Faulty defrost timer	Test and replace (p.281). ◆ ▪
Shell sweats	Exterior moisture switch off or faulty	Turn switch on (p.281). ◇ Or test and replace (p.281). ◆ ▪
	Faulty mullion heater	Have heater serviced.
Leaks inside or on floor	Clogged drain tube	Clear tube (p.282). ◇
	Misaligned drain pan	Reposition pan. ◇
	Leaky icemaker inlet valve	Tighten plumbing connections (p.284). ◇ Or replace valve. ◆
Noisy	Refrigerator not level	Level (p.280). ◇
	Tubing hitting cabinet	Gently bent tubing away. ◇
	Obstructed or faulty condenser fan	Remove obstruction. ◇ Or test and replace (p.280). ◆ ▪
	Evaporator fan faulty or hitting frost	Test and replace (p.282). ◆ ▪ If frosted, see *Doesn't defrost*, above.
Light out	Loose or burned-out bulb	Tighten or replace. ◇
	Faulty door switch	Test and replace (p.280). ◇ ▪

Degree of difficulty: Simple ◇   Average ◆   Complex ◆   Volt-ohm meter required: ▪

Gaining access

To open front grille, grasp it near the ends and gently pull it straight out. On some models, swing the bottom out and up. **CAUTION:** Always unplug the refrigerator (or turn off power to it at the service panel) before opening it for repairs.

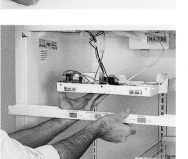

To remove rear access panel, use a nut driver or screwdriver to remove screws holding panel in place. Removing this panel allows you to reach the compressor and condenser fan and coils.

To access control panel, remove its front cover, usually held by a couple of screws and fitted into slots in the cabinet at the sides. Then unscrew the control panel from top of refrigerator compartment.

To reach evaporator and defrost heater, take out the screws in back of the freezer and carefully pull out back panel. On some models, these parts are under the floor of the freezer; to reach them, you take out the freezer's bottom panel.

279

Door repairs

A damaged gasket or a warped or sagging door makes the refrigerator run overtime (and encourages frost in a non-frost-free model). Besides the dollar bill test (below), you can check the door seal by putting a 150-watt outdoor floodlight in the compartment. Then darken the room and look for light seepage. Look at the door from different angles, moving the light cord away from the side you are checking.

When replacing a gasket, putting the new one in hot water makes it easier to handle. To keep the new gasket from bowing out at the corners, put a small bead of cord caulk (sold by refrigeration suppliers) under each corner.

A door often sags because the refrigerator is not level. Instead of adjustable casters (below), many models have threaded legs. To adjust them, tilt the refrigerator back, rest the front on a scrap 2 x 4, and screw the legs in or out.

The door light switch on some models is in the control panel, not in the door frame as shown below. To test it, open the control panel (p.279).

Condenser fan

Poor cooling, a clacking noise, or short cycling may indicate a condenser fan problem. To reach the fan, unplug the refrigerator and remove the rear access panel (p.279). Before testing the fan motor, clean the condenser coils (see *Use and care*, p.282) and look for obstructed blades. If the blades still don't spin freely, the motor has failed.

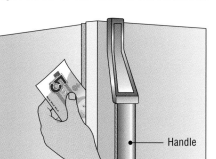

Check door seal in several places. Close door on a five-dollar bill. Look for slight resistance as you pull it out. Or put light inside and look for seeping light in dark room (see text above).

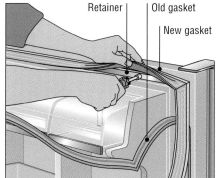

Retainer · Old gasket · New gasket

Replace gasket one section at a time. Lift old gasket edge and loosen (don't remove) screws. Pull old gasket from under retainer strip, and slip new one into place. Retighten screws.

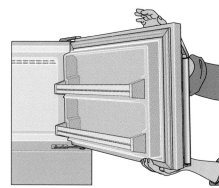

To realign warped door, loosen gasket retaining screws slightly (see left). Then grasp the door and twist it until it fits flush against frame when you close it. Retighten screws.

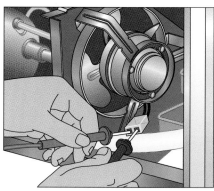

To test fan motor, trace and disconnect leads. With VOM on RX1, probe terminals. Look for reading between 50 and 200 ohms; replace if much higher or infinity.

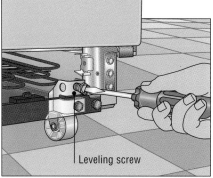

Leveling screw

To level refrigerator, place level on top. Remove grille; turn screw on each wheel (a clockwise turn raises unit). Tilting unit back slightly helps door shut better, but keep unit level if it has an icemaker.

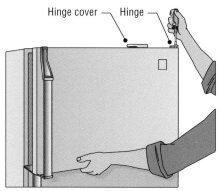

Hinge cover — Hinge

To tighten loose hinge, lift up door as you tighten hinge screws with a screwdriver or nut driver. Top freezer door hinge often has a plastic or metal cover that pops off with gentle prying.

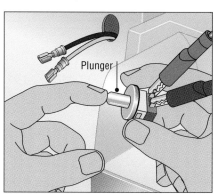

Plunger

To test door switch, unplug refrigerator, pry out switch, and take off leads. With VOM on RX1, clip probes to terminals. Look for infinity reading when you press in plunger, zero when you release it.

To replace fan motor, take out mounting bolts with socket wrench and lift out fan unit, being careful not to bend refrigerant tubing. A retainer clip usually holds blades on motor shaft.

Control panel

The control panel houses the thermostat, its sensing tube, and the dial that controls a baffle that lets cold freezer air into the refrigerator. It may also contain the door light switch, the defrost timer (below), the defrost heater test terminals (p.282), and an exterior moisture control switch. This last switch (also called an energy saver switch because turning it off in dry weather saves energy) turns on a "mullion" heater that keeps the refrigerator shell from sweating on hot humid days.

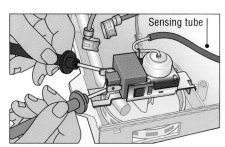

To test thermostat, take off leads and turn dial to coldest setting. With VOM on RX1, probe terminals; look for zero reading. Unmount thermostat, set on warmest setting, and put in working freezer for 30 min. Test again; look for infinity reading.

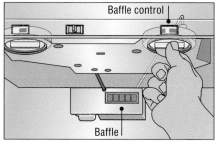

Check baffle that regulates airflow between freezer and refrigerator by moving dial that controls it. If damper doesn't move, open control panel and check mechanical linkage between control and baffle.

To test exterior moisture control switch, take off leads. With VOM on RX1, clip probes to terminals. Look for zero reading when switch is on and infinity reading when switch is off.

Testing and replacing defrost timer

This timer activates the heater that melts frost in the evaporator for 10 to 20 minutes every 10 to 12 hours. In the process, it turns the compressor off and on. If it fails, the compressor may not run. Or the heater may not go on, eventually causing a hidden ice buildup that blocks the cold-air flow and disables the evaporator fan. An access hole lets you test the timer. If the timer isn't in the control panel, look behind the front grille or behind the rear access panel.

Compressor

To reach the compressor, *unplug the refrigerator* and open the rear access panel (p.279). Take off the spring clip holding the box cover on the compressor. Then pull the overload protector and start relay off the compressor pins. On some models, the overload protector is like the one shown for an air conditioner (p.238) and the relay like the one shown for a dehumidifier (p.251). If the unit has a capacitor instead of a start relay, be sure to discharge the capacitor (p.146) first.

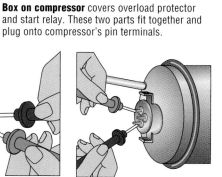

Box on compressor covers overload protector and start relay. These two parts fit together and plug onto compressor's pin terminals.

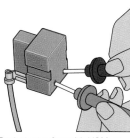

Test overload protector with VOM on RX1. Probe the wire terminal and the terminal that fits on the compressor pin. Look for zero reading; replace if infinity or high ohms.

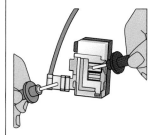

Test start relay with VOM on RX1. Remove a lead and probe terminals that fit on compressor pins. Look for reading of 20 to 100 ohms; replace if much higher or lower.

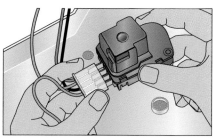

Probe all possible compressor pin pairings with VOM on RX1. Look for partial resistance on each. Test for ground on RX100: Probe bare housing and each terminal. All should read infinity.

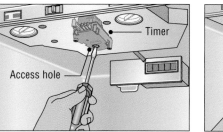

1 If compressor fails to run, turn timer until it clicks. If compressor goes on, timer is faulty. If unit isn't defrosting automatically and turning timer stops compressor or fan, timer is faulty.

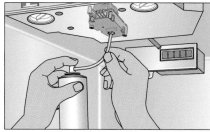

2 Before replacing timer, spray it with electrical contact cleaner through access hole and turn it a few times. Stop just before a click and wait to see if timer advances on its own.

3 To replace timer, unplug refrigerator and open control panel (p.279). Remove screws holding timer to panel and pull off leads. If wires aren't in a plug, move them one at a time to new timer.

281

Large appliances ▪ Refrigerators / frost-free

Evaporator and defrost heater

In a frost-free unit, the evaporator coils, their fan, and the defrost heater are located behind the freezer's back wall or under its floor. The fan, which circulates cold air between the coils and the two food compartments, is controlled by the door switch, the thermostat, or both. To check the fan, open both doors, wait for the compressor to go on, and hold in the door switch. If you can't hear the fan running, test the fan (below).

The defrost heater, which melts frost on the coils, is cycled on by the defrost timer (p.281). If the frost melts before the end of the defrost cycle, the defrost limit switch turns the heater off. The heater may be a metal rod, a wire wrapped in foil, or a coil inside a glass tube. All are tested the same way. Test terminals for the heater are often located in the control panel or under a doorjamb; check the wiring diagram. Or test the heater leads inside the evaporator compartment.

The evaporator compartment

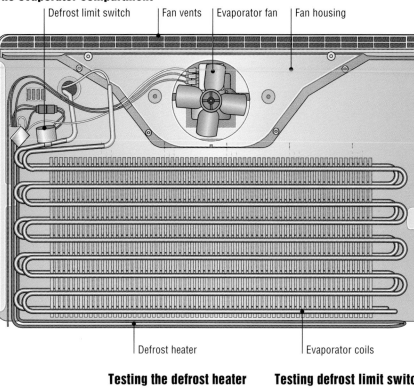

Defrost limit switch | Fan vents | Evaporator fan | Fan housing

Defrost heater | Evaporator coils

USE AND CARE

Check the temperature of both the refrigerator and freezer compartments periodically. In the refrigerator compartment, let a glass of water (right) cool near the center of the compartment for 24 hours. Then put a refrigerator-freezer thermometer in the water for a few minutes. Look for a reading between 34° and 40°F (1.1° and 4.4°C). In the freezer, put the thermometer between two food packages that have chilled for 24 hours. Look for a reading between 0° and 4°F (–17.8° and –15.5°C). If necessary, adjust the temperature setting and repeat the test.

Vacuum the condenser coils under (or on the back of) the unit regularly—more frequently if you have a shedding pet. Unplug the refrigerator and push the crevice tool as far under the unit as you can (left). Try not to bend the condenser tubing or the coil fins.

For maximum efficiency, keep the freezer compartment full of frozen items but leave room for air to circulate between items in the refrigerator compartment.

Wash the compartments, drawers, and shelves twice a year with a solution of baking soda and water. Also clean the drain pan. Wipe the gasket every couple of months. Clean spills promptly.

Clear a clogged drain tube by using a baster to flush water through the tube. Then pour in a teaspoon of ammonia or bleach to prevent a recurrence of the probable culprit, algae spores.

Testing the evaporator fan

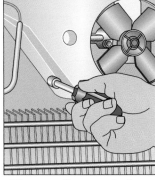

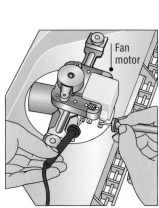

Fan motor

1 To remove the evaporator fan, unplug unit; open back panel (or floor) of freezer (p.279). Then unscrew housing holding fan, and take off leads going to fan motor.

2 With VOM on RX1, probe motor terminals (except green ground wire terminal). Look for moderate resistance (50 to 200 ohms). Replace fan if much lower or infinity.

Testing the defrost heater

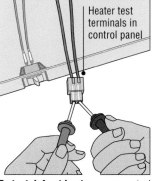

Heater test terminals in control panel

To test defrost heater, open control panel (p.279). With VOM on RX1, probe test terminals. Look for 15- to 100-ohm reading. If infinity, turn defrost timer (p.281); test again.

Testing defrost limit switch

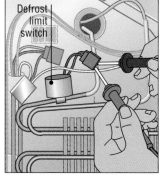

Defrost limit switch

To test defrost limit switch, trace and disconnect leads. With VOM on RX1, probe leads. Look for infinity reading when switch is warm, zero after 20 min. in working freezer.

Refrigerators / cycle-defrost

In a typical cycle-defrost refrigerator, refrigerant is pumped through evaporator plates in the back of the refrigerator compartment and in the back, top, and bottom of the freezer. The temperature is controlled by a thermostat.

In the refrigerator compartment, a defrost heater connected to the plate cycles on after each running cycle to melt any frost. (On models without a heater, the thermostat lets the temperature rise to a few degrees above freezing to melt the frost.) A tube carries the melted frost to the drain pan under the refrigerator. The freezer is defrosted manually by turning the thermostat dial to the *Defrost* or *Off* position.

Don't touch the evaporator plates. Skin oils and acids can cause spots that cause an excessive buildup of frost. To remove such spots, wash them with hot water and an automatic dishwasher detergent labeled safe for aluminum.

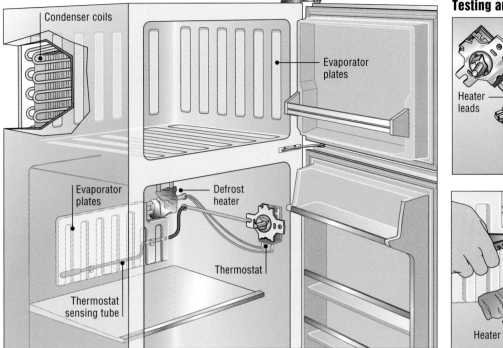

Condenser coils
Evaporator plates
Evaporator plates
Defrost heater
Thermostat
Thermostat sensing tube

Testing and replacing the heater

1 To test defrost heater, disconnect its leads from thermostat. With VOM on RX1, clip probes to leads. Look for reading between 200 and 1,000 ohms; a much higher reading or infinity indicates defective heater.

Heater leads

2 To replace defrost heater, pry off its cover (Step 3, below). Untape and cut its leads. Connect new leads with crimp-on in-line wire connectors. Fill them with silicone sealer and cover securely with tape.

Heater

Testing and replacing the thermostat

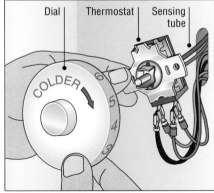

Dial   Thermostat   Sensing tube
COLDER

1 Unplug refrigerator. To access thermostat, pull or pry dial off shaft. Then unscrew thermostat and gently pull it out of wall. Take extra care not to make a sharp bend in the metal capillary sensing tube attached to thermostat.

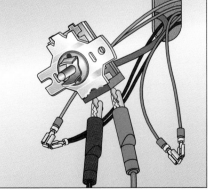

2 Test thermostat when refrigerator is near room temperature. Take off leads and turn thermostat to *Off* position. With VOM on RX1, clip probes to terminals. Look for infinity reading. Turn to coldest setting; look for zero.

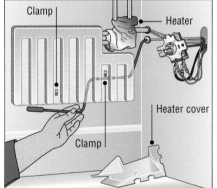

Clamp
Heater
Heater cover
Clamp

3 To replace thermostat, pry off heater cover. Then loosen (don't remove) screws that secure the clamps that holds the thermostat sensing tube bulb.

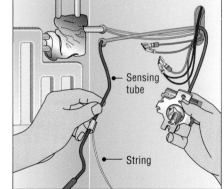

Sensing tube
String

4 Tape a string to sensing tube and pull tube out of wall. Tape string to new thermostat tube and use it to guide tube into place. Make sure to replace plastic sleeve, if any, on sensing tube, and be careful not to kink the tube.

An icemaker uses water tapped from a nearby pipe to provide a constant supply of ice cubes. The water flows through a tube to an inlet valve on the back of the refrigerator. When water is needed, the valve lets the water flow into an ice cube mold, where it freezes.

When a thermostat senses that the ice is cold enough, a heater melts the ice surface so that ejector blades can push cubes into a bin. The cycle repeats until a shutoff arm stops it when the bin is full.

Symptoms of malfunction include no ice or too much ice. Cubes with watery or hollow centers result from too little water; a layer of water or ice in the bin, from too much water. Each half-turn of the water supply screw changes the water flow by about 9 cubic centimeters (⅓ ounce); don't make more than 1½ turns in either direction.

Servicing the water inlet valve

This valve controls the water supply to the ice cube mold. Reduced supply may indicate a defective or clogged valve or filter. If you replace the valve, throw out the first few batches of ice. They may be discolored or have an off-taste.

Back of module holds motor, circuits, cam, and lever that control ejector blades.

Lever | Cam | Motor

Housing | Wiring | Ejector blades | Ice cube mold

Water inlet tube

SMALL | LARGE

Cover

Module

Thermostat

Heater terminal

Shutoff arm

Ice cube size knob (often a lever or small screw)

Water inlet valve

Water supply tube

Saddle valve

Cold-water pipe

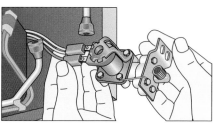

1 Turn off water supply at saddle valve on pipe. Disconnect inlet valve from refrigerator (below, left); unscrew tubes from valve, draining excess water into a bowl. Unplug wires from valve.

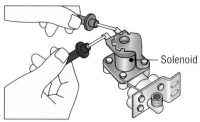

Solenoid

2 Test valve solenoid. With VOM on RX10, probe both terminals. Look for a reading between 200 and 500 ohms. If significantly higher or lower, replace the solenoid.

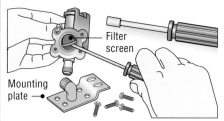

Filter screen

Mounting plate

3 Take off plate. Remove filter screen from water inlet with needle-nose pliers or small screwdriver. Wash clogged screen with toothbrush under running water. Replace if rusted.

Gaining access

To remove front cover of icemaker, unplug refrigerator and take off knob, if any. Insert a coin into slot in lower back edge of cover and turn coin to pry off cover.

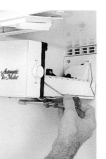

To unmount icemaker, unplug refrigerator and take out ice bin, shelves, and vertical partition. Remove top and bottom screws. Disconnect icemaker wires from harness connector or socket; remove unit from freezer.

To reach water inlet valve, unplug refrigerator, pull it away from wall, and remove back access panel (p.279). Then take out screws holding inlet valve to refrigerator.

Modular controls

An icemaker's motor and switches may be in a module that must be replaced as a unit if any one part is bad. Holes in the module let you test the parts.

CAUTION: Unplug the refrigerator before testing the icemaker motor or heater. Don't touch the jumper wire when testing the thermostat.

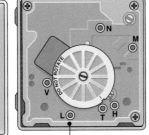

To use test holes in module, take off the ice-maker cover and insert VOM probes in the holes. The components to test are usually listed inside the cover. When testing, shutoff arm should be down and ejector blades should be in normal resting (2 o'clock) position.

Test holes

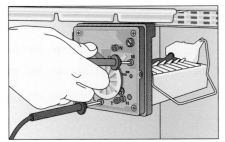

Test module motor with VOM on RX1. Insert probes in test holes L and M. Look for a reading indicating significant continuity. Test heater in holes L and H; look for reading near 72 ohms.

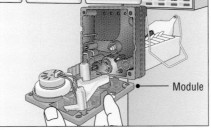

Module

To replace module, take out screws and pull off. Replace entire module. If heater tests faulty, un-mount icemaker, unscrew housing from ice mold–heater unit, and replace mold-heater unit.

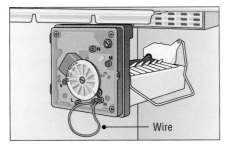

Wire

Test thermostat with freezer cold. Unplug refrigerator. Insert bare ends of an insulated wire in holes T and H. *Without touching wire,* plug in refrigerator. If motor runs, replace thermostat.

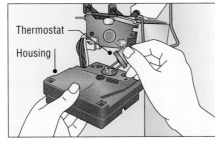

Thermostat

Housing

To replace thermostat, unplug refrigerator and unmount module and housing (above). Slip thermostat out of housing. Replace thermostat, using special metallic putty where it touches mold.

Separate controls

In a non-modular icemaker, the motor, switches, and thermostat can all be tested and replaced separately. To reach them, *unplug the refrigerator.* Then take off the front cover of the ice-maker and the mounting plate under it. There are usually three switches: The on-off switch is activated by the shutoff arm. The holding switch keeps power flowing to the ejector blades during the ice release phase. The water inlet valve switch controls the flow of water from the inlet valve. When replacing the thermostat, use the recommended heat-transferring metallic putty between it and the ice mold.

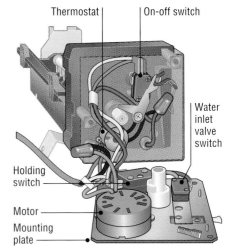

Thermostat | On-off switch

Water inlet valve switch

Holding switch

Motor

Mounting plate

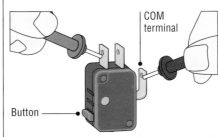

COM terminal

Button

To test on-off or holding switch, unmount it and take off leads. With VOM on RX1, probe COM terminal and other two terminals in turn. Look for zero reading on one terminal, infinity on the other. Push button in; test again. Look for reverse readings.

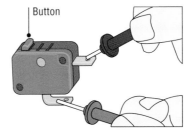

Button

To test water inlet valve switch, unmount it and take off leads. With VOM on RX1, probe both terminals. Look for zero reading with button out, infinity when you push button in.

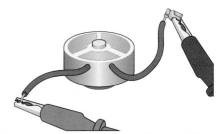

To test thermostat, unmount it, disconnect its leads, and let it warm to room temperature. With VOM on RX1, probe both leads. Look for infinity reading. Place thermostat in a working freezer, and test again. Look for zero reading.

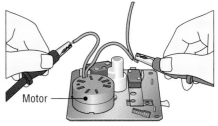

Motor

To test motor, trace and disconnect motor leads. With VOM on RX10, probe both leads. Look for a reading indicating significant continuity. Replace if infinity or zero.

A trash compactor compresses trash into easily disposable bundles. A boxlike ram inside the unit is held by two power nuts that ride down and back up a pair of threaded shafts called power screws. A chain-and-sprocket assembly driven by a split-phase motor (p.139) turns the screws. In use, the ram moves down until it stalls against compacted trash. A directional switch (triggered when the ram started down) reverses the motor's rotation, moving the ram back up. As the ram reaches the top of the unit, a top limit switch stops the motor. Both switches may be combined in newer units.

Because the ram exerts great force, the trash compactor has several safety switches. A drawer switch prevents operation with the drawer open. Most units have a keyed on-off switch. When it is not in use, keep the unit locked and the key away from children.

A freestanding model is easier to access for repair than an under-the-counter unit. Typical problems are failed switches and worn sprockets, chain, roller bearings, and power nuts. The split-phase motor may need repair or replacement (see *General troubleshooting,* p.146). When making repairs, lubricate parts following the manufacturer's directions.

Adjusting drive chain tension. Periodically check the chain's tension by pressing your thumb against it (see *Gaining access,* right). If there's more than ½ inch of play, loosen the motor mounting bolts; move the motor to adjust the chain's tension, and retighten the bolts.

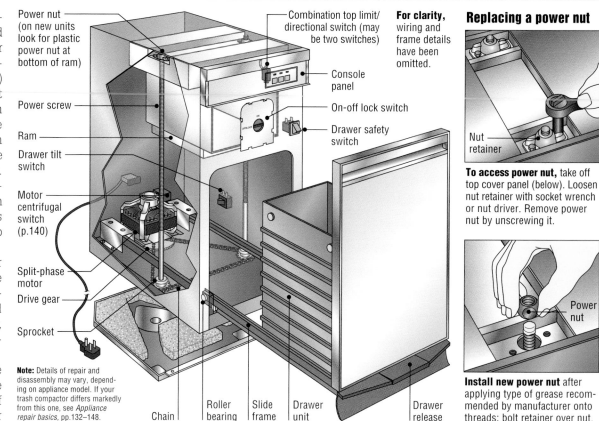

Power nut (on new units look for plastic power nut at bottom of ram)

Combination top limit/ directional switch (may be two switches)

For clarity, wiring and frame details have been omitted.

Power screw

Console panel

On-off lock switch

Ram

Drawer safety switch

Drawer tilt switch

Motor centrifugal switch (p.140)

Split-phase motor

Drive gear

Sprocket

Note: Details of repair and disassembly may vary, depending on appliance model. If your trash compactor differs markedly from this one, see *Appliance repair basics,* pp.132–148.

Chain | Roller bearing | Slide frame | Drawer unit | Drawer release

Replacing a power nut

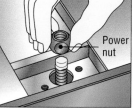

Nut retainer

To access power nut, take off top cover panel (below). Loosen nut retainer with socket wrench or nut driver. Remove power nut by unscrewing it.

Power nut

Install new power nut after applying type of grease recommended by manufacturer onto threads; bolt retainer over nut.

Gaining access

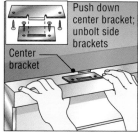

Push down center bracket; unbolt side brackets

Center bracket

To unplug an under-the-counter unit, release bracket(s) at center or side of top. Pull out and remove drawer; slide out compactor to reach plug.

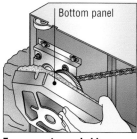

Bottom panel

To remove top and side cover panels on either unit, unbolt them with a nut driver. Before removing bottom panel, tip unit over onto blanket or padding.

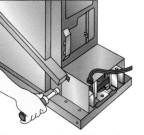

To access motor, chain, and switches on counter unit, unbolt cover panels with nut driver. To access these parts on freestanding unit, remove drive gear.

Remove console panel by unscrewing bottom of console and pushing panel up or down. You may have to remove console panel to remove top cover panel.

Troubleshooting

PROBLEM	POSSIBLE CAUSE	SOLUTION
Compactor won't start	Power off at outlet or faulty power cord	See *General troubleshooting*, p.144.
	Drawer partway open	Close drawer completely and start unit. ◇
	Faulty centrifugal, directional, drawer safety, or on-off switch	To test centrifugal and directional switches, see below; for drawer safety or on-off switch, see *General troubleshooting*, p.145. ◆ ▨
	Loose terminal or damaged wire	Reconnect loose terminal; replace damaged wire. ◆
	Split-phase motor overloaded	Let motor cool 10 min. Check chain tension (facing page); look for worn or clogged power nuts and screws. Test centrifugal and directional switches (below). Adjust or replace bad parts. ◆ ▨
	Faulty split-phase motor	See *General troubleshooting*, p.146; test centrifugal switch. ◆ ▨
Compactor starts, then stops	Drawer open during cycle; restart light on	Turn switch to *Start*. Motor should start. While holding switch, push front of drawer; release switch right away. ◇
	Split-phase motor overloaded	See *Compactor won't start*, above. ◆ ▨
	Faulty top limit switch	Test switch (below); replace if defective. ◆ ▨
Motor runs but ram doesn't move	Loose or damaged chain, faulty drive gear	Check chain tension; replace faulty chain or gear (right). ◆
	Worn power nuts	Replace both power nuts (facing page). ◆
Compactor makes odd noises	Loose or damaged chain or faulty drive gear	See *Motor runs but ram doesn't move*, above. ◆
	Dry power screws	Lubricate with grease recommended by manufacturer. ◆
	Dirty ram cover	Remove ram cover and scrape off debris with a putty knife. ◇
Drawer won't open	Faulty drawer tilt, drawer safety, on-off, or top limit switch	To test top limit switch, see below; for other switches, see *General troubleshooting*, p.145. ◆ ▨
Jammed ram	Debris in power screw, power nut, or ram	Remove debris with plastic-bristle brush or putty knife. ◆
Ram stops partway	Faulty directional switch	Test switch (below); replace if bad. ◆ ▨
	Faulty split-phase drive motor	See *Compactor won't start*, above. ◆ ▨
Compactor starts but doesn't compact completely	Debris in power screw threads or nuts	Remove foreign material. ◇
	Worn power nuts	Replace both power nuts (facing page). ◆
	Dry power screws	Lubricate with grease recommended by manufacturer. ◆
Compactor won't stop	Faulty on-off or top limit switch	See *Drawer won't open*, above. ◆ ▨

Degree of difficulty: Simple ◇   Average ◆   Complex ◆   Volt-ohm meter required: ▨

Replacing or adjusting the chain

1 Unplug the unit and access the motor (facing page). Loosen the motor mounting bolts with a nut driver; slide motor toward front of unit. Pry off the C-clip at the shaft (see *Tips from the pros*, p.189).

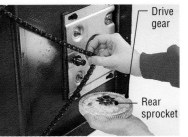

Drive gear

Rear sprocket

2 Gently pull the drive gear off the shaft. Remove the chain from the drive gear's rear sprocket. Unbolt the power screws from the frame—*do not remove the nuts on the power screws.*

Power screw

3 Without rotating them, pull the power screws just past the frame; remove the chain from the sprockets. Place a new chain around the sprockets; adjust the chain tension (facing page). Reassemble.

Testing the centrifugal switch

1 Unplug unit; access motor (facing page). Disconnect and remove switch. Set VOM on RX1. Probe opposite terminals closest to button (labeled BR and BU here; check your model's wiring diagram).

Button

2 Press button. The meter should read zero ohms. Release button; VOM should show infinity. If switch fails either of these tests, replace it.

Testing a combination top limit/directional switch

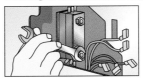

1 Remove console panel (facing page). Label and detach switch wires. Unbolt switch with open-end wrench. Set VOM on RX1. Attach one VOM clip to terminal Y, second clip to R (check wiring diagram for your model).

2 Press the switch lever or button. The VOM should show zero ohms. Move the second clip from R to each of the other terminals in turn. VOM should show infinity each time.

3 Release lever. Attach one clip to terminal Y, the other to GY. VOM should show zero ohms. Move the second clip from GY to each of the other terminals in turn; VOM should show infinity each time.

4 Attach one clip to BR, other clip to O or V; look for zero ohms with lever out, infinity when pressed. Move second clip to other terminals in turn; look for infinity readings with lever both up and pressed.

Large appliances ▪ Washing machines

Despite its many settings and cycles, a washing machine is a simple device that does just four things: it mixes hot and cold water, agitates this water with detergent and soiled clothing in a large tub, rinses the clothing in fresh water, then spins it damp-dry.

Electromagnetically controlled inlet valves regulate the mixture and flow of hot and cold water into the tub. A motor and transmission (gear assembly) drive an agitator to wash the clothes, then spin the inner basket to "wring" them out. The motor may drive the transmission directly, as in the model shown here, or by means of a belt (p.293). A pump recirculates the water through a lint filter during the wash cycle, then empties the tub before the spin cycle. A timer and selector switches control the sequence.

If a machine washes poorly, make sure you are using it properly (see *Use and care,* below, or your owner's manual). Before opening the machine to make a repair, unplug the power cord, turn off the faucets, and drain or bail out any tub or hose water.

USE AND CARE

Sort laundry into white, colorfast, and non-colorfast items and wash them separately. Also separate heavily soiled items from lightly soiled ones.

Wash lint producers, such as towels and chenille, separately from lint attractors, such as synthetics and permanent press. Turn lint producers inside out if possible.

Don't overload. Drop in items loosely. Don't pack or wrap them around the agitator. Mix large and small items for a balanced load. Judge load size by the space that items take up, not by weight. Match the water level to the load size.

If you have hard water, have a water softener installed on the hot-water line.

To avoid yellow iron stains, add a nonprecipitating water conditioner during the wash and deep rinse cycles or install an iron filter on the water line. If the iron source is your water pipes, just run the water for a few minutes first.

Use the appropriate bleach for the type of fabric you are washing (chlorine bleach for white and colorfast cottons; all-fabric bleach for synthetics and blends).

Clean the lint filter after each use (unless the machine has a self-cleaning filter).

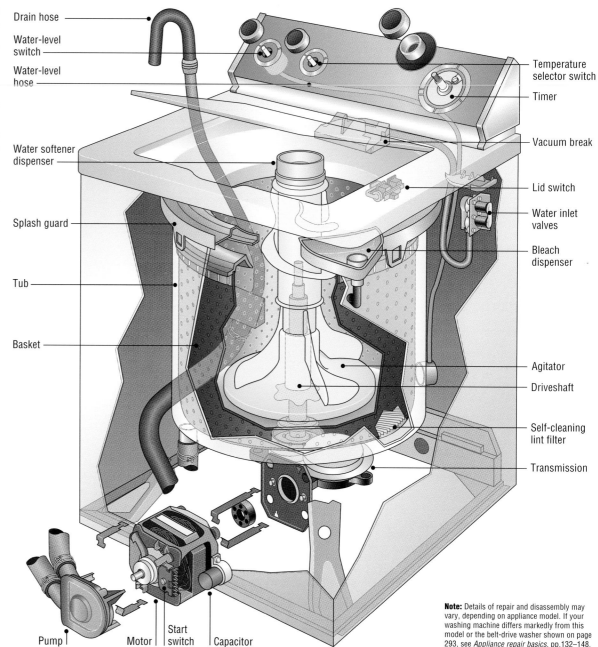

Drain hose
Water-level switch
Water-level hose
Water softener dispenser
Splash guard
Tub
Basket
Temperature selector switch
Timer
Vacuum break
Lid switch
Water inlet valves
Bleach dispenser
Agitator
Driveshaft
Self-cleaning lint filter
Transmission
Pump
Motor
Start switch
Capacitor

Note: Details of repair and disassembly may vary, depending on appliance model. If your washing machine differs markedly from this model or the belt-drive washer shown on page 293, see *Appliance repair basics,* pp.132–148.

Troubleshooting

SYMPTOM	POSSIBLE CAUSE	SOLUTION
Won't run	Power off at outlet or faulty power cord	See *General troubleshooting,* p.144.
	Faulty lid switch	Test and replace (p.291). ◆ ▪
	Faulty motor, capacitor, or start switch	Test and replace (p.292). ◆ ▪ Or have serviced.
	Faulty timer	Test and replace (p.290). ◆ ▪
No water	Kinked hoses or clogged inlet screens	Straighten hoses; clean screens (p.290). ◇
	Faulty water-level switch or timer	Test and replace (p.290). ◆ ▪
	Faulty lid switch	Test and replace (p.291). ◆ ▪
	Faulty inlet valve	Test and replace (p.290). ◆ ▪
	Faulty temperature selector switch	Test and replace (p.290). ◆ ▪
Fills slowly	Faucets partly opened or low water pressure	Open faucets fully. ◇ Have pressure checked (p.290).
	Kinked hoses or clogged inlet screens	Straighten hoses; clean screens (p.290). ◇
Water too hot or too cold	Faucets not open equally	Open both faucets fully. ◇
	Faulty temperature selector switch	Test and replace (p.290). ◆ ▪
	Faulty inlet valve	Test and replace (p.290). ◆ ▪
Won't empty	Kinked drain hose	Straighten. Or replace (p.234). ◇
	Faulty agitate/spin solenoid *(belt-drive model)*	Test and replace (p.293). ◆ ▪
	Faulty drive belt *(belt-drive model)*	Adjust or replace belt (p.293). ◆
	Clogged or faulty pump	Clean or replace (p.292). ◆
Leaks on floor	Leaky hoses or loose hose fittings	Replace (pp.234, 290). ◇ Or tighten fittings (p.290). ◇
	Clogged lint filter	Clean filter (see owner's manual). ◇
	Faulty tub gasket	Replace gasket (p.291). ◆
	Leaky pump	Replace pump (p.292). ◆
Overflows	Faulty water-level switch	Test and replace (p.290). ◆ ▪
	Stuck inlet valve	Test; clean or replace (p.290). ◆ ▪
Won't agitate	Faulty lid switch	Test and replace (p.291). ◆ ▪
	Faulty timer	Test and replace (p.290). ◆ ▪
	Clothing caught under agitator	Remove agitator to free clothing (p.291). ◇
	Faulty drive belt *(belt-drive model)*	Adjust or replace belt (p.293). ◆
	Faulty agitate/spin solenoid *(belt-drive model)*	Test and replace (p.293). ◆ ▪
	Blocked or seized pump	Free obstruction or replace pump (p.292). ◆
	Faulty transmission	Remove and have serviced (p.292). ◆
Won't spin	Wash load unbalanced or too large	Redistribute load or remove part. ◇
	Faulty lid switch	Test and replace (p.291). ◆ ▪
	Faulty timer	Test and replace (p.290). ◆ ▪
	Faulty drive belt *(belt-drive model)*	Adjust or replace belt (p.293). ◆
	Clothing caught under basket	Remove basket to free clothing (p.291). ◇
	Faulty agitate/spin solenoid *(belt-drive model)*	Test and replace (p.293). ◆ ▪
	Faulty transmission or clutch	Remove and have serviced (p.292). ◆
Noisy or vibrates too much	Wash load unbalanced or machine not level	Redistribute load. ◇ Or adjust legs. ◇
	Broken agitator	Check and replace (p.291). ◇
	Worn transmission	Remove and have serviced (p.292). ◆

Degree of difficulty: Simple ◇   Average ◆   Complex ◆   Volt-ohm meter required: ▪

Gaining access

1 Remove screws at bottom of control panel. Then swing panel up and back. (On some machines, control panel swings forward and may have screws at top or sides.) **CAUTION:** Unplug machine before accessing any internal part.

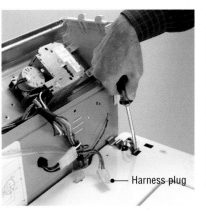

— Harness plug

2 Disconnect the electrical harness plug by squeezing side tab and pulling plug apart. Then remove clip at each rear corner: insert a screwdriver into clip's turned-up front end and pry it back to dislodge clip from hole in cabinet.

3 Tilt cabinet forward and lift it off washer base. Be careful not to snag hoses or other parts when removing cabinet. (For access to belt-drive washers, which usually have a lift-up top and a rear access panel, see page 293.)

Control panel

The timer controls the fill, drain, agitate, and spin cycles. Along with the temperature selector switch, it also opens and closes the hot- and cold-water inlet valves. The water-level switch turns them off when the tub's water reaches the set level; before testing it, check its air hose for deterioration or a loose connection. Check all controls for corroded terminals; clean with emery paper. *Unplug the washer before opening the control panel.*

Water-level switch
Temperature selector switch
Air hose
Timer

Testing the timer and temperature switch

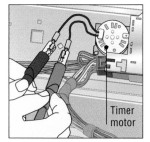

Timer motor

To test timer motor, take off leads. With VOM on RX100, probe leads. Look for reading of 1,100 to 3,000 ohms. To test timer fully, see page 234.

Test temperature switch as described in *Testing a selector switch*, p.234; test terminal pairs indicated on chart on wiring diagram.

Testing the water-level switch

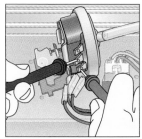

1 With VOM on RX1, probe all possible pairings of the three terminals. Look for zero reading on one pair, infinity on others.

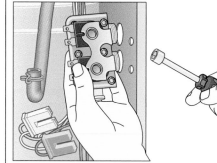

2 Disconnect air hose from tub. Test each pair again while blowing into tube until you hear a click. Look for zero reading on different pair.

Water inlet hoses and valve

Water flow or temperature problems can often be traced to the water inlet hoses or valves. But make sure your water heater is supplying water that is hot enough (p.294). Also make sure the water has sufficient pressure. If the pressure seems low, ask your water company to test the incoming supply or have a plumber check for an obstructed pipe. If you have a well, check its gauge. Most washers require 30 to 80 psi (pounds per square inch) of water pressure.

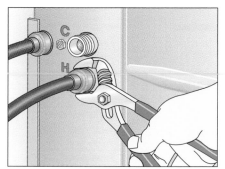

To remove and check hoses, loosen couplings with adjustable pliers, then unscrew hoses. Reinstall carefully to avoid damaging threads.

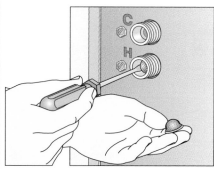

To clean screens, use small screwdriver to carefully pry their edges from ports. Use a socket that just fits inside ports to push screens back in.

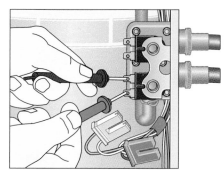

Test inlet valve solenoids with VOM on RX1. Remove leads and probe terminals. Look for reading between 100 and 1,000 ohms on each.

To remove inlet valve image and vacuum break image below.

To remove inlet valve, unclamp and take off hose to tub. Then unbolt valve from cabinet. Unscrew solenoids. Disassemble and clean valve.

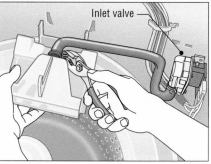

Inlet valve

To remove vacuum break, often necessary to make other repairs, unhook it and remove the hose (p.234) coming from inlet valve.

Disassembling agitator and basket

If you just want to remove the agitator, you needn't open the cabinet. But if you want to remove the splash guard and tub as well, you have to open the cabinet (p.289) and remove the vacuum break (facing page) and any other obstructions or connections. A two-piece agitator held by a recessed bolt is shown here. Many are a single unit held by a nut or bolt under a cap. Some have a side screw. If the agitator or tub is difficult to remove, apply penetrating oil and tap the edges with a rubber mallet.

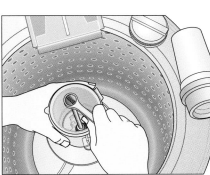

1 Lift off softener dispenser or pry off agitator lid. Take out internal cap. Remove stud and seal, using socket wrench with extension.

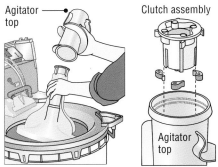

Agitator top

Clutch assembly

Agitator top

2 Lift out agitator top, then bottom (left). Check clutch assembly in top (right) for wear; replace if needed. Many agitators are a single unit.

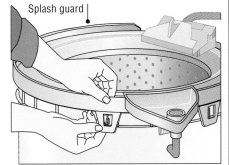

Splash guard

3 Remove splash guard by opening tabs (or prying off metal clips with a screwdriver). Replace gasket under guard if rotted or cracked.

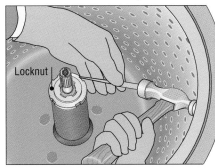

Locknut

4 *Wearing safety goggles and gloves,* remove locknut with hammer and drift punch (or use a spanner wrench). Don't hit the basket.

5 Remove basket by carefully lifting it straight up. Lint filter is inside or under the agitator in some models. Clean or replace it if necessary.

Removing the tub

A failed gasket around the agitator driveshaft can cause leaks. To remove the tub and replace the gasket, first remove the agitator, splash guard, and basket (left). Then unclamp and remove the drain hose and water-level air hose from the tub.

If the metal drive block is difficult to remove (Step 2, below), heat it slightly with a propane torch, then tap it upward with a hammer. If the tub is stubborn, apply a mild solution of soap and water to the center driveshaft.

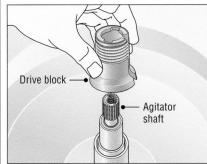

Drive block

Agitator shaft

2 Take the metal drive block off the agitator shaft. If block is stubborn, heat it with a propane torch and tap upward with a hammer.

Testing the lid switch

This safety switch turns off the machine when you open the lid. The switch shown (right) and its wires are a single component. To test it, open the control panel, disconnect the harness plug on the switch wires, and probe the terminals in the plug. To replace the switch, remove its mounting screws and pull out the switch and wires as a unit. If the lid switch has regular slide-on terminals, disconnect the wires when testing the terminals.

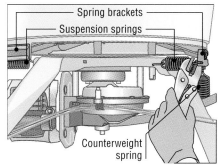

Spring brackets

Suspension springs

Counterweight spring

1 Wearing safety goggles, use locking pliers to remove springs at bottom of tub. Label spring brackets; unscrew brackets and tub from frame.

Gasket

3 Rock tub side to side and pull up. Squeeze gasket and push it out bottom. Push in new gasket from bottom. Soap shaft to reinstall tub.

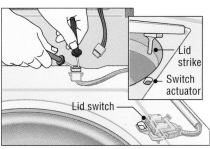

Lid strike

Switch actuator

Lid switch

Test lid switch with VOM on RX1. Probe terminals (except green ground wire) in plug. Look for zero reading with lid closed, infinity when open.

Servicing the motor components

The motor drives the drain pump and, through the transmission, the agitator and basket. To reach the motor on most models, first remove the pump (below).

The capacitor helps the motor start. If it fails, the motor won't run. If the capacitor is not mounted on the motor, look for it inside the control panel. Discharge it (p.146) before testing any part.

The centrifugal switch distributes power to the start and run windings on the motor. If it's faulty, the machine won't start. To test it (Step 3, right), you need to identify the terminals that are paired; check the wiring diagram. A terminal is usually coded with a letter indicating its wire color (for example, BU for blue, W for white, or V for violet).

If you can't isolate the source of a motor problem, take the motor to a repair shop for fuller testing. If you have to replace the motor, the new motor will usually come with a new centrifugal switch and a new capacitor. If the internal parts of the transmission are faulty, have them serviced.

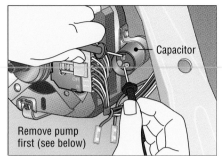

1 To test capacitor, *discharge it* (p.146). Take off leads. With VOM on RX1, probe terminals. Look for zero reading slowly moving to infinity.

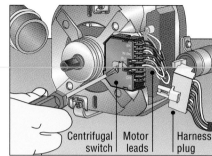

2 Remove centrifugal switch. Take off harness plug. Remove mounting screw and take switch off. Then pry off and label motor leads.

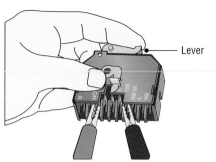

3 With VOM on RX1, probe terminals shown as switch pairs on wiring diagram. Look for zero with lever in, infinity when out (or vice versa).

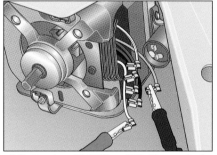

4 Test motor with VOM on RX1. Clip a probe to white lead. Clip other probe to other leads in turn. Look for reading of 1 to 20 ohms on each.

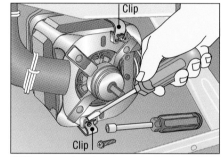

5 To unmount motor, remove screws on retaining clips, pry clips open, and pull motor out. Some motors may be mounted with bolts.

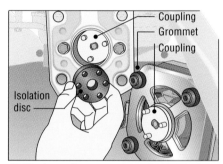

6 Check couplings on motor and transmission, and rubber isolation disc between them, for damage. Remove them and grommets for reuse.

Removing the drain pump

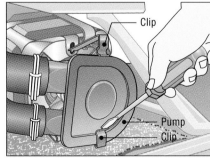

1 With a pan or towel underneath to catch water, pry open retaining clips with a screwdriver and pull pump off motor shaft.

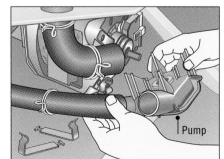

2 To remove hoses, squeeze clamps with pliers and slide clamps up hoses. Carefully twist hoses off pump. Reverse steps to replace pump.

Replacing the transmission and clutch

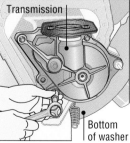

1 Remove agitator and tub (p.291), pump (left), and motor (above). Lay washer on its back to unbolt transmission.

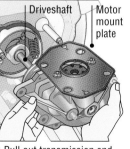

2 Pull out transmission and attached driveshaft. Unbolt and remove motor mounting plate; save for reuse.

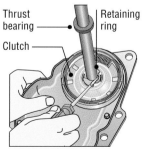

3 Pull thrust bearing off shaft. Pry off retaining ring, and slide clutch off shaft. Reassemble in reverse order.

Common variant: Belt-drive washers

Many washers, especially older ones, are belt driven. On some models you can reach the belt or belts by simply laying the machine on its back; no parts are in the way. To replace the belt on the type shown here, several parts have to be dismantled. But tightening belt tension is fairly simple. Before changing a belt, *unplug the machine,* turn off the faucets, and remove the inlet hoses.

Many belt-drive washers have a special device known as a wigwag—a pair of solenoids that control the shift between agitation and spin cycles. Test both solenoids if the unit won't switch between these cycles.

To test the wigwag or tighten the drive belt, open the rear panel. Opening it also gives access to the motor; to remove it, disconnect its leads and take out its mounting bolts. To reach the basket or tub, release the clips that open the top as on a dryer (p.259). The control panel also opens like a dryer's.

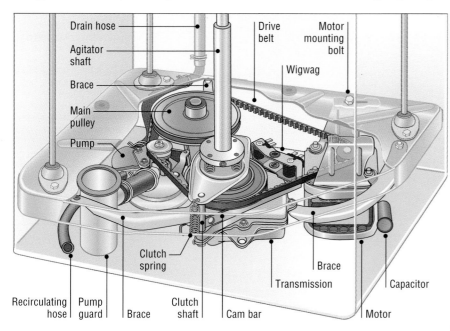

Drain hose — Drive belt — Motor mounting bolt — Wigwag — Agitator shaft — Brace — Main pulley — Pump — Recirculating hose | Pump guard | Brace | Clutch spring | Clutch shaft | Cam bar | Transmission | Brace | Motor | Capacitor

Testing the wigwag

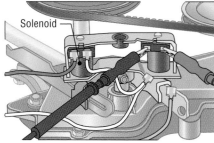

Solenoid

Test wigwag one solenoid at a time. With VOM on RX10, remove leads and probe terminals. Look for reading of 200 to 700 ohms.

Adjusting the drive-belt tension

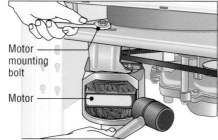

Motor mounting bolt — Motor

To adjust belt tension, open rear access panel. Loosen mounting bolt, and move motor until belt deflects ½ in. when pushed in. Retighten bolt.

Replacing the drive belt

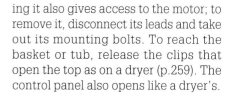

Pump — Brace — Brace — Brace — Bottom of washer

1 Loosen tension on belt (left, below), and lay machine on its back (protect inlet pipes) so that you can work on bottom of machine. Then remove bolts holding pump and braces.

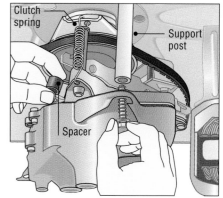

Clutch spring — Support post — Spacer

2 The front support post has a spacer. Remove bolt holding post, and take out spacer. Then unhook and remove the nearby clutch spring.

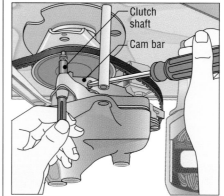

Clutch shaft — Cam bar

3 Rotate main belt pulley until cam bar begins to move out of clutch shaft. Then lift plunger on wigwag, and using large screwdriver as lever, force bar out of shaft completely. Remove shaft.

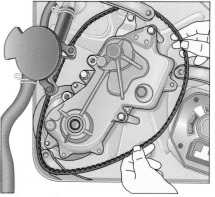

4 Rotate pulley to move cam bar back to its former position. Slip belt out. Put new belt on pulleys, reassemble parts, set machine upright, and tighten belt tension.

293

Large appliances ▪ Water heaters

A water heater is a storage tank with temperature controls and either a gas burner or electric heating elements. The tank is lined with porcelain or plastic to prevent rust. Most units also have a sacrificial anode in the tank; it corrodes over time. Any exposed steel will not rust as long as a working anode is in place. A *pressure relief (t&p) valve* lets water and steam escape if pressure builds due to overheating. A *high-temperature cutoff* shuts the heater down if the water temperature exceeds 190°F (88°C).

Drain the tank every 6 to 12 months. This maintains optimal efficiency by removing sediment particles that collect at the bottom. To drain the tank, shut off the cold-water inlet valve. Open a hot-water tap somewhere in the house. Attach a hose to the drain-cock, and let the water run into a suitable drain. To refill the tank, reopen the inlet valve; when the water runs clear, close the draincock and hot-water tap. Test the pressure relief valve every 6 months by depressing its lever to allow some water to escape. If no water is released, have the heater serviced.

Gas water heater

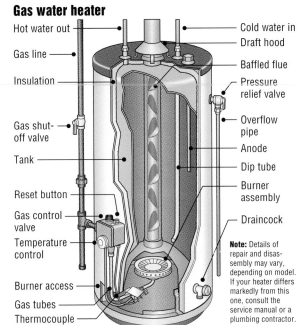

Hot water out
Gas line
Insulation
Gas shut-off valve
Tank
Reset button
Gas control valve
Temperature control
Burner access
Gas tubes
Thermocouple

Cold water in
Draft hood
Baffled flue
Pressure relief valve
Overflow pipe
Anode
Dip tube
Burner assembly
Draincock

Note: Details of repair and disassembly may vary, depending on model. If your heater differs markedly from this one, consult the service manual or a plumbing contractor.

Correcting gas heater problems

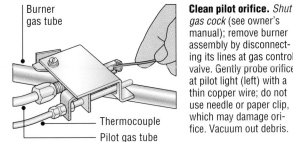

Burner gas tube
Thermocouple
Pilot gas tube

Clean pilot orifice. *Shut gas cock* (see owner's manual); remove burner assembly by disconnecting its lines at gas control valve. Gently probe orifice at pilot light (left) with a thin copper wire; do not use needle or paper clip, which may damage orifice. Vacuum out debris.

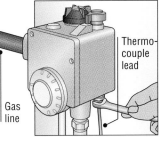

Thermocouple lead
Gas line

Check thermocouple for loose connections at control valve and verify that its bulb tip is held in pilot flame. (The thermocouple signals a shutdown if pilot flame goes out.) Don't overtighten nuts; screw them on finger-tight, then give only a quarter turn with an open-end wrench.

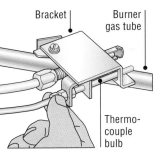

Bracket
Burner gas tube
Thermocouple bulb

To replace thermocouple, *shut gas cock* (see owner's manual); remove burner assembly; disconnect thermocouple from bracket; and attach new thermocouple. Test for leaks: apply soapy water to joints and open gas cock; bubbles indicate a leak. If ok, light pilot.

Troubleshooting: Gas water heaters

SYMPTOM	POSSIBLE CAUSE	SOLUTION
No hot water	Pilot light out	Relight pilot, following instructions on unit (p.247). ◇
Pilot light won't stay lit	Blockage in pilot orifice	Clean pilot orifice (right). ◆
	Loose thermocouple connection(s)	Tighten thermocouple connections (right). ◇
	Faulty thermocouple	Replace thermocouple (right). ◆
	Burner shut down	If pilot is lit, press reset button. ◇
Not enough hot water	Temperature control set too low	Check control; reset if necessary. ◇
	Burner flame orange, not blue	Adjust air shutters (p.247) ◇, or have serviced.
Water too hot	Temperature control set too high	Check control; reset if necessary. ◇
	Faulty thermostat	Have serviced.
	Blocked flue	Check draft hood (see *For your safety,* right) ◆ or have serviced.
Heater leaks	Relief valve venting water	Operate lever; if leak persists and temperature is OK, have valve replaced. ◇
	Tank rusted	Have heater replaced.
Heater noisy	Sediment in tank causes rumbling	Drain and flush tank (see above); then refill. ◇
	Faulty burner whistles or pops	Adjust air shutters (see page 247) ◇, or have burner ports serviced.
Hot water dirty	Sediment in tank	Drain and flush tank (see above); then refill. ◇

Degree of difficulty: Simple ◇   Average ◆   Complex ◆

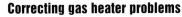
FOR YOUR SAFETY

Before repairing a gas or electric water heater, shut off its gas line or electric circuit (p.127); then drain the tank.

Never attempt to replace a gas-control valve or pipes that bring gas to it. Never replace a pressure relief valve. Call a plumber to service or replace these critical safety items.

 Poisonous carbon monoxide can leak from a faulty draft hood. With the burner on, hold your hand near the hood. Exhaust should rush into the hood; if it spills out, turn off the heater and have the vents inspected.

Electric water heater

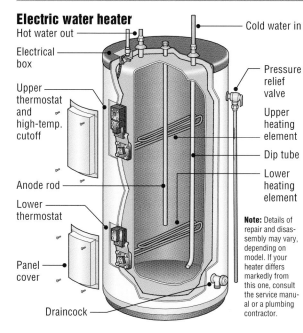

- Hot water out
- Cold water in
- Electrical box
- Upper thermostat and high-temp. cutoff
- Anode rod
- Lower thermostat
- Panel cover
- Draincock
- Pressure relief valve
- Upper heating element
- Dip tube
- Lower heating element

Note: Details of repair and disassembly may vary, depending on model. If your heater differs markedly from this one, consult the service manual or a plumbing contractor.

Troubleshooting: Electric water heaters

SYMPTOM	POSSIBLE CAUSE	SOLUTION
No hot water	High-temperature cutoff tripped	Push reset button on high-temperature cutoff. ◇
	Faulty thermostat	Test both thermostats (below); replace faulty thermostat. ◆ ▦
	Faulty heating element(s)	Test (below); replace if faulty. ◆ ▦
Not enough hot water	Thermostat set too low	Adjust settings and reset. ◇
	Faulty thermostat	Test both thermostats (below); replace faulty thermostat. ◆ ▦
	Faulty lower heating element(s)	Test (below); replace if faulty. ◆ ▦
Water too hot	Thermostat set too high	Adjust settings and reset. ◇
	Faulty thermostat	Test both thermostats (below); replace faulty thermostat. ◆ ▦
	Faulty high-temperature cutoff	Replace it if overheating occurs (below). ◆ ▦
	Grounded heating element(s)	Test and replace (below). ◆ ▦
Heater leaks	Pressure relief valve venting water	Operate lever; if leak persists have plumber check pressure relief valve. ◇
	Tank rusted	Have water heater replaced.
	Heating element gasket leaking	Tighten mounting bolts. ◇ If leak persists, replace gasket. ◆
Heater noisy	Sediment in tank	Shut off power; drain and flush tank until water runs clear, then refill. ◇
	Heating elements scale-encrusted	Replace elements (below). ◆
Hot water dirty	Sediment in tank	Drain tank (facing page); flush until water runs clear, then refill. ◇

Degree of difficulty: Simple ◇   Average ◆   Complex ◆   Volt-ohm meter required: ▦

Servicing a high-temperature cutoff

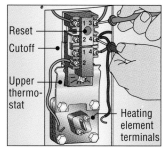

Reset
Cutoff
Upper thermostat
Heating element terminals

1 To test high-temperature cutoff, first shut off power. Remove top panel cover and push aside insulation. Disconnect leads from heating element terminals. With VOM on RX1, probe terminals on left of reset button, then on right. Look for zero reading each time. If readings are high, replace cutoff unit.

2 To replace cutoff (and thermostat), label and disconnect all wires. Pull unit from bracket. (On some models, cutoff and thermostat can be replaced separately by removing copper bus and gently prying lock tab on other side.) Fit new unit into place and reconnect wires. Press reset button; then restore power.

Servicing the thermostats

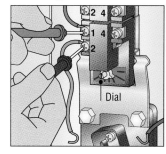

Dial

1 To test lower thermostat, shut off power; then let water in the tank cool. Disconnect leads from heating element terminals, and use screwdriver to turn temperature control dial to highest setting. Set VOM on RX1; then probe terminals 1 and 2. Look for zero-ohms reading; if higher, replace thermostat (Step 2, left).

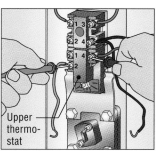

Upper thermostat

2 To test upper thermostat, disconnect leads, turn dial to the highest setting, and probe terminals 1 and 2 as described above; look for zero-ohms reading. With VOM still on RX1, probe terminals 1 and 4. Meter should read infinity. If reading is lower, replace thermostat (see Step 2, left).

Testing and replacing a heating element

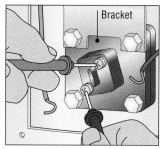

Bracket

1 Shut off power. Disconnect element leads. Set VOM on RX1 and probe both element terminals (left). If VOM reads infinity, replace element; any other reading means element is OK. To test for ground, set VOM on RX1000; probe one element screw and mounting bracket. Element is safe if reading is infinity.

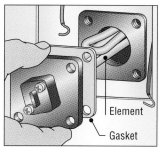

Element
Gasket

2 To replace heating element, drain tank (see facing page). Take out mounting bolts to remove heating element (or unscrew a threaded element). Clean any corrosion; then install new gasket and element. Refill tank. Check for leaks at gasket; tighten if necessary. Press reset button.

Water softeners remove minerals from water by means of an ion-exchange process. As water flows through a bed of sodium-impregnated resin beads in the resin tank, mineral ions are drawn from the water to the beads, while sodium ions leach out of the beads into the water. The unit periodically cleans and recharges the beads by rinsing them with brine, a salt (or for people on sodium-restricted diets, potassium chloride) solution. The recharging frequency affects the unit's salt consumption and is controlled by a timer or sensor that operates a motorized control valve.

Some softeners have a separate resin tank and brine tank (as below). In single-compartment models, the resin tank is inside the brine tank. Modern water softeners generally require little maintenance aside from periodic salt refill (see *Use and care*, below, right).

Troubleshooting

SYMPTOM	POSSIBLE CAUSE	SOLUTION
Motor not operating	Power off at outlet	See *General troubleshooting*, p.144.
	Motor breakdown	Call dealer for service.
Water not softened	Brine depleted	Flush tank (below); add salt. Start regeneration cycle. ◇
	Regeneration not frequent enough	Reset timer to increase regeneration frequency. ◇
	Iron content of water too high	Prefilter water or use salt with an iron control agent. ◇
	Unit in bypass mode	Set the bypass valve to *Service* position. ◇
	Water loss due to leaking pipes or running toilet	Make needed plumbing repairs (pp.110, 116, 120).
Brine not flowing	Brine line clogged	Flush out brine line (below). ◇
	Injector or filter screen clogged	Clean or replace the injector and filter screen (below). ◆
	Brine line kinked or cracked	Unkink line. Replace it if cracked. ◆
	Brine line pressure too low	Set pressure according to owner's manual. ◇

Degree of difficulty: Simple ◇   Average ◆   Complex ◆

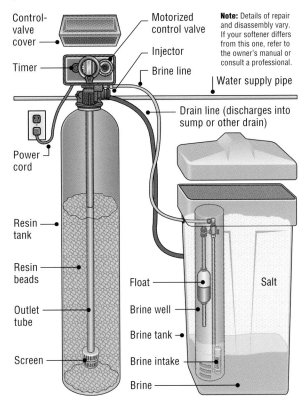

Control-valve cover
Motorized control valve
Timer
Injector
Brine line
Water supply pipe

Note: Details of repair and disassembly vary. If your softener differs from this one, refer to the owner's manual or consult a professional.

Drain line (discharges into sump or other drain)

Power cord
Resin tank
Resin beads
Float
Salt
Outlet tube
Brine well
Screen
Brine tank
Brine intake
Brine

Cleaning the injector

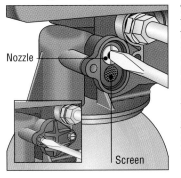

Nozzle

Screen

The injector regulates the flow of brine into the resin tank. To remove blockage, put softener in bypass mode, unscrew injector cap (inset), and remove screen and injector nozzle (left). Clean screen with warm soapy water. Clean nozzle by blowing air through it or gently clearing particles with a straightened paper clip.

Flushing the brine line

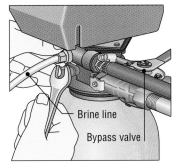

Brine line

Bypass valve

The brine line delivers brine to the resin tank. To check for clogs in the line, *unplug the softener* and put it in bypass mode. Then use a wrench to loosen the brine line fittings at the injector housing and salt tank, and remove the brine line. To clear a clog, use a turkey baster to inject warm water into the line.

Brine compartment and intake maintenance

Cleaning the brine compartment is important, especially in rural areas or areas with silty water. Wash brine intake with water and a small brush. Clean brine tank before each salt refill. Remove cover; dump out brine and any salt residue (or empty with a wet-dry vacuum). Flush tank clean with a hose; then refill with salt.

Drain lines should be installed correctly, allowing a gap for water discharge. Drain lines should be made of durable, high-quality material and should be free of kinks or restrictions.

When replenishing salt, use the recommended type and amount. Prevent salt buildup by cleaning compartment before refilling (above).

During long vacations, disconnect the timer and put the unit into bypass mode. After an extended power outage, the time clock must be reset. If there is any danger of freezing, drain the tank. Don't let the water softener operate empty.

Whirlpools and spas

Whirlpool baths and spas have adjustable water jets that massage the bather with streams of air-entrained water. A pump and a motor force from 265 to 950 litres per minute through the jet openings. Many whirlpools, and all spas, have in-line heaters that maintain the desired water temperature.

Whirlpools are essentially modified porcelain or fiberglass bathtubs, whose preinstalled pump, motor, and piping are connected to household plumbing and electrical systems. Typically designed for one or two people and located in bathrooms or master bedroom suites, whirlpools are filled for each use, then drained. Never let a whirlpool that's in use run dry; you risk damaging the motor seals or, worse, burning out the motor. Before turning on the jets, fill the whirlpool to at least an inch or two above them. Most manufac-

turers suggest that you minimize the use of soap and flush the whirlpool with clean water after use to avoid an unsanitary, hard-to-remove buildup of soap scum in the pipes.

A spa is a large fiberglass or tile-over-concrete soaking tub. It usually seats two or more people and is left filled with water for extended periods. (Because spas typically hold between 760 and 1,900 litres of water, frequent refills are wasteful and expensive.) As in swimming pools, chemicals are used both to sanitize the spa water and to maintain a proper pH level (pp.422–423). A spa may be installed indoors or outdoors and is usually filled from a hose. Most spas have external thermostats, many have digital controls, and some have two pumps, which may be similar to pumps found in a whirlpool or a swimming pool.

Gaining access

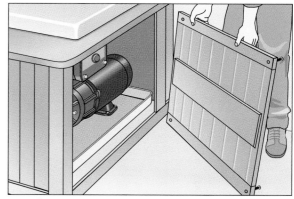

The access panel on a whirlpool or spa lets you get at the pump when it needs service. Some models have a factory-installed skirt with a pop-off front access panel. Other units are supported by a platform that is custom-built on site (above); it must have a removable panel large enough to allow easy access to the pump.

Whirlpool bath

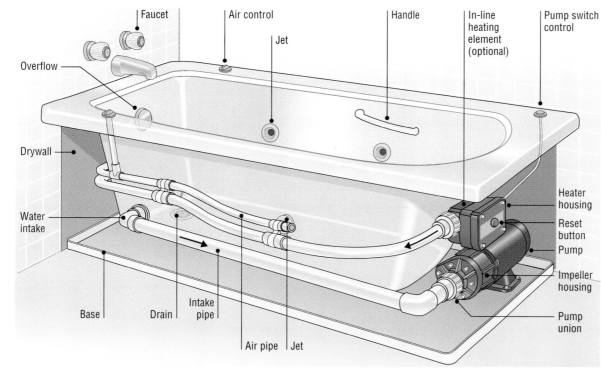

Faucet · Air control · Jet · Handle · In-line heating element (optional) · Pump switch control · Overflow · Drywall · Water intake · Base · Drain · Intake pipe · Air pipe · Jet · Heater housing · Reset button · Pump · Impeller housing · Pump union

USE AND CARE

Keep units clean. Sanitize whirlpools monthly. Add 1 cup of bleach and ⅛ cup of liquid dishwashing soap to water; run jets 5 minutes. For spas, remove filter (left) and hose off monthly. Soak it in degreaser for 24 hours every 90 days; then rinse with water.

Vacuum motor vents periodically. After long idle periods, spray motor and impeller with pump lubricant spray (sold by whirlpool and spa dealers). Don't clean the tub surface with abrasives. Instead, use a mild liquid detergent.

Large appliances ▪ Whirlpools and spas

Troubleshooting

SYMPTOM	POSSIBLE CAUSE	SOLUTION
Unit won't start	No power to pump motor	Restore power (see *Power off at outlet?*, p.144). ◇
	Pump motor failure	Check pump and motor (see *Maintaining a pump*, p.424).
	Faulty electrical connections	Repair broken wires, or loose or corroded terminals. ◆
	Defective pump switch control	Control is non-electric device to turn pump on. Have it serviced.
Jets not working	Blocked water intake	Clear the blockage (below). ◇
	Broken jet	Replace the jet (below, right). ◇
Water too hot or too cold	High-limit switch tripped	Push high-limit reset switch. ◇
	Thermostat out of adjustment	Adjust thermostat setting ◇. If problem persists, have serviced.
	Failed heating element	Test, and replace element if necessary (below). ◆ ▨
Water level drops or leakage under unit	Leaking pump union	Replace the union gasket (below, right). ◆
	Leaking pump seal	Replace seal if worn or damaged (see p.424). ◆
Jets surge or uneven	Leaking pump union	Replace the union gasket (below, right). ◆
Water drains slowly	Drain clogged	Remove clog (see *Dealing with clogs*, p.115). ◇
Spa water cloudy/smelly	Faulty water chemistry	Adjust chemistry (see *Pools*, p.422). ◇
Green corrosion on spa	Faulty water chemistry	Adjust chemistry (see *Pools*, p.422). ◇

Degree of difficulty: Simple ◇   Average ◆   Complex ◆   Volt-ohm meter required: ▨

Testing and replacing heating element

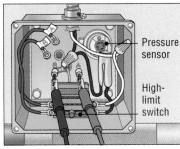

To test heating element, shut off power, then remove screws holding heater housing cover in place. Mark and disconnect element leads, set VOM on RX1, and clip probes to terminals. If meter doesn't read low ohms, replace element.

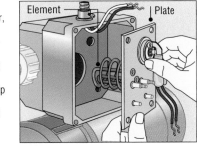

To replace element, drain water. Disconnect wires; then remove high-limit switch and pressure sensor. Pull out old element and mounting plate (left), and any gaskets. New element is attached to plate; install and remount other parts.

Clearing a blocked water intake

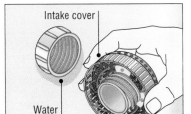

1 Water intakes have sieve-type covers that may clog with hair and particles. Remove them periodically to clean. Some intakes twist off. Others are held with a screw. (Close tub drain to avoid losing screw.)

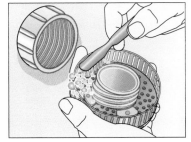

2 Clean intake cover by backflushing strainer holes with water. If inside of strainer is gummy, scrub it with a toothbrush and powdered laundry detergent. Some covers are notched to indicate proper orientation.

Replacing a pump union gasket

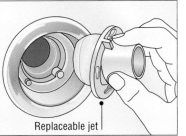

Pump unions are assemblies that join water pipes to the pump. To fix a leaky union, unscrew fitting and replace gasket. Whirlpools must be shut off and drained first; spas have valves that let you drain the union without draining the spa.

Replacing a jet

Replaceable jets on some units let you vary the air/water stream (from narrow to wide, for instance). Simply twist out old jet and twist in new. Some jets require special wrenches for removal.

Home electronics

The ever-growing capabilities of home electronics, along with the high labor costs of professional repair (even a $1.29 part may cost $100 to replace), might encourage you to buy the latest model instead of fixing the old one. But if a device that otherwise suits you breaks down, there's no reason to discard it if simple do-it-yourself servicing will extend its useful life.

These pages describe how to maintain the most popular kinds of equipment, and you'll learn the basic troubleshooting and repair skills necessary for solving common and easy-to-remedy problems. Armed with this information, you'll be able to avoid the often unnecessary (and environmentally wasteful) practice of throwing away perfectly good equipment.

Before you undertake any electronics servicing, review *Appliance repair basics*, pp.122–148, and read *For your safety*, p.301. If your equipment isn't covered specifically in this section, read the pages on tools and troubleshooting (pp.300–303), then browse through the remaining pages of the section. Many electronic products rely on a common repertoire of mechanical or electronic components; knowing how one works will help you understand others.

Electronics ▪ Tools and supplies

Cameras, telephones, audio/video equipment, computers, and a host of home electronic products operate primarily by the grace of semiconductor-based microelectronics. In the early 1950's, discrete transistors and other semiconductor devices were mounted on printed circuit boards, replacing electron tubes and a maze of wires. Further miniaturization led to the integrated circuit (IC), which is essentially a hermetically sealed capsule containing an electronic circuit along with hundreds or even thousands of semiconductors. As a result, all sorts of electrical equipment is more compact, versatile, capable, and reliable. Equipment typically will fail mechanically or become outdated by technology long before the electronic components fail (particularly if the equipment is properly cleaned, maintained, and operated).

Maintenance of electronic devices is primarily limited to general cleaning (including electrical contacts) and occasional lubrication (pp.137, 303). Testing (see *Resistance testing*, p.304) helps to pinpoint problems. The repair or replacement of components, such as fuses (p.304), worn or dirty drive belts (p.303), and faulty cables (pp.304 and 306), is usually fairly easy even for a novice.

Falling prices and the improved technology of new equipment — a VCR that cost $1,000 ten years ago might now cost about $200 and offer superior quality and features — often mean that it's better to replace a faulty unit than to spend more than a modest amount repairing it.

At minimum, electronic troubleshooting and repair calls for a trip to the library for a good electronics repair manual, schematics, and wiring diagrams (p.302) for your equipment. You must then spend some time learning to read them, and become familiar with electronic components and their coded markings so you know their test values and can order parts. Repair skills such as the precise soldering called for on electronic devices (p.305) are learned through practice. Other skills, such as repairing a cracked circuit board and solving some intermittent problems (p.302), are more readily gained.

Testing equipment

Digital multimeter (DMM) is more accurate and safer for some tests on electronic equipment than a volt-ohm meter (p.130). It performs voltage and continuity tests and has additional slots and ranges for more advanced testing. Auto-ranging is a desirable feature.

Insulated leads with probes (and plug-on alligator clips) are used with DMM.

Jumper wire with insulated alligator clip leads makes some electrical tests easier.

Resistors can be used to discharge capacitors. For most applications a 10-ohm, 10-watt, wire-wound resistor is adequate.

Component coolant is used for troubleshooting intermittent problems. Sprayed on an electronic component, it can help to track down a fault.

Disassembly and repair tools

Mini long-nose pliers and side cutter, small versions of standard electrical tools, are useful in confined spaces.

Long-nose pliers

Side cutter

Dental pick is useful for handling tiny clips, springs, and other parts.

Motor tool, a high-speed electrical tool, has accessories for sanding, wire-brushing, grinding, and other jobs.

Inspection mirror is used for exploring spaces that would otherwise require disassembly.

Magnifying glass allows you to examine small parts, solder joints, and other detail work. Hands-free models are available.

Fuse puller removes glass fuses safely.

Jeweler's screwdriver set allows you to remove tiny fasteners without damage.

Soldering tools and supplies

Soldering pen and stand. A pen for fine soldering should be between 15 and 40W (25W is ideal) and accept interchangeable iron-plated grounded tips (including a 1/16-in. or 1/8-in. tip). Ideally it should have a temperature control. The stand provides a safe place for a hot pen. The dampened sponge is used to clean the tip after every use.

Desoldering braid (left) or pump (above) removes unwanted solder. Molten solder is pumped or wicked away (p.136).

Rosin-core electronic solders, preferably small, 22 swg (standard wire gauge), are required. Never use "plumber's" or "acid-core" solder. The best solder for electronics is 60% lead, 38% tin, and 2% silver. Acceptable lead-free solder is 96% tin and 4% silver.

Cleaning supplies

Disposable cotton gloves prevent skin oils from being transferred to rubber tires and belts, and to parts that come in contact with recording tape.

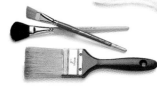

Soft new paintbrushes loosen dust and dirt during general cleaning.

Compressed air (canned air) removes dust from tight places without rubbing dirt into the components.

Swabs. Use chamois tips clean video and audio heads. For other cleaning, use cotton tips or foam tips (foam won't leave fibers behind).

Chemical cleaners. Electrical contact cleaner removes corrosion from contacts. Denatured or pure isopropyl alcohol cleans contacts, rubber belts, and many other surfaces.

Lubricants

Synthetic lubricants, such as silicone, are very durable. Used for fast-moving high-friction parts, they also are less likely to harm plastic.

Light "household" oil is petroleum-base and has many applications for medium- to fast-moving parts.

White lithium grease is preferred for slow-moving mechanisms, such as gears or tracks.

Pinpoint oiler allows user to apply a single small drop of lubricant, which is usually the amount required for mechanisms in home electronic equipment.

Equipment protection devices

Static-control wrist strap or mat discharges static electricity to ground. A mat (not shown) can be used beneath sensitive electronic equipment when making repairs.

Nonconductive plastic screwdriver reduces chances of static discharge.

Antistatic spray reduces static electricity in dry, carpeted environments. Use it if repairs are made in such conditions.

Multi-outlet surge protector protects sensitive electronic equipment from fluctuations in line voltage. Used primarily for computers, it is suitable for all solid-state electronic equipment.

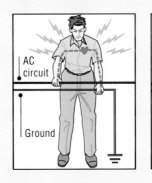

When in doubt, don't! This is the most important rule for servicing electronic equipment.

When measuring voltage with a VOM/DMM, turn the power off, clip on probes, check that they touch only the intended contacts, and restore power for test. Turn power off before removing the probes.

Always unplug equipment for repair work. If it's necessary to observe operation with cover off, unplug it for disassembly and replug for observation. Unplug again before repairs, tests, or reassembly.

Perform a current cold check (below) before plugging in equipment you have serviced. Many electronic devices have metal housings rather than plastic; so it's important to ensure there is no short circuit inside. The test applies only to AC-powered units, not to those powered by DC adapters.

Never use wire to replace a fuse, even temporarily.

Stand on a nonconductive surface when making any repair.

Don't assume that an unplugged unit is safe. Some components, notably capacitors, may hold a lethal charge (see *Disassembling a camera*, p.318). Particularly dangerous are some high-voltage capacitors found in cameras with flashes (or flash units themselves) and in audio receivers. They should be discharged by professionals only. Discharge lower voltage capacitors using a 10-ohm, 10-watt, wire-wound resistor (below). Verify discharge with a VOM set to test DC voltage; look for a zero volt reading.

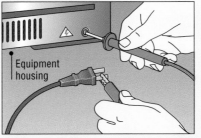

Cold check. Probe all exposed metal parts and each power cord prong with VOM set on ohms scale. Look for infinity reading, indicating no continuity/no short.

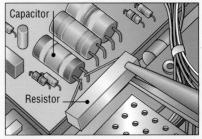

Capacitors. Use a resistor to discharge low-voltage or non-storage-type capacitors by touching resistor's leads to the component leads. See *How to test a capacitor*, p.148.

One-hand rule: Keep one hand in your pocket when touching the interior of a powered piece of equipment with the other hand. If you *accidentally* touch a live wire, significantly less current will pass through your body, especially the chest/heart area, on its way to ground than would occur if you became an integral part of the AC circuit.

Troubleshooting overview

The more complex the piece of equipment, the more important it is to troubleshoot it methodically. First, determine if the equipment is really at fault. Read the owner's manual to verify that the equipment is correctly set up and is being operated properly.

Check the obvious: Is the unit plugged in? Is the power on? Is the videotape, film, or other necessary component in place? Follow with a careful visual inspection for any obvious signs of physical or electrical damage (shorts, burn marks, foreign objects, excessive dirt, or moisture). If it seems that a problem is related to poor internal or external electrical connections, thoroughly clean all plugs, jacks, and other electrical connections (see *Cleaning,* p.303).

Next, define the problem precisely and ask yourself questions about conditions at the time of failure. What went wrong, and under what circumstances? Separate the effects from the causes; then list all the possible causes. Approach the list in a logical fashion. For a professional service technician, that means looking at the most likely cause first, but for a do-it-yourselfer, it may make more sense to tackle the symptom that is simplest to test or the least expensive to repair. Finally, test each component to verify that it is functioning. This often repetitive trial-by-error process, if methodical, will eventually locate the problem. Study block diagrams (right) to identify components that might be part of the problem.

Intermittent problems

Intermittent problems are notoriously frustrating to pin down, both because they come and go and because there are so many things that can cause such failures. Some of the more common problem sources that you can investigate (and may be able to correct) are a poor or visibly cracked solder joint (p.305); a loose, dirty, or oxidized wire/cable connection (see below and *Cleaning,* facing page); a damaged PC board or a break in board traces (see *Repairing a* *cracked circuit board,* p.305); other burned or broken components caused by rough handling during transit; variations in temperature, humidity, or voltage; and faulty components that change characteristics after the equipment has warmed up (below).

If a problem relates to a specific mode of operation, look for a dirty mode switch (a *Play* button on a VCR, for example) when operation is erratic. Clean (p.303) and test (p.304) the switch, or replace it (p.305).

Electronic road maps

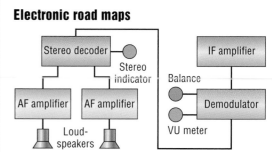

Block diagrams (and similar flowchart diagrams) help you understand how a piece of equipment operates, which is often required to make educated troubleshooting guesses. Functional subsystems of a complex device are shown in blocks; the sequence is indicated by arrows; functions that have no output are in circles. The power supply output typically would be taken to all blocks; for simplicity's sake, it is not shown here.

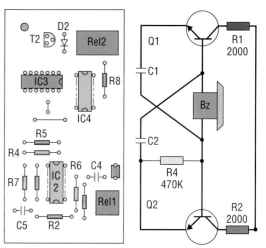

A component diagram (left) and a circuit diagram (right) both describe different aspects of components (resistors, capacitors, etc.) on a circuit board. The first identifies the mechanical arrangement of components; you need that to locate them. The second gives electrical information about the components and the connections between them, such as the voltages that should be present at particular points; you need this information for testing. Reading a circuit diagram requires an understanding of a complex language of symbols, called schematics.

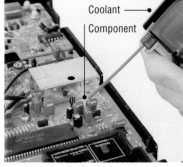

Spray component coolant on an electronic component (above) or solder joint (right) that you know is related to a malfunctioning device (learn that by studying a printed circuit board component diagram).

If cooling temporarily corrects the problem, you have located the problem source.
CAUTION: Use extreme care; coolant tests are made with power on and housing off. Unplug unit before attempting repair work.

Remove oxidation from switches and plugs: Unplug unit, and spray contact cleaner on mating parts. Then repeatedly plug and unplug connections (or operate a sprayed switch). Restore power to test.

Cleaning

Dirt interferes with the smooth operation of gears, pulleys, belts, and other mechanical components. Electrical contacts (plugs, switches, batteries, etc.) are particularly vulnerable to oxidation, which can cause complete or intermittent failure. Video and audio heads fail when there's even the slightest deposit left by tapes passing over them. Dust on electronic components insulates them, causing overheating and premature failure. Residue from spilled drinks corrodes contacts and can short out and damage components. Salt air causes corrosion problems.

A general cleaning both prevents and solves problems. Unplug a unit before disassembly (see *For your safety*, p.301). Electrical contact (or tuner) cleaners will remove slight corrosion. For more serious corrosion on exposed areas—battery and fuse contacts, for example—rub with an eraser or plain bond paper. Use only a residue-free chemical cleaner/degreaser (found in electronics stores). Less pure isopropyl or rubbing alcohol often contains oils and other additives that leave troublesome residue on critical parts. Remember that cleaners will dissolve lubricants, so be prepared to relubricate (below).

Battery contacts

To remove dust from equipment interior, use a vacuum, first agitating the dirt with a new soft paintbrush or artist's brush. Vacuums may generate static electricity; so some professionals prefer to use canned compressed air for computer interiors.

A pencil eraser removes oxidation from battery contacts and other areas of electrical contact. The slightest oxidation, entirely invisible to the naked eye, can cause complete system failure or erratic operation. Brush away debris after using eraser.

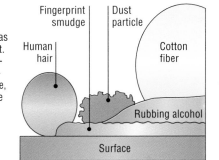

Rubber drive belts

Fingerprint smudge   Dust particle

Human hair

Cotton fiber

Rubbing alcohol

Surface

To clean rubber belts and tires, use residue-free chemical cleaners, such as denatured or 95 percent pure isopropyl alcohol. So you won't defeat the purpose of your efforts, wear cotton gloves to prevent transfer of skin oil to the rubber; it can cause them to slip.

Residue and debris can insulate electrical connections and prevent them from working; it can also harm tapes and drive belts. The relative sizes of contaminants are shown here. Use only residue-free cleaner, and wear gloves (p.301) when handling parts.

Lubrication

More durable synthetic lubricants, self-lubricating nylon bearings (nylon-to-metal contacts rarely need lubrication), and sealed bearings have reduced lubrication requirements. When in doubt, consult the manufacturer's customer service department.

Some commonsense guidelines apply. Don't over-lubricate, because this may contaminate other parts or areas and subsequently cause serious failures. For example, be careful around pulleys. You may need to oil a shaft, but you certainly don't want oil to get on the pulley or belts. Don't lubricate anything that was not factory lubricated (admittedly not always easy to tell); and conversely, if cleaning removes existing lubrication, be sure to relubricate. Don't lubricate switches, plugs, jacks, cable ends, or other electrical contacts. Doing so causes poor electrical contact.

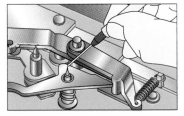

To apply a single drop of oil, use a precision oiler (squeeze a bit out while holding point up to create a vacuum so drop won't drip out too fast) or put a drop on the tip of a pointed tool or toothpick.

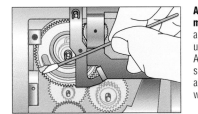

Avoid applying too much grease by placing a dab where needed, using a swab or stick. Activate the unit to spread the grease; then apply more grease only where required.

TIPS FROM THE PROS

To protect against voltage changes, have a lightning arrester professionally installed at your electrical service panel; consider placing sensitive electronic equipment, especially computers, on separate circuits; and plug such equipment into multi-outlet surge protectors.

Overheating causes premature component failure, so don't cover equipment vent openings. Never enclose electronic equipment without providing the required ventilation when operating it.

Static electricity can damage sensitive integrated circuits. To safely discharge static electricity, touch a grounding screw, the shell of a phono plug, or a metal chassis; wear a static-control wrist strap; or use an antistatic mat. When working in high-static environments, use plastic screwdrivers and try spraying antistatic aerosol on carpeting.

Resistance testing

Once you've attended to any obvious mechanical or electrical problems in a piece of electronic equipment, you'll need a volt-ohm meter (VOM) to track down less obvious problems. One of the VOM's most useful functions is the ohms resistance test. A few of the many devices or circuits a beginner can test are shown here; other applications are covered in the pages that follow.

When it comes to more advanced testing of electronic components, a digital multimeter (DMM) is preferred to a VOM because it is more accurate. A DMM may even be required if using a VOM might damage delicate components, such as those in cameras (such tests are not covered in this book, however). Before you undertake the diagnosis of any electronic appliance, always unplug the equipment and discharge any low-voltage capacitors (see *General troubleshooting*, p.146). Also see *Electrical testers*, p.125; *Circuit faults*, p.128; and *Electronic components*, p.148.

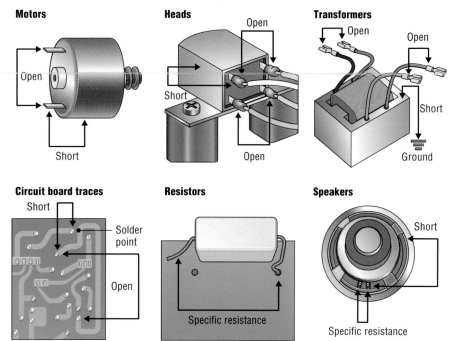

Ohms resistance tests confirm the presence or absence of electrical continuity within a device or circuit. (Arrows in the drawings above indicate contact points.) A test result that indicates infinite resistance tells you that the circuit is open. A result that indicates zero or very low resistance indicates a circuit that is closed (this *might* be due to a short circuit). When testing some devices (speakers and resistors, for example), a specific resistance (in ohms) is required to confirm proper functioning.

Fuses

A fuse consists of a wire with a low melting point enclosed in an insulating cartridge (usually glass). If the current exceeds a certain level, the wire melts, thereby opening the circuit and preventing damage to the equipment. Typically, one or more fuses are located at or near the power supply (where the power cord enters and AC supply current is converted to DC operating current). The equipment cover must usually be removed for access. Most fuses clip in place, but some are soldered. Damage may not be evident.

Blown   Fatigued

A blown fuse, usually smoked, indicates a short; inspect equipment before replacing. **A fatigued fuse** is clear, and the wire may not be visibly broken. This may not indicate a problem; just replace the fuse.

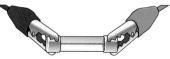

To test, set DMM on RX1 scale; probe fuse ends. Fuse should read 300 ohms or less.

Working with cables and plugs

Audio and video equipment utilizes special cables to transmit signals from antennas (coaxial cable) or between components such as a VCR and TV (phono cable). Prefabricated cables (with connectors installed) are available in various lengths and are generally worth buying. But where long runs are required or where replacement is otherwise inconvenient, you can make connections with a crimping tool and a cable cutter. Connectors may or may not have separate crimping rings.

Coaxial cable

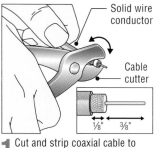

1 Cut and strip coaxial cable to expose solid wire; cut and strip outer insulation to expose braided wire. If the connector is type with a crimping ring, slide it over cable.

2 Press on connector (or tap it on with mallet); slide crimping ring (if any) over connector; use a crimping tool to crimp it in three places, working toward end.

Testing audio plugs

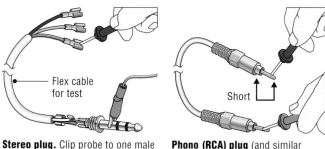

Stereo plug. Clip probe to one male plug segment; probe each wire in succession while flexing the cable. Look for continuity (zero reading) only once. Repeat for each segment.

Phono (RCA) plug (and similar coaxial cable). Probe center conductors to confirm continuity. Also probe center conductor and shell (arrows) to verify there is no short.

Repairs

Soldering techniques

Soldering provides a sound electrical and mechanical joint and prevents the oxidation that sometimes makes non-soldered connections fail. Precision soldering calls for practice. If you will be soldering electronic equipment, especially on circuit boards, practice on a damaged board first.

Proper soldering is a matter of applying the right amount of heat and solder (p.300) to a properly prepared joint. Contacts should be free of corrosion, grease, and dirt.

Appy only as much heat as required to melt the solder; then remove the iron and quickly apply the solder. Excess heat ruins the glue that bonds wiring traces to the board and can damage components. Allow the connection to sit undisturbed until the solder cools.

Solder joints

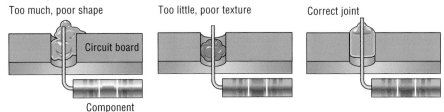

Too much, poor shape · Circuit board · Component
Too little, poor texture
Correct joint

A good solder joint is easily recognized. It should be smooth and shiny and have an even globular shape. The joint should rise just above the soldered side of the circuit board and not flow out the opposite side (where the components are located).

Soldering on a circuit board

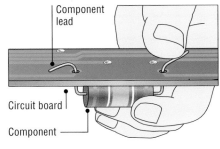

Component lead · Circuit board · Component

1 Because the slightest movement during soldering causes problems, make the connection mechanically sound by bending over the component's leads before you solder. Clamping or taping parts may also be appropriate.

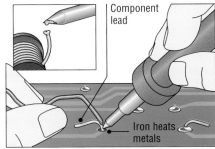

Component lead · Iron heats metals

2 Apply a drop of solder to iron tip (inset) to give additional surface area for faster heat transfer when applying heat to the joint. As soon as the joint is sufficiently heated (a few seconds), apply solder. This does not conflict with the basic rule that states "Heat the metal, not the solder."

Repairing a cracked circuit board

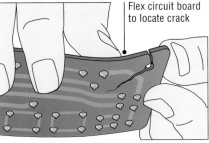

Flex circuit board to locate crack

Look for cracks around mounting screws, hinges, and rubber or plastic bumpers (some boards slide out of device; others are hinged). Flex board slightly to reveal hairline cracks.

Replacing a board-mounted part

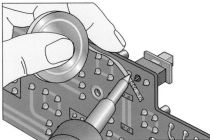

1 To replace a switch or any other visibly damaged (burned, leaking, cracked) board component, first unplug and disassemble equipment as needed to access the circuit board. Then desolder leads with braid or pump (pp.300 and 304).

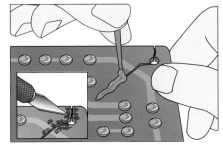

Roughen surface along crack with knife for better glue bond (inset). Mix two-part epoxy and spread it with toothpick or similar spreader. Don't use cyanurate ("super") glue; it fails when shear stress is applied.

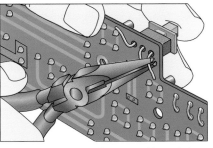

2 Be sure to remove all excess solder and clean off resin residue, using a foam-tipped swab dampened with denatured alcohol. Then insert the new component, and bend the wire leads over to secure it.

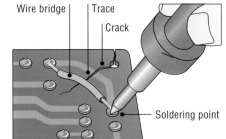

Wire bridge · Trace · Crack · Soldering point

To bypass a broken trace, strip ¼ in. of insulation off each end of a length of 24-gauge wire and tin the exposed ends. Solder wire to a soldering point at one end of trace, bridge to nearest solder connection on other side of the crack, and solder.

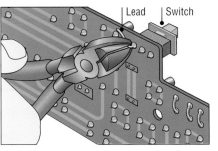

Lead · Switch

3 Solder on new component; do not apply more heat than is required to melt the solder. Clip off excess lead with side cutter (above); then clean joint with swab wetted with denatured alcohol. Reassemble unit, and restore power to test.

Home electronics ▪ Audio systems

Receivers 307
Compact disc players 308

Turntables 310
Cassette decks 312
Speakers 314

An audio system consists of a number of separate components connected by wires and cables. When linked to a TV and videocassette recorder (VCR), the components form a complete home entertainment system, or home theater. Most systems include a receiver/amplifier/tuner (facing page), compact disc player (p.308), turntable (p.310), audio cassette tape deck (p.312), and speakers (p.314).

The number of components and the maze of wires and cables connecting them may seem complex at first. In essence, however, the system consists of only three basic elements: signal sources (such as a cassette deck, a CD player, or an AM/FM tuner), a receiver/amplifier, and speakers. The TV's sound is simply another audio signal and can be routed through the stereo receiver just like the sound from a CD player.

Audio system problems can often be traced to faulty connections between or within components. This may be due to oxidation (see *Cleaning,* p.303) or to a loose or undersize wire or cable, particularly for speakers.

USE AND CARE

Allow ample air circulation. Don't stack components if this will block air vents. Vacuum dust from vent openings. Open cabinet doors when operating components housed inside.

Low-quality cables pick up hum and interference; use the best-quality cables you can afford. Don't pull them out by the wire; grasp the plug instead.

Oxidation will cause a loss of signal. Be sure to keep plugs, jacks, and speaker connections clean (see *Cleaning,* p.303).

When disassembling the system, sketch a "map" of the cable connections to make reassembly easy. Keep the original packing boxes to use when transporting components.

If they were stored in a cold area, let components warm to room temperature before use to allow any condensation inside the equipment to dry.

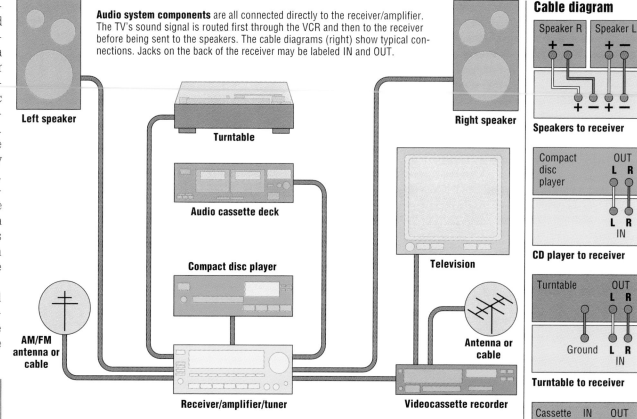

Audio system components are all connected directly to the receiver/amplifier. The TV's sound signal is routed first through the VCR and then to the receiver before being sent to the speakers. The cable diagrams (right) show typical connections. Jacks on the back of the receiver may be labeled IN and OUT.

Left speaker

Right speaker

Turntable

Audio cassette deck

Compact disc player

Television

AM/FM antenna or cable

Antenna or cable

Receiver/amplifier/tuner

Videocassette recorder

Speaker cable

Sound quality depends on keeping speaker leads as short as possible and on choosing appropriate-gauge cables (right); the larger the AWG (American Wire Gauge) designation, the smaller the wire diameter. Tin the tips of the speaker wires with solder or use crimp-on terminals (p.124), according to the type of connectors your system has at the amplifier and speaker. Doing so makes the connections more reliable, safer for the equipment, and more convenient for you when moving the speakers. To avoid damage to the system, turn the power off when making connections.

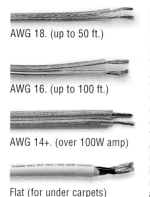

AWG 18. (up to 50 ft.)

AWG 16. (up to 100 ft.)

AWG 14+. (over 100W amp)

Flat (for under carpets)

Size speaker wire properly. Depending on the power output, the shorter and heavier the wire, the better the sound. Avoid placing any cable where it can be stepped on. Use type 14-2 UF electrical cable for exposed outdoor speaker wiring; or install 14-gauge speaker cable inside PVC tubing; also hard-wire speakers or make connections within a weatherproof box.

Cable diagram

Speaker R   Speaker L
+ −   + −
+ − + −

Speakers to receiver

Compact disc player
OUT
L R
L R
IN

CD player to receiver

Turntable
OUT
L R
Ground L R
IN

Turntable to receiver

Cassette deck
IN   OUT
L R   L R
L R   L R
OUT   IN

Cassette deck to receiver

in out video
AUDIO OUT
L R
VCR
L R
AUDIO IN

VCR to receiver

Receivers

Receivers

The heart of an audio system is the receiver, which can serve as the master control for all the audio signal sources (including sound from the TV). It selects the desired audio source, modifies and controls the signal with volume and tone controls (including surround-sound processing in more advanced units), and amplifies the signal to power one or more sets of speakers. In addition, the receiver contains an FM and/or AM tuner, which is itself a source of audio signals.

Modern manufacturing techniques combine electrical circuits formerly made up of many individual parts into a plastic logic chip the size of a postage stamp. This means that the tuning, for instance, is essentially computer controlled and must be serviced by a qualified technician. Even so, a receiver that works poorly can often be brought back to life with a thorough cleaning.

The most common cause of receiver problems is oxidation of electrical contacts and jacks (a jack is the connector used to mate a wire or plug to a circuit). The problem is made worse in large cities because of air pollution, and near the sea because of the high salt content of the air. Use a pencil eraser to clean cable pins on a regular basis. Use electrical contact cleaner (p.303) to clean the input jacks and speaker terminals.

Troubleshooting a receiver

Faulty switches can be located by jiggling each one and listening to hear if the music goes on and off. If so, spray the switch with contact cleaner. A dead receiver may mean a blown fuse. Open the housing and replace the fuse (p.304) if necessary. When an older dial-tuned receiver can't tune in radio signals, or if its tuning dial pointer doesn't move, a broken dial cord (right) is usually the cause.

Troubleshooting the power supply

Receivers typically have a primary power supply (see *Replacing the power supply unit*, p.324) that powers most of the electronic components. (Look for a fuse and component group on the main circuit board that is connected to the transformer with heavy-gauge wires.) There may also be a secondary power supply where the power cord enters; it's vulnerable to power surges. If the receiver does not power up and you have verified power at the outlet and tested the cord, the transformer or the rectifier circuit (also referred to as the power supply) may be at fault.

If a fuse is blown, isolate the secondary supply by disconnecting it from the primary transformer; then replace the fuse. If the fuse blows again, replace the secondary power supply board (right, top). If the fuse does not blow, test the transformer (right, bottom). Unplug the primary power supply from the transformer; if the fuse no longer blows, the problem is within the primary power supply.

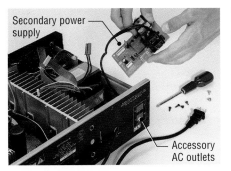

Secondary power supply

Accessory AC outlets

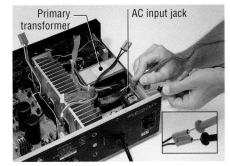

Primary transformer — AC input jack

To remove a faulty secondary power supply, unplug unit, take off housing, and remove wiring harnesses from power supply board. Unscrew circuit board and any accessory AC outlets that are attached to the rear panel. People with knowledge of schematics and diagnostic testing might test individual components, such as diodes, but more often the whole board is simply replaced.

To test transformer: Set VOM to RX1 and insert probes into plug that connects transformer to AC line (inset); similarly test wires leading from transformer to primary power supply. A zero reading in either test indicates an open winding. Probe transformer casing and chassis (ground). If there's resistance (indicating continuity), it's shorted. Unplug all wires and unscrew transformer for replacement.

Common variant: Servicing a slide tuner

Though most newer receivers are digitally tuned, many older units that may still be in service rely on a slide tuner linkage that moves a pointer across the dial. The slide tuner is a common source of problems. If the pointer sticks or jams, unplug the receiver and open the housing to investigate. The dial cord should be replaced if it is damaged or has become glazed through long use. Parts for old receivers can sometimes be found at electronics surplus outlets.

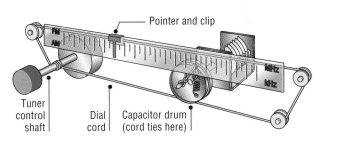

Pointer and clip

Tuner control shaft | Dial cord | Capacitor drum (cord ties here)

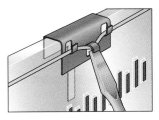

Resetting a dial pointer. Loosen spring clips and slip pointer along dial cord until station being received reads correctly; then tighten clips onto cord. Turn tuner knob to make sure the pointer does not catch anywhere along its path.

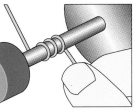

Stringing a dial cord. Wax cord with tuner cord wax or beeswax; tie it to capacitor drum; wrap it several times around tuner control shaft. Loop it around pulley and attach it to spring clips. Set pointer as described at left, and check the travel.

A compact disc, or CD, is a 12-cm-wide flat plastic disc that's stamped with a digital code representing sound. The code is aligned on a spiral track less than 1 micron wide on the underside of the disc. As the player's DC universal motor rotates the disc, a laser beam is focused on the disc and reflected back through the objective lens to the detector, which reads the digital information; circuits then send analog pulses to an amplifier.

Front- and top-loading CD players are available as portable units (p.329) or as a component in an audio system. Models for automobiles are also available. Front-loading units feature a motorized tray that slides out of the front of the player to accept one or more discs. Carousel or cartridge multiplay CD players can be programmed to play five or more discs in any order. About all you can do to service a CD player is to clean it thoroughly and perhaps replace a motor, belt, or broken tray. Fortunately, these repairs usually solve most CD player problems.

Gaining access. To access the interior, remove the housing screws, then slide the housing away from the front panel. Some models also require removal of the front panel in order to reach some parts; remove the tray front and check along the panel's edges for any tabs or screws that secure the front panel.

Note: Details of repair and disassembly may vary, depending on CD player model. If your CD player differs markedly from this one, or if you cannot clearly identify relevant components, consult your owner's manual or a service professional. Also see *Home electronics*, pp.300–305, and *Appliance repair basics*, pp.124–148.

Cleaning and servicing discs

Smudges on the clear (information) side of the disc can block the laser's view of the surface. To avoid smudges, hold a disc by its hub and outside edges, like a record. Blow dust from the surface with a can of compressed air. Clean dirt and fingerprints with a lint-free cloth dampened with CD-cleaning fluid or denatured alcohol; using a dry cloth may scratch the disc. Wipe from the center outward (not a circular motion as used for record cleaning). An abrasive particle rubbed into the CD may cause a scratch; and while scratches across the tracks can cause skips in the music, scratches parallel to the tracks can wipe out whole sections. Some scratches can be polished out using a CD repair kit, available where CD's are sold.

Though less vulnerable than records, CD's require proper handling and care.

Exploded diagram labels

- Housing
- Power supply
- Power cord
- Laser/detector/lens assembly
- CD spindle (drive motor below)
- Track
- Tray assembly
- Tray motor (brush-type DC universal)
- Belt
- Chassis (housing)
- Hold-down clamp
- CD
- Front panel
- Tray front
- Controls

Troubleshooting

Problem	CAUSE? / Solution
Player does not work	NO POWER? Verify that there's power at outlet (see *Using voltage testers*, p.123). If yes, unplug player and remove housing to test power cord (see *Faulty power cord?*, p. 144). ◇ ▨
	INTERNAL POWER FUSE BLOWN? Remove housing; examine and/or test fuse (see *Fuses*, p.304); replace if faulty. ◇ ▨
	ON-OFF SWITCH NOT WORKING? Remove front panel to test switch (see *Resistance testing*, p.304). Replace if faulty (see *Replacing a board-mounted part*, p.305). ◆
Player works but no sound	SWITCHES INCORRECTLY SET? See owner's manual. ◇
	POOR CONNECTION TO STEREO SYSTEM? Check connections; test wires and cables for continuity (see *Resistance testing*, p.304); clean connections (see *Cleaning*, p.303). ◇
	DIRTY OBJECTIVE LENS? Clean lens (facing page). ◇
Tray jams or disc ejects	CD IMPROPERLY PLACED? Pull out the tray by hand, if needed; reposition the disc, usually with label facing upward. ◆
Player skips	DIRTY OR SCRATCHED CD? Clean or repair (box, above). ◇
	DIRT ON OBJECTIVE LENS? Clean the lens (facing page). ◇
	LASER/LENS/DETECTOR MISALIGNED? Have unit serviced.
Tray won't open or close properly	DIRTY OR WORN BELT? Clean or replace (facing page). ◆
	DISC TRAY JAMMED OR MISALIGNED? Remove, clean, lubricate, and reinstall tray (facing page) ◆; or have serviced.
Distorted sound	DIRTY OUTPUT JACKS? Jacks are located on back of the CD player. Disconnect plugs; clean jacks (see *Cleaning*, p.302). ◇
	DEFECTIVE ELECTRONIC COMPONENTS? Have player serviced.

Degree of difficulty: Simple ◇   Average ◆   Complex ◆   VOM required ▨

Servicing the disc tray and belt (single-play unit)

The tray delivers the CD to the spindle. Bumping the tray when it's extended can easily damage it. In addition, forcing the tray can strip its plastic gears, or a foreign object may jam them. Always use the push button to return the tray. If the tray is stuck, suspect a faulty motor, a damaged or jammed sliding gear, or a dirty or broken drive belt. Remove the tray and inspect the gears for damage and the tray arms for cracks. Replace a damaged tray. Relubricate the gears and the travel rail, if needed, with a dab of white lithium grease.

1 Open housing (facing page) and remove any foreign object blocking tray. Press *Open/Close* control to extend tray, and unplug unit. To remove clip-on tray front (left), brace tray and slide panel to one side.

Tray front
Tray assembly

2 Unplug any cables connecting the front panel to the interior. Remove screws securing the front panel, and gently tilt it off. If the panel won't budge, check beneath it for clips or additional screws.

3 Lift off hold-down on top of the disc tray (some have a screw and a spring). Gently pull tray out of player. Clean travel rail and guides with a swab dampened with denatured alcohol. Lubricate lightly with white lithium grease.

Guide

Travel rail

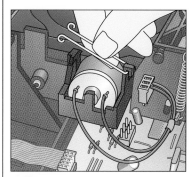

4 Remove belt to inspect for dirt, wear, or damage. Avoid touching belt with fingers; use tweezers or wear cotton gloves. Clean with lint-free cloth moistened with denatured alcohol. Replace belt if damaged. Do not pinch new belt.

Servicing the tray motor (single-play unit)

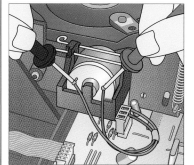
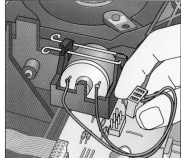

1 Unplug player and test motor resistance with a VOM set on RX1 scale. Resistance should be less than 10 ohms. High resistance indicates open windings.

2 A dirty motor plug can make tray work intermittently. To clean it, unplug and spray it with electrical contact cleaner; plug and unplug repeatedly.

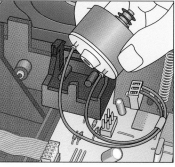

3 The motor is often clipped in place with a pair of wire bales. To remove the motor, depress the end of each bale with a finger and lift it up.

4 To replace motor, remove drive belt with tweezers or gloved hand (don't pinch belt too much or stretch it). Lift motor out of mount.

Cleaning the objective lens

Though gaining access to the lens varies from model to model, cleaning it is the same. Use a soft brush or a can of compressed air to remove heavy dust accumulations. Gently wipe with camera lens tissue or with a foam swab moistened with lens cleaner; too much pressure could damage it. Ordinary cloths or tissues may scratch the lens. **CAUTION:** Never clean the lens with the player on. An active laser can cause eye damage.

Lens
Spindle

To access the lens in a single-play unit, remove the housing and carefully lift up hold-down clamp to expose the lens.

Lens
Spindle

To access the lens in a carousel player, remove player housing and unscrew bracket secured to top of carousel; then lift bracket off.

Remove dust with canned air or soft brush; if needed, use foam swab or camera-lens tissue (not eyeglass tissue) wetted with lens fluid.

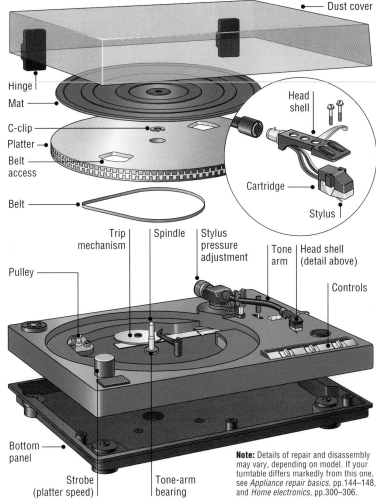

Dust cover

Hinge
Mat
C-clip
Platter
Belt access

Belt

Head shell

Cartridge

Stylus

Trip mechanism
Spindle
Stylus pressure adjustment
Tone arm
Head shell (detail above)

Pulley

Controls

Bottom panel

Strobe (platter speed)
Tone-arm bearing

Note: Details of repair and disassembly may vary, depending on model. If your turntable differs markedly from this one, see *Appliance repair basics*, pp.144–148, and *Home electronics*, pp.300–306.

Though CD players (p.308) and cassette decks (p.312) are more common, turntables are still used by people with record collections.

As a record plays, tiny variations in the walls of its grooves wiggle the stylus (needle) imperceptibly; the motion is converted to an electrical signal by the cartridge. The signal is then amplified by the receiver/amplifier (p.307) and sent to speakers (p.314).

Newer turntables are either belt-driven (as at left) or direct-drive (geared) units; older models may be driven by an idler wheel. If the platter slips or fails to turn, the belt may be dirty or worn, the idler tire may have hardened with age, or the motor may be faulty. The stylus, too, wears with use, resulting in a loss of performance. It must be replaced (facing page), in rare cases as part of a new cartridge.

Troubleshooting

Problem	CAUSE? / Solution
Power indicators light but platter doesn't spin	BROKEN OR STRETCHED BELT OR WORN TIRE? Replace belt (facing page) or idler wheel. ◆
	SPEED SWITCH OR CONTROLS DIRTY? Access controls and clean (facing page). ◆
	MOTOR FROZEN OR FAULTY? If motor is frozen, try to lubricate (see *Lubricants and lubricating*, p.137). If faulty, service it (facing page); replace motor if servicing fails. ◆
Stylus skips near end of record	TRIP MECHANISM STICKY? Access mechanism (*Disassembly*, Step 3). Clean and lubricate trip (facing page). Be careful not to overlubricate moving parts. ◆
Fuzzy sound	STYLUS OR RECORDS DIRTY? Clean stylus and records (facing page). ◇
	STYLUS WORN OR STYLUS SHAFT BENT? Replace stylus or stylus/cartridge (facing page). ◆
	STYLUS PRESSURE TOO HIGH? If cartridge rides on record, reset pressure (consult manual). ◆
Stylus skips	STYLUS FAULTY? Replace stylus or stylus/cartridge (facing page). ◆
	ANTISKATE OR STYLUS PRESSURE INCORRECTLY SET? Consult manual and reset. ◇
	TONE ARM BEARING STICKS? Lubricate bearing (see *Lubricating a turntable*, facing page). ◆
Sound weak or intermittent	CARTRIDGE OR HEAD-SHELL PINS OXIDIZED? Clean all contacts (see *Servicing the cartridge*, facing page). If cleaning fails to correct problem, cartridge may have to be replaced. ◆
	OUTPUT JACKS OR PLUGS DIRTY OR FAULTY? Clean (see *Cleaning*, p.303); or replace. ◇
Bass feedback	TURNTABLE TOO CLOSE TO SPEAKERS? Move equipment apart; place on isolated bases. ◇
Pickup (cartridge) hum	TURNTABLE TOO CLOSE TO A RECEIVER, CLOCK, OR APPLIANCE? Move equipment apart. ◇
	POOR CONNECTION? Service cartridge (facing page). Also see *Troubleshooting*, p.302. ◆
	GROUND WIRE NOT CONNECTED TO RECEIVER? Connect ground wire (p.306). ◇

Degree of difficulty: Simple ◇   Average ◆   Complex ◆

Disassembly

Access hole

1 Unplug unit. Lift off cover and mat. Rotate platter to access pulley through hole; lift belt off (see *Replacing the belt*, Step 1, facing page).

C-clip
Spindle

2 Pry C-clip off spindle (see *Tips from the pros*, p.189). Keep one finger on clip to prevent it from flying off. Protect your eyes.

3 Lift platter from spindle to expose some of the serviceable internal parts. Belt can now be removed from platter.

4 To access remaining parts, secure tone arm, install dust cover, and turn unit over. Remove bottom panel screws and lift panel off.

Servicing the stylus

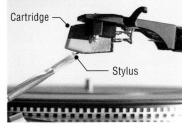

Cartridge

Stylus

Cartridge

Stylus mounted in plug-in holder

Clean the stylus with a soft brush, drawing the brush toward front of cartridge. Never touch the stylus with a finger.

If replacing the stylus, pull it out gently. Be careful not to bend new stylus when clipping it into place.

Servicing the cartridge

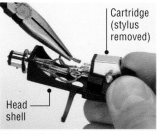

Head shell

Locking band

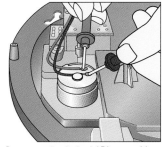

Cartridge (stylus removed)

Head shell

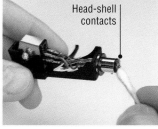

Head-shell contacts

1 Unscrew locking band by twisting it with fingers. Pull head shell away from tone arm. Remove stylus.

2 Reseat each wire to remove oxidation. If replacing cartridge, make wiring diagram before unscrewing it.

3 Spray contact cleaner on swab to clean contacts. (Spraying directly can damage cartridge and stylus.)

Cleaning the controls

Remove screws securing circuit boards to reach attached controls (here, speed selector and pitch controls). Spray electrical contact cleaner inside each control and operate it 10–20 times to clean internal contacts before reassembling. Test operation. If control is still faulty, replace control or entire circuit board (p.305).

Caring for records

Records are becoming collectible. They are increasingly hard to find and costly, so proper care is important.

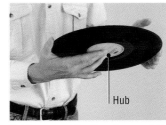

Hub

Hold a record by its edges and the center hub; never touch the grooves. Finger oils cause dirt to adhere to the groove walls.

Store records vertically in a cool dry place to prevent warping. Never leave one on a warm surface.

Insert a record's inner sleeve into its jacket with the opening at the top so record will not fall out of the jacket.

To clean a record, dampen a cylindrical record brush with denatured alcohol. Rotate record while brushing against its rotation to remove dirt and oils. To remove heavy dirt, wash record using fine-bristle paintbrush in warm water and liquid dish detergent; then rinse thoroughly and air-dry.

Replace the stylus after every 500–1,000 hours of use. A worn stylus will damage a record.

Replacing the belt

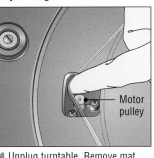

Motor pulley

1 Unplug turntable. Remove mat. Reach gloved fingertip (or screwdriver tip) into platter access hole and lift belt off motor pulley; then lift off platter (*Disassembly*, Step 3).

Gloves protect belt

2 Slip belt off underside of platter. Clean belt, rim, and motor pulley with swab and denatured alcohol, or replace belt if damaged or worn.

Servicing the motor

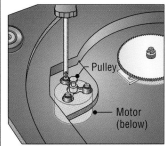

Access motor to test (*Disassembly*, Step 4). Set VOM on RX1. Probe terminals; look for low ohms reading. Probe each terminal and motor housing; motor is ok if meter reads infinity.

Pulley

Motor (below)

To replace platter motor, turn unit over; remove platter (*Disassembly*, Step 3) and motor mounting screws (above). Cut wires at the old motor and resolder them to the new one.

Lubricating the turntable

Bushing

Trip mechanism

Bearing

Apply white lithium grease to bushing atop platter gear. If platter has a ball-type bearing, remove, clean, and grease it. Clean sticky trip mechanism with denatured alcohol; lightly grease.

Lubricate tone-arm bearing with lightweight synthetic lubricant. Use just a drop or two. If you don't have a special oiler, apply a drop of lubricant with tip of a toothpick.

Home electronics ▪ Cassette decks

A cassette deck records and plays music stored on magnetic tape. Unlike a reel-to-reel tape recorder, however, the tape is contained in a housing, called a cassette, that holds the tape take-up and supply reels. The cassette deck's small size, fidelity, and convenience have made it by far the most popular music format worldwide. The deck is often used to copy music from other formats (including CD's and records) for use in car and portable tape players (pp.329–331).

Newer cassette decks feature reliable electronic circuitry, so problems are likely to be mechanical in nature. Cleaning, lubrication, and replacement of broken belts will add years of useful service. Most electronic problems are best left to a service professional.

Keep cassettes away from the magnetic fields of speakers, TV's, and computer monitors, and store them away from heat and sunlight. Take up any slack by turning the reel hub with a pencil before playing.

Note: Details of repair and disassembly may vary, depending on equipment model. If your player differs markedly from this one, contact the manufacturer for a parts list and diagram. Also see *Appliance repair basics*, pp.132–148, and *Electronics repair basics*, pp.300–305.

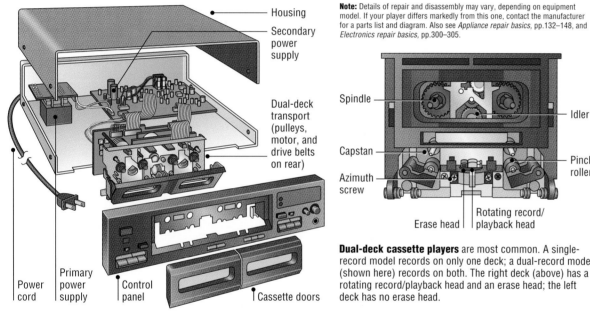

Housing
Secondary power supply
Dual-deck transport (pulleys, motor, and drive belts on rear)
Power cord
Primary power supply
Control panel
Cassette doors

Spindle
Capstan
Azimuth screw
Idler
Pinch roller
Erase head
Rotating record/playback head

Dual-deck cassette players are most common. A single-record model records on only one deck; a dual-record model (shown here) records on both. The right deck (above) has a rotating record/playback head and an erase head; the left deck has no erase head.

Troubleshooting

Problem	CAUSE? / Solution
Hiss, weak sound, no highs	HEADS DIRTY? Clean and demagnetize heads (facing page). ◇
	HEADS MISALIGNED/WORN? See *Servicing the heads*, facing page. Replace head (non-rotating type only) if grooved where tape contacts it. ◆
Tape spills out of cassette	BELT BROKEN? Replace belt (facing page). ◆
	FAULTY CASSETTE? Slap cassette flat on table to make tape lie evenly on reels. If still bad or if hubs bind, replace tape; or remove tape and install it in a new replacement cassette (below, left). ◇
	PINCH ROLLER DIRTY? Clean roller (facing page). ◇
Sound garbled	FAULTY RECORDING? Rerecord or replace. ◇
	HEADS DIRTY? See *Hiss, weak sound, no highs*, above.
	BELTS DIRTY, STRETCHED, OR SLIPPING? Clean or replace stretched belts (facing page). ◆
Deck won't rewind or fast forward	BELT BROKEN? Replace belt (facing page). ◆
	IDLER FAULTY? Remove deck (see *Servicing the drive system*, facing page); replace tire or idler (see *Servicing the idler assembly*, p.353). ◆
Deck stops unexpectedly or won't stop at end of tape	CASSETTE DIRTY OR TAPE MISALIGNED? Inspect hubs and clean off dirt; slap cassette on table to make tape lie evenly on reels. ◇
	GLAZED PINCH ROLLER? Remove deck (see *Servicing the drive system*, facing page) and unscrew from front panel. Lift roller assembly off shaft to replace (it may be secured with C-clip). ◆
	TAPE MOTION SENSOR FAULTY OR DIRTY? Access is difficult; have unit serviced.
Deck won't record	RECORD-SAFETY TAB REMOVED? Tape over tab holes on cassette to allow recording. ◇
	RECORD/PLAYBACK SWITCH FAULTY OR DIRTY? Access is difficult; have unit serviced.
Distorted, intermittent sound	DIRTY CONNECTIONS? Clean external jacks, cables, and plugs (see *Cleaning*, p.303). ◇
	HEADS FAULTY? See *Servicing the heads*, facing page. Access heads, inspect wire leads, and resolder if needed; test and replace heads if faulty. ◆
Intermittent operation	DIRTY CONNECTIONS? See *Distorted, intermittent sound*, above.
	TAPE FOULED? If tape becomes twisted inside cassette, pull out tape or open cassette to straighten (left); replace if tape is damaged. ◇
Deck shocks user	See *General troubleshooting*, p.147.

Degree of difficulty: Simple ◇   Average ◈   Complex ◆

Repairing a cassette tape

If a valuable tape breaks, use a splicing kit to repair it so you can make another copy. When possible, avoid taking the housing apart. If you must open it, remove screws or pry a bonded housing open; be careful not to let the tape unwind or fall out. Reinstall the repaired tape. Splicing kits and replacement housings that are assembled with screws are available at electronics stores.

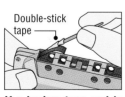

Double-stick tape

If a broken tape end is visible, fish for it with double-stick tape wrapped over a toothpick.

Pry a bonded housing open at seam, or remove assembly screws, to reach a tape you can't access otherwise.

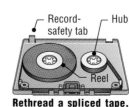

Record-safety tab
Hub
Reel

Rethread a spliced tape, or install tape reels in a replacement housing, as shown above.

Cleaning and demagnetizing the heads

A tape recorder works by magnetizing particles of metal oxide glued to the tape. Over time oxides come loose from the tape and collect on the tape guides, capstans, and pinch rollers and can push the tape off the path. The magnetic fields are weak and the particles microscopic; so even a little dirt on the head (or stray magnetism) will affect the sound. Clean and demagnetize the heads after 10 to 20 hours of use, using a cleaning/demagnetizing tape. (Usually you apply a solution and "play" the tape for 20 seconds.) If the problem persists, clean the transport (right).

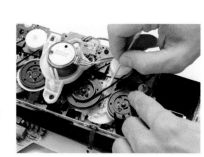

Pinch roller | Heads

Capstan

To clean tape transport and heads, open cassette door. Wipe heads with cotton swab moistened with denatured alcohol or special head-cleaning fluid. Turn player on and hold swab against each capstan and pinch roller as it turns.

Servicing the heads

Troubleshooting may suggest a problem with the heads. If your deck has a single reversing head, such as the one shown at left, servicing the head should be done by a professional. But if you have simpler non-rotating heads, you can test and/or replace them without difficulty. For adjustments only, go to Step 3. Otherwise remove the deck (see *Servicing the drive system*, Steps 1, 2, and 3, left). Remove the tape door (most clip on, others have screws) and the screws that attach the deck to the front panel. (If there's a belt from the deck to a counter pulley on the front panel, remove it first.) Then proceed as described below.

Servicing the drive system

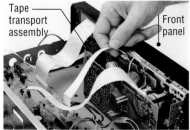

Tape transport assembly

Front panel

Transport

1 Unplug cassette deck and remove housing (facing page). Disconnect flat cables leading to front panel and transport assembly, lifting one side, then the other.

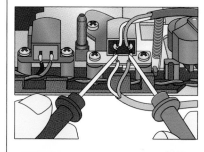

4 Turn pulleys by hand while cleaning belts with cotton swab moistened with denatured alcohol. Do not touch belts with fingers; even small amounts of skin oil can cause slippage.

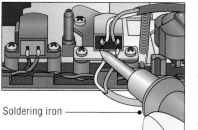

Soldering iron

1 Set VOM on RX1 and probe each set of colored wires; some heads must be removed to access contacts. Infinity means head is open (zero OK). Probe terminals and head shell; zero indicates a short (infinity OK).

2 Turn deck upside down. Remove screws holding transport assembly and front panel in place. Turn deck right side up (left), and remove front panel and transport assembly.

Belt

Motor pulley

5 To replace a worn or cracked belt, make belt path diagram; then cut or lift off old belt. Loop new belt (wear cotton gloves) and fit it over the motor pulley. Use tweezers, too, if needed.

2 Remove screws that attach head to transport. Label wires or make a diagram to facilitate installing new head; then desolder wires. Install new head. (*Note:* new head must be demagnetized before use.)

6 Thread new belt over pulleys with small screwdriver and/or gloved fingers. Don't over-stretch the belt. Rotate pulley and make sure belt isn't twisted. Reverse Steps 1, 2, and 3 to reassemble unit.

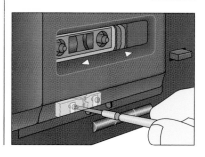

3 Unplug leads (inset) to allow partial disassembly of transport and to expose belts. Here, a circuit board is easily removed and lifted aside; in some units, however, gaining access can be quite difficult.

3 Reassemble unit; then align heads. Play a tape while you adjust azimuth screws. Listen for best treble response if using a prerecorded tape or to maximize pitch if using a special azimuth tape.

Home electronics ▪ Speakers

The typical audio system speaker is actually a collection of dependent parts. The enclosure contains a 6- to 12-inch-diameter cone woofer (for low frequencies); a 3- to 6-inch diameter dome or cone midrange driver; and a small tweeter for high frequencies (it can have various configurations). Audio signals are carried along speaker cables (p.306) to a terminal block and, in turn, to a crossover network. The network divides incoming frequencies into the appropriate ranges, sending each to the correct driver. Drivers then convert this input into mechanical movement of the cone. What you hear is actually air movement caused by the cone.

In addition to holding drivers, the enclosure can add mass to a speaker (forcing more energy into the cone) and improve bass tones. There are two principal speaker designs: bass reflex units with tuned portholes (right) and airtight acoustic suspension units.

Speakers are most likely to suffer from improper use. The enclosure is vulnerable to damage and may come unglued. For information on wood repairs, see *Working with wood*, p.57. Because the speaker is part of an audio system, a sound problem can often be traced to a faulty component in the system (such as a receiver), wiring connections between components, or an error in operating one or more of the components.

If the fault is truly with the speaker, diagnosis, disassembly, testing, and repair or replacement of parts are all relatively easy and usually require only a screwdriver and a volt-ohm meter (see *Using a volt-ohm meter*, p.130).

To disassemble:
Remove front grille to access drivers and crossover network. Grilles usually are secured with snaps or Velcro; the crossover network may be exposed on the rear of enclosure. To remove drivers in a bass reflex speaker, unscrew them; drivers in an acoustic suspension speaker may be set in sealant for an airtight fit.

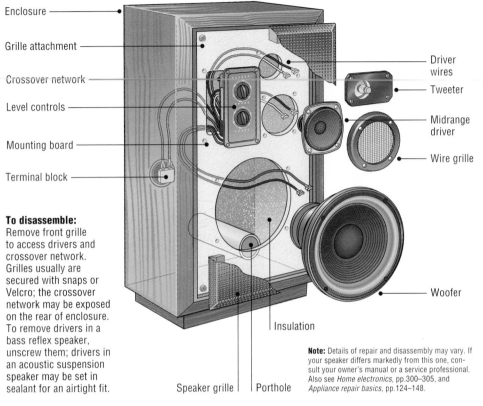

Enclosure
Grille attachment
Crossover network
Level controls
Mounting board
Terminal block

Driver wires
Tweeter
Midrange driver
Wire grille
Woofer
Insulation
Speaker grille | Porthole

Note: Details of repair and disassembly may vary. If your speaker differs markedly from this one, consult your owner's manual or a service professional. Also see *Home electronics*, pp.300–305, and *Appliance repair basics*, pp.124–148.

Repairing a damaged cone

Patch small holes in cone (paper type only) using rubber cement (apply to both surfaces); add kraft-paper patch if needed. For large holes, replace driver or have a new cone installed (called reconing).

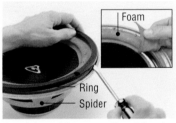

Foam
Ring
Spider

To refoam a driver, pry off retaining ring and peel off foam from cone and spider (inset). Glue new foam to cone and then to spider. Refoaming kits with instructions are advertised in stereo magazines.

Parts of a driver

Coil gap
Retaining ring
Cone
Dust cover
Voice coil
Magnet
Spider (frame)

Removing a driver

Crossover network

1 Unplug speaker cable, pry off grille, and lay enclosure on its back (above) to loosen fasteners. Lift out drivers. Crossover network on this speaker is similarly removed. On other models it may be mounted on the rear or inside. Disconnect internal wires as required.

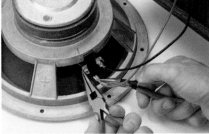

2 To disconnect wires, grasp driver terminal with long-nose pliers; use second pliers to pull off wire connector. If fit is loose, pinch connector with pliers before reattaching it. If they are soldered, place a barrier over cone when desoldering (see *How to desolder*, p.136).

Troubleshooting

Problem	CAUSE? / Solution
No sound from either speaker	SYSTEM COMPONENT PROBLEM? Make sure other audio components are properly connected and adjusted (p.306). ◇
	BLOWN SPEAKER FUSE; TRIPPED THERMAL CUTOUT OR BREAKER? Replace blown fuse; reset cutout or breaker. ◇
No sound from all drivers in one speaker	BLOWN SPEAKER FUSE; TRIPPED THERMAL CUTOUT OR BREAKER? See *No sound from either speaker,* above. ◇
	SPEAKER OR CROSSOVER NETWORK WIRING FAULTY? Test internal wires (right). Rewire if necessary. ◇ ▣
	RECEIVER FAULTY? Test with another speaker and cable; if still no sound, problem is with receiver. Have receiver serviced. ◇
No sound from one driver	VOICE COIL OPEN? Access driver (facing page); remove leads, and test driver (right). If coil is faulty, replace driver (right). ◇ ▣
	SPEAKER FROZEN OR BLOWN? Press cone lightly. If voice coil does not move in and out freely, replace driver. Cause may be too much power from amplifier circuits (see owner's manual). ◇
	CROSSOVER NETWORK FAULTY? Service network (right). ◆ ▣
	SOLDER CONNECTION FAULTY? Resolder (p.136). ◆
Mushy, distorted sound	RECEIVER FAULTY? See *No sound from all drivers,* above. ◇
	SPEAKER CABLE OR CONNECTION FAULTY? Flex cable at low volume; if sound varies, replace cable. Clean connections. ◇
	DROPPED DRIVER CONE OR LOOSE MAGNET? Remove faulty driver (facing page); have it reconed or replace it. ◇
	SPEAKERS NOT IN PHASE? Check polarity (right). ◇
	VOICE COIL FAULTY? Test driver (right); lightly press cone in and out with fingers, feeling for rubbing coil. Replace if faulty. ◇ ▣
Noisy speaker	VOICE COIL FAULTY? See *Mushy, distorted sound,* above. ◇ ▣
	DRIVER CONE DAMAGED? Repair small holes in cone (facing page); have badly damaged driver reconed professionally, or replace driver. ◇
	LOOSE ENCLOSURE PANEL, POOR SEAL? Repair (see *Working with wood,* p.55). ◆
	VOLUME CONTROL DIRTY? Clean volume control with electronic contact cleaner (see *Cleaning and lubrication,* p.137). ◆
Intermittent sound	SPEAKER CABLE OR CONNECTION FAULTY? See *Mushy, distorted sound,* above. ◇
	BROKEN LEVEL CONTROL? Test thermal cutout (if crossover network has one) as you would a fuse (see *Fuses,* p.304). ◇ ▣
	VOICE COIL FAULTY? See *Mushy, distorted sound,* above. ◇ ▣

Degree of difficulty: Simple ◇   Average ◆   Complex ◆   Volt-ohm meter required: ▣

Testing internal wiring

To test wiring, remove drivers and crossover network; set VOM on RX1 scale and probe wires from terminal block to crossover network and from network to faulty driver (left). Both should show continuity (zero reading). If faulty, rewire.

Testing a driver

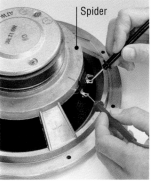

Spider

To test a driver, remove it; label and disconnect wires. Set VOM on RX1 scale; probe both driver terminals. Resistance should be close to driver's ohms impedance rating (see owner's manual). Then probe each terminal and spider; look for infinity readings.

Getting the polarity right

To maintain proper polarity (phasing), you must correctly wire the receiver to the speaker. To help, the terminals are coded red (+) and black (-); the ground wire of the cable may be coded with a white line or lettering. If the cable is not coded, verify the correct terminal by reversing the connections at the speaker to see which yields the richest bass tones. Or conduct a test: With the grille removed so you can see the drivers, clip a wire to each speaker terminal, and touch the other end of each wire to terminals on a 1½-volt battery. The cone will move out when the two positive terminals are connected to each other.

Servicing the crossover network

Capacitor

1 Remove crossover network. Pull off level control knobs and unscrew cover to access capacitors. (The capacitors block frequencies beyond the range of a particular driver.) These nonpolarized capacitors needn't be discharged as storage-type capacitors (p.146) must be.

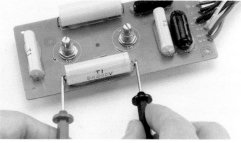

2 Test capacitor with VOM. Set meter on RX1 scale and probe both terminals. Meter should register low resistance and slowly climb to infinity. Reverse probes; results should be the same. If not, the capacitor is faulty.

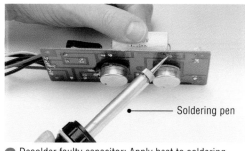

Soldering pen

3 Desolder faulty capacitor: Apply heat to soldering point with soldering pen; pull off capacitor as solder melts. Solder identical replacement to circuit board using additional solder if required (see *Soldering and desoldering,* p.136), and reassemble crossover network.

Home electronics ▪ Cameras

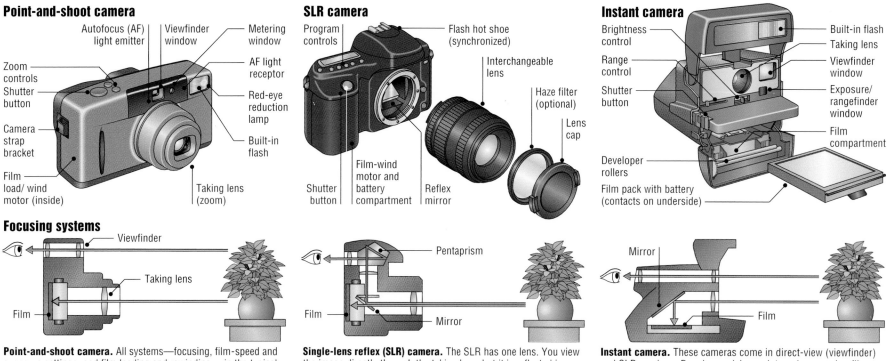

Point-and-shoot camera

- Autofocus (AF) light emitter
- Viewfinder window
- Metering window
- AF light receptor
- Red-eye reduction lamp
- Built-in flash
- Taking lens (zoom)
- Zoom controls
- Shutter button
- Camera strap bracket
- Film load/ wind motor (inside)

SLR camera

- Program controls
- Flash hot shoe (synchronized)
- Interchangeable lens
- Haze filter (optional)
- Lens cap
- Film-wind motor and battery compartment
- Reflex mirror
- Shutter button

Instant camera

- Brightness control
- Built-in flash
- Taking lens
- Range control
- Viewfinder window
- Shutter button
- Exposure/ rangefinder window
- Film compartment
- Developer rollers
- Film pack with battery (contacts on underside)

Focusing systems

- Viewfinder
- Taking lens
- Film
- Pentaprism
- Film
- Mirror
- Mirror
- Film

Point-and-shoot camera. All systems—focusing, film-speed and exposure settings, and film loading and rewinding— in the typical point-and-shoot are automatic; and the camera usually has a separate viewing and taking lens. There are single-, dual-, and zoom-lens models with manual or electric controls. The viewing lens adjusts to compensate for the different focal lengths of the taking lens.

Single-lens reflex (SLR) camera. The SLR has one lens. You view the image directly through the taking lens, but it is reflected in an angled mirror, which typically retracts momentarily as the picture is taken. A pentaprism corrects this mirror image, which is flopped (left for right, top for bottom), so it becomes right-reading at the viewfinder. The lens may be focused manually or automatically.

Instant camera. These cameras come in direct-view (viewfinder) and SLR versions. Popular models use integral processing film packs: the negative is processed and the print is produced within one piece of material. The print is either ejected from the camera after each shot or is stored internally. Some other models use two-piece, peel-apart negative and print material.

Popular still cameras fall into three main categories— 35 mm point-and-shoot, 35 mm SLR (single-lens reflex), and instant. The cameras differ in how the image is viewed (through the taking lens or through a separate viewer), how the lens is focused (automatically or manually), and how the image reaches the film. Within each of these categories, however, are hybrid cameras that incorporate features once found exclusively on other types. Modern cameras have become so complicated that there is little you can do to repair a damaged unit; instead, take it in for professional service. (A service center, in turn, may send the camera directly to the manufacturer when it comes to making complex electronic repairs.)

Most automatic cameras depend so heavily on batteries to power their internal circuitry that weak batteries (see *Camera batteries,* p.318) or poor electrical connections are, together with a variety of user errors, the most common causes of photo problems. Basic care and maintenance will usually keep a camera in good working order, however, and the techniques are much the same whatever the type of camera.

Types of film. Most popular 35 mm cameras (as opposed to some professional models) use one of several types of cassette film. Instant cameras use self-developing film; the film packets contain not only the film but also a developing solution and the batteries that power the camera itself.

35 mm camera anatomy

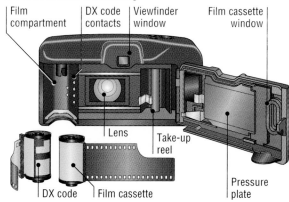

- Film compartment
- DX code contacts
- Viewfinder window
- Film cassette window
- Lens
- Take-up reel
- DX code
- Film cassette
- Pressure plate

How cameras focus

To focus a manual rangefinder (RF) camera, the user looks through the viewfinder and adjusts the lens until the two images—one from the viewfinder and one from the range-finder—are brought together to become one (right). To focus a manual SLR, the viewer looks through the taking lens and adjusts it until the image is clear.

The most common auto-focusing systems employs infrared light and geometric triangulation to calculate distance (far right). The smaller the angle, the farther away the object. Similarly, an active sonar system sends out an ultrasonic impulse instead of light, and a timer measures the time it takes for the echo to return. Both types then signal the lens motor to adjust the focus accordingly.

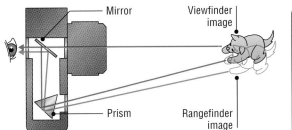

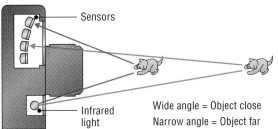

In a manual rangefinder system, a prism and mirror direct an image from the rangefinder window to the viewfinder window, where it overlaps the image seen directly through the viewfinder. When the two images coincide, the lens is in focus.

An infrared auto-focus system sends a beam of infrared light to a subject. The reflected light is picked up by one of a number of sensors—each at a slightly different angle—in the camera. The camera calculates the distance by mathematical triangulation.

Troubleshooting

Problem	CAUSE? / Solution
Camera won't operate	LENS COVER ON OR MAIN SWITCH OFF? See owner's manual. ◇
	DEAD BATTERIES OR POOR CONTACTS? Replace batteries and/or clean contacts (see *Camera batteries*, p.318). ◇
	IMPROPER BATTERY ORIENTATION? Reposition batteries correctly. ◇
	SELF-TIMER LOCKED HALFWAY? Have camera serviced.
	NO FILM IN CAMERA? Load film; some models do not operate without film. ◇
	REWOUND FILM STILL IN CAMERA? Remove film. ◇
	OUT OF FOCUS OR EXPOSURE RANGE? See owner's manual. ◇
No pictures	FILM IMPROPERLY LOADED? Load film carefully (see owner's manual). ◇
	BLANK ROLL SENT FOR DEVELOPING IN ERROR? See *Use and care*, p.318).
Blurred, unsharp photos	CAMERA OR SUBJECT MOTION? Steady camera, reduce subject motion or make shorter exposure.
	FINGER OR STRAP OVER AUTO-FOCUS WINDOW? Hold camera properly. ◇
	DIRTY AUTO-FOCUS WINDOW OR LENS? Clean window or lens (p.318). ◇
	PLASTIC FILTER USED ON INFRARED-FOCUS LENS? Remove or replace interfering plastic filter with an equivalent glass filter. ◇
	IMPROPER FOCUSING? Focus with subject centered, then recompose. ◇
	PHOTO TAKEN WITHOUT FLASH IN DARK CONDITIONS? Use flash. ◇
	FOCUS SYSTEM OR LENS FAULTY? Have camera or lens serviced.
Near in focus/ far not in focus	INFRARED-FOCUS CAMERA SHOT THROUGH GLASS/CAR WINDOW? Maintain direct contact with subject. ◇
Shutter fires and jams midway	WEAK BATTERIES OR POOR CONTACTS? Replace batteries, clean contacts, or bend contacts to increase tension (See *Camera batteries*, p.318*).* ◇
Flash fires; exposure too dark	FLASH WINDOW OBSTRUCTED? Hold camera properly. ◇
	SUBJECT OUT OF RANGE? Stay in range, often 5–10 ft. (see owner's manual).

Problem	CAUSE? / Solution
Photos too light	OBSTRUCTED OR DIRTY LIGHT SENSOR WINDOW? Hold camera properly; clean dirty window (a common problem). ◇
	WRONG FILM SPEED SETTING? Adjust setting; or use DX-coded film with DX-coding camera. ◇
Photos too dark	WRONG FILM SPEED SETTING? See *Photos too light*, above.
	WEAK BATTERY OR POOR CONTACTS? See *Blurred, unsharp photos*, left.
Light streaks, marks, or lines on photos	FILM CASSETTE EXPOSED TO BRIGHT SUNLIGHT? Handle film in dim light. ◇
	DIRT IN FILM CASSETTE? Keep cassette sealed until ready to load it. ◇
	DIRT ON CAMERA PRESSURE PLATE? Scratches on back side of film may be due to dirt on plate. Clean camera interior and pressure plate (p.319). ◇
	REWINDING TOO FAST? If emulsion (front) side of film is scratched, rewind film more slowly. ◇
	LIGHT LEAKS? Replace any missing screws; seal any holes. ◇ If camera is damaged or has worn mirror or film door seals, have it serviced.
Partial dark area on photo	FINGER OR STRAP OVER LENS? Hold camera properly. ◇
	FOREIGN OBJECT IN CAMERA? Inspect before loading film; remove object. ◇
Foggy or greenish photos	LIGHT LEAKS? See *Light streaks, marks, or lines on photos*, above.
	BAD FILM? Use film before expiration date and avoid storing it in hot places. ◇
Drive fails to stop or tears film	FAULTY MIRROR INTERRUPTER SWITCH? *(SLR only)* Have camera serviced.
	FAULTY CLUTCH? Have camera serviced.
Counter inoperative	FILM NOT ADVANCING? Make sure film has been loaded properly. ◇
	DEFECTIVE FILM COUNTER MECHANISM? Have camera serviced.
Repeated pattern on instant prints	DIRTY ROLLERS? *(Instant models only)* Clean developer rollers (p.319). ◇

Degree of difficulty: Simple ◇   Average ◆   Complex ◆

Disassembling a camera

Many professional repairs involve cameras that have been damaged by people who attempted "minor" interior repairs of their own. *Disassembling a lens or camera body is not recommended.* Most internal repairs, even thorough cleaning and lubrication inside the camera, require that you have considerable information, only some of which can be gleaned from studying repair manuals. If you feel that you are sufficiently knowledgeable about your camera to disassemble it, consider the following disassembly cautions.

⚡ **Use extreme caution** on cameras with integral flashes. Their capacitors hold 300–400 volts at sufficient amperage to kill by cardiac arrest. Unlike motor capacitors and others that can be safely discharged with reasonable care, these are very difficult to access and the slightest false move can result in death. They must be discharged by a trained professional.

Do not disassemble any camera without consulting a camera repair manual for further guidance.

Use drivers that are perfectly matched to the type and size of screw you wish to turn or you may easily damage it.

Group screws and related parts together, noting every screw and its location. Consider using a video camera fitted with a close-up lens to record the disassembly process.

Avoid using a battery-powered continuity tester or VOM on delicate electronic circuitry. The voltage from these tools can damage the camera. Use only a DMM (p.300).

USE AND CARE

Install a haze filter (if the camera accepts filters) to protect the lens in use (see *Caring for a camera lens,* above).

Always roll exposed film fully into cassette or crease the exposed end so you know the film has been exposed.

Avoid condensation that occurs when a cold camera is brought indoors. Keep it warm; or seal a cold camera in a plastic bag before bringing it indoors to warm.

Avoid using or storing a camera in a damp environment; allow a damp camera to dry thoroughly before using it.

Use a camera strap and carrying case; don't leave a camera where it's subject to falls, liquid spills, or other accidents.

Shock, moisture, extreme temperatures, and dirt are the chief enemies of any camera. Keep dirt out of the film compartment and off the lens.

Caring for a camera lens

Lenses are made of glass (or plastic), and the taking lens must be kept meticulously clean. A protective coating on the lens is easily damaged by excessive or improper cleaning, so the best course is to try to keep dirt off the lens in the first place. Never touch a lens with your fingers. Always keep the lens cap on or its cover closed when the camera is not in use. If the lens accepts accessory filters, use a haze filter to protect the lens when the camera is in use.

Clean a lens only when you must. Always blow or brush loose dust away first, so it won't be ground into the lens. Canned *moisture-free* compressed air, available at camera shops, is ideal. Use a camel-hair (or another equally soft) brush. Blower brushes do both jobs at once. If further cleaning is required, use lens chamois or lens tissue dampened with lens-cleaning fluid. Use cotton swabs to clean around the perimeter of a lens and to clean smaller viewing lenses. Never wipe a dry lens, and don't use regular cloth, facial tissues, or eyeglass lens-cleaning tissues (they may be chemically treated). If you breathe on the lens and the moisture then clears evenly, the lens is clean.

Blow or brush away loose dust with blower brush, canned air, or soft camel-hair brush. Purchase canned air from a photo shop; brands sold elsewhere may contain impurities hard to remove from a lens.

Blower brush

Lens-cleaning fluid

Lens tissue

When using fluid, always apply the fluid to the cleaning tissue, chamois, or swab; don't spray or pour it directly on the lens. Clean in a circular motion, working from the outer edges toward the center.

Camera batteries

So many camera functions depend on a reliable power source that dead or weak batteries and poor battery contacts cause most camera problems. Even new batteries may not be fresh; so have them tested when purchased. User-replaceable batteries are usually secured by a clip, but many cameras have secondary batteries for memory functions. These long-lasting batteries may be wired in place. They are harder to find; consult your owner's manual for their location.

Contacts can lose their tension and fail to make good contact with the battery. Also, the slightest corrosion on the battery terminals or contacts can cause problems even if the batteries are perfectly good. Never leave batteries in the camera when it is not going to be used for a week or more. Although it's rare, batteries can leak, causing extensive damage.

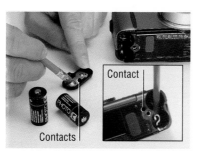

Contact

Contacts

Clean corroded contacts with an eraser. For severe corrosion, use mini wire brush in a drill. Avoid sandpaper; it's too abrasive. If contact no longer holds battery (inset) securely, bend it to increase tension.

To clean battery compartment after a battery acid leak, flood it repeatedly with electrical contact cleaner to wash out acid. Hold camera so that liquid drains out. Remove corrosion as shown at left.

Flash/strobe units

Nearly all point-and-shoot cameras, and many newer SLR's, have a convenient built-in flash. But external flash units that attach to the camera's hot shoe—either directly or via a flash cord—are still common. These units have reusable bulbs powered by high-voltage capacitors (see *Disassembling a camera,* facing page). These capacitors are charged by either single-use or rechargeable batteries (see *Cordless tools and appliances,* p.142).

The most common problem on attached flash units is a broken base (the part that attaches to the hot shoe). Such damage requires professional repair. User service is limited to battery and contact maintenance.

Be sure that the battery, the hot shoe, and the flash socket connections are clean. Simply connecting and disconnecting the flash unit or cords several times usually removes minor oxidation and dirt. If trouble persists, however, clean the contacts (below) or test the cord (bottom). If the cord tests OK and the unit still fails to operate, have the camera serviced.

Hot shoe

Clean the hot-shoe contacts if you experience flash problems. Even slight invisible oxidation can cause failures. Dampen a cotton swab with electrical contact cleaner or vinegar, and clean the contacts on the hot shoe and the base of the flash unit or the cord.

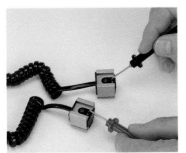

To test continuity of a synchronized-flash cord, set a volt-ohm meter on the RX1 scale and probe the mating terminals on the plug ends. The reading should be near zero. Flash cords are less used today; they are notoriously susceptible to failure.

SLR repair

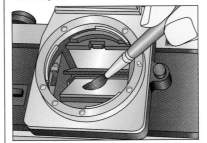

Brush any dust off a reflex mirror if it's annoying. Don't use compressed air; it may blow dust into inaccessible areas and cause problems. If necessary, follow lens-cleaning procedures shown on the facing page.

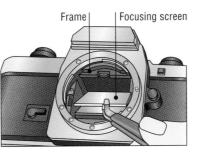
Frame | Focusing screen

To refit a focusing screen that has dropped due to impact (replaceable type only), remove lens; reposition screen in its frame using its finger hold or padded tweezers; press frame up into place.

Inside a 35 mm camera

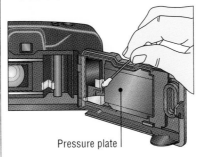
Pressure plate

Blow dust out of film compartment with canned air (don't blow delicate shutter blades). Clean pressure plate, especially its leading and trailing edges, using cotton swabs dampened with denatured alcohol.

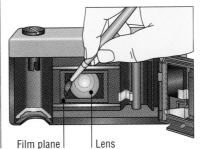
Film plane | Lens

Use black India ink to touch up matte-black coating inside film compartment of older (metal) cameras, especially between lens and film plane. Light reflected off shiny metal may cause spots on photos.

Instant-camera repair

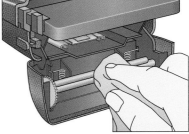

Clean developer rollers with a damp lint-free cloth. Clean lenses and windows as done with other cameras. Instant-camera batteries are renewed with each film change; they don't usually present problems.

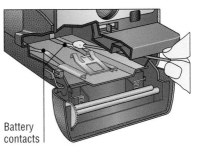
Battery contacts

Clean the battery contacts, however, if an instant camera fails to operate. They are located inside the film compartment. Use a cotton swab dampened with contact cleaner or vinegar, or use an eraser.

Home electronics ▪ Computers

A personal computer is actually a system of devices (hardware) linked by cables and controlled by programs (software). The main device is the *system unit* (sometimes referred to as the computer), which contains a silicon chip called the *central processing unit* (CPU). The CPU is the system's "brain," analyzing and processing signals from other devices, and is located on a circuit board called the *motherboard* or *system board*. Data manipulated by a computer system is contained on an inexpensive *floppy disk* or on an internal (and higher-capacity) *hard disk*. Disk *drives* "read" and "write" data to the appropriate disks. Also inside the system unit are *read-only memory* (ROM) chips, which store the computer's permanent operating instructions, and *random-access memory* (RAM) chips, which temporarily store programs and data during use.

Other common components (called peripherals) include a keyboard and mouse that enable you to enter, select, and manipulate data; a monitor (p.341) that displays the data; a printer (p.326); a CD-ROM drive; and a modem that links the computer to telephone lines.

Equipment protection. To reduce the risk of damage caused by electrical spikes, plug the system into a CSA-rated surge protector; unplug it entirely during thunderstorms. To avoid problems caused by magnetism and static electricity when servicing a computer, use nonmagnetic tools and touch grounded metal or wear an antistatic wrist strap (p.301) before touching any components.

System unit

Monitor and keyboard

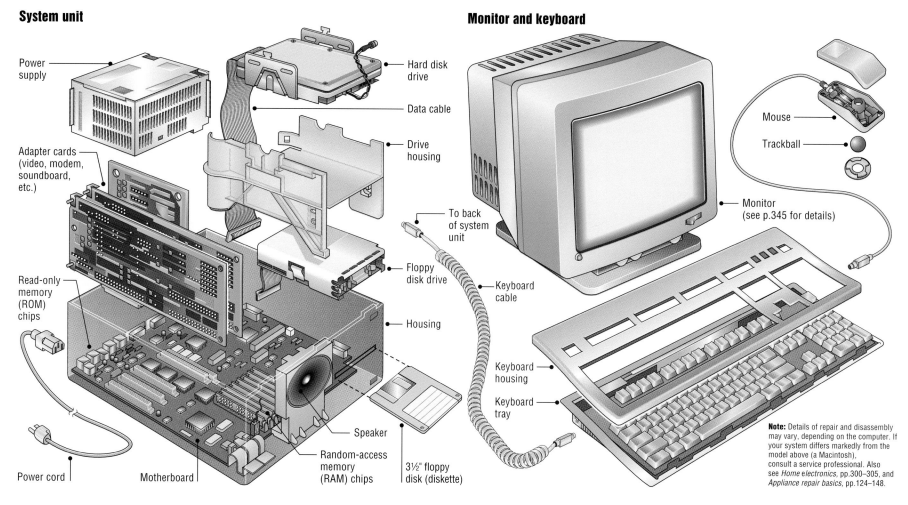

Power supply

Hard disk drive

Data cable

Drive housing

Adapter cards (video, modem, soundboard, etc.)

Read-only memory (ROM) chips

Floppy disk drive

Housing

To back of system unit

Keyboard cable

Mouse

Trackball

Monitor (see p.345 for details)

Keyboard housing

Keyboard tray

Power cord

Motherboard

Speaker

Random-access memory (RAM) chips

3½" floppy disk (diskette)

Note: Details of repair and disassembly may vary, depending on the computer. If your system differs markedly from the model above (a Macintosh), consult a service professional. Also see *Home electronics*, pp.300–305, and *Appliance repair basics*, pp.124–148.

Troubleshooting

Problem	CAUSE? / Solution
Computer does not start	POWER OFF OR FAULTY POWER CORD? See *General troubleshooting*, p.144.
	FAULTY POWER SUPPLY? Test power supply for continuity (see *Servicing the power supply*, p.324), and replace it if faulty. ◆
Computer starts, then freezes	MEMORY CONFLICT? Check for conflict using backup startup disk (see box, right). Reseat or replace chips (p.325) as needed. Add new memory if needed. ◆
Monitor, disk drive, or other device does not work, or works intermittently	PLUG LOOSE OR FAULTY? Check connections (p.322). Replace cable if needed. ◇
	EXPANSION CARD LOOSE OR FAULTY? Reseat or replace card (p.325). ◆
	DEVICE DRIVER NOT INSTALLED? Install (or reinstall) software that accompanies the peripheral (see box, right). ◇
	SOFTWARE PROBLEM? See box, right.
	MAIN CHIP FAULTY? Have unit serviced.
Monitor does not work	POWER OFF AT OUTLET? See *General troubleshooting*, p.144.
	CONTRAST AND BRIGHTNESS TURNED DOWN? Adjust controls as necessary. ◇
	MONITOR FAULTY? See *Computer monitors*, p.345.
Keyboard does not work or works poorly	KEYBOARD TRAY DIRTY? Disassemble and clean (p.324); check cable (p.322). ◆
	SWITCHES IMPROPERLY SET? Set switches on XT-style or AT-style keyboard according to manufacturer's guidelines. ◇
	KEYBOARD DAMAGED? Open keyboard housing (p.324) and check circuit board for damage; repair if possible (p.305). Blot up spilled liquid immediately; clean residue as needed (see *Servicing keyboards,* Step 2, p.324). ◆
Grinding noise inside computer	HARD DRIVE FAULTY? Grinding noise signals a hard disk about to crash. Back up all data and replace hard drive (see *Replacing a hard disk drive*, p.323). ◆
	FAN BEARING DRY? Lift out power supply (p.324) and lubricate fan bearing with spray silicone lubricant. If fan is still noisy, replace it (on some units, this might require replacement of the entire power supply). ◆
Hard drive won't read or write	HARD DRIVE FAULTY? Replace drive (see *Replacing a hard disk drive*, p.323). ◆
	CONTROLLER CARD FAULTY OR LOOSE? Some drives are controlled by a separate card mounted on the motherboard. Reseat or replace card (see *Correcting expansion card problems*, p.325), and reseat cables between card and drive. ◆
Floppy drive won't read or write	WRITE-PROTECT SLOT SET IMPROPERLY? See *Disk care*, p.323. ◇
	DISK DAMAGED OR DUSTY? See *Disk care*, p.323. ◇
	DRIVE MISALIGNED? Replace drive; see *Servicing floppy disk drives*, p.322. ◆
	DRIVE DOOR MISALIGNED ? Adjust or replace door (see *Disk care*, p.323). ◆
	READ/WRITE HEAD DIRTY? Clean it (see *Servicing floppy disk drives*, p.322). ◇
	DRIVE BELT DIRTY OR WORN? On older drives, a small rubber belt connects motor and head. Remove drive (see *Servicing floppy disk drives*, p.322). Clean belt with swab dipped in isopropyl alchohol; replace belt if damaged. ◆
	WRONG DISK DENSITY? Use correct disks (see *Disk care*, p.322).
Mouse or trackball works poorly	MOUSE DIRTY? Disassemble unit; clean ball and internal rollers (see *Servicing a mouse or trackball*, p.325). Replace mouse if cleaning fails to revive it. ◇

Degree of difficulty: Simple ◇ Average ◆ Complex ◆ Volt-ohm meter required: ▣

Gaining access

The housing of most computers either slides off or lifts up after the housing screws have been removed. Disconnect the power cord and external cables first, however. (To get inside an older Macintosh unit with a built-in monitor, lay it face down on a blanket and press down on the ports with your thumbs while lifting up on the sides.) If a computer cover jams during removal, it may be snagged on an internal cable. Be careful not to pinch or dislodge any cables during reinstallation.

Tower models. To reach internal parts of a tower-type computer, remove retaining screws on back of system unit; then lift housing up. Some units also have an access panel in front.

PC desktop model. Unplug the system unit and remove screws at the back of the housing. Slide housing backward (or forward, on some) until it stops; then lift it up to expose serviceable parts.

Macintosh desktop model. Use a nut driver or screwdriver to remove the top-cover screws on the back of the system unit. Lift cover up and remove it.

Resolving software problems

Not all computer problems are due to faulty hardware. A new program that won't run correctly may simply have been installed improperly. Reinstall the software to overwrite the previous attempt.

If the computer starts and then freezes, software may be fighting over memory (RAM). On PC's, memory-resident programs and device drivers (programs that control peripherals) are prone to such conflicts. To resolve memory problems, try shutting down unused programs; or shut down the computer *and* uplug it for 30 seconds.

If the operating system fails to start, restart the computer with a backup floppy disk that includes the startup files (every computer owner should have this disk). If it still fails, have the hardware serviced. If the computer starts properly, you have a software problem; reinstall the operating system software.

Inadequate hardware may be the cause of some software problems. You may need a faster CPU chip or more memory. If a program runs but produces no sound, you may need a different soundboard (see *Correcting expansion card problems*, p.325).

How to check external cables

When any part of a computer system fails, first check the cable connecting that part to the computer. Make sure the cable isn't loose, defective, or plugged into the wrong socket. Try unplugging and firmly reconnecting the cable several times; the friction will often clean a connection (use electronic contact cleaner to remove visible corrosion). Test a cable for continuity with a VOM (see *Resistance testing*, p.304). Hand-tighten any connection screws or secure the bales (bent-wire connectors). If the component still doesn't work, troubleshoot it further.

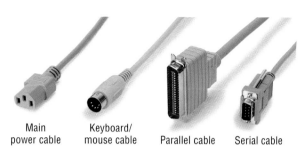

Main power cable   Keyboard/ mouse cable   Parallel cable   Serial cable

External cables. Parallel and serial cables are used to connect printers, CD-ROM drives, and other devices to the computer.

FOR YOUR SAFETY

Always unplug the computer before working on it, even before doing something as simple as detaching a keyboard or mouse. This protects delicate circuitry inside the CPU and reduces shock hazards.

Dust is the cause of many computer and peripheral problems. Protect your eyes when using canned compressed air to blow this material out.

All computer monitors, even when unplugged, are sources of high voltage and must be discharged before servicing (see page 345 and *Discharging picture tubes*, p.344).

Servicing floppy disk drives

Floppy disks (diskettes) are used to store data that can be read by floppy drives. In turn, the data can be copied onto another floppy or to the computer's hard drive. A disk drive consists of two small motors, a read/write head, and (usually) a drive belt . When you slip a diskette into the floppy drive, one motor spins the diskette while the head (driven by the second motor) moves back and forth over its surface. The head uses tiny pulses of electromagnetic energy to read and write data on the disk's magnetic coating. Newer computers come with a 3½-inch disk drive; older models may have one or two 5¼-inch drives.

If a drive tries to read a dusty disk, it could skip or scratch the surface, so protect the diskettes. Keep 5¼-inch disks in their protective envelopes, and make sure that the metal shutter on 3½-inch disks is closed when not in use (see *Disk care*, facing page). Periodically clean the drive with a head-cleaning kit.

A sure sign of a bad drive is an inability to read a disk that was formatted by the same drive. The problem in this case may be a dirty or misaligned head. Cleaning a dirty head is easy, but you may find that a drive whose head is misaligned is easier or less expensive to replace than to service.

Some floppy drives have a dust door. A broken door can sometimes be removed without affecting operation of the drive itself. If a replacement door is not available, you may have to replace the entire drive.

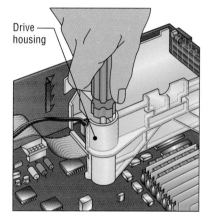

Drive housing

1 Disconnect the power cable. If the floppy drive is below the hard drive, remove the hard drive first (see facing page). Then remove screws from drive housing; they may be underneath the chassis. Their length may vary; replacing them improperly could damage the drive or nearby circuitry.

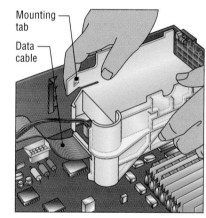

Mounting tab

Data cable

2 Pry up mounting tab with a finger. Slide drive housing forward and disconnect power and data cables. Pay particular attention to stripe on one edge of the data (ribbon) cable; when reconnecting cable, keep stripe to same side of drive. Lift drive and housing away.

Floppy drive

3 Use canned air to spray dust away from the bottom and interior of the drive. Gently clean the drive belt (if any) with a foam swab moistened in alcohol. Lift up load arm and use foam swab moistened with denatured or 95-percent-pure isopropryl alcohol to gently clean the read/write head.

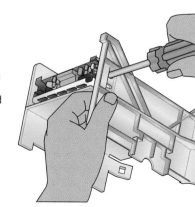

4 If the drive still doesn't work after reassembly, replace it with a new drive. To replace the drive, repeat Steps 1 and 2, above. Then remove screws holding drive to drive housing (left). Install new drive; then reinstall computer housing and test operation.

Disk care

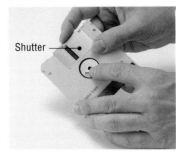

Shutter

Rotate disks by hand to look for dust (blow it off) or scratches. A 5¼-inch disk has an open window; slide back shutter on a 3-½-inch disk. Scratches and other physical damage cannot be repaired.

To eject a stuck disk from a Mac, insert a large paper clip into the emergency eject hole. If a floppy diskette gets stuck in a PC, pull it out gently with long-nose pliers.

If the floppy drive indicator light comes on when you call for a file but nothing happens, the disk itself is most likely at fault. If a disk is damaged, you won't be able to retrieve data on it. Protect floppies from excessive heat or cold, and use only felt-tip markers to write on disk jackets. Don't place disks on the system unit, the monitor, or near a telephone: their magnetic fields can corrupt data on the disk.

If you can read but not write files on a disk, check if the disk is write/protected. On a 3½-inch disk, there is a tab on the back side of the disk that must be closed for it to accept data; on a 5¼-inch disk, there must be an open notch in the edge of the diskette. If there's none (as with some program software) or if it's covered, the disk won't accept data.

What seems to be a computer problem may, in fact, be due to using an incompatible disk. Disks come in three densities: single, double, and high. High-density disk drives are required to read high-density disks. A PC can't read a Macintosh-formatted diskette, and athough a Macintosh may read a PC-formatted diskette, files usually have to be translated before use.

Use extra care in cleaning CD-ROM disks (see *Cleaning and repairing disks,* p.308); they're costly, and a tiny scratch can ruin a program that's required to read other data on the disk.

Replacing a hard disk drive

Instead of storing data on removable floppy disks, a hard drive uses a series of permanently installed, stacked metal platters called hard disks. These disks not only store more data than floppies, they also spin much faster, speeding up data retrieval. To keep your hard drive running at peak efficiency, use a defragmenting utility every month. This is a software program that rearranges the locations of files on the disk so that the read/write heads can locate them more quickly. This reorganization doesn't affect your use of the files; in fact, the only thing you'll notice is that the hard drive seems faster.

A drive failure is called a crash. When a crash occurs, the only remedy is to install a new hard drive. There are several types and subtypes of hard drives; make sure you choose the right drive for your computer. Drives for computers more than about four years old may not be readily available.

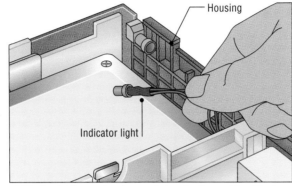

Housing

Indicator light

1 The hard drive can be above or below the floppy drive. Check for loose cables or a loose disk controller card (see *Correcting expansion card problems,* p.325). Pull indicator light from housing (above). Remove screw that secures card; then remove the card.

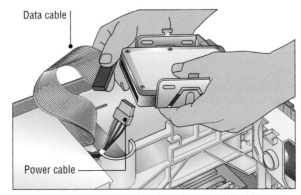

Data cable

Power cable

3 Remove any remaining cables from the back of the drive. Typically guides on the cable connector prevent improper orientation. If guides are not present, make note of the orientation of a colored stripe on the data cable for reinstallation.

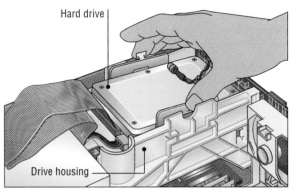

Hard drive

Drive housing

2 If any cables are readily accessible, disconnect them (tag them if they look similar enough to cause confusion during reassembly). Remove screws on each side of drive; then squeeze mounting brackets and lift drive away from drive housing.

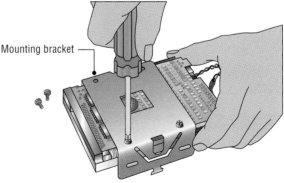

Mounting bracket

4 Separate drive from its mounting bracket by removing mounting screws. Reverse these steps to install new drive. When replacing a PC drive, run "setup" software program after installation to identify new drive for the computer. This step is unnecessary on a Mac.

323

Servicing the power supply

The power supply inside the system unit includes a transformer that reduces 115V house current and a rectifier circuit that changes it from AC to DC. It also includes a fan that cools the circuitry. Although a power supply is not user serviceable, replacing one is easy. Configurations vary widely, however.

1 Test the power supply for continuity using a VOM. Set meter on RX100 and touch probes to prongs of recessed plug. A reading of zero or infinity indicates the power supply is faulty.

2 Access interior (see *Gaining access*, p.321), and for some PC models, squeeze tab and pull out floppy drive (above) to access the screw securing the power supply to the chassis base.

Power supply

Rear

3 Remove screws holding power supply to rear and base of chassis (PC, above), or insert finger beneath the power supply to unclip mounting tab (Macintosh, see drawing p.320).

Power supply | Chassis plug

4 Disconnect any cables attached to the power supply and lift it out slowly to unplug it from the motherboard (expect some resistance). Install new unit and reassemble computer.

USE AND CARE

Dust is a computer's main enemy. Keep all components covered when not in use; periodically clean cabinets and ventilation slots with a lint-free cloth dampened with alcohol.

Don't use a vacuum cleaner to clean the inside of a computer—it may generate static. Blow out dust with a can of compressed air.

Never move a computer that's running. The read/write head of a hard drive floats above the spinning disk in use. Movement can slam the head against the disk and damage it.

Clean a monitor screen with mild glass cleaner; spray cleaner on the cloth, never directly on the screen.

Changing batteries

Desktop computers rely on a replaceable battery to keep date and time chips current when the computer is turned off. The battery, typically found on the motherboard, normally lasts about two years. If the battery is soldered in, have a service center install a replaceable-type battery instead. (To test a portable computer's rechargeable main battery pack, see page 143.)

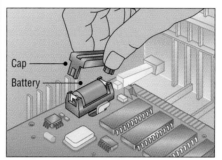

Cap

Battery

The battery in some computers is a cylindrical cell located at the edge of the motherboard and held in place with a small plastic cap. Pry cap off with your finger; then pull out cell and replace it.

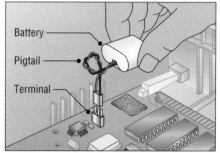

Battery

Pigtail

Terminal

Another type of battery, found in older PCs, is wired in place. To remove it, unplug pigtail from terminal on motherboard and pull out battery. Battery and pigtail are replaced together.

Servicing keyboards

Most keyboard problems, such as missing characters and stiff keys, are caused by dirt or sticky residue from liquids spilled inside the keyboard. Clean the unit as described below; then check it for faulty solder joints and damaged traces (see *Repair basics*, p.305). To protect sensitive circuitry, *always* turn off the computer before disconnecting the keyboard from it.

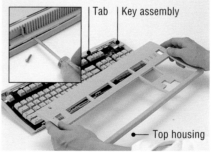

Tab | Key assembly

Top housing

1 Disconnect the keyboard and turn it upside down. Remove assembly screws; then pry apart housings (inset). Lift off top housing (above), and if required, press tabs (or remove screws) to release key assembly from tray.

Canned air

2 Shake out debris; then take keyboard outdoors and blow out interior with canned air. Use electrical contact cleaner to flush out sticky residue and to remove corrosion from keyboard cable plugs. If keyboard is still faulty, replace it.

Servicing a mouse or trackball

If the cursor on the monitor moves erratically, suspect a dirty mouse (or trackball). Keep the mouse and mouse pad free of dust and lint. The ball, easily removed for cleaning (right), rotates against tiny rollers. Any dirt or residue on either part may cause erratic cursor movement. A bus mouse is connected to an expansion card in the computer instead of to a port. If a bus mouse causes problems after cleaning, try to reseat the card itself (see below).

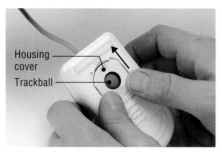

Housing cover
Trackball

1 Unplug the mouse and turn it upside down. To remove the trackball, press the ball-cage housing cover forward (some turn clockwise).

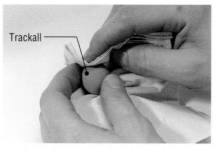

Trackall

2 Remove ball. Clean with lint-free cloth dampened with denatured or 95% pure alcohol; then air dry.

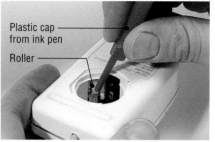

Plastic cap from ink pen
Roller

3 Scrape plaque from rollers (above); then swab them with denatured alcohol. Blow dust and debris out of ball cage; reassemble mouse.

Correcting expansion card problems

Expansion cards plug into slots inside the system unit to control devices such as a monitor, hard drive, bus mouse, or modem, among others. Symptoms of a loose or faulty card range from intermittent disk drive problems to a blank monitor. To check a card, remove it (some cards are secured with a screw) and clean its contacts; then reseat it. If the problem persists, try the card in a different slot. If it works, the first slot may be faulty; have it serviced.

To remove a card, grasp it with both hands and gently rock it back and forth while lifting. Be careful not to touch components on the card.

After cleaning pins and socket (see Step 2 below), replace card by lowering one end into place, then the other. Then press it down firmly.

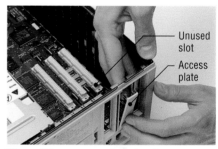

Unused slot
Access plate

When adding a new card, push out an access plate at rear of chassis, plug card into its socket, and (on a some computers) secure it with screw.

Correcting memory problems

If a computer boots and then freezes, the problem may be too little RAM, or a faulty or loose memory module. Modules (called chips) plug directly into the motherboard. If you suspect a chip problem, first try to seat the chips by firmly pressing down each one. Handle chips only by their edges, and use antistatic wrist straps when installing or removing them. Check with a chip supplier to see if any special tools, such as a chip-puller, are needed to remove chips on your computer.

Clip

1 To remove a Macintosh RAM chip (above), press clip aside and tilt chip outward. In a PC, grasp chip edges, rock it back and forth, and lift.

2 Clean connector strip contacts on edge of chip with a swab dampened with denatured or 95% pure alcohol. This may correct problems.

3 To replace a RAM chip, carefully align one end with the socket; then lower the other end and press it firmly in place.

A printer gets data from a computer through a parallel or serial cable (p.322) and converts the data into a series of small dots that form letters or images. The three principal types of printers— dot matrix, ink-jet, and laser—produce these dots in different ways. The mov-

ing printhead of a dot matrix printer has pins that strike the paper through a replaceable inked ribbon; an ink-jet printer (below) is mechanically similar but sprays ink on the paper through tiny nozzles in its printhead. In contrast, a laser printer uses a laser to "draw"

electrically charged images that attract powdered ink called *toner;* heat and pressure fuse those images to the paper. Toner cartridges are replacable. If a printer doesn't work, check for a loose connection or a paper jam. Jammed paper can usually be pulled

out from under the platen (unplug the printer first). You can solve many problems by checking the software configurations (including printer drivers), by rebooting, or by cleaning and lubricating (right). If you suspect a motor problem, have the printer serviced.

Ink-jet printer

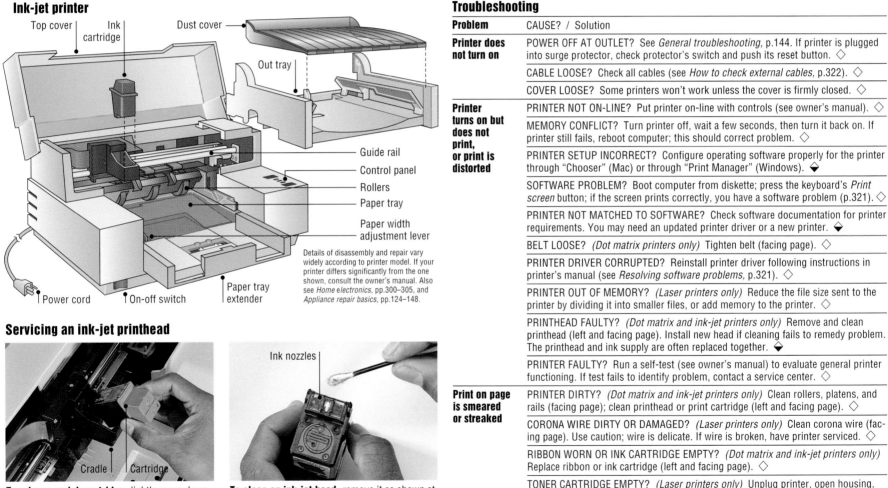

Top cover | Ink cartridge | Dust cover

Out tray

Guide rail
Control panel
Rollers
Paper tray
Paper width adjustment lever

Power cord | On-off switch | Paper tray extender

Details of disassembly and repair vary widely according to printer model. If your printer differs significantly from the one shown, consult the owner's manual. Also see *Home electronics,* pp.300–305, and *Appliance repair basics,* pp.124–148.

Servicing an ink-jet printhead

Cradle | Cartridge

To release an ink cartridge, lightly press down on it, then tip it back and out. To replace, do the reverse, snapping new cartridge into the cradle.

Ink nozzles

To clean an ink-jet head, remove it as shown at left and wipe away ink from each nozzle, using a dry or alcohol-dampened swab. Reinstall head.

Troubleshooting

Problem	CAUSE? / Solution
Printer does not turn on	POWER OFF AT OUTLET? See *General troubleshooting,* p.144. If printer is plugged into surge protector, check protector's switch and push its reset button. ◇
	CABLE LOOSE? Check all cables (see *How to check external cables,* p.322). ◇
	COVER LOOSE? Some printers won't work unless the cover is firmly closed. ◇
Printer turns on but does not print, or print is distorted	PRINTER NOT ON-LINE? Put printer on-line with controls (see owner's manual). ◇
	MEMORY CONFLICT? Turn printer off, wait a few seconds, then turn it back on. If printer still fails, reboot computer; this should correct problem. ◇
	PRINTER SETUP INCORRECT? Configure operating software properly for the printer through "Chooser" (Mac) or through "Print Manager" (Windows). ◆
	SOFTWARE PROBLEM? Boot computer from diskette; press the keyboard's *Print screen* button; if the screen prints correctly, you have a software problem (p.321). ◇
	PRINTER NOT MATCHED TO SOFTWARE? Check software documentation for printer requirements. You may need an updated printer driver or a new printer. ◆
	BELT LOOSE? *(Dot matrix printers only)* Tighten belt (facing page). ◇
	PRINTER DRIVER CORRUPTED? Reinstall printer driver following instructions in printer's manual (see *Resolving software problems,* p.321). ◇
	PRINTER OUT OF MEMORY? *(Laser printers only)* Reduce the file size sent to the printer by dividing it into smaller files, or add memory to the printer. ◇
	PRINTHEAD FAULTY? *(Dot matrix and ink-jet printers only)* Remove and clean printhead (left and facing page). Install new head if cleaning fails to remedy problem. The printhead and ink supply are often replaced together. ◆
	PRINTER FAULTY? Run a self-test (see owner's manual) to evaluate general printer functioning. If test fails to identify problem, contact a service center. ◇
Print on page is smeared or streaked	PRINTER DIRTY? *(Dot matrix and ink-jet printers only)* Clean rollers, platens, and rails (facing page); clean printhead or print cartridge (left and facing page). ◇
	CORONA WIRE DIRTY OR DAMAGED? *(Laser printers only)* Clean corona wire (facing page). Use caution; wire is delicate. If wire is broken, have printer serviced. ◇
	RIBBON WORN OR INK CARTRIDGE EMPTY? *(Dot matrix and ink-jet printers only)* Replace ribbon or ink cartridge (left and facing page). ◇
	TONER CARTRIDGE EMPTY? *(Laser printers only)* Unplug printer, open housing, and slide out old cartridge; replace with new or recycled cartridge. ◇

Degree of difficulty: Simple ◇   Average ◆   Complex ◆

Cleaning and maintaining printers

Dot matrix (below) and ink-jet printers, the most common home units, require routine maintenance. Clean and lubricate the rails if they're dirty or if the printer is sluggish. Clean the pins or ink nozzles on the printheads as required to maintain print quality. Some early models of ink-jet printers had poor-quality ink that jammed the ink nozzles; but new ink will solve that. Replace worn ribbons and empty ink cartridges (in some ink-jets the cartridge is separate from the printhead). Do not refill a cartridge unless it is so designed, and then use only the ink specified by the printer's manufacturer.

Clean the interior of printer by blowing out dust with can of compressed air (p.301); or use vacuum cleaner.

Clean guide rails with a soft lint-free cloth dampened with isopropyl alcohol; then relubricate rails.

Clean platen rollers and platen by turning platen while holding a cloth dampened with alcohol against each roller.

Lubricate rails with a drop of household oil; slide printhead to distribute. Spray silicone on cleaned gears.

Printhead

Laser printers

In a laser printer, data from the processor turns a laser rapidly on and off, directing it onto a photoconducting drum. At each point the laser strikes, the electrical charge of the drum is reversed. As the drum comes in contact with toner, the toner is attracted to only those charged locations. As the drum passes over the corona wire, the drum's original charge is restored. Dust can interfere with this process, so blow it out periodically with compressed air. Cleaning the corona wire (right) can alleviate some problems.

CAUTION: Let printer cool down completely before attempting to clean it.

Corona wire
Paper support wire

Cleaning the corona wire. Lightly rub a cotton swab along wire to clean off built-up toner and dust.

Servicing dot matrix printers

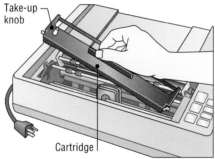

Take-up knob

Cartridge

To replace a ribbon cartridge, lift one side, then the other. To install new cartridge, turn take-up knob to loosen ribbon and insert cartridge.

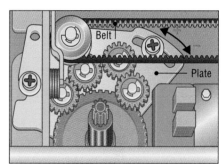

Belt

Plate

To tension printer carriage belt, loosen (do not remove) screws on gear mounting plate. Rotate plate to adjust belt tension; then tighten screws.

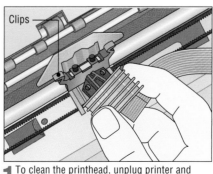

Clips

1 To clean the printhead, unplug printer and slide head to middle of platen. Unfasten head retainer clips and lift head off support pins.

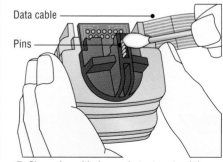

Data cable

Pins

2 Clean pins with dry swab; try to extend them first with tweezers. If any pins are missing or cleaning fails, unplug data cable to replace head.

A facsimile (fax) machine contains separate mechanisms to send, receive, and print images. It has few serviceable parts; however, most problems can be avoided or corrected with routine maintenance. Buy supplies from an authorized dealer or from the manufacturer to ensure compatiblity with your unit. Before assuming there is a problem with the machine itself, find out if the telephone line is OK (see *Telephone systems*, p.336).

The two types of fax machines—thermal (below) and plain-paper—are distinguished by the paper they use.

The printhead of a thermal fax machine heats areas of heat-sensitive paper to form printed images. The head is replaceable if it burns out but can cost nearly as much as a new machine. Most plain-paper fax machines print by fusing toner to the paper. Problems with these units usually involve the toner cartridge; follow the manufacturer's directions for replacement.

Keep a fax machine away from radiators, air conditioners, and windows. To safeguard it against power surges, plug it into a surge protector that also guards against phone-line spikes.

Servicing a thermal fax machine

Old bulb

Clean the platen using a cloth dampened with denatured alcohol. Unplug unit. Rotate the platen as you wipe it; let it dry thoroughly. Use a small artist's brush to remove dirt and dust from the paper trough.

To replace exposure lamp (bulb), unplug unit; then turn it over and remove bottom housing. Be sure bulb is cool before touching it. Twist bulb; pull it from sockets. Avoid touching new bulb during installation.

Check manual for location of exposure lens and mirrors. Unplug unit. Wipe lens and mirrors with lint-free cloth; use solvent if suggested by manufacturer. On some units, lens and mirrors aren't accessible.

To access internal components, remove housing panel screws and lift off panels as needed. To reach lens and mirror, turn unit upside down; then remove bottom housing.

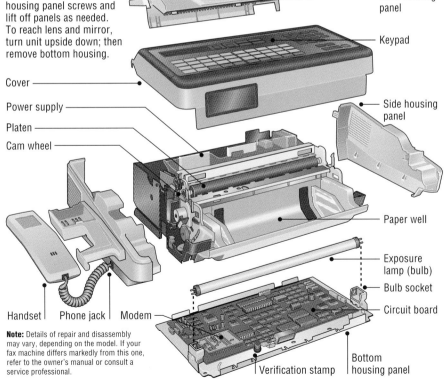

Main housing panel

Keypad

Cover

Power supply

Platen

Cam wheel

Side housing panel

Paper well

Exposure lamp (bulb)

Bulb socket

Circuit board

Handset | Phone jack | Modem

Bottom housing panel

Verification stamp

Note: Details of repair and disassembly may vary, depending on the model. If your fax machine differs markedly from this one, refer to the owner's manual or consult a service professional.

Troubleshooting

Problem	CAUSE? / Solution
ALL UNITS: Fax won't work	POWER OFF AT OUTLET? See *General troubleshooting*, p.144.
Can't send or receive documents	PHONE LINE DAMAGED OR DISCONNECTED? Check line and plugs (see *Telephone systems*, p.336). Make sure line is plugged into correct fax port. Test wall jack (p.337) and replace it if faulty. ◆
	BOARD DAMAGED? If fax has a port for an external phone, plug incoming line into it. If no improvement, or if fax has only one port, have fax serviced. ◇
Can send but not receive (or vice versa)	PHONE LINE DAMAGED? See *Can't send or receive documents*, above. ◇
	MODEM DAMAGED? Unit's modem must be serviced professionally. ◇
	EXPOSURE LAMP FAULTY? Replace lamp (above). ◇
Marks or voids on documents	EXPOSURE GLASS DIRTY? Open cover. Clean glass with a clean lint-free cloth dampened with denatured alcohol. ◇
THERMAL FAX: Fax won't print	THERMAL HEAD DIRTY? Locate thermal head. Clean head by wiping it with a clean lint-free cloth dampened with denatured alcohol. ◇
	PAPER IN WRONG? Reposition paper; only coated side will print. ◇
Marks or voids on documents	THERMAL HEAD DEFECTIVE? Remove screws securing thermal head. Replace head with duplicate. *Note:* It may be less expensive to buy a new machine. ◆
PLAIN-PAPER FAX: Marks or voids on documents	TONER SPILLED INSIDE MACHINE? Open cover; wipe up spilled toner. ◇
	CORONA WIRES DIRTY? Clean wires (see *Laser printers*, p.327). ◇
	DRUM DAMAGED? Follow manufacturer's instructions for replacement. ◆

Degree of difficulty: Simple ◇   Average ◆   Complex ◆   Volt-ohm meter required: ▣

Personal stereos

Personal stereos—radios, radio/cassette players, CD players, mini- and microcassette recorders—are compact, portable versions of their full-size counterparts. Some repairs for personal and full-size stereo devices are similar, although the personal stereos are often inexpensive enough to simply replace. Because all portable devices are particularly susceptible to mechanical problems caused by dirt and moisture, keep your unit clean and dry. If it contains rechargeable batteries, problems might also be found in the charging system, particularly plugs, contacts, and jacks.

Before attempting to repair a personal stereo, first make sure the batteries are OK and the battery contacts are clean (p.303). Also examine the headphones; breaks in the cord and loose connections will interfere with the sound quality. Headphones are essentially miniature speakers. While some styles can be repaired, most models are so small and inexpensive that replacement may be a more practical solution.

Many units have plastic tabs as well as screws to secure the housing. If you encounter resistance when separating the housing, closely examine the edges for tabs and then *very gently* pry apart the halves with a screwdriver.

Personal radios are available in digital or analog models. Digital radios usually have better sound quality; but with both types, the headphone wire acts as the antenna and clear reception may depend on its position.

Personal radio/cassette players should be kept clean and dry; sand, dirt, and water can damage the inner workings. During use, make sure the unit

Personal radio/cassette player

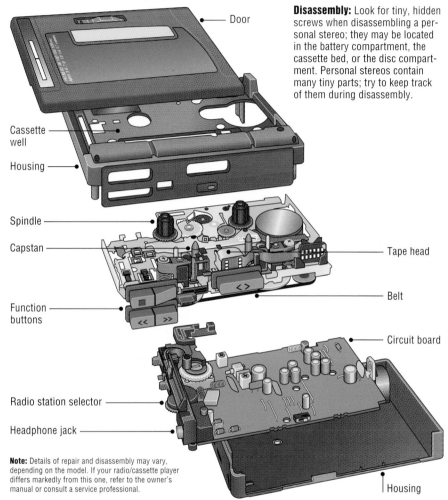

Door

Cassette well

Housing

Spindle

Capstan

Tape head

Belt

Function buttons

Circuit board

Radio station selector

Headphone jack

Housing

Note: Details of repair and disassembly may vary, depending on the model. If your radio/cassette player differs markedly from this one, refer to the owner's manual or consult a service professional.

Disassembly: Look for tiny, hidden screws when disassembling a personal stereo; they may be located in the battery compartment, the cassette bed, or the disc compartment. Personal stereos contain many tiny parts; try to keep track of them during disassembly.

is placed on a stable surface or attached securely to you. Use a head-cleaning tape regularly to prevent the oxide coating on cassette tapes from building up and reducing the sound quality.

Personal CD players can mistrack (skip) when bumped during use; try to avoid jarring the the unit too much. Some

newer models have built-in protection against skipping.

Mini- and microcassette recorders are basically cassette players that have an erase head and a record head. Periodically use a head-cleaning tape; engage the erase and record functions during cleaning so both heads get cleaned.

Gaining access

To access the interior, remove batteries; then remove all housing screws. Some models have plastic tabs along the edges where the housing meets; gently press near the tabs to unlock them.

A cassette or disc door may be screwed on (as above) or attached by plastic flanges or springs. Remove screws, gently pry up flanges with a tiny screwdriver, or pull out springs with pliers.

When removing circuit board, remove only those screws that are identified with symbols or otherwise marked. Lift out board by edges; fingerprints can harm delicate components.

Troubleshooting

Problem	CAUSE? / Solution
ALL PERSONAL STEREOS: **Unit does not work**	WEAK OR DEAD BATTERIES? Replace batteries. ◇
	CORRODED OR BENT CONTACTS? Clean corroded battery contacts with sandpaper. Slightly pry up contacts as needed to improve battery performance. ◇
	CORRODED HEADPHONE (OR POWER) PLUG OR JACK? Spray electrical contact cleaner into jack; wipe excess with cotton swab. Work plug in and out of jack. ◇
	FAULTY HEADPHONE (OR POWER) JACK? Open unit and examine jack for broken connections; resolder as necessary (see right). ◆
Sound is Intermittent	CORRODED OR BENT CONTACTS? See *Unit does not work*, above. ◇
	CORRODED HEADPHONE PLUG OR JACK? See *Unit does not work*, above. ◇
	LOOSE HEADPHONE JACK? See *Resoldering a headphone jack*, right. ◆
	BROKEN HEADPHONE WIRE? Replace headphones. ◇
Sound is fuzzy	FAULTY HEADPHONES? Try headphones in another unit; replace if faulty. ◇
	FAULTY SPEAKER? See *Speakers*, p.314. ◆
Function buttons don't work	DIRTY BUTTON MECHANISMS? Clean mechanisms with electrical contact cleaner (see *Cleaning components*, p.332); lubricate with white lithium spray. ◇
RADIO/CASSETTE PLAYERS: **Cassette loses high frequency**	DIRTY TAPE HEAD? Clean head with head-cleaning tape. ◇
	WORN TAPE HEAD? If head looks worn, have unit serviced. ◇
	MAGNETIZED HEAD? See *Cleaning and demagnetizing the heads*, p.313. ◇
	MISALIGNED HEAD? Realign head (see *Servicing the heads*, Step 3, p.313). ◆
Tape moves, no sound	OPEN TAPE HEAD? See *Servicing the heads*, p.313. ◆
	DIRTY BUTTON MECHANISMS? See *Function buttons don't work*, above.
Unit damages tapes	FAULTY TAKE-UP DRIVE? Access inside of unit. If player is driven by belts, clean them with a cotton swab moistened in alcohol. Replace broken, glazed, or cracked belts (right). If player is driven by gears, replace any that have broken or worn teeth. ◆
	DIRTY PINCH ROLLER? See *Cleaning and demagnetizing the heads*, p.313. ◇
Adjacent tracks audible	BENT TAPE GUIDES? Use needle-nose pliers to reshape guides. ◆
	MISALIGNED HEAD? See *Cassette loses high frequency*, above. ◆
CASSETTE RECORDERS: **Unit won't record**	CASSETTE SAFETY TAB MISSING? Cover hole with masking tape. ◇
	RECORD BUTTON WON'T ENGAGE? Remove obstructions that might be jamming button. Clean button mechanism with electrical contact cleaner (see *Cleaning components*, p.332); lubricate with white lithium spray. ◇
Unit does not erase	ERASE HEAD DEMAGNETIZED? *(Permanent-magnet type)* Have head professionally serviced or replaced. ◇
	MAGNETIZED ERASE HEAD? *(AC type)* Demagnetize head (see *Cleaning and demagnetizing the heads*, p.313). ◇
CD PLAYERS: **Distorted sound**	DIRTY LASER LENS? Clean lens (right). ◇
	DIRTY DISC? Clean disc (see *Cleaning and reparing discs*, p.308). ◇

Degree of difficulty: Simple ◇   Average ◆   Complex ◆   Volt-ohm meter required: ▣

Resoldering a headphone jack

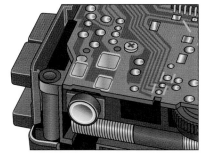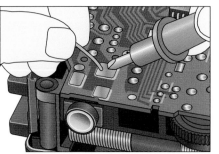

1 Open unit to access circuit board (p.329). Locate jack and inspect connection for looseness, cracks, or a frosty appearance. Avoid removing circuit board from case.

2 Resolder loose or frosty connections; fill small cracks with solder; bridge larger ones with wire (see *Soldering techniques*, p.305). Avoid disturbing other connections on the board.

Replacing a belt

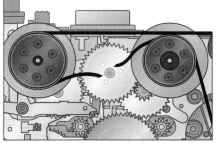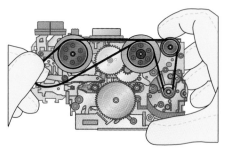

1 If needed, remove circuit board (p.329) to access belts. Look for belts that are glazed, cracked, or otherwise damaged. Some units have more than one belt; replace all of them at once.

2 Make a sketch of old belts to ensure new belts travel same paths. Belts may be slightly twisted to fit around gears; examine yours before lifting it out. Loop new belt into place.

Cleaning the laser on a personal CD player

With the player off and batteries removed, blow dust out of the disc with compressed air. Use photographic lens-cleaning fluid and a cotton swab to clean the lens. Avoid pressing on the lens mechanism. (A lens-cleaning disc, available at audio shops, can also be used.) **CAUTION:** Never look directly into the lens when it is on; it can damage your eyes.

Radios

The radio component of a portable stereo, clock radio, and table radio is basically the same in each type of device. As a result, these units share many of the same problems and repairs (see *Troubleshooting: Radios,* right).

Besides a radio, a portable stereo may have a CD player and one or more cassette decks. Repair procedures for these components are the same as for their nonportable counterparts. For more on troubleshooting and repairing CD players, see pages 308–309; for more on cassette decks, see pages 312–313.

Clock radios consist of a radio and a clock; table radios do not have a clock function. For information on clock repair, see page 158.

Digital radios have few serviceable parts. These units are quite reliable but if a part fails, take the radio to an authorized repair center.

Clock radio

Band selector switch — Housing

Function buttons

Function button contact switches

Volume control knob

— Speaker

— Digital clock

— Dial pointer

To dissasemble a clock radio, remove the housing screws; then gently separate the housing. (Wires here have been omitted for clarity). Access the internal components of a table radio in the same manner.

Portable stereo

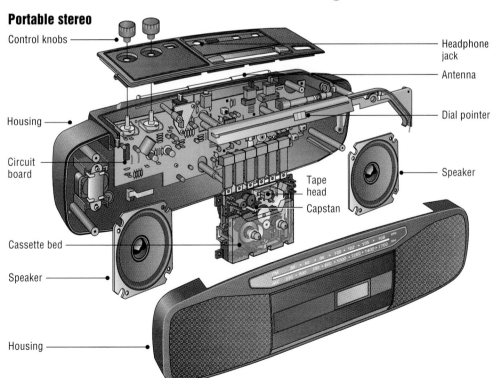

Control knobs

Housing

Circuit board

Cassette bed

Speaker

Housing

Headphone jack

Antenna

Dial pointer

Speaker

Tape head

Capstan

To disassemble a portable stereo, remove screws securing the housing; look for screws hidden underneath plastic caps or in the battery compartment. Some models have plastic tabs as well as screws securing the housing; press down on these tabs to separate the housing. Depending on the area of repair, you may also need to remove the cassette bed mounting screws.

Troubleshooting

Problem	CAUSE? / Solution
Unit won't work	POWER OFF AT OUTLET? See *General troubleshooting,* p.144, and *Troubleshooting: Personal stereos,* facing page. ◇
	WEAK BATTERIES? Replace batteries. ◇
	CORRODED OR BENT CONTACTS? See *Troubleshooting: Personal stereos,* facing page. ◇
Can't plug in power cord	PLASTIC CASE HOLDING JACK BROKEN? Reglue case (See *Repairing a cracked power jack housing,* p.332). ◇
Station indicator won't move	BROKEN DIAL CORD? *(Cord-driven units only)* See *Stringing a dial cord,* p.307. ◆
	GEARS JAMMED? *(Gear-driven units only)* Remove all obstructions. ◇
Station indicator does not show correct station	MISALIGNED POINTER? For cord-driven units, see *Resetting a dial pointer,* p.307. For gear-driven units, loosen the dial gear and realign. ◇
	LOCAL OSCILLATOR INACCURATE? Have unit professionally serviced. ◇
Fuzzy or intermittent sound	BATTERIES WEAK? Test and replace. ◇
	DIRTY OR CORRODED HEADPHONE PLUG OR JACK? Squirt electrical contact cleaner into jack. Wipe off any excess cleaner with cotton swab. Work plug in and out of jack. ◇
	DIRTY VOLUME CONTROL? Open unit and locate the volume control. Spray a little electrical contact cleaner into the control. Rotate (or slide) control several times to lubricate mechanism. ◆
	DIRTY BAND SELECTOR SWITCH? Open unit. Spray band selector switch with electrical contact cleaner; don't overspray. Move switch back and forth several times to lubricate mechanism. ◆
	BROKEN OR DAMAGED ANTENNA? See *Replacing an antenna,* p.332. ◆
Cassette on personal stereo not working properly	See *Troubleshooting: Personal stereos,* facing page; *Cassette decks,* pp.312–313; and *Receivers,* p.307. ◇
Clock on radio not working properly	See *Clocks,* p.158. ◇

Degree of difficulty: Simple ◇   Average ◆   Complex ◆
Volt-ohm meter required: ▪

Replacing an antenna

If antenna screw is on exterior of radio, remove it and pull out antenna. Slide new antenna into place and reinsert screw.

Antenna screw may be inside radio. Open unit and find base of antenna. Remove screw on mounting clip; pull out antenna.

Position base of new antenna beneath clip, with shaft going through housing. Replace screw and reassemble housing.

Repairing a cracked power jack housing

Broken jack

1 If power jack cracks, unplug radio and open housing. Align pieces of jack to check their fit.

2 Dab epoxy (p.18) onto edges of one piece at a time, using a toothpick to spread the adhesive.

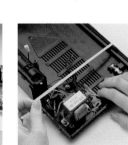

3 After gluing each piece, secure repair with an elastic band, tape, or clamp until glue sets.

Cleaning components

To clean cassette bed, wipe area with a cotton swab dipped in denatured alcohol; or use a head-cleaning tape (p.313).

To remove dust from inside unit, open case and blow any dust out with compressed air; also spray the jacks with air.

Clean button contacts with cotton swab dipped in denatured alcohol; rub with white bond paper to remove corrosion.

Car radios

A car's body usually shields the antenna from any interference caused by the spark plugs. But if interference occurs when the engine runs, the grounding connection may be faulty.

Most cars built after 1985 have noise-suppression filters built into the radio itself (or into the positive lead of the power connection) and are relatively problem-free. Older radios may experience interference from the ignition or the alternator.

Alternator noise (a high-pitched whine that gets higher as the engine accelerates) can be fixed by replacing the noise-suppression filter. Ask your auto parts dealer if the new filter is compatible with your car. To install the new filter, follow the manufacturer's installation instructions.

Ignition noise (a ticking sound that varies with engine speed) has two sources: a defective ignition coil capacitor or faulty spark plug cables. First replace the capacitor. If this doesn't help, open the hood on a damp night and start the engine; if you see small sparks arcing from the cables, replace them.

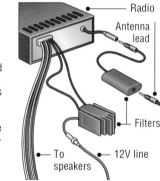

Main grounding connection may be a flexible braided strap linking engine to car's frame. In newer cars, the hood is grounded through its hinges; older cars use an L-shaped spring instead. All connections must be tight; sand off corrosion. Replace connection if necessary.

Hinge

Strap

Radio

Antenna lead

Filters

To speakers

12V line

Noise-suppression filters can solve most radio noise problems, especially on amplified systems. They are available at most auto supply stores. Line filters go on the incoming 12-volt power supply; antenna filters go between the antenna lead and the radio.

CB radios

Citizens band (CB) radios receive and broadcast voice transmissions. A typical setup consists of a microphone, a transceiver box (with speaker), and an external antenna; the system is powered by the car's battery. If you have trouble sending and receiving, look at the connections to make sure they're tight. If the CB shares the car radio antenna, fully extend the antenna (changing the length of a properly adjusted CB antenna may worsen the problem). Reception problems suggest that the volume or squelch controls are improperly set. When transmitting, be sure to fully depress the microphone's *Talk* button. If the unit does not work at all, check its power connection and fuse. A CB radio is susceptible to engine interference (see above). If problems persist, have the radio professionally serviced.

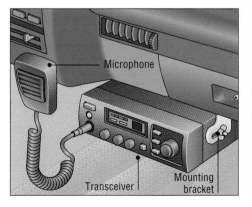

Microphone

Transceiver

Mounting bracket

Security systems

In a home security system, strategically placed sensors trigger a local and/or silent alarm when an intruder tries to gain entry. The local alarm may be a siren with a strobe light, set by a timer to run for 5 to 30 minutes. A silent alarm automatically dials the police or a security monitoring company. With some systems, the monitoring company supervises the phone line; if it is cut, the company calls the police. In other systems, the phone line has a cellular backup; if the electricity goes out or wires to the system are cut, batteries kick in to power the alarms. Users arm and disarm most security systems at a keypad installed near the entry door. Some systems can be armed and disarmed by remote control; others include a panic button that instantly triggers the alarm.

A hard-wired security system runs on low-voltage DC electricity. The sensors are wired in circuits, or "loops," that form the zones of the system. The loops originate at a central control unit, where a transformer steps down household current from 120 volts AC to 12 volts DC. A loop is either a *normally closed* circuit (current flows through closed sensor switches when the system is secure; a switch opens to set off the alarm) or a *normally open* circuit (sensor switches are open when the system is secure and trigger an alarm when they close). Most hard-wired systems are professionally installed. If your system is leased or under warranty or a service contract, test it often but call for service. Otherwise, you can test the zones and replace faulty sensors yourself (p.334).

In a wireless security system, the sensors connect to isolated digital radio transmitters. When tripped, they send out a very-high-frequency coded signal to a receiver in the control panel that sets off the alarms. Many such systems are designed to be owner-installed.

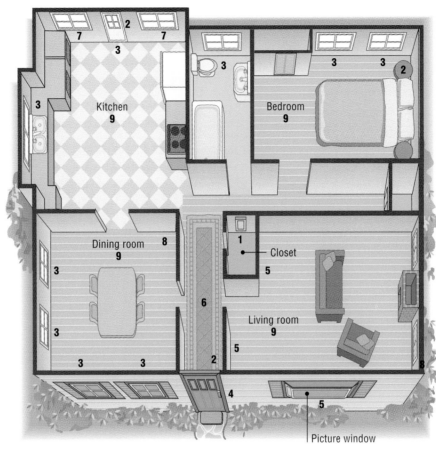

Kitchen 9
Bedroom 9
Dining room 9
Closet
Living room 9
Picture window

1: Control panel (see below).

2: Keypad lets you arm and disarm system at doorways; a portable remote model allows you to control system from other rooms and from outdoors.

3: Magnetic switch, aligned on door frame and door, or on window frame and sash, triggers alarm when door or window is opened, separating magnet and switch.

4: Plunger switch is recessed in door frame; when door is opened, plunger pops out and triggers alarm.

5: Vibration glass-break detector is attached to stationary windowpane, such as a picture window; **audio frequency glass-break detector** is mounted on wall or ceiling opposite windows; both types are triggered by breaking glass.

6: Pressure-sensitive pad under hall runner trips alarm when stepped on.

7: Wired screen appears normal but interwoven wiring forms an electrical circuit; when the screen is cut, the circuit is broken, tripping the alarm.

8: Volumetric motion detectors sense changes in a room's atmosphere that indicate an intruder: a passive infrared sensor detects heat waves given off by a body; an ultrasonic sensor detects motion with sound waves; a microwave sensor detects motion—even through walls— with microwaves.

9: Smoke detector (p.335) is activated by presence of smoke particles.

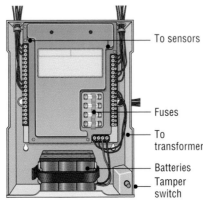

To sensors

Fuses

To transformer

Batteries

Tamper switch

The control panel is the brain of a security system. In a *wired* system (left), it is hidden from view (in a closet, for example). In a *wireless* system, the control panel plugs into a wall receptacle. Lights and test buttons on either type of panel or on the keypad will indicate if the system is working properly.

Strobe light

Alarm siren

Local alarms—sirens and strobe lights—can scare an intruder away while guiding police or firemen to the right house. Make alarm wires inaccessible to intruders by placing alarms at a gable peak or on a rooftop television antenna and running wires through the attic and down to the control panel.

Troubleshooting

Problem	CAUSE? / Solution
Frequent false alarms	USER ERROR? Wait 24 hr.; if there is no repeat, assume user error. If alarm rings again, check the wiring and sensors. ◆ ▣
	LOOSE OR CORRODED CONNECTIONS? Clean or tighten wire connections at sensors as well as at the control unit. ◆
	WORN-OUT MICROWAVE SENSOR? Replace sensor (the diodes in older microwave sensors have limited life spans). ◆
	LIGHTNING-DAMAGED ALARM SCREEN? Replace screen if you find welded contacts in the screen's tamper switch. ◆
	SENSITIVITY IMPROPERLY ADJUSTED? Check the sensitivity of all vibration- or motion-detecting sensors. ◆
	BRANCHES HITTING WINDOW WITH VIBRATION SENSOR? Trim trees and shrubs near window. ◇
	INSECTS CRAWLING ACROSS FACE OF PASSIVE INFRARED MOTION SENSOR? Check inside sensor and around it; get rid of any insects in the area. ◇
	MICROWAVE MOTION DETECTOR SET OFF BY DRAINING WATER? Microwaves penetrate walls and may be tripped by motion of water in PVC drainpipe. Re-aim microwave sensor. ◇
Siren runs all day while you're gone	TIMER SET INCORRECTLY? Check and reset timer. ◇
	TIMER FAULTY? Have timer replaced.
Can't arm system	DOOR OR WINDOW STILL OPEN? Check that all doors and windows are closed and locked. ◇
	SENSOR IN ALARM CONDITION? Isolate zone of error and check for tripped sensors. Rearm or replace faulty sensor. ◆ ▣

Degree of difficulty: Simple ◇   Average ◆   Complex ◆
Volt-ohm meter required: ▣

TIPS FROM THE PROS

False alarms are the bane of your neighbors and the police. More than 90 percent of security system false alarms are caused by user error, not faulty equipment. The following are experts' suggestions for reducing false alarms:

Practice arming and disarming the system with family members and others who must enter your house until each is expert with the process.

Invest in wireless keys that let you arm or disarm the system from outside, if you have trouble teaching the users of your system.

Sign up for verification with a security monitoring company. If the alarm goes off, the company calls the house. If you give a code word, assuring that you're not an intruder, the company won't put in an alarm.

Adjust volumetric sensors for new pets or growing children.

Finding faulty components

A faulty sensor can trigger a false alarm or make it impossible to arm the security system. Some control panels and/or keypads identify the zone that is out, narrowing your search. Others don't. On a wireless system, push any test buttons on the transmitters; if they don't respond, test the batteries (p.131). Replace low batteries. If a sensor still doesn't work, replace it following the manufacturer's instructions.

If a wired system malfunctions, use a volt-ohm meter (p.130) to test a loop or individual sensors on the loop for continuity. The test results will depend on whether the system circuits are normally closed or open (p.333). If you aren't sure, test a loop that you know is working, or consult either the manufacturer or the installer of the system.

Test each sensor on the faulty circuit. Some loops have a single sensor; two or more sensors on an open circuit are connected in parallel, those on a closed circuit, in series. When testing reveals the faulty sensor, replace it (below).

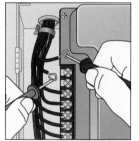

To test a loop, disconnect both leads from control panel. Set VOM on RX1 and probe leads. Reading should be near zero ohms on a closed circuit, infinity on an open circuit.

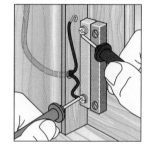

To test a wired sensor, disconnect one wire and arm sensor. With VOM on RX1, probe sensor's terminal screws. Note reading. Disarm sensor and test again. If sensor is OK, one reading will be zero, the other infinity. Replace sensor if both are zero or infinity.

Replacing wired sensors

To be sure that the new sensor will be compatible with your security system, buy an identical replacement from a security company or electronics store. Disarm and turn off power to the security system before you begin removing the faulty sensor. After installing the new sensor, test it with a volt-ohm meter (above) before rearming the whole system.

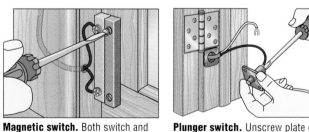

Magnetic switch. Both switch and magnet should be replaced. Attach zone wires to contacts in new switch; then screw switch onto window frame. With window closed, align magnet on sash and install.

Plunger switch. Unscrew plate of old switch in door frame and pull unit out to access contact screws. Attach zone wires to contact screws on new unit, return unit to frame, and install new plate.

Vibration glass-break detector. Use razor blade to remove old unit. Desolder unit's wires from zone wires, and solder new sensor wires to zone wires. Read label directions for mounting and sensitivity adjustment.

Testing the system's efficiency

Checking the control panel for signs of trouble doesn't insure that your security system is giving full protection. An armed sensor may stick and fail to trigger the alarm, or a volumetric sensor may not be aimed correctly. Most volumetric sensors include a *Walk test* LED (light-emitting diode); with the system disarmed, you can simulate a prowler's movements and the light will glow in response. You may find, for example, that the sensor misses a corner of the front hall and needs to be repositioned.

The tests described below check other system components. To avoid the siren's wail during these tests, make an LED tester. Buy an LED light, a 1500 ohm resistor, and wire leads from an electronics store. Solder the resistor to the short leg of the LED; then

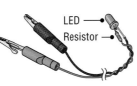

solder the red lead to the resistor (above). Add alligator clips and insulating sleeves as shown. Disconnect the siren wires at the control panel and attach the clips to the siren screws, matching the positive (red) and negative wires to the correct screws. When a sensor trips the alarm, the LED light will go on instead of the siren.

If you have a supervised telephone line, always tell the monitoring company that you are testing before you start.

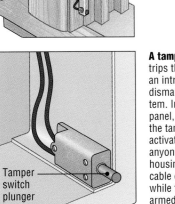

Check a magnetic switch by raising window to break connection between magnet and switch; the alarm should be triggered.

Magnet

Switch

To test an audio frequency glass-break sensor, shake some small glass jars in a plastic grocery bag next to the window. Check a vibration detector by rapping the glass—very gently—with a screwdriver.

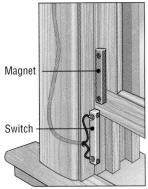

A tamper switch trips the alarm when an intruder tries to dismantle the system. In the control panel, for example, the tamper switch activates the alarm if anyone opens the housing over the cable connections while the system is armed. Test it by opening the housing.

Tamper switch plunger

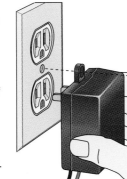

Test battery backup by disconnecting power to control panel (unscrew and unplug transformer near panel or turn off at power box). Battery power to keep system running should kick in immediately. Replace backup batteries every 4 to 5 yr.

Smoke detectors

The safest smoke detectors are hard-wired (with a battery backup) directly to a home security system and connected by telephone to a security monitoring company. When the detector is activated, an alarm sounds to waken people in the house and a digital dialer seizes the telephone line and calls the security monitoring company, which in turn calls the fire department. Such alarms protect you at home and the house when you're away. Less expensive, but effective in alerting people in a house to a fire, are stand-alone smoke detectors. Battery-powered models are easy to install yourself.

Technology. Modern smoke detectors have photoelectric or ionization sensors or both. Since each type of sensor responds more quickly to a different kind of fire, the best protection comes from using both.

Placement. At a minimum, you should have a smoke detector on each floor of your house and in each bedroom or its adjoining hallway. Install detectors on the ceiling, if possible, in the middle of the room or the hallway. Detectors can also be mounted high on walls, 6 or 8 inches from the ceiling. Avoid areas, such as corners, where air—or smoke—doesn't circulate well.

Testing. An indicator light tells you a hard-wired or plug-in smoke alarm is receiving power. A button tests the battery in a wireless smoke alarm. Check it weekly. Most battery-powered alarms emit intermittent beeps when new batteries are needed (alkaline batteries are usually preferred).

Maintenance. Dust can reduce an alarm's sensitivity to smoke particles and even trigger false alarms. Once a month use the wand attachment to gently vacuum the alarms in your home's living areas. Alarms in dustier places like the laundry room or workshop may require more frequent cleaning.

Photoelectric alarms "see" smoke particles and respond quickly to the fumes from smoldering upholstery. Install in living areas (bedrooms and hallways).and the kitchen (normal cooking smoke won't trigger them).

Ionization smoke detectors, which sense atomic particles, respond fast to hot fires with little smoke, such as those fueled by paper, wood, or fat. They are recommended for work areas and furnace rooms.

Most people today own and must maintain all the telephone equipment in their home, starting from the network interface where lines from the telephone company enter the building. (Older systems may start at a lightning protector outside instead.) To learn if a problem is your responsibility or the phone company's, plug a working phone into the jack inside the network interface. (With older systems, use the phone jack nearest the protector.) If it works there and not elsewhere, the fault is in the house wiring. Test each of your jacks (facing page). Replacing a faulty jack is a quick and easy job.

CAUTION: A phone circuit works at low voltage, but a ringing phone draws higher current and can produce a shock. To prevent ringing on a line during repairs, lift off the handset of a phone on that line or unplug the line at the interface. Use only tools with insulated handles.

A household telephone system

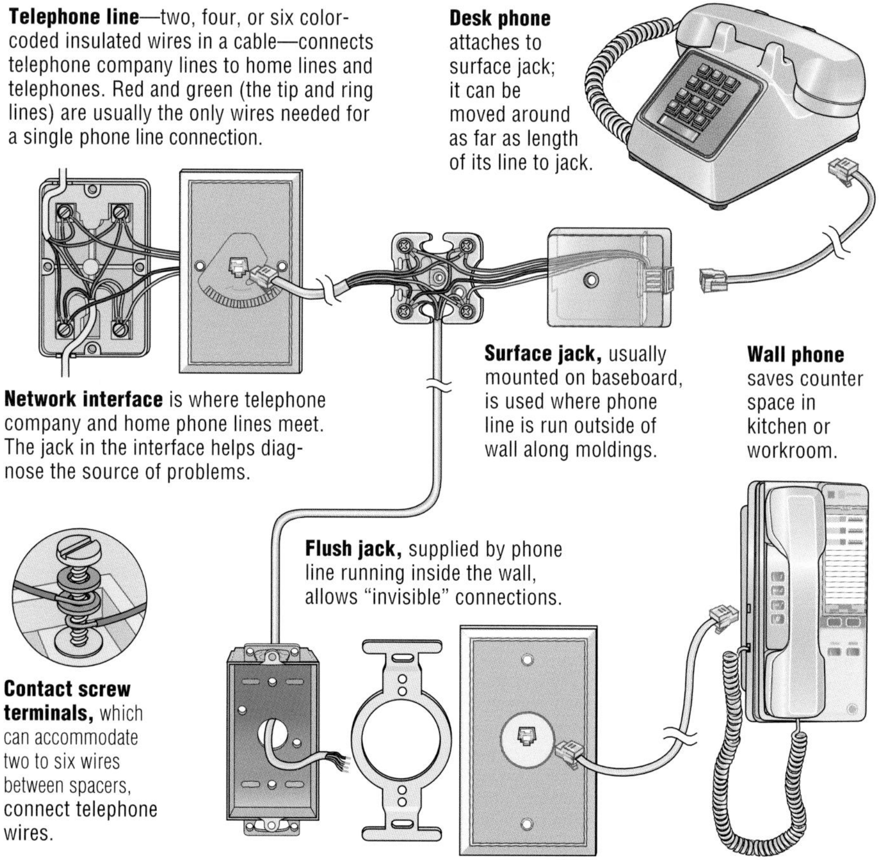

Telephone line—two, four, or six color-coded insulated wires in a cable—connects telephone company lines to home lines and telephones. Red and green (the tip and ring lines) are usually the only wires needed for a single phone line connection.

Desk phone attaches to surface jack; it can be moved around as far as length of its line to jack.

Network interface is where telephone company and home phone lines meet. The jack in the interface helps diagnose the source of problems.

Surface jack, usually mounted on baseboard, is used where phone line is run outside of wall along moldings.

Wall phone saves counter space in kitchen or workroom.

Flush jack, supplied by phone line running inside the wall, allows "invisible" connections.

Contact screw terminals, which can accommodate two to six wires between spacers, connect telephone wires.

Troubleshooting

Problem	CAUSE? / Solution
Static on line	DAMP CONNECTION IN JACK? Find and resolve moisture problem. Replace jack when conditions are dry. ⬘
	LINE CORD OR HANDSET CORD DEFECTIVE? Test and service plugs (facing page). If static persists, replace first one cord, then the other. ◇ ▣
	TOO MANY PHONES ON LINE? Unplug all but one phone; then check for static after adding each extra one. Most lines can handle five phones. ◇
	DEFECTIVE CONNECTION OR LINE OUTSIDE HOUSE? Plug good phone into diagnostic jack inside interface; call telephone company if you hear static. ◇
No dial tone	HANDSET OFF HOOK? Replace handset on hook. ◇
	MODULAR PLUG DEFECTIVE? Service or replace (facing page). ⬘ ▣
	CORDS UNPLUGGED OR DEFECTIVE? Unplug modular connections from line and handset cords, then plug back in firmly. Replace either cord if faulty. ◇
	SHORT IN LINE? Check jack for touching bare wires; repair (facing page). ⬘
	OPEN CONNECTION? Tighten loose connections in jack (facing page). ⬘
	INCOMING LINES OUT OF SERVICE? Plug good phone into diagnostic jack inside interface; contact telephone company if it doesn't work.
	SWITCH HOOK DEFECTIVE? *(Classic telephone only)* Service it (p.338). ◆
	JACK DEFECTIVE? Test jack and replace if faulty (facing page). ⬘ ▣
	SWITCH HOOK DEFECTIVE? *(Classic telephone only)* See *No dial tone,* above.
	FAULTY BELL ASSEMBLY? *(Classic telephone only)* Repair jammed clapper (p.338) or replace bell. ⬘
Bell rings, but at low volume	TOO MANY PHONES ON LINE? See *Static on line,* above.
	RINGER VOLUME SWITCH ON *LOW*? *(Electronic telephone only)* Turn volume up; switch may be located on handset or base. ◇
	DEFECTIVE PHONE ON LINE? Unplug all phones; then add them back one by one, checking for problem after each addition (have someone call repeatedly from outside). Service or replace defective phone. ⬘
No sound from handset	HANDSET CORD UNPLUGGED OR DEFECTIVE? Unplug cord, then plug back in firmly. If you suspect cord is faulty, replace it. ◇
	POOR RECEIVER CONTACTS? *(Classic telephone only)* See *Improving receiver sound,* p.338. ◇
	RECEIVER DEFECTIVE? If you cannot regain sound on classic phone by servicing receiver (p.338), replace receiver. Have electronic telephone serviced. ⬘
Called party can't hear you	MICROPHONE DEFECTIVE? *(Electronic telephone only)* Have microphone serviced, or replace phone. ◆
	TRANSMITTER DEFECTIVE? *(Classic telephone only)* Try to improve transmitter sound (p.338). If this fails, replace transmitter. ⬘
Dialing doesn't work	PULSE/TONE SWITCH SET IMPROPERLY? *(Electronic telephone only)* Set switch to mode (pulse or tone) appropriate for your phone service. ◇
	KEY CONTACTS FOULED? *(Electronic telephone only)* Access contacts and service as needed (p.339). ◆

Degree of difficulty: Simple ◇ Average ⬘ Complex ◆ Volt-ohm meter required: ▣

Phone cords, plugs, and jacks

There are three types of telephone cord: flat, which links the base of the phone to a jack; round, which links jacks to each other and to the network interface; and coiled, which connects the tele-phone's handset to the base. Cords are a common source of problems (see *Troubleshooting,* facing page), but replacement cord is inexpensive and relatively easy to install.

Modern telephone system connections are made with modular plugs and jacks. When you insert a plug correctly into a jack, an audible click indicates a complete connection.

Servicing a modular plug and jack

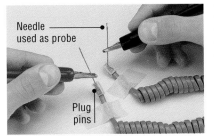

Needle used as probe

Plug pins

To test plug and cord, set VOM on RX1. Clip probes to sewing needles. Touch first pin in one plug, then touch each pin in opposite plug. In a good plug, conti-nuity (near zero ohms) will register only once (when probe touches corre-sponding pin). Repeat test with each pin in each plug.

To clean plug, dip a foam swab in denatured alcohol and run it over pins just inside plug. Use toothpick to straighten any jack pins that are bent or crossing another pin (inset).

Replacing a modular plug

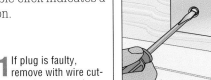

Bare wire

Insulation

Wire contact pin

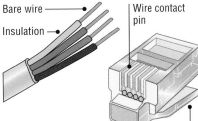

Clip

1 If plug is faulty, remove with wire cut-ters; make sure cut is straight. Strip back ¼ in. of insulation (left), using wire stripper on crimping tool. Buy crimping tool and new plug (right) at a telephone store.

2 Place new plug in crimping tool and insert stripped phone cable into plug. Squeeze handles of crimping tool firmly to set cable ends in plug (inset).

Servicing a jack

Remove jack cover. Some are held by a screw; others must be pried off. Inspect jack connections for water damage, corrosion, or shorts. A faulty jack should be replaced.

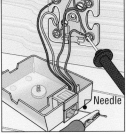

Needle

To test jack wires, set VOM on RX1. Clip one probe to needle to touch contact pin in plug. Put other probe on corre-sponding contact screw at wire end. VOM should read nearly zero on each wire.

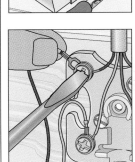

Inspect for loose wires. Re-attach each wire to its contact screw; no wire ends should protrude. Then tighten screws for a firm connection.

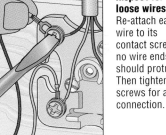

Even if only one pair of wires is being used, bare wires that touch will short out the line. Detach wires from contact screws and cut off any excess.

Replacing a surface-mounted jack

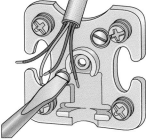

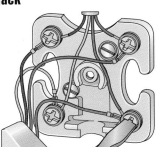

1 Remove cover of jack (pry it off if there is no screw). Loosen con-tact screws and detach line wires. To remove baseplate (above), remove screws securing it to baseboard.

2 To install new jack, attach new baseplate. Connect line wires and jack wires to terminals. Tighten screws (above) and replace cover.

Replacing a flush-mounted wall jack

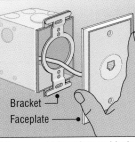

Bracket

Faceplate

1 Remove old faceplate and jack from wall box with screwdriver, leaving bracket, if any, in place. Disconnect line wires from old jack and discard faceplate assembly.

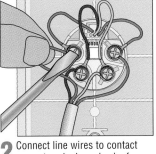

2 Connect line wires to contact screw terminals on back of new jack-faceplate assembly, matching wire colors. Screw assembly into wall-box mounting holes.

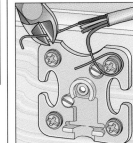

Classic telephones

The workhorse telephones with push buttons instead of dials were first introduced in the mid-1960s. You can still buy these sturdy telephones, new or reconditioned. When they need repair, you can usually do the job yourself as long as you can find parts.

The switch hook, which relies on a spring to close the switch contacts that complete a telephone circuit, is central to a variety of phone problems. Most can be solved by cleaning the switch contacts or by replacing the spring. Phones that don't ring may need a new bell assembly. Before you install one, however, make sure that the problem isn't a jammed clapper (that can be freed with a screwdriver).

CAUTION: Unplug the telephone from the wall jack before you start any repairs.

Note: For clarity, wires inside telephone have been omitted in drawing.

Earpiece cover
Receiver
Handset
Mouthpiece cover
Transmitter
Bell assembly
Bell clapper
Line cord
Handset cord
Switch hook
Housing
Switch cover
Keypad
Switch contacts
Jack
Spring

Improving transmitter sound

Unscrew mouthpiece cover; lift out transmitter. Clean off dirt with a foam swab dipped in denatured alcohol. Also clean metal contacts beneath transmitter.

Raise metal contacts slightly with a screwdriver and clean with emery cloth. Reassemble handset and make a call. If poor sound persists, have phone serviced.

Improving receiver sound

Unscrew earpiece cover and lift out receiver. Loosen terminal screws; remove wire leads. Clean leads and screws; sand, if necessary, to remove corrosion.

Reconnect each wire terminal securely to its screw. Reassemble handset. If poor sound persists, have phone serviced.

Servicing the switch assemby

1 Disconnect phone; remove housing. Remove retaining screws in push-button keypad and lift keypad out. Squeeze, then lift off plastic cover shielding switch contacts from dust and debris.

2 Clean contacts with blasts of compressed air, or wipe gently with a foam swab moistened with electrical contact cleaner. Reassemble and test phone; if still faulty, have it serviced.

Electronic telephones

Dependent on computer chips for their rich assortment of features (automatic redial, speed dialing, speakerphone capability, and other conveniences), electronic telephones contain few parts that can be serviced by the owner. Most new models are, in fact, sealed. On some older electronic phones, you can open the base—or the handset if it contains the keypad—to remedy sticky keys or dirty contacts (below, right).

Common variant: a phone with the keypad in the handset.

You can also test an electronic phone's handset and line cords (p.337) and replace faulty ones. Other repairs call for professional service. Take the phone to an electronics repair store or send it to the manufacturer (the address will be in your owner's manual). Inexpensive novelty phones aren't designed to be repaired; you're not likely to find parts to fit them.

The best preventive maintenance for an electronic telephone is to install it on a surface where it is unlikely to be knocked against or pulled down. Falls and rough treatment can loosen delicate but essential internal connections.

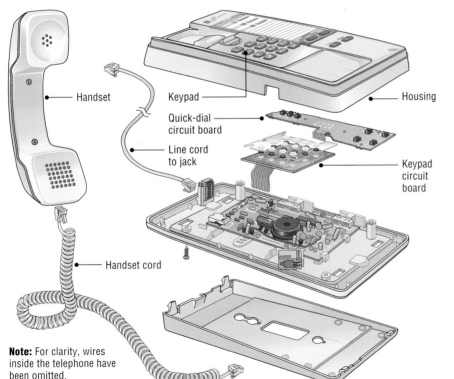

Handset

Keypad

Quick-dial circuit board

Line cord to jack

Housing

Keypad circuit board

Handset cord

Note: For clarity, wires inside the telephone have been omitted.

Cordless and cellular telephones

Line cord connects the base of a cordless phone (right) to a standard phone jack; an AC cord plugged into an electrical outlet gives the base power for recharging the handset's batteries. Recharging takes place when the handset rests on the base. The base communicates with the handset by converting electrical signals from the phone line into radio waves. Older cordless phones function within a frequency band of 46 and 49 megahertz; newer phones use the 900 MHz range.

Batteries. A low battery in a cordless or cellular phone can sabotage transmission quality. To maintain proper charging, clean the charge contacts on both the base (or charger) and the handset with a pencil eraser monthly. If a charge doesn't last long, try completely discharging and recharging the battery (p.143). You can replace the battery pack on most phones, but consult the owner's manual (some models must be returned to the manufacturer for new batteries).

Fighting interference. Cordless phones are subject to noisy interference from TV's, motors, power lines, and other telephones. Many phones automatically switch among 10 channels for the clearest signal; others must be manually switched between two channels (be sure the base and handset are set to the

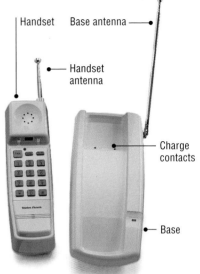

Handset   Base antenna

Handset antenna

Charge contacts

Base

same channel). If an appliance causes interference, plug the phone base into a different electrical circuit. Moving the base to an upper floor will also help curb interference.

Antenna. Replace a broken antenna. Most simply screw in. On some older models, you must unsolder a connecting wire to remove the old antenna and resolder the new one (p.136).

Servicing the keys

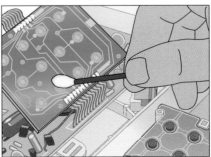

Unplug telephone from wall jack. Remove screws from housing and lift it off. Remove rubber covering from keypad circuit board. Clean contact points with a foam swab dampened in denatured alcohol.

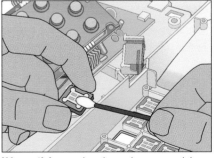

If keys stick, open housing and remove each key to check for dirt and grime. Clean each key with an alcohol-dampened foam swab before replacing it. Finally, reassemble the phone.

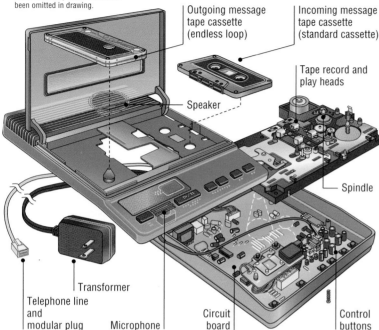

Note: For clarity some wires have been omitted in drawing.

Outgoing message tape cassette (endless loop)

Incoming message tape cassette (standard cassette)

Tape record and play heads

Speaker

Spindle

Transformer

Telephone line and modular plug

Microphone

Circuit board

Control buttons

In response to a preset number of telephone rings, a telephone answering machine plays a prerecorded message for the caller and then records the caller's response. Cassette-type answering machines store outgoing and incoming messages on one or two standard-size or small (microcassette) audiotapes similar to those used in personal audiocassette players. Newer answering machines use a computer chip to record the outgoing message or both messages. On both types of answering machines, you can replace the transformer (below) and service the modular jack connectors (p.337) and tape mechanism (p.312) yourself; faulty chips require professional service.

To keep an answering machine tape player in good working order, clean and demagnetize the tape path every 3 months. Check the drive belt when you suspect problems (see *Troubleshooting*, below, left); clean a good belt but replace a loose, stiff, or worn one (right).

Servicing the drive belt

To access drive belt, turn off and unplug machine. Turn it over and remove screws from bottom panel. As you lift off bottom panel, carefully disconnect any wires preventing its removal.

Turn over tape-player board to inspect pulleys and drive belt. Press lightly on belt with a finger; it should give slightly but fit snugly. Replace belt that feels stiff or slack or shows nicks and cracks.

To clean belt, use foam swab dipped in belt-cleaning solution from an electronics store. Cleaning prevents a buildup of dirt, which may cause slippage. Also wipe away any rubber bits on the pulley.

Install replacement belt that is exactly the same size and material as the original. Follow pathway of original installation. Make sure new belt has some give—a too tight belt can snap.

Troubleshooting

Problem	CAUSE? / Solution
Machine doesn't work	POWER OFF AT OUTLET OR FAULTY POWER CORD? See *General troubleshooting*, p.144.
	FAULTY TRANSFORMER? Replace transformer. ◇
Tape reels don't move	LOOSE OR BROKEN BELT? Replace belt (right). ◆
	FAULTY TAPE CASSETTE? Replace cassette. ◇
Machine doesn't respond to calls	TELEPHONE CORD OR MODULAR PLUG DAMAGED? Replace cord and modular plug. ◇
	FAULTY CIRCUIT BOARD? Have circuit board replaced.
Tape jams	FAULTY TAPE CASSETTE? Repair (p.312) or replace cassette. ◇
	DIRTY PLAY AND RECORD HEADS AND TAPE PATH? Clean heads and tape path (p.313). ◇
	BROKEN OR STRETCHED DRIVE BELT? Replace belt (right). ◆
Poor-quality message (hisses or other distortion)	See *Tape jams*, above.
	MAGNETIZED PLAY OR RECORD HEAD? Demagnetize (p.313). ◇
	DEFECTIVE TAPE? Replace tape. ◇

Degree of difficulty: Simple ◇   Average ◆   Complex ◆

Transformers

The transformers used with answering machines and other electronic devices reduce the line voltage from a wall receptacle –120 volts–to between 1.5 and 24 volts. Some also turn the line's alternating current (AC) into direct current (DC). Replace a faulty transformer; there is nothing you can fix, and opening it poses a shock hazard. Check the label (right). The new unit must have the same output voltage rating (10VDC on this label) as the original and the same or greater current rating in milliamperes (500mA here). The polarity of the new plug must also match the old plug (the diagram at the lower left on the label indicates that the plug's outer shell is negative and its center connector is positive).

CODE-A-PHONE
ACC-614 POWER SUPPLY

(UL) LISTED
81JI
291356

(CSA)
LR68807

MODEL NO: DV-9500-1
INPUT: 117VAC 60Hz 11W
OUTPUT: 10VDC 500mA
FOR USE WITH TELECOMMUNICATIONS PRODUCTS
⊖-(◉-⊕   MADE IN PHILIPPINES
                    0189 CM

Transformer label

Televisions and computer monitors

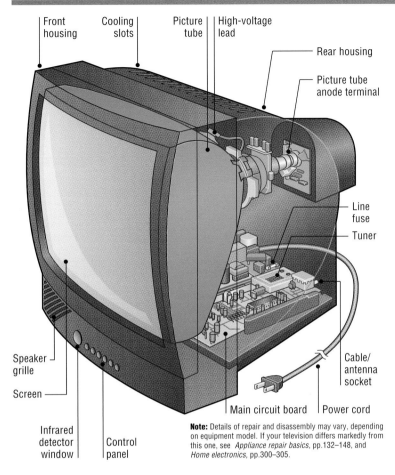

Front housing | Cooling slots | Picture tube | High-voltage lead

Rear housing

Picture tube anode terminal

Line fuse

Tuner

Cable/antenna socket

Speaker grille

Screen

Main circuit board | Power cord

Infrared detector window | Control panel

Note: Details of repair and disassembly may vary, depending on equipment model. If your television differs markedly from this one, see *Appliance repair basics,* pp.132–148, and *Home electronics,* pp.300–305.

Modern televisions, and computer monitors (p.345), rely on solid-state electronic components. TV's have an average life of three to five years of moderate to heavy use. Most problems you can fix are caused by loose connections or improperly set controls. TV's made since about 1990 are often adjusted with a hand-held remote and on-screen commands. Finer adjustments can be made using override codes that reprogram the TV's control circuitry (a job for a service technician).

Regardless of your TV's age, check a few things before calling for service. Switch to different channels or wait a few hours to see if the trouble might be with the cable service or broadcaster. Make sure the controls are set properly (see *Troubleshooting TV picture problems,* p.342, and *Adjusting for best picture,* p.343). Some TV's have a service switch behind the set; it must be set at *Normal.* Check the power cord (p.144) and cable connections, and tighten the antenna lead-in connection (p.346). Low voltage from an overloaded AC circuit (p.131) can also affect the picture. Problems that appear suddenly indicate a failed component, especially if the set has recently been subjected to shock, vibration, or excessive heat. Gradual deterioration is usually due to aging.

Servicing older TV's

Instead of solid-state components, older TV's have rows of vacuum tubes inside. If a tube-type TV has problems, about the best you can do is to adjust the controls (p.342). Though hardware stores once stocked tube testers and replacement tubes, those days are gone. Manufacturers stopped making tubes in the late 1970's, making tubes extremely costly—if you can find a source. If a tube goes bad, your only real option is to replace the set.

FOR YOUR SAFETY

⚡ **A TV can contain up to 32,000 volts** even if the set is unplugged—leave picture tube replacement and the repair of high-voltage circuits to the pros. The chief shock hazard is the picture tube anode terminal. Discharge it (p.344) before doing *any* work inside the set; stand on a rubber mat while working and always wear safety glasses. Seek professional repairs if you get a shock from a metal part or if you doubt your ability to proceed safely.

Don't block the cooling slots in the bottom and rear of the set; they prevent overheating.

Never alter the wide prong on a polarized power plug to make it fit a nonpolarized receptacle. Replace the receptacle instead (p.129).

Don't plug a TV into an overloaded branch circuit; it may operate poorly and can also be a fire hazard.

Gaining access

Unplug set and disconnect its antenna wire or cable-TV cable. Unscrew fasteners at rear of housing. Pull off back panel; at the same time, slide the power cord through its opening. On some models, the power cord may come off with back panel. **CAUTION:** An unplugged set likely contains high voltage (see *For your safety,* right).

How a TV works

A TV picture is produced when an electron beam strikes a phosphor coating on the inner surface of the picture tube. The beam covers the screen from top to bottom in a series of closely spaced horizontal lines, a process it repeats 60 times per second. As with a movie projector, the rapid sequence of frames gives the illusion of a single, continuous picture. In a black-and-white set, tones and shadows are produced by varying the beam's intensity; a color set employs red, blue, and green beams.

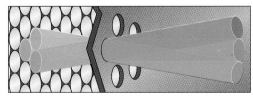

In a color tube, three electron beams pass through a shadow mask containing more than 300,000 holes. Each hole corresponds to a trio of red, blue, and green phosphor dots (these colors combined can make almost any other color). As the beams sweep back and forth, the mask focuses them on the various combinations of dots.

Troubleshooting TV picture problems

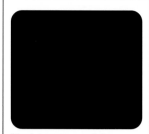

Black screen, no picture. First, make sure the TV is plugged in. Then unplug set; check the wall receptacle, the house circuit fuse/breaker and the power cord (see *Power off at outlet?*, p.144). Also check for a blown fuse or circuit breaker on or inside the TV (see *Replacing fuses,* p.344). Finally, check the horizontal circuits (see *Servicing the horizontal circuits,* p.344).

Vertical distortion. If screen shows only a single line (no height at all), reduce brightness to prevent tube damage from a burnt phosphor. Set service switch (if TV has one) on *Normal.* Turn off set and try cleaning the vertical height, linearity, hold, and centering controls by spraying TV tuner cleaner into the openings nearest them. Also check for low voltage on the circuit (see *Testing for AC voltage,* p.131).

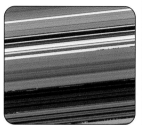

Horizontal distortion. On an older set, adjust the horizontal hold control. If you can't get the picture to lock in horizontally (or if the set doesn't have a horizontal hold control), the horizontal circuits may be faulty. Check them (see *Servicing the horizontal circuits,* p.344), or have the set professionally serviced.

Vertical roll. If the picture rolls continuously upward or downward, adjust the vertical hold (it may be a knob or a screw). If the picture is vertically stretched, adjust the vertical height and linearity control; if it also slips diagonally or breaks into diagonal rolling segments, adjust the automatic gain control, or AGC (don't confuse with the AGC delay control; see *Adjusting for best picture,* p.343).

Weak or no picture; poor sound. If screen lights up, check for loose antenna or cable connections (p.346). Try bypassing the cable converter, if there is one; if you get a picture, converter is faulty. If there is sound but no picture, adjust the AGC control. If there is no sound, set the service switch, if any, at *Normal.*

Snow in picture. Suspect a weak signal or poor connections. Tighten loose antenna wires. Rotate antenna, if motorized, to make sure the motor works. Tighten incoming cable connections. If snow appears only in rainy weather, the antenna lead-in is faulty (p.346). If TV has an AGC delay control, turn set to a weak station and adjust control for best picture.

Ghosts. Faint duplicate images are caused by signals reflecting off mountains or tall buildings. If the set has an automatic color control (ACC) button, push it to *Off.* Adjust the fine tuning until a wavy pattern appears on the screen; then turn the control just enough to clear the picture. Try different antenna positions and locations; you may need a directional antenna (p.346).

Poor focus. Turn to a channel that has a strong signal, set other controls for best picture, then adjust focus control. Reduce brightness. If picture is still poor, turn brightness to maximum, adjust brightness limiter control until images just begin to bloom (spread out), then reduce brightness control to normal.

No color. Try several solutions. Turn automatic color control (ACC) off. Adjust fine tuning until a wavy pattern appears; then reverse control enough to clear picture. Turn color killer control counterclockwise until color comes on. Look for loose connections, broken antenna wires, or interference from another appliance. If all else fails, you may need a better antenna.

Poor color. Turn the drive controls fully clockwise; then reverse them gradually to get good color quality. If color is poor only when automatic color control (ACC) is on, adjust ACC controls. If the picture has a green tint, picture tube may be worn. Check for broken antenna wires, loose connections, and interference from other appliances.

Color blotches. These are usually caused by magnetization of the TV's metal parts or picture tube. Most sets have a built-in device for demagnetizing. Turn set on for 60 sec., then off. Repeat several times at half-hour intervals. If this fails, demagnetize picture tube by running a degaussing coil (available with instructions at electronics parts stores) across the tube with set off.

Silvery bright areas. If bright areas of a picture look silvery and details are indistinct, picture tube is defective. When brightness is turned to low level, picture will appear normal but dull. With brightness up, detail in white areas is lost. The picture may improve after set has been on for an hour or more, but you'll eventually have to replace the tube.

Adjusting for best picture

The controls for picture adjustment (right) vary from model to model. Since about 1980 many controls have been eliminated or moved inside, and many recent models have on-screen controls. Since all adjustments are made with the set turned on, only on-screen or external controls should be adjusted by the owner.

Let older tube-type sets warm up for about 20 minutes to stabilize the circuits before you attempt to adjust the picture controls. If the picture has a combination of problems (see facing page), note the initial positions of the knobs before adjusting them so you can backtrack if the picture gets worse.

V LIN and V SIZE (Vertical controls)	H HOLD (Horizontal hold)	FOCUS	BRITE LIM (Brightness limiter)	SCREEN: R, B, G (red, blue, green)	DRIVE: R B G
Linearity adjusts for uniform spacing of scanning lines. *Size* adjusts height.	Stops picture from scrolling.	Sharpens picture.	Reduces bloom (spreading out of bright picture area).	These factory-set controls should not be adjusted by consumer.	Adjust for uniform color intensities.
COLOR KILLER	**PEAK PIX (Peak picture control)**	**AGC (Automatic gain control)**	**AGC DELAY**	**GRAY-SCALE TRACKING**	**SER/ NOR (Service/ Normal switch)**
Reduces color snow during B&W programs.	Limits high-frequency interference. Also called video peak or sharpness control.	Reduces diagonal rolling.	Locks out automatic gain control (AGC) to minimize snow.	Brightens color reception and maintains proper shades of gray for B&W.	Set on *normal* position; *Set up* position is only for gray-scale tracking adjustment.

Servicing tuners

A tuner identifies a TV signal. A faulty tuner can make the picture flicker, disappear, or fill with snow. Mechanical tuners are found on old tube-type sets on transistor-type sets (shown here) with separate VHF and UHF tuners (VHF for channels 2 through 13; UHF for channels 14 and above). Other than cleaning, leave service to a professional. Solid-state tuners in newer TV's must also be serviced professionally.

1 A mechanical tuner is usually held by screws on front panel. Remove metal plate protecting tuner. Wires that lead to it may have to be desoldered (p.305) if replacement is necessary.

2 To clean the contacts spray bursts of tuner cleaner (p.303) on them. Then rotate channel selector to work in the cleaner and abrade the contacts. Solid-state electronic tuners cannot be cleaned.

Servicing remote controls

Home electronic equipment, including audio components and TV's, often can be operated via remote control. These handy devices send infrared signals to a receiver inside the front panel of the equipment. The receiver converts the signals to commands that control the operation of the set. All remotes are quite similar; if you can service one, you can service others.

The very thing that makes remote controls so useful—their portability—makes them vulnerable to damage. Damage can sometimes be repaired, but a new remote is inexpensive. If the device stops working after being dropped, disassemble it and check for a cracked circuit board (p.305) or faulty solder connections (see *Intermittent problems*, p. 302). If water spills on a remote, disassemble it to let it dry. In the case of a soda spill, vigorous cleaning is called for.

1 To open control, remove any housing screws (may be hidden in battery compartment). Then insert screwdriver into seam separating housing halves (left) and twist screwdriver gently. Repeat in several locations.

3 Peel keypad away from mounting tabs. Keypad may have to be coaxed out, but do so gently to avoid damaging it. Blow out dust and debris from housing, using canned air.

2 Inspect the circuit board for damage. If wiring traces look dirty, spray the circuit board with electrical contact cleaner; swab dry. Clean battery contacts by rubbing with pencil eraser.

4 Wash both sides of keypad with soapy water and an old toothbrush. Rinse keypad with clean water; then dry it with a lint-free cloth or allow it to air-dry thoroughly before reassembly.

Discharging the picture tube

Before doing *any* work—even changing a fuse—inside a TV or computer monitor, the picture tube *must* be discharged (right). On a solid-state chassis there may be several places, called *grounding points,* through which the tube may be discharged. You must follow a schematic (p.302) to locate the proper ground because using the wrong one can destroy the TV. If not performed properly, this procedure can present a severe shock hazard.

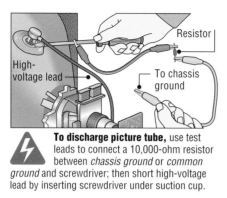

To discharge picture tube, use test leads to connect a 10,000-ohm resistor between *chassis ground* or *common ground* and screwdriver; then short high-voltage lead by inserting screwdriver under suction cup.

Servicing the horizontal circuits

The horizontal circuits guide the tube's electron beam as it sweeps back and forth across the screen. If the set is dead and the fuses test OK, the horizontal output transistor may be faulty (right). It is located near the high-voltage transformer, mounted on a large aluminum heat sink. Other symptoms, such as horizontal hold failure or sound problems, can be caused by a faulty horizontal circuit but those problems must be addressed by a professional.

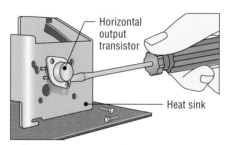

1 Remove screws on transistor; then gently pry it out of its socket with screwdriver. If transistor is soldered in place, desolder it (p.305) or have set professionally serviced.

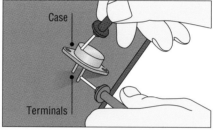

2 Test transistor: With VOM set on RX1, probe one terminal and the case; then switch leads. Resistance should be low in one direction, high or infinite in the other. Repeat for other terminal.

Servicing the sound circuits

The entire audio circuit is on an integrated circuit board, and the only owner-serviceable part is the speaker. If there's no sound or if the sound has deteriorated, unplug the TV and remove the housing (see *Gaining access,* p.341). Check the wires leading from the speaker to the circuit board; if a wire connection is loose or broken, repair it (pp.134–136). Then disconnect the speaker and test it (right). Remove the speaker for inspection or replacement (see also *Speakers,* p.314).

Replacing television fuses

Most newer TV's have at least one fuse to protect the internal circuits from power surges. (Older sets use circuit breakers; look for a manual reset button; it's usually red.) Another fuse may protect the set's high-voltage circuit. If the TV doesn't work, check the fuses. If you can't tell if the fuse is faulty or not—it isn't always obvious—test it (p.304). A fuse that blows repeatedly usually signals a faulty power supply; have the TV professionally serviced.

To remove a fuse, remove back panel (see *Gaining access,* p.341) and discharge picture tube (left). Pry fuse from fuse holder; if a fuse is soldered in place, desolder it (p.136).

USE AND CARE

Plug your TV into a surge protector (p.301) to protect it against power surges that could damage components.

Keep the TV plugged in. Programmable chips in today's sets store data in live memory and need electricity; if the TV is unplugged, reprogramming is required.

Periodically clean the screen with a lint-free cloth sprayed with glass cleaner (never spray cleaner directly on the tube).

Vacuum the cooling vents as often as needed to keep them dust free.

1 Remove rear housing of TV (see *Gaining access,* p.341). Discharge picture tube (see top); then unplug wire bundle (above) leading from input board to speaker.

2 Set VOM on RX1 and probe speaker terminals. Resistance should be close to speaker's ohms rating. Then probe either terminal and frame; zero indicates a short.

3 To remove the speaker, begin by grasping back edge of main circuit board. Lift it up slightly to disengage it from locking tab; then pull to slide the board out of the way.

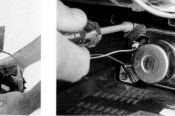

4 Use a nut driver or screwdriver, as required, to release the speaker from its mounting frame. Lift speaker away from TV, and replace it with a duplicate.

Computer monitors

Though it looks like a TV, a computer monitor processes video signals much differently, and at a higher resolution. Because the monitor depends on the computer for its signal, most servicing requires specialized equipment that lets a technician duplicate the computer's output signals. In many cases, the computer and its monitor must be tested together because the computer contains the video controller card (right).

If a problem occurs, first make sure the monitor power switch is on and all screen controls are properly adjusted. Check the power cord for continuity (p.131), and make sure the data cable leading to the computer is properly seated. Finally, check the video controller inside the computer or the fuse inside the monitor (below).

Clean a monitor screen by wiping it with a cloth sprayed lightly with glass cleaner. Vacuum the monitor's ventilation slots periodically to remove dust, or remove its housing so you can blow dust away with canned compressed air.

Replacing monitor fuses

There's one line fuse at the AC power supply and at least one other protecting the 5- and 9-volt power supplies. Pull out or desolder (p.305) fuses for testing and replacement (right). If the fuse is OK, reasssemble the monitor and check the computer's video controller card (right). If a fuse blows repeatedly, have the monitor serviced.

CAUTION: Always discharge the picture tube (facing page) before working on any parts inside the monitor, including fuses.

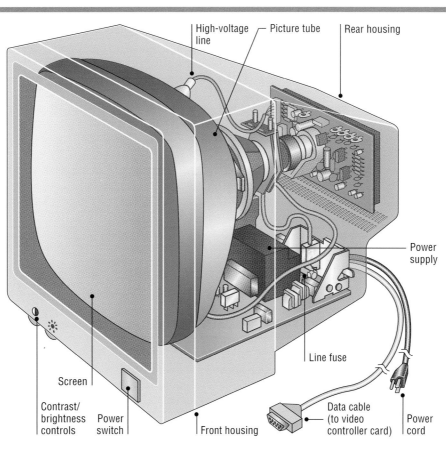

High-voltage line — Picture tube — Rear housing

Power supply

Line fuse

Screen

Contrast/ brightness controls — Power switch — Front housing — Data cable (to video controller card) — Power cord

1 Disconnect monitor, lay it face down on a padded surface, and remove housing screws (some may be under pop-out tabs). Slide rear housing off; *then discharge tube* (facing page).

Pad protects screen

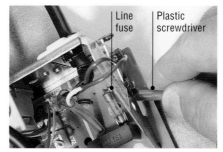

2 The line fuse is located near the power cord entrance. Pry fuse from fuse holder to test it (p.304), and replace it if faulty. If monitor has a second fuse near power supply, check it as well.

Line fuse — Plastic screwdriver

Video controller cards

A monitor gets its signal from the computer by way of a video controller card (a type of expansion card) inside the computer. A video controller must be matched to the monitor, so if you install a new monitor, you might also have to change the card. Multiscan-type monitors work with nearly any card, however. If your monitor fails to work and nothing else helps, access the card and reseat it (see *Correcting expansion card problems,* p.325). If that fails, you may have to install a new card.

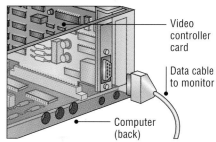

Video controller card

Data cable to monitor

Computer (back)

Most video controllers are mounted on a card (circuit board) that plugs into the computer's motherboard. Trace the data cable to its connection on the computer; that is the controller card.

FOR YOUR SAFETY

CAUTION: Unplug the monitor and *always* discharge the picture tube before working inside the monitor. A monitor can carry a lethal voltage even when it is unplugged.

Even non-lethal shocks often cause serious injuries when a hand is reflexively pulled away. You might cut your hand on sharp edges or, if holding a tool, you might break a picture tube, causing an explosion.

Beware of sharp edges on protruding screws, subframes, grounding springs, straps, and other metal parts.

A gable-mounted antenna

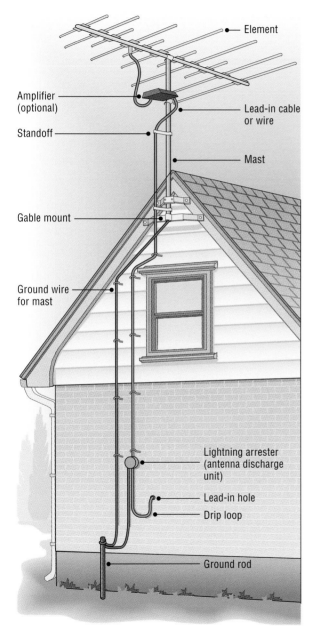

Element

Amplifier (optional)

Lead-in cable or wire

Standoff

Mast

Gable mount

Ground wire for mast

Lightning arrester (antenna discharge unit)

Lead-in hole

Drip loop

Ground rod

The best type of antenna to use is determined by several factors: the distance between the antenna and the television station, the terrain, the height and location of the antenna, and obstructions such as buildings and electric power lines. Antennas are rated for sensitivity (or gain); the higher the gain, the more sensitive the antenna is. Since the gain your antenna should have is based upon where you live, follow the manufacturer's guidelines when buying an antenna.

The lead-in (the wire or cable carrying a broadcast signal from the antenna to the television) is either flat 300-ohm twin-lead cable or 75-ohm coaxial cable (see *Troubleshooting,* p.304). Coaxial cable is shielded; so it is more resistant to interference. Older TV sets have screw terminal connectors to accept twin-lead wire; most newer TV sets have F-connectors to accept coaxial cable; some have both. If your TV terminals don't match the connections on your lead-in, install a matching transformer (facing page).

Installing a new antenna. Assemble the antenna and attach the lead-in on the ground; then secure the mount and antenna to the roof (follow the manufacturer's instructions). Attach standoffs to the house and mast every 3 feet; the lead-in must be kept 3½ inches away from metal and wood. Install a lightning arrester and connect the lead-in. For safety, wrap grounding wires from the mast and lightning arrester around a grounding rod driven into the ground. After the mast is up, align the antenna for optimum recep-

tion before locking it into position. Do this by having a helper watch the TV while you rotate the antenna.

Troubleshooting an antenna. If your TV picture is distorted with interference, examine the antenna and its connections. Start by making sure the lead-in is attached to the TV. If the connector on the lead-in is damaged, replace it (p.304). If any of the elements are broken off the antenna, install a new antenna. Check the lead-in; if it is cracked or broken, replace it. Also, the connection between the cable and the antenna should be clean and tight.

Cable boxes are used to gain access to paid television stations and are usually owned by the cable company. Your service contract with the company probably includes maintenance of the box; if you have a problem with your reception, call them for service.

FOR YOUR SAFETY

Install your antenna on a calm, clear day. Be sure the roof is dry before climbing on it; wear shoes with nonslip soles.

Keep your hands free for climbing by carrying tools to the roof in a tool belt (or hoist them up in a bucket).

Always have a helper nearby in case of an emergency.

Avoid a lethal shock: keep your ladder and the antenna clear of power lines as you work.

 Position the antenna so that the distance between it and any power lines is at least twice the maximum length of the antenna plus the mast.

Other types of mounts

Roof cone mount fits over ridge. It has a swivel foot that can be adjusted to fit roofs of different pitches. Seal all holes with roofing compound to prevent leaks.

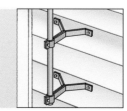

Side mounts are attached to a sidewall. (When securing a side-mounted antenna to a brick or stone house, attach the mount to a wooden eave.)

Eliminating a ghost signal

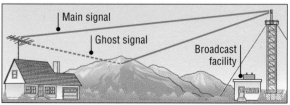

Main signal

Ghost signal

Broadcast facility

A ghost signal is reflected from a large object such as a mountain or building. It travels farther than the main signal, so arrives later; it appears as a faint copy to the right of the main image. Install a highly directional antenna and make sure that it's aimed directly at the broadcast signal.

Antenna accessories

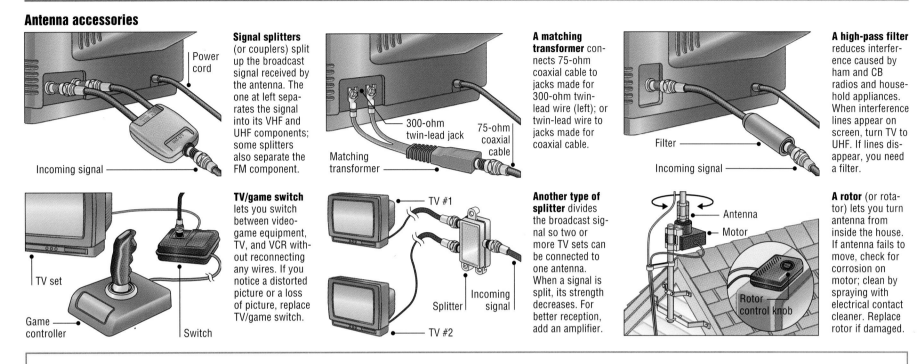

Signal splitters (or couplers) split up the broadcast signal received by the antenna. The one at left separates the signal into its VHF and UHF components; some splitters also separate the FM component.

Power cord

Incoming signal

A matching transformer connects 75-ohm coaxial cable to jacks made for 300-ohm twin-lead wire (left); or twin-lead wire to jacks made for coaxial cable.

300-ohm twin-lead jack

75-ohm coaxial cable

Matching transformer

A high-pass filter reduces interference caused by ham and CB radios and household appliances. When interference lines appear on screen, turn TV to UHF. If lines disappear, you need a filter.

Filter

Incoming signal

TV/game switch lets you switch between video-game equipment, TV, and VCR without reconnecting any wires. If you notice a distorted picture or a loss of picture, replace TV/game switch.

TV set

Game controller

Switch

TV #1

TV #2

Splitter

Incoming signal

Another type of splitter divides the broadcast signal so two or more TV sets can be connected to one antenna. When a signal is split, its strength decreases. For better reception, add an amplifier.

Antenna

Motor

Rotor control knob

A rotor (or rotator) lets you turn antenna from inside the house. If antenna fails to move, check for corrosion on motor; clean by spraying with electrical contact cleaner. Replace rotor if damaged.

Satellite dishes

An 18-in. satellite dish

Satellite dish antennas receive broadcast signals directly from orbiting satellites. This lets them pull in programming without interference, even in remote areas—provided that they have a clear view of the southern sky. Most satellite dishes are between 6 and 8 feet in diameter; newer ones are just 18 inches. Because systems differ, and tuning can be exacting, most large dishes are professionally installed; special kits are available so that the 18-inch dishes can be installed by homeowners. To receive programs, you must subscribe to a programming service. (Canadian programming is as yet unavailable, but US programming can be purchased through an American address.) If you experience a problem, first contact the programming service to make sure the signal is OK. If it is, the problem may be with the receiver or the descrambler; contact the manufacturer for repair or retuning.

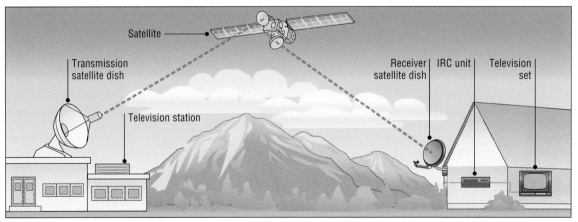

Satellite

Transmission satellite dish

Television station

Receiver satellite dish

IRC unit

Television set

How the picture gets to you: The TV station transmits the signal to a satellite. The signal is then relayed back to Earth, picked up by your dish, and brought into your house by a cable. Residential installations typically consist of the dish positioner, receiver, and descrambler. In some cases, all three components are combined into one unit called an IRC or IRD unit.

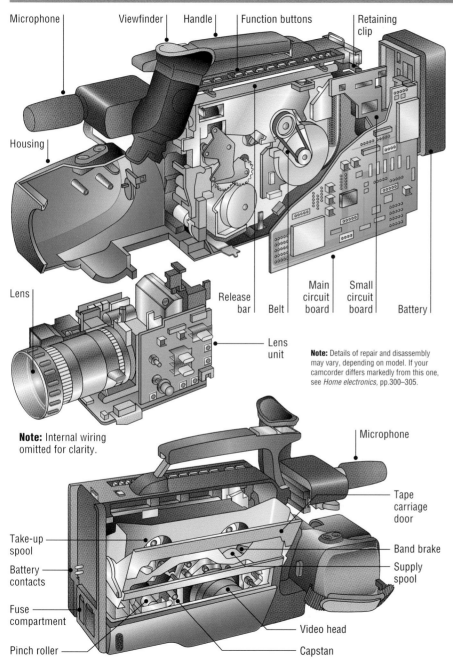

Microphone Viewfinder Handle Function buttons Retaining clip

Housing

Lens

Release bar Belt Main circuit board Small circuit board Battery

Lens unit

Note: Details of repair and disassembly may vary, depending on model. If your camcorder differs markedly from this one, see *Home electronics*, pp.300–305.

Note: Internal wiring omitted for clarity.

Microphone

Take-up spool

Battery contacts

Fuse compartment

Pinch roller

Tape carriage door

Band brake

Supply spool

Video head

Capstan

Taking video footage at home once called for separate camera and recorder units; today both functions are combined into a single compact device called a camcorder. These units may use one of several tape formats, including VHS, VHS-C (a compact version of VHS), and 8 millimeter, but are otherwise so similar that the chart below applies to any type of camcorder.

Many problems result from incorrect operation, so check the owner's manual before making any repair. Replacement parts for a camcorder may be available from an authorized dealer or from the camcorder manufacturer.
CAUTION: To avoid a shock hazard, always disconnect a camcorder from its power source (the battery or the AC adapter) before servicing it.

Troubleshooting

Problem	CAUSE? / Solution
Camcorder doesn't work	BATTERY NOT CHARGED? Recharge battery following manufacturer's instructions (consult owner's manual). If battery won't hold a charge, replace it. ◇
	AC ADAPTER CONNECTED IMPROPERLY? Disconnect; then reconnect. ◇
	CONTACTS FOULED? Clean dirty contacts on battery, charger, and AC adapter with cotton swab dipped in denatured alcohol. Remove corrosion with clean pencil eraser; then wipe area with artist's brush to remove debris. ◇
	FUSE BLOWN? Test fuse (p.304) and replace if faulty (facing page). ◆ ▆
Power goes off soon after starting	BATTERY LOW? Recharge battery following manufacturer's instructions. ◇
	SAFETY CIRCUITS DETECT MECHANICAL FAILURE? Turn camcorder power off; then turn it back on and eject tape. If problem persists, check fuse (p.304). ◆ ▆
Battery won't charge	CONTACTS FOULED? See *Camcorder doesn't work*, above. ◇
	BATTERY FAULTY? Fully discharge battery; then recharge it (p.143). If problem persists, replace faulty battery with new one. ◇
Camcorder works intermittently	FUSE NOT PROPERLY SEATED? Remove fuse, then reseat it to establish good contact. If necessary, replace fuse with one of same rating (facing page). ◆
Poor picture quality	TAPE DEFECTIVE? See *Repairing cassette tapes* (p.354) or try a new tape. ◇
	VIDEO HEADS DIRTY OR WORN? Clean with head-cleaning tape. ◇ If problem persists, have camcorder serviced professionally.
Tape doesn't run	PINCH ROLLER OR CAPSTAN DIRTY? Clean with head-cleaning tape; or wipe areas that touch tape with a lint-free cloth moistened with denatured alcohol. ◆
Tape won't load/eject	TAPE-LOADING BELT BROKEN OR DAMAGED? Replace belt (facing page). ◆
	TAPE TRANSPORT SYSTEM DAMAGED? Have unit serviced professionally.
No audio	AUDIO HEADS DIRTY? Clean with head-cleaning tape. ◇
	MICROPHONE DEFECTIVE? Have camcorder serviced professionally.
Camcorder damages tapes	FOREIGN MATERIAL IN TAPE TRANSPORT AREA? Remove carriage door and use tweezers to remove any debris from transport area. ◆
	PINCH ROLLER OR CAPSTAN DIRTY? See *Tape doesn't run*, above. ◆
	CAPSTAN BELT BROKEN OR WORN? Replace belt (facing page). ◆
Picture pulls to right In playback mode	BAND BRAKE BROKEN OR STUCK? Remove tape carriage door; remove any debris blocking brake. If brake is broken, replace it (facing page). ◆ *Note:* If brake doesn't have release clips or screws on both ends, have it replaced professionally.

Degree of difficulty: Simple ◇   Average ◆   Complex ◆   Volt-ohm meter required: ▆

Gaining access

Tape carriage

1 Disconnect power source (the battery or AC adapter). To remove the tape carriage door, remove screws securing door cover. Slide cover upward, then pull it off. *Note:* On some models, screws are concealed by rubber buttons.

Lens
Housing

2 Turn over unit. Remove housing screws (look closely; they may be hidden near lens, handle, or battery compartment); then lift off housing. If wires link housing to rest of camcorder, disconnect them at main circuit board.

Main circuit board
Ribbon cable

3 Remove screws securing main circuit board (they are painted red or otherwise marked). Once screws are out, gently fold circuit board back toward base of camera. Do not dislodge ribbon cable connecting board to unit.

Replacing belts

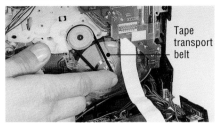
Tape transport belt

Disconnect power source; open unit (*Gaining access,* Step 3). Remove either belt if worn or damaged. Wipe new belt with denatured alcohol to remove protective coating; let dry. Then thread belt (or belts) around pulleys.

Replacing a band brake

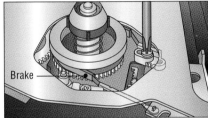
Brake

Remove tape carriage door; release carriage. If brake is held with clips, use tweezers to free it; if held by screws (as above), unscrew it. If brake is otherwise secured, have unit serviced. Install new brake with felt side around supply spool.

Replacing a fuse

FUSE
CLOCK BATTERY

1 Disconnect power source. Look for door on bottom or rear of unit; remove retaining screw. On some models, fuse is inside; remove housing and fold back board (*Gaining access,* Step 3). Fuse is in lower right corner.

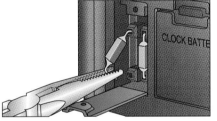
CLOCK BATTE

2 Use pliers to pull out fuse. (If fuse is inside unit, it may have to be unsoldered; see *Soldering techniques,* p.305.) Test fuse (see *Fuses,* p.304) and replace if faulty; if fuse tests OK, clean contacts (located on ends of fuse).

Releasing a stuck tape

Retaining clip

1 If *Eject* button fails, remove housing; then fold back main board (*Gaining access,* Step 3). Remove screws securing small circuit board and lift board out. (If board is also held by retaining clips, use an awl to release clips.)

Release lever

2 Look for a small release lever near top of camera. Using an awl or screwdriver, gently pull back lever; this will release the tape carriage. Carefully remove tape from the carriage.

3 Use tweezers to remove any debris (most often a tape label or adhesive tape used to defeat anti-record tab). Dust area with a soft brush and compressed air; never lubricate this area with oil or grease. Reassemble camcorder.

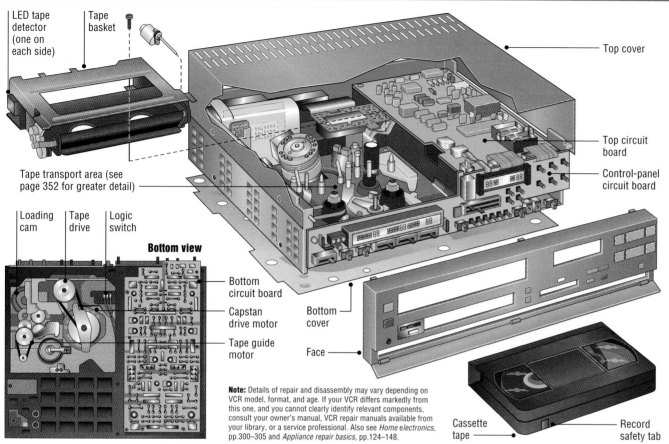

LED tape detector (one on each side)

Tape basket

Top cover

Top circuit board

Control-panel circuit board

Tape transport area (see page 352 for greater detail)

Loading cam

Tape drive

Logic switch

Bottom view

Bottom circuit board

Capstan drive motor

Tape guide motor

Bottom cover

Face

Cassette tape

Record safety tab

Note: Details of repair and disassembly may vary depending on VCR model, format, and age. If your VCR differs markedly from this one, and you cannot clearly identify relevant components, consult your owner's manual, VCR repair manuals available from your library, or a service professional. Also see *Home electronics*, pp.300–305 and *Appliance repair basics*, pp.124–148.

Gaining access

Keep track of screws.

With VCR unplugged, remove screws securing top and bottom covers. To remove face, take out face latch screws from bottom (inset); then turn VCR over and release latches while tilting off face. Align slide switches with buttons to reinstall face.

Tilt a circuit board away to access or test parts beneath it. First, remove mounting screws (usually red, circled, or otherwise marked); then release latches along edge of board opposite hinge.

Remove tape basket for better access to transport. Take out screws (usually red); disconnect plug-in power wires and any wires attached to grounding screw. Carefully lift out basket. If tape transport is shielded by a metal plate, unscrew it.

In the record mode, the video and audio heads of a videocassette recorder (VCR) store the input signals from a TV, cable tuner, camera, or another VCR on magnetic tape. In playback, the heads convert the signals into TV sounds and images. Of the eight videotape formats available (including compact sizes for camcorders), VHS is the most popular.

The basic components of a VCR are a motorized tape basket; a tape transport mechanism (rollers, capstan, etc.); video, audio, and erase heads; and electronic controls, switches, integrated circuits, and related wiring. "Cable-ready" VCR's have their own tuners. Hi-fi units have four video heads, others only two. The drive system for the tape transport comes in three varieties—belt, gear, and direct drive.

Disassembly procedures vary, depending on the model. For top-loading units, you may have to remove the cassette lid before taking off the covers (see *Gaining access*, right). Basic maintenance and repair procedures, such as cleaning, lubrication, and belt changing, however, are the same for most VCR models. Electronic components are usually reliable; when they do fail, it's often more economical to replace the VCR.

TIPS FROM THE PROS

When disassembling a VCR, use a dental pick to remove springs and tiny split rings. A magnetic screwdriver is useful too, *but keep it away from tapes.* It can ruin magnetically stored information.

Tracking down the problem

When a VCR fails to work, first check the obvious—connections, settings, and so on—then consult the owner's manual to make sure you're operating the VCR properly. Various components might faulty, so try to isolate the problem by making substitutions. For example, try another tape to see if the tape was at fault, or switch from tape to tuner. Use the chart below to identify common, easy-to-fix mechanical, electrical and image problems.

VCR-related image problems

Wiggles

Bends at top (flagging)

Dropout

Tracking error

Troubleshooting

Problem	CAUSE? / Solution
MECHANICAL/ELEC-TRICAL PROBLEMS VCR does not work	POWER OFF OR FAULTY POWER CORD? See *General troubleshooting*, p.144.
	POOR INPUT? Check cable and connectors (see owner's manual and *Working with wire*, p.304); unplug and replug cables (see *Tips from the pros*, p.354). ◇
	FAULTY POWER SWITCH? Test and replace switch (p.354; see also *Replace a board-mounted part*, p.305). ◆ ▣
	SHORT OR OPEN CIRCUIT? Inspect for loose or damaged wiring; repair. ◆
	DEW INDICATOR SHUTDOWN? If dew indicator is activated (look for a flashing light), VCR won't work. Avoid damp location or causes of condensation. ◇
VCR does not record or play back	DIRTY OR FAULTY BELTS? Clean or replace belts (p.353). ◇
	FAULTY IDLER? Inspect and service idler (p.353). ◆
	POOR INPUT? See *VCR does not work*, above. ◇
VCR plays back but does not record	POOR INPUT? See *VCR does not work*, above. ◇
	FAULTY RECORD SAFETY SWITCH? Have switch serviced.
	TAPE BAD? Try another tape cassette; if it works, first casette is faulty. ◇
	RECORD SAFETY TAB MISSING? Put tape over tab opening (see VCR drawing, p.350) to override safety feature that prevents inadvertent recording. ◇
	DIRTY HEADS? Clean heads (p.352). ◇
	MISALIGNED HEAD? Have head serviced.
Faulty or no playback; or cassette won't load	SLIPPING OR BROKEN BELTS? Clean or replace belts (p.353). ◇
	TAPE BAD? Try another tape cassette; if it works, first casette is faulty. ◇
	FAULTY PLAYBACK SWITCH? Test and replace playback switch (p.354; see also *Replace a board-mounted part, p.305*). ◆ ▣
	DIRTY OR FAULTY LOGIC SWITCH? Clean switch (p.354) ◇ or have serviced.
	FAULTY TAPE TRANSPORT? Clean VCR (p.352); inspect for defective parts. ◆
	EXCESSIVE MOISTURE? Place VCR and/or tapes in drier environment. ◇
Cassette jammed or won't eject	BASKET GEARS JAMMED? Remove and inspect tape basket (*Gaining access*, facing page). ◇
	WORN OR BROKEN DRIVE BELT? Inspect and replace belts (p.353). ◇
	BENT TAPE BASKET? Remove to straighten (see *Gaining access*, facing page). ◇
Cassette binds when ejecting	DISTORTED OR WARPED TAPE CARTRIDGE? Discard tape. ◇
	FAULTY EJECT MOTOR? Have VCR serviced.
	DIRTY OR FAULTY LOGIC SWITCH? Clean switch (p.354) ◇ or have serviced.

Problem	CAUSE? / Solution
Mangled or "eaten" tapes	POOR-QUALITY TAPE? Replace tape. ◇
	DIRTY TRANSPORT? Clean transport (p.352). ◆
	WORN IDLER TIRE? Replace tire (p.353). ◆
	TAPE GUIDES OUT OF ADJUSTMENT? Have VCR serviced.
IMAGE PROBLEMS Recording quality poor	POOR-QUALITY TAPE? Replace tape. ◇
	POOR INPUT? See *VCR does not work*, left. ◇
	DIRTY VIDEO HEADS? Clean video heads (p.352). ◆
	FAULTY ERASE HEAD? Have VCR serviced.
Poor-quality picture	POOR-QUALITY OR BAD TAPE? Replace tape. ◇
	DIRTY TRANSPORT? Clean transport (p.352). ◆
	POOR INPUT? See *VCR does not work*, left ◇.
	TRACKING OFF? Adjust tracking (see owner's manual). ◇
Wiggly picture	TAPE BAD? Try another tape cassette; if it works, first casette is faulty. ◇
	TRACKING OFF? Adjust tracking (see owner's manual). ◇
	DIRTY VIDEO HEADS OR TRANSPORT? Clean heads and transport (p.352). ◆
	TENSIONING ROD/SPRING OUT OF ADJUSTMENT? Have VCR serviced.
Jumbled picture	TAPE BAD? Try another tape cassette; if it works, first casette is faulty. ◇
	TRACKING OFF? Adjust tracking (see owner's manual). ◇
	DIRTY TRANSPORT? Clean transport (p.352). ◆
Excessive dropout	WORN, FLAKING, OR PIRATED COPY-GUARDED TAPE? Replace tape. ◇
	DIRTY TRANSPORT? Clean transport (p.352). ◆
	TRACKING OFF? Adjust tracking (see owner's manual). ◇
Picture bends at top (flagging)	TAPE GUIDES OUT OF ADJUSTMENT? Have VCR serviced.
	DAMAGED SYNC TRACK ON TAPE? Replace tape. ◇
Jumping picture	BAD OR PIRATED COPY-GUARDED TAPE? Replace tape. ◇
	DIRTY VIDEO HEADS? Clean video heads (p.352). ◆
No color	TRACKING OFF? Adjust tracking (see owner's manual). ◇
	DIRTY VIDEO HEADS? Clean video heads (p.352). ◆
	DEFECTIVE COLOR BOARD? Have VCR serviced.

Degree of difficulty: Simple ◇   Average ◆   Complex ◆   Volt-ohm meter required: ▣

Cleaning a VCR

How often you need to clean a VCR depends on the environment it's in, how often it is used, and the quality and condition of the tapes played. In general, you don't need to clean a VCR unless there's a problem. In fact, excessive cleaning can damage its heads.

Head-cleaning cassettes (available in both wet and dry types) are convenient for occasional cleaning but are neither as effective nor as thorough as a hand cleaning. For that you'll need cotton gloves, chamois head-cleaning sticks, cotton- or foam-tipped swabs, head-cleaning fluid, 95 percent pure alcohol, and an aerosol-type residue-free degreaser.

With the cover off, brush, blow, and/or vacuum loose dust from the chassis (below) but avoid brushing near the video drum and the heads. Next, clean parts that contact the videotape, leaving the erase, audio, and video heads for last. Also remove the belts and idler tire for inspection, and clean them with alcohol (facing page). Wear cotton gloves to avoid transferring skin oils to the rubber.

Liquids spilled into a VCR require immediate attention. If the power was on, a spill can easily ruin the circuit boards (a blown fuse may indicate trouble). To minimize damage, *immediately* unplug the VCR. Remove the covers to inspect, clean, and dry the unit. If clean water was spilled, mop it up and speed the drying using a fan. If soda, juice, or any other liquid that would leave a residue was spilled, spray the affected circuit boards with an electronic cleaner and brush until clean. Clean other parts with swabs or lint-free cloth dampened with alcohol. If you clean the transport area, relubricate the tape channels, cams, capstan, and mechanical sliding assemblies. Allow the VCR to dry completely before use.

The tape loop (above) describes the path of the videotape when it is being passed through the tape transport mechanism (below). Clean all parts the tape contacts. Look for dust and tape residue, using a magnifying glass.

Tape transport mechanism

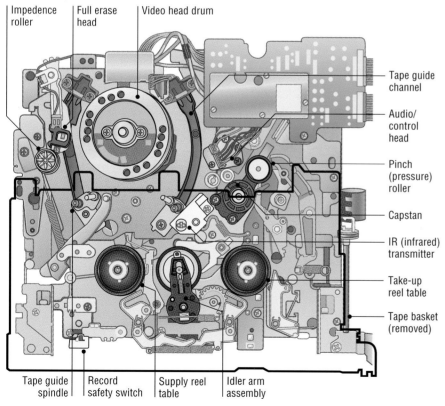

- Impedence roller
- Full erase head
- Video head drum
- Tape guide channel
- Audio/control head
- Pinch (pressure) roller
- Capstan
- IR (infrared) transmitter
- Take-up reel table
- Tape basket (removed)
- Tape guide spindle
- Record safety switch
- Supply reel table
- Idler arm assembly

Cleaning the tape transport

1 Remove general dirt and dust with a clean paintbrush (stay away from video drum area), or blow away dust with canned air (p.301).

2 Clean capstan and other tape loop components with cotton or foam swabs and alcohol. Clean video heads last to avoid recontamination.

3 Clean video head and drum with chamois-tipped swab. Hold flat against head and slowly rotate drum. Don't touch drum sides with fingers.

4 To clean stubborn residue (called a head clog), blast with aerosol head-cleaning fluid; repeat if needed. Do not stick anything into head opening.

Servicing the idler assembly

If a VCR "eats" a tape, or if *Fast forward* and *Fast rewind* won't work but *Forward* and *Rewind* do, suspect the idler (especially its tire) or bad belts (right). In some models, a faulty idler shuts down the VCR automatically. To access the idler, remove the tape basket (see *Gaining access,* p.350). Remove the idler and examine its tire under a magnifying glass for cracks or lines indicating wear. If the tire is OK, clean it (and the idler pulley), and reinstall it. Replace a worn tire (see *Tips from the pros,* p.354, for a temporary fix).

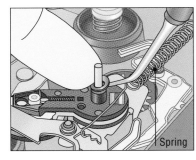

Remove the split ring holding the idler arm assembly on the shaft, using a dental pick or length of stiff wire. Use the pick to unhook the spring, noting the notch that it is in for correct reinstallation.

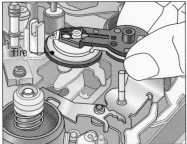

Lift idler assembly off shaft. Remove tire to inspect and clean it; replace tire if necessary. Parts are relatively inexpensive, but if they are difficult to get, it may be preferable to replace the whole idler assembly.

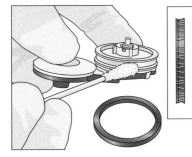

Clean idler pulley and tire with a foam-tipped swab dampened with alcohol. Wear cotton gloves. Examine tire with magnifying glass. Replace it if surface is concave (inset) or has fine lines, age cracks or other signs of wear or damage.

Cleaning and replacing belts and tires

Belts and tires in good condition should be cleaned as part of an overall servicing. Replace belts that are worn, loose, or stiff. (After you pull on a belt, it should spring back like a rubber band.) Replace tires, too, if there's any sign of wear. Service kits usually include all the belts and tires needed for a particular VCR model. Such kits, however, may be difficult to come by. Either purchase one from the manufacturer, order from a specialty electronics mail-order catalog, or buy one at an electronics repair shop.

Remove belts for cleaning if they are easily accessed. Here, the bottom cover has been removed and the bearing plate is being unscrewed. Direct-drive units don't have belts. Don't forget to clean the pulleys, too.

Wear cotton gloves when handling belts to avoid getting skin oil on them, which may cause them to slip. Clean belts with lint-free cloth dampened with denatured alcohol. Clean pulleys with foam-tipped swabs dampened with alcohol.

Use belt gauge, as printed in parts catalog, to determine size of existing belt. Replacement should be 3 to 5 percent smaller to account for old belt's stretching. It's usually best to replace all belts at the same time.

Lubrication

Sealed bearings, self-lubricating nylon parts, and durable lubricants greatly reduce the need for lubrication. *Lubricate very sparingly and only where original lubrication has failed or been cleaned off* (see *Lubrication,* p.303). Every 3 or 4 years (more often if the VCR is heavily used), apply a dab of grease to the tape guide spindle path, below, and the loading cam on the underside (p.350). Lubricate the capstan shaft reservoir, below, with a single drop of light oil from the tip of a toothpick or with a special dispenser.

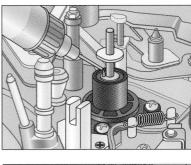

Lift up washer at base of capstan shaft. Remove foam wicking if degraded (disintegrating). Add a drop of oil and reposition the washer, which keeps oil from rising up and onto the tape.

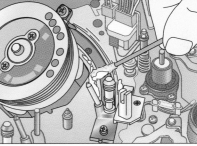

If tape guide spindle channel is dry or dirty, clean it with alcohol-soaked swabs. Apply a dab of white grease on each track (left); and activate VCR to spread grease.

FOR YOUR SAFETY

Unplug a VCR before working on it. If you need to watch internal mechanisms work, plug it back in briefly, then unplug again before continuing service.

If the cover is off when the VCR is plugged in, be especially careful around the fuses and high-voltage power supply.

Reconnect any equipment grounding wires that may have been disconnected during disassembly.

Minor electrical repairs

Troubleshooting electronics requires advanced skills and the ability to read complex schematics. Minor electrical repairs, however, such as replacing a blown fuse or testing and cleaning a microswitch, are not difficult. To access the fuse and switches, *unplug the VCR* and remove the top cover. Look for the fuses at the back of the VCR, near the power supply. Most switches are mounted on the control-panel circuit boards located behind the front face (see *Gaining access,* p.350). Tilt a circuit board to access its switch terminals.

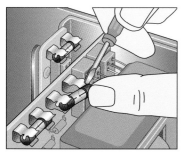

To replace a fuse, pry it out carefully with the tip of a screwdriver or a fuse puller. Fuses that blow gently (clear glass, link broken) may indicate only fuse fatigue. But fuses that blow violently (smoked glass and disintegrated link) may suggest a more serious problem.

To test switches, set VOM on RX1 scale and probe switch wires where they are soldered to circuit board. Look for zero ohms when switch is on and infinity when it is off. *Don't use a battery-operated continuity tester.* It may damage the electronics.

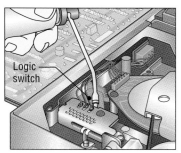

A dirty logic switch, located on the underside or above the transport area, is often to blame whenever the VCR seems "confused"— ejecting a tape that has just been inserted, for example. To clean the switch, squirt electrical contact cleaner into it.

Logic switch

Freeing a jammed cassette

If the VCR won't eject a tape, the problem may be a warped cassette or a bent basket. A foreign object may also be blocking the path or jamming a gear. To find out what's wrong, unplug the VCR and remove the top

Try to wiggle cassette free. Unplug VCR and remove its top. Using both hands, apply gentle pressure on cassette without harming tape basket. As you do so, look for places where cassette might be binding. If videotape is caught in transport mechanism, free it first. If you must touch tape, put on cotton gloves.

Repairing cassette tapes

Cotton gloves protect tape

1 To reattach a tape to its spool, remove screws securing cassette halves. Turn over cassette; prop open tape door with a stick. Lift off top. Note position of parts and tape path. Remove spools.

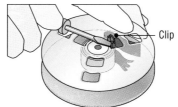

Clip

2 Pry out clip (if the spool has a pinhole on bottom, insert pin to pop out clip); remove torn tape end. Unless you're repairing a tape for one-time use, there must be 5 to 6 in. of clear tape remaining.

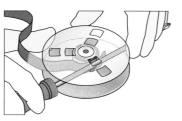

3 Press end of tape and clip against center of spool; use screwdriver to snap clip in place as shown. Reinstall spools; then thread tape. Prop door open during reassembly.

cover (see *Gaining access,* p.350). If the procedures suggested below fail, try cleaning the logic switch (bottom, left) or have the unit serviced. The loading mechanism or motor may need to be replaced.

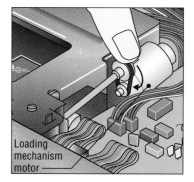

Loading mechanism motor

If you can't nudge cassette out, try activating the loading mechanism motor by hand (mechanism may be belt-, pulley-, or gear-driven). If cassette doesn't slowly rise up and out, turn motor in opposite direction. Once cassette is out, insert another to rule out a warped cassette as the cause of the problem.

TIPS FROM THE PROS

Unplugging and replugging wiring connections—to the head drum, erase head, or audio/control head, for example —can often solve VCR problems. The process scrapes off corrosion that may be causing poor contact.

For a temporary fix while you wait for a new part to arrive, try turning the idler tire inside out when one side is worn (see *Servicing the idler assembly,* p.353).

To see a VCR work without a cassette in place, use a test shell—an empty, modified cassette—that when inserted activates the VCR. You can make a test shell yourself (below) or buy one from an electronics parts supplier.

To make a test shell, open an old cassette (see *Repairing cassette tapes,* left); remove tape spools. Enlarge windows: First, score plastic with repeated light strokes; then break out plastic with long-nose pliers. When enlarging cassette window, leave a strip of material across the center. (Some VCRs have sensors that scan that area to verify that a cassette is in place.) Turn cassette over and cut away bottom the same way.

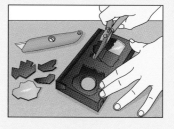

Yard and workshop tools

Proper maintenance is the best way to extend the life of yard and workshop tools and machinery. Most of these devices are powered by small engines or universal motors. While a small engine requires regular upkeep, a motor needs somewhat less attention. You'll find maintenance and repairs for small engines on pages 356–367; for motors, see *How motors work* (pp.138–141) and *General troubleshooting,* p.146.

The tools and machinery on these pages represent commonly available models. Even if your model differs from the one shown, its parts probably require similar attention. During disassembly, study the device closely so you can put the parts back where they belong. You can be sure of accurate reassembly by laying parts out in the order of removal, labeling wiring and hose connections, and even drawing diagrams of complicated assemblies.

Before beginning a repair, be sure to follow the safety tips noted here and in your owner's manual. Never work on (or use) any device when your judgment may be affected by alcohol, medication, or exhaustion.

Yard and workshop tools ▪ Small engines

Small engines power many common yard tools, from lawn mowers and tillers to snowblowers and chain saws. Like car engines, small engines produce power by the explosive combustion of gasoline vapors inside a cylinder. A carburetor mixes air and gasoline to sup-ply the vapors; a spark plug sets off the combustion. As the heated vapors expand, they push against a pis-ton within the cylinder. As the exhausted vapors exit the cylinder, the piston returns to its starting posi-tion. The back-and-forth movement of the piston is transferred to a connecting rod that turns a crank-shaft—in the same way that bicycle pedals convert the up-and-down motion of the rider's legs into the rotary motion of the bicycle's wheels.

Most larger yard machines use four-cycle engines, designed for prolonged work periods. Smaller machines, such as the chain saw and the string trim-mer, require the bursts of high-speed power supplied by the lighter and more powerful two-cycle engine.

The basic maintenance and repair procedures described on the following pages will keep an engine running smoothly, whatever its type. When replac-ing a part, make sure you get the right one for the engine you're working on. Because most equipment manufacturers assemble their products with engines obtained from other companies, look for the engine's model and type numbers on a metal plate that is usu-ally located on the crankcase casting. In some cases, you may have to look for model or type numbers on a specific component, such as a carburetor.

Four-cycle engine with vertical crankshaft

Ignition coil (new engines have electronic ignition)

Starter handle

Starter

Air cleaner

Breaker points

Governor linkage

Carburetor

Piston ring

Cylinder

Piston

Spark plug cable

Fuel tank

Spark plug

Cylinder head

Cooling fins

Intake valve

Exhaust valve

Cylinder block

Muffler

Flywheel nut

Cup

Flywheel fin (forces air across engine's cooling fins)

Flywheel key

Flywheel (keeps crankshaft rotating smoothly)

Magnet

Governor vane

Condenser

Crankshaft

Connecting rod

Crankcase casting

Oil cap

Camshaft

Cam

Tappet

Tappet box

Tappet cover

Four-cycle engine with horizontal crankshaft

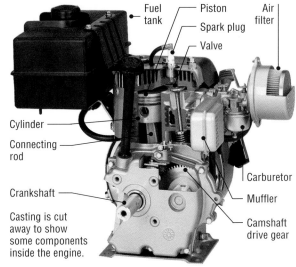

Fuel tank

Piston

Air filter

Spark plug

Valve

Cylinder

Connecting rod

Crankshaft

Carburetor

Muffler

Camshaft drive gear

Casting is cut away to show some components inside the engine.

While they may differ in design, all engines work the same way. Look for an engine with a vertical crankshaft (left) on a rotary lawn mower, one with a horizontal crankshaft (above) on a tiller.

How a four-cycle engine works

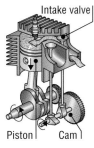

Intake valve
Piston | Cam

1 Intake stroke: An egg-shaped cam fitted on a rotating camshaft forces the intake valve open. The downward stroke of the piston in the cylinder draws gasoline/air mixture from the carburetor. The camshaft is geared to turn at half the speed of the crankshaft.

Crankshaft

2 Compression stroke: Camshaft rotation allows a spring (p.364) to close the intake valve. The piston travels back up the cylinder, compressing the gasoline/air mixture near the top of the cylinder. The tightly sealed valves prevent gases from escaping.

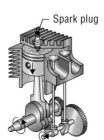

Spark plug

3 Power stroke: The spark plug ignites the compressed gasoline/air mixture. This causes the vapors to expand, forcing the piston rapidly downward, which in turn rotates the crankshaft, camshaft, and flywheel.

Exhaust valve

4 Exhaust stroke: The cycle is completed when momentum carries the piston back up the cylinder, forcing the burned gases out through the exhaust valve, which has been opened by another cam.

Two-cycle engine

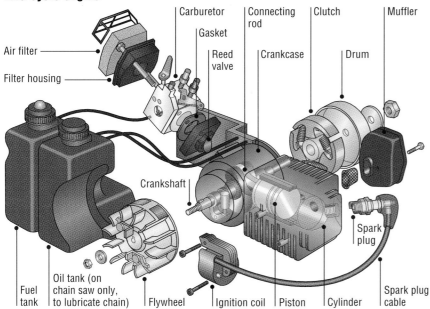

Air filter
Filter housing
Carburetor
Gasket
Reed valve
Connecting rod
Crankcase
Clutch
Drum
Muffler
Crankshaft
Spark plug
Fuel tank
Oil tank (on chain saw only, to lubricate chain)
Flywheel
Ignition coil
Piston
Cylinder
Spark plug cable

How a two-cycle engine works

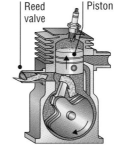

Reed valve | Piston

1 Upward stroke: As the piston moves up, it compresses the fuel/air mixture in the cylinder. The vacuum formed in the airtight crankcase by the rising piston draws more fuel/air mixture from the carburetor through the reed valve.

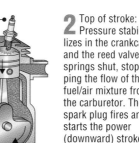

Spark plug

2 Top of stroke: Pressure stabilizes in the crankcase and the reed valve springs shut, stopping the flow of the fuel/air mixture from the carburetor. The spark plug fires and starts the power (downward) stroke.

3 Downward stroke: The descending piston transmits power to the crankshaft and compresses the fuel/air mixture in the crankcase. As the exhaust port is partially uncovered, burned gases begin to exit through it.

Fuel transfer port | Exhaust port

4 Bottom of stroke: As the piston completely uncovers the ports, the pressurized fuel/air mixture rushes into the cylinder, forcing what remains of the previously burned gases out through the exhaust port.

Periodic maintenance

The key to preventing engine problems and prolonging the life of your gasoline-powered machinery is to perform simple maintenance on a regular basis. Keeping the engine's cooling fins and air intake screen clean, for example, can prevent the engine from overheating. Described below is a general maintenance schedule for small engines; refer to your owner's manual for specific recommendations regarding your equipment.

Each time you service a gasoline-powered machine, check the mounting bolts and nuts on the engine; loose ones can cause excessive engine vibration. Before retightening, apply a medium-grade thread-locking compound to hold them in place. Also make sure that any knobs, levers, and brackets are secure.

To keep track of equipment usage, log operating hours on a piece of masking tape placed on the machine. Or estimate your yearly use of the machine and mark service dates on a calendar.

Troubleshooting. Even with regular maintenance, an engine may malfunction. To diagnose a problem in both two- and four-cycle engines, refer to the *Troubleshooting* chart on the facing page and to the owner's manual. Some repairs, such as regrinding crankshafts, boring cylinders, and complete overhauls, are best left to a professional.

Storage. Time spent on preparing your machinery for storage will pay off later on. Because fuel deteriorates quickly, be sure to add a stabilizer to it or drain it all out before storage. (Take the fuel to a service center for recycling.) Bear in mind that gasoline left in an engine can gum up the carburetor, requiring a thorough cleaning. For general storage procedures, see the facing page; refer to your owner's manual for specifics.

Before each use

Remove grass and debris from the air intake screen, muffler, oil filler, and governor linkage areas with a stiff plastic-bristle brush. Remove air intake screen to clean flywheel fins.

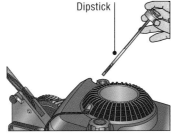

Dipstick

Check the oil level in a four-cycle engine. If there's no dipstick, open the oil fill cap; check that the oil reaches the opening or is even with the top of the slot. Add oil if necessary.

After every 25 hours of use

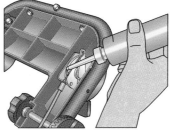

Change oil in four-cycle engine. Drain old oil into container through drain plug. If engine lacks drain plug, tip machine on its side; pour out old oil through filler hole. Refill with new oil.

Lubricate exposed cable and pivot points of any control levers, such as the clutch and throttle controls, using a few drops of light oil or white lithium grease or a spray silicone lubricant.

Clean or replace air filter regularly (p.367); more frequently if used in dusty conditions. Tap a paper air filter on a hard surface to release dirt. Wash and oil a foam filter.

After every 50 hours of use

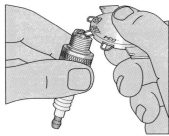

Check the spark plug. Clean it with solvent and a wire brush. Replace it if electrodes are rounded or porcelain insulator is cracked. Check and adjust gap before installing plug (p.363).

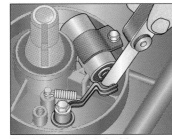

Check the electronic ignition or breaker points (p.362) only after disconnecting the spark plug. Reset the gap if necessary. Clean or replace the points and condenser.

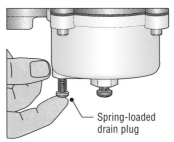

Spring-loaded drain plug

Drain fuel from float-bowl carburetor by depressing drain plug. Otherwise, remove bowl (p.360) and wash it out if the engine runs erratically, idles roughly, or releases black smoke.

After every 150 hours of use

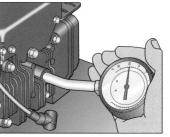

Check for low compression (p.365) if engine shows power loss, is hard to start, or stalls. Causes of low compression include worn head gasket or rings, loose spark plug, and burned valves.

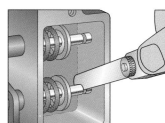

Check clearance between valve stems and tappets with feeler gauge (p.364). Disconnect spark plug first. Valve work can be complicated—you may want to consult a repair shop.

Troubleshooting engines

PROBLEM

Starter doesn't turn engine	Engine turns, will not start	Engine starts, then stalls	Runs unevenly, lacks power	Engine stalls at idle speed	Engine dies during use	Engine runs too fast	Engine runs; device doesn't	Engine vibrates excessively	Engine smokes profusely	Engine overheats	Engine backfires	Engine is extra-noisy	POSSIBLE CAUSE
●													Starter rope jammed or broken (p.366)
●													Recoil starter spring weak or broken (p.366)
●													Electric starter battery low, connections loose or corroded, or power cord damaged (p.366)
		●	●	●	●				●				Clogged air filter (p.367)
	●	●			●								Fuel tank empty; add fuel
	●	●	●	●	●								Contaminated fuel (p.367)
		●	●		●								Fuel cap breather holes blocked (p.367)
	●	●			●								Clogged fuel filter (p.367)
	●	●											Obstructed or damaged fuel line (p.367)
	●	●	●	●					●				Sticky choke; clean with solvent (you may have to disassemble the carburetor; see pages 360–361)
		●		●									Idle speed incorrect; see owner's manual to adjust
			●			●	●						Governor linkage out of adjustment (p.361)
	●	●	●	●	●	●			●	●	●		Carburetor fouled or poorly adjusted (pp.360–361)
	●	●	●		●				●	●			On two-cycle engine, incorrect fuel mixture (p.368)
	●	●									●		On two-cycle engine, faulty reed valve (p.365)
	●	●	●	●	●								Fouled spark plug or damaged cable (p.363)
					●				●			●	Insufficient oil in crankcase; add oil to oil tank
		●			●								Overheated; allow engine to cool, then restart
		●								●	●		Valves sticking, burned, or need adjusting (p.364)
	●	●	●	●					●	●			Breaker points dirty or improperly set (p.362)
	●	●	●	●	●				●				Low compression (p.365)
		●	●	●	●				●			●	Clogged muffler or exhaust port (p.367)
							●						Slipping belt (see pages on specific machinery)
							●	●					Faulty clutch (pp.370 and 379)
										●			Cooling fins dirty; clean fins
	●	●	●	●	●			●			●		Flywheel key bent, broken, or worn (p.363)
								●				●	Flywheel loose or fins damaged; tighten or replace (p.363)
●	●							●					Crankshaft bent; have engine replaced

Off-season storage

If storing equipment in a garage or shed (away from people), add a fuel stabilizer to the gas tank. For basement storage, remove fuel from tank with a siphon or cooking baster; drain fuel line and carburetor by running engine until it stalls.

Drain oil from a four-cycle engine while the engine is still warm but not running (warm oil is thinner, easier to drain). If your engine lacks an oil plug, tilt the machine (rock it gently if necessary) to drain all the oil through the filler hole.

Remove spark plug with spark plug wrench. For four- or two-cycle engine, pour 1 tsp. of fresh engine oil into spark plug hole. This prevents corrosion during storage. (Use funnel or paper cup described below, right, to pour the oil.)

To spread oil throughout the cylinder (and coat the wall and rings), turn the engine over about six times by engaging the starter—stand back to avoid spraying oil. If you have an electric starter, do this before charging the battery for storage.

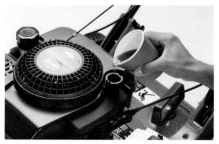

Thoroughly clean dirt and debris from all surfaces of the machine. Remove caked grass and mud with a screwdriver blade wrapped in a piece of cloth and with a stiff brush. To prevent rusting, coat bare metal with a spray lubricant.

Reinstall the spark plug; first turn it by hand to ensure threads engage properly, then tighten it with a wrench—without overtightening it. Refill crankcase with clean engine oil. To pour oil, use paper cup with a crease along one side or funnel.

Carburetors

The function of a carburetor is to mix air with fuel and feed the mixture to the engine's combustion chamber. Carburetors come in many different models but in only three basic types: float-bowl, suction-lift, and diaphragm.

A carburetor requires occasional servicing to keep it running well. If the engine stalls at low speed, loses power, or hesitates when hot, adjust the fuel mixture screws. (Refer to your owner's manual for adjustment details.) Also check the choke (p.369), which controls

the amount of air entering the carburetor; if the plate is stuck open or closed, spray it with a penetrating lubricant.

If the carburetor is fouled by the gummy residue left by evaporated gasoline, disassemble and clean it. While gaining access to the carburetor usually means simply removing the air cleaner, some devices are more complicated; refer to the owner's manual. Before disassembly, make a sketch of how the parts fit together, especially the governor linkage. Clean the parts in

a carburetor immersion-bath kit, available from auto parts stores. If the solvent is not formulated for plastic, first remove any rubber components.

When cleaning a carburetor, replace any worn springs, gaskets, diaphragms, and needles. On a float-bowl carburetor, check the float for leaks by shaking it. If you hear fluid inside the float, replace it. Carburetor replacement kits are sold at small-engine parts suppliers. To buy the right kit, supply the model numbers of both the engine and the carburetor.

The Welch plug

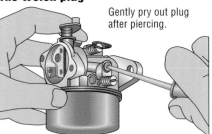

Gently pry out plug after piercing.

A metal disc called a Welch plug seals a hole in the carburetor created in the manufacturing process. If the plug isn't sealed tightly, pierce it with an awl and hammer; install a new one with a blunt punch. Seal edges with silicone gasket material.

Float-bowl carburetor

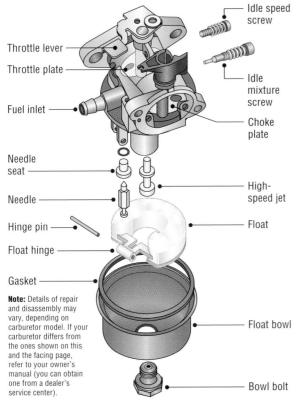

Idle speed screw

Throttle lever

Throttle plate

Fuel inlet

Idle mixture screw

Choke plate

Needle seat

Needle

High-speed jet

Hinge pin

Float

Float hinge

Gasket

Float bowl

Bowl bolt

Note: Details of repair and disassembly may vary, depending on carburetor model. If your carburetor differs from the ones shown on this and the facing page, refer to your owner's manual (you can obtain one from a dealer's service center).

Servicing a float-bowl carburetor

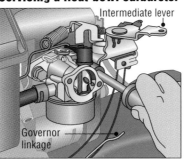

Intermediate lever

Governor linkage

1 Remove air filter. Unhook throttle cable linkage from intermediate lever. Unbolt the carburetor from the engine.

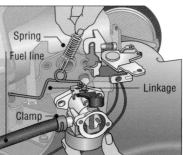

Spring

Fuel line

Linkage

Clamp

2 Detach governor linkage and spring from carburetor. Using pliers, move clamp on fuel line; pull off fuel line.

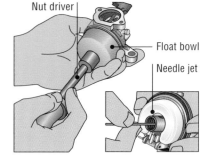

Nut driver

Float bowl

Needle jet

3 Detach bowl. Clean jet (don't remove it from Walbro models) with solvent and toothpick or broom bristle. Remove gasket.

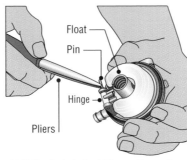

Float

Pin

Hinge

Pliers

4 Pull out pin in float hinge with needle-nose pliers to remove float. Turn parts over to let needle drop from seat or clip.

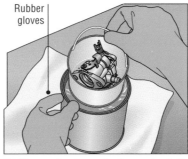

Rubber gloves

5 Clean carburetor, using immersion-bath kit. Allow pieces to dry. Reassemble carburetor with new parts from rebuild kit.

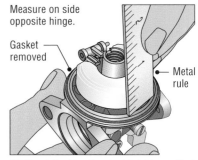

Measure on side opposite hinge.

Gasket removed

Metal rule

6 Check float level against height specified in manual by measuring from base of carburetor to float bottom. Replace gasket.

Suction-lift carburetor

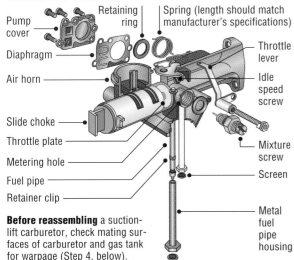

Pump cover

Retaining ring

Spring (length should match manufacturer's specifications)

Diaphragm

Throttle lever

Air horn

Idle speed screw

Slide choke

Throttle plate

Mixture screw

Metering hole

Fuel pipe

Screen

Retainer clip

Metal fuel pipe housing

Before reassembling a suction-lift carburetor, check mating surfaces of carburetor and gas tank for warpage (Step 4, below).

Diaphragm carburetor

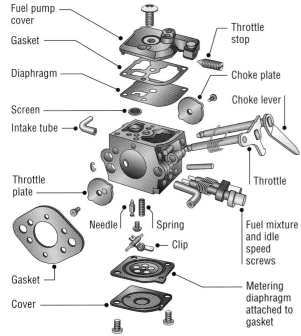

Fuel pump cover

Throttle stop

Gasket

Diaphragm

Choke plate

Choke lever

Screen

Intake tube

Throttle plate

Throttle

Needle

Spring

Clip

Fuel mixture and idle speed screws

Gasket

Metering diaphragm attached to gasket

Cover

Servicing a suction-lift carburetor

Fuel tank

1 Remove air cleaner. Unbolt carburetor and fuel tank from engine. Disengage governor linkage (below, right). Unscrew carburetor from tank. When reassembling, replace gasket with a new one.

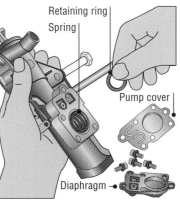

Retaining ring

Spring

Pump cover

Diaphragm

2 Make sure choke opens and shuts with ease. Unscrew and remove fuel pump cover; remove diaphragm and retaining ring to access spring. Reassemble components with new diaphragm and spring.

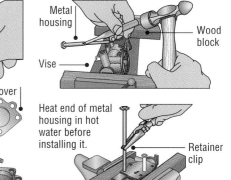

Metal housing

Wood block

Vise

Heat end of metal housing in hot water before installing it.

Retainer clip

3 To replace metal fuel pipe housing, pry it off with flat punch (top) or slide retainer clip down, freeing housing (bottom). Tap in new housing with rubber mallet. To replace plastic fuel pipe, unscrew or snap it out.

Rebuilding a diaphragm carburetor

Remove bolts in air filter housing.

1 Before unbolting carburetor on this device, remove engine (pp.368–369). On some models, just remove housing.

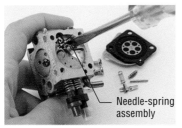

Needle-spring assembly

3 Remove needle-spring assembly; clean metal parts. Replace worn pieces; then reassemble.

Filter screen

2 Unscrew fuel pump cover; lift off with screwdriver tip. Remove diaphragm. Pry out screen with needle.

True straightedge metal rule

Feeler gauge

4 Check mating carburetor and engine surfaces. If .002-in. gauge fits under rule, insert an extra gasket.

The governor

The function of a governor is to keep an engine running at a steady speed despite changing workloads. If any part of the linkage is disconnected or damaged, the engine may stall, run poorly, or race too fast. Replace governor parts with identical ones only.

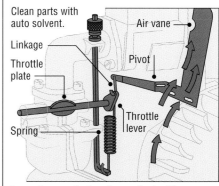

Clean parts with auto solvent.

Air vane

Linkage

Pivot

Throttle plate

Throttle lever

Spring

As engine runs faster, fins on flywheel increase air force, pushing throttle closed; as engine slows and air force lessens, spring opens throttle.

The breaker points and the condenser

In older engines, breaker points act as a switch that sends current to the spark plug at the right moment. The condenser keeps the current from burning the contact points as they open. Periodically clean the points by lightly filing off deposits with a point file. Make sure the contacting faces of the points stay flat, and don't touch the points after cleaning them. Replace the points when they become worn or pitted or during tune-ups; replace the condenser at the same time.

After disassembling the device to reach the points, rock the crankshaft back and forth. If it wobbles, you won't be able to set the gap between the points properly (see below), in which case you'll have to replace the short block assembly or the whole engine. To avoid having to service points periodically, install an electronic ignition (bottom right and facing page).

Indirect-action points

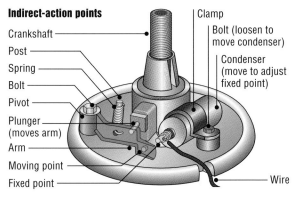

Crankshaft
Post
Spring
Bolt
Pivot
Plunger (moves arm)
Arm
Moving point
Fixed point

Clamp
Bolt (loosen to move condenser)
Condenser (move to adjust fixed point)
Wire

Direct-action points

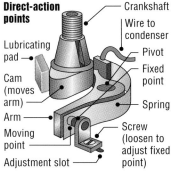

Lubricating pad
Cam (moves arm)
Arm
Moving point
Adjustment slot

Crankshaft
Wire to condenser
Pivot
Fixed point
Spring
Screw (loosen to adjust fixed point)

All breaker points have a movable and a fixed contact point. A plunger controls indirect-action points; a cam operates direct-action points. The distance between the points must be set with a feeler gauge at the gap specified by the manufacturer. After adjusting direct-action points, add a few drops of oil to pad (keep oil off points).

Servicing the breaker points and condenser

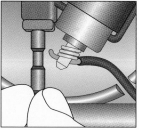

Cover

1 Remove flywheel (facing page). Clean dirt and debris from breaker point housing with compressed air. Unbolt and remove housing cover.

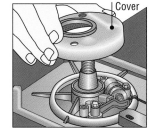

2 Open points all the way by turning crankshaft. Remove arm bolt and pivot. Detach spring from post; lift off arm. Inspect points for damage.

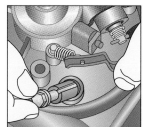

3 Pull plunger from housing; clean with electrical contact cleaner and fine emery cloth. If plunger (or arm in direct-action points) is worn, replace it.

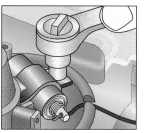

4 Unbolt clamp; remove condenser. Release wire lead; it may be held in condenser tip by a spring or nut. (If your unit has two leads, release both leads.)

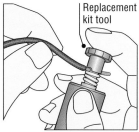

Replacement kit tool

5 To replace condenser, compress spring with replacement kit tool or pliers. Push wire lead(s) into hole in condenser; release spring. Install condenser.

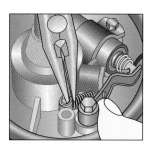

6 Fit plunger into housing with grooved end facing outward. Fit arm into groove on pivot; bolt firmly in place. Reattach spring with needle-nose pliers.

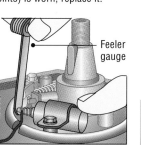

Feeler gauge

7 Rotate crankshaft to open points to widest position. To set gap, insert proper feeler gauge blade; adjust fixed point until it just touches gauge.

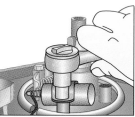

8 Tighten the condenser bolt to secure the fixed point. Turn the crankshaft; recheck the gap between points. Install housing cover and flywheel.

Electronic ignition

On newer engines, an electronic, or solid-state, ignition module mounted next to the flywheel replaces the breaker points and condenser. Little maintenance or adjustments are required with this setup. In the unlikely event that the module malfunctions, replace it. You should buy the replacement before removing the faulty module; connect the replacement to the engine in the same manner as the original.

You can set the gap between the electronic ignition module and the flywheel with a feeler gauge. If the correct gap isn't specified by the manufacturer of the replacement part or in the machine's service manual, consult your parts dealer.

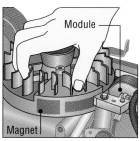

Module
Magnet

1 Remove old module and install new one, tightening its screws partway so it can slide in mounting slots. Turn flywheel until its magnets face module.

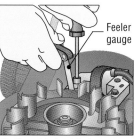

Feeler gauge

2 Place blade of feeler gauge between flywheel and module; push module gently toward flywheel. Magnets hold gauge in place as you tighten screws.

Removing the flywheel and replacing the key

To work on an engine's breaker points and condenser, you have to first remove the flywheel. You'll also have to remove the flywheel and replace it if it is cracked or has broken fins or loose magnets. To remove the flywheel without damaging the crankshaft, use a fly-wheel holder and puller. Never try to knock a flywheel off with a hammer. Once the flywheel is off the engine, inspect it for cracks.

Also check the flywheel key, located in the crank-shaft, for damage. The key is designed to bend or break if the machine hits a hard object, thereby preventing damage to the flywheel and crankshaft. Even a slight indentation in the key can throw off the engine's tim-ing, making it hard to start. Always replace a damaged key; use the model specified in the engine's manual.

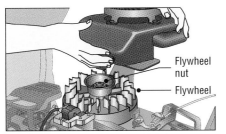
Flywheel nut
Flywheel

1 Disconnect spark plug cable. Unbolt starter housing and any other covers necessary to expose flywheel. Disconnect any linkage between housing and carburetor. Unbolt debris screen.

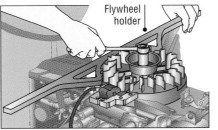
Flywheel holder

2 Holding the flywheel in place with a flywheel holder, remove the nut with a socket wrench (it may have left-hand threads). Don't steady the fly-wheel with pliers; you may damage its cooling fins.

Flywheel puller

3 To remove flywheel with puller, snug down lower nuts on puller; then alternately tighten the upper nuts a quarter turn until the flywheel is free. Bring damaged crankshaft to service center.

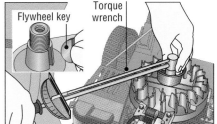
Flywheel key
Torque wrench

4 If necessary, replace flywheel key (inset). Reinstall flywheel: Hand-thread nut; then tighten with torque wrench to manufacturer's specifications. This prevents overtightening nut.

Converting to electronic ignition

With a conversion kit sold at small-engine parts suppliers, upgrading from breaker points and condenser to an electronic ignition module is easy and inex-pensive. The procedure involves first removing the coil assembly from the engine (right), then snapping the module onto the coil (below) and soldering together the right wires. Follow kit directions carefully; make sure the kit you buy is the right type for the engine.

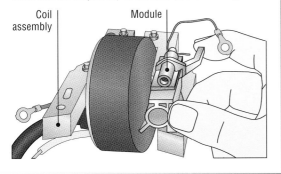
Coil assembly
Module

Reading and replacing the spark plug

A spark plug is easy to replace. Before discarding the old one, however, inspect it for clues as to how the engine is running. Light brown, dusty deposits and slightly worn electrodes mean a four-cycle engine is OK; black, powdery deposits result from a rich fuel-air mixture, a dirty air filter, or a bad ignition system. If the electrodes have black, wet deposits, suspect a poor fuel-oil mixture in a two-cycle engine or worn piston rings, a dirty air filter, or a high idle speed in a four-cycle engine. Brown, yellow, or white deposits on the electrodes signal a clogged muffler or exhaust ports. If the electrodes are worn or have a white, blis-tered look, the cooling fins are clogged, the fuel-air mixture is too lean, or the timing needs adjusting.

1 Disconnect spark plug cable; remove spark plug with spark plug socket fitted to a socket wrench. Keep the socket square on the plug or you may crack the ceramic insulator.

New spark plug

2 Test ignition coil and plug cable: Attach cable to new plug; hold threaded end of plug to metal engine block. Crank the engine. If you don't get a strong blue-white spark, replace parts.

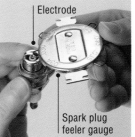
Electrode
Spark plug feeler gauge

3 Before installing new plug, use a spark plug feeler gauge to check its gap against manufacturer's specifications. The gauge should slip between electrodes with a slight drag.

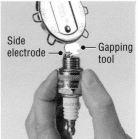
Side electrode
Gapping tool

4 To adjust the gap, bend the side electrode to the proper setting with the gapping tool on the gauge. Retest the gap, mak-ing sure that it matches the manufacturer's specifications.

Four-cycle poppet valves

In a four-cycle engine, springs hold two poppet valves closed until the camshaft pushes them open. When closed, a valve and spring in good condition form a tight seal, maintaining proper engine compression. A weak spring or bad valve reduces compression, causing the engine to stall or to run with less power.

Clean the valves and seats with an auto-cleaning solvent; then check the measurements against those specified in the engine's manual. Clearances for intake and exhaust valves often differ.

To fix minor valve defects, polish the valve head with a grinding compound and an inexpensive valve grinder (a process called lapping). Remove the compound with an auto-cleaning solvent. If a valve is badly damaged, it's best to replace it. To ensure a tight seal, lap the new valve before installing it.

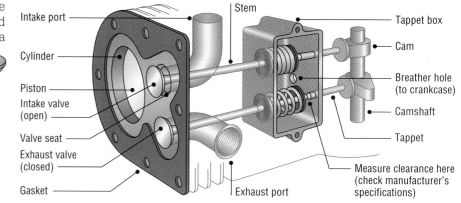

Head
Margin
Face
Stem
Cap (or seal)
Spring
Cap
Retainer

Poppet valve

Intake port
Stem
Cylinder
Piston
Intake valve (open)
Valve seat
Exhaust valve (closed)
Gasket
Exhaust port

Tappet box
Cam
Breather hole (to crankcase)
Camshaft
Tappet
Measure clearance here (check manufacturer's specifications)

Servicing poppet valves

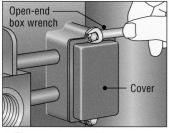

Open-end box wrench
Cover

1 Disconnect spark plug cable. Detach breather hose, if any, connected to tappet cover. Unbolt tappet box cover and remove it. Bring gasket to dealer and buy new one.

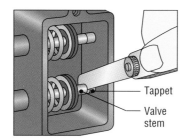

Tappet
Valve stem

2 Turn crankshaft to close valves. Check clearance between valve stems and tappets with feeler gauge. Discard valve if clearance is too great. To increase clearance, see Step 7.

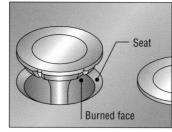

Seat
Burned face

3 Remove cylinder head (facing page); check valve faces for pitted and burned (eaten-away) metal. Inspect valve seats: if damaged, have seat resurfaced in a machine shop.

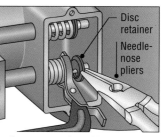

Disc retainer
Needle-nose pliers

4 Compress spring with spring compressor (from auto supply store); remove disc retainer. Pull valve out. If necessary, pry spring out with screwdriver. **CAUTION:** Wear eye protection.

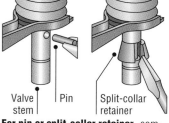

Valve stem
Pin
Split-collar retainer

For pin or split-collar retainer, compress spring; pull out pin (left) or separate collar (right). If you can't access pin, turn crankshaft to open valve. Twist stem to reach pin; close valve.

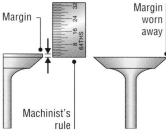

Margin
Margin worn away
Machinist's rule

5 Measure the valve margin with a machinist's metal rule or a caliper; it should be between 1/32 and 1/64 in. If margin is less than 1/64 in., discard valve. Also make sure stem is straight.

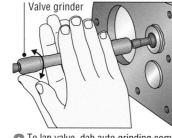

Valve grinder

6 To lap valve, dab auto grinding compound on valve face, then press valve lightly against seat and grind. Lift valve after 10 sec.; give a quarter turn; grind again. Add compound as needed.

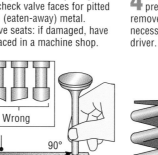

Right
Wrong
Oilstone
90°

7 Reinstall valves without springs. Close valves and check clearance (see Step 2). To increase clearance, grind valve end on oilstone. Valve end must be square.

Rotate spring; replace if height varies more than 1/64"

8 Springs should be equal length and straight; check against machinist's rule. Compare length to manufacturer's specifications. If unequal in length, skewed, or damaged, replace springs.

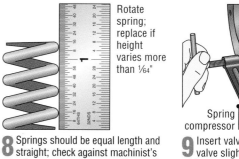

Spring compressor
Spring

9 Insert valve, spring, and caps. Lift valve slightly. Compress spring with compressor; install retainer. (Coat split collar with grease.) Install gasket and tappet box cover.

Low compression

If an engine shows signs of low compression, such as loss of power, hard starting, and stalling (for other symptoms, see *Troubleshooting engines*, p.359), check the tightness of the cylinder bolts and look for a loose spark plug. If tightening the bolts or the spark plug doesn't improve engine performance, test the compression with a compression gauge (an inexpensive device sold at auto parts stores). Check the service manual for the normal compression reading of your engine. (A 10 percent variation from the specification is often considered normal.) If the reading is low, remove the compression gauge, squirt in some engine oil, and test again. An improved reading means that the piston rings are worn and it's time to overhaul the engine. If the reading remains low, remove the cylinder head and check the gasket for cracks. (You'll need a socket wrench to unfasten the head bolts and a torque wrench to tighten them.) If the gasket is OK, check the valves and their seats for damage. Service or replace the cylinder head as necessary. Always replace the gasket; even if it doesn't look damaged, a used gasket usually leaks when reinstalled. Engine makers specify a tightening sequence and a tightening torque for the head bolts. Follow their specifications exactly.

To check compression, insert a compression gauge in the spark-plug hole and operate the starter.

Servicing the cylinder head

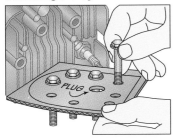

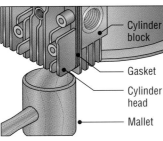

Cylinder block

Gasket

Cylinder head

Mallet

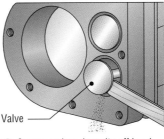

Valve

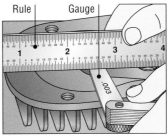

Rule   Gauge

.003

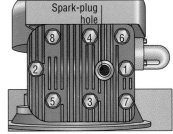

Spark-plug hole

1 Disengage spark plug cable; remove cylinder head bolts. To make sure you insert each bolt into its original hole during reassembly, make a cardboard pattern of head and place bolts in it.

2 Free cylinder head from block. If necessary, break seal by gently tapping the head with a wooden mallet. Don't pry apart block and head; this will damage them.

3 Scrape carbon deposits off head, valves, and piston with an ice-cream stick or plastic scraper. Turn crankshaft to raise valves; scrape carbon from faces, stems, and seats.

4 To check cylinder head for distortion, place machinist's rule across it; try to slip a .003 feeler gauge underneath rule. If you can, head is warped; have it trued at a machine shop.

5 Install new gasket. Insert and hand-thread bolts; tighten with torque wrench to specifications in manual. To prevent warping, tighten in 5-lb. increments in exact order shown.

Two-cycle reed valves

In a two-cycle engine, the flow of the fuel-air mixture may be controlled by a metal plate, called a reed valve, which is located between the crankcase and the carburetor. If the engine is hard to start, stalls often, or loses power, check the reed valve. Before removing the carburetor, mark the linkage so that you'll be able to replace it correctly.

Because the tempered steel of the reed can't be straightened, you'll have to replace a bent reed. Buy only the manufacturer's recommended part.

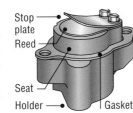

Stop plate

Reed

Seat

Holder

Gasket

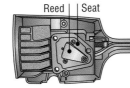

Reed   Seat

Removable valves can be found on older machines and on some new models. Unbolt the valve to remove it.

On newer models, the valve may be built into the housing. The parts may look different but the valve performs the same function.

Replacing a reed valve

Housing

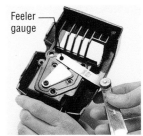

Feeler gauge

1 To test for a leak, remove the air cleaner; open choke. Hold white paper 1 in. from air intake; run engine. Fuel spots on paper means reed is leaking.

2 Remove carburetor, and if needed, housing to reach valve—reed holder may come off. In reassembling, use new gaskets on each end of holder.

3 Examine reed for bends or breaks; replace if damaged. If thinnest feeler on feeler gauge can slide between reed and seat, replace reed.

Starters

By tugging the rope of a recoil starter you engage a pulley that spins the engine's flywheel, which in turn rotates the crankshaft and starts the engine. Depending on the type of engine, the rope may be pulled horizontally or vertically. When released, a large spring automatically rewinds the rope.

Both the rope and the spring are susceptible to damage, but they are also relatively easy to replace. A rope may break because of old age; frequent breakage, however, is a sign that your replacement ropes are too short or that you're pulling the rope at an angle, causing it to rub against the housing. If the rope doesn't recoil properly, suspect a weak or broken spring.

Before starting any repair, let the engine cool completely. Accessing and replacing the starter is usually easy, although the procedure may vary from the one shown below, depending on the model. If you have to replace the spring, wear safety glasses and heavy work gloves—the spring is under tension and can fly out of the starter with great force. Even if the spring doesn't become airborne, its sharp edges can slice your hands. Because starters differ by model, purchase replacement parts that are exact duplicates of the existing parts.

Replacing a recoil starter rope

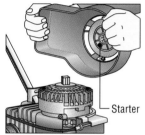 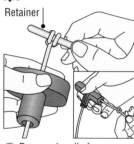 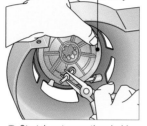 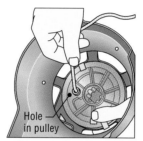 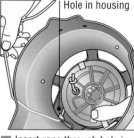 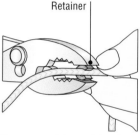

1 Remove the spark plug cable. If throttle cable is attached to housing, disengage it. To reach the starter, remove the housing and other parts as required.

2 Remove handle from rope. Look for retainer, knot (inset), or pin recessed in handle; a cover may hide them. Save handle for new rope.

3 Stretch out rope; then hold pulley firmly with thumb. Lift up knot in rope with needle-nose pliers; cut it off. Pull rope from pulley; slowly release pulley.

4 Knot end of new rope. Spin pulley counterclockwise all the way, then back off 2 turns. Hold pulley; thread unknotted rope end through hole in pulley.

5 Insert rope through hole in housing and pull tightly. Release pulley slowly, letting the rope wind around it. Attach handle. Reassemble the parts.

On some models, a retainer is attached to the rope. To remove old rope, cut it by retainer. Press retainer (you may need a new one) onto new rope with pliers.

Replacing a recoil starter spring

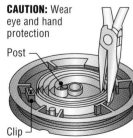 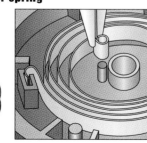 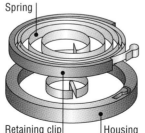

CAUTION: Wear eye and hand protection

1 Remove housing (see above), then spring cover. Release spring tension by freeing rope from pulley (see above). Pull out spring with needle-nose pliers.

2 Fasten outer end of new spring to clip on housing. Coil the spring, starting from outside and working in; then place inner hook over post.

Some springs come in a retaining clip. Insert clip into housing; push spring into place. If spring is sealed in a separate housing, replace entire assembly.

Electric starter

Powered by a small battery, an electric starter uses a gear or belt to turn the flywheel and start the engine. It needs little maintenance. If the starter doesn't work, clean the battery, starter, and switch connections (see red areas at right) with contact cleaner and a wire brush. To keep water and dirt out, coat the connections with dielectric grease during reassembly. Recharge the battery every 40 to 60 starts. If an electric starter that operates on house current doesn't work, test the power cord with a VOM (see *General troubleshooting*, p.144).

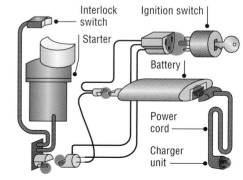

Air filters

The three basic types of air filters shown at right are all designed to trap particles of dust and debris before they enter the carburetor. Usually located in its own housing near the top of the engine, the air filter is attached directly to the carburetor or linked to it by a short hose.

While cleaning an air filter is simple, neglecting the filter can lead to a host of serious problems. The first signs of a clogged filter are hard starting, stalling, black smoky exhaust, and overheating. Complications include contaminated oil and premature engine wear. Most manufacturers of four-cycle engines suggest cleaning or replacing the filter after every 25 to 50 hours of engine operation. Filters in two-cycle engines should be cleaned every 10 hours. If you use an engine in a dusty or sandy area, clean the filter even more frequently.

Detach the spark plug cable before servicing the air filter. Replace the gasket between the filter and the carburetor if it is in poor shape. Also make sure the breather hose is in good condition.

Types of air filters

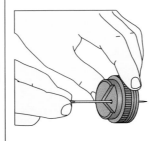

Paper filter
Cover | Paper element | Plate | Precleaner (foam) | Base

Foam filter
Foam element | Plastic insert | Cover | Screw | Housing

Foam and paper filter
Cover | Paper cartridge | Backplate | Foam precleaner

Cleaning a foam filter

1 Remove cover and lift out foam filter. Clean dirt and grease from housing interior with soft cloth. Inspect gasket for wear or distortion.

2 Wash filter with dish detergent and hot water. Rinse with clear water; then gently squeeze out excess—don't wring. Let filter air-dry.

Filter

3 Pour 1 tsp. of engine oil on the filter; squeeze filter to distribute the oil. Reassemble parts, making sure foam forms a tight seal all around housing.

Fuel lines and tank

Water in the fuel tank leads to loss of engine power and stalling. Inspect some fuel in a glass; sediment or air bubbles mean fouled fuel, as does the aroma of mothballs. Gas left in an engine for a long time forms a gummy residue in the tank and fuel line(s). If a line clogs, clear it with a pipe cleaner and petroleum solvent. Then flush the tank and line with fresh fuel, and clean or replace the fuel filter. In severe cases, clean the carburetor.

CAUTION: Detach the spark plug cable before servicing fuel lines or tank.

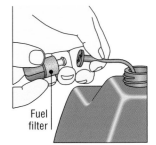

Drain plug

Fuel filter

Unclog any breather holes in gas cap with sewing needle or fine wire. Remove gasket from metal cap; then clean cap with a carburetor-cleaning solvent.

To check fuel, push drain plug on carburetor with pencil; catch fuel in a glass. Or drain fuel by disengaging fuel line. Pinch line to stop flow of fuel; reattach.

Detach fuel filter after lifting it out of fuel tank (first empty and remove tank). Or remove it from fuel line or carburetor (p.361). Wash with petroleum solvent.

Cleaning the muffler and exhaust port

A muffler reduces an engine's noise level. Clean the muffler and the exhaust port periodically on a two-cycle engine. On a four-cycle engine, clean these parts if the engine overheats or loses power. Tighten a loose muffler. It may have one threaded end that screws onto the engine or it may be bolted to the engine.

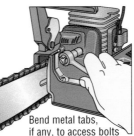

Bend metal tabs, if any, to access bolts

Wire-bristle brush

Spark arrester screen

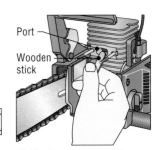

Port

Wooden stick

1 Detach spark plug cable; then remove cooled muffler. Clean off carbon deposits with wire brush; use a decarbonizing spray to free obstinate deposits.

2 If muffler has spark arrester screen, which catches burning carbon particles, clean with wire brush. Inspect for rips and corrosion; replace if necessary.

3 To clean exhaust port on two-cycle engine, move piston until it covers port. Scrape off carbon. Blow particles from port before lowering piston.

Most chain saws are powered by a two-cycle gasoline engine. The engine drives the clutch, which turns a chain of cutting teeth around the guide bar. As the chain races around the bar, it's lubricated by a thin film of oil supplied by an automatic or manual oiler.

The engine runs on a mixture of two-cycle engine oil and gasoline. Consult your owner's manual or a dealer for the correct proportions of these fluids. Always mix them in a separate container. Make sure you shake the mixture before pouring it into the tank.

Chain oil is entirely different from engine oil; use only the oil recommended in the owner's manual or by a dealer. To keep the chain from overheating during use, make sure to push the button of a manual oiler as often as directed by the manufacturer. Both types of oilers need frequent refilling.

To keep your chain saw running smoothly, service the engine regularly and make all repairs promptly (see *Small engines,* pp.356–367). Never operate a chain saw that needs cleaning, sharpening, maintenance, or replacement parts. Before starting a chain saw, make sure the fasteners are tight and the blade is set at the correct tension. Check the saw's settings before putting it to use. For example, a saw with an accidentally engaged chain brake (a safety device that stops the clutch and the chain if the saw makes an abrupt upward movement) will behave much like a saw that has a worn clutch. The saw's idle speed and fuel-air mixture screws may also need adjusting.

Some chain saws are designed so that the parts are easy to reach for repairs. Lighter, more compact models have a streamlined design that can make it more difficult to access parts—you may have to remove the whole engine, for example, to get at the carburetor. During disassembly, place the parts aside in the order that you remove them; make a note or sketch of confusing assemblies, particularly linkages and hoses. Reverse the order to reassemble the saw.

Electric chain saws. The chain of an electric chain saw is maintained just like that of a gas-powered saw. To service the universal motor and for other electrical repairs, see *Appliance repair basics,* pp.123–148.

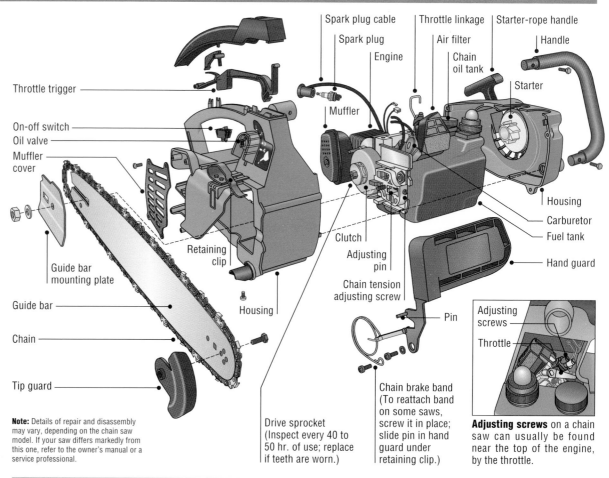

Throttle trigger

On-off switch
Oil valve
Muffler cover

Guide bar mounting plate

Guide bar

Chain

Tip guard

Note: Details of repair and disassembly may vary, depending on the chain saw model. If your saw differs markedly from this one, refer to the owner's manual or a service professional.

Retaining clip

Housing

Drive sprocket
(Inspect every 40 to 50 hr. of use; replace if teeth are worn.)

Spark plug cable
Spark plug
Engine

Muffler

Clutch

Adjusting pin

Chain tension adjusting screw

Pin

Chain brake band
(To reattach band on some saws, screw it in place; slide pin in hand guard under retaining clip.)

Throttle linkage
Air filter
Chain oil tank

Handle

Starter

Housing

Carburetor

Fuel tank

Hand guard

Adjusting screws

Throttle

Adjusting screws on a chain saw can usually be found near the top of the engine, by the throttle.

FOR YOUR SAFETY

Know your saw. Before using a saw, read all literature on safe operation provided by the manufacturer.

 Chain-saw teeth are sharp. Keep hands away from a moving chain; wear heavy gloves to handle the chain.

Protect yourself. Wear hearing protection, heavy gloves, and safety glasses when using the saw. Don't wear loose clothes or jewelry; tie back long hair. Avoid overuse of the saw; it can lead to nerve and blood vessel damage in hands and wrists.

Clear the work area of rocks, brush, and branches; make sure the area is well lighted. Never use a saw near children or pets.

Only use a saw in good working order. Make sure all fasteners are tight, the saw is clean, and the chain is sharp and properly tensioned. Never start the saw without its guards or with missing parts. Test the chain brake, if any, before each use (facing page).

Avoid kickback. Stand aside of the saw and start it before touching the wood. Avoid pinching the guide bar in a deep cut; never cut at the tip of the saw. Use kickback-reducing devices (p.371).

When refueling, remove the cap slowly; it may be under pressure. After refueling, move the saw 10 feet away before starting it. Spilled fuel can easily ignite.

Disassembly

1 Disengage the spark plug cable by pulling the boot off the spark plug. Loosen the spark plug with a spark plug wrench; unscrew it by hand.

2 Detach guide bar and chain. Unbolt nut; remove any washers and plates. Then lift chain from drive sprocket and bar from adjusting pin.

3 To disengage chain brake (if present), unscrew base of chain brake handle and band. Pull band off clutch drum; slide off handle and band.

4 To remove the exhaust muffler, unscrew its cover, then unbolt the nut holding the muffler in place. The muffler should slide out of the housing.

5 Disconnect the oil valve (oil flow indicator) by removing the screw at its base. Using tape, label the hoses attached to the valve; then pull them off.

6 With the saw set on its side, unscrew and remove one side of the housing. (On some models, you may have to unscrew the handle first.)

7 To detach the on-off switch, release it with a screwdriver or unscrew it. Label and detach switch wires; they will appear through switch hole in housing.

8 Use needle-nose pliers to disengage the throttle linkage, which is hooked to the throttle trigger. Look for the linkage above the carburetor.

9 Remove housing screws. Pull engine out of housing; make sure spark plug cable and other engine parts don't cause engine to catch on housing.

Troubleshooting

Problem	CAUSE? / Solution
Engine won't start	FUEL INCORRECTLY MIXED? Start over with newly mixed fuel. ◇
	ON-OFF SWITCH FAULTY? See *General troubleshooting*, p.145.
	ENGINE FAULTY? See *Troubleshooting engines*, p.359.
Saw runs erratically, stalls, or loses power while running	FUEL OLD OR INCORRECTLY MIXED? Start over with newly mixed fuel. ◇
	CARBURETOR FAULTY? Adjust or clean carburetor (pp.360–361). ◆
	AIR FILTER DIRTY? Clean or replace filter (p.367). ◇
	ENGINE OVERHEATING? Clean cooling passages (p.358). ◇
	VENTS IN FUEL CAP BLOCKED? Unplug the breather holes (p.367). ◇
	MUFFLER BLOCKED? Clear debris from muffler (p.367). ◆
Saw stalls when engine idles	CARBURETOR NEEDS ADJUSTING? Reset idle mix screw (see owner's manual). ◇
	CHOKE IMPROPERLY SET? Adjust it (below). ◆
Chain turns while engine idles	CLUTCH FAULTY? Inspect and repair clutch if necessary (p.370). ◆
	IDLE SPEED TOO HIGH? Adjust idle mix screw (see owner's manual). ◇
Chain stops during cutting	CHAIN BRAKE ENGAGED? Reset the brake (see owner's manual). ◇
	CLUTCH SLIPPING? Repair the clutch (p.370). ◆
Chain doesn't move when engine accelerates	CHAIN TENSION TOO TIGHT? Reduce tension (p.370). ◇
	CHAIN BRAKE ENGAGED? Reset the brake (see owner's manual). ◇
	CHAIN OR BAR WORN? Replace either or both parts (pp.370–371). ◇
	CLUTCH SLIPPING? Repair the clutch (p.370). ◆
Chain insufficiently lubricated	OUT OF OIL? Refill with oil specified for lubricating chain. ◇
	OIL FILTER DIRTY? Clean and replace the filter (p.367). ◆
	OIL HOLES IN GUIDE BAR BLOCKED? Clean out the holes (p.370). ◇
Chain cuts at angle	CUTTERS ON CHAIN DULL OR DAMAGED? Resharpen the cutters (p.371). ◆
	GUIDE BAR BENT OR WORN? Replace damaged bar (p.370). ◇

Degree of difficulty: Simple ◇   Average ◆   Complex ◆

Testing the chain brake

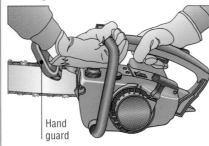

Hand guard

Test chain brake, if any, before each use. Steady saw on ground; hold with both hands. Run at full throttle. Engage brake: Carefully push left hand against guard, keeping a grip on handle. If chain doesn't stop instantly, take saw to a dealer.

Adjusting the choke

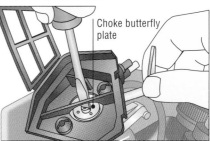

Choke butterfly plate

If choke doesn't close completely, adjust it, no matter what type of carburetor it is (pp.360–361). If choke butterfly plate is held by a screw, release it, adjust the plate, then tighten the screw. Or use pliers to slightly bend linkage controlling plate.

The centrifugal clutch

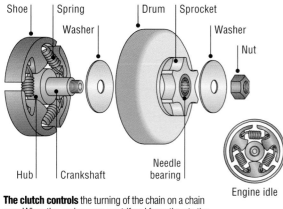

Shoe | Spring | Drum | Sprocket
Washer | Washer | Nut
Hub | Crankshaft | Needle bearing

Engine idle

Engine running

The clutch controls the turning of the chain on a chain saw. When the engine runs, centrifugal force thrusts the clutch shoes outward (right, below). The shoes grip the drum, turning it and the chain. When the engine idles, springs hold the shoes away from the drum (right, above). The drum can't rotate, so the chain stays immobile. If a properly adjusted chain moves slowly or not at all, the clutch is slipping and needs cleaning.

Servicing a centrifugal clutch

Before working on the clutch, disconnect the spark plug cable, empty the fuel tank, and remove the guide bar (see *Disassembly*, p.369). On some models, you'll have to stabilize the flywheel to remove the clutch. Place a wooden wedge between the flywheel cooling fins and against the engine, or wrap a leather belt around the fins and hold it with locking pliers.

With the drum removed, turn the crankshaft to inspect the hub-shoe assembly for irregular movement and weak springs. Run a fingernail across the grooves inside the drum; it shouldn't catch. Inspect the clearance between the drum and the shoes; it should be equal. Also inspect the needle bearing for wear. Replace any damaged or worn parts.

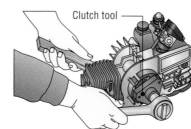

Clutch tool

1 Remove housing. Remove drum nut with a socket wrench. Using clutch tool and wrench, turn clockwise to remove hub-shoe assembly. Stabilize flywheel if needed.

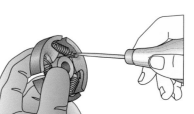

2 Dig out debris in shoes, springs, and hub with awl; clean with brake-shoe cleaner from auto parts store or with non-flammable solvent. Replace worn parts.

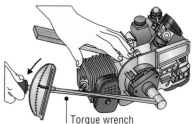

Torque wrench

3 Reassemble clutch. Tighten clutch to torque specified by manufacturer; turn torque wrench counterclockwise. Grease the bearing, but don't get grease on shoes.

Maintaining the guide bar

If the guide bar on a chain saw is reversible, equalize its wear by flipping the bar top to bottom after every 15 to 20 hours of use. To increase the life of the bar, service it before reinstalling it. When installing the bar, make sure the chain oiler hole is unobstructed and still fed by the oiler. Also make sure that the chain teeth face in the proper direction.

Before working on the bar, pull off the spark plug cable. To remove the bar and chain, see *Disassembly*, Step 2, p.369. Besides the steps below, check that the width of the groove in the bar matches the specifications in the owner's manual. Also make sure the groove is deep enough to hold the tangs of the chain. Replace a bar that is discolored (a sign of overheating caused

by improper tension, lack of chain oil, or dull teeth), worn, or damaged or that has distorted or bent rails.

Test the chain tension before each use of the saw. Using moderate force, you should be able to pull the chain up barely enough for the tangs to clear the bar. Because the chain stretches as it warms up, retest the tension 15 minutes into use and after refueling.

Use knife carefully.

1 Clear dirt from groove with a hook-bladed knife, wood stick, or screwdriver. Poke dirt from oil holes with a stiff wire.

2 Check rails for burrs that occur with saw use. Hold bar steady; file off burrs with a flat file held parallel to the rails.

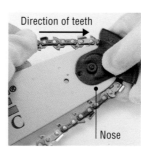

Grease gun

Nose sprocket

3 If grease fitting is present, pump automotive grease into nose sprocket until grease oozes at rail. Invert bar; repeat.

Direction of teeth

Nose

4 Wearing work gloves, install chain on guide bar. Cutters on top of bar should face bar's nose (the end with the tip guard).

5 Slip the guide bar in place with the chain around the sprocket. Tighten any mounting bolts using only your fingers.

6 Set chain tension by turning adjusting screw clockwise to tighten chain. Then tighten guide bar bolts with a wrench.

Keeping the chain sharp

A chain with sharp cutters, or teeth, is essential to make cuts that are fast, smooth, and straight; sharp cutters are also critical for safe cutting. You should sharpen your chain whenever it begins to spew fine powdery sawdust instead of chips, if it cuts at an angle, or if you have to exert more force than usual to propel the saw through the cut. If you strike an obstruction, resharpen the chain before proceeding with the job.

When sharpening a chain, use the file specified in the owner's manual and sharpen the cutters to the given angle. File on the push stroke only, using three or four light strokes for each cutter. File all cutters to one side of the chain; then turn the saw around and file the others. If you use a motorized sharpening tool, be careful not to overgrind the cutters.

You'll have to replace the chain after a number of sharpenings. At that time consider purchasing a low-kickback chain; it has specially designed cutters that reduce the chance of kickback.

Parts of the chain

Top plate
Side plate
Right-hand cutter
Tie strap
Drive link
Tang
Left-hand cutter
Depth gauge

Tools for sharpening chain-saw cutters

Flat file
Round file
File holder (with file)
Depth gauge tool
Motorized chain-saw sharpening tool

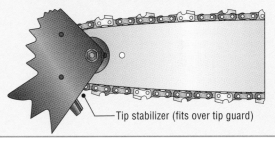
Sharpening the chain

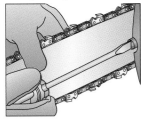

1 Inspect chain. To move chain for sharpening, relax its tension. To work on chain, set tension tighter than usual.

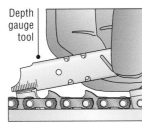

2 Measure length of each top plate. Mark shortest top plate; move chain (Step 1) to center this cutter on top of bar.

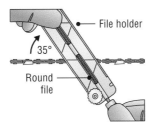

Depth gauge tool
File holder
35°
Round file

3 File cutter; use degree marks on holder to find filing angle. Remeasure top plate. File all cutters to its length.

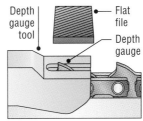

Depth gauge tool
Flat file
Depth gauge

4 After every two or three sharpenings, cut protruding gauges to uniform height with depth gauge tool and flat file.

5 After filing depth gauge, round off all corners with flat file. This prevents dragging, which creates friction and heat.

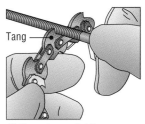

Tang

6 To reshape slightly worn tangs on drive links, remove chain from saw (p.369); lightly file tangs with a round file.

Filing diagnostics

Good cutter. Top plate angled as specified; depth gauge at right height and rounded off.

Hooked cutter. File was too small; handle was held too high. A hooked cutter will dull rapidly.

Sloped cutter. File was too large; handle was held too low. A sloped cutter will cut slowly.

Depth gauge high. Depth gauge filed above cutter height. Cutting will be hard and slow.

Depth gauge low. Depth gauge filed below cutter height. The cut will be deep and rough.

Unfiled gullet. Chips will catch on unfiled gullet. Use round file (no holder) to file gullet.

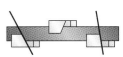

Uneven angles. Cutter angles not uniform. The chain won't cut straight and will bind.

Yard and workshop tools ▪ Chipper-shredders

Small engines **356**

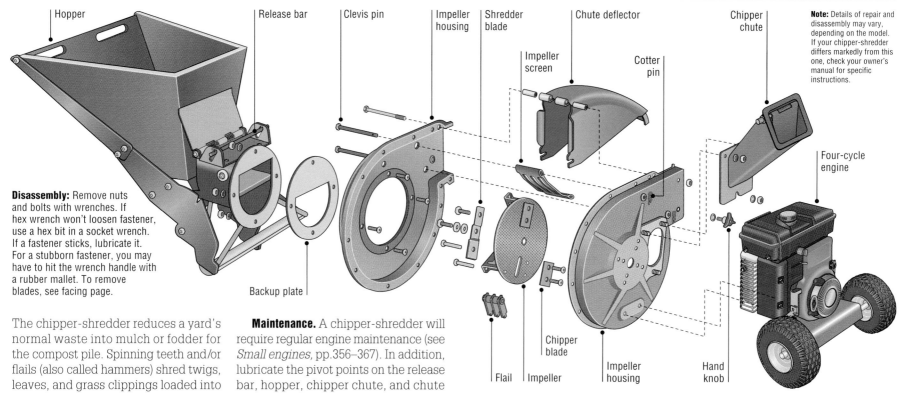

Disassembly: Remove nuts and bolts with wrenches. If hex wrench won't loosen fastener, use a hex bit in a socket wrench. If a fastener sticks, lubricate it. For a stubborn fastener, you may have to hit the wrench handle with a rubber mallet. To remove blades, see facing page.

Note: Details of repair and disassembly may vary, depending on the model. If your chipper-shredder differs markedly from this one, check your owner's manual for specific instructions.

The chipper-shredder reduces a yard's normal waste into mulch or fodder for the compost pile. Spinning teeth and/or flails (also called hammers) shred twigs, leaves, and grass clippings loaded into the hopper. Bulky debris, such as vines, stems, and branches, is dispatched by one or more blades near the base of the chipper chute. While small electric chipper-shredders can process material up to only 1 to 2½ inches in diameter, the larger engine-driven models can handle branches up to 3 or 4 inches in diameter. Some smaller units combine both the chipping and shredding functions in one compartment. Other units have a vacuum attachment that picks up leaves and feeds them into the unit for shredding and bagging.

Using a chipper-shredder is dangerous. Always follow safety precautions in the manual (see *For your safety*, right).

Maintenance. A chipper-shredder will require regular engine maintenance (see *Small engines,* pp.356–367). In addition, lubricate the pivot points on the release bar, hopper, chipper chute, and chute deflector once each season (use 20- or 30-weight oil or white lithium grease). Sharpen the cutting blades at the first sign of dullness. If the chipper blades are dull, you'll have to exert extra pressure to feed the wood; dull shredder blades will be slow or will cause the machine to spew out coarser-than-usual particles. Sharpen a blade on a grinding wheel (p.16), using its original angle as a guide and removing as little metal as possible; or take the blade to a service center for sharpening. Replace a cracked or nicked blade right away. If bolted-on flails become dull, unbolt and reverse them; if the flails are riveted, take the unit to a service center.

372

Troubleshooting

Problem	CAUSE? / Solution
Machine vibrates excessively	LOOSE PARTS? Inspect and tighten all nuts and bolts. ◆
	CHIPPER BLADE OR SHREDDER BLADES DULL? Sharpen (p.16) or replace blades. ◆
	UNBALANCED BLADE? Regrind it (p.16) ◆; or have it professionally serviced.
	IMPELLER BROKEN? Have it professionally serviced.
	OBJECT JAMMED IN MACHINE? Remove the object (see *For your safety*, facing page). ◇
Machine does not discharge	DISCHARGE CHUTE BLOCKED? Clean impeller screen (see right); clear out shredding chamber (see *For your safety*, facing page). On some models, remove screen to shred wet leaves. ◇
	OBJECT LODGED IN IMPELLER? Remove the lodged object (see *For your safety*, facing page). ◇
Discharge is slow	CHIPPER BLADES OR SHREDDER BLADE DULL? Sharpen (p.16) or replace blades. ◆
Engine stalls	DISCHARGE CHUTE CLOGGED? Remove the debris (see *For your safety*, facing page). ◇
	ENGINE FAULTY? See *Troubleshooting engines*, p.359.
Engine won't start or runs erratically	ENGINE FAULTY? See *Troubleshooting engines*, p.359.
Banging or knocking noise	LOOSE FLAIL, CHIPPER BLADE, OR SHREDDER BLADE? Tighten loose part. ◆
	OBJECT LODGED IN IMPELLER? Remove the lodged object (see *For your safety*, facing page). ◇
Vacuum lacks power *(vacuum models only)*	LEAVES TOO WET? Let leaves dry before vacuuming. ◇
	LEAF LAYER TOO THICK? Vacuum using only half nozzle width. ◇
	ATTACHMENT CLOGGED OR DAMAGED? Inspect; clear or repair. ◇

Degree of difficulty: Simple ◇   Average ◆   Complex ◆

Cleaning the impeller screen

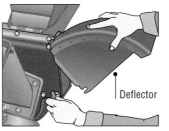

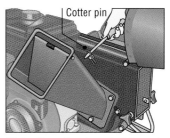

Cotter pin

Deflector

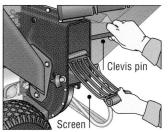

Clevis pin

Screen

1 Disconnect the spark plug cable. Secure the chute deflector out of the way by loosening the hand knobs on either side, swinging the deflector up, and tying it to the top of the hopper.

2 Pry the cotter pins out of the ends of the clevis pins, using a screwdriver. Pull out the clevis pins; remove the impeller screen from the housing, noting its position as you remove it.

3 Scrape off any debris from the impeller screen; wash the screen well with plain tap water. Replace the screen with its curved side down; then insert the clevis pins and cotter pins.

Removing the chipper blades

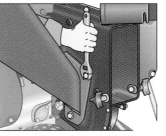

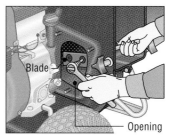

Blade

Opening

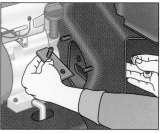

Disconnect spark plug cable. Prop up chute deflector and remove screen as described above. Unbolt chipper chute from housing. During disassembly, note placement of washers.

Turn impeller assembly by hand to position a blade in opening. Remove blade with an open-end wrench and a hex wrench (or a socket wrench fitted with a hex bit). Repeat with other blade.

After sharpening blades equally (or having them professionally sharpened), reinstall. Make sure sharp edge of each blade rests against impeller and points downward.

Removing the shredding blades

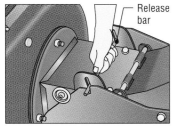

Release bar

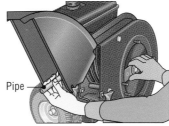

Pipe

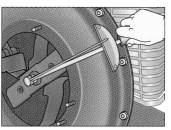

1 Disconnect spark plug cable. To lower hopper to ground, pull up on release bar and push down on hopper. Prop housing on blocks to stabilize it.

2 Unbolt any nuts and washers from hopper housing; remove the housing. Detach the backup plate.

3 Loosen knobs; tie chute deflector up out of the way. Lock impeller in place (turn it if needed) with a ½-in.-dia. pipe inserted through the impeller screen.

4 Remove fasteners on ends of blade, using open-end wrench and hex wrench (or a hex bit in a socket wrench). Unfasten center bolt and remove blade.

5 Have blade sharpened or do it yourself, grinding both cutting edges equally. During reassembly, use torque wrench (above) to tighten blade.

Inspect a garage door yearly to look for worn or loose parts. Clean the rollers, pulleys, and cables; and lubricate them with light oil. Spray or wipe a Teflon lubricant on the weatherstripping where it contacts the door.

Test and adjust the tension on the two extension springs that counterbalance the door's weight; they should hold the door steady in a half-open position, and allow it to move only slowly if door is released slightly above or below halfway. To increase the tension, shorten the lifting cable (Step 6, facing page). *Never* service a torsion spring (a large horizontal spring above the door): this dangerous job should be left to a professional door mechanic.

Testing and adjusting an automatic opener. All openers will, *if operating properly,* reverse if the garage door hits an obstruction. Openers made prior to 1982, however, do not have any backup to this system, but they can be modified with the latest equipment. Post-1982 systems will reverse instantly if a door fails to complete a close or open cycle.

Since 1993 openers have had to include a monitored backup system—typically a sensor that passes a light beam across the door opening. The door will reverse if the beam is interrupted. A door will not operate if the beam sensor is unplugged or is misaligned; the sensor can't be bypassed except by holding down the wall switch.

Check an opener monthly. Test the sensitivity first. (The force level should always be set at the minimum needed to operate the door.) Stand outside the open door with hands held at waist level and positioned to catch the bottom edge of the closing door. Activate the opener; if you can't stop (not reverse) the door with minimal effort, adjust the opener's force level control. Next, test the close limit. Place a 2 x 4 flat on the ground in the door opening. Activate the opener; if the door doesn't reverse as it hits the 2 x 4, increase the close limit (see the manual). In cold climates, a frost heave can raise the floor, causing a closing door to reverse; you may have to adjust the close limit seasonally.

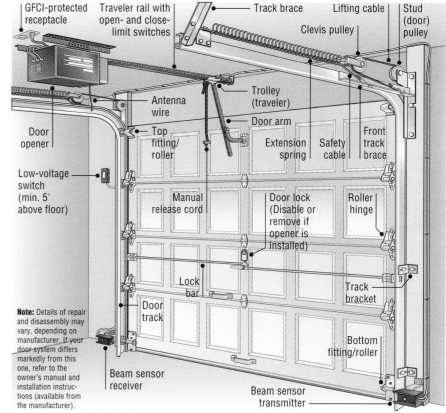

Note: Details of repair and disassembly may vary, depending on manufacturer. If your door system differs markedly from this one, refer to the owner's manual and installation instructions (available from the manufacturer).

Garage door maintenance

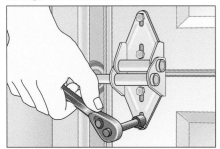

Unbolt dirty hinge rollers one at a time and clean with auto degreaser or kerosene. Replace each assembly before removing another. Plug stripped screw holes (p.76) if necessary.

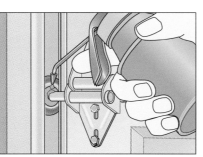

Lubricate the roller bearings and roller shaft with light oil every 6 mo. Blow or brush dirt and debris from the track, but don't lubricate it.

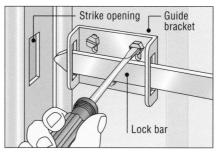

The lock bar should slide smoothly into the track's strike opening. If it doesn't, loosen the screws and move the lock-bar guide bracket up or down as necessary. Retighten the screws.

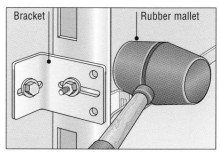

To straighten misaligned track, loosen bracket screws; tap track in or out with mallet; retighten screws. Check the door for smooth operation and a snug uniform fit with all door stops.

Replacing the extension springs and cable

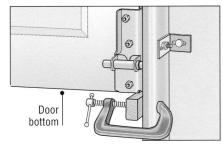

Door bottom

1 Unplug automatic opener and disengage the trolley. Open door to release tension from the extension springs and lifting cables; support with a block of wood (above) or with locking pliers clamped to *each* track immediately below a roller.

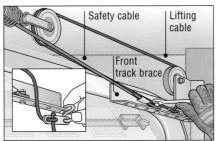

Safety cable | Lifting cable

Front track brace

2 Disconnect one end of safety cable (above); it may be bolted or tied. With one gloved hand gripping spring (to prevent it and other hardware from swinging down), detach lifting cable's fitting and S-hook from the front track brace (inset).

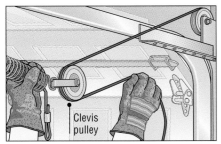

Clevis pulley

3 Wearing gloves and still holding the lifting cable, lower the spring and pull the lifting cable off the clevis pulley. Unhook spring from rear track brace and from clevis pulley. Attach new spring to pulley and to rear track brace.

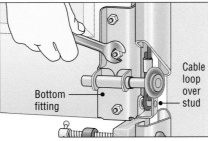

Bottom fitting

Cable loop over stud

4 Remove bottom fitting so you can release the stud that holds cable loop. (Alternatively, the loop may just lift off the stud or be secured with a cable clamp.) Check the new cable's length against the old one; attach it to door as above.

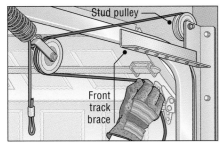

Stud pulley

Front track brace

5 Feed lifting cable up door, over stud pulley, through clevis pulley, and toward front track brace (above). Then loop adjustable fitting onto cable and attach S-hook to fitting. When cable is attached (Step 6), pulley face should be vertical.

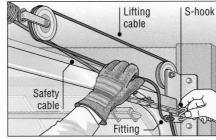

Lifting cable | S-hook

Safety cable

Fitting

6 Feed safety cable through spring and its loop, and reattach it to brace; repeat on opposite side. Adjust spring tension; move S-hook to new hole (above) or rethread cable in fitting as needed. (Shortening the cable increases tension.)

Troubleshooting

Problem	CAUSE? / Solution
Opener doesn't respond	POWER UNIT UNPLUGGED? Push plug fully into receptacle. ◇
	POWER OFF AT OUTLET? See *General troubleshooting*, p.144.
	OVERHEATED MOTOR? Check door for binding; wait 15 min. and try again. ◇
	FAULTY SPLIT-PHASE MOTOR? See *General troubleshooting*, p.146.
Opener raises but won't close door	BEAM SENSOR UNPLUGGED OR MISALIGNED? Plug in; align (see manual). ◇
	BEAM SENSOR FAULTY? Press and hold wall switch to override sensor. ◇
Opener operates by remote control but not by switch	OPEN OR INTERMITTENT SHORT CIRCUIT IN WIRING? Look for damaged low-voltage wiring (p.128) or loose connections at switch or opener. Test for continuity (p.131) or short (p.147). Rewire as needed (p.134). ◆
Remote control does not work	WEAK OR DEAD BATTERY IN TRANSMITTER? Replace battery. ◇
	ANTENNA WIRE NOT EXPOSED? Hang antenna outside housing. ◇
	BAD REMOTE CONTROL? Replace remote control. ◇
Opener runs but door won't open	WORN WORM GEAR OR CHAIN-DRIVE SPROCKET? Have serviced.
	DOOR DISENGAGED? Pull disengage cord to reset catch; activate opener. ◇
	BROKEN CHAIN, WORN GEARS? Replace chain; have gears serviced. ◇
Opener operates by itself	SHORT IN SWITCH WIRE? Replace wire from switch to receiver (p.134). ◆
	FAULTY REMOTE CONTROL? Look for stuck button; verify if remote is source of problem by removing its battery. ◇
	DOOR RESPONDING TO STRAY SIGNALS? Try shortening antenna by pushing some of it into opener; if this fails, contact installer or replace remote unit. ◇
	FAULTY CIRCUIT BOARD? Replace board ◆, or have unit serviced.
Remote-control range under 25 ft.	WEAK BATTERY IN REMOTE? Replace battery. ◇
	POOR SIGNAL? Reposition remote or extend antenna; or change remote's code to improve it's range (see manual). ◇
Door doesn't completely open	DOOR OBSTRUCTED OR BINDING? Remove obstruction; inspect door for mis-aligned tracks, loose hardware (facing page), or uneven spring tension. ◇
	OPEN LIMIT OR SENSITIVITY SET WRONG? Test and adjust (facing page). ◇
Door doesn't completely close	DOOR OBSTRUCTED OR BINDING? See *Door doesn't completely open*, above.
	CLOSE LIMIT OR SENSITIVITY SET WRONG? Test and adjust (facing page). ◇
Door reverses while closing	SAFETY REVERSING ACTIVATED? Remove obstruction, built-up snow/ice. ◇
	CLOSE LIMIT SET WRONG? Adjust and retest (facing page). ◇
Opener strains	EXTENSION SPRING MISADJUSTED OR BROKEN? Increase spring tension (Step 6, left); or replace spring (left). ◆
	WORN CHAIN SPROCKET OR WORM GEAR? Have door serviced.

Degree of difficulty: Simple ◇   Average ◆   Complex ◆

Reel mowers

A simple push-type reel mower requires little maintenance. To prevent rusting, apply a lightweight oil once a month to all cutting surfaces as well as to the reel axle and the wheels.

Hone, or backlap, the blades of a new reel mower after several seasons of use and once a season after that (far right). Automotive valve-lapping compound makes a good grinding paste. If a blade has been bent, try lightly tapping it into alignment by hammering it near the edge; check the face of the blade for straightness by laying a straightedge against it. If a blade is badly bent, replace it with a new one if you can find the replacement part.

The cutting height of a reel mower is controlled by raising or lowering the rollers. On most mowers, the two ends of the roller shaft are adjusted separately. It's time to adjust the rollers if the cutter bar scrapes the ground.

Engine power. An engine-driven reel mower has the same requirements as all gas-powered machinery. For problems with the engine, see pages 356–367; with the clutch, see page 379; with the belt or pulleys, see pages 390–391.

Adjusting the rollers

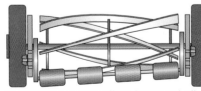

To straighten uneven rollers, loosen and adjust each end of the roller shaft to the same height; then retighten the fasteners and test the mower (see *Tips from the pros,* above). Readjust the rollers if necessary.

TIPS FROM THE PROS

Always test the mower after you straighten the rollers, backlap the blades, or make other adjustments. Insert a sheet of newspaper the same length as the reel between the cutter bar and the reel; rotate the wheel to turn the blades. All the blades should cut evenly and cleanly without binding on the cutter bar.

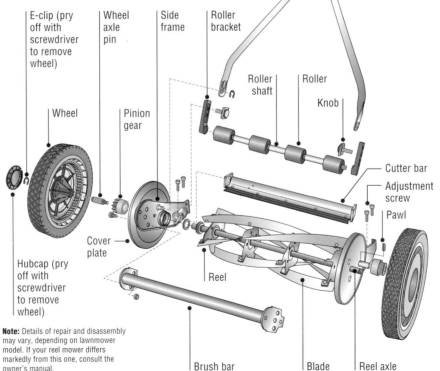

- E-clip (pry off with screwdriver to remove wheel)
- Wheel axle pin
- Side frame
- Roller bracket
- Handle
- Wheel
- Pinion gear
- Roller shaft
- Roller
- Knob
- Cutter bar
- Adjustment screw
- Pawl
- Cover plate
- Hubcap (pry off with screwdriver to remove wheel)
- Reel
- Brush bar
- Blade
- Reel axle

Note: Details of repair and disassembly may vary, depending on lawnmower model. If your reel mower differs markedly from this one, consult the owner's manual.

Backlapping the blades

1 Place mower on a work surface. Remove burrs from cutting edges of blades and cutter bar with smooth-cut flat file or flat sharpening stone—avoid sharpening edges. Adjust cutter bar so blades just graze it as they turn.

2 Try turning wheel backward. If it turns, apply grinding paste to blades' cutting edges; rotate reel backward for 7 to 10 min. This sharpens cutter bar and blades. Wipe off paste with acetone. Reassemble mower and test it, left.

If wheel won't rotate backward (or won't rotate reel backward), remove a wheel and pinion gear. Attach locking pliers to reel axle (use rag to protect axle); then continue backlapping procedure described in Step 2.

In some mowers, a pawl on each end of reel axle allows you to backlap without using pliers. Reverse direction of pawls and switch pinion gears to opposite sides. After you backlap (Step 2), return parts to normal positions.

Rotary mowers

Rotary mowers come in several styles and types: self-propelled or push-types, powered by either a gasoline engine or an electric motor (usually universal, see pages 138–141). For small-engine maintenance and repairs, see pages 356–367; for motor tests and repairs, see *General troubleshooting,* p.146. In addition, always consult the owner's manual for specific maintenance and repair procedures for your particular model. Pay special attention to the seasonal start-up and storage routines, which can help you avoid unnecessary repairs. For maintenance and repairs of blades and the drive system, see pages 378–379.

Mowers manufactured after 1982 are equipped with either a "kill switch" that shuts off the engine if the operator's hand leaves the safety bar or a blade brake that stops the blade under the same circumstances. Before each use, test either system by running the mower and releasing the handlebar; if the components do not stop within a few seconds, adjust loose connections or take the mower to a service center.

Common variant: Blade brake

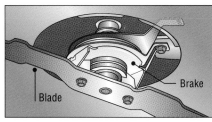

Blade

Brake

Instead of a kill switch, some rotary mowers have a blade brake located above the blade. Such mowers have two control bars: the blade brake control bar stops the blade if released; the wheel drive control bar stops the wheels if released. Either way, the engine continues to run. Check the cable and linkages regularly; keep them clean, tight, and lubricated. Have a worn brake lining replaced.

FOR YOUR SAFETY

Clear the lawn of toys, stones, branches, and other debris before mowing it.

When mowing grass on a hill, always mow across the slope.

Always disengage the spark plug cable before working on the mower.

When turning the mower on its side to make a repair, place it with the oil fill hole higher than the crankcase to keep the oil from running out.

If your mower has a grass catcher, stop the engine before emptying it.

Follow guidelines in the owner's manual.

Note: Details of repair and disassembly may vary, depending on lawnmower model. If your rotary mower differs markedly from this one, consult the owner's manual or a service professional.

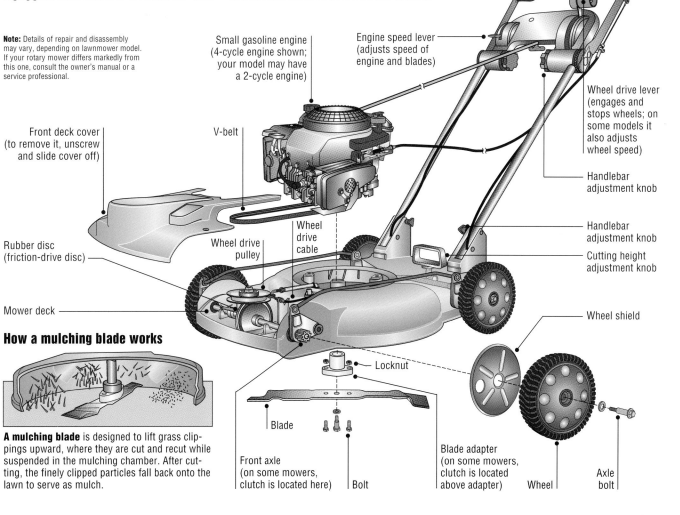

Kill switch or operator presence bar (stops engine and blades if operator releases bar while mower is in use)

Small gasoline engine (4-cycle engine shown; your model may have a 2-cycle engine)

Engine speed lever (adjusts speed of engine and blades)

Front deck cover (to remove it, unscrew and slide cover off)

V-belt

Wheel drive lever (engages and stops wheels; on some models it also adjusts wheel speed)

Handlebar adjustment knob

Handlebar adjustment knob

Cutting height adjustment knob

Rubber disc (friction-drive disc)

Wheel drive pulley

Wheel drive cable

Mower deck

Wheel shield

Locknut

Blade

Front axle (on some mowers, clutch is located here)

Bolt

Blade adapter (on some mowers, clutch is located above adapter)

Wheel

Axle bolt

How a mulching blade works

A mulching blade is designed to lift grass clippings upward, where they are cut and recut while suspended in the mulching chamber. After cutting, the finely clipped particles fall back onto the lawn to serve as mulch.

Troubleshooting: Rotary mowers

Problem	CAUSE? / Solution
ANY UNIT: Mower cuts unevenly	BLADE DIRTY? Clean off any caked mud or built-up clippings (p.359). ◇
	BLADE DULL, UNBALANCED, OR BENT? Sharpen, balance, or replace blade. ◆
	WHEELS AT UNEVEN HEIGHTS? Adjust wheels (consult owner's manual). ◇
Grass turns brown day after mowing	DULL BLADE TEARING GRASS? Sharpen or replace the blade (right). ◆
	GRASS TOO LONG? Cut no more than one-third of grass height at a time. ◇
Mower vibrates excessively or is noisy	BLADE UNBALANCED OR BENT? Balance the blade or replace it (right). ◆
	BUILT-UP CLIPPINGS UNDER MOWER DECK? Clean off (p.359). ◇
	DISCHARGE CHUTE CLOGGED? Clear chute (consult owner's manual). ◇
ENGINE UNITS: Engine won't start, runs poorly, or dies in use	See *Troubleshooting engines*, p.359.
Engine runs, but mower won't move	DRIVE BELT, CABLE, OR PULLEY FAULTY? Repair (facing page). ◆
	CLUTCH FAULTY? Adjust, repair, or replace (facing page). ◆
MOTOR UNITS: Motor won't run	See *Faulty universal motor?*, p.146.

Degree of difficulty: Simple ◇ Average ◆ Complex ◆

Rotary blades

Inspect a lawn mower blade regularly for the symptoms described at right. Sharpness is essential—once a blade becomes so dull that the original angle of its cutting edge is lost, you must replace it. Under normal use, sharpening the blade twice a season should suffice. Sharpen the blade yourself with a hand file or with a sharpening attachment on an electric drill, or have it professionally serviced. Replace a blade that's broken or badly damaged.

Balance the blade after each sharpening (or more often, as warranted) to prevent vibrations that can loosen fastenings and damage the engine.

Dull blade will tear grass instead of cutting it and will also strain engine.

Accidentally twisted blade will chop grass unevenly and probably scalp lawn in spots.

Badly nicked blade will cause lawn mower to vibrate during operation and will tear grass.

Blade in good condition has intact lift wings, which draw grass up for proper cutting.

Blade with worn or damaged lift wing won't pick up grass and will cut lawn unevenly.

Servicing the blade

1 Disconnect spark plug cable. Wedge blade in stationary position with 2 x 4. To remove blade, grasp blade with gloved hand and loosen bolts. If bolts stick, tap wrench with hammer.

2 Check the blade (and stiffener if unit has one) for damage. Replace any damaged parts with new ones specified by manufacturer. Wrong parts can cause engine-damaging vibration.

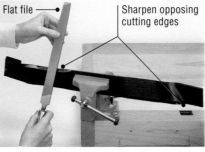

Flat file — Sharpen opposing cutting edges

3 With a medium-rough flat file, sharpen the blade along the original angle of each cutting edge. File in one direction only, toward the edge; take equal amounts of metal off each edge.

Spike-and-cone balancer

4 Check that blade balances horizontally, using a spike-and-cone balancer (available from an autoparts store) or a screwdriver. Check balance one way; then flip blade over and check again.

5 If the blade does not balance, file metal from the heavy end. Avoid filing the newly sharpened cutting edge. Check blade balance again, as described in Step 4.

6 Once the blade is balanced, reinstall it. Make sure the lift wing on each end points toward the deck of the lawn mower. This will allow the blade to cut and discharge the grass properly.

The drive system

In a self-propelled lawn mower, power is transferred from the engine to the wheels by a V-belt and pulleys or a chain and sprockets. Inspect the belt often for frays and cracks; replace a damaged belt immediately. If the mower has an idler pulley, see *Servicing the belts and pulleys*, p.387. On a chain-driven mower, care for the chain as instructed in the owner's manual. Replace the chain in the same way as for a bicycle (p.408).

The drive system may have a torsion clutch (below). You should replace the clutch if its spring breaks. If your mower offers variable speed, tighten the speed cable periodically; it can stretch after prolonged use. If your mower loses front wheel drive, adjust the wheel traction. On some single-speed mowers you can set the speed to run faster or slower (follow directions in the owner's manual).

Before starting any repairs, disconnect the spark plug cable. Disengage the wheel drive lever; on a variable-speed model, set the wheel speed to the slowest setting. To remove the deck cover, unscrew the bolts and slide the cover off.

Replacing the torsion clutch

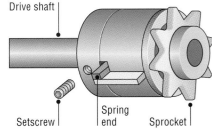

Drive shaft · Setscrew · Spring end · Sprocket

If the clutch has a broken spring, the sprocket will rotate in both directions. To replace the clutch, remove the setscrew, or on some models, force out the pin with a hammer and punch.

Adjusting the variable-speed cable

Locknut — Pulley — Disc

1 Disengage spark plug cable; remove cover. With two open-end wrenches, loosen the locknuts. Gently push the pulley toward the rubber disc until the pulley casting just touches the disc.

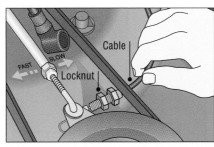

FAST · SLOW · Locknut · Cable

2 Remove all slack from the cable. Reposition the locknuts (you may have to remove the cable from the bracket). Once the cable is taut, tighten the locknuts. Slowly push the pulley toward *Fast*.

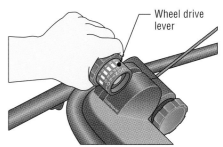

Wheel drive lever

3 To test operation, have a helper operate the wheel drive lever through all its settings. You should see the cable move at your end. If knob doesn't click in all settings, readjust the cable.

Resetting the wheel traction

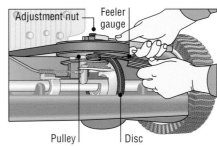

Dished nut

1 Disengage spark plug cable; grasp the nut at the bottom of the assembly with an open-end wrench. With another open-end wrench, remove the dished nut at top (note position of second nut).

Adjustment nut · Feeler gauge · Pulley · Disc

2 Insert a feeler gauge (see owner's manual for correct size) or business card between the rubber disc and the pulley. Rotate the adjustment nut until you feel a slight resistance on the gauge.

3 Reinstall the dished nut (make sure it faces same way it did prior to removal). As in Step 1, use two open-end wrenches to tighten the dished nut securely.

Replacing the wheel drive belt

1 Disengage spark plug cable; unbolt cover. Loosen nuts; tilt pulley toward engine (see *Adjusting the variable-speed cable*, above). Pull belt off pulley. Turn mower over to access blade.

Heavy work gloves

2 To remove belt, slip it over one blade tip, then the other. If necessary, rotate the blade to slip the belt over it. Position the new belt with the V of the belt facing the groove in the rear pulley.

3 Push belt end through opening. Turn mower over; slip belt onto front pulley. Position pulley and tighten nuts. Test tension by depressing belt; if it doesn't deflect ¾ in., reposition pulley.

Lawn tractor

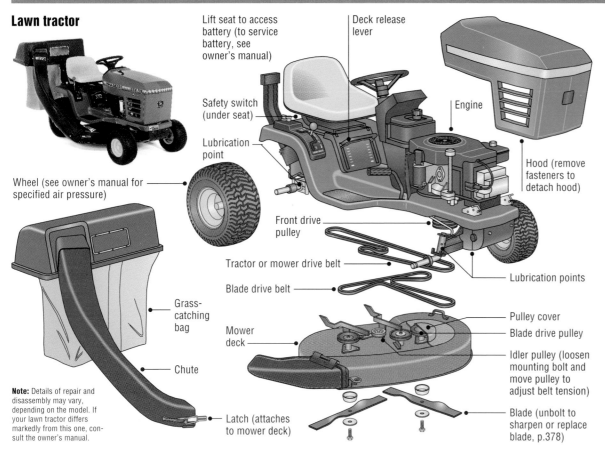

Lift seat to access battery (to service battery, see owner's manual)

Deck release lever

Safety switch (under seat)

Engine

Lubrication point

Hood (remove fasteners to detach hood)

Wheel (see owner's manual for specified air pressure)

Front drive pulley

Tractor or mower drive belt

Lubrication points

Blade drive belt

Grass-catching bag

Pulley cover

Mower deck

Blade drive pulley

Chute

Idler pulley (loosen mounting bolt and move pulley to adjust belt tension)

Note: Details of repair and disassembly may vary, depending on the model. If your lawn tractor differs markedly from this one, consult the owner's manual.

Latch (attaches to mower deck)

Blade (unbolt to sharpen or replace blade, p.378)

Riding lawn mowers and lawn tractors

A riding lawn mower is powered by a small engine with up to 8 horsepower (hp); the engine is often mounted at the rear. The similar lawn tractor (left) has a larger front-mounted engine. The features of a mower or tractor may vary; check the owner's manual for maintenance and repair procedures for your machine. For engine care, see pp.356–367. Inspect the blades regularly, and sharpen them as needed (p.378).

With use, the two V-belts on a mower or tractor stretch. The drive-belt tension must be correct for proper brake operation. Check the belts often: they should deflect only ½ inch when pressed midway between the pulleys. On some units you can increase the belt tension by moving an idler pulley; on others, move the drive pulley (see below and facing page). Eventually you'll have to replace the belts. Some tractors and mowers use chains instead of belts; they are replaced in the same way as bicycle chains (p.408).

A deck shields the blades and prevents stones and debris from hitting bystanders. On many machines, you must remove the deck to replace or adjust the belt or to change attachments.

In most units, a switch stops the engine if the driver leaves the seat without putting the transmission in neutral and setting the brake. If the engine won't start, test the switch (p.145); it should show continuity with the plunger released but not with it pressed.

Removing the mower deck

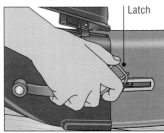

Latch

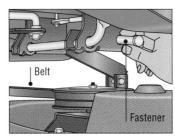

Belt

Fastener

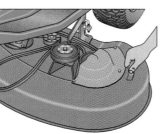

1 Lock parking brake. Push 2 x 4's under front and back of deck; lower deck lever. Remove attachments from deck, such as a grass-catching chute.

2 Remove blade drive belt from front pulley (see facing page). Remove front and rear deck fasteners, following instructions in owner's manual.

3 Raise the deck release lever to its highest position and pull out the 2 x 4's. Now you can slide the deck out from under the mower or tractor.

Adjusting the tractor drive-belt tension

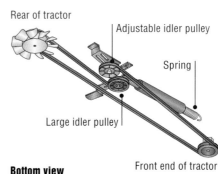

Rear of tractor

Adjustable idler pulley

Spring

Large idler pulley

Bottom view

Front end of tractor

If mower or tractor drive belt is slack, adjust tension (see text). Wearing heavy gloves, pull large idler pulley away from belt. Remove belt from adjustable idler pulley. Release large idler pulley slowly—the attached spring is under tension. Unbolt adjustable idler pulley, move it ⅜ in. toward rear, and tighten. Replace the belt; test tension. Repeat procedure if needed. If adjustable idler pulley reaches end of slot and belt is slack, replace belt.

Troubleshooting: Riding lawn mowers and lawn tractors

Problem	CAUSE? / Solution
Engine won't start, loses power, or dies in use	ENGINE FAULTY? See *Troubleshooting engines*, p.359.
	SAFETY SWITCH FAULTY? Locate the switch under the seat; test it (p.145). ◆ ▣
Mower cuts grass poorly or unevenly	TRAVEL SPEED TOO FAST? Mow at slower speed. ◇
	ENGINE SPEED TOO LOW? Adjust it; see owner's manual. ◇
	DRIED GRASS CAKED UNDER DECK? Scrape away debris. ◇
	BLADES DULL OR BENT? Sharpen or replace (p.378). ◆
	BELT WORN? *(Multi-blade decks only)* Replace belt (right). ◆
V-belt slips or comes off in use	DEBRIS IN BELT AREA? Clean. ◇
	BELT WORN, DAMAGED, OR IMPROPERLY TENSIONED? Adjust belt tension (facing page) or replace belt (right). ◆
	PULLEY LOOSE, WORN, OR INCORRECTLY ADJUSTED? Adjust and tighten fasteners; replace part or bring to service center. ◆
Belt squeals or wears excessively	IMPROPER BELT TENSION? Adjust tension (facing page). ◆
	OBJECT CUTTING BELT? Look for obstruction, such as damaged part. Repair or replace part, or bring to service center. ◆
Mower/tractor vibrates excessively when clutch is engaged	DRIED GRASS CAKED UNDER DECK? Scrape away debris. ◇
	BLADE UNBALANCED OR DAMAGED? Balance blade (p.378). Remove deck (facing page) and replace blade if needed. ◆
	BELTS FAULTY? Adjust tension (facing page). Check for wear or damage, and replace as necessary. ◆
	PULLEY OR OTHER PART IN BELT-DRIVE SYSTEM DAMAGED? Inspect and replace; or have mower serviced. ◆
Mower/tractor hard to shift; doesn't move when clutch is engaged	POOR TRACTOR DRIVE-BELT TENSION? Adjust (facing page). ◆
	IMPROPER TYPE AND AMOUNT OF LUBRICANT USED? Follow specifications for lubrication given in your owner's manual. ◇
	CLUTCH/BRAKE PEDAL LINKAGE DAMAGED OR OUT OF ADJUSTMENT? Adjust it (right) or have mower serviced. ◆

Degree of difficulty: Simple ◇ Average ◆ Complex ◆ Volt-ohm meter required: ▣

Lubrication points

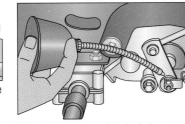

Grease fitting

Grease gun

Lubricate grease fittings on the spindle near the front wheel and on the pivot axle. Use a good-quality automotive chassis grease.

Other lubrication points include neutral gear linkage behind rear wheel. Check for specified areas in owner's manual. Use lubricant recommended by manufacturer.

Replacing the blade drive belt

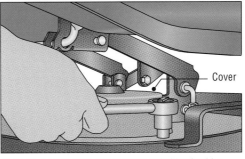

Cover

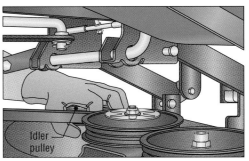

Idler pulley

1 Remove blade drive pulley cover, unbolting it with a socket wrench or nut driver. But first make sure deck is set at its lowest position (lower deck release lever), parking brake is engaged, and spark plug cable is disengaged.

2 Release tension on belt: From other side of mower or tractor, carefully pull the idler pulley toward you. You may want to have a helper push the pulley toward you and hold it in place while you continue with the next step.

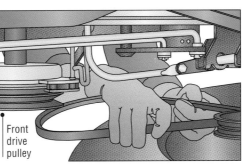

Front drive pulley

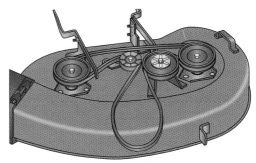

3 While still grasping the idler pulley, remove the belt from the front drive pulley (it is attached to the engine, not to the deck). Slowly release the idler pulley (it's under tension). Remove belt from the other pulleys.

4 Install new belt following the path of old belt; the V of the belt fits into the grooves of the pulleys. Fit the belt into the front drive pulley last (with the idler pulley held out of its normal position). Reattach pulley cover.

Adjusting the brake

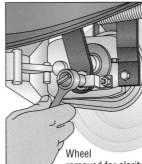

Wheel removed for clarity

If mower or tractor has a disc brake, engage brake pedal and set parking brake. With shift in neutral, push mower. If rear wheels turn, tighten hex nut near drive brake clockwise until wheels no longer turn. Release parking brake; push mower. If wheels will not turn, loosen the hex nut.

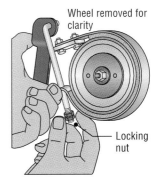

Wheel removed for clarity

Locking nut

If mower or tractor has brake band, make sure tractor drive-belt tension is correct (see text); then test brake power as for disc brake. To adjust the brake band, loosen one locking nut and tighten the other. Move the nuts toward the brake pedal to increase braking pressure, away to decrease pressure.

The various types of leaf blowers are all designed to move leaves and other light debris by pushing them with air speeds of up to 180 miles per hour. Hand-held models may be driven by a universal motor (p.139) or a two-cycle engine (pp.356–357). Backpack models are always driven by an engine. Some blowers can be converted to leaf vacuums with the addition of a vacuum tube and leaf collection bag.

Maintenance and repair. After each use, clean the leaf blower thoroughly. Remove debris from the impeller area with a small brush. At the end of the season, use mild soap and a damp cloth to remove grease, oil, dirt, and debris from the housing. Dry the housing with a clean soft rag before storing a leaf blower.

You may need to replace a worn or damaged impeller or repair a cracked impeller housing (facing page). To resolve a motor problem, see *General troubleshooting*, p.146. For engine maintenance and repair, see *Small engines*, pp.356–367. Use only replacement parts specified by the manufacturer.

FOR YOUR SAFETY

Before using a leaf blower, clear the work area of people and pets. Remove any debris, such as rocks, branches, and glass, that could ricochet and cause injury.

 Wear safety glasses, earplugs, and sturdy shoes with nonskid soles. If the work is dusty, wear a filter mask, too.

Avoid loose-fitting clothes and jewelry. Tie back long hair.

Maintain good balance and a firm footing. Don't overreach, especially when standing on a ladder to clear gutters.

Always shut off a leaf blower before putting it down or changing attachments.

Unplug the unit or disconnect the spark plug cable before cleaning or repairing the blower.

With an electric leaf blower, use only an extension cord approved for outdoor use. Don't use a cord over 150 feet long. Follow the manufacturer's guidelines for the adequate wire gauge.

Never use an electric blower in damp or wet conditions.

Prevent burns by carrying an engine-powered blower with the muffler facing away from you.

Motor-powered hand-held leaf blower

In this type of leaf blower, the airstream is directed by a blower tube that locks into the housing outlet. Some models have an additional nozzle piece that attaches to the blower tube in order to aim and shape the pattern of the airstream. To prevent accidental disconnection of the cords, knot the extension cord to the power cord as shown on page 392. Because the motor can overheat, never use the blower without the proper attachments. The model shown can accept a vacuum attachment.

Blower tube | Housing outlet | Switch | Motor | Impeller | Housing

Engine-powered backpack or harness blower

A leaf blower driven by a two-cycle engine runs on a mixture of gasoline and two-cycle oil (use the proportions specified in the owner's manual). A flexible blower tube links the engine to a rigid nozzle. To keep the engine from overheating, never run the device without its tube and nozzle attached. If using a shoulder harness strap instead of a backpack carrier, make sure the strap doesn't block the blower's exhaust outlet.

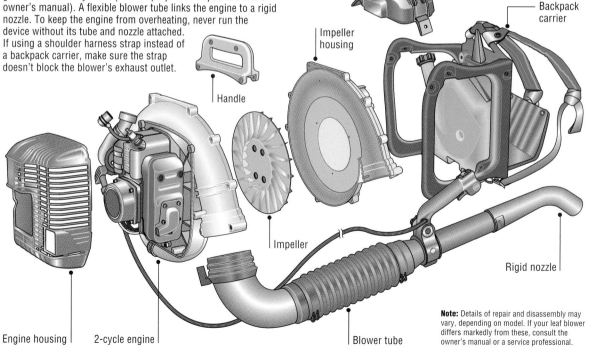

Air filter | Backpack carrier | Impeller housing | Handle | Impeller | Rigid nozzle | Engine housing | 2-cycle engine | Blower tube

Note: Details of repair and disassembly may vary, depending on model. If your leaf blower differs markedly from these, consult the owner's manual or a service professional.

Troubleshooting

Problem	CAUSE? / Solution
Blower delivers air poorly	IMPELLER LOOSE OR DAMAGED? Inspect and tighten. Replace the impeller if its fins are cracked or damaged (far right). ◆
	UNIT DOESN'T REACH FULL SPEED? *(Engine-powered units only)* See *Troubleshooting engines,* p.359.
Blower vibrates excessively	LOOSE OR WORN FASTENERS? *(Engine-powered units only)* Tighten loose fasteners; replace worn fasteners. ◇
	IMPELLER LOOSE OR DAMAGED? See *Blower delivers air poorly,* above.
Motor-powered blower doesn't work	POWER OFF AT OUTLET? See *General troubleshooting,* p.144.
	FAULTY POWER CORD? See *General troubleshooting,* p.144.
	FAULTY SWITCH? See *General troubleshooting,* p.145.
	FAULTY MOTOR? See *General troubleshooting,* p.146.
Engine-powered blower won't start, stalls often, or lacks power	GAS TANK EMPTY? Refill if necessary. ◇
	FAULTY ENGINE? See *Troubleshooting engines,* p.359.
Vacuum attachment doesn't work	VACUUM TUBE CLOGGED? Shut off blower. Remove vacuum tube and clear out debris with small stick; then reinstall. ◇
	IMPELLER HOUSING CRACKED? Inspect housing; repair crack if possible (far right). ◆

Degree of difficulty: Simple ◇   Average ◆   Complex ◆

Disassembly: Hand-held blower

Impeller cover

Unplug the blower. Detach the impeller cover. Remove the housing screws, and lift off one half of the housing. You now have access to the motor, the impeller, and the impeller housing. (On some models, you can access the impeller simply by twisting off the impeller cover.)

Disassembly: Backpack/harness blower

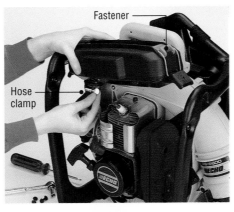

Fastener

Hose clamp

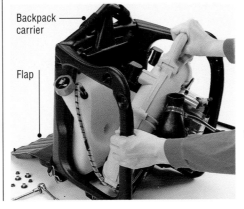

Backpack carrier

Flap

1 To prevent the engine from accidentally starting, disconnect the spark plug cable. If the engine has been running, wait until it cools down. Remove any bolts that secure the engine housing to the engine (you may have to move a hose or cable to locate a hidden bolt). Lift the housing away from the engine.

2 To remove the impeller-engine assembly, you may have to detach other parts first. On this model, remove the air filter housing by unclasping the fasteners on each end and lifting it up. Then disengage the hose to the carburetor by loosening the hose clamp with a simple turn or two of the thumbscrew.

3 Remove bolts securing impeller-engine assembly to the backpack carrier or harness. (Bolts may be hard to find; on this model, unfastening the flap reveals several bolts.) Pull the assembly from the backback carrier or harness. This may take some maneuvering. The impeller housing can now be unbolted.

Replacing an impeller

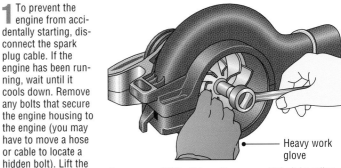

Heavy work glove

Unscrew and lift off impeller cover. Unbolt impeller with a socket wrench; to prevent impeller from rotating, hold it in place with a gloved hand or wood wedge. Pull out impeller and replace it with an exact duplicate from an authorized parts supplier. On some models, separate housing, remove motor, and pry off impeller.

Repairing a cracked impeller housing

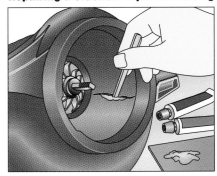

Leaf blowers that also vacuum may pick up stones or other hard objects that can crack the impeller housing and create a dangerous operating condition. Inspect the impeller housing regularly for cracks, and replace a shattered housing. To repair a minor crack, clean the surfaces surrounding the crack with a solvent such as brake cleaner or electrical contact cleaner. Roughen the crack area with coarse sandpaper. Fill the crack and cover the surrounding ½-inch area with metal-impregnated epoxy, or use fiberglass resin and cloth. After the repair dries, sand the impeller side of the housing smooth.

A cutting tool will work best when kept sharp, clean, and lubricated. Sharpen low-carbon steel blades with a fine or medium-fine single-cut flat file. To sharpen hardened steel blades, use a file or a small flat sharpening stone (see *Keeping tools sharp*, p.16).

If a cutting blade is nicked or very dull, reshape it on a bench grinder (p.16) before sharpening it. To sharpen a blade, follow the original angle of the bevel. Don't rock the file or stone, doing so can damage the bevel. After sharpening, gently rub the stone or file along the flat

Pruning shears have a curved cutting blade and a curved, square-edged hook.

Anvil-type pruning shears have a straight cutting blade and and a flat anvil blade.

Hedge clippers and **grass shears** have two cutting blades.

side of the blade (without the bevel) to remove any burrs (metal that curls under during sharpening or with use). To disassemble the shears for sharpening, you may have to hold a nut steady to remove a bolt. Make sure you lightly oil the bolt

before reassembly; tighten it until you feel a slight drag when using the tool.

Wooden handles on a tool can loosen from the metal tangs. If you feel the handles begin to wobble, tighten them immediately to prevent further damage.

Tightening a loose grip

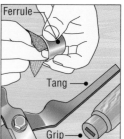

1 Separate the loose wooden grip from the tool's metal tang. Shake the grip to remove any wood particles. Rough up the inside of the ferrule with an emery cloth.

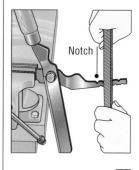

2 If the end of the metal tang tapers instead of flaring out, file a series of sawtooth notches into the tang; this will give the adhesive a surface to grip. Clean tang with an emery cloth.

Restoring the cutting edge

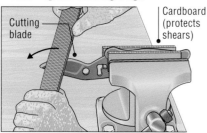

Pruning shears. To separate blades (not always possible), remove pivot bolt, pry off lock switch with screwdriver, and remove pin. Secure cutting-blade handle in vise. File along blade, following original bevel. If hook has burrs, remove them.

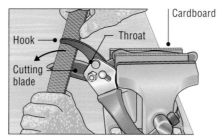

If blades cannot be separated, secure handle of cutting blade in vise. Use a file to sharpen the cutting blade, moving it from the throat toward the tip of the blade in a single motion. Gently file off burrs, if any, on the curved hook.

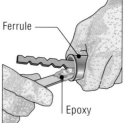

3 Test-fit the pieces. Fill any voids in grip with wood wedges or toothpicks. Slide ferrule over tang; then apply epoxy (pp.18–19) to tang, ferrule, and inside of grip.

Anvil-type pruning shears can't be taken apart. Instead, secure the cutting-blade handle in a vise; let blades spring open. Move a file in a sweeping motion along the bevel of the cutting blade, maintaining the original angle of the bevel.

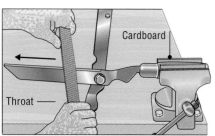

Hedge clippers. Secure handle in vise. Lay file flat against bevel and move it from throat to blade tip in a single motion. (If necessary, support tip to keep clippers from moving.) Repeat process for opposite blade.

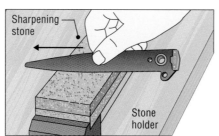

Grass shears. Disassemble shears. Draw one blade at a time across a flat stone. Follow angle of original bevel. When reassembling, tighten pivot bolt until blades close with slight drag; if bolt has a spring, tighten bolt until best cutting is achieved.

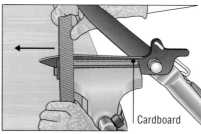

If grass shears can't be disassembled, grip one blade at a time in a vise (use cardboard or a rag to protect the blade); then sharpen along the original bevel with a file or small stone. Pull file or stone across blade, away from throat.

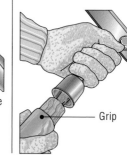

4 Push grip onto tang and seat it firmly in ferrule. If necessary, place blade tip on a wood block (to provide resistance and protect tip) and tap end of grip with a wooden or rawhide mallet.

Shovels, rakes, and hoes

With proper maintenance most long-handled tools will last a lifetime. It is best to keep the head of a shovel, rake, hoe, or other long-handled tool clean and sharp. To prevent rust, coat the head regularly with machine or motor oil. Before oiling it, remove any existing rust with a wire brush, sandpaper, or a rust-removing chemical.

If a tool handle splits, glue and clamp it back together, using yellow glue. After gluing, reinforce the repair by installing short wood screws across the split; then wrap it with heavy twine soaked in epoxy (pp.18–19). Replace a broken handle with a pre-tapered handle made of ash, hickory, or white oak. Avoid handles made of Asian woods, such as lauan; these soft woods break easily.

You should coat an unfinished handle with a 50-50 solution of turpentine and linseed oil; wipe off any excess. If a handle is badly weathered, sand it smooth and then apply the mixture.

USE AND CARE

Sharpen a digging tool by first securing the handle in a vise. Restore the original edge (usually at a 45° bevel) with a coarse 10-inch file. Sharpen the corners as well as the cutting edges on hoes and shovels.

To clean and oil a tool head in one step, fill a 5-gallon bucket with sand and add old oil from your lawn mower or car. Thrust the tool into the oil-soaked sand several times; the blade will emerge clean and sharp. You can reuse the oil–sand mixture again and again.

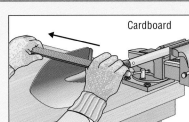
Cardboard

Replacing a broken handle

Grinding wheel attachment | Socket
Rivet

1 Grind off the head of the rivet with a grinding wheel attachment on a power drill. Drive rivet out of tool-head socket with a center punch and hammer. **CAUTION:** Wear safety glasses.

Screw

2 To extract the stub of the old handle, insert a long wood screw into the stub. Secure the screw in a vise; then hit the tool's head with a mallet to drive it off the stub.

Carbon paper

3 If new handle doesn't fit snugly, wrap carbon paper around end; insert handle into tool-head socket. Pull out handle without twisting it. Paper will leave dark marks on high spots of handle.

Common variant: handles

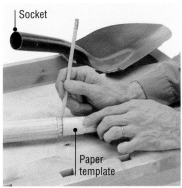
Socket
Paper template

The techniques described at left are suitable for replacing the handles of most tools. For some tools, however, you must trim the end of the handle so it fits into the tool-head socket. This is the case with old shovels and high-quality, contractor grade tools that have a forged head. If the back of the tool head is closed so you can't see the end of the handle, try this approach:

After removing the old handle, roll up a strip of paper and slip it inside the tool-head socket. When the paper fits snugly, tape its ends and use it to transfer the diameter of the socket to the handle. Mark the handle. Measure the depth of the socket and subtrate it from the mark on the handle; saw the handle at the second mark.

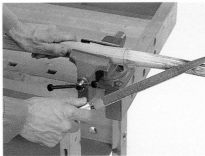

4 Remove high spots with a wood rasp or Surform tool. Rewrap the handle and test-fit it again. Continue to adjust the taper until the carbon paper leaves dark areas along entire length.

CAUTION: Never strike metal portion of tool against a hard object.

5 When the taper is correct, the handle should fit snugly into the full length of the socket. When the handle fits, strike it on a wooden block to drive it into the tool-head socket.

6 To secure the handle in the tool-head socket, drill pilot holes into both sides of the handle (at the old rivet holes) at a slight angle. Insert two round-head wood screws and tighten them.

In a two-stage snow thrower, such as the one shown below, an auger picks up snow and feeds it into an impeller, which blows the snow out of the discharge chute. (A lighter-duty single-stage snow thrower and a power shovel are not equipped with an impeller.) Many units are propelled by wheels or tracks to make them easier to push. All snow throwers are driven by either a four-cycle engine (see p.356) or a universal motor (see pp.138–139).

Periodic maintenance is crucial. Check the tautness of the V-belts that transfer power from the engine to the auger and impeller and to the drive system. Belts should give less than ½ inch when pressed with a thumb; adjust the idler pulley to decrease slack. If one belt is stretched or worn, replace both (facing page). Chains that drive wheels should have little play in them; reposition the reduction sprocket accordingly.

For smooth discharge chute rotation, grease the wormgear crank periodically; if needed, unbolt the crank to adjust it. Inspect the auger assembly after every 10 hours of use. Rotate the auger to ensure that it turns freely, and check that the shear bolts are intact. These bolts are designed to break when the machine hits an obstruction; this frees the auger from the power system, protecting it and the engine from damage. Replacing a broken shear bolt is easy, but you must use the correct replacement part. Remove the shear bolts to lubricate the auger shaft periodically. Have a damaged auger serviced professionally.

Check the scraper bar and runners occasionally. The scraper directs snow and ice into the auger, and should be replaced if worn to under 1/16 inch or damaged. The runners raise and lower the auger housing; adjust them each time you change from a paved to a gravel surface. Finally, follow the maintenance, lubrication, and storage advice in the owner's manual.

Two-stage snow thrower

Note: Details of repair and disassembly may vary, depending on the model. If your snow thrower differs markedly from this one, consult the owner's manual.

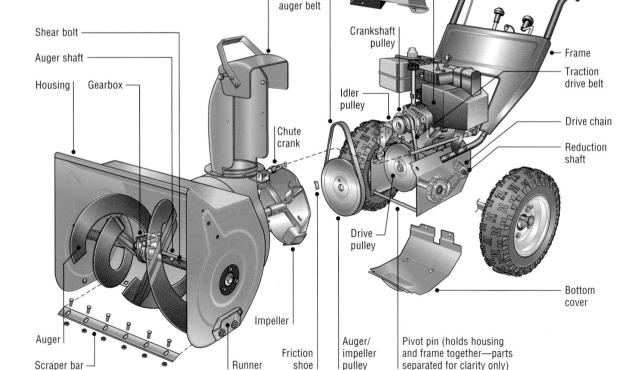

Discharge chute | Belt guard | 4-cycle engine
Impeller/auger belt
Shear bolt
Crankshaft pulley
Auger shaft
Frame
Housing | Gearbox
Traction drive belt
Idler pulley
Chute crank
Drive chain
Reduction shaft
Impeller
Drive pulley
Bottom cover
Auger
Friction shoe
Auger/impeller pulley
Pivot pin (holds housing and frame together—parts separated for clarity only)
Scraper bar
Runner

Troubleshooting

Problem	CAUSE? / Solution
Unit vibrates excessively	FASTENERS LOOSE? Tighten bolts. ◇
	PULLEYS LOOSE? Tighten (facing page). ◆
	AUGER BENT OR AUGER SHAFT DAMAGED? Have snow thrower professionally serviced.
Unit runs but doesn't throw snow	DISCHARGE CHUTE CLOGGED BY ICE? Bring snow thrower indoors to soften ice; then chip it out. To prevent new ice buildup, apply auto spray wax to auger and inside of discharge chute. ◇
	SCRAPER BAR WORN? Unbolt bar; replace. ◇
	RUNNERS AT WRONG HEIGHT? Place unit on level surface; slip spacer of desired height under scraper bar. Unbolt and reposition runners. ◇
	SHEAR BOLT BROKEN? Replace (facing page). ◇
	DRIVE BELT LOOSE OR WORN? Adjust tension; replace worn or damaged belts (facing page). ◆
	AUGER OR IMPELLER DAMAGED? Have snow thrower professionally serviced.
Unit is hard to steer	TIRES IMPROPERLY INFLATED? Inflate tires to pressure indicated in owner's manual. ◇
	DRIVE CHAINS LOOSE? Adjust chain tension (facing page). ◆
	OIL LOW IN GEARBOX? Refill. ◇
Machine doesn't start, loses power, or dies in use	SAFETY INTERLOCKS ENGAGED? Check owner's manual for the proper way to disengage. ◇
	FAULTY ENGINE? See *Troubleshooting engines*, p.359.
	FAULTY UNIVERSAL MOTOR? See *General troubleshooting*, p.146.

Degree of difficulty: Simple ◇   Average ◆   Complex ◆

Replacing a shear bolt

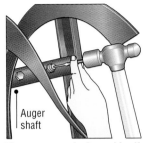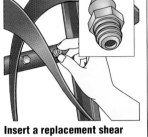

Disengage spark plug cable. If needed, drive damaged shear bolt from auger shaft, using a pin or drift punch and a ball-peen hammer. Lubricate bolt hole with a dab of white grease. **CAUTION:** Wear safety glasses when removing the bolt.

Insert a replacement shear bolt, identical to the old one, into the hole in the auger shaft. *Never use a stronger substitute bolt*—doing so can result in damage to the auger or the engine. Tighten the bolt with a nut driver or socket wrench.

Auger shaft

Adjusting the drive chain tension

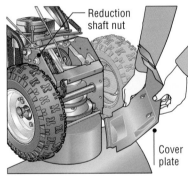

Reduction shaft nut

Cover plate

To reach the drive chains, first disconnect the spark plug cable and empty the fuel tank. Carefully stand unit up by tipping it forward, resting it on the auger housing. Unbolt and remove the bottom cover plate, using a nut driver or socket wrench.

Shaft

To test the chains, press down on each chain with your thumb; there should be little or no play. To increase tautness, loosen nuts on each end of reduction shaft; move shaft in slots, keeping movement equal at both ends. Tighten nuts to torque specified in owner's manual.

Servicing the belts and pulleys

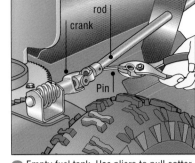

Belt guard

1 Disengage spark plug cable; unbolt guard. Check belts for wear and test tension (see text, facing page). To adjust tension, loosen idler pulley bolt; move pulley.

rod crank

Pin

2 Empty fuel tank. Use pliers to pull cotter pin from end of chute crank; then slip rod from crank. With belt guard off, pull auger/impeller belt off idler pulley.

3 With a helper supporting frame (or with handlebars securely propped up), unbolt and slowly tip apart frame and housing (the pivot pin will keep the two halves joined).

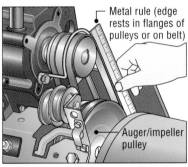

Work gloves

4 Pull idler pulley away from traction drive belt, or pull friction shoe away from auger/impeller belt. Slip belts off pulleys. Install new belts as a set, with V's toward pulleys. Test and adjust belt tension.

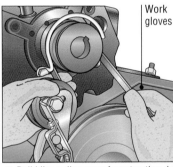

Metal rule (edge rests in flanges of pulleys or on belt)

Auger/impeller pulley

5 If belt wears often, check vertical alignment of pulleys with rule. To adjust, loosen setscrew; move crankshaft pulley. (Reassemble frame and housing to check auger/impeller pulley.)

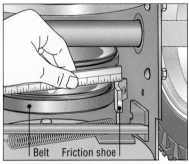

Belt   Friction shoe

6 Test the clutch after replacing the belts. Remove bottom cover; engage clutch. Use a metal rule to measure distance from friction shoe to belt; it should be $\frac{1}{16}$–$\frac{1}{8}$ in. If not, loosen and adust idler pulley.

Portable sprinklers

The sprinklers used with a garden hose are driven by water pressure to revolve or oscillate as they spray. A revolving sprinkler (right) has few parts to wear out; if kept clean, it should last indefinitely. An oscillating sprinkler (below) needs more care. Its nozzles clog with grit or hard-water deposits and the spray tube can become misaligned with the dial. All portable sprinklers require a filter washer at the hose end (you may have to buy one separately). Carry rather than drag sprinklers from place to place to keep out debris. Store your sprinklers and hoses indoors over the winter to prevent them from freezing and cracking.

Stopping leaks

Most sprinkler leaks occur where the sprinkler connects to the hose. Install a new filter washer and tighten the fitting to stop the leak. When a sprinkler leaks under the rotating arm, unscrew the bearing assembly column from the base and replace any worn washers and O-rings with exact duplicates from a hardware store.

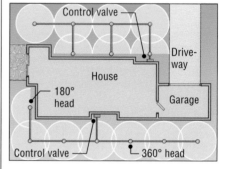

Rotating arm — Nozzle
O-ring
Column
Washer — Filter washer
O-ring

Revolving sprinkler

In-ground sprinkler systems

For an in-ground sprinkler system to work properly, there must be enough water pressure in the system of belowground pipes to force a series of built-in sprinklers to pop up and spray water in a predetermined pattern. To ensure that the water pressure is sufficiently high, system designers divide the yard into areas, or zones, that can be watered separately (below). A timer automatically switches the flow of water from zone to zone around the yard.

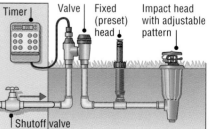

Control valve
Drive-way
House
180° head
Garage
Control valve — 360° head

A zoned sprinkler system divides the yard into separate watering areas. In this example, each zone is controlled by a separate valve. Half-circle spray heads augment full-circle heads.

A good way to check a sprinkler system is simply to watch it in operation. If sprinkler heads within a zone disperse water unevenly, clean out the clogged heads or replace them (facing page). Check nearby heads if a part of the lawn appears dry. Also look for unusually wet areas of lawn, often a sign of leaks in the pipe below. Rigid PVC pipes can be mended with a telescoping union (facing page). Use grip fittings (p.120) to patch flexible pipe.

Servicing an oscillating sprinkler

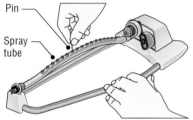

Pin
Spray tube

To clean nozzles, stick hatpin or long upholstery needle into each nozzle along the spray tube. Twirl pin to dig out any built-up dirt or debris that might be blocking nozzle.

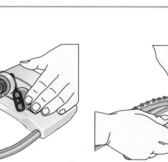

Remove nozzles to reach tough deposits. Use pliers to pull (or unscrew) nozzles. Soak nozzles in vinegar and water before clearing from both ends with a pin. Replace cleaned nozzles firmly into tube.

To adjust spray pattern, loosen setscrew on dial arm of sprinkler with screwdriver. Turn spray tube slightly and tighten screw. Test the pattern by turning on the water; repeat process if necessary.

Repairing a garden hose

1 To remove damaged piece of hose, make perpendicular cuts with utility knife to remove damage. Buy a hose coupling to match diameter of hose.

2 Soften ends of cut hose by holding them for a few moments in hot water. Repeat as necessary.

3 Insert coupling into hose ends until it seats securely. If shank of coupling is hard to insert, lubricate inside of wet hose with soap.

4 Line up clamps over hose and coupling as shown. Tighten screws until unit is secure and doesn't leak.

Sprinkler system components

Timer — Valve — Fixed (preset) head — Impact head with adjustable pattern

Shutoff valve

A control panel with a timer activates an antisiphon valve that triggers water flow to a variety of sprinkler heads along a water pipe.

Troubleshooting

Problem	CAUSE? / Solution
Sprinkler head won't pop up	LEAK IN PIPE? Repair pipe (below). ◆
	LOW WATER PRESSURE? Switch faulty unit with one closer to water source (see *Replacing a sprinkler head,* right). If head now works, check antisiphon valve; open if partway closed. ◆
	DEBRIS IN NOZZLE OR SCREEN? Clean sprinkler head (right). If cleaning does not help, replace sprinkler head. ◇ ◆
	HEAD ASSEMBLED IMPROPERLY? Remove head as if to clean (right); then reassemble following owner's manual. ◇
Uneven spray	RESIDUE OR DEBRIS IN BEARING ASSEMBLY? Clean heads (right) ◇; if cleaning fails, replace head (below, right). ◆
	HEADS MIXED? Mixing different types of heads on a line can unbalance system. Replace heads as necessary (below, right). ◆
	DEBRIS IN NOZZLE OR SCREEN? See *Sprinkler head won't pop up,* above.
Impact sprinkler head rotates part-way, then stops	DEBRIS IN NOZZLE OR CASE? See *Sprinkler head won't pop up,* above.
	STOPS SET INCORRECTLY? Stops on sprinkler head limit its rotation. Check owner's manual and reset stops as needed. ◇
	TOO MUCH WATER PRESSURE? Reduce flow at main valve. ◇
Water coming out of case	CRACKED CASE OR FAULTY HEAD? Replace sprinkler unit with duplicate (right). ◆
Unusually wet spot on lawn	LEAK IN PIPE? Dig up and repair pipe (below). ◆
	VALVE SHUTOFF FAULTY? If water seeps out of sprinkler heads when system is turned off, inspect control valve. Clean out debris and replace any damaged parts (see owner's manual). ◆
Areas of lawn overly dry	FAULTY SPRINKLER HEAD? Turn on sprinklers; clean nonworking sprinkler heads (above, right) or replace them (right). ◆
	LOW WATER PRESSURE? See *Sprinkler head won't pop up,* above.
	GRASS TOO HIGH? Tall grass may obstruct spray from sprinkler heads. Mow lawn, or clip grass away from heads. ◇

Degree of difficulty: Simple ◇   Average ◆   Complex ◆

Cleaning sprinkler heads

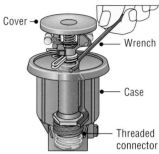

To clear a clogged fixed-head sprayer, lift out debris with the corner of a plastic credit card or other plastic device. Using a metal tool may damage nozzle.

To clean screen under fixed-head nozzle, turn off water. Remove nozzle and lift out screen. If screen has holes or tears, replace it with parts specifically made for your sprinkler brand.

To clean an impact sprinkler head, insert screwdriver between cover and case to dislodge debris. To clean case, pry up cover; remove sprinkler with special wrench.

Replacing a sprinkler head

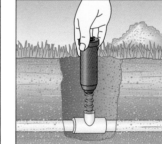

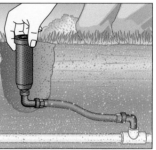

Turn off timer and close shutoff valve; then cut into grass around sprinkler head with spade, and roll back sod. Lift out dirt carefully to avoid damaging sprinkler connection fitting and pipe.

Unscrew faulty sprinkler head from nipple connector. Wrap pipe tape around threads of new head, screw it into place, and tighten joint with wrench. Test before refilling hole and replacing sod.

A flexible pipe fitting allows some variation in placement of sprinkler head. Remove old head. Screw identical new head, threads wrapped with pipe tape, into fitting and set sprinkler cover at ground level.

Patching a leaking pipe

1 Turn off timer and close shutoff valve. Roll back sod from area of leak (above, right). Dig along pipe around leak, piling dirt away from removed sod. Bail water from trench. Cut out damaged PVC pipe with a hacksaw or pipe cutter (p.122).

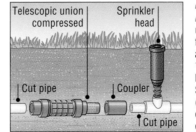

2 Patch pipe with a telescoping PVC union and coupler to fit. Compressed union and coupler should be ½ in. shorter than length of removed pipe. Solvent-weld coupler (p.122) to smaller end of union and to one end of cut pipe.

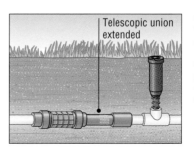

3 Extend larger end of union to overlap other end of cut pipe by 1 in. Solvent-weld the joint. Let set for 30 min. Turn on water to test repair before filling in hole.

389

Yard and workshop tools ▪ Tillers

Garden tillers come with tines in either the front or the rear. Less powerful front-tine tillers (smaller ones have two-cycle engines) can be harder to control than rear-tine models and are best for working previously cultivated soil or cramped areas with limited access. Larger, more efficient rear-tine tillers, powered by four-cycle engines, are designed for heavy-duty work; most can turn over uncultivated ground.

Tiller care. Garden tiller jobs—working compost and fertilizer into the soil, preparing garden beds for planting, or cultivating new ground—continuously expose the machine to dirt, dust, and debris. If not regularly removed, these materials can clog the tiller's air filter and cause engine strain. Use a rag to clean off the tiller's body and tines. Regularly clean the air filter, the air intake screen, the cooling fins, and the muffler (p.367). (Make sure dirt doesn't spill into the carburetor when you're removing the air filter.) Change the engine oil as often as the owner's manual recommends. Follow the general maintenance and repair guidelines for small gasoline-powered engines on pages 356–367. A problem common to all tillers is a loose or faulty drive belt; to adjust or replace the drive belt, see the facing page.

Using the tiller. Test the soil for moisture content before you bring out the tiller in the spring. Scoop up a handful of garden dirt; if you can squeeze it into a ball and then easily poke the ball apart with your finger, it is the right consistency for tilling. Tilling wet, soggy soil creates clumps that later dry into rock-hard clods. If the soil is too dry, the tiller can't dig down deep enough to be beneficial.

Raise the tines to clear the ground when you move the tiller from storage to a work site and back; this protects the tines as well as your walks and lawn. The tines are raised and lowered using the depth bar at the back of the machine. Putting the depth bar in its lowest setting raises the tines to the highest position. The higher you set the depth bar, the deeper the tines will go into the soil. When you first work new ground, make several shallow passes, increasing the depth each time, rather than trying one deep pass.

Before repairing a tiller, disconnect the spark plug cable. Upending a tiller as shown makes some repairs easier; just make sure first that the gas tank is less than half full. After completing a repair, check the oil level before starting the engine.

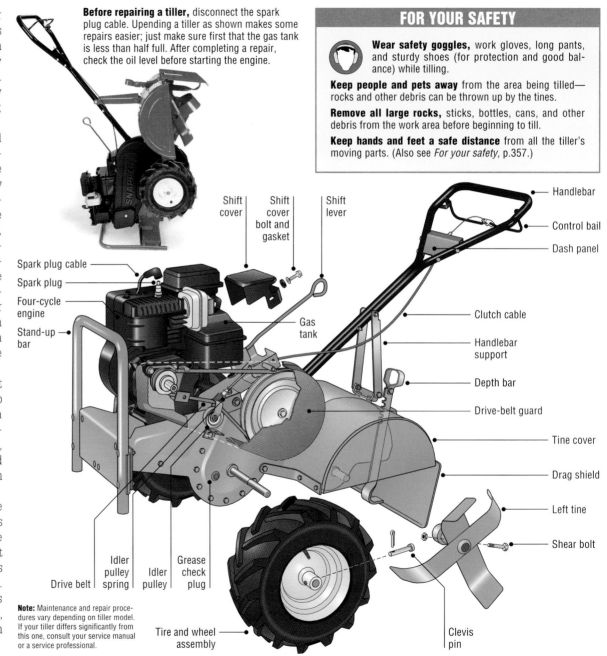

Shift cover | Shift cover bolt and gasket | Shift lever | Handlebar | Control bail | Dash panel | Spark plug cable | Spark plug | Four-cycle engine | Stand-up bar | Gas tank | Clutch cable | Handlebar support | Depth bar | Drive-belt guard | Tine cover | Drag shield | Left tine | Shear bolt | Drive belt | Idler pulley spring | Idler pulley | Grease check plug | Clevis pin | Tire and wheel assembly

Note: Maintenance and repair procedures vary depending on tiller model. If your tiller differs significantly from this one, consult your service manual or a service professional.

390

Troubleshooting

Problem	CAUSE? / Solution ◇
Tiller slows during use	AIR FILTER DIRTY? Clean filter (p.367). ◇
	OIL LEVEL LOW? Check and refill. ◇
	FUEL TANK BREATHING HOLES CLOGGED? Unblock breathing holes (p.367). ◇
	ENGINE FAULTY? See *Troubleshooting engines*, p.359.
	TINE DEPTH SET TOO LOW? Raise tines. ◇
	MUFFLER CLOGGED? Clear muffler (p.367). ◆
	WHEEL SPEED TOO FAST FOR CONDITIONS? Reduce wheel speed. ◇
Engine overheats	COOLING FINS DIRTY? Clean fins (p.358). ◇
	AIR FILTER OR MUFFLER DIRTY? Clean filter or muffler (p.367). ◇
	OIL LEVEL LOW? Fill according to manufacturer's recommendations. ◇
	ENGINE FAULTY? See *Troubleshooting engines*, p.359.
Tines don't rotate	TINES JAMMED OR DAMAGED? Check and clear, or replace (right). ◇
	DRIVE BELT LOOSE? Tighten jam nuts on dash panel or replace belt (below). ◆
	GEARBOX DAMAGED? Have gearbox serviced or replaced with new or rebuilt gearbox from the manufacturer. ◆
	BROKEN SHEAR BOLT? Remove and replace (see exploded view, facing page). ◇
Tiller vibrates excessively	DAMAGED DRIVE BELT? Replace (below). ◇
	MUFFLER CLOGGED? Clear muffler (p.367). ◆
	ENGINE FAULTY? See *Troubleshooting engines*, p.359.
Tiller pulls to one side	UNDERINFLATED TIRES? Check pressure; inflate to correct pressure. ◇
	TINES HITTING OBSTRUCTION (ROCK OR ROOT)? Remove obstruction. ◇

Degree of difficulty: Simple ◇   Average ◆   Complex ◆

Replacing the tines

1 Wearing work gloves, first remove locknut on right shear bolt with socket wrench; then pull out bolt (replace shear bolts along with tines).

2 Slide tine off driveshaft. Clean any dirt or debris off the driveshaft and the surrounding area with a slightly damp cloth.

3 Clean and smooth driveshaft by lightly rubbing it with emery cloth. Lubricate shaft as recommended in your owner's manual.

4 Align new tine as shown; then insert a new shear bolt and tighten locknut. Repeat procedure with left-side tine.

Adjusting and replacing the drive belt

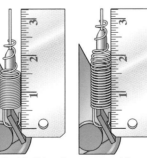
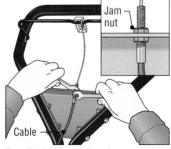
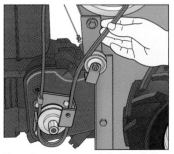

Use pliers to remove cotter pin from clevis pin on left wheel hub (inset). Remove clevis pin and wheel to access drive-belt guard. Guard is easier to remove if tiller is upended (facing page).

Loosen bolts holding drive-belt guard with socket wrench; then remove guard. Inspect drive belt for wear or damage, and replace if necessary (far right); also test belt tension.

To test belt tension, measure idler pulley spring in relaxed position (left). Pull control bail at handle; then measure extended spring (right). Difference in length should be ¼ to ½ in.

To adjust belt tension, loosen and reposition jam nuts at threaded end of cable conduit located at dash panel. Adjust idler pulley spring until desired extension is reached.

To replace a worn or defective belt, loop new belt around first drive pulley, through belt guide, over idler, and around second drive pulley. Reinstall drive-belt guard and wheel assembly.

391

Note: Details of repair and disassembly may vary, depending on the model. If your trimmer differs markedly from the ones shown here and on the facing page, refer to the owner's manual or consult a service professional.

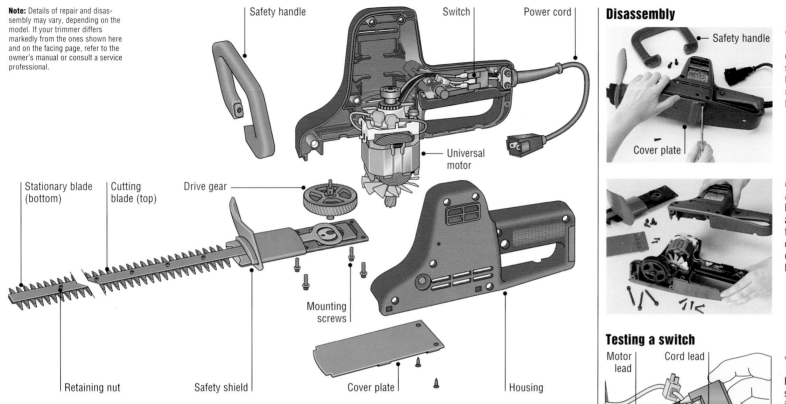

Safety handle

Switch

Power cord

Universal motor

Stationary blade (bottom)

Cutting blade (top)

Drive gear

Mounting screws

Retaining nut

Safety shield

Cover plate

Housing

Hedge trimmers

Designed to shape shrubs and hedges, a hedge trimmer has a stationary blade that catches and holds small branches in its teeth while a reciprocating blade cuts them. Most electric trimmers for home use have universal motors; some heavy-duty trimmers are powered by a small two-cycle gasoline engine (p.357).

To extend the reach of an electric trimmer, plug it into an extension cord that is rated for outdoor use; knot the cords together (left) to keep them from pulling apart.

Before each use, make sure the blade assembly is tightly secured. After each use, unplug the trimmer, wipe off the blades, and spray them with white lithium spray. Run the trimmer for a few seconds to work the lubricant between the blades. Periodically lubricate the gears and reciprocating mechanism with multipurpose grease.

Troubleshooting a hedge trimmer. If the trimmer doesn't cut well, sharpen the cutting blade (facing page); don't sharpen the stationary blade unless it's nicked. Look for loose or worn retaining nuts on the blade assembly; tighten them or replace them with self-locking nuts. If the trimmer fails to start and the problem isn't the power source or extension cord (see *General troubleshooting*, p.144), test the switch as shown at right. If the switch is OK, the motor is the probable culprit (see *General troubleshooting*, p.146).

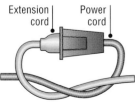

Extension cord

Power cord

Knot the cords for safety.

Disassembly

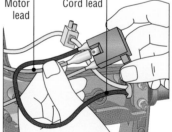

Safety handle

Cover plate

1 Unplug the trimmer. Remove safety handle; place trimmer on its side. Remove screws holding cover plate; then remove screws securing blade assembly.

2 To access internal components, remove housing screws and separate housing halves. To facilitate reassembly, carefully note locations of internal components before you remove them.

Testing a switch

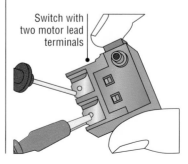

Motor lead

Cord lead

Switch with two motor lead terminals

1 With trimmer unplugged, remove housing and locate switch; note how it fits into unit. Carefully lift out switch. To make testing and reassembly easier, label cord and motor lead terminals on switch before removing leads from switch.

2 Set VOM on RX1. Clip one probe to cord lead terminal; touch other to motor lead terminal. Press switch button; meter should indicate continuity. If switch has more than one motor lead terminal, repeat test; meter should indicate continuity only once. Replace a faulty switch.

Unjamming the blades

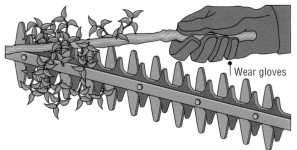

Wear gloves

To remove a twig or branch caught in trimmer teeth, unplug the tool and lay it on a flat surface. Holding the handle of the trimmer to steady it, push out the blockage with a stick. Don't use a screwdriver or another metal tool; metal may damage the blades.

Sharpening a hedge trimmer blade

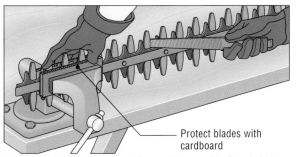

Protect blades with cardboard

Remove blade assembly from trimmer (*Disassembly,* Step 1, facing page). Place blades in a vise. File cutting blade with a double-cut flat file; follow angle of bevel. Unless they are nicked, don't file teeth on stationary blade. Replace blades if teeth are worn or missing.

Grass trimmers

Grass trimmers, or shears, are designed to trim weeds and grass in close areas. They are usually cordless and powered by a rechargeable battery. When a trimmer shows signs of losing power, recharge the battery (see *Cordless tools and appliances,* p.142).

Grass trimmers work in basically the same way as hedge trimmers (facing page): a stationary blade holds the grass while a reciprocating blade cuts it. If grass gets stuck between the blades and jams them, push out the material with a twig or other piece of wood (metal tools will nick the blades). Clean and dry the blades after each use; then lubricate them with white lithium spray. Briefly run the trimmer to work the lubricant between the blades.

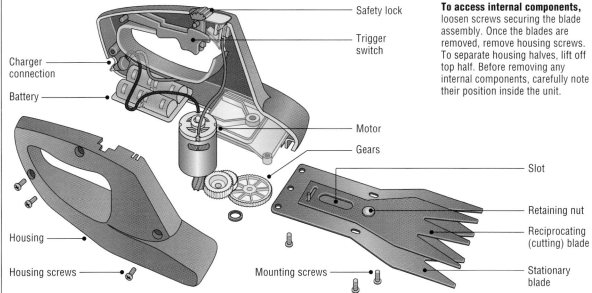

Safety lock

Trigger switch

Charger connection

Battery

Motor

Gears

Slot

Retaining nut

Reciprocating (cutting) blade

Stationary blade

Housing

Housing screws

Mounting screws

To access internal components, loosen screws securing the blade assembly. Once the blades are removed, remove housing screws. To separate housing halves, lift off top half. Before removing any internal components, carefully note their position inside the unit.

Sharpening a grass trimmer blade

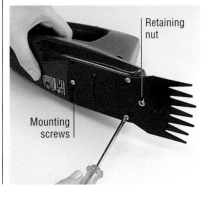

Retaining nut

Mounting screws

1 If the trimmer rips the grass instead of cutting it, the cutting blade needs sharpening. Undo blade mounting screws, and then pull off blade assembly. A loose retaining nut can also interfere with cutting action; tighten it if necessary.

Cutting blade

Stationary blade

2 Clamp blade assembly in vise. Protect blades with two pieces of thick cardboard. Sharpen the cutting blade's teeth with a double-cut flat file (follow direction of original bevel). Don't sharpen stationary blade unless it's nicked.

String trimmers

Unlike heavy-duty trimmers (facing page), which use blades to cut through plant growth, string trimmers slice through vegetation with a short, rapidly spinning length of tough monofilament line. Interchangeable heads allow some models to do the work of heavy-duty trimmers.

String trimmers come in electric, gasoline-powered, and cordless models. Electric trimmers have universal motors (see *General troubleshooting,* p.146); gas-powered models contain two-cycle or four-cycle engines (see *Small engines,*

pp.356–367); battery-powered models have DC motors (see *Cordless tools and appliances,* p.142).

Most problems with string trimmers involve the cutting head. Inspect it regularly for cracks; use only the size of monofilament suggested by the manufacturer; and check to make sure the line isn't tangled.

CAUTION: Before working on any trimmer, unplug an electric model, disconnect the battery pack of a cordless model, or remove the spark plug cable of a gas-powered trimmer.

To access internal components, remove housing screws; pull housing apart. Trigger switch may have its own housing; open it in the same way. On some models, you may have to peel off a label before you can separate the housing.

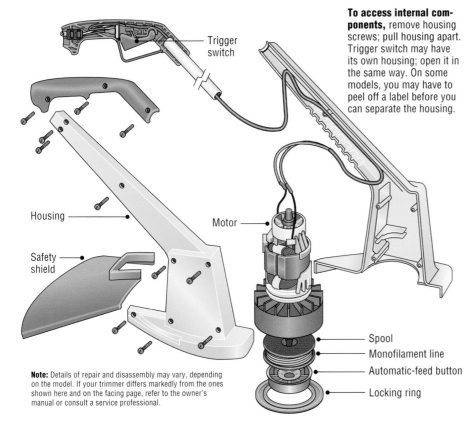

Trigger switch

Housing

Motor

Safety shield

Spool

Monofilament line

Automatic-feed button

Locking ring

Note: Details of repair and disassembly may vary, depending on the model. If your trimmer differs markedly from the ones shown here and on the facing page, refer to the owner's manual or consult a service professional.

Troubleshooting

Problem	CAUSE? / Solution
ALL TRIMMERS: Trimmer doesn't cut	CUTTING HEAD EMPTY? Install new line (facing page), or insert prewound spool (available at home centers and hardware stores). ◇
	CUTTING HEAD DAMAGED? Inspect head; replace any damaged parts. ◇
Line doesn't advance or breaks during use	WRONG LINE USED? Be sure line is correct size (see owner's manual). ◇
	LINE TWISTED OR LOOSE ON SPOOL? Rewind line (Step 4, facing page). ◇
	CUTTING HEAD DIRTY? Open head (Step 1, facing page); wipe clean. ◇
	HEAD OUTLET GUIDE BENT? Reshape guide with pliers; smooth edges with sandpaper. If needed, replace head (Steps 1 to 3, facing page). ◇
ELECTRIC TRIMMERS: Trimmer doesn't work	POWER OFF AT OUTLET? See *General troubleshooting,* p.144.
	FAULTY POWER CORD? See *General troubleshooting,* p.144.
	FAULTY SWITCH? See *Testing a switch,* p.392.
	FAULTY UNIVERSAL MOTOR? See *General troubleshooting,* p.146.
Trimmer overheats or lacks power	EXTENSION CORD WRONG SIZE OR TYPE? Replace extension cord with one rated for outdoor use; be sure its capacity is suitable for trimmer. ◇
	FAULTY UNIVERSAL MOTOR? See *General troubleshooting,* p.146.
GAS TRIMMERS: Trimmer doesn't work	CONTROLS IMPROPERLY SET? Consult owner's manual. ◇
	FAULTY ENGINE? See *Troubleshooting engines,* p.359.
Trimmer stalls or runs intermittently	FUEL SYSTEM FAULTY? See *Fuel lines and tank,* p.367.
	AIR FILTER OR EXHAUST PORT BLOCKED? See *Air filters,* p.367.
	FAULTY ENGINE? See *Troubleshooting engines,* p.359.
Trimmer overheats	MOTOR NEEDS LUBRICATION? See *Periodic maintenance,* p.358.
	COOLING FINS OR AIR PASSAGES BLOCKED? Remove debris. ◇
CORDLESS TRIMMERS: Trimmer doesn't work	FAULTY BATTERY OR CHARGER? See *Cordless tools and appliances,* pp.142–143.

Degree of difficulty: Simple ◇   Average ◆   Complex ◆   Volt-ohm meter required ▣

Installing monofilament line

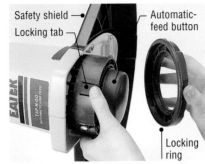

Safety shield
Locking tab
Automatic-feed button
Locking ring

1 Simultaneously press locking tab on side of spool and rotate locking ring counterclockwise. Pull off locking ring and inspect it; replace ring if damaged.

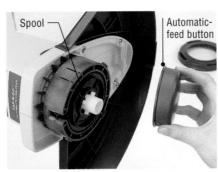

Spool
Automatic-feed button

2 Carefully pull off the automatic-feed button (sometimes called a tap button). Inspect it for cracks and other damage; replace if needed. Brush away any dirt or debris.

3 Press spool down, turn it slightly to release locking tabs, and slide it from hub. Remove spool carefully; some models have a spring beneath it that can pop out.

4 Replace spool with prewound model, or wind new line onto old spool. Fit end of line through hole in spool; it should extend no more than ⅛ in. Wind line in direction of arrow; reinstall spool.

Heavy-duty trimmers

Except for their greater power and bladed cutting heads, heavy-duty trimmers are similar to string trimmers and subject to the same types of problems (see *Troubleshooting* chart, facing page). Some heavy-duty trimmers come with interchangeable heads, allowing you to switch between a bladed head and a monofilament head. (When changing the head, be sure to install the corresponding safety shield.)

Most heavy-duty trimmers run on a two-cycle gasoline engine, although some newer models have a four-cycle engine (see *Small engines,* p.356). As a safety precaution, remember to disconnect the spark plug cable before servicing your trimmer.

Before every use, examine the blade for damage and wear, and make sure it is tightly secured. Discard a cracked or chipped blade immediately; a damaged blade can shatter, sending shards of metal flying. Use only blades recommended by the manufacturer.

To access the internal components of a heavy-duty trimmer, remove the screws securing the housing. The air filter can be reached simply by turning the access knob by hand and lifting the filter housing off. Check filter frequently; clean or replace as needed

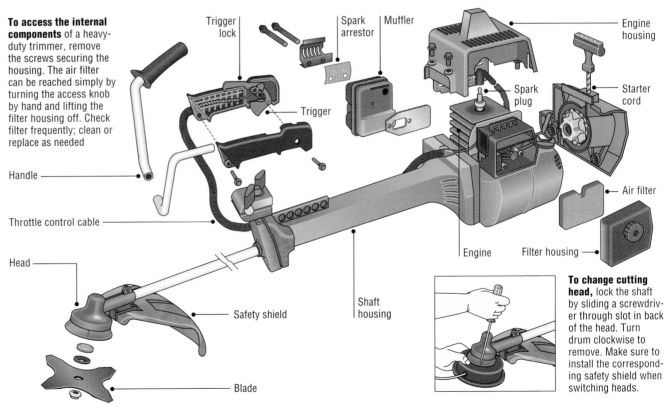

Trigger lock
Spark arrestor
Muffler
Engine housing
Trigger
Spark plug
Starter cord
Handle
Throttle control cable
Air filter
Head
Engine
Filter housing
Safety shield
Shaft housing
Blade

To change cutting head, lock the shaft by sliding a screwdriver through slot in back of the head. Turn drum clockwise to remove. Make sure to install the corresponding safety shield when switching heads.

Using a volt-ohm meter 130
Wires, cords, and plugs 134
How motors work 138

Yard and workshop tools ▪ Portable power tools

Portable power tools are available in hundreds of models for many uses. Despite this diversity, every portable power tool has the same essential components, which work, or fail, in basically the same way. If you can identify and understand those components, you'll know what to expect from them and how to keep them from failing prematurely. With this basic understanding, you'll be able to troubleshoot, maintain, and repair all sorts of portable power tools.

Troubleshooting needn't be intimidating or mysterious. In fact, it is primarily a matter of combining some basic knowledge with your own observations (see *Tips from the pros*, p.140). For example, grinding noises would suggest a mechanical problem, not an electrical one. An acrid smell, on the other hand, might be the result of overheating caused by a power system problem (perhaps a short circuit or a motor that's overheating). The smell of burning wood suggests a damaged or dull accessory (a bit or a blade).

Essential components

The table at right describes seven components common to all power tools. On subsequent pages you'll find troubleshooting information regarding five of the most common power tools.

Housing. The most visible part of any power tool is the *housing*. Though it can be damaged (look for hairline cracks), a more likely problem is that assembly screws have loosened; simply tighten them up. In some instances, you might have to replace deteriorating dust or water seals. A tool's elec-

trical parts must be insulated from the housing and from any exposed metal parts. Metal housings are grounded via the third wire in the power cord; *double-insulated* tools have a nonconducting plastic housing and do not require a grounded cord.

Electrical components. Electrical components include the *power system* and most parts of the *motor* and *controls*. Power cords are subjected to many abuses (see *Circuit faults*, p.128) and can fail where they connect to the tool or to the plug. Burnt or dirty switches and motor brushes, loose connections, and shorted motor windings are all sources of occasional problems. Internal wiring can also be faulty. On cordless tools, power system problems include weak or dead batteries and dirty or corroded electrical contacts.

Mechanical components. Dirt or lack of lubrication commonly causes mechanical components—primarily the *drive system, accessory holders,* and *accessories*—to jam, wear out, or break. Mechanical problems typically occur when the components are subjected to excessive force.

Essential components of portable power tools

Housing		The housing protects both the tool and the user. There are two types: clamshell (see *Drills and drill/drivers*, p.398, and *Vibrating pad sander*, p.399); or a combination of clamshell and stacked (see *Circular saw* and *Saber saw*, p.400).
Power system		Tools are driven either by AC power carried to the tool via a power cord, or by DC power drawn from a rechargeable battery. Internal wiring carries the current through electric controls and then to the motor. Power faults can be in the tool or in the power supply.
Controls		Controls regulate how a tool operates. Electrical controls include variable-speed and multispeed power switches and forward-reverse directional switches. The torque (turning force) setting on a drill and the in-line/orbital lever on a sander are mechanical controls.
Motor		The motor—a universal AC type for corded tools or a DC type for cordless ones—converts electrical energy to mechanical energy (see *How motors work*, p.138). Lubricated bearings or bushings at both ends of the driveshaft prevent wear.
Drive system		The drive system consists of one or more sets of gears that transfer the force of the motor shaft to the accessory holder. The gears are encased to protect them from dirt; they are greased to reduce friction between parts (some plastic gears are self-lubricating).
Accessory holder		An accessory holder, such as the chuck on a drill or the platen assembly on a sander, secures the accessories—drill bit, blade, sandpaper, etc. For the holder to function properly, the accessories must be well secured and properly aligned.
Accessory		Accessories do the work. Because they affect a tool's performance, consider them an integral part of the tool. Always use the proper accessory for the task, and be sure it is sharp, clean, and undamaged. Accessories should suit the brand and model of the tool.

General continuity test

Testing continuity on a fully assembled tool confirms that the electrical path through the cord, switch, and motor is intact. Set a VOM (p.130) on RX100, clip its probes to the tool's plug, and perform the following tests. Operate the switch (reading should be low ohms when switch is on); flex the cord (this should not cause any change); and rotate the motor manually with the switch on (a fluctuating reading suggests bad brushes; an infinity reading suggests an open brush or motor winding).

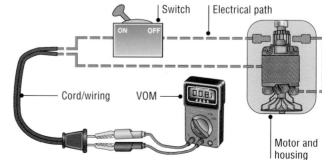

Switch | Electrical path

Cord/wiring   VOM

Motor and housing

Problem areas:

Motor: worn brushes or weak springs; loose wiring; dirty contacts; open motor winding.

Switch: contacts dirty or burnt; wire connections loose.

Cord/wiring: break or short in cord or in internal wiring.

Cordless power tools

The most common cordless tools are drills, screwdrivers, and combination drill/drivers, but cordless versions of many other tools are also available. Most are powered by rechargeable nickel-cadmium (nicad) batteries, usually in self-contained, interchangeable battery packs. To control the speed, more or less voltage is sent to the tool by multispeed or variable-speed switches; forward-reverse switches change the motor's polarity (see *How motors work*, p.138).

Cordless tools require little maintenance. Clean switch and battery contacts by spraying them with contact cleaner or rubbing them with an ink eraser. Lubricate gears and bearings with the lubricants recommended by the tool's manufacturer. A battery and its charger are responsible for most problems with cordless tools (see *Cordless tools and appliances*, p.142). Check for a faulty battery or charger. A charger's output voltage should be slightly higher than the tool's operating voltage.

USE AND CARE

Maintain any power tool regularly to keep it working smoothly, to protect yourself from injury, and to prevent costly breakdowns.

Clean tools after use with a brush or cloth.

Use an air compressor to clean tools subject to excessive dust (such as sanders). Blow air into the air *intake* while the motor is running.

Replace motor brushes as needed (p.146).

Clean the housing if you remove it during repairs. Use a cloth dampened with a mild nonammonia detergent-and-water solution. Ammonia cleansers may damage plastic.

Lubricate a tool with grease after cleaning it's gears (see manual). Lubricate sleeve bearings (p.137) with 10-, 20- or 30-weight nondetergent motor oil (see owner's manual).

To prevent rust, apply a light oil film to exposed metal parts, especially if the tool will be stored in a garage or basement.

If the battery of a cordless tool gets hot, allow it to cool before recharging it.

After 15 hours of use, and on older tools especially, add oil to any oiling holes or lubricating pads (see owner's manual for type).

Troubleshooting

Problem	CAUSE? / Solution
Motor won't run	POWER OFF / FAULTY CORD? See *General troubleshooting*, p.144.
	SWITCH(ES) FAULTY? First, try to determine which switch is faulty by operating them all. Then test switch (see *General troubleshooting*, p.145). ◆
	BRUSHES DIRTY, WORN, OR DAMAGED? Inspect; clean or replace as needed (see *General troubleshooting*, p.146). ◆
	MOTOR DIRTY? Disassemble tool and clean motor. ◆
	COMMUTATOR OR ROTOR FAULTY? Unplug tool; turn rotor; then try tool again. If tool then works, commutator or rotor is faulty. Test and service motor (see *General troubleshooting*, p.146) or replace tool. ◆ ▨
	CONNECTING WIRING BROKEN? Inspect and rewire (see *Wires, cords, and plugs*, p.134). ◆
	BATTERIES DEAD? *(Cordless tools only)* Recharge or replace (p.142). ◇
	BATTERY CONTACTS DIRTY? *(Cordless tools only)* Clean contacts (p.143). ◇
Motor hums or runs slowly	GEARS JAMMED OR BROKEN? Clear jam; replace damaged parts. ◆
	BEARINGS DRY OR FROZEN? Lubricate (see *Cleaning and lubrication*, p.137). ◆
	ROTOR STRIKING FIELD COIL? Check motor mounting. If shaft is bent, replace motor if economical; otherwise replace tool. ◆
	COOLING FAN BENT? Inspect; straighten or replace fan. ◆
	FIELD COIL SHORTED? Test field coil (see *General troubleshooting*, p.146); replace defective motor if economical, otherwise replace tool. ◆ ▨
	BRUSHES OR ARMATURE DIRTY? Access motor and brush off carbon dust. ◆
	BATTERIES WEAK? *(Cordless tools only)* Charge batteries (p.142). ◇

Problem	CAUSE? / Solution
Motor overheats or smokes	BEARINGS / GEARS DAMAGED, DRY, OR FOULED? Clean, lubricate, or replace as needed (see *Cleaning and lubrication*, p.137). ◆
	FIELD COIL SHORTED? See *Motor hums or runs slowly*, left.
	AIR VENT HOLES CLOGGED? Brush or blow off dust; remove obstructions. ◇
	EXCESSIVE LOAD? Apply less force; be sure accessory is sharp. ◇
Motor sparks excessively, stops, or smokes/smells	FIELD COIL SHORTED? See *Motor hums or runs slowly*, left.
	BRUSHES DIRTY, WORN, OR DAMAGED ? See *Motor won't run*, left.
	TOOL OR MOTOR DIRTY? Disassemble to clean tool and motor. ◆
	COMMUTATOR OR ROTOR FAULTY? See *Motor won't run*, left.
	BRUSH SPRING FAULTY? Stretch a weak spring or replace it. Replace brushes as well if part of spring assembly (see *General troubleshooting*, p.146). ◇
	OIL ON COMMUTATOR? Access motor; clean commutator with degreaser. ◆
Tool shocks user	GROUND FAULT? Disassemble tool to inspect for damaged wiring insulation or loose connections; service motor (see *General troubleshooting*, p.146). If tool is wet, disassemble and allow parts to dry. ◆
Tool is unusually noisy	MOTOR SHAFT BENT? If bent, replace motor if economical, or replace tool. ◆
	PARTS LOOSE? Tighten fasteners; secure with thread-locking adhesive (p.18). ◆
	BEARINGS WORN? Disassemble tool and replace worn bearings. ◆
	COMMUTATOR OR ROTOR FAULTY? See *Motor won't run*, left.
	BEARINGS DRY? Lubricate bearings (see *Cleaning and lubrication*, p.137).
	DEFECTIVE MOTOR? Service motor (see *General troubleshooting*, p.146). ◆

Degree of difficulty: Simple ◇   Average ◆   Complex ◆   Volt-ohm meter required: ▨

Yard and workshop tools ▪ Portable power tools

Drills and drill/drivers

A wide range of accessories (bits, sanding discs and drums, pumps, etc.) makes the electric drill one of the most versatile of power tools. An electric drill typically includes a variable-speed switch and a reversing switch that allows the tool to drive and remove screws. A drill/driver is similar to a drill but includes a clutch that disengages the motor at a preset torque.

Cordless drills that operate on 7.2 volts or less, as well as older models, may have integral batteries. More powerful tools (9-volt and above) come with interchangeable battery packs and chargers (right). Some cordless drills and drill/drivers have a safety switch that prevents you from turning the tool on accidentally.

Troubleshooting. A drill is usually the most heavily used power tool in the home or workshop. Although it's subject to the same problems as other tools—faulty cords and switches, worn brushes, bearings, and gears, and burnt

Charger and battery

motors—it may require repair or maintenance more often because of frequent and often demanding use.

The accessory holder on a drill—its chuck—secures a drill bit or other device. Cordless drills and smaller corded models may have keyless chucks, but many heavy-duty tasks require the tight grip only a keyed chuck can provide. Turn the key in each of the three holes for an even, secure fit. If the chuck doesn't tighten, the assembly may be rusted, jammed, or bent, or the chuck fingers may be broken. Wobbling or snapped bits and irregularly shaped holes may indicate a worn chuck. Replace a damaged or worn chuck (facing page). Chucks on newer drills are typically threaded onto the driveshaft. Older drills may have a tapered chuck that must be pried off with a pair of opposing steel wedges. Chucks on all reversing models (and a few non-reversing ones) are secured with a left-handed retaining screw.

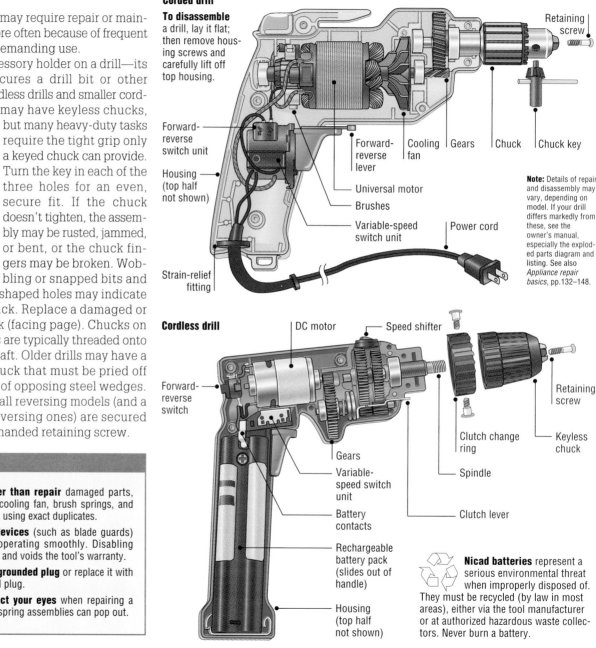

Corded drill

To disassemble a drill, lay it flat; then remove housing screws and carefully lift off top housing.

- Forward-reverse switch unit
- Housing (top half not shown)
- Strain-relief fitting
- Forward-reverse lever
- Cooling fan
- Gears
- Chuck
- Chuck key
- Retaining screw
- Universal motor
- Brushes
- Variable-speed switch unit
- Power cord

Note: Details of repair and disassembly may vary, depending on model. If your drill differs markedly from these, see the owner's manual, especially the exploded parts diagram and listing. See also *Appliance repair basics,* pp.132–148.

Cordless drill

- DC motor
- Speed shifter
- Forward-reverse switch
- Gears
- Variable-speed switch unit
- Battery contacts
- Rechargeable battery pack (slides out of handle)
- Housing (top half not shown)
- Clutch change ring
- Spindle
- Clutch lever
- Retaining screw
- Keyless chuck

Nicad batteries represent a serious environmental threat when improperly disposed of. They must be recycled (by law in most areas), either via the tool manufacturer or at authorized hazardous waste collectors. Never burn a battery.

FOR YOUR SAFETY

Read the owner's manual before attempting to service any power tool.

Never operate a corded power tool while standing on a damp or wet surface.

Disconnect the power cord (or remove the battery) before fixing a tool or changing accessories. Turn the switch off before plugging a tool in.

Test a metal-housed tool for continuity before using it after disassembly (p.396).

Replace rather than repair damaged parts, especially the cooling fan, brush springs, and internal wiring, using exact duplicates.

Keep safety devices (such as blade guards) in place and operating smoothly. Disabling them is unsafe and voids the tool's warranty.

Never alter a grounded plug or replace it with an ungrounded plug.

 Protect your eyes when repairing a tool; spring assemblies can pop out.

Drill repairs

To remove chuck, open jaw and remove left-hand retaining screw (inset). Lock hex wrench in chuck and tap it sharply, usually counterclockwise, with mallet. Unscrew chuck by hand.

Regrease disassembled gears with excess grease scooped from gear case. Replace dry or dirty grease, using white lithium grease (p.137) or packets available from the manufacturer.

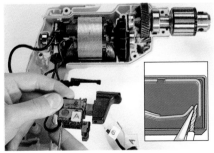

To replace a switch, tag and diagram wires. To remove push-in wire (inset), insert awl tip and press spring to release wire. Some switches may be pried open, but reassembly can be tricky.

Vibrating pad sander

Vibrating pad sanders are usually defined by the size of sandpaper they accept—half-, third-, quarter- and sixth-sheet sanders are common. Better models have lever-controlled dual action, sanding *in-line* to reduce scratching or *orbitally* for faster cutting.

Troubleshooting. In addition to the problems common to all power tools (see *Troubleshooting portable power tools,* p.397), sanders are vulnerable to fine dust; switch and brush failure caused by dust is particularly common.

(Switches may be sealed in a plastic boot for protection.) Clean a sander after every use, preferably by blowing out dust with compressed air. Remove the platen as needed to clean it (right).

Most sanders have permanently lubricated bearings. Clean and grease open bearings if they get dirty. Some sanders have oiling ports, which require a few drops of light oil after every 15 hours of use. If the motor hums but the pad doesn't vibrate, a jammed helical gear assembly is the likely culprit.

To disassemble tool, remove housing screws; lay tool flat and carefully lift off top housing. To remove platen, remove platen screws.

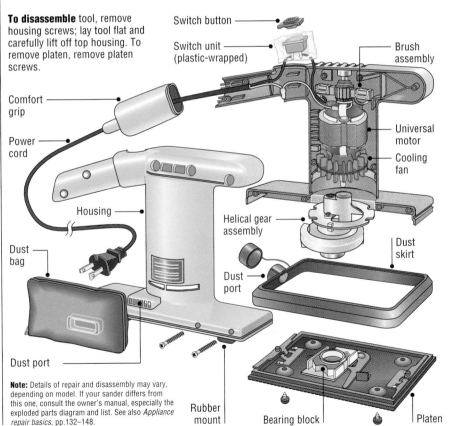

- Switch button
- Switch unit (plastic-wrapped)
- Brush assembly
- Comfort grip
- Power cord
- Universal motor
- Cooling fan
- Housing
- Helical gear assembly
- Dust skirt
- Dust bag
- Dust port
- Dust port
- Rubber mount
- Bearing block
- Platen

Note: Details of repair and disassembly may vary, depending on model. If your sander differs from this one, consult the owner's manual, especially the exploded parts diagram and list. See also *Appliance repair basics,* pp.132–148.

Cleaning the platen

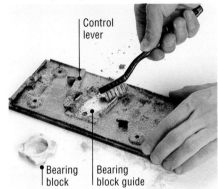

- Control lever
- Bearing block
- Bearing block guide

Clean caked dust from platen, especially around bearing block guide and orbital/in-line control lever. Grease cleaned guide sparingly.

TIPS FROM THE PROS

Cover your work surface with a cloth so small parts won't bounce off or roll away.

To minimize contamination of a tool's internal parts, blow any dust off before beginning disassembly.

For an extensive disassembly, follow a parts list and an exploded diagram (or draw your own) as you disassemble.

Lay a tool flat on your workbench when removing its housing. This helps to keep the gears and other parts from falling out.

Organize fasteners as you remove them by grouping them by component or by type of fastener. This makes reassembly much easier. Be particularly vigilant when removing housing fasteners because they may be of different sizes.

To avoid damaging brushes and brush holders, remove motor brushes as soon as they become accessible, and before disassembling the motor.

Use removable thread-locking compound for metal-to-metal fasteners, especially if you notice that it was used during manufacturing (evidenced by dabs of colored material on a fastener's threads).

Circular saw

Note: Details of disassembly and repair may vary, depending on the model. If your saw differs from this one, consult the owner's manual. See also *Appliance repair basics,* pp.132–148.

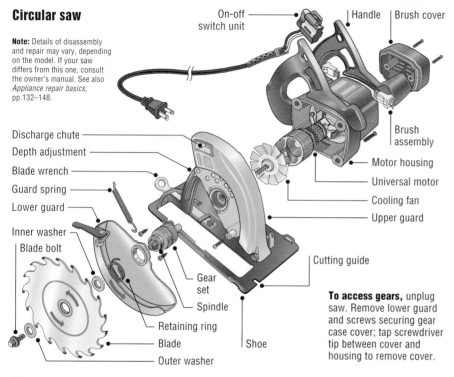

On-off switch unit
Handle
Brush cover
Discharge chute
Depth adjustment
Blade wrench
Guard spring
Lower guard
Inner washer
Blade bolt
Brush assembly
Motor housing
Universal motor
Cooling fan
Upper guard
Gear set
Spindle
Retaining ring
Blade
Outer washer
Shoe
Cutting guide

To access gears, unplug saw. Remove lower guard and screws securing gear case cover; tap screwdriver tip between cover and housing to remove cover.

Circular saws are available in sizes defined by the maximum blade size the saw accepts (7¼-inch is the most common). Saws are prone to the same problems afflicting other power tools. In addition, however, the blade guard is a critical safety feature that must be maintained in perfect order. The lower guard may have to be removed (right) for a thorough cleaning. Remove resin from the blade guards with a commercial blade cleaner or a solvent such as turpentine, or use oven cleaner and a brush. Lubricate the lower guard at its hub. Keep saw blades sharp, and clean them with the same solvents.

Gaining access. To reach the motor for service, unplug the saw. Remove the brush cover, brushes, and the screws that secure the motor housing to the guard assembly. With the saw resting on its blade side, slowly lift the housing and note the position of any washers.

Servicing the blade guard

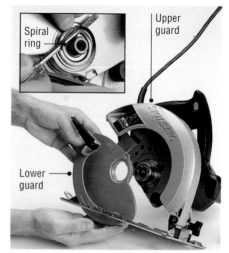

Spiral ring
Upper guard
Lower guard

To remove lower guard, unplug saw and remove blade. Remove the inner washer and guard retraction spring; pry off spiral ring (inset) with small screwdriver (split in ring may be difficult to see); place finger over ring to keep it from flying away. Pull off guard; clean and lubricate with silicone spray. Reassemble guard.

Saber saw

Saber saws (sometimes called jigsaws) make straight or curved cuts in wood, metal, tile, and many other materials depending on the blade used. Most saber saws have a variable-speed switch, and some also have a mechanical switch or lever that adjusts the cutting action of the blade.

In addition to the standard maintenance required for other power tools, pay particular attention to cleaning and lubricating the rear motor bearing (the front bearing is sealed). You should also wipe or scrape off caked grease from inside the shaft assembly; then relubricate. Adjust the blade guide so that it supports the blade without binding.

Note: Details may vary. If your saw differs from this one, consult the owner's manual. See also *Appliance repair basics,* pp.132–148.

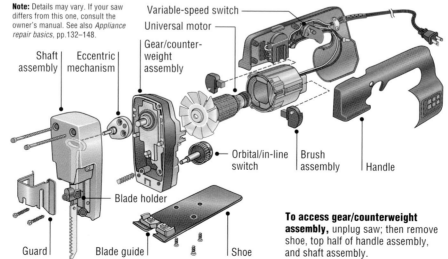

Shaft assembly
Eccentric mechanism
Variable-speed switch
Universal motor
Gear/counterweight assembly
Orbital/in-line switch
Brush assembly
Handle
Blade holder
Guard
Blade guide
Shoe

To access gear/counterweight assembly, unplug saw; then remove shoe, top half of handle assembly, and shaft assembly.

Servicing the gears

To service the gears and counterweight assembly, position a screwdriver across the face of the eccentric mechanism to keep it from rotating as you loosen the screws securing it. Thread-locking compound prevents screws from vibrating loose.

Sports and recreation gear

Whether you are a biker, a fisherman, a skier, or a camper, nothing spoils an outing more than faulty equipment. Your safety can also be threatened, as when a boat leaks or a swimming pool contains murky water. In most cases, performing the regular maintenance chores outlined in the following pages will keep your sports and recreation gear in good working order. But wear and tear can take a toll. Bicycle tires go flat and canoe hulls get dented. Gas grill connections work loose. Springs wear out on fishing reels. Ski bases get gouged by rocks, and zippers on sleeping bags break. These are among the many mishaps that you can set right by following the step-by-step instructions found throughout this section.

Sports and recreation gear ▪ Bicycles

Mountain bike

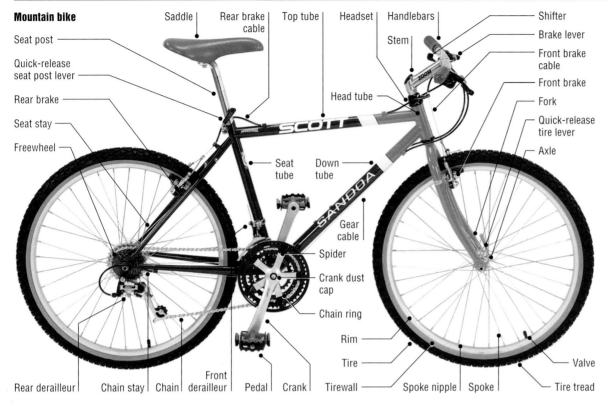

Saddle
Rear brake cable
Top tube
Headset
Handlebars
Stem
Shifter
Brake lever
Front brake cable
Front brake
Fork
Quick-release tire lever
Axle

Seat post
Quick-release seat post lever
Rear brake
Seat stay
Freewheel

Head tube

Seat tube
Down tube

Gear cable
Spider
Crank dust cap
Chain ring

Rim
Tire
Valve

Rear derailleur
Chain stay
Chain
Front derailleur
Pedal
Crank
Tirewall
Spoke nipple
Spoke
Tire tread

Types of bikes

Designed for off-road riding in the California mountains, mountain bikes, or all-terrain bikes (ATB's), like the one shown above, have become best-sellers in North America. Its sturdy frame, knobby tires, straight handlebars, and wide padded seat make the mountain bike a comfortable vehicle for traveling over bumpy country lanes and urban potholes. The traditional road bike (left), with its lighter frame, thin tires, drop handlebars, and narrow seat, is better suited for pure speed or long trips

Road bike

on smoothly paved roads. Hybrid bicycles combine the lightweight materials and some of the efficiency of a road bike with the durability and comfort of a mountain bike. All three types of bicycle are available with as many as 24 speeds for easy pedaling over any kind of topography.

Three-speed bikes with enclosed hub gears have given way to a new breed of bicycles equipped with a sophisticated system of derailleurs, freewheels, and chain rings (p.407) that allows the bike to run seamlessly through a range of gear combinations at the touch of a precision index shifter. Single-speed bicycles with pedal-controlled coaster brakes are still available in the juvenile market; this continues to be the first two-wheeler most children learn to ride.

Fitting a bike

Good fit makes a bike work and feel better. Standing over the frame, the distance between your crotch and the top tube should be 3 inches on a mountain bike, 2 inches on a hybrid, and 1 inch on a road bike.

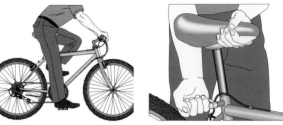

To find the correct saddle height, sit on the bike in your stocking feet. Your heel should rest on the pedal when your leg is extended. To raise or lower seat, loosen seat post nut or quick-release lever. Adjust seat, making sure you don't raise it above 2½-in. safety mark; tighten nut or lever.

To find the best saddle position, sit on the bike with cranks horizontal. With the seat parallel to the ground, a plumb line from your kneecap should bisect the forward pedal axle. Loosen seat screw to adjust tilt or to move seat forward or back. Retighten screw.

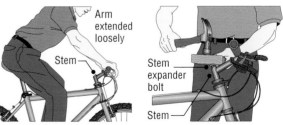

Arm extended loosely
Stem
Stem expander bolt
Stem

For comfortable handlebar height, top of stem should be 1 to 3 in. below saddle. To adjust height, loosen stem expander bolt 3 or 4 turns with hex wrench. Place wood block on bolt head and tap it with a hammer until bolt head is flush with stem. This loosens wedge inside stem, allowing you to raise or lower handlebars. Retighten bolt.

Periodic checks

Riding over rough terrain—whether urban or off-road—is tough on a bike. To minimize problems and to ensure a safe ride, regularly perform the tests and make the adjustments described below.

Press down on the headset with front brake engaged, and roll wheel back and forth. If you hear a clicking noise, tighten locknut and top cup on headset (p.404).

To test headset bearings, pick up front of bike and turn the handlebars. If the motion is rough, grease the bearings or replace them (p.404).

To check front hub, grasp frame and wheel. Try moving wheel from side to side. A click means axle bearings are loose. Have bike repaired professionally.

Check back hub by trying to move back wheel from side to side. If you feel bearings click, they're too loose. Have bike repaired professionally.

Spin pedals and cranks; grinding or clicking indicates worn pedal bearings or loose bottom bracket bearings. Both repairs require bike shop equipment.

Align cranks horizontally and push down hard. If there is any movement, tighten crank mounting bolts. Models vary; consult your owner's manual.

Bicycle-repair tools

A chain tool enables you to push out a link pin and remove a bike chain for servicing.

A chain washer cleans a chain while it is still on the bike.

A third hand is a stiff wire used to hold brakes closed when replacing or adjusting a cable.

A chain whip aids in removing the freewheel cassette.

A freewheel remover slides onto the axle to loosen the compression-fit freewheel.

A spoke key adjusts and removes spokes. It can be round or horseshoe-shaped.

A tire lever helps work a tire off the rim. Used together, three are usually sufficient.

A pressure gauge tells you if your tires are properly inflated.

A biodegradable cleaner and a polish keep bike exterior shining.

A small adjustable wrench fits many bike nut sizes.

A multi tool contains an array of the most commonly used hex-head wrenches needed for bike maintenance.

A foot pump is the most efficient way to inflate tires.

Regular maintenance and lubrication (p.404) will prolong the life of your bike and can prevent mishaps on the road. You can make most adjustments yourself. Some repairs, however, such as truing a wheel after an accident, straightening a bent wheel, or calibrating the tension on the wheel spokes, require special equipment available only at a good bicycle shop.

General care. Store your bike in a dry place to discourage rust. Never lay a bike on its right side; you could damage the freewheel, chain rings, and derailleurs or throw them out of alignment. Use a rack to transport your bike by car, rather than laying it in the back cargo area. Be careful with gas-station air pumps; they can blow out the tube on a badly seated tire.

Before every ride, make sure the wheels are securely attached, the tires are inflated to the pressure listed on the tirewalls, and the brakes are operating properly. Check that the wheels are straight and have no loose spokes. Bounce the bike and listen for the rattle of loose nuts or bolts. Tighten fasteners by tool size. Use a 4-millimeter wrench to tighten all the 4-millimeter nuts and bolts; then change to a 5-millimeter wrench. (Consult the owner's manual for instructions; overtightening nuts and bolts can damage some alloys.) Secure bags and panniers; nothing should hang down that could catch in the spokes.

After every ride, brush mud and debris off the tires. Wipe dirt and moisture off the frame, seat, handlebars, cranks, and pedals with a soft cloth. If the chain is wet, dry it and lubricate it lightly (p.404). If the bike is extremely muddy, wash it with hot soapy water and a sponge. Rinse and towel off the bike; lubricate affected areas. Don't use a high-pressure washer to clean the bike; a strong blast in the wrong direction could drive water and dirt into a set of bearings, causing considerable damage.

Every month, lubricate the bike (p.404). Check for loose bearings and mounting screws and worn cables and brake pads.

The headset

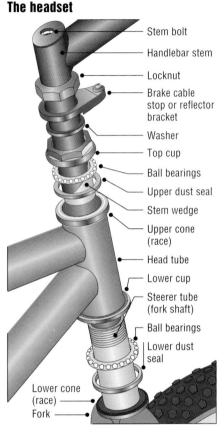

- Stem bolt
- Handlebar stem
- Locknut
- Brake cable stop or reflector bracket
- Washer
- Top cup
- Ball bearings
- Upper dust seal
- Stem wedge
- Upper cone (race)
- Head tube
- Lower cup
- Steerer tube (fork shaft)
- Ball bearings
- Lower dust seal
- Lower cone (race)
- Fork

A headset takes a lot of impact stress as you ride your bike. Service it once a year or whenever the fork binds or clicks as you steer.

Using a bike stand

A good stand holds the back wheel above the floor for repairs. Buy a folding model (left), or use a bench vise to keep the bike at a comfortable working height.

Cleaning and lubricating the headset

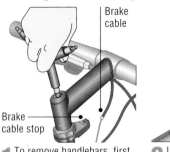
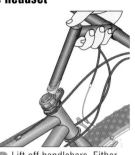

Brake cable

Brake cable stop

1 To remove handlebars, first lift brake cable out of stop. Loosen stem bolt with wrench; tap with hammer and wood block (p.402) to free stem.

2 Lift off handlebars. Either disconnect the brake and gear cables to free handlebars or rest handlebars on frame without straining cables.

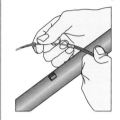

Locknut
Top cup

3 Loosen locknut at top of headset with a wrench. If locknut won't turn, hold top cup beneath it steady with second wrench while you turn first one.

4 Lift off locknut, cable stop or reflector bracket (if any), washer, top cup, bearings (they may be loose or caged), and dust seal. Lay out in order.

5 Check all parts for wear. Clean metal parts with solvent. Replace pitted or flattened bearings with a new set of same number and size.

6 Lift head tube off steerer tube and fork to get access to bottom bearings. Clean metal parts with solvent. Replace bearings and misshapen or pitted parts.

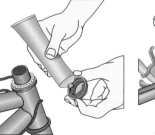

7 After applying grease to lower cup, slip head tube back over steerer tube, taking care not to dislodge new bottom bearings.

8 Pack new bicycle grease into top cup. Put bearings and any dust seals back in place on steerer tube. Replace top cup, washer, and cable stop.

9 Hand-tighten top cup over bearings. Reverse a quarter turn and hold in position with a wrench. Then tighten locknut over top cup with wrench.

Other lubrication points

Remove brake and gear cables from their bolts and pull them out of housings. Rub cables with grease; then slip them back into housings.

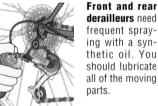

Lubricate brake pivot points on each arm with synthetic oil, such as Finish Line or Tri-Flow. Keep lubricant off brake pads and wheel rims.

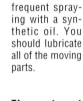

Front and rear derailleurs need frequent spraying with a synthetic oil. You should lubricate all of the moving parts.

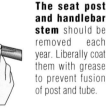

The seat post and handlebar stem should be removed each year. Liberally coat them with grease to prevent fusion of post and tube.

A chain should be lubricated with a synthetic oil as you turn the crank backward. Wipe up excess oil or it will attract dirt. Keep oil off rim.

Bicycles / wheels

A bike's wheels and tires are subject to more wear and tear than any other part. For comfort and speed—and to ensure maximum tire longevity—check the tire pressure often; it should match the pressure imprinted on the side of the tires. Underinflated tires cause more damage to wheels than potholes do; a properly inflated tire protects the rim and is less likely to suffer punctures.

A Presta valve (left) has a nut that must be loosened before inflation; a Schraeder valve (right) resembles a car tire valve.

There are two types of tire valves (left), so make sure the pump you carry matches the valve on your tire. Keep the tires clean and free of materials that might cause a puncture. Loose spokes also threaten tires. Use a spoke key to tighten them evenly all around (this is a skill you should practice at a bicycle shop).

Fixing a flat tire

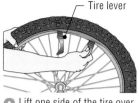

Tire lever

1 Remove wheel (below) and let out the rest of the air. Unscrew a Presta valve and push it in; use a pen or other small instrument to release air from a Schraeder valve.

2 Lift one side of the tire over the rim with your hands, or use tire levers to carefully pry one tirewall off the rim. Be careful not to puncture the tire or the inner tube.

3 Lift the valve out through the valve hole and remove the inner tube. Look for the cause of the puncture inside the tire. Remove glass or a nail; tape a protruding spoke nipple.

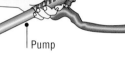

Pump

Bead

4 Patch tube (far right) or unpack a replacement tube. To prevent wrinkles and creases, partially inflate new or fixed tube before installing it in tire.

5 Press valve through valve hole in rim, and tuck rest of tube into the tire. Deflate tube slightly before you begin tucking tire edge back into the rim with your thumbs.

6 You may have to reach across the wheel and yank the last few inches into place. Reinflate tube slowly, and check that the tire bead seats properly around the rim (inset).

Patching a tube

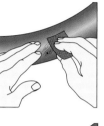

Find the puncture hole if you can, and mark it. If you can't locate it right away, put the tube in water: the leak is where the bubbles come out.

Dry the area and clean it with the abrasive in your kit. Apply a light, even coat of the adhesive. Let it dry until it becomes tacky (about 5 min.), or follow kit instructions.

Peel patch backing and apply patch, sticky side down, to glued area. (Your kit's instructions may differ slightly.) Smooth firmly from middle out. Wait 5 min. to reinflate and test tube.

Removing the front wheel

1 Release front brake by depressing the arm and taking out the cable nipple as shown. If your bike has a different release mechanism, check the owner's manual for directions.

2 If your bike has a quick-release lever, flip it to the open position. You may then have to unscrew it 4 to 6 times to completely release the wheel.

3 If your bicycle has axle nuts, loosen them equally on both sides without removing them completely.

4 Holding the handlebars in one hand, slip the front wheel free of the fork slots with the other hand. Reverse these procedures to install the front wheel.

Removing the rear wheel

1 Shift gears so that the chain rests on the smallest chain ring and the smallest cog of the freewheel. Lift the chain off the freewheel.

2 Loosen the back brake by depressing the brake arm and removing the cable nipple. (Release mechanisms differ depending on bike model; check your owner's manual.)

3 Flip the quick-release lever on the rear hub to the open position, and unscrew if necessary. If your bike has axle nuts, loosen them equally on both sides.

4 Bracing the bike by the seat with one hand, give the back wheel a sharp rap with your other hand to release it from the frame. Guide the wheel down and out, avoiding the chain.

The brakes are your bike's main safety feature; maintaining them properly, with the brake pads correctly positioned on the wheel rim, is essential. The front brake is usually cabled to the lever on the left handlebar, the back brake to the lever on the right handlebar. (Left-handed people often prefer to reverse this lever placement.) Position the brake levers so that you can grip them easily with two fingers. When squeezed, the levers shouldn't touch the handlebars. Replace frayed or kinked cables (below) with cables of similar weight and material.

To determine the condition of the brake pads, check the wear indicators, such as notches or grooves. When these indicators start to disappear, replace the pads.

The cantilever brake

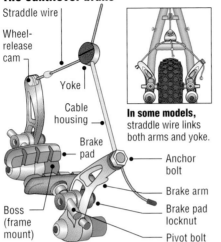

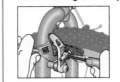

In some models, straddle wire links both arms and yoke.

- Straddle wire
- Wheel-release cam
- Yoke
- Cable housing
- Brake pad
- Anchor bolt
- Brake arm
- Brake pad locknut
- Boss (frame mount)
- Pivot bolt

Cantilever brakes have two arms mounted on pivot bolts. One arm is linked to brake cable, the other to a straddle wire. Squeezing brake lever draws arms up, forcing brake pads against rim.

Replacing a brake cable

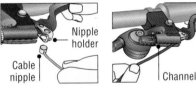

- Nipple holder
- Cable nipple
- Channel

To remove cable, loosen anchor bolt and adjuster screw, if any, at wheel (see brake drawings at right and above right). Pull cable out of housing, stops, and brake lever. Start new cable by securing nipple in holder and feeding cable into lever channel.

- Cable stop

Grease new cable, thread it through housing, and follow stops along bike frame to brake. Thread cable through yoke of cantilever brake and into anchor bolt. On side-pull brake, housing end goes into adjuster screw, cable end into anchor bolt.

The side-pull brake

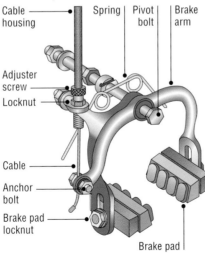

- Cable housing
- Spring
- Pivot bolt
- Brake arm
- Adjuster screw
- Locknut
- Cable
- Anchor bolt
- Brake pad locknut
- Brake pad

On side-pull brakes, squeezing the brake lever raises one brake arm, forcing the brake pad against the rim. Tension between the anchor bolt and the locknut makes the other arm—and pad—move.

Positioning brake pads

To position brake pads, loosen pad locknuts. Set each pad ⅛ in. from rim, toed with front closer to rim; retighten nut.

Squeeze brake lever to test if pads grab the center of the tire rim. A brake that squeaks may not be toed properly.

Adjusting cantilever brakes

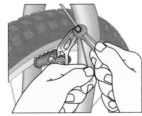
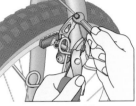

1 To adjust tautness of brakes, first loosen anchor bolt holding brake cable.

2 Loop a third-hand tool over brake pad ends to hold brake pads in place on tire rims.

3 Pull cable taut while you tighten anchor bolt. Remove third hand; test brake.

Adjusting side-pull brakes

1 To tighten cable, first try hand-turning adjuster screw clockwise. For more effect, loosen the anchor bolt.

2 Apply third-hand tool to hold brakes firmly on tire rim. Rings on either side of third hand fit over brake pad locknuts.

3 Pull lower end of cable taut through anchor bolt with pliers. Tighten anchor bolt.

4 Release third-hand tool. If brake pads remain closed, loosen cable tension slightly.

You can also adjust brakes by loosening pad locknut and repositioning pad (see top of page).

5 Center adjusted brake over wheel by tapping spring with screwdriver and hammer.

Bicycles / gears

Most modern bicycles feature 10 to 24 speeds. This variety is achieved by a rear freewheel cluster of five to eight cogs combined with a front cluster of two or three chain rings. Connected by cable to the shifter on the left side of the handlebars or frame, the front derailleur shifts the chain from one chain ring to another. The rear derailleur, controlled by a similar shifter on the right side of the bike, moves the chain from cog to cog on the freewheel.

Shifter levers come in a variety of designs (see right) and two basic types. A friction shift lever allows you to feel your way from one gear to another. Index shifters (which are sometimes made to also operate with friction) shift gears automatically, clicking from gear to gear. (Most bicycles made after 1987 are equipped with index shifters.)

A derailleur that fails to operate smoothly or that causes the chain to jump gears requires immediate attention. Use the tension adjusters on the shifter and the derailleur to tighten or loosen the cable. Or you can adjust the cable at the anchor bolts on the derailleurs. Replace worn or damaged cables (see below).

Shifters

Down-tube shifters, used on road bikes, are either clamped to the bike's frame or mounted on soldered (braze-on) studs called bosses.

Adjusting the front derailleur

The front derailleur cage should be positioned so that it is ⅛ in. above, and parallel to, the largest chain ring. Use a wrench to loosen and tighten clamp bolts that hold derailleur in position.

To tighten a cable, shift chain to smallest chain ring. Then loosen the cable anchor bolt. Pull the cable taut with pliers and tighten the bolt.

To set derailleur, shift chain onto large chain ring. Position cage so that it clears the chain without forcing it to override chain-ring sprockets. Tighten high gear screw. Move chain to smallest chain ring and repeat process with low gear screw.

High gear screw

Low gear screw

Anatomy of a rear derailleur

A rear derailleur serves three functions: It holds the chain in position; at a signal from the shifter, it moves the chain from cog to cog on the freewheel; and it keeps the chain taut. Two pulleys in the spring-loaded cage guide the chain and control its tension.

Positioning the rear derailleur

High screw

1 Place right shifter in friction mode, if possible. Shift chain onto largest chain ring and smallest freewheel cog. Then turn high adjustment screw until center of guide pulley aligns with smallest freewheel cog, as shown at left.

Low screw

2 Shift chain onto smallest chain ring and largest freewheel cog. Then turn the low adjustment screw until the guide pulley aligns with the largest freewheel cog, as shown at left.

Thumb shifters, found on mountain and hybrid bikes, are handlebar mounted. They feature one or two levers and sometimes a switch for changing from index to friction mode.

Dual-lever shifters under handlebars may be thumb operated, or have both a thumb-operated main lever and a release lever operated by the index finger.

Replacing worn cables

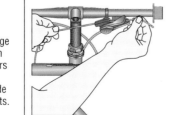

1 With chain on smallest cog, remove old cable. Feed new cable completely through shifter hole, securing nipple.

2 Grease new cable, and feed it through housing and shifter cable stops in same pattern as old cable.

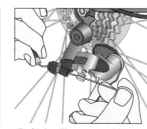

3 At derailleur, run cable between anchor bolt washer and lip. Pull cable taut and tighten anchor bolt. Cap cable.

Grip shifters, designed for mountain and hybrid bikes with straight handlebars, allow you to change gears with a twist of the wrist.

Servicing the chain

A worn chain can jump out of gear or break in use. To preserve a chain, keep it dry, clean, and lubricated. After riding through puddles, for example, wipe off the moisture and relubricate the chain. To make chain cleaning easier, use a chain washer (see *Bicycle-repair tools,* p.403). Otherwise, remove the chain and soak it in a solvent, such as kerosene.

One- and three-speed bikes require a ⅛-inch-wide chain; bikes with derailleurs use a ³⁄₃₂-inch-wide chain. When replacing a chain, consider installing a new free-wheel and chain rings (facing page) as well. Check the compatibility of replacement parts at your bike shop.

Spotting a worn chain

A new chain sits snugly on the teeth of a chain ring for maximum efficiency when pedaling.

A worn chain stretches, exposing part of the gear teeth. Gear slippage is often the result.

Checking for proper chain length

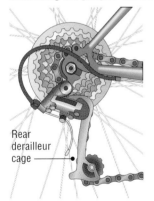

To make sure chain is the right length, shift it onto smallest freewheel gear and largest chain ring; rear derailleur cage should hang perpendicular to ground.

Another way to check chain length is to shift chain onto largest freewheel gear and largest chain ring; length is OK if rear derailleur cage is almost parallel to chain stay.

Opening a chain

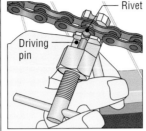
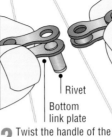

1 To open a chain, first set a link in the chain tool so that the tool's driving pin lines up directly with a chain rivet.

2 Twist the handle of the chain tool about six turns. The rivet should barely clear the bottom link plate.

Putting on a new chain

1 To make removal easier, loosen the old chain by shifting it onto the smallest freewheel cog and smallest chain ring. Break the chain with a chain tool (above).

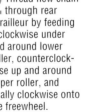

2 Thread new chain through rear derailleur by feeding it clockwise under and around lower roller, counterclockwise up and around upper roller, and finally clockwise onto the freewheel.

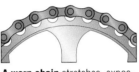

3 Set new chain on smallest freewheel cog and largest chain ring. Holding chain together by hand, check its length (see left). Use chain tool to add or take off links as needed for proper fit.

Common variants: Chain linkages

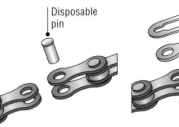

A HyperGlide chain link has disposable pins. To break a chain, push pin completely out; keep extras for repairs.

Master link with retaining clip joins chain on a single-speed bike. Closed end of clip faces front of bike.

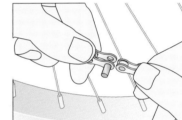

4 To join the chain, bring the ends together, lining up the link that has the protruding rivet with its mate on the other end of the chain.

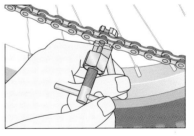

5 Use the chain tool to drive the rivet through the link plates. The rivet tip should protrude as far as the tips on the adjacent links.

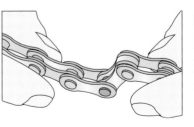

6 Loosen up the newly joined link by flexing it with your fingers. Lubricating the chain and riding the bike should loosen the link further.

Bicycles / freewheels and chain rings

Freewheels

Hard use and abrasive dirt can damage the cogs, or sprockets, that make up the freewheel. Clean a freewheel regularly with a rag, old toothbrush, and cleaning solvent (don't let solvent drip into the moving parts). Change a freewheel if a cog's teeth look worn or if a bad spill results in bent or chipped teeth. You may also want to install a new combination of gears to improve your bicycle's performance.

Cassette freewheels slip as a unit into splines, or slots, around the hub; standard freewheels screw onto a threaded hub. Manufacturers' designs differ; be sure that a replacement freewheel will fit your bike.

Changing a cassette freewheel

1 Remove rear wheel (p.405). Hold quick-release lever while unscrewing axle nut, turning it counterclockwise.

2 Install remover tool on axle over freewheel locknut; replace axle nut to hold remover in place.

3 Lean over wheel and wrap chain whip around a large freewheel cog. Slip wrench on remover and press down hard.

4 Turn chain whip clockwise; turn wrench counterclockwise to loosen locknut. Unscrew axle nut, remover, and locknut.

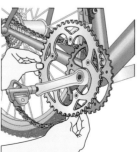

5 Slip old cassette off hub. Line up wide spline on new cassette with wide spline on hub. Slip cassette into place.

6 Install remover tool. Tighten locknut using wrench and chain whip. Replace remover with axle nut or quick-release.

Changing a standard freewheel

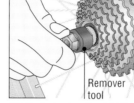

Axle nut

Locknut

1 Remove rear wheel (p.405). Remove axle nut. Slip correct remover tool for your freewheel over locknut.

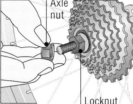

Remover tool

2 Reattach axle nut and tighten by hand (or close quick-release over removal tool to hold it in place).

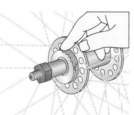

3 Lean over wheel (freewheel facing away from you). Brace wheel and turn removal tool counterclockwise with a wrench.

4 Unscrew old freewheel to remove it. Grease threads of new freewheel and hub before screwing on new freewheel.

TIPS FROM THE PROS

To remove a grip, pry it up with a screwdriver as you apply hair spray inside. Pull off old grip; clean handlebar. Apply hair spray to ease on new grip. Let dry 30 minutes.

Chain rings

An integral part of a bike's power drive, chain rings are subject to the same stresses as chains and freewheels. The primary cause of wear is gritty, abrasive dirt. Clean the chain rings as often as you do the chain and freewheel. A dirty chain gets the chain rings grimy as soon as you start to pedal again.

An accident can bend a chain ring. To check, rotate the cranks backward while you look straight down on the chain ring. Any wobbling suggests a bend, which a bike shop may or may not be able to correct. Regular wear and tear can also cause chain-ring teeth to bend or break; if this happens, replace the chain ring.

Changing a chain ring

1 Remove chain by shifting to smaller chain ring and turning cranks backward while you push chain off chain ring.

Hex wrench

2 With chain off, unscrew chain-ring bolts in alternating pattern with the proper-size hex wrench.

3 Slip off each chain ring and place on a smooth, flat surface. If a chain ring doesn't lie flat, have it repaired or replace it.

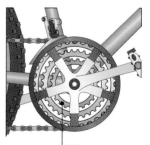

Third ring

If there's a third ring, check owner's manual. You may have to remove crank first; or rings and crank may be one unit.

When a bike mishap occurs on the road, having a repair kit with you can mean the difference between a brief stopover and hours of trudging with the bike in tow. The kit shown below can help you perform the most common repairs such as fixing a flat, mending a broken chain, or tightening loose nuts. Bike shops sell combination tools that can simplify the basic tool kit even further.

Some bike repairs call for improvisation, especially if the accident has also damaged the frame pump. The quick fixes suggested below will at least get you home or to a repair shop.

On-the-road repair kit

A tire lever helps work a tire off the rim. (The job may require as many as three levers.)

A puncture kit should include patches, abrasive pads, and liquid cement.

Plastic ties are useful for many temporary fixes, such as securing a broken spoke.

A five-dollar bill is tough enough to hold an inner tube within a split tire (see below).

A small roll of cloth tape comes in handy for many bike repairs.

A snap-on chain link allows you to make a quick chain repair.

A combination tool includes an adjustable wrench, fixed wrenches, hex wrench, chain and spoke tools, and freewheel remover.

A frame pump fits between brackets on the down tube of your bike and provides adequate pressure to fill tires. The pump head must match your tire's valve type.

Improvising a bike stand

Balance a road bike for repairs as shown, if there is no fence post or tree limb to hang it on. Upend a mountain bike on seat and handlebars.

Quick fixes

To fix a bent rim while on the road, find a tree or pole to push against. Remove wheel from bike and tire from rim (p.405). With rim bent toward you, press wheel against support with both hands. Remount tire and return wheel to bike. Ride carefully.

A flat tire won't roll as well as one that's even partially filled. If you can't fix a punctured tube on the road (p.405) or if the pump won't work, fill the tire with soft debris. Use tire levers to work one side of tire off rim. Stuff the inside with leaves, paper, or dirt. Return tire to rim.

A gash in a tire may cause the tube to pop through and blow out. To get home safely, deflate the tube, work the side of the tire near the gash off the rim, and place a folded five-dollar bill against the gash inside the tire. Reinflate the tube and return tire to rim.

A flapping spoke can jam up a chain or freewheel, causing serious problems. If a spoke breaks, immediately secure the loose ends to an adjacent spoke with tape. If you have no tape, try to tie up the broken spoke with string or a plastic tie.

With a snap-on chain link, you can quickly fix a broken chain while on the road. After removing (p.408) and discarding the broken link, join the ends of the chain with the snap-on link, which literally snaps into place when you press the parts together.

Boats

Anatomy of a small pleasure boat

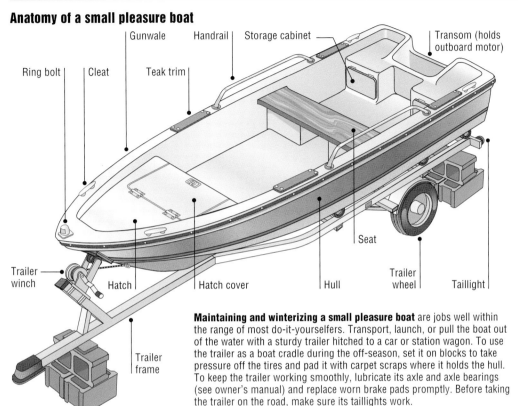

Gunwale · Handrail · Storage cabinet · Transom (holds outboard motor)

Ring bolt · Cleat · Teak trim

Trailer winch · Hatch · Hatch cover · Hull · Seat · Trailer wheel · Taillight · Trailer frame

Maintaining and winterizing a small pleasure boat are jobs well within the range of most do-it-yourselfers. Transport, launch, or pull the boat out of the water with a sturdy trailer hitched to a car or station wagon. To use the trailer as a boat cradle during the off-season, set it on blocks to take pressure off the tires and pad it with carpet scraps where it holds the hull. To keep the trailer working smoothly, lubricate its axle and axle bearings (see owner's manual) and replace worn brake pads promptly. Before taking the trailer on the road, make sure its taillights work.

If you live in an area where pleasure boats are pulled from the water for the winter, you can extend the life of your boat and simplify its spring launching by cleaning and maintaining it properly before storage.

Once the boat is out of the water, remove and winterize the outboard motor (p.414). Use a power washer or a scrub brush to remove all marine growth and stains from the hull. Wash down the wood and metal trim, and apply protective coats of paint, sealer, or varnish (right). Clean the interior surfaces, lines (ropes), life jackets, and seat cushions.

Inspect and repair the hull (p.412). Repaint a hull that needs it, or prepare the bottom for a copper- or tin-base anti-fouling finish, which prevents marine organisms from attacking the hull. (Finishes and other boat supplies are sold at marine stores.) When painting, follow the package advice on sanding, undercoats, compatibility of paints, and work temperature and humidity. Protect a clean fiberglass hull and metal hardware with automobile paste wax.

Tie down a plastic cover over bumpers hung from the gunwales so air can circulate under the cover to prevent mildew. To avoid sags where water can accumulate, extend the cover with a frame made of bowed flexible slats fitted into sockets attached to the gunwales. Buy frame materials at a marine store.

Oiling teak trim

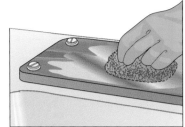

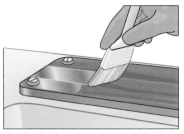

Clean teak trim with a commercial teak-cleaning solvent and a nylon scrubber or soft-bristle brush. Wear protective gloves and goggles.

Use brush or rag to apply several coats of teak oil or sealer. Let each coat dry completely before sanding lightly and adding the next layer of preservative.

Applying anti-fouling paint

Smooth hull by cleaning, scraping, and sanding. Use masking tape at the waterline for a clean painted edge. An undercoat may be needed to help paint adhere.

Apply paint with brush or short-nap roller, following manufacturer's recommendations for a good working temperature range and drying time between coats.

Setting up a protective cover

Bow frame · Bow frame socket · Carpet scrap · Bumper · Tie-down line

Secure cover over bowed frame and bumpers, allowing bumpers to hold cover out between tie-down lines for ventilation. Create vents at boat ends by leaving cover untucked. Put carpet scraps under tie-down lines to prevent chafing on hull.

A fiberglass boat hull is made of layers of reinforcing fabrics bonded with epoxy or polyester resin. Blisters form when moisture seeps through the outermost resin (gel coat) and reacts with water-soluble materials within the lamination. The blisters contain acidic material; wear gloves, goggles, and a mask as needed when making repairs.

Minor scratches can be sanded and filled with color-matched gel coat; patch gouges and holes with epoxy resin filler or layers of fiberglass mat and resin. (Buy repair materials at marine supply stores.) Proper surface preparation (cleaning, drying, and sanding) is essential for a professional result. Work in the shade; most resins need low humidity and an ambient temperature of about 70°F (21°C) to cure. Mix resins carefully according to the label.

Repairing deep scratches

Scrape out scratch with a can opener, chisel, or similar tool to create a V-shaped groove. Clean work area and mark it off with masking tape. Mix epoxy resin and hardener, following label instructions.

Push mixture firmly into scratch with putty knife, cover patch with plastic wrap, and remove air bubbles with dowel. Wet-sand cured patch with 400-grit paper. Finish with 600-grit paper; buff.

Repairing fiberglass blisters

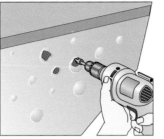

1 Open blisters with a countersink bit on an electric drill. Clean out the blister pockets with a sanding attachment, and flush with water.

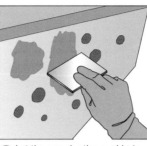

2 Let the area dry thoroughly (a week or more). Fill blister holes with a resin-hardener-filler mixture, applied with a stiff spreader.

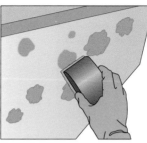

3 After mixture has cured, wet-sand the patch with 400-grit paper. Repeat the process until the repair is level with the surrounding area.

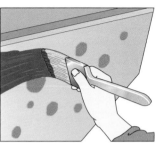

4 Wet-sand with 600-grit paper until the surface is glossy. Protect an under-the-waterline repair with anti-fouling paint.

Repairing holes in the hull

1 Using a keyhole saw or an electric saber saw, cut a rectangular opening around damaged area from the outside of the hull. Holes larger than 10 in. in length require professional repair.

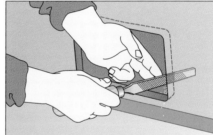

2 Use a file to create a 45° bevel around repair from outside. If hole will be patched from the inside, bevel should flare toward the interior, as shown here. Sand edges with 80-grit paper.

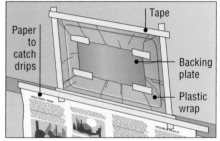

3 Make a backing plate out of cardboard, wood, or aluminum large enough to cover hole; wrap plate with plastic wrap. Tape plate (plastic side toward hole) over hole on outside of hull.

4 From inside hull, apply thick layer of gel coat to backing plate. Cut several successively larger pieces of fiberglass mat to fit the size of hole and beveled edge. Use a brush to saturate each piece of mat with resin mixture.

5 Start rebuilding laminate by applying smallest mat to still-tacky gel coat. After adding each mat, squeegee it to remove any air bubbles. Add successive layers of saturated mat to hole until patch is as thick as the hull.

6 Let layers cure according to directions on resin label (some require an airtight covering). Remove backing plate. Wet-sand both sides of patch with 400-grit paper; finish with 600-grit paper. Buff gel coat on exterior until it shines.

Boats / inflatables

With proper handling and maintenance, modern inflatable boats—made of PVC or Hypalon—can provide 10 years or more of enjoyment. Consult the owner's manual for instructions on inflating the boat—the sequence of chambers to be filled and how to test for proper infla-tion. For a quick check, push down on the boat; if the fabric ripples, the cham-ber probably needs more air. Under-inflation is more of a problem than overinflation. Too little air allows a boat to flex and causes premature wear; it is difficult to overinflate a boat chamber, particularly if you use a foot pump.

Abrasion can also shorten an inflat-able's useful life. Avoid dragging your boat across sharp shells or gravel, and try to keep sand from accumulating under the floor or in crevices. Don't let rough docking or mooring lines rub across the surface of the boat.

Use only a mild detergent or soap and water to clean modern inflatables. Silicone- or petroleum-base products prevent the glues used for repairs from adhering properly.

When your boat is not in use, keep it out of the sun (cover it if you keep it out-side). For long-term storage, clean and dry the boat thoroughly, then deflate and fold it. If an inflatable is stored in freez-ing temperatures, allow it to thaw in a warm room for several hours before unfolding it.

Painting an inflatable

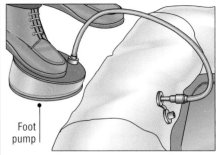

1 Use a foot pump or an electric pump to give the boat shape without bringing it up to full pressure. Follow the manufacturer's instructions for the proper inflation sequence.

Foot pump

Finding and fixing punctures

1 Low air pressure in any of the chambers of the boat suggests a leak. Brush soapy water on valves, seams, and surfaces of the suspect chambers; leaking air will cause the solution to bubble at the source. Use a wax china marker (grease pencil) to identify any holes.

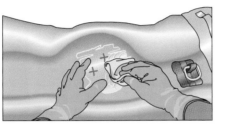

2 To patch a boat, first deflate it and place damaged area on a smooth work surface. Wearing rubber gloves, clean around the hole on a PVC boat with methyl ethyl ketone. Sand a Hypalon boat first to create a slightly tacky sur-face, and then clean with acetone.

3 Consult the owner's manual to determine compatible fabric and glue for patching. Cut a patch 2 in. larger all around than hole. For small holes in close proximity, one large patch is preferable to several tiny ones. Round corners on patch, using a coin as a template.

2 Clean boat with mild detergent and water (above). When boat has dried, wipe it down with solvent recommended by paint manufacturer to improve adhesion of the paint or coating.

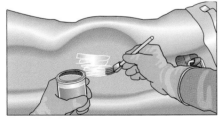

4 Work in a well-ventilated area, out of direct sunlight, and wear gloves. Follow manufac-turer's directions for applying glue to patch and boat in several thin coats. Allow each coat to dry the full time specified (5 to 10 min.). Glues cure best at temperatures close to 70°F.

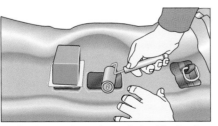

5 Carefully apply patch over hole while the glue is still tacky. Press hard on the patch, and use a roller or a flat scraping tool to eliminate any air pockets from the glue. To help get a strong bond, place a weighted object on the patch while it is curing.

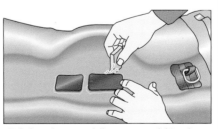

6 Before glue cures fully, remove weight and use a rubber gum eraser (sold at art supply stores) to clean off any excess glue that has seeped out from underneath the patch. (Glue left on the boat's surface discolors in the sun.) Replace weight; let glue cure completely before using boat.

3 Use disposable brushes to apply the recom-mended coats of paint. Some inflatable boat paints need a week or more to dry. Never launch or fold up a boat until the last coat is fully cured.

Though it isn't entirely accurate, the term "outboard motor" is generally used to describe the portable engine that propels a boat. Most small outboards feature a two-cycle engine similar to those found in yard tools (for basic troubleshooting and maintenance procedures, see pages 356–367). Because it takes a lot of power to move a boat through water, a boat engine, particularly a two-cycle engine, is geared to run nearly full blast all the time. More than other engines, it requires clean, well-filtered fuel and plenty of water circulation to keep it cool. In addition to its own vibration, an outboard is also subject to buffeting by water and weather, which can loosen fasteners, snap wires, and corrode metal parts. Preventive maintenance starts with frequent inspections of the wiring, cables, fasteners, fuel filter, and hoses. To gain access to the engine, simply unhinge the cowling (cover) and remove it. Replace defective wires or cables promptly, and tighten loose connections with a wrench or a screwdriver. Regular lubrication, as outlined in your owner's manual, is crucial.

Anatomy of an outboard

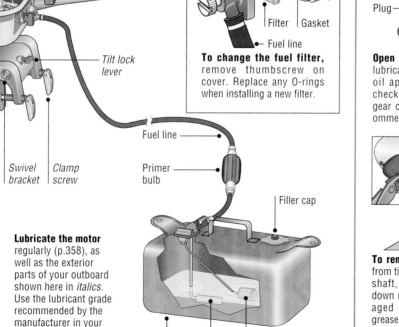

Engine | Cowling | Starter | *Throttle shaft* | Tiller

Fuel filter

Shift lever and shaft

Tilt lock lever

Note: Details of design and disassembly may vary, depending on model and manufacturer. If your outboard has a four-cycle engine or otherwise differs from the outboard shown here, see pages 356–367 and consult your owner's manual.

Swivel bracket | *Clamp screw*

Anode

Propeller

Gear case

Lubricate the motor regularly (p.358), as well as the exterior parts of your outboard shown here in *italics*. Use the lubricant grade recommended by the manufacturer in your owner's manual.

Fuel line

Primer bulb

Filler cap

Fuel tank | Filter | Cork float

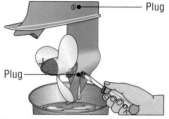

Thumbscrew

Cover

Filter | Gasket

Fuel line

To change the fuel filter, remove thumbscrew on cover. Replace any O-rings when installing a new filter.

Winterizing an outboard

For winter layup, pull the outboard motor from the water. Wash off mud, grass, and salt with soap and fresh water, and perform the maintenance chores below. Finally, lubricate the engine and exterior parts of the outboard (see *Anatomy of an outboard,* left). Store it upright (an unheated garage is OK). After cleaning off any corrosion and checking the fluid levels, store the battery in a warm dry place. Fuel tanks should be rinsed out with fresh gasoline and emptied; you can add fuel stabilizer to a partially full tank so long as you store it away from heat sources and flammable materials.

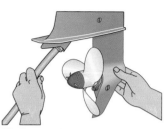

Flush out cooling tube by attaching a garden hose to the intake (some outboards require an adapter, available at any marine store). Idle the motor for 10 min. while fresh water circulates through the cooling system.

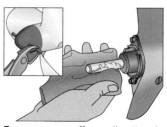

Plug

Plug

Open both plugs to drain gear case lubricant from the lower unit. If the oil appears milky, have a dealer check the unit for leaks. Refill the gear case only with a lubricant recommended by the manufacturer.

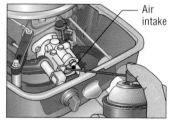

Air intake

To clean carburetor, inject fogging (rust-inhibiting) oil into the carburetor air intakes with the motor operating at a fast idle. Disconnect the fuel line, and continue fogging until the engine dies.

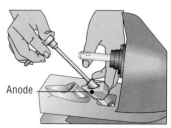

Anode

To remove propeller, pull cotter pin from tip (inset), remove solid pin from shaft, and slide off propeller. File down minor nicks but replace a damaged propeller (wipe waterproof grease on shaft before reinstalling).

Inspect the sacrificial anode and replace it if the zinc has been reduced by half or more. To ensure good contact, scrape off all paint and oxidation where the new anode will be attached.

Canoes

Most canoes today are constructed of aluminum, fiberglass, or plastic. Canoes made of wood, or of wood covered with canvas, are becoming rare. Whatever materials they are made of, all canoes require similar handling. Never drag a canoe—empty or loaded—along the ground. Never load a canoe unless it is afloat. On land, canoes should be turned upside down and tied securely to prevent lifting—and possible bashing—by the wind.

Aluminum canoes. Use duct tape or epoxy putty to make temporary fixes on an aluminum hull. For permanent repairs, use silicone rubber caulking to fill small holes and a fiberglass cloth and epoxy resin patch to cover larger holes (p.412). Leaks near or below the waterline require a fiberglass patch. Dents in aluminum hulls can often be knocked out as shown at right. When storing an aluminum canoe for the winter, remove all metal tools and gear from the interior to prevent electrolytic corrosion.

Fiberglass canoes. Built from layers of polyester or epoxy resin, fiberglass fabric, and other lightweight woven materials, these canoes are sturdy and easy to handle. Repair scratches, gouges, and small holes in a fiberglass canoe in the same way you would similar damage in a fiberglass boat hull (p.412).

Plastic canoes. Damage to hulls with a foam core can also be repaired with fiberglass patches. Dents in single-thickness plastic canoes, however, may not need any special attention. If left in the sun, or heated gently with a light bulb, many plastic canoes will return to their original shape.

Repairing dents in an aluminum hull

Place a hardwood block over a large dent and hammer gently from the inside with a rubber mallet. Start at the outside edges and work toward the center.

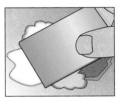

Fill gouges with epoxy auto-body filler (apply with plastic scraper). Sand area between coats, using finer and finer paper. Finish with aluminum or marine paint.

Straightening a buckled aluminum keel

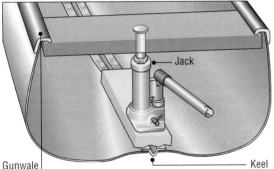

1 Unbend a buckled keel using a hydraulic auto jack and scrap lumber. Place one board over the keel at center of buckle and the other under gunwale; then position jack.

Jack

Gunwale

Keel

2 Slowly pump jack against boards until the hull regains its original shape. Don't jack too hard or wood will splinter. The keel should run straight and even from bow to stern.

Hanging a canoe for storage

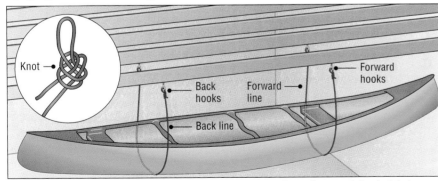

Knot

Back hooks

Forward line

Forward hooks

Back line

For safe storage, suspend a canoe from the rafters of a garage. Screw four sturdy hooks into two parallel rafters as shown above. Tie a line from the two forward hooks to hold canoe nose above car level. Tie a second line of the same length to one back hook. Slide nose of canoe through forward line loop; holding rear of canoe up with one hand, slip back line under canoe and secure over hook.

Tying a canoe to a car

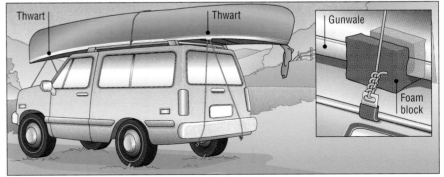

Thwart

Thwart

Gunwale

Foam block

To carry a canoe on a car, lash it to luggage rack and bumpers or undercarriage with nylon line as shown above. If you don't have a rack, slip foam blocks over canoe gunwales (inset) to protect car; secure line to hooks on window rain channels. Taut rear lines from thwart to car's undercarriage prevent canoe from sliding forward during stops.

Sports and recreation gear ■ Exercise machines

Stationary bikes

Other than minor adjustments, little servicing is typically required on a belt-flywheel stationary bike (below). A new stationary bike may come with a belt that's too taut, or the belt may loosen with time and use. If the belt tension knob no longer works, check the belt adjustment clasp. If the chain on a stationary bike is too loose, replace it as you would the chain on a regular bike (p.408). Belt and chain adjustments may require removal of the flywheel case.

Handlebars

Control panel

Seat

Tension knob

Flywheel

Belt

Chain

Crank

Pedal

Belt adjustment clasp

Flywheel case (must be removed in most models to access belt)

Removing the flywheel case

1 Locate and remove side screws from case. Check bottom for screws as well.

2 Loosen bolt holding crank and pedal to bike, using a socket wrench. Remove bolt.

3 Lift off pedal and crank; remove case side. Some cases slip over crank and pedal.

Adjusting belt tension

A belt is correctly tensioned if it gives about ½ in. when you try to lift it off the flywheel with a screwdriver.

Adjustment clasp

Set tension knob to lowest setting. Unhook belt adjustment clasp and adjust belt. Rehook clasp when you achieve proper tension.

Treadmills

Time and use can cause the running belt on a treadmill to become skewed on its platform and/or to lose tension. You can fix both problems by adjusting the positioning bolts at the end of the platform.

A loose-feeling running belt may be a sign that the drive belt is loose. If tightening the running belt two or three quarter turns doesn't work (don't overtighten it), unplug the unit and open the motor case. Follow the directions on page 213 for adjusting the motor's position to take up drive-belt slack.

Adjusting the running belt

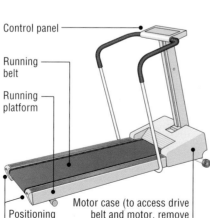

Control panel

Running belt

Running platform

Positioning bolts

Motor case (to access drive belt and motor, remove screws and lift off housing)

Running belt is properly tensioned if you can lift its edges 3 to 4 in. off the platform while the middle stays flat. For good performance, the belt should also be centered and run straight down the center of the platform.

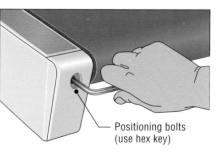

Positioning bolts (use hex key)

To tighten belt, unplug unit; give each rear positioning bolt a quarter turn clockwise. Repeat if needed. To center belt, set unit to run at 5 mph. Give a clockwise quarter turn to bolt on side where belt's too close. Wait 30 sec.; repeat if needed.

Fishing tackle

Fishing rods

After a day of fishing, always check your tackle—rods, reels, lines, hooks, lures, nets, and leaders—for damage and loose fittings. If you have been fishing in salt water, rinse your tackle thoroughly with fresh water to prevent corrosion. After freshwater fishing, use a damp rag to clean off grit and scum. Dry your gear with a soft cloth.

Clean fiberglass ferrules with cotton swabs and soapy water; clean metal ferrules with pipe cleaners dipped in acetone. (Don't use oil; it attracts dirt.)

Mend frayed guide wrappings in the field with tape or a coat of clear nail polish. For permanent repairs, rewrap the guides (right). A nicked guide can break a line and should be replaced.

To avoid a permanent bend, or "memory," in a fiberglass rod, never store it with the tip leaning up against a wall, particularly in warm weather.

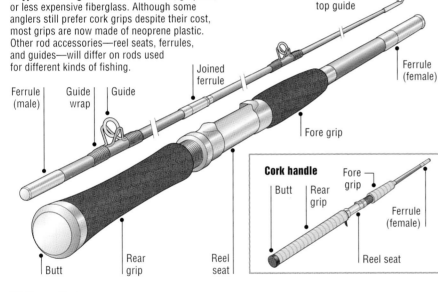

A typical fishing rod is made of boron, graphite, or less expensive fiberglass. Although some anglers still prefer cork grips despite their cost, most grips are now made of neoprene plastic. Other rod accessories—reel seats, ferrules, and guides—will differ on rods used for different kinds of fishing.

Tip-top, or top guide

Ferrule (female)

Joined ferrule

Fore grip

Ferrule (male)

Guide wrap

Guide

Butt

Rear grip

Reel seat

Cork handle

Butt

Rear grip

Fore grip

Ferrule (female)

Reel seat

Fitting a tip-top

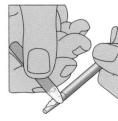

Select a tip-top fitting with an inside diameter slightly larger than that of rod tip. (Sanding the tip to make it smaller weakens it.) Dab ferrule cement (sold at tackle shops) on tip.

Squeeze ferrule cement into tip-top socket. Join the parts, then gently twist tip-top to align it with the other guides. Remove excess adhesive with a toothpick and acetone.

Wrapping a guide

Tackle shops sell guides, wrapping thread, and clear epoxy finishes.

For wrapping a guide, the rod must be placed so that it will rotate freely—preferably in a holder, which you can buy or make (right). Remove any damaged wraps or guides. Taper the feet of new guides with a file for a smoother fit. Before starting a wrap, fold a length of thread to make a pull loop, and set it aside. Position the guide on the rod, and secure one of its feet with masking tape. Start wrapping the free foot. To anchor the thread, lay the loose end lengthwise along the rod so that the first few windings will hold it. To wrap, hold the spool of thread in one hand and rotate the rod with the other. After finishing the free foot, untape and wrap its mate. Coat each wrap with epoxy, turning the rod as you do so to keep the epoxy from sagging.

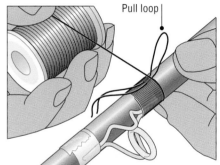

Notched holder

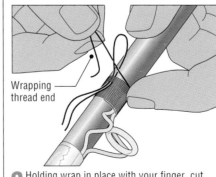

Free end of thread

Tape

Pull loop

1 Lay end of spool thread along rod and wind over it, securing it firmly. After several wraps, push threads together with blunt end of spoon.

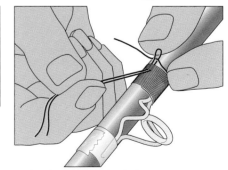

Pull loop

2 Keep wrapping and pushing threads together until you're 6 or 8 turns from the end. Lay pull loop over wrap, and finish winding over it.

Wrapping thread end

3 Holding wrap in place with your finger, cut thread from spool, leaving a loose end about 1 in. long. Push end through pull loop.

4 Pull the loop completely through wraps; it will take loose end of thread with it. Trim protruding end of thread so it is flush with wrap.

Fly reels

Of the four basic types of fishing reels—fly reels, open-face spinning reels, closed-face spinning reels, and bait-casting reels—the fly reel with its revolving spool is the easiest to disassemble and service. In many models, just pressing a catch will release the spool from the frame.

Like all fishing gear, a fly reel is vulnerable to grit and sand. After each fishing trip, open the reel and clean the inner surfaces with a cloth dipped in kerosene or alcohol. Use pipe cleaners to wipe the axle cylinder. Lubricate the axle with a dab of waterproof grease; use lightweight oil to lubricate other parts of the reel. Because salt is corrosive, reels used for saltwater fishing should be rinsed thoroughly in fresh water before you clean and lubricate

them. Keep lubricants away from the line, however; oil and grease can ruin the line's finish.

Most problems with fly reels involve worn or broken parts. The spring on the spool catch can become fatigued, causing the spool to loosen. Replacing the spring (right) is a simple procedure. The spring-and-pawl mechanism, which keeps the spool from turning on its own in the frame, may wear out or break and have to be replaced (below, right).

If you can't find a reel part at your local tackle shop, write the manufacturer. Reel makers usually keep a large inventory of spare parts. Always keep the booklet that comes with a new reel; in it, you'll find an exploded view of the reel that identifies the parts and tells how to order them.

Replacing a spool catch spring

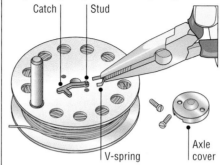

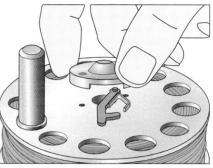

Remove axle cover and old spool catch V-spring. With spool catch on stud, place straight side of new V-spring against catch.

Replace axle cover, aligning screw holes in cover with those in spool. Hold cover firmly as you tighten screws.

Replacing a broken spring and pawl

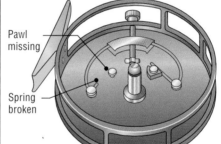

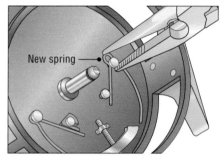

1 If a fly reel is not working properly, lift off the spool and examine the parts in the frame. Here a spring is broken and a pawl is missing.

2 Remove broken spring; clean reel frame with a kerosene-soaked rag. Use needle-nose pliers to squeeze head of a new spring onto stud.

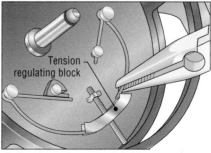

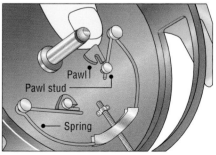

3 Note how other spring is held against the tension regulating block. Using pliers, snap long end of new spring onto right end of block.

4 Put pawl on stud, straight edge against spring. Replace spool; test reel. If action is wrong, rotate pawl so rounded side is against spring.

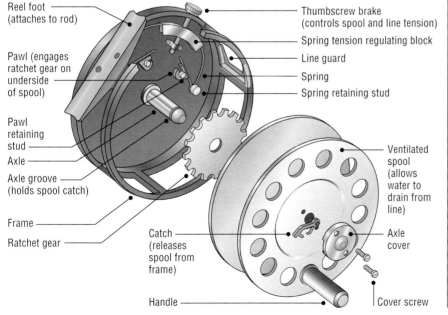

- Reel foot (attaches to rod)
- Pawl (engages ratchet gear on underside of spool)
- Pawl retaining stud
- Axle
- Axle groove (holds spool catch)
- Frame
- Ratchet gear
- Thumbscrew brake (controls spool and line tension)
- Spring tension regulating block
- Line guard
- Spring
- Spring retaining stud
- Ventilated spool (allows water to drain from line)
- Axle cover
- Catch (releases spool from frame)
- Handle
- Cover screw

Open-face spinning reels

Technically, a spinning reel has a fixed spool that doesn't rotate. The spool of an open-face spinning reel, however, does move back and forth in conjunction with the rotating head and bail. The bail, which bears the brunt of winding the fishing line, may break at either of its ends and require replacing (below).

Regularly oil the exposed parts of an open-face spinning reel. Once a year, disassemble the reel to clean and relubricate the gears.

Line roller — — Reel foot

— Antireverse lever

Bail arm

Line spool

Line spool nut

Bail

Rotating head

Handle

Servicing a closed-face spinning reel

Plate

Inner cone

Spool

Shaft

In a closed-face spinning reel, the line passes through the front cover plate. To disassemble, first remove plate with a half turn.

Remove inner cone, which rotates to wind line onto spool, by turning clockwise and lifting out.

Clean out old lubricant with kerosene or alcohol once a year; regrease cover plate, cone, spool, and spool shaft.

Installing a new bail on an open-face reel

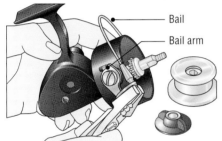

Bail

Bail arm

1 For convenience, remove line spool by unscrewing nut that holds it. To loosen old bail, use pliers to remove locknut securing bail to bail arm.

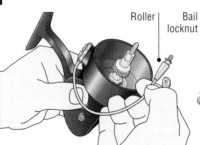

Roller | Bail locknut

2 Check the roller as you remove it from the bail; if it is corroded or nicked, replace it along with the bail.

Bail arm screw —

3 To release other end of bail, remove bail arm screw and bail arm; don't lose spring that is under bail arm. Remove old bail and discard.

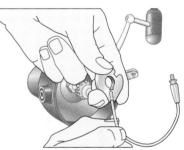

4 Start new bail through bail arm. Replace spring (below). Slip roller onto other end of bail and mount in opposite bail arm. Tighten locknut.

Replacing a bail spring

Two springs at either end of the bail are essential to the retrieval of line on an open-face spinning reel. They make the bail snap over and catch the line in a collar on the way to the spool. If either spring breaks or becomes fatigued, the bail won't work properly. Replacing a bail spring is a simple procedure (right); the only tricky part, which gets easier with practice, is repositioning and holding the bail arm against the tension of the spring while tightening the screw.

1 Remove screw securing bail arm (there is a bail arm and spring at both ends of bail).

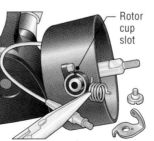

Rotor cup slot

2 Pull out old spring with needle-nose pliers and discard. Position new spring so that its tail fits into slot in rotor cup.

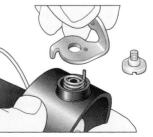

3 Place bail arm over spring so that tail of spring fits into hole in arm. Position bail arm correctly (there will be tension from spring) and hold in place.

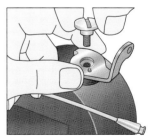

4 Screw bail arm tightly into place over spring, making sure tail is still in bail arm hole. Procedure is same for spring at other end of bail.

Bait-casting reel

A rapidly revolving spool distinguishes the bait-casting reel from the spinning reel and the much slower fly reel. Most big saltwater reels are simply giant versions of the bait-casting reel with powerful star drags. Whatever the size of a bait-casing reel, moisture from a wet fishing line continuously sprays its spool and side plates. To prevent rusting and corrosion of metal parts, regularly wash the reel with fresh water and keep it lubricated.

After every day of fishing, wipe your reel, add a small amount of light household oil to the oil ports on either end of the spool axle, and lightly oil the star drag, handle, and handle shaft. If the reel has a level wind guide, lubricate the groove into which its top fits.

Thoroughly clean and lubricate a bait-casting reel once a year. Remove the handle and clean sand out of the threads. Soak the line-winding gears in solvent to remove old grease. Let the reel dry completely; then regrease. At the same time, look for and replace worn drag washers and broken springs (below). To avoid mix-ups, store parts in a compartmented tray (or egg carton) in the order in which they were removed.

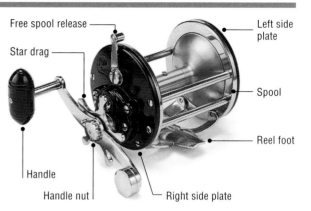

Replacing drag washers and springs

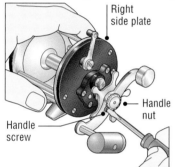

1 Remove screw on handle with screwdriver, and loosen handle nut with wrench provided with reel.

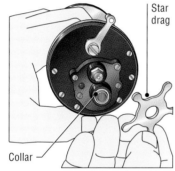

2 Remove handle; then lift off star-shaped drag washer, or star drag, and the cylindrical collar beneath it.

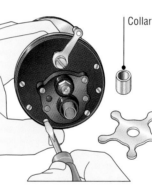

3 Remove outside screws on right side plate, and lift off left side plate and spool. Set these pieces aside.

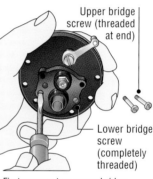

4 First remove two upper bridge screws from top of right side plate; then remove two lower bridge screws.

With bridge screws removed, turn over right side plate to find brass bridge that holds main gear in place.

5 With bridge screws removed, turn over right side plate to find brass bridge that holds main gear in place.

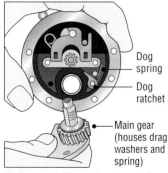

6 Remove bridge and main gear. Dog spring and dog ratchet will pop out or loosen; remove these parts.

7 Lift main gear off shaft; take out round drag washers and round spring for cleaning and lubrication.

8 Keep washers and spring in order of removal. Clean and grease. Replace worn parts. Reassemble on bridge shaft.

9 Replace dog ratchet and spring. Reposition bridge gear unit so that it holds dog ratchet and spring in place.

10 Holding bridge firmly with right thumb, turn it to align bridge screw holes. Install screws and reassemble reel.

Gas grills

Tune up a gas grill at the start of each outdoor cooking season. With the gas off and the burners removed, scrape and wire-brush the interior and the cooking and fire grates. If the igniter won't spark, you should adjust, clean, or replace it. Clean stone briquettes by burning them, soiled side down, for 30 minutes. If the grill uses a home gas line, inspect the connection for corrosion. Have your gas supplier repair potential leaks.

Routine maintenance

Inspect all gas connections regularly. Brush hose fittings and valves with soapy water; bubbles indicate leaks. Tighten connection and test again. Replace fitting if necessary.

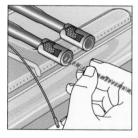

To clean blocked venturi tubes, remove burner and venturi tubes from burner gas valve. Turn over burner and push a pipe cleaner into each venturi tube until it hits the end.

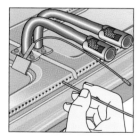

Open clogged burner ports, one by one, with coat hanger wire or toothpick. Flushing burner with water through a venturi tube will show you which ports are still closed.

Close top of grill after each use and turn both burners on high for 10 min. When grill cools, you'll be able to brush briquettes clean.

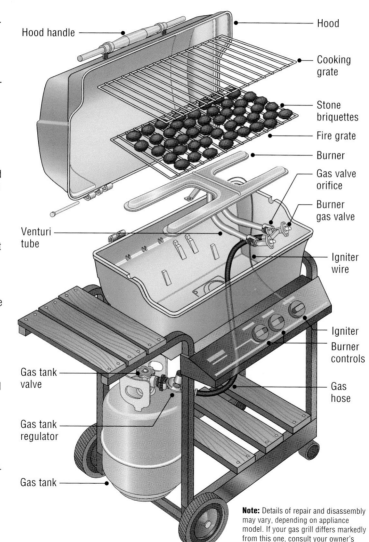

Hood handle

Hood

Cooking grate

Stone briquettes

Fire grate

Burner

Gas valve orifice

Burner gas valve

Venturi tube

Igniter wire

Igniter

Burner controls

Gas tank valve

Gas hose

Gas tank regulator

Gas tank

Note: Details of repair and disassembly may vary, depending on appliance model. If your gas grill differs markedly from this one, consult your owner's manual or a service professional.

Portable camp stoves

A compressed-gas stove seldom requires repair, but it is heavy to carry and unreliable in cold weather. A liquid-fuel stove (below) is lighter and more reliable in every temperature. To keep a liquid-fuel stove working, use fresh fuel and dismantle and clean the generator with alcohol regularly (but keep a spare on hand in case the old one fails). Oil the fuel pump—a plunger connected to a leather cup—with light machine oil annually to keep the cup pliable. **CAUTION:** Keep the tank away from heat when servicing it.

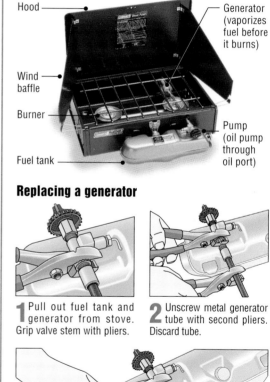

Hood

Generator (vaporizes fuel before it burns)

Wind baffle

Burner

Pump (oil pump through oil port)

Fuel tank

Replacing a generator

1 Pull out fuel tank and generator from stove. Grip valve stem with pliers.

2 Unscrew metal generator tube with second pliers. Discard tube.

3 Unscrew and discard old needle. Install new needle in valve; hand-tighten, then give needle quarter turn with pliers. Slip new generator tube over needle. Tighten with pliers.

Sports and recreation gear ▪ Pools

Local building codes dictate the installation standards for home swimming pools. In your town, a pool may have to be set back a minimum distance from the property line and/or be surrounded by a fence. You may also need building and electrical permits, inspections, a certificate of occupancy, and possibly even a new property survey.

Aboveground pools are more popular than inground pools. They cost less, can be installed and maintained by a handy do-it-yourselfer, and can be taken down and reassembled elsewhere if you move. The basic water chemistry, winterization, and maintenance procedures for filters, pumps, and vinyl liners are similar for both types of pools.

Pool chemistry. Water purity in a home pool is maintained by a filter (facing page) and chemicals. Filtering removes dirt, sand, and other solids that are blown or tracked into the pool. Chemicals, mainly chlorine, kill bacteria, neutralize unfilterable wastes, and impede the growth of algae. The amount of chemicals needed to disinfect a pool depends on the water's acidity or alkalinity, its hardness or softness, its temperature, and the hygiene of the swimmers. For chemical treatment to be effective, pool water must have the proper balance of potential hydrogen (pH), total alkalinity (TA), and calcium hardness (CH). The pH level is measured on a scale of 0 to 14; 7 is neutral. A slightly alkaline pH, between 7.2 and 7.6, is best for pool water. Total alkalinity is a measurement of all alkaline chemicals in the pool water—typically bicarbonates, carbonates, and hydroxides. If the TA is too high—more than 120 parts per million (ppm)—the pH will resist adjustment to the desired range. Calcium hardness measures the water's mineral content. When the CH is too high (500 ppm or more), scale forms and the pool equipment corrodes; when the CH is too low, the liner suffers damage.

When chlorine is added to pool water, a certain portion (chlorine demand) is immediately used to

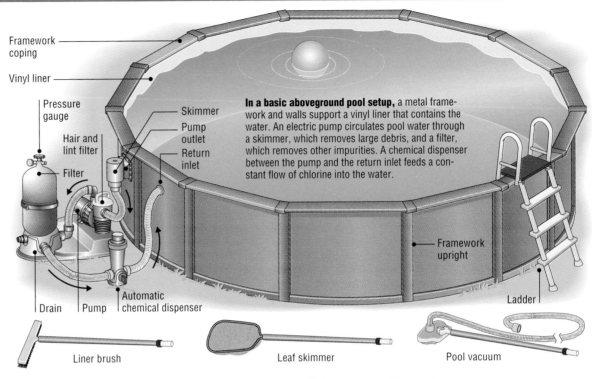

Framework coping

Vinyl liner

Pressure gauge

Hair and lint filter

Filter

Skimmer

Pump outlet

Return inlet

In a basic aboveground pool setup, a metal framework and walls support a vinyl liner that contains the water. An electric pump circulates pool water through a skimmer, which removes large debris, and a filter, which removes other impurities. A chemical dispenser between the pump and the return inlet feeds a constant flow of chlorine into the water.

Framework upright

Drain | Pump | Automatic chemical dispenser

Ladder

Liner brush

Leaf skimmer

Pool vacuum

destroy bacteria, algae, and other organics. The remaining chlorine (chlorine residual) will destroy bacteria and algae in the future. The chlorine residual should be between 1.0 and 1.5 ppm.

Testing the water. At the start of the pool season, have a pool dealer analyze your water for calcium hardness. Buy a reagent kit (right) to test the pH, TA, and chlorine residual levels.

Collect test water away from the return inlet at a depth of 18 inches or more (arm's length). Test the pH before adding chlorine to the water (chlorine raises the pH and alkalinity of the water). For the first 2 weeks of pool use, test and adjust the water chemistry every day. When the water chemistry has stabilized, test it twice a week.

QUICK FORMULAS

The volume of water in a pool determines the amount of chemicals needed for purification. To find the number of litres in a rectangular pool, multiply length by width by average depth (in feet) by 7.5; for a round pool, multiply surface (πr^2) by average depth (in feet) by 5.9. In each case, multiply the result by 3.8.

Using a reagent test kit

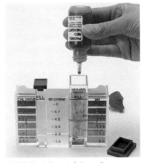

1 Wait at least 6 hr. after adding chemicals before testing pool water. Rinse test tube in pool, then fill to line. Hold bottle of reagent erect and add correct amount, according to the instructions that accompany the kit.

2 Cover tube with cap (not a finger—skin oils affect readings) and shake. Match test colors to shade of sample to determine pH, TA, or chlorine residual level. Discard water samples (reagent dirties pool). Store kit out of sunlight.

Troubleshooting

Problem	CAUSE? / Solution
Cloudy water	EARLY ALGAE GROWTH? Add chlorine. ◇
	HIGH pH? Lower pH with acid (sodium bisulfate). ◇
	HIGH TA? Add acid to lower TA. ◇
	POOR FILTRATION? Clean filter and skimmer. ◇
Algae, slimy bacteria	LOW CHLORINE RESIDUAL? Adjust pH; shock with chlorine (see *Preventive maintenance*, below). Run pump until water clears, then add algaecide. ◆
Eye and skin irritation	LOW pH? Raise pH with sodium carbonate. ◇
	TOO MANY CONTAMINANTS? Shock with chlorine to raise chlorine residual level. ◆
Chlorine odor	TOO LITTLE FREE CHLORINE? Shock with chlorine to raise chlorine residual level. ◆
High chlorine reading	HIGH CHLORINE LEVEL? Dilute sample with distilled water; retest; don't swim if level tops 3 ppm. ◇
	OLD REAGENTS USED FOR TEST? Retest with new regeant; add chlorine as needed. ◇
	HIGH CHLORINE RESIDUAL? Let dissipate; swim when level falls below 3 ppm. ◆
Foaming	BUILD UP OF ORGANICS? Shock with chlorine; run pump until water clears. ◆
Scaling	HIGH pH or TA? Add acid to lower pH and TA. ◇
Corrosion	LOW TA? Add sodium bicarbonate to raise TA. ◇
Scum ring	CONTAMINANT BUILDUP? Use cleaner/degreaser; make swimmers bathe before swimming. ◆

Degree of difficulty: Simple ◇ Average ◆ Complex ◆

Preventive maintenance

To keep pool water healthy with a minimum of chemicals, make it a family rule to shower and use the bathroom before swimming. Body oils, sweat, suntan lotion, and urine eventually clog filters. As they accumulate, they make the water murky. To neutralize these organics, try a chlorine shock treatment: Put 5 to 10 times the normal amount of chlorine in the deep end of the pool with the pump running. Allow the pump to run as long as the chlorine manufacturer suggests before allowing swimmers in the pool.

Always keep the pump running when people are swimming. The circulating water holds debris in suspension, so that it will get trapped by either the filter or the skimmer basket.

Cleaning the filter

A pool pump circulates water through a filter that collects large dirt particles. When the filter becomes clogged, water flow is restricted and the back pressure, measured in pounds per square inch (psi), rises above normal. Check the filter pressure gauge every day; when the pressure exceeds the level suggested by the manufacturer, shut off the pump and clean the filter. Three media may be used in pool filters—diatomaceous earth (DE) in a fabric grid, pleated cartridges, or sand. Each requires a different cleaning method, as shown below. **CAUTION:** Open the air valve and let the pressure drop to zero before unclamping a filter unit.

Cleaning a DE filter

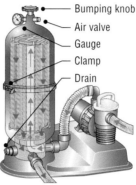

Bumping knob
Air valve
Gauge
Clamp
Drain

Clean a DE filter when pressure gauge rises by 10 psi. Stop pump. Turn bumping knob back and forth one stop; repeat 4 times. (Some models have a bumping lever instead of a knob.)

Change DE if bumping fails. Shut off pump. Open air valve. Let old DE drain out with water. With pump running, add new DE (amount manufacturer recommends) through skimmer.

Pump

Clean fabric grid once each season. Shut off pump. Open air valve, and drain water and DE. When filter has finished draining, unhinge clamp, lift off top of filter unit, and remove filter grid.

Hose loose dirt off filter grid. Scrub fabric with brush and filter cleaner (available at pool stores). Rinse grid; then reassemble filter. Turn on pump and add new DE.

Cleaning a cartridge filter

A cartridge filter is a pleated cylinder that traps dirt as pool water is pumped through it. Clean a cartridge filter when the pressure gauge reading rises 10 psi over the initial clean-filter reading. Turn off pump and open air valve. Let filter drain; then unhinge clamp and lift off top of filter unit.

Pull out cylinder and hose it off, or if body oils and minerals have accumulated in the filter, soak it overnight in the cleaning solution recommended by the manufacturer (check your owner's manual). Filters usually must be replaced every 2 years.

Cleaning a sand filter

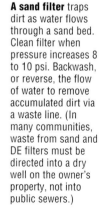

A sand filter traps dirt as water flows through a sand bed. Clean filter when pressure increases 8 to 10 psi. Backwash, or reverse, the flow of water to remove accumulated dirt via a waste line. (In many communities, waste from sand and DE filters must be directed into a dry well on the owner's property, not into public sewers.)

Patching a vinyl liner underwater

1 Wearing goggles and carrying a scrap of vinyl, look for leak underwater. When you find it, cover it with vinyl. Suction will hold patch in place temporarily.

2 Cut a permanent round or oval patch from vinyl in patch kit. Patch should be twice the size of gash. Coat one side of patch with kit adhesive.

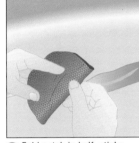

3 Fold patch in half, sticky sides together, to keep adhesive dry; then carry it underwater to leak.

4 Remove temporary patch; unfold and apply permanent patch. Smooth out bubbles with hand or flat tool to ensure full adhesion and speed drying.

FOR YOUR SAFETY

Turn off the power before investigating the source of any problem in your pool system.

Handle pool chemicals with care: read labels and heed warnings. Date chemicals as you buy them. Use a separate, clean scoop for each. Don't mix chemicals—old and new versions of the same chemical or different types of the same chemical can ignite, produce toxic gases, or explode.

Don't add chemicals to the pool if people are swimming.

Store chemicals in a cool, dry, well-ventilated area out of the reach of children. Don't stack containers; separate liquid and dry chemicals.

Maintaining a pump

Centrifugal pumps are used to circulate pool water, drain basements, and circulate hot water in heating systems. In a centrifugal pump, an electric motor rotates an impeller to move the water. Most pumps are self-priming (the housing automatically fills with water when you turn the motor on), but check the owner's manual to be sure.

The most common pump problems are a worn impeller and a leaking shaft seal assembly; either part can be replaced (see below). To avoid trouble, keep the air vents on the pump motor clear of debris and regularly clean out strainers or filters in the suction and delivery lines. To prevent cavitation (noisy air pockets in the moving water), keep lines and valves into and out of the pump clear and fully open. For motor repairs, see pages 140–141.

Strainer basket cover · Connecting band · Outlet pipe to filter · Seal assembly · Shaft · Capacitor cover · Split-phase induction motor · Pump support · Impeller · Diffuser · Strainer basket · Inlet pipe

Replacing a pump impeller and shaft seal

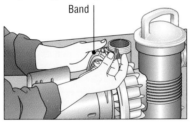

Band

1 To disassemble pump, turn off pump motor and shut suction and discharge valves. Loosen screw (or nuts and bolts) that secure band connecting pump and motor.

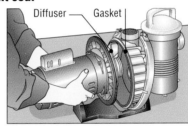

Diffuser — Gasket

2 Pull motor away from pump housing. You may first see a gasket and the diffuser, a vaned plate that helps the impeller move water. Not all pumps have diffusers.

Diffuser

O-ring

Back-plate

3 Using a screwdriver, remove screws holding diffuser to backplate. Check the diffuser and its O-ring for signs of wear. Replace a badly gouged or pitted diffuser.

4 To access the shaft and remove the impeller, turn motor around and pry cover off shaft bottom with a screwdriver. If screw holds shaft to impeller, remove it.

5 If there is no screw in shaft, use one hand to hold shaft bottom securely with groove-joint pliers while you unscrew impeller from shaft top with the other hand.

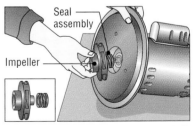

Seal assembly

Impeller

6 Slip impeller and seal assembly off shaft. Replace with identical parts (protect carbon face on seal as you work). Lubricate with waterproof grease. Reassemble pump.

Winterizing a pool

Pools can't survive subfreezing temperatures without special preparation. Because ice expands upward and exerts little extra pressure on the sides of an aboveground pool, the water is left in it. (Actually, the water protects the pool from ground freezes, which can buckle or cave in the sides.) Water that seeps under the pool bottom, however, can cause frost heaves that will stretch the liner, ruin the sand filler supporting it, and weaken the sides. Check carefully for liner leaks and make permanent repairs (p.424) before winterizing the pool.

The winterization process begins with a thorough cleaning of the pool (below). Test and balance the pool water and then treat it with a chemical winterizing kit, available from a pool store. Clean the filter (p.423). Drain all the plumbing lines and store hoses in a protected place. Drain and disassemble the pump and the automatic chemical dispenser. Drain the filter, filter valves, and the line to the gauge. Store the pump, filter, and chemical dispenser in a warm, dry garage or basement. Shut down or disconnect all the electrical lines. Finally, cover the pool as shown at right.

Installing a cover

A winter cover keeps dirt and debris out of the pool and slows the growth of algae. It also protects a vinyl liner from punctures caused by wind-blown ice. Buy a pool cover that can be locked into place. A woven mesh cover keeps out leaves, snow, and most dirt but allows rainwater and melting snow to enter the pool. (Excess water flows out through the skimmer.) Solid covers keep out water but, because they tend to puddle, are hard to remove without dumping debris into the pool.

1 Always clean pool before balancing the water for winter. Use a leaf skimmer (left) to lift leaves and debris from the surface. Remove scum at the waterline with a sponge and the type of cleanser recommended by the liner manufacturer.

2 Scrub vinyl-lined pool walls with a liner brush to remove algae and dirt. Always work from the top down, so that the debris collects on the bottom of the pool, where it can easily be vacuumed.

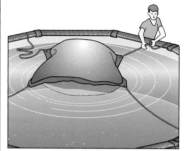

1 Buy a vinyl pillow with grommets in each corner at a pool shop. Inflate and float the pillow in the center of the pool, securing it with slightly slack tie-lines attached at the corners. The pillow prevents the cover from accumulating pockets of rainwater and snow.

3 Several hours before vacuuming, turn off the filtering system. Dirt and suspended solids will then settle to the bottom of the pool. Fill the vacuum hose with water by holding it to the return inlet. Assemble vacuum, and clean pool bottom.

4 Remove catch basket from skimmer and discard debris. Store basket indoors. Lower pool water level to just below the skimmer. Place a block of Styrofoam in the skimmer to prevent damage during a freeze.

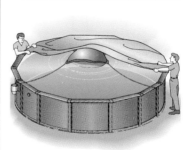

2 A pool cover must be large enough to accommodate the inflated pillow and still be held down securely around the sides of the pool. Before positioning the cover over the pillow and the pool, use a leaf skimmer to remove last debris from the pool.

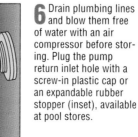

5 Turn off pump. Remove and clean the filter basket. Store pump indoors if possible. A pump that stays outside in subzero temperatures must have all moisture removed. Refer to the owner's manual for how to winterize a pump for outdoor storage.

6 Drain plumbing lines and blow them free of water with an air compressor before storing. Plug the pump return inlet hole with a screw-in plastic cap or an expandable rubber stopper (inset), available at pool stores.

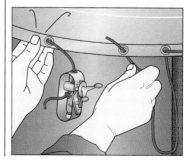

3 Secure the cover around the sides of the pool by threading cable under the cover between closely spaced grommets and over the cover between widely spaced grommets. Tighten cable with a turnbuckle. As winter temperatures drop, retighten turnbuckle.

In-line skates

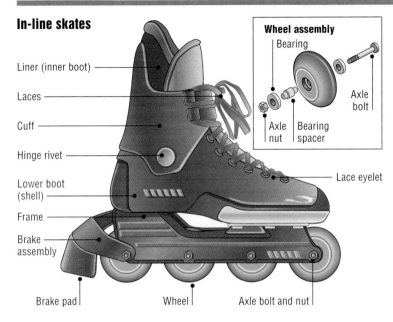

Liner (inner boot)

Laces

Cuff

Hinge rivet

Lower boot (shell)

Frame

Brake assembly

Brake pad

Wheel

Axle bolt and nut

Wheel assembly

Bearing

Axle bolt

Axle nut

Bearing spacer

Check the wheels, bearings, and brakes of in-line skates before each use. The nuts that hold the wheels on the axle bolt should be tight enough for security but loose enough for the wheels to roll freely. (Never use power tools on skate nuts.) Reverse a slightly worn wheel (below); then rotate it with the other wheels in one of the patterns shown at right (the pattern depends on the number of skate wheels). Wheels on skates used outdoors should be rotated after 6 to 8 hours of

Wheel rotation patterns

Three-wheel

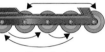
Four-wheel

Five-wheel

skating. Replace badly worn wheels.

If a skate's wheels bind as you turn them, the bearings are probably defective. Skating through sand, gravel, or water can damage bearings and shorten their life.

Open-type bearings (the balls are visible) can usually be serviced at home. Take the bearings out of the wheels and disassemble them, keeping the parts in order. Use solvent to clean the parts and dry them with a lint-free cloth. If any balls are pitted, misshapen, or missing, replace them all. Repack the balls with bicycle grease or another recommended lubricant. If the bearings are sealed (you can't see the balls), have them adjusted or replaced by a skate dealer. As a matter of routine, wipe off the bearings after every outing.

Brake pads also wear down with use; replace them as needed (below, left).

Reversing and rotating a wheel

Worn area

Check wheels regularly and reverse them when one side shows wear. At the same time, change their position in line (see *Wheel rotation patterns*, above).

To remove a wheel, loosen axle bolt and nut with tools that came with skates. Turn wheel over so that worn side faces in opposite direction.

To return a wheel to the frame, fasten axle nut securely without over-tightening. Follow the same procedure when rotating wheels.

Changing brake pads

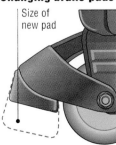

Size of new pad

1 Periodically inspect brake pads for wear. On some skate models, you must remove rear wheel along with brake assembly to change pads.

2 Remove brake assembly with tools that came with skates; use screwdriver to loosen screw from center of brake pad. Remove pad.

3 Slide new brake pad into brake assembly so that screw holes align. Screw pad to assembly; reinstall assembly on skate frame.

Other skates

All skates—ice, in-line, roller, and skateboards—need regular care. Check axle nuts and action nuts for tightness. Rotate roller-skate and skateboard wheels in an X pattern. Service bearings as needed (above). Replace worn wheels, stops, truck cushions, and pivots. Shield wheels and bearings from cleaners used on the boot. Dry ice-skate blades after each use; have them sharpened professionally.

Roller skate anatomy

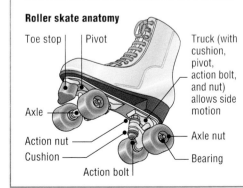

Toe stop

Pivot

Truck (with cushion, pivot, action bolt, and nut) allows side motion

Axle

Action nut

Cushion

Axle nut

Bearing

Action bolt

Skis

Taking good care of your skis will not only make them last longer but also make you a better skier. Skis that are properly tuned, sharpened, repaired, and waxed tend to be faster and more responsive than skis that are poorly maintained

In addition to drying your skis thoroughly after each day on the slopes, pay special attention to the condition of the base, or underside, of the skis.

Base configurations

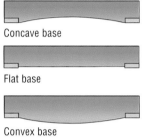

Concave base

Flat base

Convex base

Advanced skiers may prefer a curved base, but most skiers get the best results from skis with flat bases. New skis are usually delivered from the factory with their bases flat. As skis are used, the bases tend to develop either a concave or a convex curve. As a result, your skis will need to be tuned flat periodically (see *Tuning skis*, below, right). How often depends on how much you ski. Racers, for whom as little as j second can mean the difference between first and second place, tune their skis before each run. At the beginning of every ski season, have your skis tuned and structured (patterned) at a ski shop where professional equipment is used. After that, check the bases periodically with a true bar, and tune them as needed. Sharpen the skis' edges and fill any gouges (p.428) at the same time.

Waxing. All skis, even so-called waxless skis, benefit from waxing before every ski trip (p.428). Because newer skis have highly porous bases, they absorb wax better but require more frequent waxing. Special ski waxes have been developed for every kind of snow and weather condition. Picking the right wax not only makes skis perform better, it protects them from ultraviolet rays and the chemicals in man-made snow.

Bindings. Bindings are important safety devices. Clean and dry your bindings after every day of skiing, but leave their repair or adjustment to a shop that knows your particular brand.

Tools for ski repair

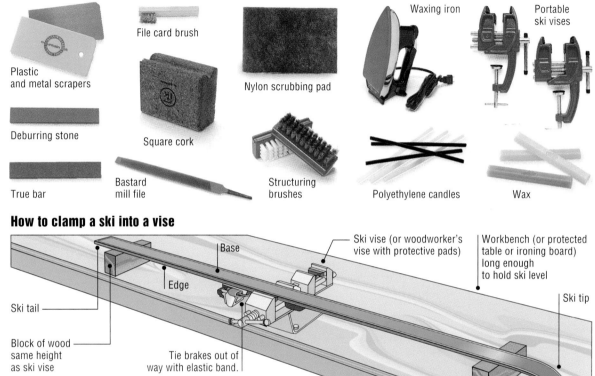

Plastic and metal scrapers

File card brush

Nylon scrubbing pad

Waxing iron

Portable ski vises

Deburring stone

Square cork

True bar

Bastard mill file

Structuring brushes

Polyethylene candles

Wax

How to clamp a ski into a vise

Base

Edge

Ski tail

Block of wood same height as ski vise

Tie brakes out of way with elastic band.

Ski vise (or woodworker's vise with protective pads)

Workbench (or protected table or ironing board) long enough to hold ski level

Ski tip

To work on a ski, attach it firmly to a long surface, such as a workbench or an ironing board, with a vise. Support the ski's ends with blocks.

Tuning skis

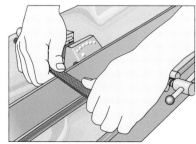

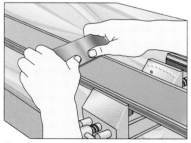

Check base for flatness by holding a true bar across it in several places and sighting down it. If you see light at the bar's edges, the base is convex; in the middle, concave.

To flatten a concave base, clamp ski, base side up, in vise. Using a 10-in. bastard mill file, make firm overlapping strokes from toe curve to tail until edges and base are even.

Correct a convex ski base with a metal hand scraper, held at a 30° angle as shown. Push scraper from tip curve to tail along the base until base surface is even with edges.

Sharpening skis

Sharpened edges make a ski more responsive and easier to handle. Clamp the ski, base side up, in a ski vise (p.427). Hold a 10-in. mill bastard file flat against the base with both hands. Working from tip to tail and applying constant pressure, make several long strokes until the edges are flat and sharp.

Ski vise

To sharpen side edge, turn ski sideways in vise. Hold file flat against edge with one hand while steadying ski with the other. Make several long strokes down edge from tip to tail. Repeat procedure on the other edge.

Deburr bottom edges with a diamond stone. With ski still on its side, hold stone in one hand and gently press it along edge to remove metal burrs. Turn ski over and deburr the other edge.

Detune tip and tail to eliminate sharp edges at points where ski enters and exits snow. Work on tail and tip of one side, then the other. With ski in vise, base side up, hold diamond stone at a 45° angle. Move it gently against edge along last 2 to 3 in. of tail (left). Repeat motion on tip, moving stone down 6 to 9 in. on each side of ski.

Filling a gouge

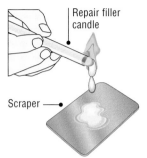

1 Clamp ski (p.427). Clean with biodegradable cleaner and wax remover. Dry with lint-free towel. Clean out gouge with utility knife.

Repair filler candle

Scraper

2 Light a polyethylene repair filler candle. Burn it over scraper until candle produces clear drops.

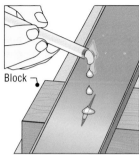

Block

3 Drip clear filler into gouge until it fills completely. If filler is too hot and flows too fast, blow out flame and start over.

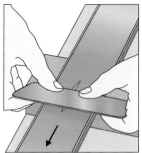

4 Let repair cool 30 min. Plane area with a metal scraper to remove excess filler and create a smooth surface.

Waxing skis

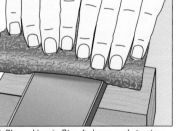

1 Clean ski as in Step 1 above, and structure (roughen) base for accepting wax. To structure base, put ski in vise, base side up, and rub base from tip to tail with a nylon scrubbing pad.

2 Melt ski wax candle on waxing iron over base (turn down iron temperature if wax begins to smoke). All-purpose and specialized ski waxes are applied the same way.

3 A medium-hot iron makes the wax fluid and forces it into the porous base material. Iron in generous amounts of wax from tip to tail. Let fresh wax cool as long as overnight.

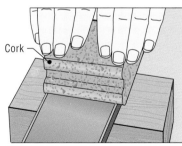

4 The longer you wait to scrape off excess wax, the better the wax is absorbed. Hold a plastic scraper at a 35° angle and pull in long strokes the length of the ski.

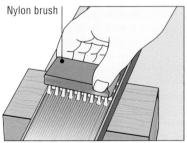

Cork

5 Polish wax finish by rubbing base gently with a nylon scrubbing pad from tip to tail. Finish polishing (above) by rubbing base vigorously with a rectangular piece of cork.

Nylon brush

6 Run a nylon brush from tip to tail to structure base for dry, cold skiing conditions; use a brass brush for wet conditions (the deeper grooves displace more moisture under the ski).

Tents, backpacks, and sleeping bags

Tents

The canopy of a modern tent is made of uncoated taffeta or ripstop nylon. The uncoated fabric lets moisture from breath and perspiration escape to the exterior. The floor of the tent and the rain fly—the tent's outer wall—are made of a urethane-coated waterproof nylon. An insulating dead air space separates the rain fly from the canopy.

Although nylon tents are lighter and usually more durable than older canvas tents, they do have weaknesses. Sparks and heat can melt nylon, and rocks can tear it. Patching tears is not difficult (right), but to avoid problems in the first place, pitch a tent well away from fires and stoves, and sweep the ground clear of rocks before setting up the tent. The corners that hold tie-line grommets are subject to wear; replace the grommets and reinforce the fabric as necessary.

Rain fly —
Tie-line grommet
Canopy
Door zipper —
Tie-line
Door | Sidewall | Peg

Permanent patch for a torn tent

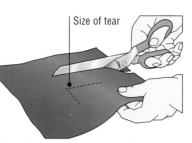

1 Use duct tape or other pressure-sensitive tape to make a temporary patch in the field. To preserve the tent's shape, don't overlap sides of tear when you make the permanent patch after returning home.

Size of tear

2 At home, cut a nylon patch 2 in. larger than the tear (or hole) on all sides; it should match the fabric you're mending: Use uncoated fabric for the canopy, waterproof nylon for the floor and rain fly.

3 Cut nylon usually unravels. To prevent this, heat-seal edge of patch by passing its cut edges along a candle flame. (An alternative technique is to cut patch with the hot point of a wood-burning tool.)

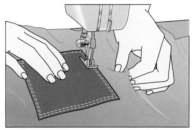

4 Center patch over exterior side of damage; sew two rows of stitches around patch edges. Use No. 46 nylon thread and, preferably, a sewing machine. If hand-sewing, use a needle no larger than needed to pierce fabric.

Cut tent fabric at corners to create flaps
Patching material
Fold flap under and stitch edge

5 To finish inside of patch, turn tent inside out. Cut, fold, and stitch raw edges of tear to back of patch as shown. This will keep tear from spreading to stitch line of new patch.

6 After sewing any part of a tent or backpack, spread seam sealant on both sides of all stitch lines for waterproofing. Work in a well-ventilated area; sealant smell gives some people a headache.

Replacing a grommet

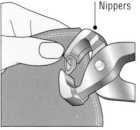
Nippers

1 If a damaged or loose grommet is still in place, pry it apart with pliers or wire nippers. Work alternately on both sides of fabric until the two pieces are separated.

Webbing

2 Cut a piece of nylon webbing to reinforce the fabric around the grommet hole. Heat-seal the cut edges of the webbing (Step 3, above).

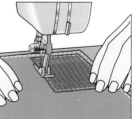

3 Slide webbing over hole and secure it with a line of stitches. Heat tip of an awl over flame and burn a hole through webbing where grommet will go.

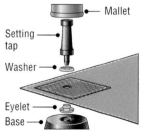
Mallet
Setting tap
Washer
Eyelet
Base

4 Align parts of grommet setting tool as shown, with hole in fabric over eyelet, and washer, rounded side up, on top. Hit setting tap into hole with mallet until grommet is tightly set.

Replacing a backpack's strap and buckle

Backpacks are designed to help you carry heavy loads as comfortably as possible. Waist and shoulder straps, which bear the greatest burden, are the most likely to fail by pulling out of their seams. Strap repairs are easy to make as long as you have a sewing machine.

A backpack's plastic buckles are designed for quick hooking and unhooking. To replace a damaged one, remove the buckle's strap from the pack and discard the old buckle. Thread the strap through the replacement buckle, and reattach the strap to the pack as shown below.

Exterior-frame backpack

Frame   Loaded pack

Seam ripper

1 To replace a buckle, or to secure a strap that's pulling loose, open up the seam, being careful not to cut strap or pack. Remove strap.

Pin

Tail

2 Slip strap back into seam, leaving 1 in. or more of tail inside. Tape or pin strap in place, setting it at same angle as it was originally.

3 Machine-sew seam to hold strap; reinforce with a second row of stitches. Use a size 20 commercial sewing needle and No. 46 nylon thread.

Stitch here first

4 Secure strap with another double row of stitches. If tail is inside a seam on pack body, anchor tail to body fabric.

On-the-trail repairs

Problems with camping gear often don't show up until you are well underway. Trail repairs may not be permanent, but they can save an outing. Essential emergency items for tents, backpacks, and sleeping bags:

Duct tape for quick patch of tears in nylon tents, packs, or sleeping bags. (Tape later reminds you to make a permanent repair using matching fabric.)

Nylon thread (No. 46) or dental floss and a needle to repair pulled-out straps.

Plastic disc-clamp loop set to replace a torn tent peg loop. Insert the plastic disc into the tent corner from the inside. Secure with plastic clamp on the outside. The clamp holds a loop of twine as a temporary peg loop.

Neoprene seam sealant to stop small seam leaks, particularly along the edges and at the corners of tent floors.

A heat-and-melt patch stick to repair small tears, abrasions, and punctures in fabric. Heat the stick and, using a knife, spread on area to be patched.

Sleeping bag care

Most sleeping bags are covered with taffeta or ripstop nylon and filled with down or another insulator. Down bags can be washed by hand in a bathtub but are best handled by an experienced dry cleaner. Lifting a wet down-filled bag can ruin the baffles that hold the down in place. Machine-wash other sleeping bags, following the manufacturer's instructions. Patch sleeping bag holes and rips with duct tape to prevent loss of insulation. Store clean sleeping bags loosely folded in a dry closet.

The long zippers on sleeping bags are the major source of problems. You may be able to repair a zipper (p.30), but replacement (right) is easy.

Down sleeping bag

Replacing a sleeping bag zipper

Open a few stitches in the zipper seam. If down pops out, pin or sew an extra seam behind the zipper seam to hold the down in place.

Remove old zipper, one stitch at a time, with a seam ripper or embroidery scissors (a razor blade could cut the fabric).

If the new zipper might be used to join two sleeping bags, try it out on mating bag before sewing it in place.

Pin zipper in place. Machine-sew one side at a time, using a zipper foot to guide the needle an even distance from the teeth.

Shortening a zipper

If you can't find a zipper of the right length, you can buy plastic-toothed or nylon coil zippers by the yard from a sewing center. Cut one to size with scissors.

To form stops at top and bottom, use a soldering iron (p.136) to melt two plastic teeth together (insert). Fold tape to make stops for a coil zipper.

Home emergencies

You can avoid many home emergencies by making safety part of your routine. The hazard symbols used throughout this book (and explained in the following pages) alert you to the potential shock, fire, and poisoning risks associated with some repairs. For additional precautions to take when making repairs, be sure to read any *For your safety* boxes found with the specific repair instructions in this book.

Learn the proper use of your tools, and always read the manufacturer's instructions before you try out new equipment. Wear appropriate protective clothing and gear. Keep first-aid supplies on hand, and review the emergency procedures in this section *before* an injury happens. These procedures have worked successfully in the past, but improvements are introduced now and then. Contact a reputable first-aid organization, such as St. John Ambulance, to update your knowledge of the latest procedures.

Electricity

Make sure everyone in your house knows the location of the service panel and which parts of the house are controlled by each circuit breaker or fuse (see *Correcting circuit overloads*, p.127). Mark the circuit breakers or fuses on the service panel (p.127) so all household members can quickly turn off power to any part of the house when needed.

Use only safety-tested and listed electrical appliances (see *Canadian Standards Association*, p.125). Read the owner's manual before operating a new appliance, and keep the manual for reference. Unplug power tools and small electrical appliances when not in use and store them out of the reach of children. If any electrical device trips a fuse or circuit breaker, smokes, has an unusual odor (see *Tips from the pros*, p.140), or causes a tingling sensation when touched, unplug it at once. Either identify and solve the prob-

lem (see *General troubleshooting*, pp.144–147) or have the device serviced before using it again.

Prevent electrical fires by keeping electrical equipment in good repair: Replace frayed or damaged cords and faulty plugs (p.144); avoid overloading outlets with too many plug adapters; and don't coil appliance cords (coiled cords can get hot enough to ignite).

Before repairing an electrical device or doing any other electrical work yourself, read the *Appliance repair basics* section of this book (pp.125–148) carefully and follow all the safety precautions contained in it. Above all, *always unplug the appliance or turn off power to the circuit before doing any work on an appliance or circuit.*

Water and electricity can be a fatal mix. Never touch electrical appliances, switches, sockets, or cords if your hands or feet are wet or if they are in contact

with a water faucet or a grounded pipe. Install ground-fault circuit interrupters (p.128) in all areas where water may come in contact with electrical appliances or cords: the kitchen, bathroom, laundry room, and garage.

Don't touch a shock victim until you're sure you won't endanger yourself. If victim is still touching electrical source, shut off power at service panel (p.127). Standing on a dry surface, disengage victim from source with a wooden broom handle or other dry nonconductive object. Call for emergency help. Give artificial respiration (p.434) or cardiopulmonary resuscitation (p.435) if it's needed and if you are trained.

Fire

Prepare for a fire emergency by installing smoke detectors (p.335) and by learning how to operate a fire extinguisher before it's needed (facing page). Have alternative exits (doors or windows) mapped out for each room, and rehearse an emergency escape plan with your family (prompt evacuation is crucial in order to avoid smoke inhalation, the primary hazard of residential fires). Prearrange an outside meeting place.

If you are caught in a fire and must travel through smoke, keep low to the ground. If you are trapped, open a window at the top to let heat and smoke out, and at the bottom to breathe fresh air. Never open a door that feels hot to the touch.

Prevent a fire from starting by observing fire safety practices. Store flammable liquids in closed containers away from any source of ignition, such as a furnace or a water heater. Keep oily rags in a closed metal container to avoid spontaneous combustion until you can properly dispose of them as a hazardous waste. Don't fill fuel tanks of gas-powered tools while the engine is running or still hot. Clean grease from

the kitchen stove and vents. Keep pot handles turned inward when cooking, and never leave anything on the stove unattended.

To safely clean up an oil or gas spill, apply an absorbent material—vermiculite or cat litter—to soak up as much as possible. *Don't use sawdust; it is combustible.* Wash area with detergent and water. Put oil- or gas-soaked material in a metal container with a lid to prevent fire. Oil- or gas-soaked materials are hazardous wastes; call your recycling center, health department, or environmental agency for disposal information.

Fight a small fire with an extinguisher. In the absence of an extinguisher, douse burning wood, paper, or cloth with water. Keep a watch on sofas or chairs that have caught fire, however, even after thoroughly dousing them—fires in upholstery can smolder and reignite. If a grease fire erupts in a frying pan, smother it with the pan's lid or a liberal dose of baking soda or sand. When a fire involves electricity, shut off the power at the main service panel. If a small fire can't be put out immediately, evacuate the house and call the fire department from a neighbor's telephone before trying any further measures.

Stop, drop, and roll

If your clothes catch fire, don't run for help; the air you stir up will feed the flames. Instead, cover your face with your hands to protect your throat and lungs, and "stop, drop and roll." Stop immediately; drop to the ground; and roll over and over to smother the flames.

Types of fire extinguishers

A quick defense against small home fires, a fire extinguisher is rated for use against various type of fires. A multipurpose fire extinguisher, rated A-B-C, is effective against all of the most common fires in homes and is a good choice if you have only one. Larger models have more capacity. Read the instructions and learn how to use an extinguisher (below). Check the pressure gauge monthly; if it is low, replace the extinguisher or have it recharged.

A Class A extinguishers are designed to fight blazes in wood, paper, rubber, and most plastics. Use near fireplaces, and in living areas and bedrooms.

B Class B extinguishers contain dry chemicals to smother fires fueled by oil, solvents, grease, gasoline, kerosene, and other flammable liquids. Use in kitchen, workshop area, and garage.

C Class C extinguishers also contain dry chemicals to smother fires in electrical equipment. Use in workshop area and near the electrical service panel.

To operate a fire extinguisher, first pull the pin or other release mechanism. Aiming at the base of the fire (not the top), squeeze the handle and sweep from side to side until the flames are out. Be sure that the fire is not between you and an exit; you may need to leave quickly if the fire persists or suddenly gets out of hand.

Gas

To prevent a buildup of gas that can result in a fire or explosion, utility companies add a scent to odorless natural gas and liquid propane gas. If you smell even a slight gas odor, evacuate the house and call the utility company from a neighbor's telephone. Don't smoke, light matches, or even flick on a light switch if you suspect a gas leak.

Fumes from combustible devices—gas stoves, gas or kerosene space heaters, gas water heaters, oil furnaces, or woodstoves—contain carbon monoxide (CO), an odorless and lethal poison. If such appliances are not properly vented or develop combustion chamber leaks, they can cause illness or even death (see *Gas poisoning,* p.438). An annual inspection of your heating system and flues by a professional heating contractor is your best defense against CO poisoning. Installing CO detectors near the furnace and on each floor of your house is an added precaution.

Never use equipment intended for outdoor use—charcoal or propane grills or camp stoves, for example—indoors, not even when a storm interrupts your regular supply of gas or electricity. The result can be carbon monoxide poisoning. Exhaust from gasoline engines also contains CO. Don't run your car engine in a closed garage under any circumstances. Always start gas-fueled equipment such as lawn mowers and tillers outside the garage.

Shutting off the gas

Locate shutoff valve for each gas fixture in your home. If an appliance malfunctions or you smell gas, shut valve by turning handle perpendicular to pipe.

The main gas shutoff valve in a house is usually located near the gas meter. Keep groove-joint pliers (p.14) nearby so you can turn it off quickly in an emergency.

Plumbing

For common emergency plumbing repairs, see page 109. If your furnace goes out in freezing weather, you can protect the pipes from freezing by turning on all the taps and running the water at a slow, steady rate. This works, of course, only if the drains are running freely. To protect toilet plumbing, shut off the water supply and flush the toilet to empty the bowl and tank. If a pipe does burst, try to sop up the water as quickly as you can to prevent floor damage.

If a washing machine or dishwasher floods, place rolled beach towels, rugs, or other absorbent rags around the appliance to contain the flow of water. Soak up the standing water with a mop or sponge.

To pump out basement water, rent a portable pump. Wear rubber boots in a flooded basement, and be careful not to touch any electrical outlets or appliances. Plug pump into a ground fault interrupter receptacle, and direct water to a drain or out a window.

Home emergencies ▪ Basic first aid

The first-aid kit

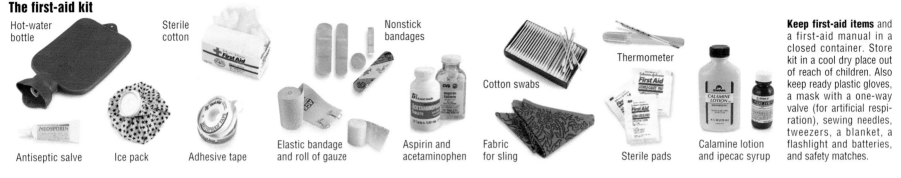

Hot-water bottle

Sterile cotton

Nonstick bandages

Antiseptic salve

Ice pack

Adhesive tape

Elastic bandage and roll of gauze

Aspirin and acetaminophen

Cotton swabs

Fabric for sling

Thermometer

Sterile pads

Calamine lotion and ipecac syrup

Keep first-aid items and a first-aid manual in a closed container. Store kit in a cool dry place out of reach of children. Also keep ready plastic gloves, a mask with a one-way valve (for artificial respiration), sewing needles, tweezers, a blanket, a flashlight and batteries, and safety matches.

The recovery position

1 To prevent unconscious person from choking, kneel beside victim and loosen tight clothing. Turn head toward you. Tuck near arm under body; put far arm over chest. Lift far ankle over near one.

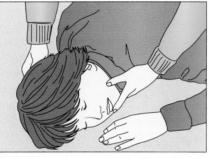

2 Grasp victim's clothing at far hip; carefully cradle the head with your other hand as you support the torso with your knees. Gently roll the victim onto the stomach.

3 Tilt the head back to open the airway. Then bend the arm near you to prop up the victim's upper body, and bend the leg near you to prop up the lower body.

4 Pull other arm from under victim and lay it beside the body. Cover the victim with a coat or blanket. **CAUTION:** Don't move anyone with a head, neck, or back injury.

Artificial respiration for an adult or child

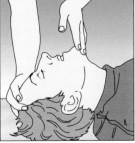

1 Lay victim on back. Gently tilt the forehead back and lift the chin to open airway, which may be all that is needed for the victim to start breathing.

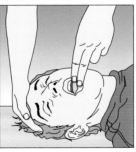

2 If victim doesn't begin breathing, turn head to side and clear the mouth of any foreign matter with a sweep of two fingers. Repeat Step 1.

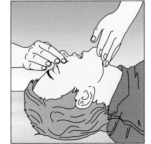

3 If victim still isn't breathing, pinch nose shut with your index finger and thumb. Open your mouth wide and take a deep breath.

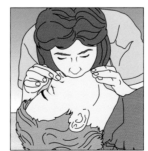

4 Seal your lips around victim's mouth. Exhale fully. Feel for victim's breath on your neck. Repeat every 5 sec. for adult; every 3 sec. for a child.

Artificial respiration for an infant

Place infant on back on a firm surface. Clear airway. Covering baby's nose and mouth with your mouth, give two slow breaths (1 to 1½ sec. each) using just enough air to make the chest rise. (The chest should rise if the air goes in.) Remove your mouth and inhale; repeat procedure at a rate of 1 breath every 3 sec.

CPR

Cardiopulmonary resuscitation, or CPR, is a technique that alternates artificial respiration (facing page) and chest compressions to revive victims who have no pulse. Artificial respiration supplies oxygen to the blood; chest compressions restore blood circulation.

CAUTION: This guide is meant as a memory aid for someone who's had formal CPR training. Don't try this technique without training; improperly administered chest compressions can injure ribs and internal organs. Also, do not administer CPR unless the victim has no pulse; chest compressions can cause a faintly beating heart to stop.

CPR for an infant up to 12 months

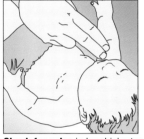

Check for pulse in brachial artery (left). To compress chest, place two fingers on chest, a finger width below nipples. Press down 1 in., five times. Resume artificial respiration. Repeat procedure; check breath and pulse after 1 min., then every few minutes thereafter.

CPR for a child from 1 to 8 years

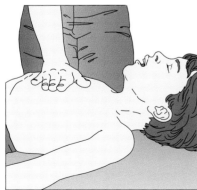

Feel for pulse in a carotid artery (see *CPR for an adult,* Step 1, right). Depress child's chest 1 to 1½ in. with only the heel of one hand. Give five compressions, then one breath. Check breath and pulse after 1 min. and then every few minutes thereafter.

CPR for an adult

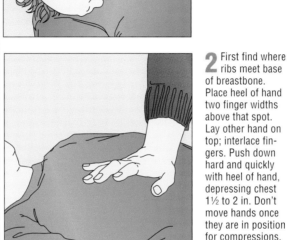

1 After two breaths of artificial respiration (facing page), feel for the victim's pulse in one of the carotid arteries on either side of the neck. If you don't feel a pulse, begin chest compressions.

2 First find where ribs meet base of breastbone. Place heel of hand two finger widths above that spot. Lay other hand on top; interlace fingers. Push down hard and quickly with heel of hand, depressing chest 1½ to 2 in. Don't move hands once they are in position for compressions.

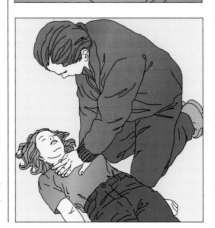

3 Press 15 times, counting "One and two and . . ." up to 15. Then release your hands and give two breaths of artificial respiration. Repeat the cycle four times, which should take about 1 min. Check pulse. Continue cycles and check for return of pulse every 3 min.

Bleeding

Severe bleeding can lead to shock (p.439) or even death. To control the blood flow, press down firmly on the wound for 5 minutes with a clean cloth. Raise the injured area above the heart, except if the victim has broken bones. Have the victim rest. As a last resort, after you call for medical help, try to stop bleeding from an arm or leg wound at one of the body's main pressure points—places where arteries can be pressed closed against the underlying bone.

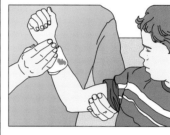

To stop bleeding from a lower-arm wound, hold victim's arm at right angle to body. With your thumb on outside of upper arm and your fingers on inside, press hard against bone. Alternate 5 min. of maximum pressure with 5 min. of reduced pressure.

To stop bleeding from the leg, lay the victim down. Bend the injured leg at the knee. With one thumb on top of the other, press firmly in the fold of the groin against the rim of the pelvis. Alternate 5-min. periods of maximum pressure and reduced pressure.

Bruises

A bruise is a sign of bleeding beneath the skin. At the first sign of a bruise, apply cold compresses to the area, 15 minutes on and 15 minutes off, to minimize pain and swelling. On an arm or a leg bruise, reduce swelling by raising the limb above heart level. Consult a doctor when a bruise occurs on or near the abdomen, on the back, or when the victim has difficulty moving the bruised area. Also check with a doctor if a bruise doesn't start to fade within a week.

Home emergencies ▪ Treating injuries

Burns

You can treat a small (half-dollar-size or less) first-degree burn at home (below), but larger or more severe burns require prompt professional attention. Never put ice or butter on a burn. Keep the burn site above the heart (a face-burn victim should sit up). Remove jewelry and tight clothing from the burn area before swelling occurs.

First-degree burns are red and painful but do not produce blisters.

Second-degree burns are red and painful with blisters and swelling.

Third-degree burns are deep. Skin is white or black; pain is severe if nerves aren't destroyed.

Treat minor burn by soaking area in cool (not icy) water or by applying cool wet cloths. Cover with a sterile nonstick dressing and bandage.

Chemical burns

Caustic chemicals such as bleach, lye, and acid can cause severe damage to tissues. To treat chemical burns, first remove clothing from the burned area (the clothing may still be contaminated with the chemical and cause further damage); then flush the area with slowly running cool water for 15 to 20 minutes. Use a hose, or pitchers of water. Cover the burned skin with a sterile nonstick dressing and bandage; get the victim to a doctor quickly.

To treat an eye that has been splashed with a caustic chemical, flush the eyeball with cool water for 15 minutes or more. Cover with a sterile nonstick dressing and bandage. Seek immediate medical help.

Choking

Choking happens quickly and can be fatal. The Heimlich maneuver—and several variations described here—is an emergency procedure for unclogging a completely blocked airway. If a choking victim can talk, however, don't interfere; he is getting oxygen and can cough up the obstruction himself.

When an infant is choking

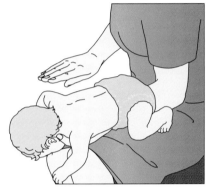

Place infant across arm on your lap with head lower than chest. Support the head at the chin. Use the heel of your hand, give five back blows between shoulder blades. If back blows fail, turn infant over.

Give five quick thrusts, with two fingers, to chest. Check the mouth. Use little finger to sweep out object, but only if you see it. Try to give breaths (p.434). Repeat the cycle of back blows, chest thrusts, and breaths.

Cuts and abrasions

To prevent infection, clean minor cuts and abrasions with soap and water; then dress with sterile bandages. Press down on a wound to stop the flow of blood. If a wound continues to bleed after 5 minutes of pressure, seek medical help. Very long or deep incisions, those still containing debris, and those caused

When an adult is choking

To perform the Heimlich maneuver on a conscious victim, stand behind him, your arms around his waist. Place your fist, thumb against the abdomen, just above the navel. Hold fist with other hand. Give a quick, forceful, upward thrust to expel obstruction. Repeat as needed.

If victim isn't breathing but has a a pulse, place her on the ground, face up. Kneeling astride hips, put heel of one hand slightly above the navel. Place the other hand on top and keep the fingers raised. Holding arms straight, deliver up to five thrusts. Check mouth for expelled object. Repeat if necessary.

If you are alone and choking, place your fist on your own stomach as described above. Perform up to five thrusts on yourself. An alternative is to press your stomach forcefully over the back of a chair (left). Repeat until object is expelled.

by a dirty object should also be seen by a doctor (you may need a tetanus booster shot). After tending the wound, look for signs of infection—redness, heat, or swelling at the site or red streaks leading from it—usually starting 24 to 72 hours after the injury. See a doctor at the first hint of infection.

Drowning

Don't attempt a swimming rescue unless you recently have taken a lifesaving course. Throw a lifeline from the shore or a boat. If you do pull a victim out of the water, get someone to call for help while you check the person's breathing and pulse. If breathing has stopped, begin artificial respiration (p.434). If there is no heartbeat, and if you have the training, start cardiopulmonary resuscitation (p.435). If the person is breathing and there is no reason to believe he has a back or neck injury, put him into the recovery position (p.434); cover him while you wait for a doctor.

To rescue someone from a pool, brace yourself and reach out a hand, life preserver, or pole to pull person to safety. Entering the water to attempt a solo rescue is dangerous; a panicky drowning victim can pull you both under, even in shallow water.

Offer an oar to a drowning person from a boat, and pull victim boatside. Tie victim to a towline so that you can row him to safety. Don't try to pull victim aboard without help; a capsized boat jeopardizes both of you.

Eye injuries

Eyes are vulnerable to injuries and require prompt attention. If an object such as a splinter or piece of glass penetrates the eye, don't try to remove it. Make a temporary eye patch with a piece of gauze or cloth and adhesive tape, and immediately seek emergency medical treatment. Check with your doctor after any eye injury, especially if you experience a direct blow to the eye or to the head near your eyes.

To remove a speck or an eyelash from an eye, first wash your hands. Gently pull upper eyelid down until tears form, which may wash out object. If not, pull down lower eyelid and use a moistened clean tissue or cloth to remove speck.

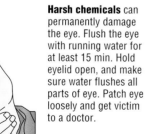

Harsh chemicals can permanently damage the eye. Flush the eye with running water for at least 15 min. Hold eyelid open, and make sure water flushes all parts of eye. Patch eye loosely and get victim to a doctor.

Fractures

Fractures most often occur at the narrowest—and weakest—point of a bone. When a bone breaks, you may actually hear or feel the snap. The fracture site will be painful, and possibly swollen and blue from internal bleeding. Call for medical help; then try to immobilize the broken bone (below and below right) before the victim is moved. If the fracture involves a head, neck, or back injury, don't move the victim. Never try to reset the fractured bone, and don't let the victim put weight on it. A doctor will reset the bone and put it in a cast; let the doctor know if the cast is uncomfortably tight or if it causes numbness.

A simple fracture, also known as a closed fracture, is one that doesn't pierce the skin. The bone may be cracked or broken into several pieces.

In a compound fracture, also called an open fracture, one or more pieces of the broken bone break through the skin.

Use a sling to support a broken arm only if the injured arm bends without undue pain. Secure sling to chest by tying a broad bandage around the arm and torso. Do not tie over the fracture.

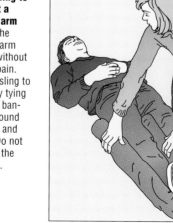

To immobilize a broken leg, improvise a splint with a rolled-up blanket. After the blanket is in place, bind the injured leg to the other one—gently—by tying feet and knees together with strips of cloth or rope.

437

Gas poisoning

Inhaling carbon monoxide and other poisonous gases that interfere with the absorption of oxygen into the bloodstream can result in suffocation. Signs of carbon monoxide poisoning include headache, nausea, vomiting, dilated pupils, and flushed skin. The victim may become confused and lose consciousness; without treatment, the victim will die. Move a person who has inhaled a poisonous gas into fresh air immediately and call for emergency medical help. Loosen any tight clothing at the neck and waist to make breathing easier. If the victim is not breathing, open the airway and begin artificial respiration (p.434). If the victim has no pulse and you are trained, administer CPR (p.435) until a medical team arrives.

Head injuries

Because a blow to the head may damage the brain or the spinal cord, always seek medical attention. Don't move the victim of a head injury unless he is in serious danger—from fire or drowning, for example. Suspect a head injury if blood or clear fluid is leaking from the victim's nose, mouth, or ears.

A concussion occurs when a blow causes the brain to strike the inside of the skull. Concussion victims may lose consciousness briefly and may later experience headache, nausea, confusion, inappropriate sleepiness, and/or agitation. Paralysis, weakness, seizures, and unequal pupils may also occur. Monitor the victim of even a minor hit to the head for 24 hours and report symptoms of concussion to a doctor.

Poisoning

If you believe a person has been poisoned, call your local poison control center for first-aid instructions. Some poisons can be ejected through vomiting; others need dilution in the stomach. You may be told to have the victim's stomach pumped at an emergency room. Try to identify the poison specifically. If a child, for example, drinks solvent in the workshop, read the container label (which may say not to induce vomiting) and the list of ingredients to the poison control representative. If you are told to induce vomiting, use 2 tablespoons of syrup of ipecac for an adult, 1 tablespoon for a child, or 2 teaspoons for an infant. Follow this with 8 ounces of water or milk. Keep the victim sitting up to prevent choking when the induced vomiting does occur.

Puncture wounds

When the skin is punctured by a sharp object, there is often little bleeding. This increases the chance of infection because bleeding helps to flush bacteria and debris from a wound. Always flush a puncture wound with running water to help clean it out. Don't remove deeply embedded objects yourself; let a doctor do it. Also see your doctor if the wound is more than ½ inch deep or if the puncture was caused by a dirty object, such as a rusty nail. Deep puncture wounds can damage tendons, nerves, and blood vessels. When a tendon is injured, there may be partial or even complete loss of function in an extremity. For that reason, puncture wounds of the hand, wrist, arm, leg, and foot should be checked as soon as possible for internal damage.

Removing a fishhook

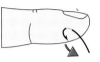
Anesthetize the fingertip with ice; then push the hook forward until the barb, point first, breaks completely through the skin.

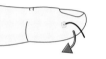
Use pliers or other wire cutters to snip the barb off the hook. Carefully start pulling the remaining shaft of the fishhook back out of the finger.

Wash both entry and exit wounds with soap and water, apply antiseptic, bandage the finger, and seek medical advice about the need for a tetanus shot.

Bandaging a head wound

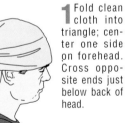

1 Fold clean cloth into triangle; center one side on forehead. Cross opposite ends just below back of head.

2 Bring the same ends around to the front of the head and tie. Keep victim's head steady while you are working.

3 Place one hand on the bandage to keep it from slipping. Use other hand to draw the point downward at back of neck.

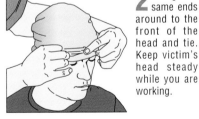

4 Lift point of bandage up to crown. Fix it in place with a safety pin or adhesive tape, or tuck it into edge of bandage at forehead.

Saving a severed digit

Lay the victim down with the head lower than the heart. Elevate the injured hand or foot. Stop the bleeding (below) and treat the victim for possible shock (facing page). Wrap the severed digit in a clean moist cloth and put it in a plastic bag. Seal the bag, pack it in crushed ice, and take it to the hospital with the victim. Severed digits can often be reattached by microsurgery.

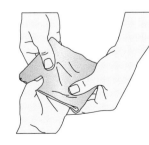
Hold clean cloth against wound, adding more layers as necessary to halt bleeding. Bandage cloths in place.

Shock

A lack of sufficient blood to the body's organs and tissues may result in shock. After a heart attack or major injury, particularly one involving a severe loss of blood, watch for the signs of shock—cold clammy skin, confusion, dizziness, weak, rapid pulse, and fast, shallow breathing—and call for medical help at once. While you wait, try to open the victim's airway (p.436) and control bleeding (p.435). Raise the feet to improve circulation unless the head, neck, or spinal cord is injured. Check the victim's pulse. Administer CPR (p.435) if needed and if you have the training. Loosen tight clothing. Keep the victim warm but not overheated. Do not give him anything to eat or drink.

Splinters

For splinters under skin, use needle sterilized over a flame for a few seconds to open the skin; pull splinter out at same angle it entered.

To remove a splinter, wash the skin around the wound with warm soapy water. Sterilize tweezers in boiling water for 5 minutes. Use the tweezers to pull out the splinter at the same angle it entered the flesh. Wash the wound with soap and water and apply a sterile bandage. If pain or swelling persists, or if the splinter is too deeply embedded to get out with home methods, see your doctor.

Sprains and strains

A *strain* is a pulled muscle. A *sprain* involves stretched or torn ligaments around a joint. Both cause pain, swelling, and bleeding under the skin. First aid for either involves rest, ice, compression, and elevation (remember the acronym RICE). Rest allows tissue to heal. Ice numbs pain and reduces swelling. Apply an ice pack, 15 minutes on and 15 minutes off, every few hours for the first 2 days. Wearing a compression bandage (right) for at least 2 days also helps control bleeding and swelling. Keeping the injured area elevated above heart level for as long as possible reduces internal bleeding.

Strained back

Hard physical exertion or an awkward movement can result in severe low back pain. For the first day or two, apply cold compresses to the strained muscle for 20 minutes at a time. (Use a towel soaked in cold water or a plastic bag of crushed ice or frozen vegetables wrapped in a towel.) If the pain persists, consult a doctor about medication to ease the discomfort and inflammation.

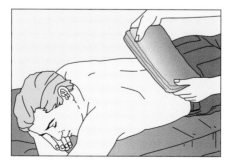

After applying cold compresses to a sore back to reduce tissue swelling, switch to a hot-water bottle or heating pad to relax tense muscles.

Bandaging a sprain

1 Wrap a sprained ankle with a compression bandage in a figure-8 pattern. Make two loops around the instep; then stretch bandage diagonally across the foot.

2 Bring the bandage around the ankle to the front of the foot, and then wrap it diagonally across the instep and under the arch.

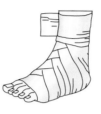

3 Continue wrapping the bandage in figure-8 turns. Each turn should overlap the previous turn by about three-fourths of the bandage's width.

4 When the foot and ankle are wrapped, secure the bandage with a pin. Leave toes bare. If they become numb or discolored, the bandage is too tight.

Moving heavy objects

Use a dolly or cart whenever possible. Otherwise, push and slide large objects into place. If you must lift something heavy (an air conditioner, for example), enlist a friend's help. If you are alone—and fit enough to try a solo lift—make sure your footing is stable and your body is centered over your feet. When you lift from a low height, bend your knees and keep your back flat. Get a good grip and pull the object close to you. Lift with your legs, not your back. Move your feet to turn; never twist your back while lifting or carrying a heavy load.

Unconsciousness

An unconscious person may slip in and out of a state of drowsiness, maintain a drunkenlike stupor, or fall into a coma. No matter what the symptoms may be, a person who is unconscious—even for a short period of time—requires immediate medical attention. If you know for sure that the victim has not sustained a head, neck, or back injury, put him or her in the recovery position (p.434). Otherwise, don't move the victim. Make sure the victim's airway is clear (p.436), and keep checking that it remains clear (vomit, blood, or saliva may block the top of the windpipe or the tongue may slide over it). If the victim has stopped breathing, perform artificial respiration (p.434), taking care not to twist or rotate the head. If there is no pulse and you have the proper training, begin administering CPR (p.435). Try to stop any bleeding while you await the ambulance.

Consumer information

Most of the tools, supplies, and parts needed for the repair and maintenance tasks described in this book can be found at hardware stores, home improvement centers, and other retail outlets. (The availability of some brand-name tools may vary across the country.) To locate more specialized or unusual items, consult the Yellow Pages of your telephone directory under headings such as "Electrical Appliances—Small, Repairing," "Refrigerators and Freezers—Servicing," "Plumbing Supplies" or "Electrical Equipment."

Manufacturers often sell parts and accessories by mail order, and frequently include listings of service centers with their instruction manuals. These listings come in handy if a product requires repairs. Some firms maintain customer service departments that give advice about proper usage and care of your appliance. They may also be able to replace a lost owner's manual. If you have difficulty finding a product locally, you may be able to track down the right service center or parts supplier by asking the counter staff at a local hardware store for suggestions. National electronic "phone books" on CD-ROM can be consulted, and you can also search the Internet for a source.

Many companies, sometimes referred to as third-party or aftermarket suppliers, sell servicing tools and replacement parts for appliances they don't manufacture. Aftermarket parts are typically sold by mail order or through large parts supply houses. When ordering these parts (or any others), be sure to have the model number and any other identification numbers available; they might be stamped on the part or on a tag attached behind or beneath the appliance.

Another ally in the effort to find a particular company or product is your local public library. Most have a variety of excellent reference resources, including such publications as *Brands and Their Companies, Canadian Trade Index, Fraser's Canadian Trade Directory, Sweet's Canadian Construction Catalogue File,* and *Scott's Directories.* Some libraries also subscribe to consumer or trade magazines that carry repair information and parts source listings. If you can't find anything that helps, ask the reference librarian for help.

In some cases, even after you've made a substantial effort, finding parts or information can be difficult because companies go out of business, change hands or locations, or are headquartered overseas. Sometimes parts for older models are discontinued. If you've tried without success to locate parts or servicing information, look for a repair shop that's willing to help. If someone at the first shop you call says, "Throw it away and buy a new one," check with at least one other shop to verify this advice. Someone may know of a parts distributor for your product, or may be able to assist in locating a hard-to-find manufacturer by checking the Canadian Standards Association numbers, or other identification markings on the product. As a last resort, you might even be able to find a part at a secondhand shop, but it probably won't be covered by a warranty of any sort.

Consumer complaints. If you have a problem with a product, check to see if it is still under warranty. If so, follow the guidelines and procedures established by the dealer or manufacturer. If the product warranty has expired, contact the dealer and describe the problem clearly and calmly. Keep copies of contracts, receipts, letters, etc.; note whom you talk to and when. If the dealer does not solve the problem to your satisfaction, contact the manufacturer. If that doesn't help, the following organizations can provide you with useful advice: The Consumer Association of Canada (613 238-2533) and Industry Canada, Consumers Branch (800 348-5358). Other organizations worth contacting include your provincial office of Consumer Affairs and your local Better Business Bureau.

FOR YOUR SAFETY

Awareness and knowledge are the keys to preventing accidents. Various organizations provide safety information for consumers. Obtaining and studying their materials is a good way to help you and your family prevent injuries. Another useful resource is your local fire department, which may provide guidance on fire prevention and emergency preparation.

Child safety. The Canadian Institute of Child Health (885 Meadowlands Drive, Suite 512, Ottawa, ON K2C 3N2) provides information about injury prevention, playground safety and other subjects. Contact them by telephone (613 224-4144) or fax (613 224-4145). Child safety information is also available from the Ottawa-based Canadian Paediatric Society. Their tele-

phone number is 613 737-2728, and their fax number is 613 737-2794. The Canadian Tire Protection Foundation offers materials to groups involved with child-safety programs. Write to P.O. Box 770, Station K, Toronto, ON M4P 2V8, or telephone 800 748-8903.

Product safety. The Canadian Safety Council (1020 Thomas Spratt Place, Ottawa, ON K1G 5L5) publishes literature about safety issues. Their telephone number is 613 739-1535, and their fax number is 613 739-1566. The Canadian Standards Association (178 Rexdale Boulevard, Etobicoke, ON M9W 1R3) also provides useful consumer information. Contact this association by telephone (416 747-4129) or fax (416 747-4292).

Safe tool use starts with proper protective equipment such as goggles and dust masks. You'll be much more likely to use these items if you store them within easy reach.

The Construction Safety Association of Ontario (21 Voyager Court South, Etobicoke, ON M9M 5M7) is dedicated to promoting the safe operation of electrical and hand tools used outdoors, in workshops, and on commercial sites. This association distributes information throughout Canada. Their telephone number is 800 781-2726, and their E-mail address is info@constructsafety.on.ca. The Hand Tools Institute (25 North Broadway, Tarrytown, NY 10591) is a trade association that provides information about the safe use of nonpower

hand tools to organizations, colleges, and consumers all over North America.

Reducing bicycle hazards. The Canadian Cycling Association publishes a booklet about bicycle safety and pamphlets that address safety issues concerning cyclists and motorists. Write to 1600 James Naismith Drive, Gloucester, ON K1B 5N4.

Safety on and around the water. The Canadian Power and Sail Squadron directs consumers to local squadrons across Canada that offer courses in safety and navigation. For information, call 888 227-2628. The Watercraft Training Centre (800 336-2628) is concerned with the safe use of personal watercraft and directs consumers to local instructors.

Index

Index

Index

Index

Index

ACKNOWLEDGMENTS

*The editors are especially grateful to the following individuals and organizations
for their help in providing or reviewing information for this book.*

Abu Garcia
Advanced Water Conditioning
Almost Heaven, Ltd.
American Gas Association Research
American Lawn Mower Company
Ames Lawn and Garden Tools
Art & Ray's Lock and Safe
Associated Locksmiths of America, Inc.
Association of Home Appliance
 Manufacturers
B&B Pool and Spa Center
Best Chairs, Inc.
Black and Decker
Broan Manufacturing Company, Inc.
Campmor
The Carpet and Rug Institute
Chemical Engineering Corporation
The Coleman Company
John Deere Company
Dremel
Echo Inc.
EdgeCraft Corporation
The Eureka Company
Fedders North America
Fiskars, Inc.
Fyrnetics, Inc.
Garrett Wade Company, Inc.
Gaz Métropolitan
GE Wiring Devices
Gil's Grills, Inc.
Gleim Jewelers
Granado Appliance
Hamilton Beach/Proctor-Silex, Inc.
A.P. Henricks Co., Inc.
Homelite
Honeywell Inc.
Husqvarna Forest & Garden Company
International Cutlery, Inc.
Keystone Appliance Company
Kline & Company, Inc.
KPM Distributors
Inflatable Boats
Interlace Productions
Lennox Industries, Inc.
Leviton Manufacturing Co., Inc.
Lightolier, Inc.
Lux Products Corporation
Makita U.S.A., Inc.
Manier: Kistner, Inc.
Metal Industries Inc. of California
National Fire Protection Association

National Spa and Pool Institute
David P. Nick & Associates
Nikon, Inc.
North American Assoc. of Mirror Manufacturers
C.S. Osborne & Company
Outboard Marine Corporation
Pac Fab, Inc.
PDI Inc.
Pegasus Products Inc.
Penn Fishing Tackle Mfg. Co.
Phifer Wire Products, Inc.
Polaroid Corporation
Portable Rechargeable Battery Assoc.
Poulan/Weed Eater
Pressure Sensitive Tape Council
Price Pfister, Inc.
Princeton Ski Shops
Rain Bird Sales Corp.
S-B Power Tool Company
SANYO Energy (USA) Corporation
Sears, Roebuck and Co.
Sharp Electronics Corporation
Simply Speakers
Ski Barn
SMC Marketing Corporation
Snapper Power Equipment
Sony Electronics Inc.
Spear and Jackson/Neill Tools
Specialty Coffee Association of America
Star Water Systems/Flint and Walling, Inc.
Strongridge, Ltd.
Tecumseh Products Company
Teledyne Water Pik
Thomson Consumer Electronics
3M
The Toro Company
TROY-BILT Manufacturing Company
TSP Enterprises
Underwriters Laboratories Inc.
Unique Finds Antiques, Inc.
Vermont American Tool Company
White Sewing Machine
Xymox Technologies, Inc.
Zoller's Marine Center, Inc.

PHOTO CREDITS
cover: Stephen Mays
 Michael Molkenthin
p. 342: © Peter Grumann/The Image Bank.
p. 351: © Norman/Zefa